Robert M. Boynton
UNIVERSITY OF CALIFORNIA, SAN DIEGO

HOLT, RINEHART AND WINSTON
New York   Chicago   San Francisco   Dallas
Montreal   Toronto   London   Sydney

To my father and to Sherry and Mike

Library of Congress Cataloging in Publication Data

Boynton, Robert M.
  Human color vision.

  Bibliography: p. 406
  Includes index.
  1. Color vision.   2. Color—Psychological aspects.
3. Visual perception.   4. Visual discrimination.
I. Title.
BF789.C7B66   152.1'45   78-26443
ISBN 0-03-084682-X

Copyright © 1979 by Holt, Rinehart and Winston
All rights reserved
Printed in the United States of America
9 0 1 2 3   038   9 8 7 6 5 4 3 2 1

Preface

Through the application of scientific method for about four hundred years, substantial progress has been made toward an understanding of how human beings are able to appreciate and gauge the colors of things. Before that, such understanding had been wholly lacking. The principal aim of this book is to put forth some of our current concepts about the nature of such color perception.

With the general reader as well as the formal student in mind, I have tried to build each chapter from fundamentals without assuming any special background beyond that furnished by some lower-division study of general science and mathematics. My approach is scientific and rather theoretical. Nevertheless it is hoped that those who are concerned with color esthetics and color technology will find my treatment of human chromatic mechanisms to be of some value. (Such a group would include artists, interior decorators, optometrists, ophthalmologists, illuminating engineers, architects, textile and ceramics workers, graphic arts designers, and color TV and photographic engineers.)

Despite our inability to solve the mind-body problem, it is scientifically productive to suppose that a definite anatomical and physiological substrate underlies all that we see, colors included. Similarly, it is important to be convinced that a physical world exists, one which would persist without the need for humans or other creatures to populate and perceive it. To be consistent with these essential assumptions, my approach necessarily utilizes concepts drawn freely, and in roughly equal proportions, from physical, biological, and behavioral science.

I propose no radically new theory. Instead, because I am convinced that we have by now achieved a substantial number of solid concepts about color, these are the ones that are developed and stressed. Although these ideas will undoubtedly require substantial modification and elaboration in the future, they seem unlikely to be completely overthrown by some paradigmatic revolution. Still, at the frontiers of research, theoretical ideas vary considerably and these must be held tentatively. For pedagogical purposes I have not hesitated to use models that I prefer, and to which I have occasionally contributed, without confusing the issues by discussing all possible elaborations or an excessive number of alternatives. Despite such simplification, fact and fancy should be discriminable. Moreover, enough references are given, many of them quite recent, to enable the interested reader to pursue various theoretical issues in the light of the conceptual framework provided here, and to learn more about the experimental evidence upon which these ideas rest.

Experimental data are presented mainly to illuminate theoretical ideas that are distributed throughout the book. In an effort to illustrate the nature of modern empirical visual science, a few experiments are described in considerable detail. In the early chapters, readers are invited to try a few simple experiments of their own; these appear in boxes. And by means of historical examples, it is made clear that theory not based upon experiment is vacuous.

There are many people to thank. An initial draft was read by my colleague, Donald MacLeod, to whom I am especially indebted for his penetrating and scholarly suggestions. After revision, each chapter was reviewed by at least one expert of my choosing. This permitted the correction of many errors and led to some substantial re-writing. While he was on leave at UCSD from Santa Barbara, Jack Loomis volunteered to read these penultimate revisions and made many helpful suggestions, as did an anonymous reviewer selected by the publisher.

The following are the scholars who reviewed one or more chapters: Howard Baker, John Boles, Frank Clarke, Julian Hochberg, Carl Ingling, Naotake Kambe, Lloyd Kaufman, Donald Kelly, Yves LeGrand, John Mollon, Walter Makous, Dirk van Norren, Thomas Piantanida, Joel Pokorny, and Vivienne Smith. They gave freely and generously of their time and expertise, and I thank them all. Please do not blame any of them for deficiencies that remain. I am also indebted to W. David Wright, one of the founding fathers of modern colorimetry, for his help in producing an abridged version of some delightful reminiscences about his role in that development, to be found in the appendix.

At Holt, Rinehart, and Winston, I wish to acknowledge the support and assistance of Joan Greene, psychology editor, as well as that of four patient predecessors with whom I interacted over nearly a decade: Tom Davies, Deborah Doty, Terry O'Reilly, and Roger Williams. For improving my efforts in many ways, and for coordinating the production of this book, a very special vote of thanks is due to Brian Heald.

Thirty years ago, Lorrin A. Riggs introduced me to visual science, and I owe much to him. On a pair of sabbatical leaves I learned a great deal from W. S. Stiles, F. J. J. Clarke, K. T. Brown, and D. N. Whitten. On the home front, two major sources of inspiration and tolerance have been my wife, Allie, and my father, Merrill H. Boynton.

For more than twenty years, my research has been supported by the National Eye Institute (NEI) or by one of the institutes of the U.S. Department of Health, Education, and Welfare from which NEI eventually evolved. I very much appreciate this support. Because doing research provides insights and perspectives attainable in no other way, my own work is cited disproportionately in this book. NEI has also supported many graduate students and postdoctoral fellows who worked in my laboratories at the University of Rochester and the University of California, San Diego. From them, I have learned more than I could teach. I hope that they will enjoy this book, because every one of them contributed to it.

La Jolla, California   **R. M. B.**

Contents

1
A Brief History of Color Science
1
EARLY GREEK CONCEPTS	2
NEWTON'S BREAKTHROUGH	10
TOWARD EXPLAINING THE APPEARANCE OF THE SPECTRUM	13
TRICHROMACY	15
OPPONENT-COLOR THEORY	18
THE CIE SYSTEM	19
ANATOMY AND PHYSIOLOGY	19
CHROMATIC CONTEXT	20
SUMMARY	21
NOTES	22

2
Subjective Color Phenomena
25
THE COLOR OF OBJECTS	25
DIMENSIONS OF CHROMATIC EXPERIENCE	27
MISCELLANEOUS COLOR PHENOMENA	33

v

vi   Contents

SUMMARY   41
NOTES   41

3
Physical Concepts
43

NEED FOR A PHYSICAL DEFINITION OF THE STIMULUS   43
LIGHT   46
SOURCES OF LIGHT   50
REFLECTION   54
DIFFRACTION, REFRACTION, AND SCATTER   55
THE FATE OF A PHOTON   58
THE IMPORTANCE OF DIRECTION   60
WAVELENGTH, PHOTON ENERGY, AND RETINAL IRRADIATION   64
DISPERSION AND CHROMATIC ABERRATION   65
SUMMARY   68
NOTES   69

4
Retinal Anatomy Underlying the Perception of Form and Color
72

THE MOBILE EYE   73
OPTICAL ELEMENTS OF THE EYE   75
THE RETINA   80
EVIDENCE OF ELECTRON MICROSCOPY   89
SOME SPECULATIONS ABOUT FUNCTION   93
SUMMARY   94
NOTES   95

5
Color Matching and the Visual Pigments
97

THE MATCHING OPERATION   99
METAMERIC MATCHING AND THE SPECTRAL SENSITIVITY OF ROD
    VISION   101
ON THE NARROWNESS OF THE VISIBLE SPECTRUM   105
MONOCHROMACY AND THE MOLECULAR BASIS OF VISION   106
TRICHROMATIC COLOR VISION AND ITS BASIS   113
RETINAL DENSITOMETRY   118

COLOR MATCHING	128
DATA FROM ACTUAL COLOR-MIXTURE EXPERIMENTS	144
SPECTRAL ABSORPTION CURVES OF HUMAN CONE PIGMENTS	149
SUMMARY	154
NOTES	155

6
Sensitivity Regulation
159

PHOTOGRAPHY AS AN ANALOG	163
LIGHT AND DARK ADAPTATION	166
BLEACHING AND REGENERATION KINETICS	169
RECEPTOR ADAPTATION BY RESPONSE COMPRESSION	173
HOW THE THREE FACTORS SHRINK THE RANGE OF CONE RESPONSE	176
OTHER MECHANISMS OF RECEPTOR ADAPTATION	179
RAPID ADAPTATION AND RESPONSE COMPRESSION	183
CHROMATIC ADAPTATION	183
SPECTRAL SENSITIVITY: VARIATION OF TEST WAVELENGTH	187
TVI CURVES	196
π MECHANISMS: WHAT ARE THEY?	200
SOME EVIDENCE FOR POSTRECEPTOR CHROMATIC ADAPTATION	203
SUMMARY	204
NOTES	205

7
The Encoding of Color
207

OPPONENT-COLOR THEORY	208
AN OPPONENT-COLOR MODEL	211
SOME METHODOLOGICAL NOTES	215
HUMAN VISUAL ELECTROPHYSIOLOGY	217
RECEPTORS	219
HORIZONTAL CELLS	226
PROJECTIONS TO THE BRAIN	228
SINGLE-UNIT ELECTROPHYSIOLOGY	231
CHROMATIC MECHANISMS IN THE LATERAL GENICULATE NUCLEUS	232
RECEPTIVE FIELD ORGANIZATION	238
RECEPTIVE FIELDS AND THE CHROMATIC CODE	240
VISUAL CORTEX	244
SUMMARY	246
NOTES	249

8
Chromatic Discrimination
251

CHROMATIC VS ACHROMATIC COLOR DIFFERENCES	253
INTRODUCTION TO WAVELENGTH DISCRIMINATION	255
THEORETICAL DEVELOPMENT: PRELIMINARIES	257
CRITICAL QUESTIONS ABOUT CHROMATIC DISCRIMINATION	259
MODELING WAVELENGTH-DISCRIMINATION FUNCTIONS	268
INTERACTIONS BETWEEN R-G AND Y-B CHANNELS	274
EXPERIMENTAL DATA: CHROMATICITY DISCRIMINATION	275
THEORETICAL CONSIDERATIONS FOR EXTENDING MACADAM'S RESULTS	279
ADDITIONAL STUDIES OF CHROMATIC DISCRIMINATION	282
METHODOLOGICAL NOTES	284
MEASUREMENT OF LARGE COLOR DIFFERENCES	288
SUMMARY	291
NOTES	292

9
Some Temporal and Spatial Factors in Color Vision
296

SPATIAL AND TEMPORAL BEHAVIOR RELATED TO R, G, AND B CONES	297
DIRECT HETEROCHROMATIC PHOTOMETRY	299
FLICKER PHOTOMETRY	301
THEORETICAL BASIS OF FLICKER PHOTOMETRY	306
SINUSOIDAL FLICKER	308
SPATIAL PROPERTIES OF THE THREE KINDS OF CONES	324
TEMPORAL RESPONSES OF CONES AND THEIR PATHWAYS	327
COLOR INFORMATION FROM EDGES	331
A TEMPORAL CODE FOR COLOR?	331
SUMMARY	332
NOTES	333

10
Variations and Defects in Human Color Vision
337

VARIATIONS IN NORMAL COLOR PERCEPTION	338
HOW COLOR VISION CAN GO WRONG	341

DICHROMACY ON A CHROMATICITY DIAGRAM   344
THE ANALYTICAL ANOMALOSCOPE   346
GENETIC BASIS OF COLOR BLINDNESS   351
SOME CONTROVERSIAL ASPECTS OF RED-GREEN DEFICIENCY   358
RESIDUAL RED-GREEN DISCRIMINATION IN DICHROMATS   364
OTHER FORMS OF COLOR BLINDNESS   366
COLOR VISION TESTING   371
WHAT DO RED-GREEN–DEFECTIVE OBSERVERS REALLY SEE?   380
VARIATIONS IN NORMAL COLOR VISION   382
SUMMARY   384
NOTES   386

Appendix
390

PART I. CIE SYSTEM   390
PART II. THE ORIGINS OF THE 1931 CIE SYSTEM   397
PART III. SMITH AND POKORNY (1975) CONE SENSITIVITY
         FUNCTIONS   405

References
406

Index of Names
427

Index of Subjects
432

1
A Brief History of Color Science

From our experience with black and white photographs, we know that we can see an object without knowing its hue. Moreover, an object need not be perceived in order for the experience of hue to arise. Place an opaque screen before the eye and punch a small hole in it: there is then no way to discern anything much about the nature of an object seen through that hole.* Instead one perceives a disembodied filmy hue, localized in the plane of the screen, which is usually very different from the hue that would be seen if the screen were removed. There are other situations where hues can be seen though definite objects are not. We can gauge the hue of point sources of light or of diffuse disks of uncertain size and distance in an otherwise dark surround. For a few seconds, before it fades, we can also judge the hue of full-field illumination of the sort that can be produced by placing half a Ping-Pong ball over the eye.*

But such conditions are contrived. Usually we see objects rather than disembodied lights, and most objects have seemingly inherent colors that we can describe by means of familiar color names. This process seems so simple that

*An asterisk draws attention to a nearby description of a simple experiment that can be carried out with very common equipment. These experiments will illustrate and amplify the points raised in early chapters of the text. Numbered superscripts refer to notes that are collected at the end of each chapter.

> Construct a reduction screen by cutting a small square hole, about 1/16″ (1.5 mm) on each side, near the center of a sheet of construction paper. Very interesting effects can be observed if papers of several colors are used in turn. Cover one eye and look at the hole, holding the paper at arm's length, perpendicular to the line of sight, so that it occludes the areas surrounding the hole. Notice the appearance of various areas of the visual environment seen through the hole, as compared with normal viewing. Notice also how the appearance of what is seen through the hole varies depending upon the color of the construction paper that is used.

it is hard to believe how complicated it really is. In order to understand the problem of color perception it is therefore necessary to ask how we are able to perceive objects in the first place. For this reason we must be concerned with spatial as well as with chromatic vision.

EARLY GREEK CONCEPTS

How are we able, through the sense of vision, to discern the nature and color of objects far removed from our bodies—objects with which we are obviously not in contact? The ancient Greek philosophers correctly reasoned that something must pass between our eyes and the objects that are visually apprehended. The basic elements of nature at that time were conceived to be earth, air, fire, and water. Empedocles, who suggested in the fifth century B.C. that the "eye is like a lantern," evidently was referring to the fact that, under certain circumstances, the eyes of animals appear to be self-luminous. (This is an illusion, the basis of which will be explained in Chapter 5.) Assuming this to be true, Plato developed an emanation theory of vision, according to which an inner fire gave rise to visual rays shooting outward from the eye in the direction of a perceived object.[1]

It was not considered necessary to do experiments in those days, but even so it was obvious that, for man at least, no vision occurred in the total absence of light. So Plato was forced also to propose the existence of outer rays of light that were supposed to interact somehow with the visual rays.

Epicurus later rejected the emanation theory, preferring instead some rather wild ideas about what was transmitted from external objects to our eyes. He specifically considered and rejected the notion that rays of any kind were involved. Instead he thought that tiny husks (replicas) "maintain the similarity of the objects in colour and form, enter into our sight and into our thought according to the proportion of their size and with very rapid motion."[2] Not a very useful proposal, surely.

Among the ideas about which most of these early philosophers agreed, were the notions that black and white should be regarded as basic opposites, and that other hues are derivable from a limited number of more fundamental ones.

> Take an ordinary sheet of typing paper and wrap it around the front part of the head, holding it against the side of the face on each side while pulling it as close to the eyes as possible. Now aim the head at the sky, or other uniform area of the visual field. Although some structure will be seen, because of the grain of the paper, this is a fair approximation of a *Ganzfeld*—a fully filled, structure-free visual environment. With the paper still in position, move the head or (if you dare) walk around the room. This provides an idea of what vision (including color vision) would be like for a person who has light perception, but no pattern vision.

But there was no agreement about what these basic hues were. Although the notion of color mixture was prevalent, there was little understanding or agreement concerning just what was being mixed, or where, or why.

The following statement, by Plato, seems especially remarkable:

". . . neither that which impinges upon, nor that which is impinged upon, but something which *passes*—some relation—between them, and is peculiar to each percipient. For the several colors can scarcely appear to a dog or to any animal as they appear to a human being; nor, indeed do they appear to one man as they do to another; or even to the same man at one time as they do at another (Beare, 1906, p. 55)." This statement contains a remarkable series of early insights about species and individual differences in color perception (Chapter 10), with an added hint of awareness of the process of chromatic adaptation (Chapter 6).

That the physical nature of surfaces had something to do with their color was also widely appreciated: Democritus thought that hard surfaces appeared white and rough ones black, while Plato wrote of the "surface limit of the diaphanous in a determinately bounded body (Beare, 1906, p. 60)" as being important. He also correctly thought that the degree to which light penetrates a surface was significant for the purpose of color rendering. Aristotle was especially specific in believing that reflection was an important process for the production of color.

But despite such occasional flashes of insight, wrong ideas abounded, and no effort was made to settle disputes by experiment. The following quotation is offered as a horrible example of some of Plato's ideas that were very wide of the mark:

> That which dilates the visual current is *white*, the opposite is *black*. When a more rapid motion [than that of white], belonging to a different kind of fire, impinging on and dilating the visual current right up to the eyes, forcibly distends and dissolves the very pores of the eyes, causing a combined mass of fire and water—that which we call a tear—to flow from them, and being itself fire meeting the other fire right opposite: then, while the one fire leaps forth as from a lightening-flash, and the other enters in and becomes extinguished in the moisture, colors of all varieties are generated in the encounter between them, and we feel what we call a *dazzling* sensation, to the external stimulus of which we apply the terms *bright* and *glittering* (Beare, 1906, p. 51).

The importance of the brain in perception was appreciated very early, for example by Plato, although some (like Aristotle) preferred the heart as a sentient center. Dissection was practiced by the Greeks and the gross anatomy of the eye had been explored. The more obvious internal ocular components, including lens, vitreous, and various layers of the eye (with the retina) were known,[3] and the optic nerve was recognized as the connection between eye and brain. But the idea of probing a system to test its response was one whose time had not yet come.

Much of Greek anatomy and physiology was incorporated into the teachings of Galen. Judged by the length of time his views were accepted—about 1,500 years—he was the most influential physiologist ever known. Galen was a strong proponent of a specific form of emanation theory. He stated that the brain was "an organ where all sensations arrive, and where all mental images, and all intelligent ideas arise." He believed that rays were discharged in the direction of an object: these emerged through the pupil, interacted with the object, and then returned to the eye. He taught that the brain was in communication with the eye by means of a visual spirit flowing back and forth through a hollow optic nerve. The visual rays, entering the eye following their return from the perceived object, interacted with the visual spirit in the lens of the eye. The latter, having come from the brain, was now flushed back into it, carrying with it the replicas of objects seen.

Even if true, the foregoing would explain little unless one understands what happens in the brain. What would permit the replicas of the outer objects, carried into the brain by the visual spirit, to be interpreted there? Although Galen was not specific on this point, there emerged over the years the concept of the "sensorium," still popular with some sensory physiologists as late as the twentieth century A.D.

The sensorium is a hypothetical place in the brain where input from the sense organs is presumed to be delivered in order to give rise to our sensations and perceptions. *Sensorium* is a concept that makes little sense unless it is tacitly assumed, not very usefully, that some little creature exists there who can look at, and thus interpret the meaning of, the incoming replicas. Even today it is exceedingly difficult to think clearly about what is involved here. Our knowledge about the final, interpretive stages of the visual process is still very rudimentary. Concepts such as "association cortex" and "integrative centers" represent no real advance. The final stages are so bound up in the seemingly insoluble "mind–body" problem that they may forever resist experimental analysis. To the historians of the future, it is likely that the early Greek ideas about these matters will look no worse than some of our current concepts.

THE MIDDLE AGES

Following the decline of Greek civilization, records of what had been learned were to some degree retained and utilized in the Arab culture. During the middle ages, when little of scientific interest was going on elsewhere, there lived among the Arabs a remarkable natural philosopher named Abu Ali Mohammed Ibn Al Hazen, mercifully known also as Alhazen (965–1039 A.D.), who rejected the emanation theory of vision. In agreement with the first Arab philosopher-scientist, Alkendi, Alhazen became convinced that an optical image of the sort produced by a pinhole camera (with which he experimented) was produced in the eye. Upon viewing the image formed by a pinhole camera obscura, one can see that it contains much important information about the external world.* Although the image is two-dimensional, very dim, and usually lacking in fine detail, objects nevertheless can be perceived in their proper geometrical relation to other objects and their surrounds. Moreover, the colors of objects appear to be retained in such a reproduction.

> It is easy to build a pinhole camera, and for those not familiar with this device (widely heralded as the proper way to view a solar eclipse), the following description may be helpful. Take a shoebox and cut two holes in one end, each of about a quarter inch (6.25 mm) in diameter. One of these holes should be near the edge, the other about in the center. Take a piece of aluminum foil and punch a small hole in it with the tip of an ice pick, or one end of an unbent paper clip. Tape this over the center hole, so that the hole in the foil is within the hole in the box. Take the box out of doors on a sunny day; stand with the sun at your back, so that its light shines on the pinhole. Use the second hole to look into the box. An image of the sun will be seen on the opposite wall of the box. If the hole is not too small, images of artificial lights can also be seen, and it will be noticed that they are inverted.

In Alhazen's time, it was by no means clear that the pinhole camera had anything in common with the eye. It was correctly believed that light entered the eye through the pupil, but the diameter of the eye's pupil (at least 2 mm) is much too large for it to act as a pinhole. Because dissection was prohibited in the Arab culture, Alhazen was forced to depend heavily upon recorded Greek anatomy. Alhazen suspected that an image was present somewhere in the eye and he presumed, following the teachings of Galen, that it would be located in the crystalline lens in the middle of the eye. Although mistaken about this, Alhazen had the important insight that there must be points in the eye corresponding to points on perceived objects. He was also correct in supposing that light from an object was reflected to the eye following illumination by a source of light, and that the apparent color of an object depended to some extent upon the color of the light, as well as upon some property of the object (see Fig. 1.1).

Much later, during the Italian Renaissance, the great scientist-painter Leonardo da Vinci (1452–1519) turned his brilliant mind toward some of the problems of vision. He was a leader in the development of perspective drawing, which had been completely unknown to the Greeks. He also realized that a pinhole, located in an otherwise opaque screen, is capable of producing behind it an image of objects out in front. Assuming that light travels in straight lines,

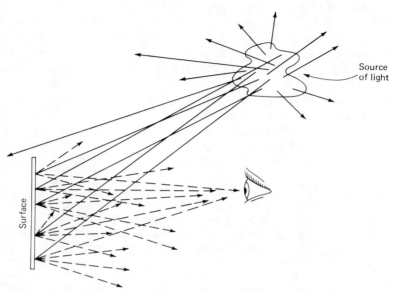

FIGURE 1.1 Alhazen apparently knew that the color of a surface depends in some way upon the color of the light incident upon it, as well as upon some property of the surface, which scatters the light incident upon it in various directions, including toward the eye. This differs importantly from Galen's idea, which was believed for 1,500 years, that something is discharged from the eye toward the surface.

he reasoned that there must also be a plane in front of the screen that corresponds to the one behind, excepting that geometrical relations in the forward plane will be normal, whereas the image to the rear is inverted. Leonardo found that, by placing a plane of glass before the eye and tracing carefully an outline of perceived boundaries in the visual field, the eye itself somehow assumed the role of the pinhole: a replica so derived appeared to the eye as being in proper perspective (see Fig. 1.2). Leonardo also became convinced that there was some kind of image inside the eye, and he made drawings in which he unsuccessfully attempted to sketch just how the image-forming rays might behave.

But his efforts proved fruitless because nothing was yet known about the laws of light refraction (Chapter 3), and for all his genius, Leonardo was not destined to discover them. He was also seriously hampered in his efforts by a curious and irrelevant preoccupation, one that Alhazen had also suffered from: Leonardo thought that the image in the eye must be right side up. This fact should give us pause. He was assuming that, in order for the world to appear right side up, the ocular image must be oriented in the same way. Many philosophers have been troubled by this problem. But this assumption is necessary only if one holds to an old view of perception, which Boring (1948, p. 224) describes as follows:

FIGURE 1.2 Principles of perspective, according to which the three-dimensional object with corners ABCDE is rendered in the window EFGH by the points abcde. The latter are located as if taut strings from ABCDE are drawn toward the eye and allowed to intersect the plane of the window. Illustration is from Pirenne (1970), who attributes it to Brook Taylor (1811), **New Principles of Linear Perspective.**

The older theory of perception regarded the mind (the soul, the sensorium) as a personal entity within the head, shut off from the external world but seeking information about it and perceiving the representatives (images, copies) of objects that the nerves bring to it. This was the common-sense theory: a cranial homunculus able to perceive directly anything that comes within range of its apprehension. The mind, according to such a view, would see the image *on the retina* and would see it inverted because it *is* inverted. Thus, since the mind does not see objects without inversion, there was a problem [to account for the perceived right-side-up world, despite the upside-down retinal image].

Today the view is widely accepted among experimental psychologists that the concept of mind is not particularly useful. Furthermore, one perceives objects, not images. The term "image" is a very slippery one, whose referent is somewhat obscure even in optics. As applied to brain processes or conscious events, it becomes a hopelessly vague notion. The idea of a sensorium, with a little creature inside to view what is coming in, seems related to a kind of naive faith that the end product of vision, as it appears in the brain, must somehow represent—in some more or less obvious way—the geometry of visual space. This viewpoint is with us yet today. It is common to find, in introductory treatments of vision, statements implying that although the retinal image is upside down, we are spared the perception of an inverted world thanks to the heroic effort of the brain, which turns it right side up again.[4] The error contained in this kind of thinking is at least as serious as the earlier error of the emanation theory of vision. For surely the brain does nothing at all to the retinal image, if that image is regarded, as it must be, as a purely optical phenomenon. As Johannes Müller pointed out[5] in the nineteenth century, the brain receives nerve signals, not light. These messages have their origin in the patterning of light received at the retina, but neither the amount nor the quality of information contained in the retinal image is in any sense altered by transformations of that image such as inversion or left–right reversal.

KEPLER AND THE RETINAL IMAGE

The seventeenth century marks the start of the modern era for the study of light and vision. Gradually, though with much difficulty, the habits of speculation and of appeal to ancient authority began to be replaced by more astute natural observation, experimentation, and a willingness to challenge established views. There was surely much to learn about color, a subject about which total confusion still prevailed in 1600.

Descartes (1596–1650) would soon promote an influential and scientifically useful philosophy that treated humans partly as machines, drawing a clear distinction between objective and subjective domains. Without microscopes, microelectrodes, or radiometers, investigators lacked the means by which to understand or measure either the physical light stimulus or the response of the eye. It was still not clear whether color was embodied in light, object, eye, or soul. Despite a knowledge of ocular gross anatomy and a growing suspicion that rays of some kind caused an image to be formed somewhere in the eye, spatial vision was not yet correctly understood any more than it had been by the Greeks or Arabs.

Spectacle lenses had been discovered by 1285, and positive lenses had been used to improve the performance of the pinhole camera by G. B. Della Porta in 1589. But the study of lenses had a curious history: they were considered not to be scientifically respectable. To use lenses, it was thought, would lead to distortions of perception that must be carefully avoided by the objective investigator. For a very long time the manufacture and use of lenses was left to artisans and practitioners, who used them without understanding how they worked.

Johannes Kepler was a noted astronomer who believed in the heliocentric theory of Copernicus. In the field of optics, he was the first to understand how positive lenses work, and why their use permits enlargement of the aperture of a pinhole camera, leading to the double benefits of increased brightness and improved quality of the image. There had been substantial resistance to Kepler's early observations with his telescope, related to the fact that his crude lenses had produced severe chromatic aberration, giving rise to the perception of colors where none were otherwise evident. (Chromatic aberration is discussed in Chapter 3, p. 67.) A respected philosopher of the time wrote: "the telescope shows images larger than the real objects or nearer; it shows them coloured and distorted [and] therefore it misleads us and cannot be used as an instrument of observation."

In addition to being forced to live with this kind of "scientific" negativism, Kepler was also concerned with the ever-present danger of persecution by religious zealots. The accomplishments of early scientists such as Kepler cannot be fully appreciated without taking into account the inhibiting effects of this kind of epistemological and social climate. Today the science of physics provides a way of describing the world that is grossly at odds with biblical descriptions, as well as with the way we perceive it. Now we take for granted that science advances with the development of instruments that extend human senses, permitting the measurement of that which otherwise is too small to be seen, or of radiation or matter to which human end organs are wholly insensitive.

Proceeding from his understanding of optical relationships, Kepler reasoned that the crystalline lens within the eye was required to form an image in the eye, and so the image could not be in the lens itself. He inferred instead that the receptive layer for image reception was at the back of the eye, in the retina. He seemed keenly aware, more than most of his predecessors had been, that this is the end of the trail so far as light is concerned in the visual process. Some other substance or process must intervene at this stage, one that is somehow capable of appreciating the light. But Kepler's speculations about how this might work were woefully wide of the mark, being clearly influenced by a religious and mystical turn of mind that was still natural even for men like Kepler, who were beginning to stake out the territory of modern empirical science.

Kepler was also mistaken about a basic fact of purely optical importance, believing incorrectly that no light refraction takes place at the cornea of the eye, which is in fact the principal refractive interface. Despite this error, Kepler was correct in believing that the retinal image was small, inverted, and systematically related to points in space. Moreover, it was colored: "Green is depicted green, and in general things are depicted by whatever colour they have."

In 1595, according to Polyak (1957), an Italian named Aranzi actually had cut a hole in the back of an animal eye, and by placing a translucent screen there, he had directly observed the colored image that Kepler was later to imagine. Kepler was apparently unaware of Aranzi's work, which was too far ahead of its time to create much attention. In 1625, long after Kepler had drawn his conclusions, Christoph Scheiner repeated Aranzi's experiment in Germany. Its significance was immediately recognized, and Scheiner is usually cited today as the one who first accomplished the demonstration. Descartes, in his *Dioptrique* (published in 1637), also reports having done this experiment.

The formation of retinal images may seem to have relatively little to do with color vision. Therefore it is worth stating again that a proper explanation of color vision is not possible without a general understanding of the visual process, in particular the physics and physiology underlying its spatial aspects. After all, if Democritus had been correct that color is something inherent in tiny replicas entering the eye, then the task of color science today would be to capture and dissect these replicas, and to perturb them in order to discover which of their features contains information that is specific to color. Instead, the problem becomes one of analyzing the distribution of light on the retina, and of understanding what aspect of this light is capable of giving rise to sensations of color.

NEWTON'S BREAKTHROUGH

Throughout the period of history so far described, nothing was known about the physical nature of light, although the science known as geometrical optics was gradually being developed. This is a branch of optics that treats light as being comprised of rays that move in straight lines and suffer refraction when passing from one optical medium to another (see Chapter 3). These concepts are mainly useful for predicting the location of images, which is done these days by computer. But geometrical optics fails to describe many important features of physical reality and is unable to deal with most of the physical aspects of color. To do this requires an understanding of the physical nature of light (physical optics) and this work did not advance rapidly until the nineteenth century.

Almost everyone knows about Isaac Newton's famous experiment in which he broke white light into its special components by passing a beam through a prism. Newton understood geometrical optics very well, as a perusal of his *Opticks* (1730) will show, and his experiments with prisms were probably the most important in the history of color science.

Newton's biographers are fond of pointing out that he purchased his prisms at the Stourbridge fair, almost as if to imply that he was on a lark and might accidentally have discovered spectral dispersion while looking through one of them on his way home. So far as the source of supply is concerned, he was not, after all, able to order them from Edmund Scientific or Bausch and Lomb. And Newton was by no means the first to disperse white light with a prism, or to note that colors resulted.[6] But when he got his prisms back to his rooms at Trinity College he set up his experimental conditions with care and precision, and was masterful in interpreting the observations that followed.

If a thick beam of white light is dispersed by a prism, a continuum of overlapping spectra is produced and these mainly recombine to produce white: only at the edges are residual fringes seen. Newton reduced the size of his incident light beam to dimensions small enough to minimize the overlapping spectra, but he kept the beam large enough to allow sufficient light for clear visual observation of the spectrum that was formed. Newton's light source, the sun, was of course the most intense available; his aperture—used to limit beam size—was a small circular opening in an otherwise opaque shutter. The prism that he used, a regular triangular one, was set at the precise angle of minimum dispersion. According to already established principles of geometrical optics, this condition should have produced a perfectly circular spot of light on his receiving screen. What Newton observed instead was a shape of the sort that would be traced out by a continuous succession of overlapping circles, consisting overall of a splotch of light with straight sides and rounded ends, longer than its width by a ratio of about five to one, and changing gradually in color from violet at one end to red at the other.

Newton extended his experiment in important ways. A narrow colored band was selected from the spectrum and was passed through a second prism, as shown in Figure 1.3. Newton reported that there was no further dispersion or change of color. In another experiment, he recombined the dispersed rays of the initial spectrum and found that white light was thereby restored. From these and other observations, he concluded that white light was in fact a mixture of colored lights, and that the rays corresponding to each color took different paths through the prism.

Newton appreciated the continuous nature of the spectrum. In his *Opticks*, he wrote:

The Spectrum did appear tinged with this Series of colours, violet, indigo, blue, green, yellow, orange, red together with all their intermediate Degrees in a continual Succession perpetually varying. So that there appeared as many Degrees of Colours, as there were sorts of Rays differing in Refrangibility.

Here, although Newton identified certain regions of the spectrum in terms of "ROY G. BIV" (the eponymous acronym that many of us learned in school),

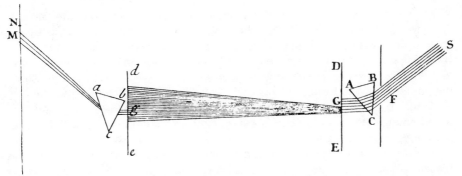

FIGURE 1.3 Newton's diagram of one of the experiments described in the text. Light from the sun, coming in at the right, is dispersed by prism **ABC** and a small part of the beam is selected by aperture **G** in screen **DE**. The dispersed spectrum is seen along de. Another small aperture **g** picks off a narrow part of the spectrum and delivers it to a second prism **abc**. If **g** is sufficiently small, no further dispersion is seen.

his perception of graded colors in the spectrum led him to conclude that the hypothetical rays of spectral light were also graded continuously—an idea that turns out to be correct (see Chapter 3). Newton also was careful to point out that the light rays themselves are not colored, but should be regarded instead as providing only a disposition for eliciting one or another color sensation if delivered to the eye.

Yet when Newton said that white light was a mixture of colored lights, it was not clear whether the mixture was to be regarded as being a physical affair or if it depended also upon the eye for its occurrence. Given that he felt that a continuous appearance of spectral colors implied a continuous series of sorts of rays, it appears that Newton leaned toward the presumption that color mixture is in the light, since if it were in the eye, as we now know it to be (see Chapter 5), a few discrete types of rays could nevertheless produce a subjectively continuous appearance of the spectrum. It is characteristic of Newton that, lacking any definitive evidence about where color mixture occurs, he chose not to take a firm stand on this important matter. Probably for the same reason, Newton did not speculate about visual mechanisms that might be responsible for rendering the colors of his rays.

What is most impressive about this work is that it removed color from the perceived object, where it had for so long been assumed to reside. Instead Newton placed the stimulus for color perception in the rays reflected from the object. And he went a step further, showing experimentally that the color of an object was related to its ability to reflect the colored rays of the spectrum selectively, also making the critical observation that monochromatic light, approximated by isolating just one part of the spectrum, is only more or less reflected by a surface, but is not otherwise changed in character.

The idea that white light is comprised of a mixture of colored lights was so contrary to common sense that, although it was widely adopted by post-Newtonian physicists, it absolutely outraged the famous German poet-scientist Johann Wolfgang von Goethe,[7] who had become infatuated with the colored appearance of things as seen through prisms. He repeated some of Newton's experiments and did many of his own, concluding that Newton's conclusions were mistaken and could only have been reached under the bizarre and contrived circumstances of Newton's experiments. This kind of dispute has been common in the history of science. It arises between those who favor difficult and controlled experiments and those who, like Goethe in his time and the Gestalt psychologists of a later era, tend to favor a more naturalistic form of observation. While the latter claim that the whole of a complex process can never be understood by taking it apart, their opponents find it difficult to imagine how progress can occur by any other route.

Some of Goethe's objections were not without foundation. Since Newton had claimed that there was no further dispersion when a small part of the spectrum was passed through a second prism, there could be no further appearance of color fringes. In repeating the experiment, Goethe noted that faint color fringes did in fact appear. Today we know that this happens because a narrow spectral band is not the same as pure monochromatic light. Newton had either failed to observe this variation in color, or he may have decided to ignore it as a second-order effect. Given that he had just invented the calculus, we must assume that he understood the nature of limiting conditions. If so, he reached the correct conclusion by ignoring effects that, though inevitable in real experiments with finite wavebands of light, would not occur at the theoretical limit.

There is an important history lesson here. The foregoing illustrates a style of research that can sometimes lead quickly to strong and important inferences. Yet when deviations from an expected result occur, one ignores them at great peril. In another instance, Newton himself was not so fortunate. By using crossed spectra he had attempted to determine whether white light could be produced in the overlapping square by the mixture of only two colors. He failed to find this, observing instead a slight residual color.[8] From this he concluded that it would not be possible to get white from a mixture of only two pure spectral colors. This time he had no theoretical basis for what to expect in the limiting case, and he guessed wrong. Nevertheless, there was nothing otherwise incorrect about what he reported, and in this case, where he did not understand so well what to expect, he was careful to report exactly what he observed.

Newton had also asserted that chromatic aberration in telescopes could never be corrected. This would follow if, as Newton had thought, all kinds of glass had the same characteristics of chromatic dispersion. But they do not (see Chapter 3, p. 67), and multiple-element color-corrected lenses were in fact developed during Newton's lifetime. Goethe, who was born 22 years after Newton's death, took this as evidence that Newton had been wrong not just about optical glass, but about almost everything. Although Goethe's diatribe against Newton was of unusual intensity, such scientific conflict is not itself unusual. Helmholtz and Hering (see pp. 15–18) were to be at odds later, and there are plenty of unmentionable examples that could be cited from the present era of color science.

TOWARD EXPLAINING THE APPEARANCE OF THE SPECTRUM

For much of his life, Newton favored a corpuscular theory of light. It sometimes happens with the greatest of scientists that they eventually carry out themselves, sometimes perhaps without intending to do so, the very experiments that prove most damaging to their cherished beliefs. Working with juxtaposed plates of glass, one flat and the other just slightly curved, he produced and carefully studied what are now called "Newton's rings." Although Robert Hooke had previously done this experiment, once again it was Newton who performed the quantitative analysis, through which it proved possible more fully to understand the implications of these rings.

Vasco Ronchi, in his fascinating book on the history of light and vision (1970, p. 176), writes: "Newton's measurements and calculations established that the dark rings were always formed where the thickness of the film [of air between the two glass layers] was a multiple of a given value, namely 1/89,000 part of an inch (0.285 μ) for light of a bright yellow and that the bright rings occurred where the thickness had a value which was between those of the dark colour . . . [and] that the ratio of the thickness required to produce red and violet rings was 14 to 9." Here Newton had almost in his grasp the relation between wavelength and hue, but it eluded him. His results are easy to understand by wave theory. The rings are caused by interference, which in turn depends upon the wave nature of light and the occurrence of constructive and destructive interference (Chapter 3). Destructive interference would create dark rings in the condition where the transmitted and reflected waves are 180° out of phase, or shifted by half a wavelength. This occurs at a separation of 0.285 μm in yellow light. The full wave would then be 0.570 μm, or 570 nm, and this turns out be an accurate estimate of the wavelength of yellow light.[9] The ratio of 14 to 9 corresponds to that between 650 to 417 nm, wavelengths that appear red and violet as they should. Thus Newton was the first to develop a method for measuring the wavelength of light, although he failed to recognize it as such.

Earlier Newton had done the first experiment relating the wavelength of light to the appearance of hue. His procedure was to mark the places in the spectrum that corresponded to the midpoints of his seven zones of hues, and then to ask others to do the same. He concluded from this that there was reasonable agreement among observers. Although a correlation between degree of refraction and hue was accepted from this time forward, attempts to measure this correlation—even to the extent that Newton had—seem not to have been made until very recently.

There are perhaps three reasons for this delay: (1) It is controversial whether sensations can be measured. For example, neither Hering nor Helmholtz would attempt such measurement in the nineteenth century, although both were keen introspectionists who understood the physical nature of light. Hering described the appearance of colors and how they should be arranged in a proper color diagram. Helmholtz went to great lengths to select color terms that satisfied him as being proper descriptors of the points of the spectrum marked by Fraunhofer's solar lines, but his description was qualitative only. (2) The appearance of the spectrum depends upon its intensity. This is known as the Bezold-Brücke hue shift, about which Helmholtz had earlier commented, especially with respect to the loss of reddishness when violet lights are raised to high brightnesses. (3) The appearance of any color depends, to a surprising extent, upon its surroundings. The appearance of one part of a spectrum is influenced by the rest of it.

To judge spectral colors properly, it is necessary for a narrow spectral band to fill a visual field of the desired size with light of uniform quality. The effects of context and surround on color perception are exceedingly important (see Chapter 2 and the concluding section of this chapter).

TRICHROMACY

According to Helmholtz (1924, v.2, p. 162), "Pliny tells us that the ancient Greek painters knew how to prepare all colours with four pigments . . . and even in the celebrated fresco, The Marriage of the Aldobrandini, dating from Roman times, the profusion of pigments is very small, as Davy's chemical investigations showed." In addition to mixing lights, Newton had also mixed pigments, but he attached little significance to the critical difference between these two operations. During the eighteenth century, a number of physicists, including Tobias Meyer (whose work is most often cited), attempted to understand color by means of experiments in which as few as three pigments were mixed. But the prevailing view was that colors and their mixtures were properties of external manipulanda, not of the eye. It remained for Thomas Young in 1801 to propose a trichromatic theory that included physiological as well as physical terms:

As it is almost impossible to conceive each sensitive point of the retina to contain an infinite number of particles, each capable of vibrating in perfect unison with every possible undulation, it becomes necessary to suppose the number limited; for instance to the three principal colours, red, yellow, and blue, and that each of the particles is capable of being put in motion more or less forcibly by undulations differing less or more from perfect unison. Each sensitive filament of the nerve may consist of three portions, one for each principal colour.[10]

This statement embodies all of the important ideas of modern trichromatic theory, for which there is now overwhelming experimental support, as will be seen in Chapter 5. It contains the implication that the wavelength of light (which, as we will see in Chapter 3, is reciprocally related to its frequency of vibration) varies continuously across the spectrum, consistent with what Newton had supposed. Young explains that the relation between wavelength and hue depends essentially upon the ratios of activation among three processes: this is the basic idea of trichromacy. The alternative hypothesis that each receptor (or "sensitive point of the retina") could respond in some differential way to each wavelength is rejected, with the substitution of the idea (now known as the principle of univariance—see Chapter 5) that a receptor can respond only more or less vigorously, depending upon how well it resonates with the frequency of the incoming light. Since light comes in a continuous series of frequencies, it is not possible to conceive of an infinite number of receptors, each sharply tuned to only one frequency. Three types of receptors might do, if these were to have overlapping spectral sensitivities such that each wavelength produces a different ratio of responses among them. It should be recognized that these prophetic ideas were developed before anything at all was known about the physiology of the retina: the argument was largely a logical one, being no more than a plausible hypothesis based upon known physical facts.

The development of color science has often profited from the part-time efforts of some very great physical scientists. Bertrand Russell states without qualification that, in his opinion, Newton was the greatest scientific genius of all time. If so, Thomas Young could surely qualify as a very close second. His work on vision had begun early. For his study of visual accommodation (focus of the eye) he was elected to fellowship in the Royal Society in 1793 at the age of twenty-one (nine years younger than Newton). Young worked in an astounding variety of scientific fields, and color vision was for him only a minor interest. Perhaps for this reason he did not choose to spend much time promoting trichromatic theory. Perhaps he was not convinced that it was correct: the number three was, after all, offered very tentatively; no proof that this was the correct number of particles was given; and none was sought. More important than the number of postulated color receptors was the idea that no one class of them could, by itself, carry a message from which hue could be deduced. But Young had no proof of this, either.

In any event, Young's ideas on color were not very widely accepted; this fact is illustrated by noting that David Brewster, a very respectable optical physicist, seriously proposed as late as 1855 that there were but three fundamental kinds of light, called red, yellow, and blue, and that all physically realizable lights—including spectral ones—contained mixtures of these three.

It was Hermann von Helmholtz who revived Young's idea in the second book of his monumental three-volume *Handbook of Physiological Optics,* which stands as the greatest work in the history of visual science. Helmholtz almost defies classification.[11] He studied medicine at the Friedrich-Wilhelm Institute in Berlin, where he came under the influence of the world's first professor of physiology, Johannes Müller. While a very young man, Helmholtz was the first to measure the velocity of nerve conduction. He authored the principle of conservation of energy, invented the ophthalmoscope, did almost as much work in audition as in vision, and was absolutely first-rate as a physcist, mathematician, psychologist, and physiologist. He eventually became professor of physics at the University of Berlin.

The *Handbook* was first published from 1856 to 1866, when Helmholtz was between 35 and 45 years of age; a second edition appeared 30 years later, during the last decade of his life. A third German edition was posthumously published from 1909 to 1911, with editorial additions by A. Gullstrand, J. von Kries, and W. Nagel. The work was considered so important that it was translated into English by J. P. C. Southall and others in 1924, and was published by the Optical Society of America, with additional appendices and editorial comments.

In his second volume, Helmoltz wrote:

Young's theory of the colour sensations, like so much else that this marvelous investigator achieved in advance of his time, remained unnoticed, until the author himself [Helmholtz] and Maxwell again directed attention to it. It is sufficient to assume that the optic nerve is capable of sensations of different kinds, without trying to find out why the system of these visual sensations is just what it is.

Helmholtz refers here to James Clerk Maxwell, another nineteenth-century physical genius, who is probably best known for his vector equations describing electromagnetic fields.

Helmholtz's first sketches of overlapping spectral sensitivity curves are shown in Figure 1.4. It is probably unfortunate that he talked about fundamental sen-

---

1. The eye is provided with three distinct sets of nervous fibres. Stimulation of the first excites the sensation of red, stimulation of the second the sensation of green, and stimulation of the third the sensation of violet.

2. Objective homogeneous light excites these three kinds of fibres in various degrees, depending on its wave-length. The red-sensitive fibres are stimulated most by light of longest wave-length, and the violet-sensitive fibres by light of shortest wavelength. But this does not mean that each colour of the spectrum does not stimulate all three kinds of fibres, some feebly and others strongly; on the contrary, in order to explain a series of phenomena, it is necessary to

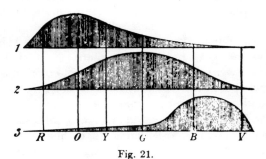

Fig. 21.

assume that that is exactly what does happen. Suppose that the colours of the spectrum are plotted horizontally in Fig. 21 in their natural sequence, from red to violet, the three curves may be taken to indicate something like the degree of excitation of the three kinds of fibres, No. 1 for the red-sensitive fibres, No. 2 for the green-sensitive fibres, and No. 3 for the violet-sensitive fibres.

FIGURE 1.4   Helmholtz's three overlapping spectral sensitivity curves, and the text that goes with them, from Helmholtz (1924). This is a basically qualitative account, as indicated, for example, by the use of color names to identify the spectrum. Curves like these, representing the results of actual measurements, will be found in Chapter 5. Note that Helmholtz has plotted the spectral colors in an order that is reversed relative to the modern convention.

sations, rather than *receptor processes,* because curves of this kind (although they explain color matches) do not explain color sensations—a point that will be elaborated shortly. Maxwell, after doing some ingeniously simple experiments using reflecting surfaces on a spinning top (the ancestor of the modern color wheel) conducted the first color-mixture experiments that made use of spectral light and was thus the first to provide quantitative data that we would today relate to the absorption spectra of the three kinds of cone photopigments in the retina (Chapter 5).

OPPONENT-COLOR THEORY

In the late nineteenth century, a German physiologist named Ewald Hering[12] developed a viewpoint about color vision that was largely based upon the subjective appearance of colors, rather than upon physical experiments, like those of Maxwell, that had involved only color matching. The trichromatic theory, as put forth by Helmholtz, is inadequate to account for the way colors appear. It cannot reasonably explain, for example, why red and green lights mix to produce yellow (a color qualitatively different from each of the components in the mixture), or why this yellow, if mixed with blue, can produce a perfect white. Helmholtz did not consider it worthwhile "to find out why the system of these visual sensations is just what it is." Ever since, most trichromatic theorists have been physicists, for whom the appearance of colors often is regarded as being of little scientific interest.

But the appearance of colors did concern Hering, who also wanted to show why one never sees reddish greens or yellowish blues. Hering speculated that the answer might lie in an "opponent-color" process. More than a half century would pass before there was a shred of direct physiological evidence to support this idea, but abundant evidence has been developed since 1950 (see Chapters 4 and 7). Hering suggested that the visual system might be capable of generating signals of two opposite kinds, depending upon wavelength. This is an idea that was not favorably received by either the physicists or physiologists of that era, being squarely at odds with both the Young-Helmholtz theory of color and the doctrine of specific nerve energies of Müller.

Opponent-color and trichromatic theory competed for a long time. The resolution of the conflict between them began in the 1920s, presaged in 1905 by von Kries. The psychologist G. E. Müller and the physicst Erwin Schrödinger worked out plausible zone theories to handle the problem. According to such models (of which there have been many since) the initial trichromatic color separation, of the sort that Young had proposed, leads next to an opponent-color stage. The direct evidence that has been provided to support this conciliatory idea will be considered in Chapter 7.

The past 40 years have seen a rapid development in color science. This period is too recent to qualify as history, and the work is too technical to permit a simple summary. Nevertheless this chapter will be concluded with a very brief overview of a few modern developments.

THE CIE SYSTEM

Until 1931, the concept of color had no precise scientific basis and colors could be specified only by appeal to physical samples. In that year, the International Commission on Illumination (CIE)[13] adopted a system of color specification which has lasted to the present time. The basic data with which the founding fathers of colorimetry worked were color-mixture functions of the sort that Maxwell had originally obtained. A standard set of color-mixture values, based mainly upon extensive experimental investigations by W. D. Wright and J. Guild in England, was adopted. The idea was to reduce any spectral radiance distribution (Chapter 3) to only three variables, and to state that, for color vision, any two stimuli describable by the same values of each of these variables, no matter how physically different, would be defined as colorimetrically identical. Because the color of a surface does not seem to change very much if intensity is changed without change in spectral distribution, it proved possible to reduce the description of color to only two variables that could be represented on a two-dimensional chart known as a *chromaticity diagram*. The properties of such a diagram will be explained in Chapter 5. The particular one adopted by the CIE, which will be minimally utilized in this book, is discussed in Appendix I (p. 405).

Although very useful, there are many limitations to this system. For one thing, the color matches that it predicts apply only to a hypothetical standard observer, and not exactly to any particular human being. It is valid only for restricted conditions of viewing with small fields that are neither too bright nor too dim. The chromaticity diagram does not represent color appearance very well, and although there is really no reason why it should (see Chapter 8), it has often been used for this purpose.

ANATOMY AND PHYSIOLOGY

The improvement in the nineteenth century of the light microscope and histological procedures permitted the discovery of rods and cones as the photoreceptors in the eye, and provided the basis for the duplicity theory that will be described in Chapter 4, according to which cones are the receptors for color vision. Yet it has proved impossible to the present day to show clear anatomical differences between the three cone types that are believed to exist in primates, or to extract their photopigments, which are believed responsible for absorption of light. Fortunately, it has proved possible to examine cone pigments by less direct techniques (Chapter 5).

Biological tissue is electrically active, and the recording of such activity (electrophysiology) began in the nineteenth century and has advanced to a fine art. Direct physiological evidence to support the notion of three classes of cones, and of opponent-color responses at subsequent neural stages, now exists (Chapters 4 and 7). Many workers today are recording from the visual brain, presumably a step closer than the retina to visual consciousness.

Whereas inferences about mechanisms of color perception could until recently be made only indirectly on the basis of psychophysical evidence (for example, experiments on color matching using human subjects and behavioral measures), a wide spectrum of research techniques now exists that should, in the years ahead, move us closer to a complete description of how the human color-vision system actually works. Much of this book is devoted to an examination of the state of such evidence today, considered in terms of what it seems to imply for how we see color. As the subject advances, psychophysical experiments continue to add to our knowledge of color vision, and these will be stressed. Many of these experiments could have been done many years earlier, although some depend heavily on technical advances in the area of stimulus presentation. But even where they were technically possible at an earlier time, the state of anatomy, neurophysiology, and photochemistry would not have suggested the usefulness of some of the experiments of today, which test implications of theories rooted in the more direct techniques, but not fully testable by them. Conversely, the data of the psychophysicist, together with theories developed from such data, provide a framework within which the electrophysiologist conducts his research.

CHROMATIC CONTEXT

In the spring of 1958 a student in my physiological optics class at the University of Rochester showed me a clipping from the *New York Times* describing a demonstration by Edwin Land, president of the Polaroid Corporation, that had been done the previous day at a meeting of the National Academy of Sciences. According to the newspaper account, Land had photographed a scene with two cameras, one of which had a red filter in front of its lens, the other, a green one. Positive black-and-white slides were prepared from the resulting negatives and placed in two slide projectors. One of these delivered its light to the screen through a red filter, whereas the other was used without any filter at all. With the images in perfect registration, a full gamut of color was seen in the resulting reproduction. The student wanted to know what I thought about this report.

My reply was that there was probably a mistake in the *New York Times* account. I was wrong: the description of what Land had *done* was entirely accurate, and it was also true that Land had *claimed* that a "full gamut" of color experience had resulted. As a conclusion to this chapter, I wish to expand upon this incident for a variety of interrelated reasons.

- In his report of this work, Land (1959a) begins by stating (p. 115): "We have come to the conclusion that the classical laws of color mixing conceal great basic laws of color vision. There is a discrepancy between the conclusions that one would reach on the basis of the standard theory of color mixing and the results we obtain in studying total images." My orientation toward color had indeed been in the classical tradition. Given my reaction to the *Times* account, I conclude that there is truth in what Land said.
- Nevertheless, there is no logical reason why the classical laws of color mixing

(see Chapter 5) should conceal anything about the effects of chromatic context. If they do, it is because someone has inappropriately extended these classical laws. Helmholtz was guilty of this, and the modern tradition of associating particular regions of chromaticity space with particular hues perpetuates the error.
- Despite a great deal of work from his and other laboratories, the "great basic laws of color vision" to which Land alludes are very far from being fully formulated. When Land and McCann later stated (1971) that "there is no predictable relationship between flux at various wavelengths and the color sensation associated with objects" they could have meant (a) that to predict the appearance of a color, one must *in principle* know about the colors in the surround, (b) the "great basic laws" are not yet known (so that even if the surround colors are specified the prediction cannot be made), or (c) if the surround colors are known, the prediction of color appearance can be made.
- I agree with (a) and (b) above, but reject (c). Land and his associates have formulated some of the necessary principles and are able to make some reasonable predictions. Many such predictions are not very accurate, even in a completely abstract situation, and they ignore the effects of memory color and psychological context that must eventually be taken into account. Much of what Land did was not so new as he thought, nor were his predictions of color appearance superior to some earlier ones (see Judd, 1960, and Walls, 1960, for reviews).
- Nothing like "a full gamut" of color is possible in the Land demonstration. McCamy (1960) demonstrated this beautifully by putting Land and Kodachrome images side by side; in the same talk he induced members of the audience to shout out the color names of various objects as an assistant gradually and surreptitiously dimmed one of the projectors, and the names kept coming even after the light had been turned off entirely.

I have decided not to deal with the very difficult topic of chromatic context in this book. I have made an attempt elsewhere (Boynton, 1978) to discuss "color in contour and object perception" and there is no point in reproducing that material here. So far as Land's work is concerned, the reader is referred to two *Scientific American* articles (Land, 1959c, 1977), to the pioneering work of Helson (1938, 1963), of Helson and Michels (1948) and Judd (1940), to Land's two original papers (1959a, b) and to McCann, McKee, and Taylor (1976) for a recent account of the "retinex" theory.

SUMMARY

The question of how, through the sense of vision, we are able to discern the nature and color of remote objects, has been raised repeatedly throughout recorded history. Speculations of the Greek philosophers, who did not indulge in experimentation, were clever but mostly wrong. For example, it was widely believed that rays were discharged from the eyes (emanation theory) and that tiny replicas of perceived objects could be released by such rays, to be delivered through the pupil of the eye and from there flushed through the hollow optic nerve to the sensorium in the brain.

In the middle ages, Alhazen rejected emanation theory. Instead, he argued that an image of some kind, perhaps similar to that formed in a pinhole camera, was passively formed within the eye. Later, Leonardo da Vinci came close to a full understanding of visual optics, but he failed because of his conviction that the retinal image could not be inverted. The German astronomer Johannes Kepler was the first to understand the basis for image formation by positive lenses, and was thereby able to conclude that there must be an inverted retinal image.

Visual science has profited greatly from the part-time efforts of some great physical scientists. For example, although not the first to disperse the spectrum, Isaac Newton fully understood the implications of this experiment (when properly executed) for color vision. He demonstrated that the colors of objects relate to their spectral reflectances. He also stated correctly that the rays of light are not themselves colored; rather they contain a disposition to elicit color percepts in an observer.

By studying the rings formed by juxtaposition of plates of plane and slightly curved glass, Newton also demonstrated the wave properties of light and pointed the way toward the measurement of wavelength. Johann Wolfgang von Goethe rejected Newton's analytical approach and objected to most of his conclusions. Such conflict between analytic and holistic approaches is still present today.

Thomas Young laid down the basic principles of trichromatic vision in 1801, although he had remarkably little to go on. He was not an especially vigorous promoter of these ideas, which were elaborated later by Hermann von Helmholtz, who made the first sketches of three overlapping curves of spectral sensitivity conceived to provide the initial physiological basis for color perception.

Opponent-color theory, which dealt with color appearance rather than color matching, had its origins with Ewald Hering; opponent-color and trichromatic theories competed for a long time. Coalescence of these theories started in the 1920s and has continued to the present time.

A set of standard color matching curves was adopted in 1931 by the CIE, along with a chromaticity diagram upon which to represent colors. Anatomical and physiological work had its beginnings in the nineteenth century and has advanced over the years as new techniques have been developed.

The chapter concludes with a brief discussion of chromatic context (the appearance of a color depends importantly upon its surroundings). Despite the importance of this topic, it will not be further developed in this book.

NOTES

[1] To obtain information concerning the early Greek concepts about color, I have relied mainly upon the following sources: Beare (1906), Boring (1942), Helmholtz (1924), Polyak (1957), and Ronchi (1970). The Greek philosophers and writers whose ideas

are summarized here lived at approximately the following times: Democritus, 460–370 B.C.; Plato, 427–347 B.C.; Aristotle, 384–322 B.C.; Epicurus, 342–270 B.C.; Galen, 130–200 A.D.

[2]This is part of a longer passage described by Ronchi (1970, page 27) as "controversial." Another translation is given by Hernnstein and Boring (1965, p. 90) as follows: ". . . models, similar in colour and shape, leave the objects and enter according to their respective size either into our sight or into our mind; moving along swiftly, and so by this means reproducing the image of a single continuous thing and preserving the corresponding sequence of qualities and movements from the original object as the result of their uniform contact with us, kept up by the vibration of the atoms deep in the interior surface of the concrete body." The need to rely on translation, wherever it occurs, inevitably raises added ambiguities in attempting to understand the original author's intent.

[3]See Chapter 4, especially Figure 4.1 on page 73, where current conceptions of these and other structures are considered.

[4]In the slim and generally rather neat *Golden Library of Knowledge* book on *Vision*, Rainwater (1962) puts it this way: "The image formed on the retina is upside down and is reversed from right to left. We are not aware of this inversion and reversal, as our brains are able to decode the information from the retina and keep our world from seeming topsy-turvy" (p. 10). Somewhat better (but not much), Lawson et al. (1975), in one of the standard introductory psychology texts, write: ". . . the lens of the human eye . . . produces an inverted retinal image so that if we were looking at a person he would be imaged on our retina with his head down and his feet up. . . . Inasmuch as we never see directly our retinal image and because the entire image is inverted, we see the world upright by ignoring the inversion information in the retinal image produced by the human lens" (p. 147). The point that is missed by Lawson et al. is simply that there is no "inversion information" to be ignored: this would be available to us only if we did "see directly" our retinal image. As they correctly state, we do not.

[5]This is known as Müller's "doctrine of specific nerve energies." Today we know that all nerve fibers are fundamentally alike. It is not "nerve energies" that are specific: rather, it is something very special, about which we still know very little, about the specific regions of the brain to which specific nerve fibers project and the type of chemical released at the termination of each fiber.

[6]In a letter to me, Dr. J. D. Mollon of the University of Cambridge has passed along the following information: "Prisms (long thin ones, with knobs on, such as Newton used) were probably sold widely at fairs, being intended to be hung up at windows or on chandeliers, to produce colours. I recall a letter from Newton to Oldenburg published in the *Philosophical Transactions* of the Royal Society for 1671 in which he speaks of buying a prism 'to try therewith the celebrated Phaenomena of Colours.' I hope that by the time you're next in Cambridge we'll have set up in the Science Museum the recombination experiment with two of the original prisms."

[7]A very nice review of the scientific side of Goethe's work is given by Magnus (1949).

[8]Very narrow spectral bands are needed to get white from two components; with bands as wide as Newton used, some inhomogeneity would be expected.

[9]A dark spot is always observed at the point of contact between a glass plate and the slightly curved surface of the glass that contacts it. This is evidence of phase reversal, since if such reversal did not occur in the wave reflected at the point of contact, the center spot would be light, not dark. In order to achieve the first dark ring concentric with the central dark spot, the separation must be increased so that the full distance

traversed by a wave, in the space between the curved and flat surface, is exactly one wavelength. Since this space is traversed twice, the physical distance must be exactly half a wavelength. For more detail about Newton's rings, see Strong (1958, p. 222).

[10] Quotation originally from Young (1802) as given by MacAdam (1970, p. 51). In 1777, George Palmer had published a book on *Theory of Colors and Vision* (London: Leacroft, 1777) in which his first "principle of vision," as given by MacAdam on page 41 of his book, is: "The surface of the retina is compounded of particles of three different kinds, analogous to the three rays of light; and each of these particles is moved by his own ray." Trichromatic theory in this form apparently accepts the doctrine that light rays exist in discrete classes, and misses the point so clearly elucidated by Young (and which had also been understood by Newton), according to which light exists in a continuum of frequencies and is responded to by sensitive elements having broad and overlapping tuning curves.

[11] Crombie (1958) has published a very readable short biography of Helmholtz.

[12] L. M. Hurvich and D. Jameson (1964) have done a noble service for visual science by translating Hering's *Theory of the Light Sense*, originally published in 1905, 1907, and 1911. This is also a good source of biographical material about Hering.

[13] The letters "CIE" stand for "Commission Internationale de l'Éclairage," which is the French version of "International Commission on Illumination."

2
Subjective Color Phenomena

THE COLORS OF OBJECTS

Among the properties with which objects seem to be endowed are included such things as shape, weight, and color. The shape and weight of an object clearly can be specified physically with rulers and balances; such specifications correlate with our judgments about the size of objects (whether visually or tactually obtained) or with their felt heaviness when the objects are lifted.

The appreciation of the color of an object differs from the discernment of its size, in that vision is the only sense through which color can be judged.[1] Whereas it is possible to judge the shapes of objects by our visual impressions of them, and to compare these with tactual experiences involving the same objects,[2] such associations in the case of color are manifestly impossible. There is no way that a person who has been blind from birth can have any appreciation of what is meant by the color of an object.

Is there, for color as for length, a physically measurable property of an object that is related to its perceived color? The answer is yes: this property is called the *reflectance* of the surface of the object. As Newton correctly observed, a spectral light can only be more or less reflected from a surface; otherwise it remains qualitatively unchanged. Thus, when white light[3] shines upon a surface, the various wavelengths of which it is comprised are reflected more or less equally. Such reflection, if it is not differential with wavelength, produces a surface that has a neutral appearance—black, gray, or white, depending upon the percentage of light that is nonselectively reflected. Differential reflection with wavelength, when it occurs, is usually correlated with the perception of hue. For example, if long wavelengths are reflected more than short ones, the surface will appear yellow, red, orange, or brown. These relationships will be discussed in much more detail in the following chapter. For now, it is helpful to know at least this much about the physical basis for the perception of an object's color.

We tend to take for granted that color is a property of the surface of an object. When we change the color of a surface by painting it, it is difficult to avoid the impression that the color which was originally in the paint can has now simply been applied to the surface. Moreover, we recognize that, should we scrape the surface of an object, its color may change, as when we scrape the yellow paint from a pencil, and see the more neutrally colored wood beneath. On the other hand, similar scraping of a red crayon will reveal that its color resides not only on its surface, but also within it. Thus we note that the inside of an object may have a color also, but one which is rendered manifest only by exposing it to light and to our vision. The color that we see apparently depends upon some property of the surface of objects, as these are exposed to light seen by reflection to our eyes.

If color is somehow on the object, being an inherent property of its surface, one would not expect it to change according to the conditions under which the object is viewed. To a first approximation, including many of the important conditions of ordinary viewing, this appears to be the case. For example, take a yellow banana initially seen under artificial light, and look at it outside in the bright sunlight.[4] Its color does not seem to change very much under these two drastically different conditions of viewing. When the perceived color of an object does not change, despite such changes in lighting or viewing conditions, the phenomenon is called *color constancy*. It is related to the more general fact that many different physical stimuli can give rise to the same or similar sensory impressions.

From the standpoint of evolution and survival, color constancy is obviously a very good thing, since only to the extent that color is in fact a stable property of the surface of an object may we discern this important property of that object. We can, for example, tell whether a banana is ripe or not, and do so whether we are indoors or outside. The physician may judge the pallor of a patient's skin. The secretary knows that the yellow copy is to be filed. The cartologist can designate whether areas of his maps are to be regarded as land or water. In the context provided by examples such as these, color does seem to be an important property of objects, in accord with a commonsense view that is hard to deny.

But there are serious problems with this view. If color is a property of a surface, how can we explain the following facts?

- Almost all colors disappear under low illumination (for example, under the light of the quarter moon).*

- For some observers (the so-called "color-blinds" discussed in Chapter 10) objects that appear very different in color for the normal observer may appear hopelessly alike.
- Objects that are seen as highly colored, and easily discriminable in daylight, lose their color when viewed under sodium vapor light, even at very high intensity.

> Take a magazine outside on a moonlit night; try to tell which of its illustrations are reproduced in color and which in black and white.

We will explain these facts later. For now, let us note that color is a latent property of a surface which may or may not become manifest. Suppose that I see a red book on my bookshelf. I cannot reasonably doubt that the book will still be there, as red as ever, if I leave the room. If I turn the lighting down to a very low level, its redness will disappear, though I still see the book. The typical observer under this condition will probably maintain that a red book is still there, in the same sense that he would also argue that the fine print on its cover, no longer visible in the dim light, is still present, continuing to form words and sentences as before. In referring to the *latent* content of what is on the book's surface, the observer will say that not only is the book itself still there, but that there is yet fine print on the cover, and moreover that the book is red. He could of course be wrong, but if the book is a familiar one, by turning on the lights he will confirm his expectancies.

We must be sympathetic with the commonsense viewpoint just described. Indeed, it is pointless to suppose that a book disappears when the room is made totally dark, or when an observer leaves the room: the book is presumed to have a physical existence that transcends the view of any particular observer. Similarly, it does somehow seem useful to suppose that, as the light level is lowered, the book is still red and the fine print on its cover, although no longer visible, is still there. What is needed, where color is concerned, is a physical description of those qualities of the surface of the book that are responsible for the appearance that it has for a normal observer under appropriate viewing conditions. These qualities could be supposed to survive even under conditions that abolish the sensation of color. The key to this, as previously noted, is *reflectance*. The way that reflectance supplies the physical basis for color vision will be discussed in the next chapter.

DIMENSIONS OF CHROMATIC EXPERIENCE

The nature of color experience depends to a very significant degree upon the mode of perception. Evans (1964), who has written extensively on this subject, distinguishes between what he calls a "light mode" and a "surface mode" of perception. This distinction corresponds closely to one that has long been in the literature, between the perception of "aperture color" and of "surface color" (sometimes also called "unrelated and related" colors). Surface color is the normal mode of color perception, where colors apparently belong to the surfaces of objects. Aperture color results whenever the color is presented in such a way as to make its localization impossible with respect to an object. One way to do this is with a "reduction screen,"[5] which permits a view of only a small element of a surface, eliminating all cues that could relate it to some portion of a real object.

As an example of the profound difference between what is seen in these two modes of perception, imagine a scene in which a chocolate bar is brightly lit by an obvious and visible spotlight, whereas there is a ripe orange in another part of the scene that is seen under more general and dimmer illumination. There is no doubt that the colors of the chocolate and the orange are very different indeed when they are seen as object colors, in the total context of the overall scene. Suppose now that a reduction screen is placed between the observer and the scene, with two small holes cut in it, so that by moving his eye the observer can first see (as an aperture color) only the chocolate, and then (also in aperture mode) the surface of the more dimly lit orange. It is quite possible for these two aperture colors to appear identical. A more exact test could be made by using a telescope having a very narrow field of view, and by arranging for it to pick up a semicircle of light from one or the other of the objects, depending upon how it is aimed. By adding an adjacent and variable comparison field (to form a full circle) it would be possible to match the color of the chocolate, and then to verify that the match held also with respect to the orange.

The use of a reduction screen or a telescope provides a percept that is highly correlated with the actual light distribution coming from the object being sampled. When a full scene is viewed, the context effects that arise are of two sorts. One effect, which is very complicated, results from the fact that real objects are seen, together with the various sources of illumination that are present. The other effect, somewhat simpler, has to do with the action of colors in the surrounding field; these effects can occur also in a completely abstract setting.

The aperture mode of perception is by far the simpler to deal with, and for this reason, the focus of this book will be upon it. The concept of the aperture mode of viewing can be enlarged, after Evans, to include not only a central circular spot—the primary stimulus—but also a uniform concentric surround (Fig. 2.1). As noted, the appearance of such a central spot will depend not only upon the physical characteristics of the light contained within it, but also to a surprising extent upon the characteristics of the light in the surrounding region. (The nature of the surround's influence is discussed in Chapter 7.) To allow good experimental control of such fields, they are produced with projectors or special optics; nevertheless, it is legitimate to consider them as aperture colors, devoid of reference to any particular object, because this is how they are seen.

To begin with the simplest of all possible cases, let us consider first the

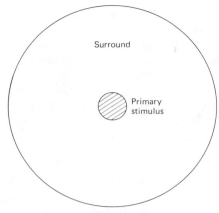

FIGURE 2.1 General appearance of the simplest stimulus configuration possible that permits the assessment of a surround field upon the appearance of an aperture color, called here the "primary stimulus." The appearance of the primary stimulus varies enormously, depending upon the color and intensity of the surround.

aperture mode of perception, in the special case of zero surround. What should be visualized here is a single, circular spot of light, having a rather etherial appearance, imprecisely localized in depth, seen in an otherwise completely dark environment. Although it requires a carefully contrived laboratory situation to produce a stimulus having such an appearance, a distant signal light, seen at night, is a common example that comes fairly close. Such a stimulus is perceived as self-luminous, probably because our experience teaches us that this is most probably the physical case. It should be noted, however, that a white piece of cardboard, carefully illuminated with a spotlight, could also produce the same appearance—provided that the light source were shielded from view, the light scattered from the illuminating beam were too weak to be directly visible, and any light escaping around the edges of the cardboard were absorbed in a suitably contrived light trap.*

> A related experiment is to project a small spot of light (using a slide projector) onto a dark screen, such as a piece of black cardboard. It helps to trace carefully around the outline of the projected spot with a black felt pen, particularly if the spot's edges are at all fuzzy. Try varying the intensity of the spot by filtering out some of the light by putting your fingers in front of the projector (very close to it). The spot can easily be seen as if it were a piece of white paper attached to the black cardboard, provided that it is not too bright; at brightness higher than an actual piece of white paper could reflect, it will appear self-luminous.
>
> This works especially well if the projector can be kept out of sight, and if observed by someone who has no idea of how the demonstration was set up. But even when you know what is happening, the sensory effects are quite compelling.

It is generally agreed that such a disembodied stimulus has a color that can be described as varying along three dimensions: *hue, brightness,* and *saturation*. The dimension of brightness is easiest to understand. At one extreme, the stimulus is just barely visible; at the other extreme it is dazzlingly bright and painful to regard; further increases in physical intensity will not necessarily make it appear brighter, and it may be dangerous to look at, as would be the case if the central portion of the sun were viewed through a reduction screen. There are many discriminable steps of brightness along the continuum between these two extremes; it is a continuum that correlates most highly with the physical intensity of the light.

Although hue is generally considered to be a single dimension of color experience, it is actually more complicated than that. For the aperture color with dark surround, combinations of four color names plus white are sufficient to describe the chromatic content of what is seen: the color names are red, yellow, green, blue, and white. All combinations are possible excepting those including red and green, or yellow and blue. For example, blue-greens are common experiences, and a given blend of blue-green can vary from a very pastel, or pale, hue (almost white) to one that is much more richly chromatic. But reddish greens and yellowish blues are never seen.

Because whiteness can coexist with any of the hues, and because white somehow does not seem to be a color in the same sense as are the other four, it is conventional to denote as *hue* the experiences of red, green, yellow, blue, and the permissible blends of pairs of these, and to introduce the term *saturation* to signify the relative white content of a stimulus perceived as having a particular hue. The dimensions of hue and saturation can be conveniently represented in a two-dimensional color diagram as shown in Figure 2.2 (p. 35). The circle represents each hue at high saturation.

Hue varies continuously around the circle, for example from red counterclockwise, through yellowish reds (oranges) to pure yellow; then through a gradation of yellowish greens until pure green is reached; next through a succession of progressively more bluish greens culminating in pure blue; and finally back to red through a range of reddish blues (purples). For any particular hue—for example pure blue—the white content can vary gradually from the very high saturation shown on the outer circle, to zero at the center. Hues of equal saturation, but less than that represented on the outer circle, would be represented upon concentric circles having smaller radii.

Such a diagram has no necessary referent whatever to the domain of physics. A color circle of this sort could be put together by giving observers a sample of colored papers, including those shown in Figure 2.2 and some intermediate steps, whose physical properties could be completely unknown. The instructions to the subjects might be merely: "Arrange these chips of colored paper in some reasonable and ordered way." Given enough time and patience, most people would order them according to the kind of diagram of Figure 2.2, although the orientation is arbitrary, and the counterclockwise ordering of colors described above could just as well be clockwise instead.

Dimensions of Chromatic Experience 31

Some additional remarks should be made about the concept of pure hue (sometimes called *psychologically unique* hue). The explanation of such a conception requires an appeal that is wholly to subjective experience. Most people agree, for example, that there is a "pure" yellow which has the following properties: (a) it cannot coexist with blue; (b) it is neither reddish nor greenish. (Most yellows are tinged with one or the other of these, though never both at the same time.) Similar arguments can be made for three other pure hues, and can be summarized as shown in Table 2.1.

In terms of the color diagram of Figure 2.2, these rules can have a geometrical representation. The hues that potentially can be present with any particular unique hue on the circle are those that are adjacent; those which cannot coexist are opposite. Color space, so represented, divides itself into four quadrants as shown in Figure 2.2. The first quadrant (upper right) consists of red-yellow mixtures of various saturations, containing a quarter of the total possible color experience. Within this quadrant, color changes are continuous, and qualitatively alike in that all colors are reddish, yellowish, and whitish, to varying degrees. At the border defined by unique yellow, which separates the first quadrant from the second, there is a qualitative change, since red on the right side of this border is replaced by green on the left, separated by a narrow band of unique yellow.*

> Look carefully at the other three quadrants of Figure 2.2, and work out analogous statements to describe the color sensations that are represented there. There are also four "balanced hues," one of which is orange (located midway between unique red and unique yellow). What color names can be used to describe the other three balanced hues?

A purely subjective, or psychological, diagram of this sort is not a satisfactory point at which to leave the description of color experience, but it is the best that we can hope to do without recourse to physical measurements. Such a representation does, nevertheless, seem to give an ordered account of color experience, and it is one that has proved useful to interior decorators and artists, as well as to color scientists.

Table 2.1 Rules for Pure Hues

Name of hue	Cannot coexist with	Also is devoid of hues shown, with which it can potentially coexist
red	green	yellow or blue
yellow	blue	green or red
green	red	blue or yellow
blue	yellow	red or green

Effects of Surrounds

We turn now to a consideration of what happens when a surround is introduced, as in Figure 2.1. If we confine our attention strictly to the central spot in the center, we will find that three surprises are introduced, and that each of these corresponds to a new dimension of subjective experience. Consider first the case of a white spot with a white surround. If the white surround is made brighter than the central test spot, the spot will darken in appearance. If the surround is made bright enough, the central spot will appear black. If the surround is then suddenly removed, it will once again be evident that there is light physically present in the central spot, and it appears white, not black. Without the surround, the central spot never appears black, even when reduced in intensity until it is nearly invisible.

As the central spot is progressively reduced in intensity, for a given intensity of the surround, a point will be reached where the spot appears as black as it can possibly appear, so that further reductions in the intensity of the spot will not make it appear any blacker. This is called the point of subjective black, and it depends upon the ratio of intensities of central spot and annular surround, as well as upon other factors, including the size of the spot.

For an intermediate level of the ratio of surround to spot intensity, the spot will be darkened, but not made black. Evans writes of this as the introduction of a "gray content." This terminology seems satisfactory, so long as we recognize that the gray content may become so strong as to yield black. The appearance of the central spot is so critically dependent upon the surround that it is sometimes difficult in the laboratory to tell whether the surround intensity has been increased or the spot intensity decreased, since either will result in a darker spot and—to a lesser extent—a brighter-appearing surround. But by using a reduction screen, the two possibilities can easily be distinguished.

Let us consider next the case where the surround is white, and the center spot is highly chromatic. Evans describes the appearance of such a chromatic field, as its intensity is varied relative to a fixed surround, as follows:

At some low value of luminance, relative to the surround, of the order of 1% or less, the color is seen as black. . . . For all colors, as this ratio is increased the appearance of the color passes through a predictable series. At first the blackness decreases, the hue appears at low saturation mixed with black or dark gray. As the ratio continues to increase, gray decreases and saturation increases, until a point is reached at which the gray has disappeared. This point is usually considerably below and in some cases very much below a luminance match with the surround. As luminance is still further raised, the color becomes flourent[6] and saturation continues to increase. The saturation and this fluorence continue to increase up to and slightly beyond a luminance match with the surround. Above this, brightness continues to increase but the fluorence disappears and saturation decreases. The color takes on the appearance of a light source (Evans & Swenholt, 1967, p. 1319).

A further complication in the case of dark colors is the introduction of at least one completely new experience of hue, namely brown, which is produced by surrounding a yellow or orange with a brighter annulus of white light. This helps us to understand how the chocolate bar and the orange, viewed through a reduction screen as previously described, could look alike. Brown, like black, is a sensation that seldom appears without a surround field.[7] Other dark colors, such as maroon, olive green, and navy blue, appear to be qualitatively more similar to their brighter counterparts than brown is to yellow and orange. The existence of the dark colors adds a great deal to the entire range of possible chromatic experiences, and greatly complicates their description.

Even more impressive and more complicated effects can occur when chromatic fields are used both in the test spot and the surround, or in more complicated ways in the visual array.

MISCELLANEOUS COLOR PHENOMENA

In this section, a variety of interesting phenomena having to do with color perception will be described. Some will be illustrated with color plates, but many will not; some are demonstrations that can be set up easily in the laboratory, or even at home; others require special materials or techniques that would make this difficult. All are chosen because they make some contribution to our appreciation of human color perception, but not all of the points that they make can be made clear in this chapter, since only after an exposure to some of the physical and physiological principles of color is this possible.

Effects of Lighting

Figure 2.3 (p. 36; from Evans, 1948, p. 55) shows a collection of marbles illuminated under two extremely different conditions. Looking at the top set, the experienced observer will recognize immediately that (a) the marbles are shiny, and (b) they are illuminated by a concentrated source of light—perhaps the sun or a flashbulb. Looking at the bottom set, he will not be so sure of what he sees. Although he may be looking at the same kinds of marbles seen in the top set, the possibility exists that the balls in the bottom set are diffuse—possibly made of cloth, painted with a very flat paint, or cut from Styrofoam. These possibilities would appear more likely if all of the balls were uniform in color, for example like the white one half-seen at the far left, which indeed appears as if it could be made from Styrofoam. The variegation of color on most of the other marbles, and some of the highlights that remain (despite the attempt at diffuse illumination) provide clues that the objects almost certainly are marbles seen under diffuse illumination, and not discs or Styrofoam balls painted to look as marbles do when seen under diffuse illumination. The latter illusion could be greatly enhanced by blackening in the shadow areas, making them look more like the ones in the top picture. Its appearance could be duplicated by taking a photograph of actual Styrofoam "marbles."

There is much less ambiguity about what is seen in the top picture. Although these objects could conceivably be Styrofoam balls with specks of white paint on them, placed just so (to imitate highlights), the dark and well-defined shadows—unless also faked—make this possibility unlikely. In the real-world situation, it is of course most unlikely that such a collection of objects would have upon them white specks located in just the positions where they would have to be, were they actually highlights.[8]

For most observers, the colors of the marbles in the top picture will appear somewhat more saturated than those in the bottom one. It would be very surprising to reach out to touch one of the marbles at the top, and not find it smooth and hard to the touch. One may not be quite so sure about the balls at the bottom, especially the white one at the left. It could be soft and squashy, or at least quite roughly textured.

The highlights seen in the collection of marbles at the top are, of course, images of the source of illumination, seen by reflection from the convex surface of the marbles. In one case, the bluish marble at the far left, a very poor image of the source is also formed underneath the marble, providing information that this object is at least partially transparent. The hard surface of a marble, as we shall see in Chapter 3, reveals its hardness by means of the mirrorlike (specular) reflection from its surface, and its color by diffuse reflection of light from the layers just underneath. The specular reflection does not alter the distribution of wavelengths in the reflected light, relative to those that are incident. Thus one can actually gauge the color of the source from these highlights; therefore it is by no means necessary to look directly at the source of illumination in a scene to know what its color is. This is undoubtedly an aid to color constancy, and one which would be lost under diffuse illumination, or if all surfaces reflected only in a diffuse manner. Most illumination is a mixture of concentrated and diffuse: this is what we get on a sunny day, from the combination of direct sunlight and skylight. This is also what the professional photographer often chooses to use for best form and color rendition. Many surfaces also reveal a mixture of specular and diffuse reflectance.

The marbles of Figure 2.3 may also be used to illustrate again some of the effects of using a reduction screen, associated with the differences between aperture and object color. A reduction screen that permitted the viewing of only the highlight from one of the marbles at the top would, of course, obscure all information about the color of the marble.

Physical Analysis of Complex Scenes: Color Television

Starting with Chapter 3, we will be concerned with the physical specification of the stimulus for color perception. A major purpose of this book will be to explain our perceptions of colored objects as these relate to an objective description of these objects, one that can be given through the use of physical measuring instruments (see Chapter 3). Because they are simpler, laboratory

Miscellaneous Color Phenomena   35

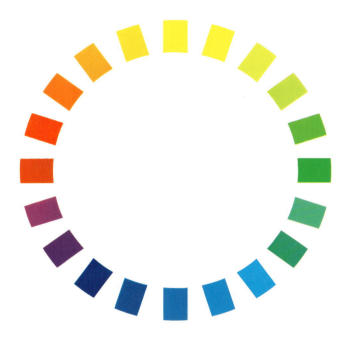

FIGURE 2.2 This illustration depicts the arrangement of saturated colors around a closed circle, where the psychologically unique hues are represented at the cardinal points as shown. Other colors, not shown, would be located inside the circle, showing progressively greater desaturation of each until white is reached at the center.

situations involving stimuli such as discs, annuli, and split fields will be greatly stressed. But the real world is much more complicated, as, for example, in the case of the marbles just discussed.

Is there any hope of achieving a purely physical description of such a complex scene? The answer is yes, and the trick is to break the scene up into a large number of elements, each of which is homogeneous and therefore amenable to a simple physical description. This is exactly what lies behind the illusions created by color television. A color TV screen consists of about a million phosphor dots of three types. When irradiated from behind by an electron beam, one type glows red, another glows green, and a third type glows blue. (There are no dots that are white, or of any other color.) In a physical sense, the color TV image is nothing more (or less) than this collection of glowing dots, each of which can vary in brightness, but not in hue.*

36   Subjective Color Phenomena

FIGURE 2.3   The marbles at the top were illuminated by a concentrated light source; those at the bottom, by diffuse and uniform lighting. (After Evans, 1948).

> With the aid of a magnifying glass, carefully examine these elements. Note the spatial arrangement of the three phosphor types, and the absence of any white or yellow dots.

In a static scene, the illusion of color TV depends upon the limited ability of the retina of the eye to resolve spatial detail. The impression of continuous temporal flow in a changing scene depends upon the limited ability of the visual system to keep track of time. (These matters will be dealt with systematically in Chapter 9.) Where color vision is concerned, special interest attaches to the fact that these elements need be of only three different colors, rather than continuously variable as in the actual scene. A larger point to be gleaned in the present

Miscellaneous Color Phenomena 37

FIGURE 2.4 The four urns depicted here are all printed with ink exactly the same color, and will yield the same color sensation if a reduction screen is used. The striking differences in color among the four urns are due entirely to the surrounds against which they are depicted. (After Evans, 1948.)

discussion is this: to the extent that color TV can simulate impressions that would be received by looking directly at the scene the camera sees, then to this extent one can legitimately consider the visual scene to be comprised of a very large number of homogeneous elements.

Each of us who has seen TV can judge this for himself. A major concern of artists is to understand the extent to which such simulation works, and to learn the tricks that are needed to compensate for the fact that viewing a painting or a motion picture or a TV tube cannot exactly simulate the experience of viewing the scene being reproduced. But even if we had never seen television, we could conclude a great deal from watching the behavior of others. That people will sit transfixed for hours, watching a million dots of three colors whose individual intensities are changing, reveals at once that something much more interesting than a mere collection of dots is represented there.

Successive Contrast and Afterimages

In his Ives Medal address to the Optical Society of America in 1958, Deane B. Judd demonstrated that the color one sees may depend upon colors, no longer in the scene, to which the eye has previously been exposed. A section of the written summary of his talk is reproduced below. (In this quotation, the phrase "orchid plaque" is used to describe a patch of light on the screen, probably circular in shape, having an "orchid" [light purple] hue.)

... a slide was projected that consisted of red, yellow, green, and blue quadrants. The members of the audience were requested to fixate the center of the slide for about

38   Subjective Color Phenomena

FIGURE 2.5   Evans caption reads: "As there is no overlapping of inked areas in these designs, they consist only of three colors in addition to the white of the paper: a red, a blue, and black. The visual appearance of any area of red or blue, however, depends in part on the colors of the adjacent areas. The blues surrounded by black appear darker and more saturated than those surrounded by white, and different in hue from those surrounded by red. The shifts in brightness are opposite to those that would be predicted on the basis of contrast effects. This phenomenon is called the 'spreading effect.'" (The opposite of contrast is also known as "assimilation.") (After Evans, 1948.)

15 sec, then the slide was removed, and after a second or two there appeared (apparently to each member of the audience) the after-image complimentary of the four hues: that is, by means of the retinal areas previously exposed to the red quadrant, the white screen appeared blue-green, similarly, other segments of the white screen appeared purplish

blue, red-purple, and orange. This is the classic demonstration of successive contrast, or the projection of a negative after-image onto a white surface. This after-image requires fixation for several seconds for its appearance. It moves with the eye, and has no object character.

To show that there is an instantaneous type of adjustment in chromatic sensitivity of the visual mechanism, an orchid plaque was shown against a gray background under which conditions the color perception was that of a light purplish red of moderate saturation. Then it was presented against a brilliant magenta background. The color perception was then reported by many in the audience as gray. It was noted that the transition from orchid to gray took place without perceptible time delay, and that the color was stable. Furthermore, the color was perceived as belonging to the plaque in the same sense that the light purplish red color of moderate saturation was perceived to belong to it when viewed against a gray background (Judd, 1959, p. 326).

Simultaneous Color Contrast

Figure 2.4 shows examples of the effect of surroundings upon the apparent color of an object. The four urns illustrated in Figure 2.4 (from Evans, 1948, facing p. 178) are all printed with exactly the same ink. Note the changes in both lightness and hue which are caused by the simultaneous presence of differing backgrounds. And finally, in Figure 2.5 (Evans, 1948, facing p. 192) is an excellent illustration of the von Bezold "spreading effect."

Perceived Nonuniformity from Surrounds

Figure 2.6 shows a series of steps, each of which, incredibly, is physically uniform within the boundaries that delimit it. To prove this, cover all but one of these areas with opaque pieces of paper or cardboard. As soon as the paper is removed, allowing more than one step to be seen, the scalloped effect appears. The more steps that are seen at once, the more compelling is the effect. In this example, it is the lightness of each patch that varies from one side to the other; each appears lighter at the left, contrasting with the darker panel to the left, and brighter at the right, contrasting with the lighter panel to the right.

Effect of Intensity

The perception of the color of objects depends importantly upon the amount

FIGURE 2.6 Each sector of this step-tablet is of uniform intensity, as can be confirmed by masking the adjacent sectors. The extreme nonuniformity of brightness is related to the influence of adjacent areas that are either lighter or darker than the one being examined. Lateral inhibitory mechanisms in the retina and brain are believed to be responsible. (From the Kodak gray scale, © Eastman Kodak Company, 1977.)

Here is a demonstration that can easily be done at home. A variable intensity of light source, such as a dimmer, is helpful, but it can be done anyway by turning lights off and on, and shielding them in various ways. The demonstration will be described as if done with tungsten light, varied in intensity by means of an inexpensive dimmer. Use it to operate a 15W bulb, and place it, exposed, somewhere in the corner of an ordinary room filled with ordinary objects. The entire room should be without windows, or have heavy enough drapes to exclude the evening light. A bookcase filled with books is particularly suitable. Have available some magazine illustrations, some printed in color, some in black and white, and spread them around on the floor—or better, have someone else do this for you. Set the dimmer at a very low setting, so that the lamp itself can barely be seen, and enter the room, having first exposed yourself to a high level of interior illumination in an adjoining room.

At first, nothing will be seen. Then, gradually, the outlines of the contours that are longest and of highest contrast—such as the edge between a white doorframe and an adjoining dark wall—will be seen. Gradually, smaller objects will become visible, including the books in the bookcase. However, if the conditions are set properly, none of the books on the shelf will have any color, although they will vary in lightness, which will permit them to be discriminated. Introspection will reveal that visual sensations under this condition are totally achromatic—black, white, and gray—possibly tinged with a bit of bluishness. It is impossible to tell which of the illustrations spread on the floor are printed in color. Now, as the intensity of the light source is slowly increased, all objects in the room will be seen more clearly. The first hue to be perceived will be red—not very strong or distinct, but definitely present. Red areas of the colored illustrations on the floor will appear dull-reddish, and a basis for discrimination between the two types of reproduction will be evident.

As the intensity of the lamp is increased further, more and more hues will be seen. The distinction between the illustrations on the floor will become obvious and, at the highest level, chromatic perception will become more or less normal. But a single 15W bulb in the corner of a room is not really sufficient to mediate good color perception, which can be easily demonstrated by switching on all the regular lights in the room.

One of the important phenomena to be observed as the level of illumination is increased is the reversal of brightness relations that takes place between some adjoining objects. Specifically, if a red and a blue book are located side by side on the shelf, the blue one will look much lighter than the red one (which will probably appear black) at the lowest level of illumination, although neither will have any hue. So long as hue is not present, this relation will remain. When the level of illumination is reached that first permits the perception of red to be associated with the red book, its lightness will begin to increase relative to the blue one. At some higher level, they will appear equally light and of different color, and at the highest levels, there will be no doubt (if the books are properly chosen) that the red book now appears brighter than the blue one. Why are brightness relations affected in this way by changing the light level? And why does color vision fail totally at very low levels of illumination? It turns out that both these phenomena have their origin in a remarkable peculiarity of the eye, which will be considered in Chapter 5.

of light that is available to illuminate them. The exercise on the opposite page is designed to illustrate some of the perceived changes in color that occur as a function of intensity.

SUMMARY

A variety of subjective color phenomena has been described, and some simple experiments have been discussed that are easily done without specialized equipment and can be used to illustrate some of these phenomena. Such observations should provide convincing evidence that color vision is a very complex phenomenon, and that the color of an object depends not only on the nature of the paint on its surface, but also on the color of the light used to illuminate it, the intensity of that light, and the chromatic characteristics of other surfaces located nearby. There are many more demonstrations that could be provided, but the ones recommended in this chapter should be sufficient to prove the complexity of color perception and to develop an increased awareness of one's sensations, where color is concerned. But an eternity of such demonstrations would not suffice to explain the mechanisms within the eye and brain that are responsible for what is perceived. For this, it is necessary to study the physics and physiology of the subject. This study will begin in Chapter 3.

NOTES

[1] We will return to this point again in the next chapter. See especially footnote 2 on page 69.

[2] The seemingly reasonable idea that visual perception depends for its development upon tactual experience seems, by and large, to be a false one. When the two senses are put into conflict, vision nearly always predominates. As Gregory and Wallace (1963) have pointed out, one cannot draw any safe conclusions about normal visual development based upon the kinds of difficulties that are experienced when pattern vision, lacking from birth because of defects in the optical system of the eye, is through surgery rendered possible for the first time in adulthood. In a recent textbook, Rock (1975) summarizes a great deal of evidence to show the primacy of visual over tactual perception.

[3] As Newton first noted, the light itself is not colored. The use of color names to describe light is therefore technically incorrect. Such usage will nevertheless be permitted in this book, but Newton's caveat, "the rays are not coloured," should be kept in mind.

[4] Artificial light (for example, tungsten incandescent) and daylight are physically quite different. As a result, the light reaching the eye, after being reflected from the banana, contains a very different physical mixture of wavelengths, depending upon whether it is viewed under daylight or artificial incandescent illumination.

[5] The use of the term "reduction screen" is due to Katz (1935), who spoke of "surface color" and "film color." See also the exercise on page 2.

[6] Evans uses the term "fluorent" to describe an appearance similar or identical to that experienced when viewing fluorescent (Chapter 3, p. 70) surfaces. The color appears

to glow and has an exceptionally vivid appearance. Along with the gray content induced by bright surround fields, the appearance of "fluorence" adds a second new dimension to the test spot when it is seen within a surround.

[7] Hochberg (personal communication) has called attention to the fact that sensations of brown can sometimes arise by successive as well as by simultaneous contrast. See Bartleson (1976) for an interesting article entitled "Brown."

[8] This, of course, is precisely what artists do in order to represent highlights and thus create the illusion of a shiny, hard surface with the use of their diffusely reflecting paints.

3
Physical Concepts

NEED FOR A PHYSICAL DEFINITION OF THE STIMULUS

Through the use of our various senses, as these interact in the process of perception, we infer that there is a world outside our own bodies, one that is filled with objects that seem to have a physical reality. But there are major differences between the world as most of us perceive it, and the world of a physical scientist as he conceives of it—at least during a substantial part of his working hours. Most of us see desks, tables, people, animals, automobiles, and so forth—objects seemingly arranged in meaningful ways in an external world. The physical scientist, in addition, "sees" molecules, photons, subatomic particles, fields of magnetic flux, and so forth. Most of these physical entities are difficult to visualize, and can be seen only in the same cognitive sense that a blind man might say "Yes, I see what you mean."

For most of us, such physical concepts are almost impossible to understand unless we at least make *some* attempt at visualization. We learn to diagram an atom as having a spherical nucleus surrounded by little whirling balls, although we are cautioned (if we are well taught) that this is only a model—nothing more than a metaphorical visual crutch, crudely representative of mathematical relations that provide a more accurate and truthful description.

Part of the need for the concepts of physics is related to a person's limited ability to perceive directly that which is very large or very small. From a single vantage point, using unaided sensory equipment, we can see very little of the world about us, and can know almost nothing about the nature of the universe. The astronomical notion of the earth as merely a small planet in one solar system, revolving about a single star among billions, separated from one another by unimaginable distances, is not something that occurred to primitive man or that we can plausibly ascribe to the perception of monkeys. The development of the telescope (once the initial suspicions about it were overcome) increased man's ability to observe far distant objects and proved very helpful in the development of these new concepts. But even less direct, less "visual" observations, such as the inferences that are made from the data of stellar spectroscopy, were needed. Sophisticated inferences about the interrelations among stellar bodies, derived from very careful measurement of their behavior as a function of time, were also required.

Looking in the other direction, it has long been clear that objects exist that are much too small to be seen with the naked eye. Some of these can be brought up to visual dimensions with the use of a microscope. Diffraction sets a limit to the performance of a light microscope, and the electron microscope can take us down only a few orders of magnitude further. There is nothing about the overwhelming amount of detail still visible at the level of electron microscopy to suggest that, if the process could be extended again by several orders, there would be any less detail to observe.

It is perhaps not easy to accept the idea that the kind of reality yielded by our direct perception is of such a limited and special kind, but it will be very helpful for our understanding of color perception if we can force ourselves to do so. Considered within the framework provided by the theory of evolution, it is perhaps not particularly difficult to understand why we should be so limited and yet at the same time so gifted. Our perceptual abilities have presumably evolved, along with our other capacities, according to what is important in the external environment from the standpoint of adaptation and survival. If, say, static fields of magnetic flux carried significant information for us, we probably would have evolved magnetoreceptors. That we have not done so may be taken as evidence that there are other forms of physical disturbances available in the sea of energy within which we live that are more significant for our survival: we have developed specialized receptive equipment that is specifically tuned to what is most important.[1]

Survival on earth is not dependent upon an accurate perception of the universe or, until very recently, even upon what is happening on the other side of the mountain. We usually survive without being able to see microorganisms, although occasionally they are lethal. It must be emphasized that those perceptual powers that we do possess, utilizing our unaided sensory capacities, are impressive indeed. We may suppose that, if we could see the microscopic world, or react directly to static magnetic fields (as some birds apparently do), the capacity to do so would only have evolved at the expense of the significant and presumably more important perceptual powers that we possess instead.

Although we cannot directly perceive the world in a way that accords with its description in physical terms, there is no reason to deny the physical existence of ordinary objects, such as a blue book I now see upon my desk. I can, after all, confirm its existence in many ways: by feeling it, by lifting it to discern its heaviness, by blowing on its surface in order to sense the reflected wind, by slapping it hard so as to hear the sound that this makes and to feel a sting in my fingers. I can hold the book to the light and note that it is impossible to see through it. I can try to bend it in order to gain an impression of its physical resistance. All of these events interact to confirm my perception, initially based upon the remarkable act of vision at a distance, that there is indeed a book lying on my desk. Only a fool (or a philosopher) could deny it. Yet of all the properties that the book seems to possess, its color is something special because I am unable to confirm it by any of these other operations: only my eyes can tell me that the book is blue.[2]

As I pointed out in the first chapter, it is obvious that we are not in direct contact with such remote objects, whose forms we can recognize and whose colors we can identify. We seek in this book to deal with current conceptions of how such visual perception is possible. We have seen that prescientfic efforts to gain such understanding led to concepts that were necessarily very speculative and usually untrue. It is evident that we are not in contact with the visual object that is perceived. Rather, light—reflected from the object—enters our eyes, stimulates our retinas, indirectly activates our brains. Somehow, from this activity, we gain an appreciation of the presence of the object, and of its color.

It is tempting to fall into a trap, as the Greek philosophers did (and much more recently some of the Gestalt psychologists) of defining the object that is perceived as constituting a "stimulus for vision." To say that I perceive a pen lying on my desk because the "pen" stimulates my eyes is not to solve the problem of perception, but merely to state that perception occurs. What we require instead is a description of the object that is, to the highest degree possible, independent of how the object looks to us. Anything less inevitably begs the question.

The abstract world of physical science represents a system that is already available to describe the universe in this very special way. As already noted, physical descriptions may be characterized by saying that, to the highest degree possible, they account for nature in a manner that is independent of the limitations of man's unaided sensory processes.

It has frequently been pointed out (for example, by Pratt, 1948), as if doing so somehow destroyed this special status of physics, that sensory perception is also necessary in order for the physical scientist to go about his business. There is no denying that scientists of all kinds require sensory perception, but the argument that this fact somehow destroys the special status of physics as a scheme for objective descriptions of the world is a specious one. To understand why, we must consider the nature of the sensory discriminations that physical scientists make. Typically these are of the most elementary sort, like the discrimination of the portion of a scale at which a pointer is aimed. In principle (and with increasing frequency also in practice) such discriminations can be replaced by nonhuman machinery. A digital voltmeter can replace the pointer, and finally the output of the meter can be delivered directly to a computer. Where this is not yet possible, as for example in the interpretation of complex features of an electron micrograph, the interpretations gleaned therefrom are partly science, but they are also partly art. Human ingenuity and intelligence of a high order are always required to set up an experiment and to interpret it. Yet to the highest degree possible, the data themselves should prove capable of being handled automatically, without the need for human perception to intervene.

Ideally, physical descriptions are free of the raw power of man's sensory processes. This power is so important in everyday life, and is so vital to certain fields of endeavor, such as art and literature, that it may be difficult to accept the view that, for the clear understanding of this power itself, a different (and more difficult) description of the stimulus is required. The physical environment so conceived has a nature and presence that does not depend upon whether anyone is around to perceive it. The tree falling in the forest produces a physical sound whether or not anyone is there to hear it. And a description of the pen on my desk should be possible using concepts which do not presume that the pen necessarily will be perceived by anyone, but which *do* assume that it has a physical existence that can be given an independent description.

LIGHT

In 1792, the *Encyclopaedia Britannica* stated[3] that: "It is obvious . . . that whatever side we take concerning the nature of light, many, indeed, almost all the circumstances concerning it, are incomprehensible, and beyond the reach of human understanding."

One hundred and seventy-six years later, writing in the September 1968 special edition of *Scientific American* on "Light," Gerald Feinberg wrote:[4] "At present the photon theory gives us an accurate description of all we know about light. The notion that light is fundamentally just another kind of matter is likely to persist in any future theory. That idea is the distinctive contribution of 20th-century physicists to the understanding of light, and it is one of which we can well be proud."

The quotations just sampled provide us with a starting point for our discussion of light, the stimulus for color vision. We see from them that an earlier view that light could never be understood has given way to a modern conceptualization according to which particles of light, called *photons,* can be regarded as "just another kind of matter." This modern view immediately removes some of the mystery from the act of vision by making manifest the connection between the object being perceived, and our eyes.

When a photon is emitted from a source it moves instantly at the speed of light (about 3×10^8 m·s^{-1}) in a direction that is more or less randomly determined. Light differs from most other particles of matter by having a *zero rest mass*: despite this, photons are never at rest, and in their actual state of motion they possess energy and momentum. It is thus to be expected that a beam of light should be capable of exerting pressure upon a physical object, and it is reassuring to find that this actually happens.[5] But the momentum possessed by photons is exceedingly small, despite their velocity (which is the highest known in nature). For most purposes, including vision, the pressure that light exerts is negligible and has nothing to do with the extent of its stimulating capacity.

During the lifetime of a photon, the energy that it possesses is maintained at an exact value, and to a first approximation it moves in a straight line. In a vacuum, it would continue to do so forever. As discussed below, other fates are possible for photons that move within environments containing other particles of matter with which photons may interact. Photons that emerged from distant stars, hundreds or even millions of years ago, reach our eyes unchanged. It is conceptually important, and even a bit awe-inspiring, to realize that an ancient particle of light is in no sense "tired" and loses none of its energy or capacity to stimulate the eye during its long journey to earth. What is seen in such a case is an event that occurred many years ago. This is a significant problem in astronomy, but not for visual science: even for the longest terrestrial distances over which vision is possible, the speed of light is, for all practical purposes, infinite. For example, optical contact with a mountain located 50 miles distant is established in 0.00027 s. We will see in Chapter 9 that the physiological latencies involved in visual information processing are orders of magnitude greater than this, meaning that even if light did travel with infinite velocity—as the ancients believed—there would be very few situations where one could tell the difference.

Because photons often move in straight lines, inferences can be made about the place of origin of a photon, provided that some kind of machinery exists which can be used to gauge the direction of photon incidence. We have already seen something of how the eye does this, by mapping all photons that originate from a given point in space upon a restricted region of the retina. The flight path of a photon corresponds to what is called, in geometric optics, a *ray*. One photon is sufficient to describe the path of a ray, though a ray could be defined by billions of photons, each following the same path.

A typical environment containing a source of illumination is packed solid with such photon paths, or rays. Given a reasonable sampling time, an arbitrary point in such an environment would have rays passing through it in all possible directions. If the numbers of photons per unit time defining these rays were all equal, there would obviously be no basis for pattern vision: such a situation exists in a perfect *Ganzfeld* and is approximated in an arctic whiteout, or in the center of an integrating sphere.[6] In the real world, sources of light are nonuniformly distributed, and their output varies with direction; also, surfaces vary in their reflectivity. Consequently, if one were able to sample a given point in the environment, he would find that the rate of photon flow in certain directions would exceed that in others. At each location in the environment where an eye might be, the proximal basis for visual perception lies in the distribution and directionality of the photon flow that enters the pupil of an eye located there.[7] And the color of the object, as we shall now see, is related to the distribution of wavelengths of these photons.

The idea that the wavelength of light can be associated with the behavior of an individual photon has developed relatively recently. One might suppose that the wave properties of light apply instead to collections of photons, in much the same way that the waves in water do: the latter are in no sense attributable to individual water molecules moving along the waves. But the analogy is not a good one. Individual water molecules bob up and down but do not move laterally as a wave sweeps across the water. On the contrary, individual photons travel very fast and their wave properties are intrinsic to each particle. As they travel, they vibrate in a plane perpendicular to their primary path.[8]

If a particle vibrates with a frequency f in a plane perpendicular to its direction of travel, and is moving at the speed of light c, then some distance λ will be traversed during the time required for the particle to vibrate through one cycle. Thus *wavelength* is inversely proportional to the frequency of vibration: $\lambda = c/f$ (Fig. 3.1).

An experiment proving that the wavelength of light must be associated with individual photons, rather than a collection of them, goes as follows: Imagine a collection of photons, all of the same wavelength, vibrating in phase, and moving parallel to one another (a collimated beam of coherent, monochromatic

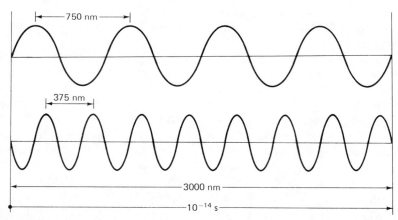

FIGURE 3.1 Relations between wavelength and frequency of vibration. In 10^{-14} s, light will travel about 3,000 nm. Extreme violet light (375 nm) vibrates through 8 cycles during this time, so the distance λ that it travels during one cycle is $3,000/8 = 375$ nm. Extreme red light vibrates more slowly, covering 4 cycles during this time; the distance that it travels per cycle is $3000/4 = 750$ nm. The distance that light travels during one cycle of vibration defines its wavelength.

Light   49

light). Assume that these are incident upon a pair of very narrow slits (Fig. 3.2). The distribution of light that results was first shown by Thomas Young. It results from considering that the two slits act as sources that emit photons vibrating in phase; as they move outward a variety of phase relations occurs, depending upon the distances of various points in space relative to the two slits. Along the plane that is shown in Figure 3.2, bright areas are seen where the light is in phase (called constructive interference) and dark areas are seen where the light is out of phase (destructive interference). This result would be predicted if the wave properties of light applied to aggregates of photons, and it seems most reasonable to suppose that the interference patterns reveal interactions between different photons—some passing through one slit, and some through the other. But this is wrong.

In 1967, Pfleegor and Mandel reported doing this kind of experiment under conditions where the rate of photon arrival at the receiving plane was so slow that no two photons could possibly interact.[9] Very sensitive detectors were used to register where each photon arrived at the plane behind the slits. Over a very long period of time, the distribution of photon incidence that built up was the same as that obtained under the more usual high-intensity conditions where interactions between photons seemed possible. The implication, as Dirac had earlier expressed it,[10] is clear: "Each photon then interferes only with itself." Dirac went on to say that "Interference between two different photons never occurs." Although Pfleegor and Mandel's experiment fails to prove the second statement, their result is consistent with it.

A bothersome aspect of Pfleegor and Mandel's result is that individual photons must somehow pass through both slits! It is conceived that photons are not

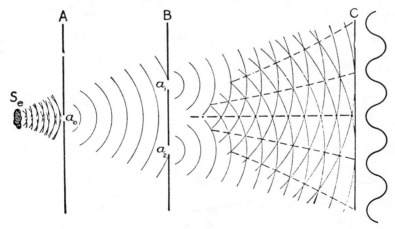

FIGURE 3.2   Interference produced by coherent light passing through a pair of slits. Where light is vibrating in phase, amplitude is doubled (dashed lines); amplitude is less everywhere else and is zero in the center of regions flanked by dashed lines. A receiving screen at C results in an amplitude distribution as shown at the far right. (After Ditchburn, 1976, p. 105.)

precisely localized in space (sometimes called the "fuzzy ball picture" of the photon). Even so, it is almost impossible to visualize how a single photon, supposedly a quantum affair, can divide itself, pass discretely through two slits, and then interact with itself on the other side. This is a classic case of where intuition and efforts to visualize fail. Nevertheless, one cannot reject physical concepts merely because they seem to violate common sense.

As a consequence of the foregoing, optical phenomena can legitimately be treated in terms of probability statements that pertain to single photons. The concept of light intensity therefore relates to the numbers of photons involved, there being no interaction between them. (Actually there is a very small interaction of light with light, but like the pressure of light, it is too small to be of any practical importance.) For our purposes we may safely assume that beams of light do not interact with one another because their components (photons) do not. Among other things, this idea rules out any possibility that the mixture of colors is something that occurs in light itself.

The wavelengths of photons to which the eye is sensitive are in the range of about 380 to 750 nm. Although the perception of hue cannot be reliably mediated by a single photon, the use of large enough numbers of them (high intensities) under otherwise appropriate conditions leads to a reliable correspondence between wavelength and hue. The shortest perceptible wavelengths appear violet, or reddish blue. As wavelength is increased, the reddish component diminishes and disappears at about 470 nm, at a point called *psychologically unique blue*. (Recall, from Chapter 2, that this is a blue that is neither reddish nor greenish.) As wavelength is further increased, the blue becomes progressively more greenish; a balanced blue-green is achieved around 490 nm and then the green component predominates and unique green is reached in the range of about 500 to 515 nm.

The longest wavelengths of the spectrum appear to be nearly a pure red. Shortening of wavelength here introduces a yellowish component; a balanced red-yellow (orange) is seen at about 600 nm. Further shortening of wavelength causes the red component to diminish until psychologically unique yellow is reached at about 575 nm. The range between about 515 and 575 nm consists of yellow-green blends, balanced at about 550 nm.*

SOURCES OF LIGHT

No creature—not even a cat—can see in the dark. All visual perception demands that a source of illumination be present to irradiate the objects that are seen. Sunlight, which has presumably always been available to guide the evolution of eyes, is still very important. The light of the sun begins as gamma radiation comprised of wavelengths at least a million times too short to see. This radiation is spread out into longer wavelengths "by absorption and re-emission processes throughout the sun's bulk (Henderson, 1970, p. 15)." The distribution of wavelengths in sunlight is further altered following interaction with the

Sources of Light   51

> Refer to the color diagram of Figure 2.2. Using the information provided here in Chapter 3, indicate around the color circle the wavelengths that correspond to the psychologically unique hues and the balanced blends. Note that there is no wavelength corresponding to the balanced sensation of reddish blue.

earth's atmosphere. Figure 3.3 shows how extraterrestrial sunlight has its spectrum altered by absorption and scatter. By the time sunlight reaches the earth, all wavelengths are still richly represented throughout the visible spectrum.

The production of artificial light originally required that something be burned in open air. The flame of a candle is an example of such a source. Its spectral output is very deficient, relative to that of daylight, in the shorter wavelengths of the visible spectrum. In general, the same is true for incandescent lamps (ordinary light bulbs) in which a controlled combustion of an electrically heated filament occurs within a gas-filled enclosure designed to preserve the life of the filament. When operated at very low temperatures, no visible radiation is produced by such a lamp. As the applied voltage is increased, causing an increase in the flow of current through the filament, its temperature is raised and the

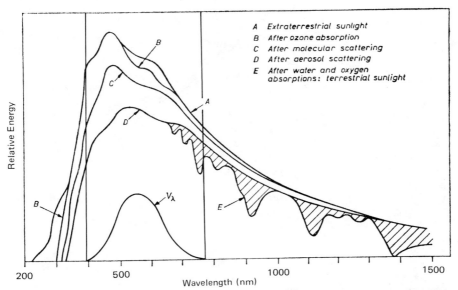

FIGURE 3.3   The topmost curve (**A**) shows the spectral disbribution of sunlight as it enters the earth's atmosphere. The other curves show how the amount of light is reduced, and its spectral distribution altered, by additional factors as shown. The relative spectral sensitivity of the eye, under conditions where color vision prevails, is given as V_λ at the bottom. This shows that the eye is sensitive to a region of the spectrum where the radiation reaching the earth from the sun is most plentiful. (After Henderson, 1977, Fig. 1, p. 48.)

52   Physical Concepts

spectral distribution of the emitted light changes in the manner depicted in Figure 3.4. Associated with increased voltage is a change in the apparent color of the filament, or of a white object illuminated by it, that varies from dull to bright red and then through orange to yellowish white and finally to a definitely bluish white. The deficiency in the shorter wavelengths is eliminated at the highest temperatures, but at the cost of a drastic shortening of the life of ordinary light bulbs. The quartz-iodide lamp, now used in many slide projectors (and

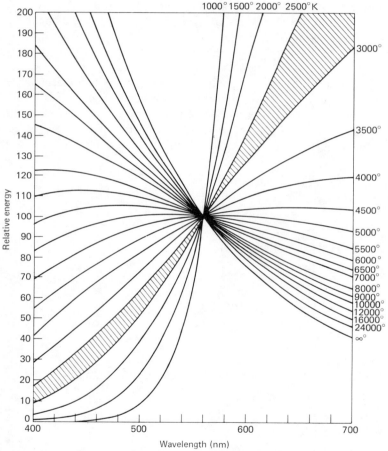

FIGURE 3.4   Spectral distribution of light emitted from a "complete radiator" (which tungsten closely approximates) as a function of temperature. These curves are normalized at 560 nm and therefore do not show that the absolute amount of energy emitted grows, at all wavelengths, as temperature is increased. Ordinary tungsten lamps operate in the range (shaded) from 2,500° to 3,000°. Over this small range, the efficiency of such lamps increases from about 8 to about 22 lumens per watt. (From **The Science of Color**, 1953, p. 261.)

laboratories), solves this problem by causing much of the tungsten that leaves the filament to redeposit itself upon the filament, rather than upon the inside wall of the lamp enclosure. Such lamps are, however, much too expensive to use for ordinary illumination.

Good "color rendition" depends upon a continuous spectrum like that provided by sunlight or incandescent lamps. The latter generate large amounts of infrared radiation, resulting in more heat than light. This limits the efficiency that can be provided by this kind of artificial light, as measured in "lumens per watt." The lumen is a measure of the amount of visually effective light, and is directly proportional to the troland unit (to be defined shortly). The watt, a unit of physical power, refers in this case to that supplied as input to the lamp, which is of course what the consumer pays for. It is not surprising that, when fluorescent lights (which are much more efficient) were developed in the 1930s, they almost immediately started to become popular for commercial lighting, and are now widely used for this purpose.

A fluorescent lamp contains a mercury vapor. When energized electrically, its atoms emit ultraviolet radiation that itself is invisible. The manner in which this radiation is converted into visible light is explained by LeGrand as follows:

> ... the inside of the envelope, or tube, [is coated] with a *fluorescent* layer, which absorbs the 253.7 nm radiation and emits, as a result, a continuous spectrum of longer wave-lengths. ... [T]he spectral emittance of the fluorescent light is a maximum at about 440 nm for a coating of calcium tungstate, 480 for magnesium tungstate, 525 for zinc silicate, 595 for cadmium silicate, 615 for cadmium borate and 665 nm for magnesium germinate. Usually about 16% of the energy consumed by the lamp reappears as fluorescent light (1968, p. 25).

This corresponds to about 60 lumens per watt (see Figure 3.4 for data on tungsten incandescent sources). The spectral lines of a fluorescent tube, which may contain a mixture of these substances, are smeared so that there is a continuity of radiation throughout the spectrum. Especially for the most efficient lamps, which are deficient in longwave radiation, fluorescent lamps are poor for color rendering. The subtle colors of human complexions are not improved. Incandescent sources are often used to spotlight roast beef in areas otherwise lit by fluorescent light. Otherwise an expensive red roast looks like a cheap overcooked cut, and even the completely uncooked meats in the supermarket look grayish and unappetizing.

There are many other light sources in common use these days. A full treatment of these is not necessary here, and can be found, for example, in the Illuminating Engineering Society *Handbook*.[11] These other sources include arc lamps, like the xenon source used for commercial motion picture projection (and in many vision labs) and the sodium vapor lamp, sometimes used for highway illumination because of its exceptional efficiency. The spectral lines of the xenon arc are greatly smeared under pressure, resulting in an excellent spectral distribution for color rendering. The low-pressure sodium vapor lamp, on the other hand, emits mostly yellow light from a narrow band of the spectrum and only very weakly elsewhere; virtually total color blindness occurs when objects are seen illuminated by its rays. High-pressure sodium, which is becoming increasingly popular for street-lighting, has better spectral properties because of the smearing of the spectral lines.

REFLECTION

Most of the time we see objects only because they reflect light to a greater or lesser degree than their backgrounds. Offhand it might seem that reflection should be a rather simple matter. From the subjective view of Chapter 2, glossy surfaces reflect light at the same angle of incidence and without any change of color. Matte surfaces diffuse light and somehow have the ability to change color. Having now reviewed some physical principles we can appreciate that the character of light that comes back from a surface is the same as that of the light incident upon it (recall that Newton first appreciated this). We explain this now by stating that individual photons have frequencies of vibration, and therefore wavelengths, that are basic to their quantal nature.

Most writers who deal with the topic of reflection, even at the highly technical level that is necessary to understand the principles of color printing or photography, assume that the reflected light from a surface is some portion of that which was incident. Light is incident upon the color print: some of it passes through the outer glossy surface and through the layers of selectively absorbing dyes. The spectral distribution of the light (numbers of photons as a function of wavelength) is altered by the double transfer through the dyes, both before and after reflection from the white paper beneath. There may be internal reflections, there is a problem of scatter, and there are many other technical problems to deal with, but surely the light reflected from the print is the same light that illuminated it.

On the contrary, the physicist Victor Weisskopf writes:

The overwhelming majority of things we see when we look around our environment do not emit light of their own. They are visible only because they *reemit* part of the light that falls on them from some primary source, such as the sun or an electric lamp. What is the nature of the light that reaches our eyes from objects that are inherently nonluminous?

In everyday language we say that such light is reflected or, in some cases, transmitted. As we shall see, however, the terms reflection and transmission give little hint of the subtle atomic and molecular mechanisms that come into play when materials are irradiated by a light source (1968, p. 60).

Reemission implies that the photons reflected from an object are not the same ones that are incident upon it. Nevertheless, with the relatively rare exception of fluorescent materials,[12] such physical theory states that the wavelength of the emerging photon is exactly the same as that of the incident one.

The numbers of emerging photons never exceed the numbers of incident ones. The time delay involved in the substitution of one photon for another is too short to measure. Therefore, so far as the potential visual effects of emerging photons are concerned, they might as well be some of the same ones that were incident upon a surface. No conceivable detector, whether eye or otherwise, could tell the difference. We shall therefore assume that any emerging reflected photon is the same as one of those that were incident, meaning that individual photons reflect without losing their identity. Making this assumption allows us to trace the fate of a hypothetical individual photon as it interacts with matter, both outside and inside the eye.

Recall from Chapter 2 that the most important property of a surface for perceiving its color is diffuse spectral reflectance. This is a statement about how the probability of a photon being reflected from a surface, in an unpredictable direction, varies depending upon the wavelength of the incident photon. Although much remains to be learned about how surfaces in nature manage to do this, the fact that they do is crucial for color perception.

DIFFRACTION, REFRACTION, AND SCATTER

Diffraction

If a photon crashes into an opaque (nontransparent) object, it will be either absorbed or reflected. If it passes the edge of such an object at a considerable distance, the presence of the remote object will have no ability to influence the flight path of the photon, and it will sail by just as it would if the object were completely removed from the scene. But if a photon passes very near the edge of a surface, its vibrating, fuzzy nature permits an interaction with the edge: metaphorically speaking, it "kicks off" the edge, and the direction of its travel will be changed.

To predict the result of this kind of interaction of light with edges, each element of an edge can be treated as a new source of light: this was first done, very successfully, by Huygens in the seventeenth century.

This kind of interaction of light with edges is called *diffraction*. It is important in vision mainly because diffraction sets an upper limit on the ability of any optical system, including that of the eye, to image each point as a point. In the pinhole camera, diffraction is very great and the image quality is poor. As the pupil of the eye becomes larger, the image blur due to diffraction becomes less. This relates to the fact that opening the pupil allows a smaller proportion of the incoming light being processed by the eye to interact with the edge of the pupil.

So far, we have had nothing to say about the effect of the medium through which light travels. Except for a vacuum, there is no such thing as a perfectly transparent medium. The fact that light requires no medium for its transport is a fact only grudgingly conceded by physicists in this century: the idea of an "ether" that supposedly existed for this purpose, even in a vacuum, had long been in vogue. Experimental evidence capable of testing, yet failing to support, the ether concept finally led to its demise (the famous Michelson-Morley experiment).[13]

Transparent media have an effect on light because they contain atoms that interact with photons. Some of the atoms absorb photons, but we will not deal further with absorption here. Others change the flight path of a photon, and this is called *scatter*. The flight paths of photons that are able to pass through a medium without change of direction define the *image-forming rays,* and these are almost always the ones that are important for vision. Image-forming rays that pass through the atmosphere are little altered by it; it is also the case that photons traveling along these paths do so with negligible reduction of speed compared to that in a vacuum. Apparently these photons get through the widely spaced molecules of the atmosphere without interacting with them.

Transparent media other than the atmosphere, such as glass, have a much higher molecular density, and it is not possible for photons to pass through (even though very few of them may be absorbed) without interacting with the atoms of the glass. These are regularly arranged in such a way as to permit repeated interaction without change of direction, once a photon is completely within the glass. But these interactions produce in addition a very important result, namely a reduction in the velocity of the photon compared to what it would be in air. This is not a small effect: ordinary glass or water will reduce the speed of light by about a third. The speed of light in a vacuum divided by the speed of light in a medium defines the *index of refraction* of that medium (1.33 for water).

Refraction

Refraction refers to a change in the direction of light as it passes from one medium to another. Consider, as in Figure 3.5, a photon obliquely approaching a block of glass, coming from air. A part of the fuzzy photon gets into the glass first and must slow down; the part still outside continues at its original rate. The only way that a photon can enter the glass, and maintain its integrity, is to change its direction. An analogy may help here: imagine two wheels, mounted on roller bearings on opposite ends of an axle, entering sand from a concrete roadway. If the direction of entry is perpendicular to the edge of the roadway, both wheels will leave the roadway at the same time, and will be slowed in the sand by the same amount, so that the unit as a whole, defined by a line perpendicular to the axle, will continue to move in its original direction. But if the entrance is oblique, the sand will slow the rotation of the inner wheel before the outer one is affected. In order to preserve its integrity, the unit must change direction as it enters the sand.

Refraction is what allows images to be formed in eyes and cameras. As Kepler first understood, positive lenses can be used to cause bundles of diverging light, incident upon one surface of a lens, to converge again on the other side to form an image, which must be upside down, as shown in Figure 3.6. (Refraction will be dealt with again at the end of this chapter).*

> The inversion of the image in the eye can be directly appreciated by pressing gently, though the eyelid, on the lateral surface of the eye, with the eye turned inward and the pressure applied as close as possible to the lower orbital ridge. The pressure phosphene that results will be perceived in space up and opposite, localized in that part of space where a light source must be located in order to form an image on the retina at the region where the external pressure is applied.

Scatter

Scatter occurs whenever the reradiation of photons by the molecules of a transmitting medium is other than in the forward direction. Such photons become useless for, and often degrade, spatial vision. The light that we see when a beam pierces a smoky room is visible only because of scatter: in a perfectly transmitting medium, beams of enormous intensity could pass just before our eyes and we could not see them. There is appreciable light scatter over long distances even in clear atmosphere, and a great deal of it occurs under other conditions, especially in fog. There is a surprisingly large amount of scattered light in the eye itself, which has significant effects for vision.

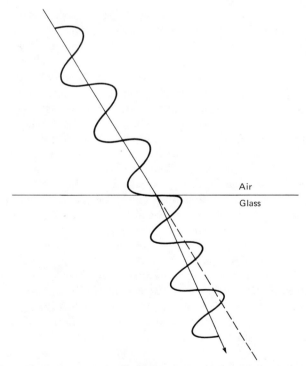

FIGURE 3.5 Refraction of light at an air-glass interface. The change of direction of a photon is associated with a reduction of velocity and a decrease in wavelength.

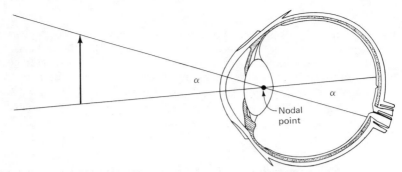

FIGURE 3.6 Nodal point system for determining the location of a retinal image.

When scattering particles are large, as they are in the eye, scatter is largely independent of wavelength and is concentrated in a forward direction. When the particles are small, as in the atmosphere on a clear day, shortwave photons are much more likely to be scattered than longwave ones; this is the physical basis for the blue of the sky.

THE FATE OF A PHOTON

Consider now a photon, on its way toward the earth from the sun, which ultimately might enter the eye of an observer, thus contributing to his vision. What is the probability that this will happen, and upon what factors does this probability depend?

To begin with, unless the photon is traveling through outer space in the direction of the earth, the initial probability that it will enter into an earthling's vision is nearly zero. To a first approximation, outer space is a perfect vacuum: therefore the path of a photon will be in a straight line (neglecting weak magnetic field effects) and it will miss the earth. Photons that miss the earth in this manner are most unlikely to have a second chance, with the exception (which we shall ignore) of some of those that travel in the direction of the moon or other objects in the solar system (see path a in Figure 3.7) from which they may reflect.

Consider next a photon, b, which is headed for the earth at a grazing angle. The greatest probability by far is that it will pass unmolested through the relatively enormous spaces that separate the molecules of gas and particulate matter in the atmosphere. If so, it will emerge from the other side of the atmosphere and cannot possibly contribute to visual stimulation. For such a photon, then, its direction of travel must somehow be altered in order for it to be a potential contributor to vision. This happens fairly frequently. If a photon interacts with an atmospheric molecule, two major possibilities exist. It may be absorbed by the molecule, increasing the latter's agitation and thereby adding its tiny share to atmospheric temperature. Such a photon will travel no farther and no longer is in contention as a visual stimulus. A second possibility is scatter, which can occur in any direction within the full 4π steradians of solid angle surrounding the molecule, including straight ahead (in which case the scatter would be undetectable and might as well never have occurred) and straight back along the path of incidence. Where scatter is concerned, the probabilities involved are very complex and depend upon the wavelength of the photon as this relates to the properties of the molecule with which it collides. For a photon incident upon the earth's atmosphere at a grazing angle, the result is that the photon, which would almost certainly have missed striking a planet free of atmosphere, instead has a finite probability of being scattered toward the surface of the earth (c,c' in Figure 3.7).

Consider next a photon d headed directly toward the earth. It may also be absorbed or scattered before reaching the earth. If scattered, it may be directed into space (d') or toward a different terrestrial point than that toward which it started (d). On a clear day, the greatest chance is that the photon will escape collision with atmospheric molecules and continue its trip to earth.

From the standpoint of an observer on earth, then, a group of photons that all originate from the same place may reach the eye in more than one way. Imagine, first of all, that the eye is pointed straight toward the sun (e). Given the origin of a photon at a particular point on the sun, there is a certain probability that, having traveled through space and having avoided collision with atmospheric molecules, it will continue directly to the eye. We do not, of course, frequently look directly at the sun (although its rays very often enter the eye in peripheral vision while we are trying to look somewhere else). More important

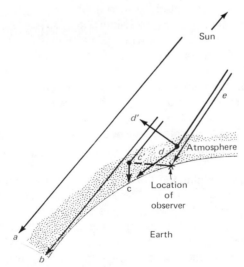

FIGURE 3.7 Various ways in which a photon coming from the sun might, or might not, reach the eye of an observer.

is the fact that sunlight illuminates everything around us, and a certain percentage of this light is reflected toward our eyes. Few objects are self-luminous; most are seen as a result of reflection. So this is a second path that an individual photon might take: from sun to object to eye. A third photon may start out in a direction deviant from that which would stimulate the eye directly. Instead, it is scattered in the atmosphere, and therefore appears to be coming from some place other than its original source. Scattered light is what makes the sky light up. Almost everyone has seen by now, on television or in photographs, the effect of an absence of such light scatter on the moon, where the sky is jet-black even at midday because the moon lacks atmosphere.

A fourth and final possibility is a scattered photon that strikes an object and is then reflected into the eye. Most objects that are seen in the shade on a sunny day owe their visibility to this effect: on the moon, they generally would not be visible. On a cloudy day, *all* objects owe their visibility to illumination provided by scattered light.

THE IMPORTANCE OF DIRECTION

A prerequisite to gauging the color of an object is to discern that the object exists in the first place. To gain the action-at-a-distance that is characteristic of such object vision, it is necessary somehow to extract salient information from the dense pattern of rays that are found in any complex real-world environment. To do this requires spatial vision, which may be defined as an ability to detect the discontinuities in such patterns of rays caused by the presence of the object.

Imagine yourself in a classroom which, being filled with the usual sorts of people and objects, is illuminated by a combination of light from the window and overhead fluorescent fixtures. Consider that you are sitting somewhere in the middle of this room, and that a white piece of cardboard is attached to the wall at the front of the room. At the location of the pupil of (say) your right eye, there will exist a complex array of photon flight paths, or rays—some coming directly from the sources of radiation, others reflecting from the various surfaces in the room, including the cardboard. Suppose now that an arrow, about two feet long, base down and tip up, is drawn on the cardboard with a green felt pen. If anyone were to ask you or others in the room "what has just been drawn on the cardboard?" all will agree that it is a green arrow. This seems simple. It is not.

The usual textbook explanation of how this happens is shown in Figure 3.6. The arrow is shown at the left with just two rays emerging from it—one from the base and one from the tip. These rays cross in the eye and produce an image, which is upside down, upon the retina. The image is green, and the arrow is seen and this explanation is inadequate in the extreme. In the first place, the green arrow, which is not self-luminous, does not have the capacity to reflect photons only in the direction of the eye. Second, the light reflecting from it comes from all along the length of the arrow, not just from the ends.

Third, the retinal image must be processed: its existence does not "explain" vision.

Pretending for the moment that the arrow is self-luminous, let us concentrate on the light coming from its tip. A critical point is that photons emerge from this point in space in all possible directions within the half-sphere in front of the cardboard. There is not just one ray headed magically toward the middle of the eye as shown in Figure 3.6. (If this were so, moving the head slightly would cause the arrow to disappear; actually, of course, one can move freely around the room and see the arrow from just about any vantage point.) A truer situation is diagrammed in Figure 3.8. With the eye in any particular location, the rays of interest are the diverging ones which strike the cornea of the eye over a range of locations such that the rays passing through the cornea also pass through the pupil of the eye. We ignore, for purposes of analysis, all other rays.

We have known, since Kepler, that the optics of the eye bring this bundle of rays to a focus on the retina where the so-called retinal image of the arrow tip will be formed. Because of the diffraction limitation and other factors, it is both theoretically and practically impossible for an optical system to image a point exactly as a point. Instead, the point will be imaged on the retina as a more-or-less Gaussian (bell-shaped) spread function. Nevertheless, it will be convenient to imagine that there is a point image on the retina, keeping in mind that this represents a serious oversimplification.

What then is the meaning, if any, of the diagram of Figure 3.6? The explanation has to do with the concept of the *nodal point* in optics. The behavior of any coaxial optical system, however complex, can be predicted by a model of the type shown in Figure 3.9. Given the object point, two nodal points, and a known location of the image plane, the approximate location of the image can be calculated by drawing a line from the object to the first nodal point, and another line from the second nodal point, parallel to the first line, until it intersects the image plane. The eye is an unusual optical system, because the rays

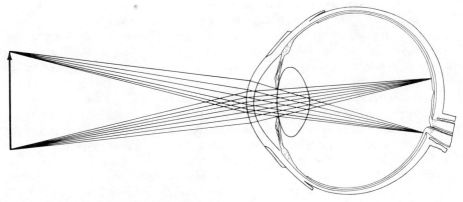

FIGURE 3.8 Actual path of rays through the eye.

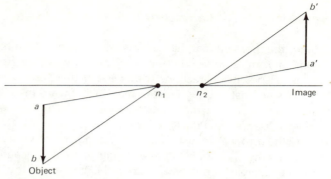

FIGURE 3.9 Use of the nodal points of an optical system to determine image location in a known plane.

entering it from air proceed to a denser medium from which they do not again emerge. Partly for this reason, the two nodal points of the eye are very close together, and although their locations vary slightly depending upon the state of accommodation of the eye, they may be considered for many practical purposes as being coincident, located about 7 mm behind the vertex of the cornea of the eye. This is very neat: it means that the location of an image on the retina of the eye can be very easily determined, at least to a first approximation. Simply draw a line from the object, through the nodal point, and determine where it strikes the back of the eye. *But no photon actually follows such a path,* unless it passes along the optical axis of the eye. The actual path is usually much more complicated, because refraction takes place at the corneal surface and at a number of other places within the eye, where there is a sudden change in the index of refraction. To represent the formation of an image in the eye as if actual light rays cross at the nodal point is a useful concept for first-approximation calculation of retinal image location, and for defining the *visual angle* subtended by an object. If taken with respect to the nodal point, visual angle is the same outside as inside the eye.

The fact that the arrow on the cardboard is not self-luminous complicates the matter considerably. Imagine a nondirectionally sensitive photocell[14] at the location of the eye, and suppose that a reading of its output is taken before the arrow is drawn on the cardboard. After the arrow is drawn, the number of photons per unit time received at the photocell is decreased. But by how much?

It is worth taking time out to do the calculation—at least approximately. To simplify the problem, we will imagine a black object on a white background, the latter consisting of the half-sphere of Figure 3.10 with a nondirectional photocell located 10 meters from the back of the half-sphere. Assume that the surface of the sphere is uniformly illuminated and, for the moment, that the green arrow is replaced by a nonreflecting black line, 0.2 cm wide and 30 cm in length. All areas of the sphere will affect the photocell equally, except the area that is black. The area of the black region is 0.0006 m^2, while that of the

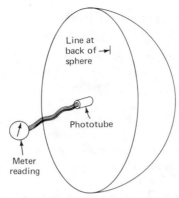

FIGURE 3.10 Adding the line at the back of the sphere, though it is clearly visible, would not cause any significant change in the output of the nondirectional phototube.

hemisphere is $2\pi r^2$, which is slightly more than 600 m². The result is that the decrease in the rate of photon incidence upon the photocell, caused by the black line on the sphere, is less than 1 part in a million.

But the eye can do better than this. The line so far described subtends a visual angle of about 0.35 minutes of arc. A black line of this width can be discriminated very easily. Hecht, Ross, and Mueller (1947) reported that under ideal conditions they could see a wire 1/16 of an inch in diameter at a distance of one mile. This works out to about 0.5 *second* of visual angle. Thus, for an easily visible line, a reduction in the amount of light received at the photocell could be less than 1 part in 10 million. No nondirectional device could possibly discriminate such a small difference; the ability of the eye itself to discriminate variations in the intensity of a uniform field is more like one part in a hundred (see Chapter 6). The remarkable fact that the observer easily sees such a line must therefore be critically dependent upon the ability of the eye to sort out photons according to their direction of incidence, and to disregard most of these as irrelevant to the task at hand. In essence, this is what the formation of a retinal image accomplishes, by translating differences in angle of incidence of photons upon the eye into spatial location upon the retina.

There is, of course, much more that could be said on the matter of spatial vision. For example, how do we localize an object in depth? How do we judge the size of an object? How does the visual system deal with the inevitable blur of the retinal image caused by the fact that points are not exactly imaged as points? In this book on color, we will not deal much further with these interesting issues. It is hoped, however, that the following point has by now been well established: without pattern vision, there could be no vision of real objects; since color is usually a perceptual property of real objects, then there can be no study of the color of real objects without becoming involved to some extent with the problems of pattern vision.

WAVELENGTH, PHOTON ENERGY, AND RETINAL IRRADIATION

One of the triumphs of twentieth century physics has been the clarification of the relation between the wavelength and the energy of the photons that make up light at that wavelength. (The reader is reminded that each photon also has wave properties.)

The quantitative relations between the wavelength of a photon and its frequency of vibration have already been mentioned. Given that all photons travel at the same velocity, whatever their frequency of vibration, it is perhaps intuitively clear that those photons which vibrate faster are more energetic than the ones which vibrate more slowly; it turns out that the two quantities are directly proportional to each other. This, then, is the picture to bear in mind: longwave photons vibrate relatively slowly and are less energetic than shortwave photons.

Probably the most basic property of a photon is its frequency of vibration. This does not change as a photon enters a medium of higher index of refraction. Since the photon now moves more slowly, its wavelength must shorten. No energy is lost. Therefore a photon of red light at 650 nm will have its wavelength shortened to 487 nm inside a medium, such as the eye, with an index of refraction of about 4/3. Frequency of vibration, which is 4.6×10^{14} s^{-1} outside the eye, is the same inside. Despite the fact that frequency is a better metric for measuring the spectral aspect of light than is wavelength, the use of wavelength in visual science is very well established, and the convention will be followed in this book.

In describing various experiments to be reported in chapters to follow, it is necessary to decide in what units of intensity to report the visual stimuli that have been employed. A bewildering variety of units has been used for this purpose. The subject of photometry deals with the definition of such units, and this is required because the eye has a sensitivity that differs very much depending upon the wavelength of the photons that are absorbed in the retina. To specify the visual stimulus strictly in terms of the numbers of photons incident upon the retina would be meaningless, unless the wavelength distribution of these photons were known, so that their visual effectiveness could be evaluated.

There exists a unit of retinal illuminance, which is the density of light incident upon the retina, called the *troland* (td). The usual definition of the troland requires first that the entire system of photometry be developed. Readers are referred to other texts for such a treatment.

We shall avoid such agony here simply by noting that, at a wavelength of 555 nm, where each photon vibrates 5.4×10^{14} times each second and has an energy of 3.58×10^{-12} erg, approximately one million photons per second per square degree of visual angle,[15] incident upon the retina, are required to produce a retinal illuminance of 1 td. The general equation for the number of trolands N(td) is:

$$N\,(\text{td}) = \frac{8 \times 10^{-7}}{Q_\lambda^*} N\,(\text{photons} \cdot \text{s}^{-1} \cdot \text{deg}^{-2}) \qquad (3.1)$$

where Q_λ^* is a measure of the relative sensitivity of the eye that varies with wavelength, as will be discussed in Chapter 5. Q^* has a value of 1.0 at a wavelength of 555 nm, and because this is the wavelength of highest sensitivity for the light-adapted eye, Q^* has a value of less than 1 at all other wavelengths. The total variation of wavelengths of visible photons is less than two to one. Late in the nineteenth century it was established that the visible spectrum is but a narrow band in a total spectrum of electromagnetic radiation that covers some 22 logarithmic units (decades), as shown in Figure 3.11. To deal with very long wavelengths in a manner analogous to the way it handles visible ones, an eye would have to be scaled upward proportionally in size. To deal with very short wavelengths, an eye would have to be microscopically small. Moreover, it is not likely that X-rays, which pass easily through most objects that are significant to us, would be effective messengers about the outside world. Visible light apparently has just the right wavelengths to reflect from objects in useful ways, and to permit the evolution of a compact and efficient pickup device, the eye.

DISPERSION AND CHROMATIC ABERRATION

Although Kepler was the first to understand in a general way how lenses work (as we saw in Chapter 1), the principles of light refraction that underlie their function were not quantitatively understood until very late in his lifetime. In notes that were not discovered until their author's death, Willebrord Snell wrote in 1621 that "the place of the image follows in each case a well-defined perpendicular in such a way that always the incident ray observes to the place of the image from the point of incidence its own perpetual proportion" (Sabra,

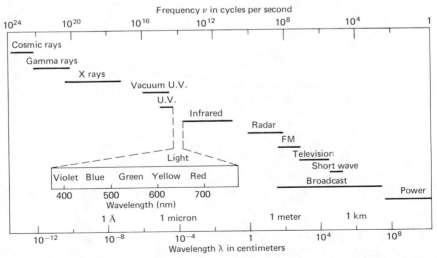

FIGURE 3.11 The visible spectrum is a relatively narrow band in the total spectrum of electromagnetic energy, as shown here. (From Riggs, 1965.)

1967, p. 99). What this means[16] is illustrated in Figure 3.12a. Ray AB, incident upon interface MN (for example, that between air at the top and glass at the bottom) is refracted as shown. If a perpendicular to the interface is erected anywhere to the right of B, the ratio BD/BE is constant, no matter what the angle of incidence of AB with respect to the interface MN. In 1637, Descartes published the law of sines, usually called today "Snell's law," in the form that we now know it.[17] For this purpose, the simpler construction shown in Figure 3.12b was used; the relations that Snell discovered can be expressed instead as:

$$n_1 \sin \theta_1 = n_2 \sin \theta_2$$

where n_1 and n_2 are designated as, and in fact define, the relative *refractive index* of each medium.

Snell's law permits an extremely accurate calculation of the direction of the refracted ray, provided that the indices of refraction of the media are known. Conversely, measurements of the deviations of such rays provide an easy and practical way to measure the relative indices of refraction of any two optical media. It will be recalled that these relations can, in principle, also be determined by measuring the relative speed of light in the two media. But this is not easy to do, and nothing was known anyway about the speed of light at the time Snell made his discovery.[18]

Newton's dispersion of white light into its spectral components shows that refraction varies with wavelength. When light slows down, for example when entering glass from air, the photons that comprise that light slow to different

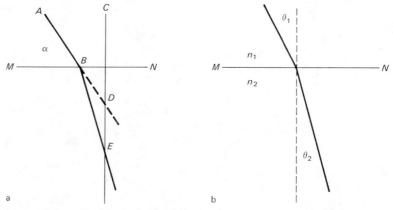

FIGURE 3.12 a. Snell's law in the form that he discovered it: BD/BE is constant, no matter what the angle of incidence, α. b. Snell's law in the form given it by Descartes: $n_1 \sin \theta_1 = n_2 \sin \theta_2$.

degrees, depending upon their wavelengths. The photons that vibrate fastest (and which therefore have the shortest wavelengths) slow down the most, and show a larger change in direction than those that vibrate more slowly. Therefore, the "index of refraction" of an optical medium is not a single value, but is instead a continuous series of values that vary as a function of the wavelength of the light.

But the full story is yet more complicated. The rate at which the refractive index varies with wavelength differs from one optical medium to another. The more rapid this variation, the greater is the *dispersive power* of the medium. Because refraction varies with wavelength, whatever the dispersive power, a simple lens always refracts shortwave light more than longwave light, causing *chromatic aberration* to occur. It is common to correct for this in man-made optical systems by judiciously selecting optical glasses of particular refractive and dispersive powers which can be used together in multielement lenses.[19]

Perhaps because eyes are not made of glass, no such correction for chromatic aberration has evolved. If the *eye* is accommodated (focused) on a distant red target of wavelength 700 nm, a distant violet one of 400 nm will be seriously blurred (Fig. 3.13). If focus is held on the distant red target, the violet one must

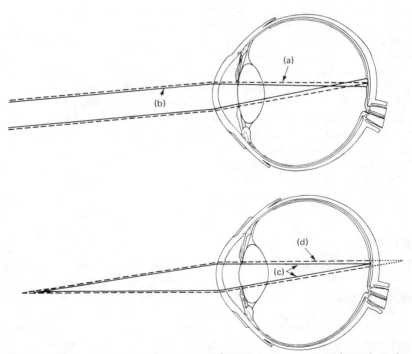

FIGURE 3.13 Chromatic aberration in the eye. Distant targets can never be in focus for violet light (b). Near targets can be (c), but not simultaneously for red light (a) (d).

be brought to within about a half meter of the eye before good focus is achieved. This means that normal eyes are seriously myopic—in the vernacular, "nearsighted"—for distant blue targets, and so there is no possibility that the mixed rays from a white target can all be optimally focused upon the retina. Since there is no way to accommodate for distant violet targets, it is not surprising that the eye tends to accommodate instead for longer wavelengths than this, allowing the shortwave components of the retinal image to be seriously blurred.

Yet we do not ordinarily perceive the expected effects of such chromatic aberration, which would be a visual world whose edges are tinged with chromatic fringes. Why not? This is an important problem for color vision, and we shall return to it in subsequent chapters. Leaving the details for later, the following factors seem to be involved in the attempt to understand this interesting problem.

- Selective absorption occurs in the eye media, reducing the effectiveness of blue light and thereby effectively shortening the visible spectrum (Chapter 5).
- The blue-sensitive cones enter importantly into the perception of hue, but very little into the perception of contour. Since these cones absorb mostly shortwave light, this is in effect another spectrum-shortening device, but one that is selective for contour (Chapters 5, 8, and 9).
- The Stiles-Crawford effect, attributable to the directional sensitivity of the cone photoreceptors, reduces the effectiveness of rays entering the margins of the pupil (Stiles & Crawford, 1933a); these marginal rays produce the greatest amount of chromatic aberration (Figure 3.13).
- When prisms are mounted before the eyes, the chromatic fringes that they produce upon the retina are at first very evident in sensation. But if the prisms are worn for a long time, the fringes become very much less evident and may even disappear. This indicates that neural machinery exists which is capable of compensating for consistent relations between fringes and contours, somehow expelling the part of the message that carries no real information about the outside world (Kohler, 1962).

SUMMARY

The concepts of physics provide a description of reality that is independent of how the world is perceived by humans or other organisms. The use of physical concepts to help explain human color vision is very important, because doing so avoids a tautology that is inevitable if, as is often done, the stimulus for vision is described in commonsense terms, based upon how things look.

Light mediates between perceived objects and our eyes. Of the various ways to regard light, its conception as a collection of swiftly moving and vibrating photons is especially useful for vision. The vibration of each photon occurs at a specific frequency that is inversely related to its wavelength; this vibration carries the initial chromatic message. Among the properties of light that are important for vision is its tendency to move in straight lines except when scattered, diffracted, refracted, or reflected. The optical system of the eye causes diverging light from points in visual space to converge at the retina to form an image there. Spatial vision, thus mediated, is essential to color vision since the latter normally relates to, and is affected by, specific regions of space. Furthermore, all vision, including color perception, fades in the absence of boundaries.

Reflection is important because the visual properties of object surfaces, including their colors, depend upon it. Diffraction limits the optimal quality of any image, including the one in the eye. Scatter is helpful because the diffuse light that it provides from the sky helps to fill dark shadows. Refraction is essential for image formation in eyes and cameras.

The direction of photon travel is critically important for vision. As an example, it is shown that, unless the directions of incident photons can be sorted out, the percentage of change in the total number of photons reaching the eye, from an easily visible target, is orders of magnitude too small to register.

The relation between the wavelength and energy of photons is easily and clearly understood within the framework of modern physics. The energy of a photon does not change as it moves from one medium to another, nor does its frequency of vibration. In passing from air to glass, for example, a photon slows down and its wavelength decreases.

The standard unit of light intensity to be used in this book is the *troland*, which is proportional to the number of photons per second per square degree incident upon the retina, and inversely proportional to the quantized photopic spectral sensitivity of the visual system.

The eye is subject to a serious amount of chromatic aberration, which nevertheless seems to have no seriously deleterious effect upon spatial vision.

NOTES

[1]There is no way to be certain that fields of magnetic flux could not tell us a great deal about what we require to know about the physical world. However this may be, we certainly know that vision provides much of our information about the outside world, though perhaps not quite the 90 percent once claimed by the American Optometric Association. Because vision is in fact so important, it is reasonable to expect that light interacts with objects in especially useful ways, and that we have been able to evolve sensory devices that are able to extract whatever is most important from the radiation patterns in which we find ourselves imbedded.

[2]From time to time, one sees reports that colors can be discriminated by some people through the tactile sense. A blindfolded person surely could tell the difference, say, between a white cat and a black cat in the sunlight because the black cat would feel warmer than the white one. The discrimination would then be based on a correlation: cats that absorb the most infrared radiation (heat) are also those that tend to absorb the most visible radiation, so hot cats also tend to be black. If the light reflected from objects is restricted to the visible spectrum, there is no scientifically acceptable evidence that colors are discriminable by touch (see Makous, 1966).

[3]According to Henderson (1970), p. 1.

[4]An article by Feinberg (1968) is the lead article in the September 1968 issue of *Scientific American,* devoted exclusively to light. The eleven articles in the issue have been republished, along with a number of additional articles from other issues of *Scientific American,* in *Lasers and Light,* with introductions by Arthur L. Schawlow (San Francisco: Freeman, 1969).

[5]See, for example, the textbook by Strong (1958), p. 58. I will not give references for all of the physical concepts introduced in this chapter, all of which are treated in detail in standard texts. I have tried to eliminate most of the mathematics and to encourage visualization of optical concepts. As a result, my treatment is not entirely rigorous.

[6]An integrating sphere is used in photometry to measure all of the light in a beam (for example that passing through a filter that scatters light) or to mix two beams. If the inside of a sphere is painted white, light admitted through a small hole will be diffusely reflected many times and will appear to "light up" the sphere uniformly.

[7]See Boynton (1974) for an elaboration of these ideas.

[8]There are two orthogonal components to this vibration, which vibrate in phase, called the electric and magnetic vectors. If light is unpolarized, the electric (and magnetic) vector assumes random orientations. If light is plane polarized, the electric vector is constrained to assume only one orientation: in other words, the vibration of the photon is fixed in one direction. When light is circularly polarized, the angle of vibration changes as the photon moves, something like the slot of a turning screw. Some animals are sensitive to the angle of light polarization but humans are not.

[9]According to Feinberg (1968), G. I. Taylor of Cambridge University had produced interference patterns on a photographic plate 50 years before Pfleegor and Mandel, using extremely low exposures and several months of exposure.

[10]Dirac (1958, p. 9); also quoted in Scully and Sargent (1972).

[11]Kaufman, J. E. (ed.), *IES Lighting Handbook* (5th ed.) New York: Illuminating Engineering Society, 1972.

[12]Here and in the discussion to follow, *fluorescence* is ignored. Surfaces that exhibit this phenomenon are widely used these days in advertising displays, producing very vivid colors that seem to glow almost as if self-luminous. Fluorescence occurs when light is absorbed by the surface and is then reradiated at a longer wavelength. If this is to be regarded as reflected light, then clearly it is not inevitable that the wavelength of incident photons is preserved in reflection. Fluorescence plays a very minor role in object perception.

[13]See for example, Ditchburn (1976), p. 404, or almost any other optics textbook.

[14]A nondirectional photocell is one that will react in the same way to any photon incident upon its receiving surface, whatever the angle at which it strikes that surface. Most detectors are directionally sensitive: photons incident perpendicular to the surface are more likely to register than those striking at a grazing angle. This is true of the cone photoreceptors of the human eye (the so-called *Stiles-Crawford effect.*)

[15]A square degree of visual angle would result, for example, from the viewing of a square that subtends one linear degree of visual angle on each side. It could also be produced by a circular spot having a diameter of $(2/\sqrt{\pi}) = 1.128°$. One square degree is also equivalent to 3.046×10^{-4} steradian.

[16] According to Kingslake (1974, p. 799). Snell's use of the word "image" to describe the intersection of ray paths and construction lines is not at all in accord with modern usage.

[17] Descartes gave Snell no credit and was later accused of plagiarism. It is, however, entirely possible that Descartes arrived at "Snell's law" independently.

[18] The prevailing view held that the speed of light was infinite. Newton thought it finite, but predicted incorrectly from his corpuscular theory that light should travel faster in glass than in air.

[19] Typically only three wavelengths in the visible spectrum are corrected and some deviation of the others is allowed.

4
Retinal Anatomy Underlying the Perception of Form and Color

Since the time that Kepler first understood the optics of the eye, it has been realized that the *retina*, and not the lens, constitutes its photoreceptive component (Fig. 4.1). The basic structure of the retina has been known since the 1870s, when staining techniques were developed that rendered some of the critical retinal structures visible under the light microscope.[1] Two huge volumes by Stephen Polyak (1941, 1957) summarize a wealth of detail about the structure of the retina at the level of magnification that light microscopy permits. However, because the light microscope left many details unclear—in particular the connections (synapses) between nerve cells—correlation between structure and function was not easy.

The application of the electron microscope to the study of the retina, which began about 1950, has led to greatly improved understanding. But microscopy, however detailed and suggestive it might be, cannot hope to provide ultimate answers about the relation between structure and function. The major advances in this respect have arisen through the application of the techniques of electrophysiology, which depend upon the fact that biological activity produces electrical signals, and the correlation of that class of evidence with anatomy.

For vision, electrical records first appeared in 1860, when the electroretinogram (ERG) was obtained using an electrode applied to the cornea of a frog.[2] Nowadays, signals can also be recorded from single units in the visual system

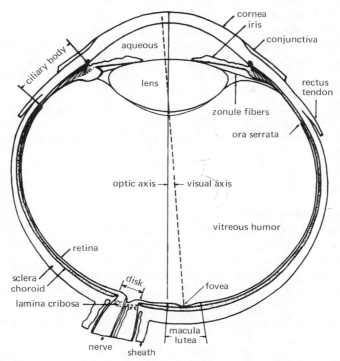

FIGURE 4.1 This cross section of the eye was originally prepared by Salzmann (1912) and, with modifications, has been widely reproduced. This figure is reproduced from Rodieck (1973, p. 3). Not all of the features that are labled here are discussed in this chapter.

of animals by the insertion of tiny recording electrodes that nestle close to active cells (*extracellular recordings*) or in some cases impale the cells (*intracellular recordings*).[3]

In this chapter we shall consider some of the basic findings about the nature of the retina, especially those that have been revealed by optical and anatomical methods. This will provide the background necessary to consider concepts about sensitivity regulation (Chapter 6) and neural mechanisms of color vision, including those in the brain, in Chapter 7. The photochemistry of vision will be considered separately in Chapter 5.

THE MOBILE EYE

The retina cannot effectively function independently of the eye that contains it, or of the other structures in and around the eyeball that allow an image to be formed, permit the eye to move, and thereby enable it to sample the visual environment. The human eye, one of the most complex structures in the body, is just a little less than an inch in diameter. It deviates from a sphere in that its posterior part is somewhat flattened, and there is also a pronounced bulge in front caused by the transparent cornea, which for optical reasons, in an eye of this size must have a radius of curvature less than that approximated by the eye as a whole.*

> The corneal bulge can easily be verified by closing the eyelids and lightly touching the outer surface of the eyelid with a fingertip while rotating the eye slowly from side to side.

Each eye[4] is located in the *eyesocket*, or *bony orbit*, a cone-shaped cavity that points slightly outward relative to the midline of the head. The eye, thus recessed, is also cushioned by surrounding fatty tissue. The functional significance of such an arrangement may be threefold: (1) Being located high in the body, the eyes have a good vantage point from which to survey the environment. (2) The eyes are located very close to the brain, which permits the transmission pathways from eye to brain to be both short and well protected. (3) The recession of the eyeballs into the bony orbit, together with the surrounding fat and the covering lid, minimize to an important degree the probability of serious injury to this vital organ.

Movement of each eye is controlled by three pairs of extraocular (outside-the-eye) muscles that determine the position of the eyeball within the socket. (The insertion of the rectus tendon, attached to one of the six extraocular muscles, is shown in Figure 4.1.) Each time we change our point of fixation, an exquisitely coordinated relaxation and contraction of these muscles causes a change in eye position. When the position of the head is fixed and there is no predictable motion of objects in the visual world, only *saccadic* eye movements can be made.[5] These so-called "saccades," of which we are typically unaware, are ballistic and largely preprogrammed, meaning that once such an eye movement is under way, little modification of it is possible. If the head is turned from side to side while an object is fixated, the eyes roll smoothly in the opposite direction, tending thereby to remain fixed in space. With the head fixed, smooth eye movements can occur that permit the tracking of external objects, providing that these are moving in predictable ways over distances that are not too large. An act such as following the flight path of a tennis ball also requires head movements, controlled by muscles in the neck, upon which tracking movements of the eyes are superimposed. Small errors of this tracking system are compensated by saccadic eye movements that are superimposed upon the smooth ones.

The literature on eye movements is enormous;[6] a great deal is known about their neurophysiological underpinnings. For most of the basic experiments on human color vision the head is not free to move, and the subject is instructed to fixate upon a black dot, a point of light, or on the center of a more complex target. However, the ability to fixate is limited by small eye movements, called *physiological nystagmus*, that occur even during the most intense effort to fixate. These small movements have been found to be necessary to maintain vision; the entire visual world appears to fade away if eye movements are artificially eliminated.[7]

The Act of Fixation

Whenever we wish to pay visual attention to an object we fixate it, with little awareness of what we are doing, by moving our eyes so that the image of that object will fall on a specialized region of the retina, the *fovea centralis*. This is a depression in the retina represented near the bottom of Figure 4.1. Though it comprises a trivial percentage of the total area of the retina, the fovea is critically important for the perception of visual detail* and also for color vision. The signals leaving this region of the retina activate a disproportionately large part of the visual brain. The act of fixation is important not only in everyday life but also in the vision laboratory, where, by assuming that a subject can follow the instruction to look at a fixation target, the experimenter can know to which part of the retina a stimulus is directed.

While looking squarely at one of the words near the center of this page, attempt to read some of the others without moving fixation from the original word. Although many words are visible, only those quite near the fixation word can be recognized. It is an interesting fact of perception that we are normally unaware of the impreciseness of our peripheral vision. (See also p. 89.) Most people with substantial blind areas in the peripheral retina, such as can be caused, for example, by glaucoma, fail to notice them, whereas blind spots in the central retina, which can be caused by looking at laser beams, are immediately obvious.

OPTICAL ELEMENTS OF THE EYE

Cornea

The cornea, through which light enters the eye, is transparent despite a complex lamellar structure. At the outer corner of the eye is the *lacrimal gland*, which secretes tear and mucus solutions. Tears are necessary to help maintain the normal exchange of oxygen and to control the water balance within the cornea, which otherwise will become cloudy, scattering so much of the incoming light as to seriously degrade the retinal image. Blinking of the eyelids helps to maintain the distribution of tears across the cornea, filling in its microstructure and thereby improving its quality as an optical interface. The cornea is also richly endowed with pain receptors, which function, along with the eyelids, to help protect the eye.

The cornea is the primary refractive element of the eye because its index of refraction is substantially greater than that of air; the refractive indices of other structures in the eye are more similar to that of the cornea than to air. Thus, the smoothness of the corneal surface, and its index of refraction, are very important. Recall from Chapter 3 that, by Snell's law, the greater the difference in refractive index between two optical media, the greater is the amount of refraction that will occur. The indices of refraction of the ocular media relative to air are approximately as follows:[8]

cornea	1.37
aqueous	1.33
lens (cortex)	1.38
lens (core)	1.40
vitreous	1.33.

Vision is unclear under water because water (1.33) and the cornea have nearly the same refractive index. The optical power of the cornea is nearly lost and severe "farsightedness" (hyperopia) results. The use of watertight goggles permits air to intervene and restore normal corneal function. When contact lenses are worn to correct refractive errors in air, the anterior surface of the contact lens, which together with the intervening fluid has about the same refractive index as the cornea, simply replaces that of the cornea.

Unlike man-made optical surfaces, which for ease of manufacture are usually sections of spheres, the radius of curvature of the cornea is less at the margin than at the center. This is a type of aspherical curve that a lens designer can use to help eliminate spherical aberration, which otherwise results because spherical surfaces refract the marginal rays too much relative to those passing near the center of the lens.

Iris and Pupil

The iris controls the entry of light into the eye. The variable opening within it, the *pupil*, determines the amount of light that can pass through to the retina, doing so without altering the field of view. In other words, light can reach any region of the retina having passed through any region of the pupil. The annular iris, which determines the "color of the eye" when viewed from the front, varies in width to alter the size of the pupil as a function of the level of illumination of the retina. However, its size depends also upon a host of other factors, including the size and region of the retina stimulated, spectral and temporal characteristics of the light, and emotional reactions having nothing necessarily to do with vision. The constriction of the pupil that occurs with increasing external illumination is not nearly sufficient to keep the illumination of the retina constant (see Chapter 6).

The quality of the retinal image depends upon the size of the pupil. When the pupil is very small, the image is degraded by diffraction; when it is very large, the effects of spherical and chromatic aberration are most serious. The neural organization of the retina changes as a function of retinal illuminance, to provide one of the mechanisms of light adaptation to be discussed in Chapter 6. The pupil appears set for a slightly clearer image than the neural processing machinery can use (Campbell & Gregory, 1960). For example, at very low levels of external luminance, very little detail is perceptible because the low rate of photon incidence upon the retina is sufficient only to excite a few rod receptors. The rods are organized into very large *receptive fields*, meaning that photons falling as far as a degree apart (0.3 mm) on the retina have effects that summate spatially. Visual resolution in dim light is therefore limited by the receptive field spacing and cannot be modified by changes in pupil size. At high levels of external luminance, optical aberrations are perceived if pupil size is artificially enlarged, as will be recognized by anyone who has had an ophthalmological examination during which a drug was used to enlarge the pupil. The spatial resolution of the neural processing machinery is finely tuned for high illumination, so optical aberrations introduced by an inappropriately enlarged pupil are resolvable.

The response of the iris muscle depends upon the action of light upon the same photoreceptors that mediate vision. Some of the signals derived therefrom are sent to the midbrain for processing and lead to signals that are directed back to the iris musculature. The pupils of both eyes move together in what is known as the *consensual* pupillary response; this means that both pupils grow smaller when light is delivered to only one of the eyes.

Much of the experimental evidence to be discussed in this book has been derived from studies in which the subject's head is fixed as he bites on a dental impression; he is instructed to regard a fixation point; and light is beamed through the pupil of the eye in what is known as the *Maxwellian view* (Boynton, 1966; LeGrand, 1968; Westheimer, 1966). For such research, the pupillary response is an unwanted nuisance, because it causes the amount of light entering the eye to vary no matter how exactly the external stimulus may be controlled. The effects of pupillary fluctuations can be eliminated in Maxwellian view by making the light beam, as it passes through the pupil, smaller than the smallest pupil (about 2 mm in diameter). If Maxwellian view is not used, a small *artificial pupil* (a hole in a thin metal plate) can be positioned immediately in front of the eye.

An important advantage of a small pupil over a large one relates to the *depth of focus*. In the middle panel of Figure 4.2, the eye is accommodated for distance, resulting in a *blur circle* on the retina, as explained in the figure legend. If the pupil were made smaller, the entire bundle of rays that are shown converging toward a point behind the retina would be made smaller; in the limit there could be a very narrow pencil of rays constrained nearly to the visual axis. Reducing the size of the pupil therefore decreases the size of blur circles on the retina, whether these are caused by inappropriate accommodation or by aberrations, thereby increasing the range within which objects will be in reasonable focus for a particular state of accommodation. This improvement in depth of

78 Retinal Anatomy

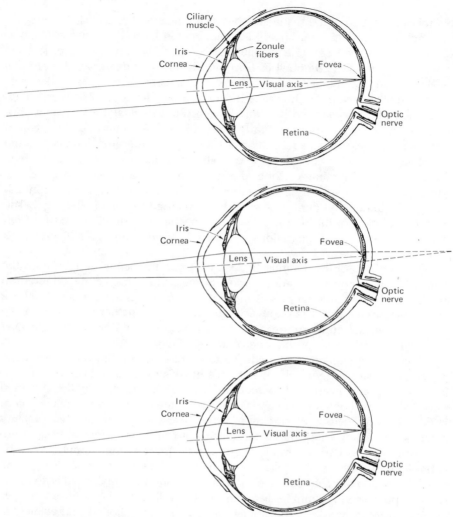

FIGURE 4.2 **Top**: The lens of the eye is held in a flattened position by the action of the zonule fibers that support it. Light from a distant source provides parallel rays, seen entering from the left. The cornea provides most of the refraction needed to bring the rays to a sharp focus at the fovea. **Middle**: The fixated object has been brought close to the eye. The shape of the lens has not changed, and the refraction at the cornea is no longer sufficient, because the rays striking it are now divergent, to form a point image on the retina. Instead, a circle of light intersects the retina and the image is blurred. If a hole were cut in the back of the eye, an image would be formed behind it, as shown by the dotted lines. **Bottom**: Contraction of the ciliary muscle releases some of the tension of the zonule fibers. This is the act of accommodation. The lens changes shape, especially at its anterior surface. This added refractive power is now sufficient to restore a sharp image at the fovea.

field will be familiar to many photographers, since the same principle applies to cameras. One pays a price for it, however, in loss of retinal illumination and increased blur due to diffraction. For the eye, a 3-mm pupil usually produces optimal image quality.

Lens

The lens of the eye is a complex multilayered structure whose shape changes during the act of *accommodation*. This process allows objects at various distances from the eye to be clearly imaged, though not all at the same time. If removed from an eye, the lens assumes its maximally curved shape. The extracted lens selectively absorbs shortwave light and appears yellow, more so for older eyes than younger ones. This selectivity of transmission influences the color vision of an observer in ways that will be discussed in the next chapter.

Most of the change of shape during accommodation takes place at the anterior surface of the lens, which in the intact eye is in contact with the iris. When the eye is focused for a distant object, the *zonule fibers*, which hold the lens taut, exert their maximum pull. As an object is brought nearer, the retinal image will blur unless an adjustment is made (Fig. 4.2). Contraction of the ciliary muscle, which rings the eye, is able to release some of the tension that otherwise is exerted by the zonule fibers, allowing the front surface of the lens to bulge. This action adds optical power to the total system, restoring the focus of the image. Maximum accommodation occurs when the ciliary muscle is sufficiently contracted to reduce the tension exerted by the zonule fibers, allowing the lens to assume its maximum bulge. With aging in humans, a condition known as *presbyopia* gradually sets in; although the ciliary muscle remains active, the lens loses its capacity to bulge. By age 60 or so, it usually becomes "stuck" in the flattened shape, making near vision of fine detail impossible without correcting spectacles or contact lenses.

Sclera

The white *sclera* which constitutes the tough outer tunic of the eye is contiguous with the transparent cornea. Unlike the cornea, which is exquisitely sensitive to pain and has no blood supply at all, the sclera is heavily vascularized, has few pain receptors, and is somewhat more difficult to penetrate. The sclera is contiguous at the back of the eye with the sheath of the optic nerve.

Vitreous and Aqueous

A photographic camera has rigid walls, but the eye would collapse were it not filled completely at an intraocular pressure greater than that of the surrounding atmosphere. About two-thirds of the eyeball is filled with the *vitreous body*, a thin jellylike substance interlaced with peculiar fibers. The *anterior chamber* of the eye, between cornea and lens, is filled with an exceptionally clear fluid called the *aqueous humor*. The aqueous is continuously generated and absorbed. It controls the intraocular pressure, which must be high enough to maintain the integrity of the eye, but not too high, or the cells of the retina will be destroyed.

THE RETINA

The retina is the only structure in the central nervous system that is directly visible, this being possible with the aid of an *ophthalmoscope* which the examiner uses to look into the eye through the pupil. In truth, however, the sensory structure of the retina cannot be visualized this way, since the retina is largely transparent and its critical features are of microscopic dimensions. What is seen is called the *fundus*; it has an orange-red hue that is characteristic of the vascular supply of the retina. Upon this background, the vessels that supply the circulation of blood to the retina are easily visible. To learn anything about the microstructure of the retina, it must be removed from an eye, subjected to histological procedures (fixing, staining, slicing, and so forth), and viewed microscopically.

The human retina is about 250 μm thick over most of its extent, which is about the thickness of four or five sheets of typing paper. It contains a total area of about 1100 mm^2, about that of a silver dollar (Taylor & Jennings, 1971), and has a volume of about .25 cm^3. Within this small volume are found something like 200 million nerve cells that are directly involved with the processing of visual information, distributed across the retina in a very highly organized fashion.

Most of the volume of the retina is contained within the *inner* and *outer limiting membranes* (Fig. 4.3). The inner limiting membrane separates the retina from the vitreous humor, which is shown at the bottom of the figure.[9] The outer limiting membrane is located about four-fifths of the way toward the top surface of the retina, which in turn is separated from the outside surface of the eye by about 500 μm of tissue that includes the sclera and *choroid*. The latter is a pigmented layer lying just inside the sclera, whose function is to absorb much of the light that passes through the sclera, which otherwise would reach the retina from the wrong side.*

The retina also contains radially oriented cells, not shown in Figure 4.3, that extend all the way from the inner to the outer limiting membrane. The function

---

By pulling the lids wide apart with the fingers on a sunny day, the effects of stray light entering the eye through the sclera can be directly appreciated. The effects are most easily seen if sunlight directly strikes the eye while the observer is looking at objects seen in the shade. The resulting stray light casts an apparent veil over everything and reduces contrast. Other important sources of stray light in the eye include scatter from the cornea and lens, but these are harder to demonstrate.

The Retina   81

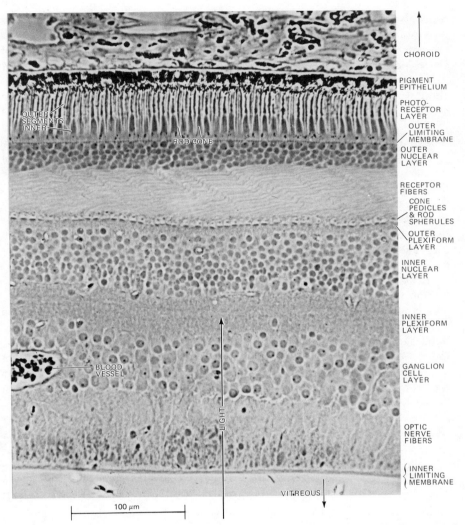

FIGURE 4.3 Cross section of the human retina about 4° from the fovea. (From Boycott and Dowling, 1969.)

of these so-called *Müller* cells is probably structural. They have processes extending laterally along their length that fill up much if not all of the space of the inner retina not occupied either by nerve cells or blood vessels.

Photoreceptors

The outermost parts of each photoreceptor extend beyond the outer limiting membrane as if punched through it; the membrane helps to hold the receptors in position. *Rods*, the receptors for low-intensity, colorless vision, differ from cones, both morphologically and functionally. Rod outer segments consist of a large number of laminations, usually referred to as *discs*. Each disc contains an estimated 10,000 molecules of rhodopsin and each molecule is capable of absorbing a photon of light. Rhodopsin molecules do not move from one disc to another, or between receptors. There are about 1000 discs in each rod and about 10^8 rods in the eye, so the total number of rhodopsin molecules in the eye is on the order of 10^{15}.

The structure of the outer segment has been known only since the work of Sjöstrand in 1953; the estimates of the numbers of molecules per disc are indirect (see Wald, Brown, & Gibbons, 1963). It has also been established that the discs of rod outer segments are continuously replenishing themselves. New discs are formed at the base of the outer segment, near a constricted region (*cilium*) that connects the outer and inner segments. The discs move upward (toward the outer surface of the eye) at a rate of about 10 μm per day, eventually reaching the end of the outer segment, where they are sloughed off and are "eaten" by the *pigment epithelium*, into which the outer tips of the photoreceptors project (Young, 1971).

Rhodopsin is easily extracted from rod outer segments (see p. 106). Although the extraction of cone photopigments has never been accomplished, their characteristics have been examined by physical techniques to be described in the next chapter, and they are of the expected three different kinds. Cone outer segments also have discs, but upon close examination it is found that, rather than being self-contained as in rods, they are formed by an infolding of the cone membrane as shown in Figure 4.4. Evidence that cone discs are also replaced has recently been reported (Young, 1978); this occurs at different times for rods and cones during the diurnal cycle.

Another difference between rods and most cones is the shape of their outer segments, as seen in Figure 4.4. Except for the ciliary region, the overall shape of rods is cylindrical; they were appropriately named on the basis of their shape by early anatomical workers. The inner segments of most cones, by contrast, are much fatter, and taper near the outer segment to give them their conical form. However, the cones in the central fovea are rodlike in shape and actual dimensions, suggesting that shape is probably not the most critically distinguishing feature by which to classify rods and cones.

The remainder of each photoreceptor lies inside the outer limiting membrane. Rods have a connecting cilium separating their outer segments from the cell nucleus, from which another fiber leads to the termination of the rod, called the *spherule* because of its form. Cones, again, are different: the nucleus is more immediately juxtaposed with the inner segment; from it runs a long fiber connecting the nucleus to the foot of the cone, known as the cone *pedicle*. Cone pedicles differ from rod spherules in a number of respects. They lie somewhat deeper in the retina, they are much larger, and they are considerably more complex. These features are visible with the light microscope; the detailed nature of their complexity will be discussed shortly in connection with the evidence provided by electron microscopy.

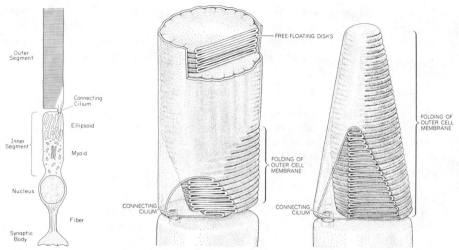

FIGURE 4.4 At the left is a generalized conception of the important structural features of a vertebrate photoreceptor cell. At the right are shown the differences between the structure of rod (left) and cone (right) outer segments. These diagrams are from Young (1970) and Young (1971).

Other Retinal Layers

The pigment epithelium, shown near the top of Figure 4.3, is not usually considered to be a part of the sensory retina; this begins instead with those portions of the photoreceptors lying outside the outer limiting membrane. The collection of rod and cone nuclei lying below the membrane is known as the *outer nuclear layer*. In the *outer plexiform layer*, near the cone pedicles and rod spherules, are the dendrites of the *bipolar* and *horizontal* cells. The cell bodies of the bipolar and horizontal cells lie in a thick region of the retina known as the *inner nuclear layer*, which also contains the cell bodies of the *amacrine cells*. These, unlike the horizontal and bipolar cells, make no direct contact with the photoreceptors. Although there are some exceptions, the horizontal cell bodies tend to be located outermost, the amacrine cell bodies innermost, and the bipolar cell bodies intermediate in the inner nuclear layer.

The *centripetal* (direct through) pathway for carrying visual information is from *receptor* to *bipolar* to *ganglion* cell. The nuclei of the latter form a third nuclear layer. The region between the ganglion cell and the inner nuclear layers, containing the various connections among bipolar, amacrine, and ganglion cells, is known as the *inner plexiform layer*. Recently, Dowling and Ehinger (1975) have discovered, in both fish and monkey, cells that connect the inner and outer plexiform layers. Their function is believed to be centrifugal—from inner to outer layers—and these have been called *interplexiform cells*.

The ganglion cell axons that emerge from the inner end of the ganglion cell bodies are the *optic nerve fibers* that connect eye and brain. In order to exit from the eyeball, all of these fibers course laterally in the eye (Fig. 4.5) as far as may be necessary to reach the *optic disc*.* This innermost layer of the retina is known as the *nerve fiber layer*. The full collection of optic nerve fibers, about a million of them, leaves the eye at the optic disc; they are contained outside the eye within the sheath of the *optic nerve*.*

> The blind spot is the sensory counterpart of the receptor-free optic disc, and is one of the easiest so-called *entoptic* phenomena to demonstrate. On a piece of white paper, draw a horizontal line about 15 cm long and lay a penny at the right end of it. With the left eye covered, look squarely at the line, using the right eye at a viewing distance of about 30 cm. Look first at the penny, and then shift fixation along the line to the left. A point will be reached where the penny disappears. For this condition, the image of the penny will be upon the nasal retina, about 16–18 degrees from the fovea, corresponding to the location of the optic disc. Continued movement of fixation leftward along the line will cause the penny to reappear as its image comes out of the blind spot on the other side. If the penny is removed and the experiment repeated, the blind spot is not perceived. Nor is it seen in everyday life.

The details of the connections among the six sensory cell types just described are of vital importance for understanding, or even speculating about, spatial and chromatic information processing in the retina. We shall return to a discussion of these connections presently. Before doing so, it will be useful to describe the anatomy of the *fovea centralis*, which differs from the rest of the retina in several important respects.

The Fovea Centralis

It is a curious feature of the vertebrate retina, implicit in what has already been discussed, that light must pass through so many retinal layers before finally reaching the photoreceptors. Moreover, there is an extensive vascular system in the retina that invades the inner nuclear, inner plexiform, and ganglion cell layers. (Part of one blood vessel is visible at the bottom left in Figure 4.3.) With the exception of the blood vessels, the other retinal structures are relatively transparent to light, so that to be clearly visible by light microscopy they must first be stained. A variety of staining techniques is available, some of which selectively invade neural tissue.

The blood vessels are not transparent; therefore they cast shadows on the receptor layer of the retina. These shadows normally are not seen, for two reasons. First, there are no blood vessels in the central fovea, where we see most critically. Second, the vessels occupy a fixed position, buried within the retina, so that their shadows upon the photoreceptors are stationary under normal conditions of seeing. This constitutes a natural form of stabilized retinal "image" which prevents the retinal vasculature from being seen except under unusual circumstances such as those of the previous exercise.

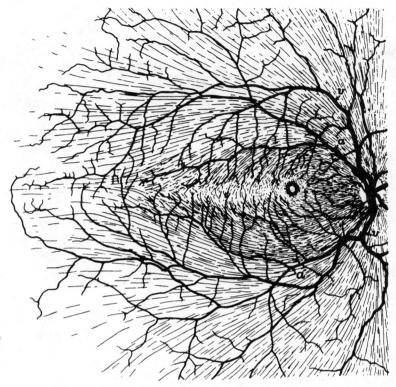

FIGURE 4.5 The thin lines show the pathways of the optic nerve fibers. The heavy lines are the blood vessels of the retina (see box below). The optic disc is at the far right; the fovea centralis appears as the encircled region to the left of the disc. This drawing is based on the anatomy of the rhesus macaque monkey, but is very similar to that of the human. (From Brown, 1965, and Polyak, 1941.)

Figure 4.6 illustrates the curious specialization that exists only in the fovea. First, the retina there is less than half as thick as in the remainder of the eye. The change in thickness creates the depression, or pit, from which the term *fovea* derives. Despite the thinness of the foveal retina, the outer segments of the photoreceptors are actually longer than anywhere else. They are also thinner and therefore more closely packed than elsewhere in the retina. All other neural

> Using a flashlight (a penlight will work best), shine the light obliquely upon the sclera in an otherwise dark room. Wiggling the light slightly is helpful. What should be seen is a map of the retinal vasculature, like that of Figure 4.5, seen as if projected outward in space. It should be possible to discern, with practice, that there are no vessels at the point of fixation (corresponding to the fovea). This subjective vascular map will, of course, move with the eye.

Retinal Anatomy

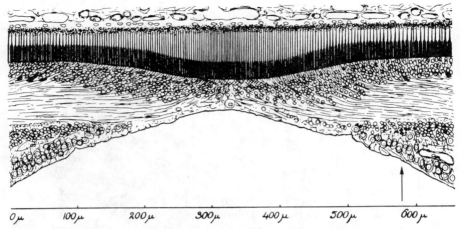

FIGURE 4.6 Central fovea of the human retina. (From Polyak, 1957.)

tissues in the fovea, including the cell bodies of the foveal cones, are laterally displaced.

If one were somehow to insert an electrode radially into the retina at the location shown by the arrow in Figure 4.6 in order to stimulate the ganglion cell body located there, the apparent location of the light that would be seen would differ from that caused by photic excitation of the receptor at the point along the retina toward which the arrow points. The result of such electrical stimulation would appear as if nearer to the point of fixation, because the electrically excited ganglion cell is one that normally would be excited by photons striking near the center of the foveal pit.

This hypothetical experiment illustrates an aspect of the law of specific nerve energies that was mentioned in Chapter 1: the brain must interpret the meaning of incoming messages along a particular neuron according to the location of the receptor that, if stimulated in the normal way by light, would give rise to activity in that neuron. A phenomenon known as the "blue arcs of the retina" serves further to demonstrate this point.*

It is likely that the blue arcs are caused by excitation provided by neurons somewhere between receptors and ganglion cells, lying near the path of ganglion cell axons whose origins are near the fovea (Moreland, 1969a). The arc-

---

To see the "blue arcs of the retina" a small red or orange light is best (Moreland, 1968b). The display of numbers on a pocket calculator will work. The arcs are best seen about 1–3 minutes after extinguishing normal room lighting, in a dark room, with the gaze directed just a bit to one side of the red light. It may help to move the light a bit, or to interrupt it. A faint bluish-white arc will be seen to flash in the visual field.

like paths of these fibers are anatomically well established (Fig. 4.5), and the perceived arcs are the exact projections of these paths. Although it has been hypothesized that bioluminescence from these fibers might activate the underlying rods with light, experiments by Alpern and Dudley (1966) and Moreland (1968) have shown this to be unlikely. (See Moreland [1968b, 1969] for additional references and data related to the blue-arc phenomenon.)

The anatomy of the foveal pit has important implications for the resolution of fine visual detail. In order to dissect a highly detailed optical image, it is necessary to have a high density of photoreceptors. There are about 150,000 cones per mm^2 in the central fovea, a far greater concentration than elsewhere in the eye. To have a retinal image of excellent optical quality formed upon the photoreceptors, it is necessary to reduce the scattered light in the retina as much as possible; this is neatly accomplished with the foveal depression. The improved spatial resolution that results is not accomplished at the expense of sensitivity to light. On the contrary, the fovea of the light-adapted retina is its region of highest sensitivity.* In addition to the better optical image at the fovea, this sensitivity is probably also due to the structure of foveal cones and the larger numbers of pathways to the brain that the foveal cones enjoy by comparison with the remainder of the retina.

> Using a hard pencil, make a very light gray dot in the center of a sheet of blank white paper. Under strong illumination, move the point of fixation away from the dot and notice that it disappears. This is not a general result, however. The dimmest perceptible spots of light that can be seen in the dark, when the eye is well dark adapted (see Chapter 6), are seen by rods alone and disappear when directly fixated. To see them, one must shift the point of regard slightly to one side. This is quite easy to demonstrate on a starry night.

Figure 4.7 permits a visualization of how the cones are arranged in the central fovea, and the *parafovea* which surrounds it. The small circles in the bullseye are cross-sections of cone outer segments. This "central bouquet" of cones, numbering only a few hundred, is the region of visual fixation. As one moves from the center of the bullseye, the diameters of the cone inner segments begin to increase at once, and have at least doubled at only 0.05 mm from the center, corresponding to less than 10 minutes of visual angle. The first rods are seen as small dots starting at about 0.1 mm, meaning that there is a region of about two-thirds of a degree in diameter within which there are no rods whatever, called the *rod-free area* of the fovea. Farther out, the cones continue to fatten and the rods to increase in number. At the margin of the foveal pit, which roughly corresponds to the end of the diagram at the right, there are many more rods than cones per unit area, although the fat cones still occupy more space than do the slender rods.

A quantitative estimate of the distribution of rods and cones in the human

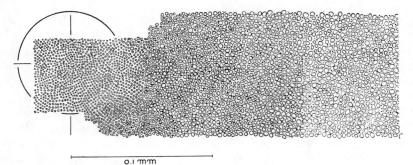

FIGURE 4.7 Horizontal section through a region of the human retina containing the fovea, whose exact center is at the intersection of the straight lines at the left. The section is through the inner segments. Cones appear as open circles whose diameter enlarges toward the parafovea; rods are seen as small black dots. (From Pirenne, 1948, Fig. 28, p. 28-29.)

retina is given in Figure 4.8. Note that the peak densities for rods and cones are nearly equal, but that the maximum rod density lies well out in the periphery. The declination of the rod function to zero at the fovea is quite steep. The decline of cone density from the exact foveal center is even steeper; beyond about 10 degrees, the density of cones becomes roughly uniform across the retina.

The emphasis upon the importance of the foveal region of the retina should not be permitted to obscure the importance of cones in the peripheral retina. From Figure 4.8 it may be estimated that only about 4 percent of the cones are in the fovea. Moreover, when considering the relative densities of rods and cones in the peripheral retina, account must be taken of the much larger cross section of the peripheral cones relative to the rods. In attempting to estimate the relative probabilities that a photon will be absorbed in a rod or cone, the density values of the cone curve of Figure 4.8 would need to be multiplied by something like a factor of ten.*

> Take a long mailing tube, and while covering the left eye, try to move about in a room while looking monocularly through the tube. It would be easy enough to read the "20/20" line on an acuity chart this way, and by that criterion be judged to have normal vision. But the actual visual loss is almost catastrophic: as the head moves, the world appears to sweep by the end of the tube in the opposite direction; orientation is difficult and walking very dangerous. Even in a very familiar room, it is hard to direct the line of sight toward a known object designated as the target; with the full visual field this occurs rapidly and easily, and clearly depends upon peripheral vision. Remove the tube (or open the other eye) and note that the perception of color in the peripheral visual field, corresponding to the peripheral retina, is very evident.

Electron Microscopy 89

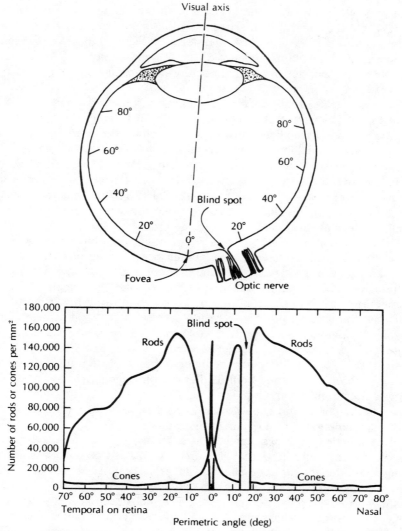

FIGURE 4.8 Rod and cone density as a function of retinal location. (From Cornsweet, 1970, Fig. 7.2, p. 137.)

EVIDENCE OF ELECTRON MICROSCOPY

In a pair of important papers, Dowling and Boycott (1966) and Boycott and Dowling (1969) systematically developed a number of indicators that made it possible to identify certain important features in electron micrographs of retinal tissue. Often, using these indicators, one can tell which region of the picture belongs to what type of cell and discern where synaptic connections exist. The use of this and other information, including that of other workers, allowed them to assemble the summary diagram of Figure 4.9. By comparing Figure 4.3 with Figure 4.9, it is evident that the sizes of various structures, and the thicknesses of the retinal layers, are considerably distorted in Figure 4.9, which is essentially a diagram of connections and not of literal neuroanatomy. It also lacks an example of the sixth type of retinal neuron, the recently discovered interplexiform cell.

Photons are absorbed in the outer segments of the rods and cones, shown at the top of Figure 4.9. A single such event, at least in a rod, is all that is required to elicit a useful signal from that receptor. Such an event therefore must produce a signal that is somehow transmitted down the length of the rod. The signal also must be communicated to a bipolar cell, since a half-dozen or so such events, occurring in different rods, are sufficient to arouse a visual sensation (Hecht, Shlaer, & Pirenne, 1942; Sakitt, 1972). Thus rods must also be able to excite the bipolar cells to which they connect, and through them the ganglion cells that carry the message to the brain.

The cone pedicles, which are 5 or 6 μm in diameter, have between 15 and 30 indentations, called *invaginations*, at their base. A triad of processes inserts into each invagination. The central one of these leads to a bipolar cell, always of the same type, originally called a *midget bipolar* by Polyak (1957). (An exception to this has been reported by Stell, Lightfoot, Wheeler and Leeper [1975] in the goldfish retina, where the central process sometimes is from a horizontal cell—see Fig. 7.9.) The lateral processes come from horizontal cells. In the centripetal pathway, midget bipolars synapse exclusively with *midget ganglion cells*. A second type of cóne bipolar, the *flat bipolar*, makes its contacts on the flat portions of cone pedicles between invaginations; recent evidence suggests that some midget bipolars may also do this. A flat bipolar connects from 7 to 12 cones and cannot therefore be supposed to carry information specifically attributable to any particular cone.

Electrophysiological evidence indicates that the signals produced by receptors, bipolar cells, and horizontal cells are slow, graded potentials, which differ in amplitude depending upon stimulus intensity. Such potentials are very different from action potentials of the sort that occur in many parts of the nervous system, which were once thought to be universal. Amacrine cells produce transients at the onset of a light stimulus, and again when the light is extinguished. Ganglion cells that produce transient bursts of spikes may receive their input largely from amacrine cells (see MacLeod, 1978, for discussion and references). The ganglion cells generate true action potentials capable of carrying the visual message over the relatively long distance to the brain. A word of caution is in order regarding these generalizations about retinal signals, because the evidence so far has come mostly from nonprimate and cold-blooded material. Some of it is from the mud puppy (*Necturus*), a creature whose retinal cells are considerably larger than those of primates, but are organized in much the same way (see Fig. 4.10). It has proved possible to impale all five kinds of retinal neurons in *Necturus* with microelectrodes, to record from them, and finally to inject a

Electron Microscopy 91

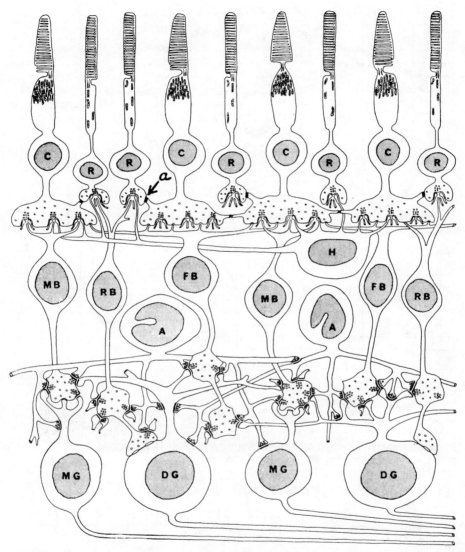

FIGURE 4.9 The schematic retina of Dowling and Boycott Z1966). **R**, rod; **C**, cone; **MB**, midget bipolar; **RB**, rod bipolar; **FB**, flat bipolar; **H**, horizontal cell; **A**, amacrine cell; **MG**, midget ganglion cell; **DG**, diffuse ganglion cell.

dye through the electrode in order to verify later, histologically, the cell whose response has been recorded. Similar intracellular records from fish and turtles, relevant to their color vision, will be discussed in Chapter 7. No such intracellular records have as yet been possible in primates, excepting spike discharges of the ganglion cells.[10]

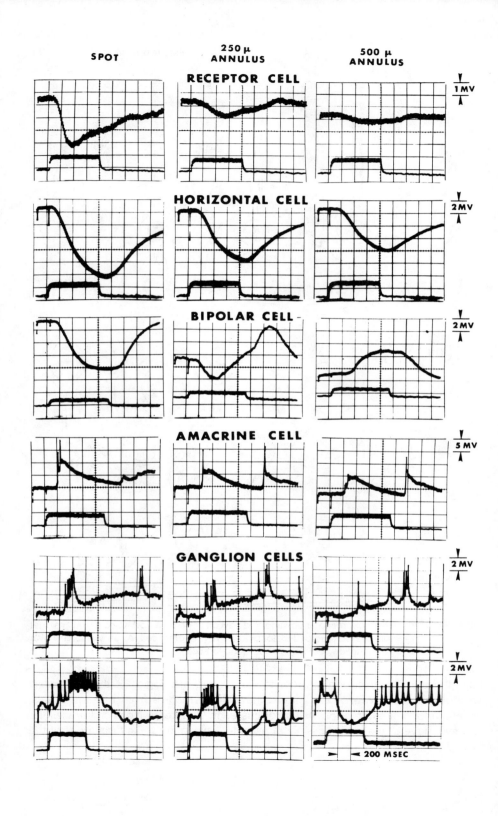

We are not overly concerned with rods here because rods cannot, by themselves, mediate color discrimination (Chapter 5). However, to the extent that rods are functional in the same eye that contains cones, they potentially complicate color vision. Therefore it is interesting to note the following:

- There are direct contacts, in some cases, between rod spherules and cone pedicles, as shown at *a* in Figure 4.9.
- Horizontal cells connect to both rods and cones.
- Bipolar cells connect only to rods or to cones, depending upon type, but bipolar cells of both types connect to the same amacrine and ganglion cells.

It seems apparent that the retina is replete with possibilities for interactions between rods and cones.

At the light levels required for good color vision, rods do not contribute to vision to a significant extent, at least in the central retina. In the central fovea this is true because no rods are stimulated there by a small light source; elsewhere the rods saturate (Aguilar & Stiles, 1954) at luminances corresponding roughly with those provided by good indoor illumination, where the cones of course continue to react discriminatively. The structures in Figure 4.9 that seem to be concerned exclusively with rod vision include the rods themselves, and the rod bipolars, which connect only to rods.

SOME SPECULATIONS ABOUT FUNCTION

As shown in Figure 4.9, horizontal cells connect only to receptors. The diagram is misleading because it shows no horizontal cell input via the central process of any cone invagination, and because the single horizontal cell depicted there is shown as if it connects to cones and rods not far separated from one another. Horizontal cells that contact both rods and cones do so in a peculiar way. The primary contact is with cones in the neighborhood of the horizontal cell body. The contact with rods is quite distant, mediated by a very long axon (*telodendron*) whose terminal arborization makes contact with rods (Kolb, 1970). Horizontal cells are estimated to cover as much as 1000 μm laterally in the retina. A typical cell has seven groupings of dendritic terminals, believed to represent connections with seven cones. It also seems likely that any given cone is in contact with from two to four horizontal cells. Horizontal cells have not been shown to make contact with one another in the primate retina.

FIGURE 4.10   These records are taken with electrodes inside the cells of retinal neurons of the **Necturus** retina. Light stimulates the eye for 200 ms, as shown at the bottom. Receptors, horizontal cells, and bipolar cells respond with slow potential changes that build while the light is on, and diminish afterward, with some delay. The first action potentials, or "spikes" are seen in the amacrine cell. The response of the gnaglion cell that carries the visual message to the brain consists of the action potentials and not the slow waves upon which they are superimposed under these conditions of recording (Werblin & Dowling, 1969).

It is speculated that horizontal cells receive information from cones and pass it back again to cones. Their synaptic relations with the cones—the way that their processes flank the centripetal contact that cones make with the bipolar cells—suggest that they exert some sort of modulating influence upon the signals being passed from cones to bipolars.[11] Another possibility is that, by feeding back upon the receptors, they actually influence the potentials generated by the receptors themselves. In any case, horizontal cells appear to tie groups of receptors together.

That horizontal cells are probably involved with the processing of chromatic information is suggested by the fact that, in fish and turtles, some horizontal cells are found that produce a response whose polarity depends upon the wavelength of the light stimulating the retina (first discovered by Svaetichin in 1956; see Chapter 7).

In *Necturus*, the amacrine cells are the first to respond preferentially to transients, by producing large signals to the onset and offset of illumination (Fig. 4.10). They may have a role to play in visual adaptation but they are also likely to be involved, because they connect directly to one another, in long-distance lateral effects of the sort described in Chapter 2 that occur in color perception.

Very likely the centripetal pathway from receptor to bipolar to ganglion cell in primates is subject to influences from (1) connections of flat bipolars with many cones; (2) collection by diffuse ganglion cells of signals from many bipolars; (3) the presence of two types of lateral cells in the retina (horizontal and amacrine cells), which presumably modify the function of the centripetal pathways in important respects. It is not yet known exactly how these cells interact to process chromatic information, though it is virtually certain that they do. It seems likely that the more diffusely organized cells are of special importance for color vision, whereas those with more limited lateral organization, particularly the midget bipolars and ganglion cells, are likely to be particularly concerned with the preservation of signals that are essential for pattern vision.

SUMMARY

The major focus of this chapter is upon the retina, where receptors (rods and cones) absorb photons and produce the first signals of vision, now known to be slow potentials quite unlike ordinary nerve action potentials. But the retina comprises only a tiny part of the mobile eye, which normally samples the visual environment in a complicated series of saccadic and smooth movements. The eye is always in motion, even during the act of fixation. Nevertheless, a cooperative observer can fixate well enough to localize, within reasonable limits of accuracy, the region of the retina being experimentally stimulated.

The optical elements of the eye, which allow the formation of the retinal image, are described. Most light refraction occurs at the optical interface between air and cornea. The iris controls the entry of light into the eye, helping to maintain an image quality that the retinal nervous system can fully utilize, while serving also as one mechanism of light adaptation. The act of accommodation allows the lens of the eye to change its shape so as to modulate the optical power of the eye, keeping objects at various distances from the eye in good focus.

The various layers of the retina, as revealed by light and electron microscopy, are described. The outer segments of the rods and cones contain the essential photosensitive pigments that react to the absorption of light. The fovea centralis is an important and highly specialized retinal region lacking in blood vessels, where the other structures that cover most of the retina are laterally displaced so that a high quality image can be formed there. This is also the retinal region of highest spatial acuity, greatest light-adapted sensitivity, and optimal attention value. The central part of the fovea is devoid of rods, and the density of the long and slender cones is at a maximum there. The remainder of the cones in the eye are literally cone shaped, have a much larger cross section, and are found in the peripheral retina.

Electron microscopy has begun to reveal in detail some of the elaborate connections among the nerve cells of the retina. Of particular interest are the horizontal cells that interconnect the cones. That horizontal cells are probably involved with the processing of chromatic information is indicated by the opposite polarity of response exhibited by some of them, depending upon the wavelength of the absorbed light.

The centripetal pathway from receptor to bipolar to ganglion cell is affected by lateral influences from (1) connections of flat bipolars with many cones; (2) the collection by diffuse ganglion cells of signals from many bipolars; and (3) the two types of lateral cells of the retina (horizontal and amacrine).

NOTES

[1] The Golgi stain proved to be especially valuable. It has the curious property of selectively staining only a small proportion of neurons. The use of the new staining techniques was taken up most vigorously by the famed anatomist S. R. Cajal, whose work on the vertebrate retina has been translated into English by R. W. Rodieck (1973) as an appendix to his comprehensive and highly recommended textbook, *The Vertebrate Retina*. Cajal was the first to show that all vertebrate retinas contain the same basic elements in about the same configuration.

[2] We shall return to the electroretinogram, though only briefly, in Chapter 7. A comprehensive summary of this subject, including its early history, has been provided by Armington (1974).

[3] A summary of bioelectric recording techniques is available in a three-volume set edited by R. F. Thompson and M. M. Patterson (1973, 1974).

[4] Although it is important that there are two eyes rather than only one, monocular color vision differs little from the binocular variety. Most of the time, in this book, we will pretend that vision occurs through only one eye.

[5] Saccadic movements of the eyes are very rapid (up to $800°/s^{-1}$), therefore the accelerative forces that they produce cannot be negligible. Richards (1968) has suggested

that a decrease in visual sensitivity occurs during a saccadic eye movement, due to shearing forces acting upon the receptors. The neural machinery of the eye must be able to withstand such forces. Since the tissues of the eye are not rigid, this means that there can be no empty space in the eye. Most people have a perceptible amount of debris in the vitreous, which is free to move to some degree within the vitreal jelly; these are called *muscae volitantes*. They appear subjectively as "floaters" in visual space, whose motion can be induced by making eye movements. Donders reported floaters that remained in the visual field for 17 years (Zoethout, 1947, p. 105).

[6] For a brief and readable summary of the eye movement control system, see Robinson (1968). For a recent multiauthored survey of the subject, see Monty and Senders (1976).

[7] An encylopedic coverage of research on the fading of vision with stabilized retinal images has been published by Ditchburn (1973).

[8] These values are from Zoethout (1947, p. 55). They refer to a schematic eye developed by Gullstrand.

[9] Figure 4.3 displays the retinal cross section in the conventional way, with the outside of the eye at the top, and the inside at the bottom. In this representation, light is incident upon the retina from the bottom of the diagram and travels toward the top. The top of the retina, as shown here, is also called *distal* or *scleral*; the bottom, *proximal* or *vitreal*. Near the fovea, a line drawn from the center of the eye would pass vertically through Figure 4.2; for that reason such a direction is called *radial*.

[10] Much of the evidence cited here has been nicely summarized by Dowling (1970) in the published version of the Jonas M. Friedenwald Memorial lecture, delivered to the Association for Research in Vision and Ophthalmology.

[11] See Tomita, Kaneko, Murakami, and Pautler (1967). See also MacNichol and Svaetichin (1958). In an earlier report, Svaetichin mistakenly thought that his records were from receptors. In the 1958 study, a dye injection technique was used to show that the potentials came from "more proximal structures," presumably horizontal cells. This presumption has proved to be correct.

5

Color Matching and the Visual Pigments

To attain an understanding of color vision we must consider complex events at three different levels. First there is the great variety of subjective color phenomena such as those mentioned in Chapter 2; these are what must be explained. In searching for an explanation, a natural place to start is with the physical events leading to the stimulation of the eye, since it is here that the process of color vision begins. Yet a consideration of the physics of color (Chapter 3), far from accounting for what we see, confronts us with a strangely complicated situation that does not seem to correspond in any simple or direct way with our visual experience. Newton's experiments with prisms (Chapter 1) illustrate this: a surface that appears white may be sending to the eye a stimulus compounded of photons of every possible wavelength, and yet the resulting sensation of a simple uniform white gives no impression of any such complexity. To establish this requires more than an eye: it also requires physical instrumentation. In this sense, our sensations fail to do justice to the physical reality of the observed events. Certainly they do not represent these events in all their aspects.

And yet color vision would be impossible if there were not some relation between the physical stimulus and what is subjectively experienced. The complexity of the physical stimulus warns us, however, that the relationship cannot be a simple one. To understand color vision, we must understand this relationship, and the key to such understanding lies in the processes that intervene between reception of the physical stimulus on the one hand, and visual experience on the other. These processes occur in the intricate machinery of the visual pathways whose description began in Chapter 4. A considerable portion of the remainder of this book will be devoted to tracing the visual signals as they are transmitted through the visual pathway, and to examining what is known or hypothesized concerning the nature of these signals and of their transformations in retina and brain.

The guiding assumption behind any attempt to understand vision in terms of its physiological underpinnings is that visual experience depends at any particular time upon the specific events that are taking place in the visual pathway. Suppose, for example, that the eye were removed and a pattern of action potentials could somehow be sent down each of the million fibers of the optic nerve (in the direction of the brain), which is exactly the same as that produced by viewing a natural scene with eye and nerve intact. What will be seen as a result of the artificial stimulation of the optic nerve should, according to our guiding assumption, be indistinguishable from the natural scene as perceived with the visual system intact.

Suppose that we knew in minute detail the exact state of someone's visual pathway at a particular instant: would we then be able to characterize the nature of his visual experience? The answer is "no," unless we would also have available a catalog of all possible states of the visual pathway and their corresponding sensations. But we do not possess such a catalog and we never shall, because the number of possible states of the visual pathway is inconceivably large; so is the variety of possible visual experiences.

That the catalog required to document the relationship between pathway-states and sensation would be impossibly cumbersome is illustrated by a simple calculation based on the analog of color television. The red, green, and blue phosphor dots that make up the color TV picture (recall the exercise on page 36) number altogether about a million. Thirty separate pictures are delivered each second in order to provide a convincing illusion of motion and seemingly continuous visual input. Although brightness varies continuously in natural scenes, a reasonable depiction of brightness in a scene can be had with as few as eight discrete levels (R. E. Graham, 1958). Therefore, to specify the character of a color TV picture for only 1 s would require a table of $1,000,000 \times 30 \times 8$ or 240 million values. The situation in the visual pathway where the optic nerve leaves the eye is roughly the same: about 30 specifications per second of one of eight quantized levels of spike frequency in each of about one million optic nerve fibers would be needed to characterize the visual message.

In fact, our only knowledge of physiological events is based upon general principles and we have no means of determining in any detail what is actually happening in a particular individual's visual pathway at any particular time. Response indicators such as the electroretinogram or the evoked cortical potential, which will be described in Chapter 7, are orders of magnitude too crude to qualify. Therefore, progress in understanding vision must be based on the discovery of general principles in the subjective realm that can be related to what we know, or can hope to learn, about the operation of the visual pathway.

Because they are directed toward the discovery of simple general principles, basic experiments in visual science often make use of stimulus displays that may at first seem to be ridiculously simple. Yet it has been repeatedly shown that simple general principles will best reveal themselves in such perceptually impoverished situations, and that the principles discovered there are also applicable to vision in more complex everyday environments. To readers who are trained in physical science, this will be recognized as a normal way to proceed. (If there are any readers left at this point whose roots are in the visual arts, the approach will probably seem to them incredibly alien.)

The general class of investigation that has proved most useful for providing a bridge between physiology and sensation is the *psychophysical experiment*. In this type of study, the physical stimulus is kept simple, as just discussed, and so is the response: the observer (often called a *subject*) is not free to describe what he sees in just any way that he chooses. As we shall see in numerous examples to follow, his behavior is very much constrained. Simplification of procedure on the response end of the experiment carries with it the same kinds of advantages that accrue from simplifying the stimulus.

In attempting to build a bridge between physiology and sensation, it helps very much to have the stimulus specified in purely physical terms. The paradigm below illustrates this:

Psychophysics: Physical stimulus →Behavioral response
Physiology: Physical stimulus →Physiological response

This procedure allows a correlation to be made between the behavioral and physiological responses, especially when exactly the same physical stimuli have been used in both cases.

THE MATCHING OPERATION

One of the simplest and most fundamental experiments in color vision proceeds as follows. The subject is asked to fixate the center of a small disc, divided into two halves that can be separately illuminated. When the two halves of the disc are illuminated with light of the same spectral composition (so as to produce, for example, a white appearance in each half) the subject then sees the two halves merge so that the disc appears as a uniformly filled circle. This is not surprising, for the disc is now actually physically uniform. Suppose now that the spectral composition of the light illuminating the left half-circle is altered, without any change being made on the right. It is not surprising that the fields will now differ in color, since the discrimination of color has its physical basis in the composition of the spectrum, as we saw in Chapter 3.

Sometimes the expected fails to happen: in such cases an appreciable change in the spectral composition of one half of the field will go undetected by the subject, who continues to see a uniform white circle. In failing to perceive the physical difference between the two halves, the observer behaves as if he were "color-blind." Such apparent failures are not due to inattention but rather to inherent limitations of normal color vision.

To illustrate the fact that normal subjects may be regularly fooled, the two lights A and B, whose spectral distributions are shown in Figure 5.1, are matches for normal subjects under conditions where normal cone vision is operative. Two such stimuli are called *metamers*; stimuli that physically match, and for that reason also look identical, are called *isomers*. A trivial special case will serve to illustrate that there is no limit to the number of metamers that a stimulus may have: stimuli with identical spectral compositions within the visible spectrum may differ arbitrarily in their spectral composition in the ultraviolet region of the spectrum without being visually distinguishable. For stimuli that differ within the visible spectrum, however, metamerism is the exception rather than the rule; exact or even near metameric matches seldom occur outside the laboratory. This is fortunate, and it suggests that the amount of color discrimination that we possess is sufficient for all practical purposes.[1]

Two physically different lights will constitute an exact color match only under certain mathematically specifiable conditions. These constraints governing color matching are the most precisely established of the general principles relating to

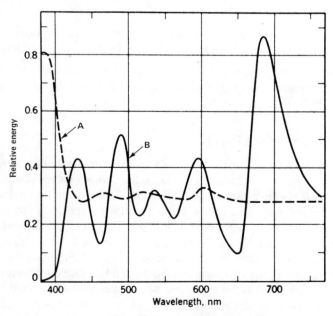

FIGURE 5.1 An example of two colors that will match for a typical observer, despite very great differences in the way that they reflect light as a function of wavelength. (Wyszecki & Stiles, 1967, p. 351.)

vision, and they have proved to be of cardinal importance for understanding the nature of the physiological processes involved in color vision.

METAMERIC MATCHING AND THE SPECTRAL SENSITIVITY OF ROD VISION

In Chapter 2, the point was made that color vision fails totally under dim illumination. As a preliminary to the analysis of true color vision, it is instructive to consider first the characteristics of colorless night vision (also known as *scotopic* vision). Scotopic vision, as it turns out, is mediated by rods, whereas daylight vision, including color vision, depends upon the activity of cones (this is called *photopic* vision). Because these two varieties of photoreceptors share certain basic characteristics, rod vision can be considered as a prototype for cone vision, one that is simpler and easier to analyze.

The failure of color vision at low light levels is not directly due to any impoverishment of the physical stimulus. Objects retain their characteristic spectral reflectance whatever the illumination level, and moonlight differs little from sunlight in terms of its relative spectral distribution. Our incapacity to distinguish between different colors in rod vision is a consequence of a fundamental limitation in the rods themselves, which fail to distinguish between physically different radiations for reasons that will shortly be explained.

Although in rod vision we are totally color-blind, we still manage to distinguish between some differently colored objects. This is possible because objects may still vary in their relative *lightnesses*.[2] Otherwise night vision would be impossible and we would be totally blind, rather than merely color-blind. But the lightness difference between two objects can be eliminated for rod vision merely by reducing the amount of light reaching the eye from the lighter object without any change in relative spectral distribution.

A Matching Experiment

We can bring this problem into the laboratory and examine it, for example by using the bipartite field of Figure 5.2. Suppose that each half of the field is illuminated by monochromatic light, with different wavelengths in the two halves—λ_1 for the left side, and λ_2 for the right. Suppose further that the intensities of the fields are set at such low levels that only the rods can see them. What appearance will the split field now present to the subject? Since the difference in color between the two halves of the field is not detected by the rods, the field might appear as a uniform circle. In fact, this happens only under rather special circumstances, namely when the relative intensities of the two half-circles are such as to exactly eliminate any difference in brightness between the two. Normally the two half-circles will differ in brightness; therefore, in order to investigate the color-matching properties of rod vision, the experimenter must make arrangements to eliminate that brightness difference. This is most conveniently done by giving the subject a means to control the light intensity[3] in

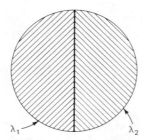

FIGURE 5.2 The appearance of a bipartite, or split, field as seen by an observer. The two halves of the field radiate monochromatic lights of different wavelengths. If the fields are dim it is always possible to adjust the intensity of one half of the field so that the two halves match exactly: the border disappears and the field is visually homogeneous.

one of the half-circles. If the subject is instructed to adjust the intensity so as to abolish any difference in brightness between the half-circles he finds that, once the brightnesses are equated, the two halves merge to form a uniform circle. This is what it means to be totally color-blind. There are some abnormal subjects (see p. 347) who would be able to produce a uniform circle for lights of any two wavelengths even at high intensities. Whereas these subjects are totally color-blind all of the time, all of us are totally color-blind under conditions where rods alone are functional.

Precisely what relative intensities are required to eliminate brightness differences and produce these matches for rod vision? This can be determined experimentally by placing a light detector in place of the subject's eye. By occluding first the left and then the right half-circle, the number[4] of photons impinging on the eye from each half-circle can be measured separately. It turns out that two lights of equal brightness for rods are by no means equal in any physical sense. For instance, when one half-circle is illuminated with light from the longwave end of the spectrum (that would appear red at high intensities) and the other is illuminated by blue or green light, the red half-circle must provide more than 10,000 times as many photons to the eye in order to match the other light. Rod vision, then, is not equally sensitive to photons of all wavelengths.

Spectral Sensitivity

The matching experiment may be used to define the relative sensitivity of rod vision to various wavelengths of monochromatic light. This is done by having the subject make matches between a fixed standard light in, say, the right half-circle and each of various test wavelengths delivered in turn to the left half-circle. Each time that a new wavelength is introduced on the left, the subject adjusts its intensity to make it match the standard, and then a physical light detector is used to measure the number of photons provided at the matching intensity. The results of these measurements specify the numbers of photons required at each of the wavelengths tested in order to produce a constant effect for rod vision.

The relative sensitivity of rod vision for the various wavelengths can now be defined as follows. At each wavelength of the test (left) field, take the *reciprocal* of the number of photons required to match the standard; the resulting number defines the *relative spectral sensitivity* of rod vision for that wavelength. Relative sensitivity is highest for wavelengths near 500 nm, since it turns out that in this spectral region the number of photons required for a match with the standard is least. Relative spectral sensitivity values are usually standardized by expressing each sensitivity value as a fraction of 1, with the unit value being assigned to the wavelength of greatest sensitivity. Lights of all other wavelengths therefore have a relative sensitivity less than 1. Sensitivity measured in this way is sometimes called *quantized* spectral sensitivity to distinguish it from *energy-based* spectral sensitivity. The latter depends upon measures of energy, rather than of photons.

Energy- vs Photon-Based Sensitivity

We have just seen that quantized sensitivity depends upon measuring the numbers of photons required for a constant effect. More often energy-based sensitivity is measured instead, and since the energy of a photon varies with wavelength, as we saw in Chapter 3, these measurements are not equivalent. For instance, when a red light includes 10,000 times as many photons as a blue one, the energy supplied by the red light is less than 10,000 times that supplied by the blue (recall that the longwave photons are vibrating more slowly). Since the energy of individual photons is inversely proportional to wavelength, a red light at 660 nm supplying 10,000 times as many photons would supply only about 7,000 times the energy of a blue light at 460 nm. Since sensitivity is reciprocally related to the amount of stimulation required for a certain visual effect, energy-based sensitivity (the reciprocal of energy required) is relatively greater in the long wavelengths than is photon-based sensitivity. The ratio of energy-based to photon-based sensitivity is proportional to wavelength. In this book we will describe the eye's spectral sensitivity both ways, with emphasis on the photon-based measure. Since the visible spectrum covers less than an octave of variation in wavelength, the two measures of sensitivity do not differ very much.

Need for a Logarithmic Ordinate

Spectral sensitivity for rod vision is shown two ways in Figure 5.3. At the top are shown at the reciprocals of the energies required for a match, normalized to 1.0 at the peak. This is exactly as described earlier in this chapter. At the bottom, the logarithm of sensitivity is plotted instead. Since the logarithm of 1 is zero, the curve assumes this value at its peak, and all other values, because they represent fractions, are negative. At wavelengths where the tails of the curves at the top appear to have run into the baseline, and whose ordinate

104 Color Matching and the Visual Pigments

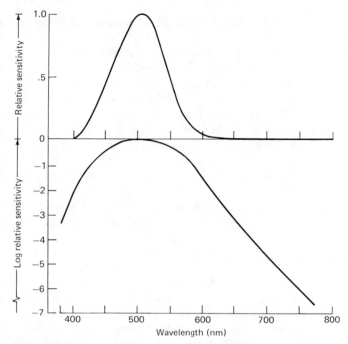

FIGURE 5.3 **Top:** Relative spectral sensitivity for rod vision, measured as described in the text, using a field like that of Figure 5.2. **Bottom:** The same curve, except that the ordinate values are scaled logarithmically. Note the way in which this brings out the details in the tails of the curve, which are lost in the top curve. Values are plotted on an energy basis. Wavelength scale is linear with its reciprocal, which is proportional to the frequency of photon vibration.

values therefore could be mistaken for zero, a finite sensitivity actually remains which is much more accurately represented on the logarithmic curve at the bottom. We will see later in this chapter that the tails of cone spectral sensitivity curves are critically important for understanding color vision; in order to achieve an accurate graphical impression, the logarithmic ordinate is essential.

It is only in a loose sense that we can refer to the "ends" of the visible spectrum. If radiation in the near infrared or ultraviolet is intense enough, it can be seen. Nevertheless, the notion that the visible spectrum has limits is valid because of the very rapid descent of spectral sensitivity at extreme wavelengths. Outside the range from 385 to 645 nm, more than 10,000 times as many photons would be required to stimulate rods, compared to the wavelength of maximum sensitivity. Outside these limits, therefore, photons are so unlikely to be effective that they can usually be ignored.

ON THE NARROWNESS OF THE VISIBLE SPECTRUM

Why is the eye sensitive only to a narrow range of wavelengths within the electromagnetic spectrum? Like many questions about vision, this one can be interpreted in two different ways. First it could be taken as a purely physical question: why are photons of infrared and ultraviolet light so unlikely to be effective upon rods? In the case of ultraviolet light, the answer is simple; it is because these photons are heavily absorbed by the lens and are thereby prevented from reaching the retina. In young people, the lens is almost transparent to long-wavelength light, with absorption increasing progressively toward the shorter visible wavelengths. During life, the lens grows thicker and less transparent, especially at the shorter wavelengths.[5]

Since photons of infrared radiation do reach the retina, why are we so insensitive to them? It has been shown that the decline in spectral sensitivity near the red "end" of the spectrum can be attributed to the lower energy values that are associated with the more slowly vibrating photons at longer wavelengths. (This will be elaborated shortly.)

A second way to answer the question about why the visible spectrum is so narrow is to consider the consequences for vision if the range of detected wavelengths could somehow be enlarged. This seems to pose a query about the purpose of the system, an approach to understanding that would be branded as "teleological" by some, and dismissed out of hand. This approach to biological questions, though admittedly risky, often produces interesting insights. It is not necessary to decide, or even to ask about, whether the "design" of the system has been provided by trial and error through evolution, or is due to the efforts of some Great Designer. However it may come about, the design of the visual system is so clever and exquisite that one cannot examine it without concluding that, at the very least, Nature is no fool.

From the standpoint of design, then, we note first that the yellowness of the lens, which is associated with its selective absorption of blue light, is not preordained. For example, cats and the African primate *Galago* (bush baby) have much more transparent lenses than humans, that transmit most of the incident light even at 400 nm.[6] The longwave limit is not absolutely fixed either, since a variety of cold-blooded animals have higher sensitivity than we to the near infrared. Why then have these enlarged visual capacities been denied to man?

Consider the benefits and disadvantages of ultraviolet vision. The benefits are limited because ultraviolet radiation in the usable range of wavelengths is sparsely represented in the natural environment, so that sensitivity to these very short wavelengths would increase the effective intensity of the retinal image by only a small amount. Probably more important is the harm that the added shortwave light would do because of the eye's marked and uncorrected chromatic aberration (p. 67).

What about the infrared limitation? Pirenne has suggested (1948, pp.

53–54) that very high sensitivity to infrared would be undesirable because the human body continuously radiates a quantity of infrared radiation commensurate with body temperature. This body heat is present inside the eyeball, so if we were sensitive to infrared light we would probably see it as a luminous fog that would tend to obscure the visibility of external objects. Thus we may have evolved a low infrared sensitivity in order to avoid this fog, along with a lens that screens out ultraviolet light that would otherwise obliterate details because of chromatic aberration.

MONOCHROMACY AND THE MOLECULAR BASIS OF VISION

Rhodopsin: The Rod Pigment

To generate a visual sensation, light must be absorbed within the retina, and the retina must somehow register that absorption by itself undergoing a change that will initiate the process leading to sensation. With this in mind, many investigators have looked for signs that light can affect the state of the retina. The first successful experiments were reported by Franz Boll in 1876 (see also Hubbard, 1977). He found that if he removed an eye from an animal and aimed it at a brightly-lit window, subsequent examination of the retina under dim light showed an image of the window still present on the retina as a kind of photographic record which Boll called an "optogram." Where it had not been exposed to light, the retina appeared purplish pink, but the part where the image of the window had fallen had become almost transparent. From this demonstration Boll concluded that the retina contained some kind of pinkish substance that became transparent when exposed to light.

Not long after Boll's first observations, this substance was isolated by chemists from retinal extracts and was given the name *rhodopsin*, from the Greek words *rhodos*, meaning red, and *ops*, the eye. The fact that this stuff was present in the retina at a considerable concentration, and underwent a change (becoming relatively transparent when light fell upon it) at once suggested that rhodopsin might play a critical role in the process of vision. Subsequent experiments have confirmed this, and have established a link between the pinkish color of rhodopsin and the spectral sensitivity of night vision.

The pinkish color is characteristic of rhodopsin from the eyes of many animals, including man. The color is determined by rhodopsin's *absorption spectrum*, based on the variation with wavelength of the probability that a photon will be absorbed in rhodopsin. Photons that are not absorbed are mostly reflected, and the purplish-pink color is seen because rhodopsin reflects more of the spectral extremes than of the middle portion of the spectrum.

Because only absorbed light can cause a change in rhodopsin, visual sensitivity is greatest for the wavelengths that are most absorbed by it. The correlation between the sensations of night vision and the absorption spectrum of rhodopsin is so close as to make it virtually certain that the effects of light upon rhodopsin, rather than upon other substances, are responsible. In terms of the paradigm mentioned earlier:

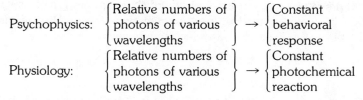

It should be emphasized that these relations do not absolutely prove that a photochemical reaction is the basis for the constant behavioral response. But the highly quantitative nature of the agreement strongly supports the hypothesis of a causal link.

Rhodopsin is not, as we shall soon see, the only visual pigment, and it is not involved at all in normal color vision at high light levels. Nevertheless, because the principles of its reactions are probably the same as for cone photopigments and it has proved much easier to examine, some further examination of the photochemistry of rhodopsin is worthwhile. What is the nature of the change that rhodopsin undergoes when exposed to strong light? Thanks principally to the investigations of George Wald, for which he was awarded a Nobel prize,[7] we know that rhodopsin passes through a long sequence of separately identifiable states before reaching the colorless condition in which Boll first observed it.

Mechanisms of Absorption in Rhodopsin

When a rhodopsin molecule absorbs a photon, it will be effective for vision only if it can raise the internal energy of the system of electrons in the rhodopsin molecule so that it exceeds a critical level. The gap between the baseline energy level and the critical energy level is usually too large to be bridged by a very long-wavelength photon. If the baseline energy level were constant, we might expect the visible spectrum to terminate abruptly at some long wavelength beyond which photons are suddenly too feeble to be effective. But the random variation of the baseline, which is caused by thermal fluctuations of electron energy, allows any long-wavelength photon some chance of producing a molecular effect, even if this chance be very small. For this reason, lights of long wavelengths can be seen if they are strong enough to provide enough photons to counteract the high odds against success for any one of them.

Infrared vision has been demonstrated at least to one micron of wavelength (1000 nm) (Griffin, Hubbard, & Wald, 1947). For wavelengths in the range from about 660 nm and beyond, it has been observed that sensitivity varies with wavelength according to a simple function compatible with the physical explanation just provided:

$$\log S_\lambda = k + a/\lambda \qquad (5.1)$$

where S_λ is the sensitivity at wavelength λ, k is a constant independent of wavelength, and a is another constant having a value of about 14,600 if wavelength is in nm. This equation means that sensitivity in the far red part of the spectrum (700 nm) changes by a factor of about 7 percent per nm. This value varies slightly with wavelength. But if we rewrite Equation (5.1) in terms of frequency of vibration, f, instead of wavelength, we get

$$\log S_\lambda = k + a'f \qquad (5.2)$$

which means that, as the frequency of vibration of a photon increases (which shortens the wavelength), log sensitivity rises linearly. Because the x-axis of Figure 5.3 is linear with wavelength according to the more common convention for visual research, the function exhibits a slight upward concavity at long wavelengths.

Equation (5.2) holds good for both cone and rod vision. Physical considerations suggest that the value of the constant a' should depend upon the individual's temperature. Brindley and Lewis (cited in Brindley, 1960), following a lead from the Dutch scientist Hessel De Vries, heated and cooled themselves over a small but sufficient range to produce corresponding changes in spectral sensitivity.[8]

Rhodopsin and Human Spectral Sensitivity

The identification of rhodopsin as the visual pigment for human night vision was first firmly established by Helmholtz's most illustrious student, Arthur König, in 1894. For his experiments, König constructed a sophisticated spectrophotometer, a device that could direct a beam of spectral light of any chosen wavelength into a solution, in order to measure the quantity of light passing through it. König had planned to begin his experiments using animals, but chance presented him with a pair of fresh human retinas just after he had gotten his apparatus ready. Being very careful not to bleach any, he extracted the rhodopsin from the retinas and put the pinkish solution in his spectrophotometer. He then passed light of several wavelengths through the solution, doing this in turn as he spanned the visible spectrum and recorded how much light of each wavelength was transmitted.

Next, König bleached the rhodopsin and made a similar set of measurements on the bleached solution. In this second set of measurements, rhodopsin—having been fully bleached—was not absorbing any light. The difference between the measurements before and after bleaching therefore represented light lost by absorption in the rhodopsin before bleaching. It was then possible to estimate the absorption spectrum of rhodopsin in the following way: Denote the tested wavelength by λ and the intensities of the light passing through the rhodopsin solution, before and after bleaching, by $I_1(\lambda)$ and $I_2(\lambda)$ respectively. The amount of light absorbed by rhodopsin at each wavelength is $I_2(\lambda) - I_1(\lambda)$.

Expressed as a fraction of $I_{2\lambda}$, the absorbed amount is

$$\frac{I_{2\lambda} - I_{1\lambda}}{I_{2\lambda}}.$$

The variation of this fraction across the spectrum traces out the absorption spectrum. If what matters for vision is the amount of light absorbed in rhodopsin, the absorption spectrum of rhodopsin must determine the spectral sensitivity of rod vision. König found this to be true within experimental error: absorption was maximal at about 500 nm, and fell off progressively on either side of that wavelength.

König put the comparison between the absorption spectrum of rhodopsin and human spectral sensitivity on a quantitative basis. Consider again the spectral sensitivity of Figure 5.3, which was obtained by asking an observer to choose the intensities that made each wavelength, taken in turn, look the same as a fixed standard stimulus. If it is true that the observer detects these lights according to the effects that they have on rhodopsin, a prediction can be made about the absorption spectrum, based upon the visual matches. At any given wavelength, the amount of light absorbed in rhodopsin is proportional to the intensity of the incident light, with a constant of proportionality given by the absorption spectrum of rhodopsin. This proportionality depends upon the probability that any individual photon will be absorbed, multiplied by the numbers of such photons that are available. The amount of light absorbed by rhodopsin from stimuli of different wavelengths can be made equal by setting the intensities to be inversely proportional to the values of the absorption spectrum at the wavelengths in question. For example, if a change in wavelength reduces the probability of photon absorption to a tenth of what it had been before the change, the initial absorption can be regained by pouring in ten times as many photons. Since spectral sensitivity as measured psychophysically is by definition the reciprocal of the amount of light required for a match to the standard, the prediction is simply that the spectral sensitivity of night vision and the absorption spectrum of rhodopsin should be proportional.

A complication, recognized by König, is that a significant amount of shortwave light is lost in vision by being absorbed, mainly by the lens, before it can reach the visual pigment. When this is taken into account, König found the proportionality principle to hold within experimental error: visual spectral sensitivity was found proportional to the absorption spectrum of rhodopsin multiplied by the spectral transmittance of the eye media.

The Principle of Univariance

König's observation, that similar sensations result when rhodopsin absorbs equal amounts of light at different wavelengths, would not be logically inevitable even if rhodopsin were the only operative visual pigment. We need one further assumption to make it so, which the visual physiologist William Rushton has called the *principle of univariance*. According to this principle, the effect of absorbed photons upon the visual pigment is independent of their wavelengths. The biochemical evidence supports this assumption by showing that the initial action of light upon rhodopsin is to cause a conformational change in the rhodopsin molecule of the sort depicted in Figure 5.4, known as *photo-isomerization*. If visual sensations are generated as a result of such actions, equal numbers of molecules isomerized must lead to indistinguishable sensations. The photopigment molecule does not know anything about the wavelength of the photon that isomerized it: only the fact that the event has taken place is signalled. Because of this, lights of any two wavelengths can cause equal amounts of isomerization, provided that their intensities are adjusted to take into account the relative probabilities that photons of these two wavelengths will cause isomerization to occur. Without the limitation imposed by the principle of univariance, we might be able to distinguish colors by using only one visual pigment; because of univariance, we fail.

Additional Complications

The problem of prereceptoral absorption has been considered as one factor that would be expected to cause a difference between spectral sensitivity as found psychophysically and that obtained in the chemistry lab. There are other complications which must also be taken into account.

- It is important to be precise about the units in which the amounts of light at various wavelengths are measured. Because the number of molecules isomerized depends upon the number of photons absorbed, and not upon the energy of each absorbed photon, the light must be measured in numbers of photons (rather than in energy units).

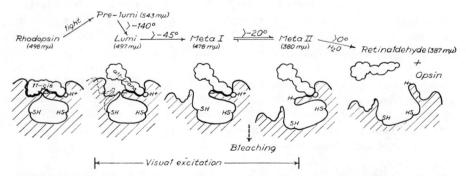

FIGURE 5.4 **Isomerization** refers to a change in the configuration of a molecule, with other changes of its constituent atoms or linkages. In this depiction, from Wald (1968, p. 234), the absorption of a photon is shown to cause a change in the configuration of the chromophore of rhodopsin, which initially in the **11-cis** form and is locked onto the protein base of the molecule as shown at the far left. As it straightens to the **all-trans** form and is dissociated from the protein base, the chromophore has participated in the process of bleaching.

- Spectrophotometry on whole retinas suggests that the absorption spectrum of the rhodopsin retina exhibits a "red shift" when compared to the absorption spectrum in solution, with the wavelength of peak sensitivity moving slightly toward the longer wavelengths.
- In extracting visual pigments, solvents must be used and these selectively absorb some light as a function of wavelength: this places a selective "filter" in the test-tube that must be taken into account in the chemistry lab, just as the preretinal absorption must be dealt with in the psychophysical experiment.
- The products of bleaching also absorb light, and although their concentration depends upon the amount of bleaching that has occurred, the light which these photoproducts absorb does not contribute to vision.

The red shift of whole retinas is not yet understood, although it is possible that the fraction of incident light that is retained within the receptor may vary with wavelength. More can definitely be stated about the matter of units. Even a photon of relatively high energy will isomerize only the particular molecule that absorbs it. This has been established by experiments comparing the absorption spectrum of a rhodopsin solution with its *action spectrum*. If the amount of light is measured in photons, the action spectrum is proportional to the absorption spectrum. But if the amount is measured in energy units, the two functions differ by a factor proportional to wavelength. The visual matching experiment is, in effect, a determination of the action spectrum, and exact agreement with the absorption spectrum can be expected only if the light is measured in photons.

It is probably just as well that König was not aware of all of these complications. He measured energy, since photons were unknown at the time. Using rhodopsin in solution, his measurements could not reveal the red shift of receptors *in situ*. It is doubtful that his rhodopsin extracts were perfectly pure. Individually these complications introduce errors that are small and to some extent compensatory; in the end, the agreement between photochemistry and psychophysics turned out to be within his experimental error.

Matches of Monochromatic Lights

The principle that when lights of different wavelengths isomerize equal quantities of rhodopsin, the resulting sensations are indistinguishable, leads to a concise mathematical statement of the conditions for a visual match between two spectrally dissimilar lights in night vision. The sensitivity of rhodopsin in the eye (including the effects of preretinal absorption) may be defined by the average number of molecules isomerized per photon of wavelength λ incident upon the eye. This quantity will of course be less than 1.0 (often much less); denote it by S_λ. Similarly, let S_μ stand for the sensitivity at wavelength μ. Suppose now that in a split field like the one in Figure 5.2, one half of the field is illuminated with wavelength λ and the other with wavelength μ. The intens-

112 Color Matching and the Visual Pigments

ities of these two fields may be represented by the numbers of photons incident upon the eye (per unit time) from each field, and these quantities may be labelled I_λ and I_μ respectively. The number of photopigment molecules isomerized per unit time will then be $I_\lambda S_\lambda$ on the side of the field illuminated with wavelength λ, and $I_\mu S_\mu$ on the other side. The two halves will be visually indistinguishable if these products are equal—that is, if the following equation is satisfied:

$$I_\lambda S_\lambda = I_\mu S_\mu. \tag{5.3}$$

Matches with Complex Spectral Distributions

Equation (5.3) makes a statement only about the condition for a match between two monochromatic lights. Most objects stimulate the eye with a continuous spectral distribution, where light of all wavelengths is represented. Can the principal that "equal isomerization means equal sensation" be generalized to predict the conditions for a match between spectrally complex stimuli? The answer is "yes." Recall from Chapter 3 that photons act independently of each other. This is also true for the act of absorption: individual absorptions occur between individual, noninteracting molecules of rhodopsin. This means that the total number of isomerizations may be obtained simply by adding together the contributions from each wavelength that is present in the stimulus. This *additivity* in the action of photons upon pigment has important consequences for visual matching that can be tested experimentally and found to hold. If stimulus A is indistinguishable from B, and C is indistinguishable from D, then $A + C = B + D$. In fact, all of the rules of algebra work: as another example, if $A = B + C$, then $2A = 2(B + C)$. This rule is especially important, because it states that a match made at one intensity level will hold at another intensity level, and it turns out that color matches for cone vision also follow these rules within rather wide limits.

The principle of univariance makes it possible to treat spectrally complex stimuli in the same way as monochromatic stimuli. In each case the visual effect of a stimulus can be represented by a single number, which stands for the number of molecules of photopigment that are isomerized by the stimulus.

To determine the effect of a spectrally complex stimulus, the spectrum must first be divided into narrow bands, and the effect of photons within each such band must be found separately by multiplying the intensity provided by the stimulus within each band by the sensitivity of the photopigment to that band of wavelengths, just as was done for monochromatic lights in deriving Equation (5.3).

The total effect is then found by adding together the effects of each spectral band. Stimuli of different spectral composition will match if their total effects on the pigment are the same. In the limit, where the spectral bands are extremely narrow, this process may be summarized for matching fields by writing

$$\int^\lambda I_\lambda S_\lambda d\lambda = \int^\mu I_\mu S_\mu d\mu,$$

where the limits of the definite integrals cover the visible spectrum, usually taken to be from 380 nm to 750 nm.

TRICHROMATIC COLOR VISION AND ITS BASIS
The Shift from Rod to Cone Vision

Having completed a long digression into the realm of rod vision, where we are all color-blind, we are ready now to tackle the more complex problems of trichromatic cone vision. Superficially, the phenomena of color vision at high light levels, where the cones are active, seem to be very different from those of scotopic vision. For example, the transition from color-blind night vision to colored cone vision involves a dramatic breakdown in the additivity of visual matching that has just been described for rod vision. A red and blue light that look the same at a low light level will not continue to match, but will appear in their true colors, and at different brightnesses, if the intensities of each are increased by the same factor. The brightness difference occurs because of a dramatic change in the spectral sensitivity of the eye that is associated with the advent of color vision: whereas in rod vision sensitivity is greatest near 505 nm, in cone vision it is greatest at about 555 nm. If red and blue lights match for night vision and both are increased proportionally in intensity so as to stimulate cones, the blue light will appear exceedingly dim. An additional increase of its intensity, by as much as a hundredfold, may be necessary to restore a brightness match, after which the two fields will continue to differ in hue.

One way to measure the difference in spectral sensitivity between photopic and scotopic vision is to determine thresholds under conditions designed to favor the exclusive stimulation of cones in the one case, rods in the other. (The concept of *threshold* and a discussion of psychophysical methods useful for measuring thresholds, will be found in Chapter 6, starting on page 168.) Cones can be uniquely stimulated by confining the stimulus to the rod-free foveal region of the retina. Rods can be preferentially stimulated by imaging the stimulus on a peripheral part of the retina, where rods dominate. Wald published the results of such an experiment in 1945; these data are shown in Figure 5.5. The rod curve has the expected shape and a straightforward interpretation along the lines just discussed. The interpretation of the cone curve, because three different kinds of cones are involved, is more complicated (see Chapters 6 and 9). The curve for cones 8° from the fovea is based upon the initial perception of hue.

The ordinate values in Figure 5.5 are the reciprocals of the radiometric amounts of lights (energies) required for threshold visibility. For example, at 500 nm, the rod curve has a sensitivity value of about 2.4 log units, corre-

Color Matching and the Visual Pigments

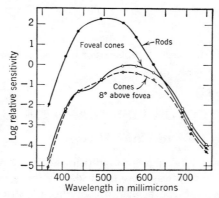

FIGURE 5.5 The curve labeled "Foveal cones" was obtained by determining the intensity required for threshold visibility of a 1° foveal test flash (on an energy basis) and plotting the log reciprocal of that value, normalized to 0 at the peak. The curve labeled "Rods" was obtained using a stimulus of the same size, positioned 8° in the periphery, with the sensitivity units on the same scale as those for the cone curve. As the energy of the peripheral stimulus is increased (downward on the graph), the peripheral stimulus eventually appears colored; the threshold for the perception of hue is shown by the dashed curve. The distance from the solid curve at the top to the dashed curve is the photochromatic interval, which is highly dependent upon wavelength. (From Judd, 1951, p. 811; originally from Wald, 1945.)

sponding to a threshold energy value of -2.4 log units. As energy is increased at that wavelength, the stimulus appears progressively brighter, but no color is seen in the periphery. Finally, when an energy level of about 0.7 log units is reached, which is about 1000 times higher than the threshold for rods, only then does the blue-green hue of the stimulus finally become apparent. Shifting its retinal location to the fovea again reduces the stimulus to threshold. The range between the absolute threshold for rod vision and the first appearance of hue is known as the *photochromatic interval*. This interval, expressed as a ratio, is about 1000:1 (3 log units) at 500 nm; it is virtually nonexistent at long wavelengths.

This change in the relative brightness of blue and red objects was first described in 1823 by Purkinje, a Czech physiologist and follower of Goethe who made many subtle observations that have helped in the understanding of the visual process. The shifting of the eye's spectral sensitivity toward longer wavelengths as the light level is increased, or toward short wavelengths when it is decreased, has been termed the *Purkinje shift*.*

The failure of additivity in the transition from colorless night vision to colored day vision, and the change of spectral sensitivity associated with it, are not due to violations of the principles of either univariance or of additivity at the pigment level. Rather they are signs that visual pigments other than rhodopsin are com-

> Take two pieces of colored paper, one blue and one yellow, each about two or three inches square. Select the colored papers so that the yellow member of the pair is definitely lighter than the blue one when viewed under daylight. Then, after the eyes have become dark-adapted under conditions of very low illumination (moonlight would be excellent), note that the blue member of the pair appears much lighter than the yellow. Both will now appear colorless.

ing into play in vision. Cone color vision, as it turns out, has the same relation to the properties of the cone photopigments that colorless rod vision bears to the properties of rhodopsin.

In night vision, spectrally dissimilar lights can be matched to one another simply by varying the intensity of one of them. What it means to have color vision is that no such match generally can be made. If a split field has a standard white on the left-hand side and a monochromatic red on the right, the two halves cannot be made to match by adjusting the intensity of the red, provided that the light level is high enough to ensure cone vision yet not so bright that discomfort, glare, strong and persistent afterimages, and marked bleaching of the cone pigments occur. Cone color vision has limitations, less drastic than those of rod vision, but similar in principle. Even the cones can be fooled into allowing a metameric match between spectrally dissimilar lights.

Complementary Colors

A special case of metamerism occurs when complementary monochromatic lights are mixed to match white. For example, this can be done with a red light that is mixed with just the right amount of monochromatic light of a suitable wavelength from the blue-green range of the spectrum. Despite their visual similarity, the white that is created from monochromatic complementaries is physically very different from the matching white that may include significant amounts of light from every region of the spectrum. The possibility of making white by mixing complementaries illustrates a limitation of human color vision. But it is a limitation that reveals itself only under such precise circumstances that Newton, as we recall, thought it impossible. For the match to occur, the following three conditions must be met exactly:

- For a fixed wavelength of the red light, the blue-green light must be of the appropriate wavelength.
- The amount of blue-green light relative to the amount of red must be correct, so that the mixture exhibits no tinge either of blue-green or red.
- The intensity of the resulting mixture must be such that it does not look brighter or dimmer than the standard.

With an apparatus like that of Figure 5.6, capable of creating uniformly colored fields of nearly monochromatic light and mixtures of colored lights with

Color Matching and the Visual Pigments

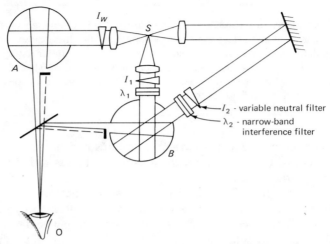

FIGURE 5.6 An apparatus that could be used to make color matches of spectral complementaries vs. white. Light from source S enters integrating sphere **A**; a half circle defined by a second opening in the sphere is seen by the observer **O**. Source directs light of wavelength λ_1 through one opening of integrating sphere **B**, and that of wavelength λ_2 through a second opening of the same sphere. Lights completely mix inside the sphere. Observer **O** sees the back side of sphere **B** through a third opening in that sphere, as a half circle juxtaposed with the one in **A**.

precise intensity control, a good white can be obtained without any difficulty. A complementary wavelength can be found, not only for red, but also for most spectral lights. However, green and yellowish green spectral lights (495 to 570 nm) have no exact spectral complementary: they yield yellowish tints when mixed with long wavelengths and bluish tints when mixed with short ones. They do have complementaries, but these are not in the spectrum; it turns out that purples (mixtures of long and short wavelengths) are required to produce them. The explanation for this is related to the spectral sensitivities of the cone photopigments, as will be explained shortly.

If there is too much of one complementary in the mixture, the result will be a color resembling more or less the hue of whichever component is present in excess. When this happens, the match can be restored by adding, to the near-white, a suitable amount of the spectral complementary of the hue that dominates the mixture of spectral colors. This has led to a way of specifying colors where each color is described by (1) the wavelength of the spectral light that must be mixed with white in order to produce that color, and (2) the proportion of the spectral light that must be introduced in order to produce it. These quantities are respectively called the *dominant wavelength* and the *purity* of the colors specified. It should be noted that conditions (1) and (2) must both be met. If (1) is met but (2) is not, the perceived hue will be more or less correct, but the saturation will be wrong. If (2) is met but not (1), the saturation will be more or less correct, but the hue will be wrong. For purples, no dominant wavelength can be specified. Instead, the complementary wavelength is given.

For nonspectral colors, where purity is less than 1, the units in which the white and spectral lights are measured must be specified. The units that seem to be the most natural ones—numbers of photons, or energy, or trolands— have not proved convenient in practice, and other units have been developed. (The particular units adopted by the CIE will be explained in the Appendix.) A second important ambiguity in the specification of colors by dominant wavelength and purity is that the choice of white is somewhat arbitrary. Several physical definitions of white have been proposed. One is to define it as a light that provides the same energy in each band of wavelength across the spectrum. Another is to define it as a spectrum that provides the same number of photons in each band of vibration frequency. It turns out that neither of these physical "whites" is truly white, because when presented in a dark surround, they look bluish to most observers. The less bluish is the equal-energy white, and in color specification it has been most often used as the reference for specifying dominant wavelength and purity. In any event, it is not correct to refer to dominant wavelength, purity, or complementary colors unless the context makes clear the nature of the reference white.

Physiological Basis for Metameric Whites

Why must three conditions be met in order to match an equal-energy white with a mixture of complementary colors? We have already seen the answer in the prophetic statement of Thomas Young on page 15: a white matches a mixture of spectral complementaries providing that both stimuli have identical effects on the three different cone photopigments. When this happens, each pigment in turn behaves in accordance with the principle of univariance, and none of them can tell that there is any difference between the two stimuli. When all three pigments cannot tell, then any possible basis for distinguishing two colors as being different is lost. If the spectral sensitivities of the three classes of pigments were known, then it would be possible to calculate, from any known physical intensity distribution, the relative rates of photon absorptions in each of the three classes of pigment. From this it would be possible to specify any color in terms of three values that are proportional to the absorption rates in the three kinds of pigments.

All this has been appreciated in a general way since the time of Maxwell and Helmholtz, but the absorption spectra of the three classes of cone pigments were not known to them, nor did they know that pigments were specifically involved. It is surprising to learn that the extraction of cone pigments has so far proved virtually impossible,[9] whereas we recall that Boll first did it for rhodopsin more than a hundred years ago. One consequence of the lack of direct evidence about cone pigments has been the emergence of quite a few "doubting Thomases" who have proposed various schemes to explain color perception that either ignore the principle of univariance, or flatly deny it. Common to most of these theories has been the claim that all cones are alike, and that any individual cone can sort out wavelength from intensity.[10]

The Search for Cone Spectral Sensitivity Curves

No aspect of color theory can rest on a firm footing without knowledge of the actual cone absorption spectra. Because this information is so important, the search for these has been an intense one. In Chapter 7, we will see that it is now possible to impale single cones in fish and turtles, where it has been shown by this very direct means that the expected three classes of cone receptors do exist. Although this result is important, and obviously provides direct support for the idea of trichromacy, it does not prove it for man. Moreover, the absorption curves of the pigments of these cold-blooded animals definitely are different from human ones. Another direct physical technique is called *microspectrophotometry*, which is basically the method that König pioneered, but refined to the point where the absorption of light in the outer segment of a single cone can be measured. This has been done by building spectrophotometers with beams so small, and sensitivities so great, that the tiny amounts of absorption that are involved can be detected. During the early exploitation of this technique during the 1960s, a handful of primate cones (including a few human ones) were examined. So far as they went, these results were consistent with the trichromatic view. Most of those who worked originally with the method seem to have given it up. Paul Liebman, who has stayed with it, has offered no evidence on human cones, and has had discouraging things to say about the accuracy of the method. Very recently, however, a British research team has reported more accurate data for rhesus monkeys. Of about 80 cones measured, almost exactly half were R cones, the other half G. No B cones were found.[11] We turn next to the one physical method that has worked for man, and which has been fully exploited: this is retinal densitometry, the topic of the next section.

RETINAL DENSITOMETRY

The process of bleaching in the retina is to some extent similar to exposing a photographic film. But unlike the optogram formed by bleaching, what is stored on the retina cannot be meant to serve as a permanent record: fresh visual pigment must replace what has been bleached so that the eye can keep signalling new images as they fall upon the retina. In retinas dissected away from the eye, the supply of rhodopsin is never completely replenished after bleaching. But it must be replenished somehow during life or else a few hours of exposure to daylight would lead to permanent blindness.

Retinal densitometry depends upon the fact of bleaching, and the principle of the method, as used by Robert A. Weale, Rushton, and their respective collaborators,[12] is not difficult to understand. A beam of light is delivered to the eye. Some of this light will be absorbed in the visual pigments of the retina, some will pass through unabsorbed, to be reflected from the back of the eyeball. If this light escapes absorption again during its outward passage from the retina, some will emerge through the pupil of the eye, where it can be measured with a photodetector.

The intensity of the emerging beam serves as an index of visual pigment concentration in the retina, for the following reason. Suppose, for instance, that the retina contains enough visual pigment to absorb half the light at each passage through the retina. In that case the reflected beam apparently will emerge at only one quarter of the intensity that it would have had in an eye with no visual pigment present. If the retina is now flooded with a very strong light— one strong enough to bleach nearly all of the visual pigment—the intensity of the reflected beam will increase by a factor of four, and the fact of this increase can be used to gauge the amount of bleaching that has taken place. Having said all this, the reader is now cautioned not to take the foregoing quantitative example literally, because the actual situation is far more complicated.

Why Retinal Densitometry Is Difficult

The following are four reasons why the technique of retinal densitometry cannot yield a result so simple as that just described.

- Not all of the light that passes through the retina the first time has a second chance to be absorbed after reflection by the pigment, since much of it is absorbed first behind the retina, mainly in the pigment epithelium or choroid.
- Some light reflects back from optical interfaces, blood vessels, or spaces between the receptors. The amount of this light is unaffected by bleaching, and its effect is to superimpose a steady intensity upon the change in the returning light due to bleaching. This reduces the percentage of change due to bleaching compared to what it would be in the absence of these and other sources of stray light.
- Some light is reflected back after passing through only some of the photopigment molecules in the receptors.
- Only a tiny percentage of the light passing into the pupil will reemerge from it, because most of the light that is not absorbed is diffusely reflected and thus scattered to irrelevant parts of the eye. This fact does not affect the percentage change that is measured due to bleaching, but it reduces the absolute levels to the point that very sophisticated methods are required to measure even the largest percentages of change that bleaching can produce.

Since little of the incident light reemerges from the pupil, it is not surprising that the pupil of the eye typically appears intensely black, except for the specular reflections that produce highlights at the cornea and lens. Some animals have a retroreflector called the *tapetum* behind the retina that seems obviously designed to give the receptors a second chance to catch the light that is not absorbed on the initial passage; by directing it back toward the pupil, the added absorptions occur in the appropriate receptors to help form a reasonably good image. (Examples of retroreflectors are some of the surfaces used on license plates in some states, labels on the sides of boxcars, and road signs.) Retroreflection causes the eyes of cats to appear to glow under conditions where those of humans do not, and it is also why the light in the cat's eye can be seen only from a vantage point close to the source that illuminates the eye.*

> In a dim room, and with the subject looking straight at the camera, take a flash photograph. If the flash bulb or lamp is located near the camera lens, the pupil of the eye of the subject will appear a brilliant red in the resulting photograph. Moving the flash away from the optical axis of the camera will eliminate this. Doing this in an initially dim room ensures that the pupil will be large, permitting more light to be reflected from the fundus than would be true for a smaller pupil. To see the fundus of another eye under continuous illumination requires a high-intensity source of light and some means to put the observer's eye on the optical axis of the eye being scrutinized. Helmholtz (1924, pp. 249 ff.), invented the ophthalmoscope, which is commonly used by eye-care practitioners for this purpose. Cornsweet (1970, p. 447) tells how to build an ophthalmoscope with inexpensive components.

The Range from No Bleach to Full Bleach

Because of the technical difficulties just enumerated, the maximum difference between the amount of light reflected from the human eye after a "full" bleach,[13] compared to a dark-adapted reference condition of no bleach, is about 0.2 log unit (approximately a 60 percent increase); when measurements are made for cone pigments, to be discussed shortly, the range is more nearly 0.15 log unit, or about a 40 per cent increase.

Retinal Densitometry on Rods: Regeneration Kinetics

Earlier in this chapter we approached the subject of cone color vision by first considering the principles underlying color-blind rod vision. We now do this again for retinal densitometry, where one of the simplest questions to be answered by the technique is: how quickly can the eye supply the rods with fresh rhodopsin? To investigate this, Rushton and his collaborators caused the measuring beam to fall on a portion of the subject's retina that was well populated with rods. If the eye had not recently been exposed to light, the intensity of the reflected beam was to be found to be at its minimum, owing to the presence in the retina of a full complement of unbleached rhodopsin, with all molecules available to absorb light. Then Rushton flooded the relevant retinal region with enough strong light to bleach nearly all the visual pigment there. The bleaching light was then extinguished and the measuring light (itself too weak to bleach very much rhodopsin) was once again exposed to monitor the amount of unbleached rhodopsin in the retina. Over time, the intensity of the measuring beam declined as expected, indicating that the retina's supply of unbleached rhodopsin was indeed being replenished.

The replacement of rhodopsin, it was found, is a relatively slow process, but not so slow as the recovery of sensitivity in dark adaptation as measured psychophysically (see Chapter 6, p. 170). Most of the rhodopsin returned in about five minutes, whereas dark adaptation takes at least half an hour. The precise time course of the recovery of rhodopsin offers a considerable degree of insight into the process involved. Because this insight is critical to the understanding of dark adaptation, but not for understanding the cone spectral sensitivity curves, it will be developed in Chapter 6. For now, what has been described is offered as evidence that the technique of retinal densitometry is capable of doing what it purports to do. An outcome of the quantitative work that needs to be anticipated here is that the intensities that are required to bleach a large fraction of the photopigment, even with steady viewing, are quite high—around 25,000 td, both for rhodopsin and the cone pigments. (This is a level of retinal stimulation that would be provided by looking at a white piece of paper under sunlight on a moderately bright day.) Most of the pigment irradiated by the retinal image of a naked tungsten lamp filament can be bleached in one second. In nature, only the sun's disk, or its direct reflection, are strong enough.

The Stability of Relative Spectral Absorption Curves

The percentage of light absorbed in a solution of pigment molecules depends upon three factors: (1) the probability that a pigment molecule, if it encounters a photon, will absorb it; (2) the concentration of the solution, which depends upon the density of pigment molecules (which is a function of the concentration of the solution) and (3) the path length through which the measuring beam is allowed to pass. For the discussion that follows, assume a fixed path length and assume that the concentration may be varied. If the concentration is low, the probability that a pigment molecule near the end of the path will absorb a photon is little different than for one near the beginning. The absorption spectrum depends only upon the characteristics of the constituent molecules. So long as this is true, increases and decreases in concentration will not alter the relative absorption spectrum. If the pigment concentration is high, the probability that a photon will reach molecules near the end of the path will be selectively changed, as a function of wavelength, depending upon how much absorption has already taken place in the molecules nearer the front of the path. This has been called *"self-screening"* (see Dartnall, 1962, p. 339, for an excellent treatment of the details of this argument).

Over a considerable range, color matches are independent of the intensity of the light. On the basis of the considerations just outlined, it is to be expected that these matches should fail if the concentration of cone pigments is high and can be varied due to bleaching, because these matches depend upon relative spectral sensitivity curves whose shapes would change. Retinal densitometry tells us that little bleaching occurs over the normal levels of photopic vision where most of our color vision occurs, and where most color matching experiments have been done. Because of this, the intensity of the light within this range is not an important variable: it is the *relative* degree of stimulation of the three kinds of cone photopigment that matters. On the subjective side, the apparent hue and saturation of lights does not change very much over the intensity range under discussion here (although the changes that do occur are of considerable theoretical interest).

Various estimates of the densities of cone photopigments suggest that they are high enough to cause a significant change in spectral sensitivity curves with strong bleaches,[14] and it is found that metameric color matches do begin to fail at bleaching intensities. But we cannot deal further with these interesting issues here. Rather we will assume that the relative spectral sensitivity curves of cone pigments are, for practical purposes, invariant.

Retinal Densitometry and Cone Pigments: General Considerations

Recall from Chapter 4 that the foveal region of the retina contains the highest density of cones, but very few rods. It was therefore reasoned by Rushton and his associates that, by testing within this region, it should be possible to investigate the behavior of cone photopigments. This is a more difficult task than for rhodopsin; there were some false starts and at last count Rushton and his collaborators had used six different densitometers, gradually improving the technique over 20 years of investigation. A major problem, of course, is that in the study of cones one presumably has three pigments to contend with, rather than just one. Rushton (1963, 1965b) gave these the names *erythrolabe, chlorolabe,* and *cyanolabe*, which derive from the Greek and stand for red-, green- and blue-bleached pigments respectively. These pigments are housed primarily, and perhaps exclusively, in the cones of three types, which will hereafter be called R cones, G cones, and B cones for short. If one can assume, as it is probably safe to do, that very long wavelengths are much more absorbed by erythrolabe than by the other pigments, it might seem that progress toward the study of this pigment in isolation could be achieved by using longwave bleaching lights. But this does not work out well because strong bleaches are required to establish the upper limit of the measuring range, and these are very likely to bleach a significant but unknown amount of chlorolabe as well.

Retinal densitometry has never revealed any clear evidence of the existence of the putative blue-sensitive pigment, cyanolabe. This is a bit disturbing for two reasons: (1) one would like to have this objective evidence as part of the full story about human cone pigments; (2) the fact that the stuff cannot be found raises a reasonable doubt about the sensitivity of the technique in general. We shall see later that there are probably very few blue cones in the foveal retina, which affords the most likely explanation for the inability of retinal densitometry to find their pigment; moreover, this cloud of failure has a silver lining. Because there are only two cone pigments to be measured where retinal densitometry is concerned, the job of sorting them out is considerably simplified.

So far as the determination of cone spectral sensitivities is concerned, the most progress has come from applying it to the examination of two classes of color-defective observers whose characteristics will be examined in Chapter 10. One of these, called a *protanope*, apparently lacks erythrolabe and perhaps also the R cones (or the cones may be filled instead with chlorolabe). Protanopes constitute about 1 percent of the male population and are therefore easy to find. Their availability opens the door for the densitometric study of the only remaining pigments that can be seen by this method. Another class of color-defective observer, the deuteranope, is equally common but more controversial. Deuteranopes may lack chlorolabe, but some investigators believe that they possess the normal complement of both cones and pigments: if so, their problem would be associated with a fusion of the outputs of the R and G cones (see Chapter 10). It seemed likely that retinal densitometry could help settle this issue and, if chlorolabe were lacking, permit the examination of the remaining pigment.

Retinal Densitometry with Deuteranopes

The studies of deuteranopes have been difficult, to say the least. At first Rushton tentatively concluded that they possess both erythrolabe and chlorolabe, in apparent agreement with the fusion hypothesis. But later, on the basis of better evidence, he recanted and has unequivocally concluded that "There is no chlorolabe in the deuteranope" (1964, p. 276). We will not review this evidence here, because it appears equivocal, Rushton's final statement notwithstanding. The method simply does not permit any such unqualified statement: if it did, one would also be forced to conclude that "There is no cyanolabe in any human eye."

Densitometry with Protanopes: Details of Procedure

There is widespread agreement that protanopes are lacking virtually all of the red-sensitive pigment, erythrolabe. The application of retinal densitometry by Rushton to the measurement of the remaining pigment, chlorolabe, has been described by Robert A. Weale, another leading exponent of retinal densitometry, as "in many ways a classic as regards experimental technique and there is little doubt that his experimental findings satisfactorily account for observations made by other, chiefly sensory, methods" (1965, p. 81). The experiment is worth reporting in some detail.

The layout for the densitometer is illustrated in Figure 5.7. The bleaching beam originates from light source S_2, the test beam from source S_0. The bleaching light is delivered to the eye as a series of flashes separated by dark intervals

124   Color Matching and the Visual Pigments

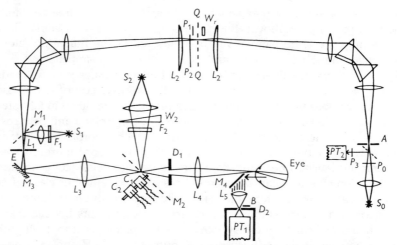

FIGURE 5.7 Layout of the retinal densitometer used by Rushton (1963) for the examination of the cone pigment of the protanope. Details are given in the text.

of equal duration, delivered by reflection from a rotating "windmill" mirror M_2 that revolves fast enough to deliver 135 flashes each second, which is equivalent to a steady light of half the intensity; it appears steady to the observer. When the windmill mirror is not reflecting the bleaching beam into the eye, its open sectors permit the transmission of light from the test channel.

The major part of the optical system supplying the test light is identical to one of three such channels in a precision colorimeter designed by W. S. Stiles, for research on color matching to be described later in this chapter. Note, in the upper-right and upper-left corners of the diagram, that symmetrically arranged pairs of prisms are depicted. The purpose of the first pair at the upper right is to disperse the white light into its spectral components, while causing the beam component at 486 nm to turn at exactly 90°. The various lenses allow the spectrum to be sharply focused in the plane $Q-Q$, where narrow bands of light of any desired wavelength can be selected by blocking the undesired portion of the image of the spectrum which is sharply focused here. The prisms at the upper left recombine the spectral components of the light into a beam that is white (if none of the spectrum is blocked at $Q-Q$) or of whatever spectral distribution is created by a template placed at $Q-Q$. All spectral components of this emerging beam travel the same path, in exactly the opposite direction (downward on the diagram) relative to the initial beam of white light.

Diaphragm D_1 and lens L_4 are used to deliver the light through the edge of the dilated pupil of the eye. The light falls on the central retina, imaged as a spot of 3° diameter, concentric with the fovea. Light reflected from the fundus passes out through the other half of the pupil and is reflected by mirror M_4 into the phototube, PT_1, to provide a measure of the intensity of the light reflected from the eye. An additional aperture picks out only the central 2° of the 3° field that otherwise would be provided.

The purpose of one part of the experiment is to determine, for each of a variety of bleaching wavelengths, the intensity of the light required to produce a 50 percent bleach of chlorolabe. It is important that measurements be made only during the time that the test light is delivered to the eye through the spaces of the windmill mirror, since the equipment is set to be responsive to the test light, which itself is too weak to bleach much pigment. If light from the adapting beam were allowed to reach the phototube, this would saturate its response and make measurements impossible. To eliminate this problem, one of the commutators C_1 on the shaft supporting the windmill mirror closes a shutter at B whenever the bleaching light is being delivered to the eye.

The signals derived from retinal densitometry are so weak that one cannot rely upon the absolute intensity of the returning test beam, which could fluctuate slightly from time to time for various reasons, including fluctuations in the output of the lamp that provides the measuring light. To improve the sensitivity of measurement, there is a comparison beam of very long wavelength (700 nm) which is negligibly absorbed by any pigment. The actual experimental measurements consist of varying the intensity of the comparison beam, by means of a neutral density wedge W_r, to keep the intensity of that beam equal to the test beam, whose intensity is affected by the bleaching. (There are many other details about this complex apparatus that will not be described here.)

The experiment then proceeded in the following way. The subject was carefully aligned and instructed to fixate as well as possible. A dental impression of his teeth was made, and the subject bit upon this in order to control the position of his head. A recording galvanometer was adjusted to read zero whenever the amount of light reflected from the eye by the test beam was that previously established as indicating a 50 percent bleach.

The experimenter moved the wedge W_r in a direction intended to bring the galvanometer reading to zero. This was done in the presence of various wavelengths of the bleaching light (achieved by placing narrow-band interference filters at F_2) after having adjusted their intensities by means of another wedge W_2, with W_r set for the position of 50 percent bleach. Any deviation of the galvanometer reading from zero was indicative of an incorrect setting of W_2 relative to the desired 50 percent value, with the direction of the error indicated so that W_2 could be adjusted to achieve the desired result.

With a bit of trial and error, it proved possible in each case to find the energy of the bleaching light required to bleach 50 percent of the pigment. To do this, a test beam of 540 nm was used, near the expected sensitivity peak of chlorolabe. Using seven spectral lights, ranging from 615 to 492 nm, plus an unfiltered white, Rushton established an excellent agreement between the action spectrum of chlorolabe, as measured in this way, and the perceived brightness of the bleaching lights. Specifically, lights that bleached 50 percent of the pigment all appeared equally bright, whatever their spectral composition. This of course is the expected result if only one pigment is being bleached.

To test further that only one pigment was involved, another experiment was conducted in which the wavelength of the test stimulus, rather than that of the bleach, was varied. Figure 5.8 shows the result of that experiment. The test wavelength is plotted on the x-axis; the y-axis shows the change of density of wedge W_r that resulted from bleaching. Rushton's figure caption (1963, p. 352) explains the rest:

> Circles plot at six wave-lengths the change in . . . density when the dark-adapted fovea was bleached by the red light transmitted through Ilford 205 gelatin filter (small circles), followed by bright white light (large circles). Small squares show a similar experiment where the bleaching light passed through Ilford 623 (bright spectrum blue-green) filter; large squares, bright white light. The white lights were strong enough to bleach fully, the coloured lights were adjusted in intensity to bleach 50%. Since red and blue-green result in the same difference spectrum, only one photosensitive pigment is present. Curves: protanope spectral sensitivity (Pitt, 1944).

The logic of this test, which is a familiar one for chemists, is important and will carry over to the analysis of psychophysical experiments to be considered in the next chapter. If two pigments are in solution, then the spectral transmittance of that solution can be selectively altered by bleaching it with different wavelengths of light. This happens because the pigment with the greater sensitivity to the bleaching wavelength will be more affected by the bleaching light than the one with lesser sensitivity. Such a solution, for example, might exhibit a two-peaked curve of spectral sensitivity before bleaching. A bleaching light corresponding to the wavelength of the shortwave peak would selectively depress that peak before having much of an effect on the other one, and *vice versa* for a longwave bleach. In Rushton's experiment, then, if two pigments had been present, the shapes of the curves obtained by using two such very different bleaching wavelengths should be different in shape, and clearly they are not.[15]

Limitations of the Evidence of Retinal Densitometry

Retinal densitometry has confirmed that there are cone photopigments, and that there are two kinds of these that can be measured in normal and color-blind eyes. It has supplied critically important evidence about the intensity levels that are required to bleach significant amounts of rhodopsin and cone pigments, and about bleaching kinetics. But for the purpose immediately at hand, that of determining the spectral sensitivities of the cone pigments, it is necessary to conclude that the value of the method has been very limited. In the experiment just described, Rushton certainly demonstrated that the action spectrum of what-

Retinal Densitometry

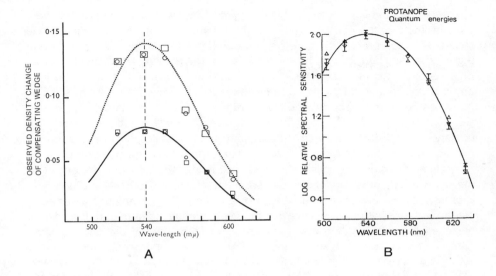

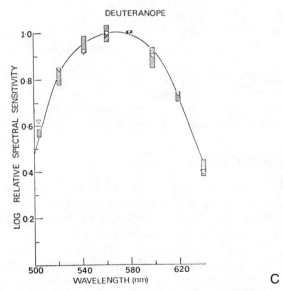

FIGURE 5.8 A shows Rushton's 1963 measurements that show changes in the amount of light reflected from the eye of the protanope, for two very different colors of the bleaching light. In B and C are the more recent (1971) data of Mitchell and Rushton, showing the action spectra of the protanope's and deuteranope's remaining pigment. The triangles in each case plot spectral sensitivity values measured psychophysically, and the curves are for protanopes and deuteranopes investigated by Pitt (1935).

ever absorbed the light from the bleaching stimulus was equivalent to the spectral sensitivity of the eye as established by brightness matching over the range tested. The experiment of Figure 5.8, though it purports to prove that only one pigment is bleached, can by no means rule out the presence of a small amount of a second pigment undetected by the method. One might argue that an amount so small could be of no importance for vision, but this is not so. The point has been made before, and will be made again, that the tails of the special sensitivity curves of cone pigments are critical. We will shortly see, from the evidence of color-mixture experiments, that relative absorption of less than 1 percent in a second pigment can be very important for color perception.

Retinal densitometry fails in the tails. In Figure 5.8, for example, not even the wavelength of peak sensitivity—somewhere around 540—is very clearly established. Moreover, this curve is not an action spectrum, but a series of wedge settings where the linearity between wedge setting and fraction of bleached pigment is taken mostly as an act of faith. Even if the densitometric data were very accurate, which they are not, the comparison of those points with Pitt's curve proves very little. Finally, retinal densitometry is unable to provide any measurements at all for wavelengths less than 500 nm, whereas the shapes of the spectral sensitivity curves for erythrolabe and chlorolabe at short wavelengths are critically important for color vision.

More recent data by Mitchell and Rushton (1971) are also shown as part of Figure 5.8. These are based on the preferred method of establishing the photon intensity required at each wavelength for a 50 percent bleach. There has been a substantial improvement upon the earlier results and the new data are consistent with the interpretations based upon the earlier, less adequate data. Relative to psychophysics, however, the method still fails to reveal much about the lower portions of the action spectrum.

COLOR MATCHING

In subsequent chapters, we will see that very precise specifications of the shapes of the cone pigment curves are required in order to understand chromatic discrimination (Chapter 8) and color deficiencies (Chapter 10).

Accurate shapes for these curves are now available, a fact that may seem surprising in view of the limited contributions of the objective methods just discussed. The detailed evidence has not been achieved by chemical or biophysical techniques, but instead through psychophysical methods. It might seem incredible that the use of procedures that involve the intact human subject could reveal such curves more accurately than the direct methods, but it is true. The most important psychophysical experiments have been those on color matching; as we saw in Chapter 1 this work began with Maxwell more than 100 years ago. The remainder of this chapter will largely be concerned with this evidence, and with showing how it relates to the action spectra of the three types of cone photopigments.

Hypothetical Curves

To introduce this topic we deal first with sets of hypothetical spectral sensitivity curves. For convenience it will be assumed that the three classes of photopigments are uniquely contained in R, G, and B cones, and that phenomena such as the "red shift" of rhodopsin (p. 111) can be ignored, so that the spectral curves of the pigments and those of the receptors are proportional. The curves to be sketched in this section are wrong, but they prove useful for pedagogic purposes. We will work our way through a few sets of them that will gradually take us fairly close to the real ones. This will help to introduce various principles that are difficult to make clear when starting with the real curves.

Curves That Fail to Overlap

The most obvious respect in which the curves of Figure 5.9 differ from the real cone absorption curves is that they fail to overlap. Curves of this sort imply that a photon of any particular wavelength can be absorbed in only one of the three types of cones. This arrangement would be disastrous for good discrimination of spectral colors: the principle of univariance applies separately within each of the spectral bands covered by the three pigments, so within each of these ranges there could be no discrimination at all of stimuli whose wavelengths are restricted to this band. From the standpoint of efficient photon collection (especially near 500 nm and 600 nm where the tails of the curves descend to zero) this is also a very poor arrangement.

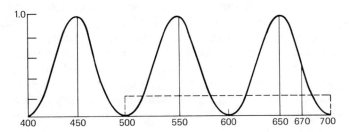

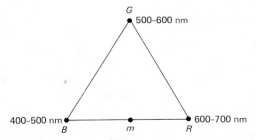

FIGURE 5.9 An initial set of hypothetical sensitivity curves that do not overlap. In the color triangle at the bottom, spectral colors plot only at the corners.

A major purpose of a color mixture experiment is to specify any arbitrary stimulus, called the *test*, in terms of a mixture of three components (often called *primaries*). As previously noted, two such stimuli will match whenever the photons delivered to the eye from the mixture field are absorbed in all three classes of cones in the same way as those delivered by the test stimulus. From the curves of Figure 5.9, it should be intuitively clear that the choice of usable matching wavelengths is at once both arbitrary and constrained. Each must fall somewhere within a spectral band defined by the sensitivity curve of one of the cone types; although these locations are not critical, it is necessary that no two of them fall within a single such band. (A fourth stimulus would of necessity fall in the same band as one of the original three; within that band an infinite number of combinations of relative intensities of those two stimuli could cause the same absorptions to occur, and thus the color match would not be a unique one.) By adjusting the intensities of the three components in turn, there should be no problem about producing in this way an equivalent stimulation of all three types of cones, thereby to achieve a match with any test stimulus.

The Mixture Experiment from the Subject's Perspective

Such an experiment requires an apparatus capable of delivering the test stimulus to one half of a bipartite field, and the components of the mixture field to the other. Recall that photons do not physically mix, so what is actually needed is a means for causing the entire mixture field to radiate its photons, for all three component wavelengths, uniformly toward the eye. There are a variety of ways to accomplish this, one of which has already been considered in Figure 5.6 in connection with the special case of mixtures of complementary colors. Figure 5.10 is intended to represent all possible methods schematically. If it helps to have something definite in mind, recall and extend the use of the integrating spheres of Figure 5.6, or imagine that the mixture field is built up from the superimposed images of half fields delivered from three slide projectors. With the latter arrangement, narrow-band interference filters could be placed in front of each projector to select the matching wavelengths, and the intensity of each component could be continuously varied by means of variable transformers supplying the lamps of each projector. A fourth projector, with its semicircular image reversed, could be used to provide the adjacent test stimulus.[16]

Consider 450, 550, and 650 nm as the wavelengths of the three matching components (primaries). These happen to fall at the peaks of the hypothetical sensitivity curves: call them blue, green, and red for short. As an example to show how the experiment goes, attempt to specify a test stimulus of 670 nm by a mixture of these three mixture components. The subject's task is to manipulate the three intensities of the mixture field in order to produce an exact match with the 670-nm test. A bit of trial and error would establish that the appropriate amounts of the blue and green primaries must be zero, since no

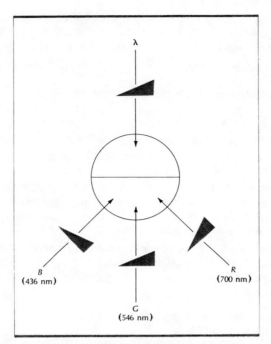

FIGURE 5.10 Schematic arrangement of stimuli for a color-mixing experiment. A test stimulus is delivered to the top of a split field, while a mixture of three primaries is delivered to the bottom. All are adjustable in intensity by means of neutral wedges. An arrangement must also be provided so that any one of the primaries can, in turn, be added to the test stimulus in the top field. (From Boynton, 1971.)

match can be made if any finite amounts are tried. This is true because the 670 test stimulus fails to stimulate either the B or G cones, so it is necessary in making a match that the mixture field should also fail to do so. Once this is discovered, then the task that remains is easy to understand, being identical in principle to the single-pigment matches of rod vision (p. 101). After the match is made, physical measurement would reveal only half as many photons in the matching field as in the test. This difference compensates for the greater sensitivity of the red cones at 650 as compared to 670 nm; the argument is the same as that for rod vision discussed earlier.

The test stimulus need not be monochromatic in order to be matched. Suppose that it consisted instead of a continuous range of photons covering the range from 500 nm to 700 nm, as shown by the dotted lines in Figure 5.9. It can be seen at a glance that such a stimulus causes equal activation of both the R and G cones. In attempting to match it, the subject would discover once again that the blue primary is useless; but both of the remaining two would be needed. The match would now require equal numbers of photons to be absorbed from each component of the mixture, in order to cause equal stimulation of the red and green cones, just as for the test. If the test stimulus were further extended at the same photon level to include the remaining spectral region from 400 nm to 500 nm, then the subject would also require the blue mixture component to make the match.

The primaries used in the matching experiment need not be monochromatic either. For the curves of Figure 5.9, one of them could, for example, be of any spectral distribution confined to the range of wavelengths from 600 to 700 nm. No matter what this distribution might be, such a stimulus could only serve to activate the R cones. Suppose that it overlapped a bit into the adjoining spectral region: could a match then still be made? If the test stimulus were monochromatic, the answer would be "no," because such a test stimulus would activate only one kind of cone, whereas the assumed primary would activate two of them. This is similar, as we shall see, to what happens with spectral primaries when the sensitivity curves overlap.

A final comment about these nonoverlapping curves is that they would permit a fair discrimination of colors that depend upon continuous curves of reflectance covering the entire spectrum, which is in fact a reasonable description of most naturally reflecting surfaces.

Necessary Relations between Stimuli and Sensations

An important psychophysical assumption that underlies the matching operation now needs to be made explicit. The relationship between physics and sensation must permit the subject to converge upon a solution when making a color match. It surely would not do, for example, if low levels of activation of R cones yielded sensations of red that suddenly changed to green at higher levels. Further, it seems necessary for the correlation between physical intensity and brightness, as delivered via one type of cone, to be monotonic over the range being examined; otherwise there would be at least two physical intensities that could cause the same sensation and unique matches could not be made. Although the psychophysical relationships may be complex (in particular, there is no need to assume that private pathways exist, for example, from red cones to a red sensorium) the sensations that are generated as a consequence of photon absorptions in the three cone types must relate in some sensible and continuous way to the amounts of these absorptions.[17]

The Trilinear Triangular Color Diagram Introduced

Newton first suggested that colors could be represented on a two-dimensional diagram. Maxwell (1855) later made this idea more explicit by introducing the use of trilinear coordinates to describe the results of his early color experiments, carried out with a spinning top upon which sectors of colored papers were attached. Although (as Maxwell fully realized) such coordinates are ideal for the representation of color mixtures, trilinear coordinates have seldom actually been used for that purpose. For example, the CIE has officially adopted the use of Cartesian coordinates for its chromaticity diagram (see Appendix I). Yet the use of a triangular chart instantly clarifies relationships that are otherwise obscure, and for that reason the color triangle will be introduced here.

Consider the equilateral triangle of Figure 5.11. The colors represented by the unique activation of each of the three kinds of cones are plotted at the corners of the diagram. Side BR is positioned horizontally and therefore has an appearance similar to the x-axis of the more familiar Cartesian coordinate system. The proportion of G-cone activity required in a color match is represented as the perpendicular distance above the BR axis, in the same way that an ordinate value is represented in Cartesian coordinates. The proportions contributed by the other two types of cones are represented in the same way (to appreciate this it might help to rotate the diagram so that the primary under consideration is in each case at the top). Thus there are three coordinates obliquely related to each other; the proportion of total activation represented

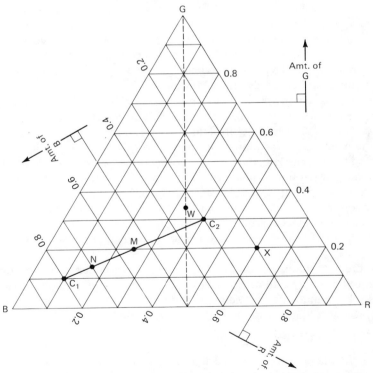

FIGURE 5.11 Color diagram in trilinear coordinates (color triangle). The features illustrated by this diagram are explained in the text.

by a particular kind of cone is represented as the distance along a perpendicular erected from the opposite side of the triangle.

This triangular diagram has a special property that makes it ideal for representing color matches: Given any point within it, such as x in Figure 5.11, the sum of the distances from that point to the three sides is always the same.[18] For the point shown, $r = 0.6$, $g = 0.2$, and $b = 0.2$. A limiting case occurs when x is located at one of the corners. For example, if it is at G, this implies that the color match requires only the stimulation of G cones. If one of the components of the mixture field were able to stimulate only G cones, then the other two components of the mixture would have to be extinguished in order to make the match. This amount of G, whatever its actual intensity (which would depend upon that of the test field being matched) is specified as 1.0, since this is a diagram to represent proportions of the three mixture components, not their absolute intensities. The dotted line from BR to G therefore has a unit length and divides BR into two equal parts. The locus of all stimuli that require equal amounts of B and R in the match is given by this line; at G, these amounts are zero, whereas at the other end of the line—at a point midway between B and R on the line BR—they are 0.5.

A point W at the very center of the diagram is equally far from each side, the distances therefore being 1/3 in each case. These examples help to demonstrate that the position of any color in this diagram shows very nicely the relative activations of the three kinds of cones caused by any stimulus.

Such a triangular diagram is shown in Figure 5.9, under the nonoverlapping spectral curves. All spectral stimuli between 600 and 700 nm are represented at R. Those between 500 and 600 nm are all at G, and the remainder are plotted at B. Although no spectral light can plot anywhere except at the corners, complex stimuli that activate both R and G cones (but not B) can be represented along the side RG of the triangle according to a "center of gravity" principle. According to this principle, mixtures lie along the side of the triangle at a location that depends upon the relative amounts of each component required to make the match. For example, a color at m (Fig. 5.9) would be one that requires equal amounts of B and R components to match it. A color that requires four times as much R as B will be located four-fifths of the distance from R toward B on the line RB. All possible mixtures of R and B plot somewhere along that line.

The proof of the center of gravity principle is fundamental and requires that color equations be written. Such equations summarize the information contained in the triangular color diagram, and apply similarly to diagrams in Cartesian coordinates that express the same information.

Color Equations

It was mentioned on page 112 that the operations of color matching obey the rules of ordinary algebra. In this relation, the "=" sign of algebra translates to "matches with" in the laboratory, and the "+" sign implies the superposition of lights by one or another of the methods already described. Negative quantities of light cannot be produced in a colorimeter, but the algebraic equivalent is to add that amount to the other side of the equation: we have already seen how this is done in the laboratory to permit matches that otherwise would not be possible.

A few examples may help. Suppose that a match is made between a spectral yellow Y and a mixture of red and green primaries (R and G). We may write

$$y(Y) = r(R) + g(G),$$

where (Y), (R), and (G) stand for the stimuli being used, whose amounts are y, r, and g. Read this equation: "y units of (Y) are matched by a mixture of r units of (R) and g units of (G)." (For now, we will not worry about the units.) Suppose now that we add some other color, say b units of (B), to both sides of the colorimetric field. Algebraically:

$$y(Y) + b(B) = r(R) + g(G) + b(B),$$

and the two sides of the equation, having been equal before, remain equal since the same quantity has been added to each side. This could be tested experimentally by adding a veil of blue light to the previous match, for example by reflecting it to the eye from a piece of glass so that it covers the entire field. Experimentally, as well as algebraically, the match will hold.

Suppose that the intensity of both halves of the field were increased by the same factor, say 2. The equation will now read

$$2y(Y) = 2r(R) + 2g(G)$$

and the equation remains valid. Experimentally, what is required is to double the numbers of photons reaching the eye from both halves of the field, without altering their relative spectral distributions. This is most easily done by making the match initially with a neutral filter in front of the eye, one which absorbs exactly 50 percent of the photons incident upon it without regard to wavelength. After the match is made, the filter is removed, and although both halves brighten, the match holds.

These properties of color matches are what should be expected by the trichromatic theory introduced earlier in this chapter. The original match exists, by this view, because photons are absorbed at the same rates by all three classes of photopigments despite the physical differences represented by the two sides of the equation. In the first example, the addition of blue light of the same amount to both halves of the field would be expected to cause additional photons to be absorbed by the three photopigments in the same way for both halves of the field, and there is no reason why this should destroy the match. In the second example, provided that the action spectra of the three cone types are not altered by the added light, the doubling of the numbers of photons will not alter the physiological identity[19] originally implied by the two sides of the color equation.

136   Color Matching and the Visual Pigments

As a final example of a property of color matches that makes their mathematical expression useful, consider their stability under conditions of chromatic adaptation, a subject to be discussed more fully in the next chapter. Suppose that, following the match $r(R) + g(G) = y(Y)$, the eye is strongly adapted to a red light, after which the original fields are viewed. The Y half of the field, which previously looked yellow, will now appear decidedly green. But the R + G side of the field, which also previously looked yellow, also now looks green. The fields in fact will continue to match, although their appearance is grossly changed. This example illustrates that, although color equations express the conditions for a color match, they do not tell us anything directly about what the matching colors look like.

Center of Gravity Principle

Now we can examine the center of gravity principle using color equations and Figure 5.11, which gives a geometrical meaning to these equations. Start with unit amounts of two colors C_1 and C_2 as follows:

$$C_1 = r_1 (R) + g_1 (G) + b_1 (B) \qquad (r_1 + g_1 + b_1 = 1) \quad (5.4)$$
$$C_2 = r_2 (R) + g_2 (G) + b_2 (B) \qquad (r_2 + g_2 + b_2 = 1) \quad (5.5)$$

and a third color

$$C_3 = r_3 (R) + g_3 (G) + b_3 (B) \qquad (5.6)$$

Suppose that C_3 is the additive mixture of m units of C_1 and n units of C_2:

$$C_3 = m(C_1) + n(C_2) \qquad (r_3 + g_3 + b_3 = m+n) \quad (5.7)$$

The first two equations are unit equations; Equation (5.7) expresses an amount of C_3 that is the sum of the m and n units of its two components. Equation (5.7) can be rewritten:

$$C_3 = \frac{m}{m+n} (C_1) + \frac{n}{m+n} (C_2) \qquad (r_3 + g_3 + b_3 = 1) \quad (5.8)$$

which now, like Equation (5.6), expresses a unit amount of the mixture. If Equations (5.4) and (5.5) are substituted into (5.8), it can be seen by comparing the result with Equation (5.6) that

$$r_3 = \frac{m}{m+n} r_2 + \frac{n}{m+n} r_2,$$
$$g_3 = \frac{m}{m+n} g_1 + \frac{n}{m+n} g_2, \text{ and} \qquad (5.9)$$
$$b_3 = \frac{m}{m+n} b_1 + \frac{n}{m+n} b_2.$$

The Equations (5.9) imply, for example, that if r_1 and r_2 are known, the value r_3 can be computed as the weighted sum of r_1 and r_2, where these weights must add to unity and correspond to the proportions of the two components of the mixture. The same rule applies also to g_3 and b_3, meaning that r_3, b_3, and g_3 all increase in the same proportion as the mixture varies from C_1 to C_2; the only way that this can happen is if the mixture always falls along the straight line connecting C_1 and C_2 in the color diagram.

These relations may be seen in Figure 5.11, where examples are given to illustrate how this works out. Suppose that for

$$C_1 = \begin{cases} r_1 = 0.1 \\ g_1 = 0.1 \\ b_1 = 0.8 \end{cases} \text{ and } C_2 = \begin{cases} r_2 = 0.4 \\ g_2 = 0.3 \\ b_2 = 0.3. \end{cases}$$

As required for representation on the color triangle, unit amounts of each color are indicated by these values, and the colors C_1 and C_2 that they represent are shown in Figure 5.11 in their appropriate locations.

Suppose first that these two colors are mixed in equal amounts. By means of Equations (5.9):

$$r_3 = \tfrac{1}{2} r_1 + \tfrac{1}{2} r_2 = 0.05 + 0.20 = 0.25$$
$$g_3 = \tfrac{1}{2} g_1 + \tfrac{1}{2} g_2 = 0.05 + 0.15 = 0.20$$
$$b_3 = \tfrac{1}{2} b_1 + \tfrac{1}{2} b_2 = 0.40 + 0.15 = 0.55.$$

This point is located half way between C_1 and C_2 at M.

Suppose that C_1 and C_2 are unchanged, but that they are now mixed in the proportion $4C_1$ to $1C_2$. Now

$$r_3 = 0.8 r_1 + 0.2 r_2 = 0.08 + 0.08 = 0.16$$
$$g_3 = 0.8 g_1 + 0.2 g_2 = 0.08 + 0.06 = 0.14$$
$$b_3 = 0.8 b_1 + 0.2 b_2 = 0.64 + 0.06 = 0.70$$

This point is located one-fifth of the way from r_1 to r_2, one-fifth of the way from g_1 to g_2, and one-fifth of the way from b_1 to b_2, meaning that it must also be located one-fifth of the way from C_1 to C_2, at N.

Trichromatic Units

By definition, if equal "amounts" of R, G, and B stimuli are mixed, the mixture falls at the center of the color triangle. These amounts could be expressed in terms of photons, ergs, or trolands, but none of these turn out to be convenient. Another possibility is to let the position of a point in the color diagram represent the relative probabilities of photon absorption in the three kinds of cone photopigment. But this could be done only if these relative probabilities were known. Although, as we shall see, the shapes of the relative spectral sensitivity curves are now fairly well known, their relative heights are not, so that such a specification is at present not possible.

It is important to understand that color matches do not depend upon these relative heights. Suppose, for example, that a color match were made and that the numbers of molecules of erythrolabe in the retina were suddenly halved. A given stimulus, say one at about 580 nm that appeared yellow before, would now activate the R cones relatively less than before and the appearance of the color presumably would change toward green, in much the same manner as in the case of adaptation to red light mentioned earlier. But, again, both sides of the field should change in the same way, providing no basis for upsetting the color match. Indeed, *all* of the erythrolabe could be removed without upsetting the match, as in the case of the protanope (Chapter 10), who will accept the match of a normal observer.

If two fields match exactly, then each will in turn match the same additive mixture of red, green, and blue components of a mixture stimulus. If the units of measurement for the red component of two identical stimuli are the same, equal numerical values imply equal amounts of that component. The same is, of course, true for the green and blue components. But the units in which the red component is measured need not be the same as those for the green or blue. It would be bizarre to do it, but it would be permissible to measure the red component in ergs/sec, the green one in photons/sec, and the blue one in trolands.

One scheme that is used in practice is to abandon all of the familiar units and introduce new ones, known as trichromatic, or *T-units*. One could decide that the center of the color triangle should represent a white that matches an equal-energy spectrum. If so, the decision implies that equal "amounts" of the red, green, and blue mixture components produce this white. The T-units are specified by an auxiliary experiment in which the subject is asked to match an equal-energy white using a mixture of the three mixture components. The amounts of each of the components of that mixture are then defined as equal under the matching condition, no matter how different they might be in radiometric or photometric units. A consistent result of this type of match is that the number of trolands of blue light is quite small relative to the numbers of trolands of the red and green primaries. This correlates with the fact that an amount of blue that adds very little to the brightness of a preexisting red–green mixture has the capacity to greatly alter the hue of the field.

R and G Curves That Overlap

We can move a step closer to reality by broadening the absorption curves of the assumed R and G pigments so that they partially overlap, as shown in Figure 5.12. If these curves implied the same probabilities of photon absorption at their peaks, then the crossing of the R and G curves at 600 nm would imply that a photon of that wavelength would stand an equal chance of being absorbed by either pigment. The curves have been drawn so that there is a range from 500 nm to 510 nm where the probability of absorption by the R cones (and the B cones as well) is zero, and another range from 690 to 700 nm, where only the R cones can absorb photons. Test stimuli falling within either of these ranges can therefore be matched by using only a single primary pro-

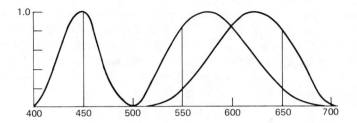

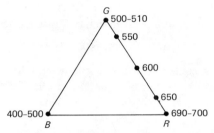

FIGURE 5.12 A second set of hypothetical spectral sensitivity curves. These differ from the first set (Fig. 5.9) in that the R and G curves now overlap. The result is that spectral stimuli from 500 to 600 nm are now represented continuously along the **RG** side of the color triangle.

vided that it is chosen to fall also within the same band of wavelengths as the test stimulus to be matched.

Suppose instead that the primaries are chosen to be 550 and 650 nm as before. In this case there will be some test wavelengths that can still be matched by a mixture of the two primaries, namely those that fall in the range from 550 to 650 nm. A test stimulus at 600 nm, which stimulates these two types of cones equally, can be matched by equal amounts of the two components, assuming that the R and G absorption curves are symmetrical as shown. Note that each component of the mixture is absorbed to some degree by the "wrong" type of cone, which did not happen in the initial example of Figure 5.9, where the R and G curves were not permitted to overlap. With the new curves, test stimuli in the range from 650 to 700 nm, and from 500 to 550 nm, cannot be matched by a mixture of 550- and 650-nm primaries because these test stimuli produce a greater imbalance in the relative stimulation of the two types of cone than do either of the components of the mixture. For example, a test stimulus at 695 nm uniquely activates R cones, whereas the red mixture component at 650 nm does not. To make a color match in this case, the green primary must be placed on the "wrong" side of the field, to be added to the 695-nm test.

Letting R' stand for the red primary, G' for the green one, and T for the test, we can state the conditions for the match as

$$T + g'(G') = r'(R') \qquad (5.10)$$

What is the amount g' of the green primary that must be added to the test? It must be an amount that, when mixed with the test, will reduce the ratio of R to G cone activation to 4, since this is the ratio produced by the 650-nm component acting alone on the other side of the field. To find this value, first express the test stimulus and the two primaries by their relative absorptions by the red and green cones:

$$R' = 0.8(R) + 0.2(G)$$
$$G' = 0.8(G) + 0.2(R) \qquad (5.11)$$
$$T = 1.0(R).$$

If we translate the requirement for a match of Equation (5.10) into these terms:

$$1.0(R) + 0.8g'(G) + 0.2g'(R) = 0.8r'(R) + 0.2r'(G) \qquad (5.12)$$

The value g' must be such that the two coefficients for (R) sum to four times that for (G) on the left-hand side of Equation (5.12). This condition is achieved when

$$\frac{1 + 0.2g'}{0.8g'} = 4 \qquad (5.13)$$

The value of g' that satisfies Equation (5.13) is .33. Therefore the relative amount of G' that must be mixed with the test in order to allow a match with the red primary is .33.

If it be assumed that the corners of the color triangle have the same significance as before, we can replot the spectral colors as required by the new curves. The point R still represents the location of a stimulus that would activate R cones exclusively, which now covers the range from 690 to 700 nm. Since the red primary, at 650 nm, now stimulates the R cones 4 times as much as the G, it therefore plots four-fifths of the way from G toward R. Similarly the green primary at 550 nm plots four-fifths of the way from R toward G. A stimulus of 600 nm, which stimulates R and G cones equally, plots midway between; by measuring ordinate values everywhere between 500 and 700 nm, the R/G ratios for all other spectral colors in this range can be determined and plotted in Figure 5.12 according to the center of gravity principle.

Broadening the B Curve

The foregoing curves are still very fanciful because of the failure of the B-cone sensitivity curve to overlap with the others. To remedy this, the B-cone curve has been broadened in Figure 5.13. Over the range from 400 to 500 nm, all spectral stimuli continue to plot at the B corner of the diagram, since it is still true that B cones are exclusively activated by stimuli in this range. But the range from 510 to 600 nm reveals something new and interesting, since for the first time in this series of examples all three types of cones are assumed to be activated by spectral lights within this band of wavelengths. As an example of what this implies for the color triangle, consider where a stimulus at 550 nm

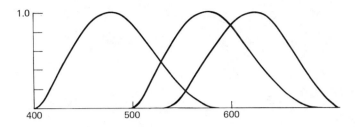

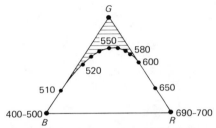

FIGURE 5.13 In this third set of hypothetical spectral sensitivity curves, the B curve has been broadened to overlap the other two in the spectral region from 500 to 600 nm. These wavelengths are represented along the curved locus shown crossing the color triangle.

will plot. This wavelength is assumed to be absorbed equally by R and B cones, but by G cones 5 times as much as for either of the others. If a photon is absorbed, the probability that it will happen in the G cones is then 5/7. For the R and B cones, this probability is 1/7. This point plots as shown in Figure 5.13.

The locations of a number of other spectral stimuli have also been shown in Figure 5.13. Stimuli from the longwave end of the spectrum to 600 nm, which activate only R and G cones, fall along a straight line connecting R and 600 nm. In the region from 600 to 510 nm, the spectral locus is curved, and this turns out to be characteristic of any part of the spectrum where three kinds of cones are stimulated. Below 500 nm, all stimuli again plot at the B corner. Since mixtures of any two stimuli fall along a straight line that connects them, we can see at a glance that in the region of the spectrum where all three curves overlap to generate a curved spectral locus, no monochromatic light can be matched by a mixture of any two lights of other wavelengths. Note also that the G cones can no longer be uniquely stimulated by any real light.

A Final Set of Curves

One more set of curves (Figure 5.14) will take us fairly close to reality. We now extend the R and G curves farther into the short wavelengths. (If there is to be wavelength discrimination in the short wavelengths, then at least one of these curves must extend to 400 nm.) In Figure 5.14 the tails of the R and G

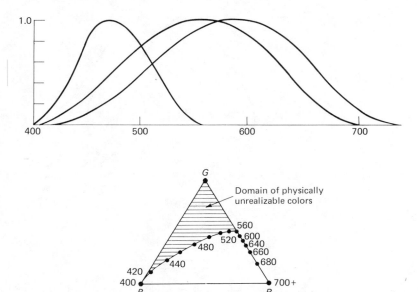

FIGURE 5.14 A fourth and final set of hypothetical spectral sensitivity curves. These approach those of real human cones in their qualitative aspects.

curves have been extended so that they overlap throughout most of the visible spectrum, and the B curve has been given a breadth intermediate between the shapes that were assumed in the previous examples.

These curves are qualitatively similar to the real ones to the extent that the R and G curves are similar in shape and lie relatively close together, whereas the B curve is different in shape and is rather well separated from the other two. The consequences of assuming these revised curves may be seen in the color triangle of Figure 5.14.

Physical-mixture Components at the Corners of the Diagram

Maxwell, who first used the triangular color diagram, had no information about cone pigments; therefore he plotted the *physical* components of his matching field at the corners of the triangle. This differs from what has been done in the foregoing examples, where each of the corners has represented the unique activation of one type of cone. The spectral sensitivities of the cones overlap. Therefore, the colors represented at the corners of our diagram cannot match real lights that always activate more than just one type of cone. For this reason, the colors represented at the G-corner of Figure 5.14 (and for that matter all colors in the shaded region) can be called "imaginary."

If physical mixture stimuli (R',G',B') are specified instead at the corners of the diagram, a stimulus that would uniquely activate G cones would be represented along an extension of the line RG, beyond G to the upper left in Figure 5.14. This would imply that some R' must be added to G in order to allow a real stimulus to match it.

We can provide a further physical interpretation of the meaning of imaginary matching stimuli with the help of Figure 5.15. This time we will suppose that none of the three types of cones is capable of being uniquely stimulated by a real light. Let the triangle R'B'G' enclose the domain of real colors that can be generated by mixtures of three physical lights. The larger triangle RGB represents the enlarged domain of colors encompassed by a set of imaginary primaries, perhaps those corresponding to the spectral sensitivities of the three types of cones. Consider, as an example, the representation of the imaginary component G in terms of the real stimuli. The line labelled "+g" is drawn as a perpendicular from B'R' to G. The length of this line specifies the proportion of G' that is needed. It implies that the proportion of G' is much greater than the unit amount (+g') that can be physically achieved.

To determine the proportion of R' needed in a match for G, first extend the line B'G'. The short perpendicular from this line to G is in a negative direction, since G falls above and to the left of the extension of B'G'. A similar construction

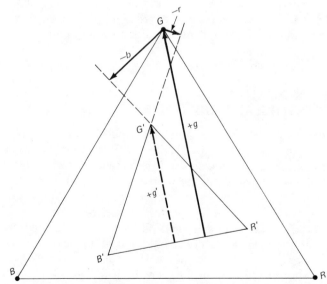

FIGURE 5.15 R, G, and B are imaginary primaries, lying outside the domain of real colors and those that can be matched by an additive mixture of real primaries R', G', and B'. This construction shows how imaginary primary G can be represented in terms of the real primaries.

reveals a need for an even larger negative proportion of the B' component. These three proportions are now represented as distances labelled $+g$, $-r$, and $-b$. These show the proportions of the three primaries needed to make the match with G. As before, the sum of the three values is unity.

Place a mixture of the negative components B' and R' in one part of a split field, say on the left, where they will be seen as a purple. Place the G' component on the right side of the field. Now the meaning of the imaginary primary G is this: if a unit amount of the imaginary primary G could somehow be added to the purple mixture in the left side of the field the result (with suitable intensity adjustment) would permit a match with G' on the right side of the field. In other words, the purple mixture specifies a physical light that would be required in order to desaturate the imaginary primary G until it matches the real G'. Since light cannot be physically subtracted, G is physically unrealizable, and it is in this sense that it is imaginary.

Transformations from One Set of Primaries to Another

Given a set of color-mixture curves that are based upon one set of primaries, it is possible to calculate the color matches that these curves imply for any other set of primaries. The primaries, or mixture components of the two sets, are assumed to differ in their spectral distributions; these may or may not be monochromatic. Such a transfer from one set of primaries to another is possible because, as previously indicated, the laws of color mixture follow the laws of ordinary algebra. The problem is best handled in the context of matrix algebra, where the solutions of the simultaneous equations required for the transfer are routine.

DATA FROM ACTUAL COLOR-MIXTURE EXPERIMENTS

Accurate sets of color-mixture functions were obtained long ago by J. Guild (1925–1926) and W. D. Wright (1928–1929) in England. Wright's curves indicated the amounts of three spectral primaries that were required to match other spectral colors throughout the visible spectrum. In 1931, the CIE settled upon a standardized set of functions, derived by change of the assumed wavelengths of the primaries into a new system said to represent the color matches of a "standard observer" (Judd, 1933). When it became evident that there was a problem with the CIE values in the blue end of the spectrum, Judd (1951a) published a correction that raised the values of all three functions somewhat at wavelengths shorter than about 450 nm. In 1955, W. S. Stiles reported the results of a very careful investigation, carried out under CIE sponsorship at the National Physical Laboratory, the basic standards laboratory of Great Britain. The work yielded results that fell midway between the CIE values and Judd's corrected curves in most cases.

Stiles's Mixture Curves

The results of Stiles's determinations are shown as the solid curves of Figure 5.16. These are drawn through 49 data points which fall so accurately upon the smooth functions that in most cases they cannot be seen. Also shown for comparison are the original CIE values and Judd's corrections of these. Stiles's curves show the amounts of three spectral primaries at 644, 526, and 444 nm, required to match 46 other wavelengths in the spectrum. The functions are presented in separate panels, one for each component of the mixture field. These show the relative energies that are required to match the test wavelength indicated on the x-axis. The relative energy values are scaled independently for each light so that the amount of a primary used, when it matches its own wavelength, is taken as 1.0 no matter what the actual energy. Most of the determinations were made at 500 td, although somewhat less light than this was available at the spectral extremes. It should be recalled that, within limits, color matches do not depend upon the absolute intensity level that is used; Stiles's intensities mostly fall within these limits.

Each function is plotted on a logarithmic ordinate. Although this is unconventional for representing color-matching data, it is necessary to show accurately values that are small relative to the peaks of the curves (recall the discussion of log scales on page 104). It is clear that, unlike the objective methods, color matching is not a procedure that "fails in the tails." There is no indication, even for points that fall a thousand or more times below the peak of a curve, that any appreciable increase in measurement error has occurred. By comparison, recall that values obtained by physical methods do not even reliably exist below 25 percent of the peak value: to see what this means on the logarithmic plot of Figure 5.16, horizontal lines have been drawn 0.6 log unit from the top of each curve: physical methods at best can only skim off the top. The fact that the lower values can be accurately measured by the psychophysical method of color matching means that very small amounts of light absorption have very important effects upon color matching, as well as on the perception of color upon which such matching depends. We hope that it is now very clear what was meant by the earlier emphasis upon the importance of the "tails" of the curves.

In Figure 5.16, each panel shows functions that are interrupted at three places by vertical lines. These represent the wavelengths of the primaries. Where the test stimulus is of the same wavelength as one of the primaries, the ordinate value is, by definition, zero (the logarithm of 1). Within each panel, the spectrum is therefore divided into four regions. In four of the resulting twelve regions, negative proportions of a primary are represented; since negative numbers do not have logarithms, Stiles chose to indicate the logarithm of absolute values, together with the sign of the original values whose logarithms are plotted within each section of the curve.

From the shortest wavelengths tested to the wavelength of the blue primary, positive amounts of blue and red stimuli are required for a match, while small

146 Color Matching and the Visual Pigments

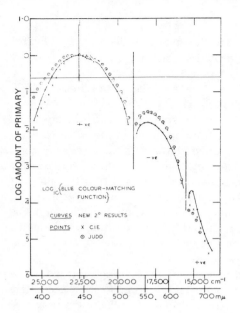

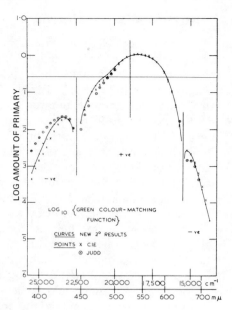

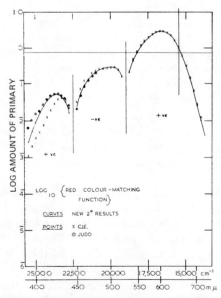

FIGURE 5.16 Color-mixture curves for 2° fields as determined by Stiles (1955). Each panel represents the amounts of one of the three primaries used in mixtures matching the spectral wavelengths shown. Horizontal lines are drawn 0.6 log unit below peaks.

amounts of the green primary must be added to the test wavelength. In the next region of the spectrum (between the wavelengths of the blue and green primary components of the mixture field) positive amounts of the blue and green are required, while small amounts of red must be added to the test field. In a third region between the wavelengths of the green and red primaries, positive amounts of red and green are needed in the mixture field with small amounts of blue added to the other side. Beyond the wavelength of the red primary at the right, the red stimulus accounts for most of the mixture, together with a small negative amount of green and a tiny positive component of the blue.

Unit Coordinate System of Plotting

A way of plotting color mixture data that has proved very useful is shown in Figure 5.17. In this plot, the amounts of the three primary stimuli required to match each spectral wavelength are adjusted so that the ordinate values always sum to unity. The proportions of the red, green, and blue components are thereby directly given, and these can be used to represent colors in a color triangle or a chromaticity diagram. They are known as *chromaticity coefficients*. The details of the procedure used to obtain these particular curves are clever and worth understanding.

Earlier in this chapter (p. 138) it was noted that the units in which the primaries of a color match are specified are not ordinary ones. The system used in Figure 5.17 was developed many years ago by W. D. Wright (1928–1929). It makes use of two reference wavelengths that are located about midway between pairs of primaries (in this case at 488 and 580 nm). We will call these the blue-green and yellow reference wavelengths respectively. A color match is made, independently of the spectral determinations, in which the yellow reference is matched with a mixture of the red (645) and green (526) primaries. By convention, the amounts of the red and green are stated to be equal for this condition. A similar but separate operation is carried out for the blue (444 nm) and green lights which are adjusted to match the blue-green reference; this defines equal amounts of these two stimuli. The fact that the green stimulus is used twice permits it to serve as a bridge between the units of red and blue. Here is a step-by-step example to illustrate how this works.

- Select some amount of the red primary, say 100 td. The subject is given control of the intensity of the green stimulus and of the yellow (580 nm) reference.
- The subject adjusts the amount of green in the mixture with red, in order to produce a yellow that matches the yellow reference. To make the match exact for brightness as well as hue, he simultaneously adjusts the amount of the yellow reference. Suppose that it turns out that 200 td of the green primary stimulus is needed for the match. (A very small amount of the blue stimulus may be required, added to the reference, in order to make the match exact.)

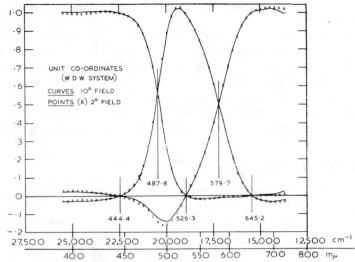

FIGURE 5.17 Data of Figure 5.16 plotted on unit coordinates (see text for explanation). The curves are for matching with a 10° field and are not discussed in the text. It will be seen that color-matching functions expressed this way vary only slightly with the area of the matching fields over this range.

- The 200-td green primary is mixed with the blue. The blue-green reference is the main component of the other half of the field, but a modest amount of the red stimulus will be needed to desaturate it. The subject therefore adjusts three stimuli (all except the green) to make a match. Suppose that 5 td of the blue component is required in the match.
- The troland amounts of the red, green, and blue mixture components in the two matches are in the ratio of 100 : 200 : 5. To specify the amount of a mixture component in any subsequent color match, in trichromatic units, the troland values are reciprocally adjusted: the red troland values are multiplied by 2, the green by 1, and the blue by 40.

The clever part of this scheme is that it eliminates from the color equation the effects of prereceptoral absorption, which vary considerably from one subject to another. The method works because the quality of a monochromatic light cannot be changed by the action of an absorbing medium; as Newton demonstrated, only the amount is altered. For an observer with very yellow (blue-absorbing) lens, for example, the energy required to achieve a unit trichromatic amount of the blue component will be higher than for an observer with a clear lens. Yet for both subjects, a unit trichromatic amount of each of these lights implies the same stimulating power at the retina.

When this procedure is followed, the agreement between observers is very good. A set of curves for 10 observers tested by Wright (1946) is shown in Figure 5.18.[20] Although the wavelengths of the primaries used by Wright are

Spectral Absorption Curves   149

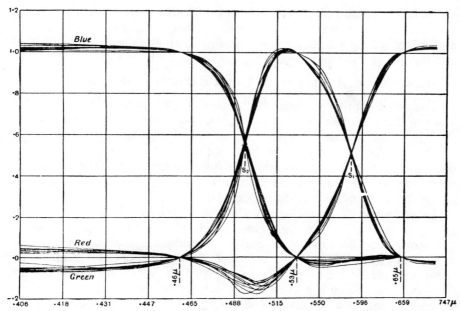

FIGURE 5.18 Color-matching data of W. D. Wright, plotted in the unit-coordinate system. Note that the primaries are different from those of Figure 5.17, but that the curves appear similar. (Wright, 1946, p. 130.)

slightly different than those that yielded Stiles's curves of Figure 5.16, the general features are the same.

SPECTRAL ABSORPTION CURVES OF HUMAN CONE PIGMENTS

We have seen that color-mixture curves have shapes that depend upon the choice of wavelengths of the primaries used to determine them, but that all such sets of curves represent the same color-matching behavior. "Imaginary" components of a mixture field cannot be physically realized because they imply a degree of selectivity of absorption in cone photopigments that cannot be achieved by real lights because of the overlapping nature of the spectral absorption curves of real cones. There are many triads of imaginary primaries that yield color-mixture curves whose values are all positive; if the domain of real colors plots entirely inside a color triangle whose corners define the components of the mixture field, an all-positive set of curves is indicated.

The actual absorption curves of human cone pigments must be related to the data of color-mixing experiments, since a color match implies equal absorptions for each member of the metameric pair within the three kinds of cone pigment. The absorption curves of the actual pigments must also be all-positive, since negative absorption has no physical meaning. Therefore, of all the possible sets of imaginary mixture stimuli enclosing the domain of real colors in the color diagram, there is one (and only one) such set that specifies the relative absorption spectra of the actual pigments contained in the outer segments of R, G, and B cones of the human eye.

Importance of Data from Color-defective Observers

The search for these curves, which has been a long one, has nearly ended. The key that has unlocked their hiding place has been found within the eyes of certain color-defective observers (see Chapter 10). It depends upon the finding that the color vision they exhibit is not different in principle from that of normal subjects, but is impoverished specifically because they lack one or another of the normal cone photopigments. Not all color-defective observers meet this requirement; those who do are called *dichromats*.

Left with but two types of cones, the dichromat needs only two primary components in order to make a color match. If given three knobs to adjust, each controlling the amount of one of the components of the mixture, his matches are neither unique nor reproducible, and it is only by chance if the resulting match is also acceptable to a normal observer. There will be much more to be said about abnormal color vision in Chapter 10, but the facts mentioned here should be sufficient to make it clear why the dichromat is so important for the understanding of normal cone pigments.

Dartnall's Standard Shape

In 1953, H. J. A. Dartnall demonstrated that a wide variety of photopigments that had been extracted from many different species had absorption spectra having the same shape,[21] if plotted on the basis of wavenumber (proportional to frequency of vibration). Although many different wavelengths of peak sensitivity could be found, a template based on the curve shape for any one of them could be used to represent any of the others, simply by shifting it laterally along the wavenumber axis.

The shape of the standard curve is shown in Figure 5.19, where it will be seen to have a smooth principal peak. If extended to shorter wavelengths, the curve would continue its rise, producing a secondary maximum called a *cis-peak*. For a pigment like human rhodopsin, the cis-peak is in the ultraviolet and can play no role in vision. If there were a cone pigment of this shape with a peak sensitivity at a wavelength longer than about 600 nm, the cis-peak surely could play a role in color vision—it might even account for the resurgence of redness in the violet end of the spectrum.

Dartnall's standard curve is an empirical generalization. There exists no adequate chemical theory to show exactly why it should be true that discrete shifts of curves having the same shape, if plotted in this particular way, should occur. We will not deal here with any theoretical ideas that have been advanced, except to say that the explanation for the shape of the linear longwave slope, which was dealt with on page 108, is consistent with Dartnall's template. The

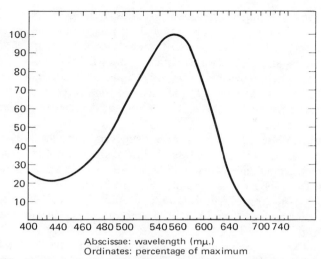

FIGURE 5.19 Dartnall's (1953) standard curve for a pigment with peak sensitivity at 560 nm.

important point is that it works, and if the concept could be extended to the treatment of the pigments of human cone vision, then their exact shapes would be known if the wavelengths of peak sensitivity could be established with sufficiently high accuracy.

This hope has been frustrated. In the first place, there is a bad fit between the Dartnall template and the spectral sensitivity curves of protanopes and deuteranopes. The most careful analysis of this discrepancy is due to Smith and Pokorny (1972) and Stiles and Wyszecki (1974). The latter authors posed the question: Is it possible to find a set of Dartnall pigments such that, with preretinal absorption taken into account, they are adequate transformations of color mixture data? The answer is "no." Most of the difficulty seems related to the shape of the longwave pigment (erythrolabe). Smith and Pokorny approached the problem by taking a careful look at protanopic and deuteranopic spectral sensitivity data available in the psychophysical literature (all of it consistent with the physical evidence of retinal densitometry). Figure 5.20 illustrates what they found. When the data are plotted on a wavenumber scale, the data for protanopes and deuteranopes coincide. The dashed curve in this plot represents the Dartnall template. The discrepancy is mainly at the long wavelengths, and although it is not large, it is highly significant for color vision. Again, the tails of the curve prove to be important. When Smith and Pokorny had a retrospective look at the pigment absorption data in the literature, they found many other instances where their curve shape fitted the experimental data somewhat better than did that of Dartnall.

Cyanolabe, on the other hand, seems definitely to be a pigment of the original type. It is a curious fact that, despite the elusive nature of this "blue-catching" pigment from the standpoint of physical measurement, its characteristics have been the easiest of all to reveal by psychophysical methods. Some of these methods will be discussed in the next chapter; the most obvious data once again have come from a class of color-defective observer, the blue-cone monochromat. These subjects apparently have only B cones and rods (see Chapter 10), so it is easy at high intensities to measure the spectral sensitivity of their B cones psychophysically. The resulting curve is excellently fitted by Dartnall's original curve shape.

Smith and Pokorny's finding strongly suggests, though it does not prove, that deuteranopia is caused by a loss of chlorolabe and not by fusion: it seems unlikely that a single template could be used to fit the sensitivity curves of protanopes, from whom it is virtually certain that erythrolabe is missing, and deuteranopes as well, if in fact the deuteranopes possessed both kinds of pigment. Rushton's revised view (p. 123), based on retinal densitometry, is therefore supported.

The smooth curve drawn through the data in Figure 5.20 is due to an earlier analysis by Vos and Walraven (1971). The set of cone sensitivity curves derived by these authors is very similar to a set proposed by Smith and Pokorny. Both are probably very close to the actual curves.

This section will be concluded with a brief description of considerations leading to the curves that are shown in Figure 5.21 (also given in tabular form on page 405). Before itemizing the facts that these curves attempt to predict, one additional concept needs to be elaborated.

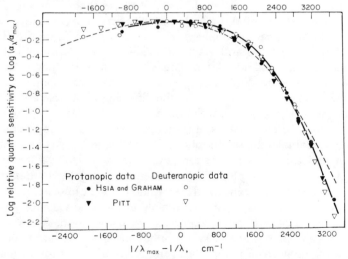

FIGURE 5.20 Log relative quantal sensitivity as a function of wavenumber for protanopes and deuteranopes. All curves have been scaled to unity at their maxima and they have been shifted laterally for best fit. The dashed line is Dartnall's standard shape; the solid line is from Vos and Walraven (1971). (Smith & Pokorny, 1972.)

Spectral Absorption Curves 153

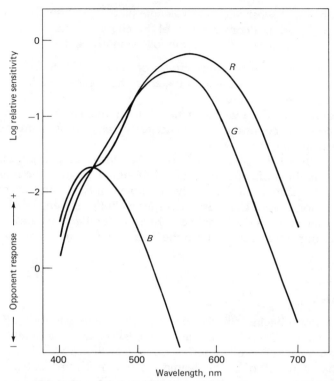

FIGURE 5.21 The spectral curves of Smith and Pokorny. These come very close to representing the relative spectral sensitivities of the red-, green-, and blue-absorbing photopigments of the human retina. The relative heights of the curves are discussed in the text. The values of these curves are given in Appendix III.

Luminosity Functions for Photopic Vision

Spectral sensitivity for rod vision can be unambiguously obtained, as we saw on page 108, since a metameric match is achieved and both halves of the field therefore appear identical. The measurement of analogous functions for photopic vision is a more difficult problem, one that will be discussed more fully in Chapter 9. These functions, which are also called *spectral luminous efficiency functions*, or "luminosity functions" for short, are ambiguous for cone vision because, as noted earlier, two wavelengths of equal luminosity for cones are perceived as being qualitatively different. Luminosity functions have nevertheless been obtained for normal subjects at photopic levels of intensity, and these have been compared with the less ambiguous curves that come from dichromats. Vos and Walraven used luminosity data of normal subjects not only to help specify the relative spectral sensitivity curves for the three types of cones, but also to suggest where these curves should be displayed vertically, relative to one another, in a sensitivity vs wavelength plot. Otherwise, their analysis also depends heavily upon a consideration of the characteristics of dichromats.

The curves of Figure 5.21 have the following properties:

- They account for color-mixture curves of normal subjects.
- If the R and G curves are added together, they predict the luminosity function of the normal observer.
- If either the R or G curve is eliminated, the remaining curve sums with the B function to account for the luminosity curves of protanopes and deuteranopes respectively.
- If it is assumed that the heights of these curves are proportional to the relative numbers of cone receptors of the three types in the retina, then a reasonable estimate of the relative numbers of R, G, and B cones in the foveal region is about 32 : 16 : 1 respectively (Walraven, 1974).
- The B cone curve is reasonably consistent with other estimates of its shape, as for example that derived from the data of blue-cone monochromats (see p. 369).

SUMMARY

Human vision begins with the absorption of photons in four different kinds of photopigments. One of these, rhodopsin, is found in the outer segments of rods. When a photon is absorbed, it isomerizes the rhodopsin molecule and initiates the sequence of events leading to vision. The probability of photon absorption varies with wavelength, but once a photon is absorbed, all information about its wavelength is lost. Any two arbitrary spectral distributions may therefore be matched for their effects upon rhodopsin simply by varying the intensity of one of them. Since rods contain only rhodopsin and operate over a low range of intensities below the cone threshold, rod vision is color-blind. Color vision depends upon the absorption of photons in the three kinds of cones, which contain different pigments. Unlike rhodopsin, these have resisted direct chemical analysis.

It appears likely that a given type of cone contains only one kind of pigment. Stimuli that differ in their spectral distribution may also appear identical in cone vision; these metameric matches are much more restricted than for rods and most spectral distributions that differ physically cannot be made to match at any adjustment of relative intensity. Metameric matches occur in the special cases where the same rates of photon capture occur in each of the three types of cones, by being absorbed at the same rate by erythrolabe (the R-cone pigment), chlorolabe (G cones) and cyanolabe (B cones). As for rods, once a photon is absorbed by a cone pigment molecule, the visual system has no information about its wavelength. The initial basis for color perception therefore lies, as Thomas Young suspected long ago, in the relative rates of light absorption by the three types of photopigments.

The exact shapes of the pigment absorption curves are critically important for understanding color vision. The method of microspectrophotometry permits direct measures of the transmittances of cone photopigments, but primate data are scarce and noisy, serving only to confirm the trichromatic view in a general way. Retinal densitometry, which can be practiced on living human subjects, measures the change in light reflected from the back of the eye as this varies with the bleaching of the photopigments. Although more extensively used than microspectrophotometry, it has suffered from two limitations: (1) cyanolabe, though certainly present, cannot be observed by this technique; (2) the method "fails in the tails" for erythrolabe and chlorolabe, since the important lower limbs of their absorption spectra cannot be assessed accurately.

Nevertheless, the shapes of the absorption curves of human cone photopigments are known with reasonable accuracy from inferences drawn from human psychophysical experiments. Color-mixture experiments with normal and dichromatic subjects have been especially helpful in this regard. In principle, any light can be represented by a point in a color triangle, as Maxwell first showed, where distances from the three sides specify the proportions of the three components of the mixture. If the corners of the diagram represent the physiological primaries, then a given location in the triangle can specify, at least in principle, the relative probabilities that a photon will be absorbed by each of the three types of pigment. These probabilities are the same for all metamers that are represented by that point.

The power of color-mixture data for revealing physiological facts lies first of all in the discovery that the numerical data and operations of color matching are isomorphic with the numbers and operations of ordinary algebra. This permits the writing of color equations to express the results of color-mixture experiments. Depending upon the choice of primaries that are used in such calculations, the colors of the spectrum can be specified by an infinite number of sets of three curves. Only one of these can represent the set of three physiological primaries whose values are proportional, if preretinal absorption is taken into account, to the action spectra of the three types of cone photopigments. This choice has been made mainly on the basis of the data from dichromats who lack one or another of the normal cone pigments.

NOTES

[1] Slight metamerism often occurs when parts of a manufactured object are made from different materials, causing different formulations of colorants to be used in achieving a color match. Metameric surface color matches usually break down a little when viewed under some of the variety of common illuminants (daylight, incandescent lamps, fluorescent tubes, and various other types of discharge lamps).

[2] The word *lightness* is used to refer to the perceived correlate of the reflectance of a surface, as opposed to the *brightness* of a disembodied aperture color. It will be recalled from Chapter 2 that there is a profound difference between these two modes

of viewing. Most of the basic color science under discussion in this book is based on experiments where aperture colors have been viewed, as these are simpler to interpret.

[3] Whereas the word "intensity" is used here (and elsewhere in the book) in its generic sense, it will always stand for a physical measure. Strictly speaking, what is under discussion in this section is radiometric intensity per unit (projected) area of the field, known as *radiance*.

[4] If the fields are continuously exposed, the significant measure is not the number of photons in the exposure, but their rate. It will be seen in Chapter 9 that the number of photons is the physical correlate which determines the threshold visibility and suprathreshold brightness of very brief flashes. The word "number," as used here, could stand either for the number of photons per unit time (rate) in an extended stimulus presentation, or the total number presented during a very brief flash.

[5] Weale (1963). For a review, see Ruddock (1972).

[6] Cooper and Robson (1969).

[7] Wald's Nobel lecture, delivered in Stockholm on December 12, 1967, has been published in *Science* (Wald, 1968). This provides a good review of his work, including that concerned with human color vision and color blindness.

[8] Brindley's discussion of this subject is on page 251 and 252 of the first edition of his book, published in 1960. The topic has been dropped in the second edition (Brindley, 1970).

[9] Wald (1937) extracted a cone pigment called *iodopsin* from the chicken, and Bridges (1962) reported extracting two cone pigments from the pigeon. No primate pigments have ever been extracted.

[10] A recent example is the theory of Biernson (1966). Some comments of Rushton (1966), specifically in reaction to the type of modeling done by Biernson, make choice reading. For example (p. 1130): "Vision is a subject infected by a type of speculator from which most subjects are immune—the speculator who delights in suggesting what is fantastically improbable, and then challenging the world to prove his particular fantasy impossible. . . . Speculators are concerned to conceal the cracks in their structure. Scientists study the relevant observations at first hand. . . . Speculators rely on popular sources, review articles, student textbooks, etc. . . . Most important of all, the scientist's theory leads to predictions that can be tested experimentally, and which he generally is employed in testing: by means of this his theory may be improved. The speculator is not concerned with experiments or indeed in meeting the reality behind his speculation at all. His speculations seldom lead to new and testable predictions and consequently remain a patch of sterility in the fertile forest of experimentation."

[11] In his excellent review article in the *Handbook of Sensory Physiology*, Liebman (1972) makes the following statement on page 515, at the end of his discussion of primate data. "In conclusion then, primate data have not been improved upon in the five years since their promulgation. At best, they suggest the existence of three cone pigments in separate cones in confirmation of previous theory. Although arguments for knowledge of greater accuracy can be given and ancillary information has been cited, the MSP data alone cannot be regarded as accurate to better than 20-30 nm, and published densities cannot be regarded as indicative in the least of what exists in the living eye." The recent success of the British research team of Bowmaker, Dartnall, Lythgoe, and Mollon (1978) suggests that Liebman, as well as this author,

may have been overly pessimistic. Also, the British group has finally found a couple of B cones, which is very reassuring. They are reported to look, superficially, just like R and G cones. It seems clear that there are very few of them in the primate retina.

[12] Although Brindley and Willmer (1952) had described a retinal densitometer, they did not successfully measure the effects of bleaching, and the first full papers from the Cambridge laboratory were those of Campbell and Rushton (1955) and Rushton, Campbell, Hagins, and Brindley (1955). In 1953, Weale described an application of the method to the observation of "Photochemical reactions in the living cat's retina" in the *Journal of Physiology*. He first described the procedure in the *Annual Report of the Institute of Ophthalmology, 1950–51* (p. 18).

[13] Because these end points are known and interpretable, the problem of stray light can be more or less ignored and a linear relation assumed between the amount of bleaching and the measured values that are obtained for intermediate bleaches. (Over such a short range, logarithms are nearly proportional to their numbers, so if the full range is 0.2 log unit, then a change of 0.1 log unit can be taken as corresponding roughly to a half bleach.) If one does not want to make this assumption, it is sometimes possible to determine the energies required (for example, at various different wavelengths) to produce a criterion amount of bleaching. For this purpose, the middle of the range is a good point at which to aim, and a valid action spectrum can be measured even if the percentage of bleaching to which that point corresponds is not exactly known.

[14] Working the other way round, Miller (1972) estimated the density of erythrolabe and chlorolabe by measuring the effects of bleaching on the spectral sensitivity of protanopes and deuteranopes. His density values fall in the range from 0.4 to 0.6.

[15] In retinal densitometry, complications due to stray light can sometimes lead to double-peaked curves even though a single pigment with a single peak sensitivity is present (Rushton, 1965b, p. 34).

[16] Colors may also be "mixed" by repeating them in rapid succession (Chapter 9) or by presenting them as large numbers of interlaced tiny dots, each too small to be resolved by the eye. This is the principle used in "pointillist" painting and color television.

[17] Grassman anticipated this in part long ago when he wrote (Helmholtz, 1924, p. 133 v. 2) "When one of two kinds of light that are to be mixed together changes continuously, the appearance of the mixture changes continuously also" (Grassman's second law). It may be helpful for some readers to appreciate that color matching is akin to solving three simultaneous equations by iteration. To be successful at this, it is necessary to know whether a change from what has gone before in one of the coefficients has allowed one to move closer to, or farther from, a solution. Similarly, when the subject changes the amount of one of the primaries in the mixture, he must be able to tell whether that change has caused the fields to appear more or less similar than before.

[18] I am indebted to A. Eisner for the following proof, which requires that it be shown that the sum of the lengths of the perpendiculars erected from the three sides of an equilateral triangle to any point inside the triangle is a constant equal to the altitude of the triangle. If a is the length of an altitude and s is the length of a side, the area of the equilateral triangle $A = \frac{1}{2} as$, since all three sides are equal. Now divide the full triangle into six right triangles by means of the dotted lines from the internal point

to the three corners. The area of the full triangle must be equal to the sum of the areas of these six triangles. Therefore:

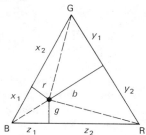

$A = \frac{1}{2}gz_1 + \frac{1}{2}gz_2 + \frac{1}{2}by_1 + \frac{1}{2}by_2 + \frac{1}{2}rx_1 + \frac{1}{2}rx_2$
$= \frac{1}{2}g(z_1 + z_2) + \frac{1}{2}b(y_1 + y_2) + \frac{1}{2}r(x_1 + x_2)$
$= \frac{1}{2}gs + \frac{1}{2}rs + \frac{1}{2}bs$
$= \frac{1}{2}(g + r + b)s.$

Therefore

$\frac{1}{2}as = \frac{1}{2}(g + r + b)s$
$a = g + r + b.$

[19] The expression "physiological identity" was coined by F. J. J. Clarke (1960), p. 376.
[20] Starting on page 126 of his book *Researches on Normal and Defective Colour Vision*, Wright (1946) explains the special system that he developed for specifying the trichromatic coefficients as described here.
[21] Two such curves are in fact required, depending upon animal species. It was not revealed earlier in this chapter that the photochemical process in the eye depends upon a store of vitamin A from which one of the important components needed for regeneration is derived. Humans possess one type of vitamin A called vitamin A_1; some other animals (for example, fish) possess vitamin A_2.

6
Sensitivity Regulation

People with normal vision are capable of making visual discriminations, including those concerned with color, over an enormous range of light intensities. Although it is not pleasant to do so, one can, for example, read in midday under direct summer sunlight, and yet see well enough on a hazy night to avoid large objects while walking around under feeble, filtered starlight. For these extremes of seeing conditions in everyday life, the ratio of intensities is about 10^{10}, or ten thousand million, to 1. On a logarithmic scale, this enormous range is about equally divided between scotopic (rod) and photopic (cone) vision. When rods alone are stimulated there is no color vision, for reasons given in the previous chapter. Accordingly, this chapter will mainly deal with visual discriminations that occur within the photopic range. Nevertheless, it will again prove instructive to consider the simpler rod system as a prototype.

Before beginning a discussion of the technical aspects of visual sensitivity control, a pair of illustrations from everyday life will help set the stage. Consider first that none of the thousands of stars of the clear night sky can be seen during the day. Yet the increment of light added to the retinal image, as a result of light from a star, is unchanged when the sun rises. The difference must therefore have something to do with the nature of the visual system, regarding the ways it responds to such increments with and without a background. Scattered light from the sun, which illuminates the sky, will add to the light from a star. The increment of retinal illumination provided by the star, by itself sufficient to render that star easily visible against the dark background of the night sky, becomes insufficient to allow the perception of the same star against the bright daytime sky. The effect is not absolute, for brighter objects can still be seen. The moon, for example, has an intensity at night that is roughly equal to that of the sky by day. In the daytime, the luminance of the moon adds to that of the sky. The ratio of intensities of moon-plus-sky to sky alone is approximately two to one— easily sufficient to allow the moon to be seen. In fact, an object the size of the moon could still be detected (though just barely) even if its intensity were only about 1 percent that of the sky.

Although the increment provided by a star in the daytime is the same as at night, the percentage of light that it adds is decidedly not. The invisibility of stars in the daytime could easily be understood if the sensitivity of the eye were found to depend upon ratios, rather than increments. The idea that sensory systems react in such a way is captured in "Weber's law," which states that "$\Delta I/I =$ constant." This is perhaps the oldest law in visual psychophysics. More than one hundred years ago Fechner wrote in his *Elements of Psychophysics* that "The law as applied to vision had, in the past, been stated by Bouguer, Arago, Masson, and Steinheil in connection with other investigations, and later by myself and Volkmann, without, however, anyone's paying much attention to it."[1] It turns out that for vision Weber's law applies only at high intensities and not always perfectly even then. Nevertheless, there is more truth to it by far (except at extremely low levels of illumination) than to a law stating that the sensitivity to increments is what remains constant. Later in the chapter we will explore the failure of Weber's law as expressed in "threshold vs intensity" curves (p. 196).

A second example from everyday life will serve to illustrate a crucial point about such shifts of visual sensitivity: they take time. Because of this, entering a dimly lit enclosure, such as a theater on a bright day, can be an almost devastating experience. At first it is difficult to know where an aisle is, and quite impossible to tell whether a seat is occupied, or for that matter even whether there are seats. This situation gradually improves. At first, gross outlines become discriminable, for example the boundary of an aisle. Later it is possible to tell whether a seat is occupied, and eventually a familiar face can be recognized. Vision in the dimly lit enclosure will gradually improve and eventually reach a state that is optimal for that amount of illumination. (Recall the exercise on page 40.) This process is called *dark adaptation*. The reverse process, which occurs upon leaving the dimly lit enclosure, is called *light adaptation*.

Chromatic Adaptation: A Triple Problem

The basic information about color received by the brain derives initially from the relative degree of activity among three types of cones. If we lived in a world where illumination never varied, we could forget about the problem of adaptation. But instead there is at least a million-to-one range of luminances for the cones to contend with; a problem that is deftly handled, it would seem, by a system whose sensitivity automatically shifts from one time to another in order to keep itself within a sensitive range. We will see that there are many mechanisms needed to accomplish this, and that doubtless there are others yet to be discovered. All these somehow manage to work in concert and with such incredible precision that the colored appearance of things changes relatively little over the whole range of stimulus intensities. Where color vision is concerned, then, it is not just the sensitivity of a unitary photopic system that is under continuous adjustment, but rather that of a system with three inputs.

The mechanisms of adaptation are nevertheless easily capable of changing apparent color. This is an aspect of what is called *chromatic adaptation*. Try the exercise described on this page,* and the subjective effects of chromatic adaptation will become evident. Underlying this demonstration there are parallel mechanisms, existing independently within each eye, that orchestrate a delicate process of sensitivity adjustment that normally keeps all three components of two tripartite systems precisely tuned, preserving the very delicate balance required for stable chromatic perception. Most of these mechanisms work independently within each eye. This is true of the photopigments that absorb the light, of the cones that contain them, and of all the retinal machinery that was discussed in Chapter 4. The demonstration shows that the colored appearance of things can easily be upset by adapting the eye to unusual conditions. But if the two eyes receive almost the same input, as they normally do, the adaptive machinery is so precise that there is normally no difference at all in the perceived color of objects as they are viewed alternately with the two eyes.

Normally we see colors about the same way with each of our eyes. Test this by covering one eye at a time, switching your view of various colored surfaces seen in the environment. (For a few readers there may be slight differences which probably will not have been noticed before.) Now, while covering the left eye, stare for 15 to 30 seconds at a bright light, such as an incandescent lamp or the sky. Upon repeating the original experiment, definite differences will be seen depending upon which eye does the looking; these will fade over time as the exposed eye recovers its original state of sensitivity. During the period when the two eyes differ, looking with both eyes will result in an intermediate sensation. This demonstration shows that a major part of the balance of the mechanisms in the eye that determine perceived hue is independently determined within each eye. The fact that the two eyes normally mediate the same sensations results from the fact that they are normally in the same state of adaptation (for example, both eyes are exposed to a bright source); it also shows the almost incredible precision of identical control by the separate eyes.

Numbers of Photons Involved

For a good appreciation of the need for adaptational machinery, it is helpful to develop some conception of the numbers of photons that fall upon the retina over the range of conditions under which color vision occurs. If the photons from an external field are beamed through the central part of the pupil, the smallest amount of light needed for foveal vision is about 0.1 td. By Equation (3.1) (p. 64) this corresponds at 580 nm to 125,000 photons per square degree on the retina during each second. In order to see such a "threshold" light, an exposure of only 100 ms is as effective as one that lasts a second. Therefore, 12,500 photons in the briefer exposure are sufficient to arouse a visual sensation.

Since there are about 10,000 cones in a square degree patch at the fovea, the numbers of photons arriving in 100 ms at threshold are on the same order of magnitude as the number of cones. Since not all arriving photons are absorbed, there are evidently fewer photons absorbed than there are cones.

Suppose that a white page reflects 80 per cent of the incident light, and the black print 4 percent. A few calculations will show what this implies at three levels: (a) threshold, (b) a good level of illumination for reading, and (c) outdoor sunlight.

	Trolands (completely reflecting surface)	Photons per 100 ms per square degree of retina (page)	Photons per 100 ms per square degree of retina (print)	Print–page difference	Print to page ratio
Threshold	0.1 td	10,000	500	9,500	0.05
Reading light	1,000 td	1,000,000	50,000	950,000	0.05
Sunlight	100,000 td	1000 million	50 million	950 million	0.05

The percentages of light reflected from page and print do not depend upon illumination level because they relate directly to the probability that each incident photon will be reflected, and this probability, although it differs for print and page, is not affected by light level. Thus the ratio of print to page luminance is 0.05, whether the values that enter into the calculation of this ratio (itself dimensionless) are expressed in trolands, numbers of photons, or whatever units. From the table one can see how, as illumination level is raised, the print-page *difference* in photon density at the retina increases from 9500 to 950,000,000 photons per square degree of retinal area during each 100 ms. A difference of 950,000 photons, provided by reading light, would under sunlight result only if the print to page ratio were reduced to .00095. This could be done by using a *very* light gray ink, but such letters would be invisible under any light. A ratio like 0.05 is called *contrast*, and it is very often expressed as a percentage (5 per cent contrast, in this example). This definition of contrast is a good one to use when the critical (test) area to be discriminated—in this case the letters—is small relative to the background, because positive contrasts (test area brighter than the background) and negative contrasts (test area darker) produce nearly equivalent visual effects (Blackwell, 1946).

Sensitivity to contrast improves as illumination is increased, in violation of Weber's law, and our ability to see objects against their backgrounds in fact improves—as we all know from everyday experience—as the level of illumination is raised. But our ability to see an object of fixed intensity, such as a star or traffic signal, decreases.

The Use of Background and Test Fields

In Chapter 5, we saw that a simple bipartite field, used for color matching, has unexpected power for generating data useful for understanding the spectral sensitivities of the cones. For studying adaptation, a different stimulus configuration has often been used, one that is equally simple. A *background field* is used to control the state of adaptation of the eye. The size of this field does not matter very much, so long as it subtends about six degrees or more of visual angle. In most experiments the background is presented steadily and the subject looks at it until his adaptive state stabilizes. Then, while he is still looking at the field, a *test flash* is superimposed upon the field. If a small flash appears at the point of fixation, it can easily be confined to the rod-free area of the fovea. The most often measured characteristic of the foveal test flash is its *threshold*, defined as that intensity of the flash required for it to be just barely visible. The test flash is too brief and feeble to affect the state of adaptation being probed. With this technique many things can be varied, including especially the intensity of the background field. When the spectral composition of the background and test fields differs, the technique is called the *two-color threshold method*.

Background fields, if presented steadily, can raise the threshold of perception for superimposed test flashes (recall the stars). But backgrounds near threshold intensities have no such effect: only when their intensities are about 30 times threshold do they begin to elevate the threshold of the added flash. Such a background would, in a 100-ms period, deliver nearly 400,000 photons to the flash area, corresponding to about 40 photons per cone. At 100,000 td, the trillion or so photons involved would provide about 100,000 photons per receptor in 100 ms. These threshold statistics show that an individual cone is able to register, at least some of the time, the arrival of a single photon. Yet that same receptor must also be able to withstand the assault of more than a million photons in a 1-s exposure. The ability of the eye to adjust its sensitivity so that it can respond effectively over such very wide ranges of light intensity is called *visual adaptation*. Subsumed within it are the specialized problems of light, dark, and chromatic adaptation.

PHOTOGRAPHY AS AN ANALOG

In order to make good black-and-white photographs, the exposure of the film must be appropriate to the amount of light falling on the external scene, which in turn is proportional to that imaged by the optics of the camera at the film plane. As many would-be photographers have learned to their sorrow, seriously underexposed film leads to photographic prints that turn out black all over, whereas severe overexposure leads to photographic whiteout.

The potential amount of information in a photograph is related to the number of discriminable spatial elements that comprise it, multiplied by the number of discriminable steps of brightness that can be provided by each element. Extremely inappropriate exposure, whether too great or too small, thus causes the loss of all information that the photograph otherwise might have conveyed.

Because cameras and eyes look at the same scenes, both are faced with the same problem of attempting to respond appropriately to the amount of incoming light. Faulty exposure of the eye can also cause loss of information. Because of the incredibly sophisticated "design" of the eye, this happens relatively seldom, and then usually only to a modest degree. Because cameras are simpler than eyes, and most readers will have had some experience with photography, the principles of proper photographic exposure will be described in order to provide background for what follows on the sensitivity regulation of the eye. Despite the usefulness of the eye—camera analogy, the reader is warned that eyes and cameras do not usually solve their problems in the same way. It is the problems, not their solutions, that are common in the two cases.

First it is necessary to pause for a moment to introduce one more photometric concept, to be added and related to the troland unit that has been used to this point. *Luminance* is a technical term that refers to the intensity per unit area of light coming from a surface toward the eye. In referring to quantitative measures of luminance in this and chapters to follow, the unit of "candela per square meter" (cd/m^2) will be exclusively used. For the purposes of this book, all we need to know about this unit is its relation to the unit of retinal illuminance, the troland (introduced on page 64). By definition, a surface xternal to the eye having a luminance of 1 cd/m^2 produces a retinal illuminance of 1 td if the area of the pupil of the eye is 1 mm^2. For an external surface of fixed luminance, the retinal illuminance produced by it increases in proportion to the area of the pupil. Neither the area of the surface nor its distance from the eye affects either luminance or retinal illumination.[2]

In order to produce a photograph that depicts real objects, the luminances of various areas in the scene must differ. Objects stand out because they are either brighter or darker than the backgrounds against which they are seen. (For the moment, we neglect the role of color differences.)

Since most scenes do not depict actual sources of light, we consider here only those that depend upon reflected light for their rendition. We shall ignore also certain problems in connection with the "highlights" caused by specular surfaces. Assuming uniform illumination and a "flat" scene (recall the marbles at the bottom of Figure 2.3), the total range of luminances depends entirely upon the range of reflectances of the objects that are there.

Some objects reflect more than 90 percent of the light incident upon them. No matter what the illumination, those that reflect about 70 percent or more appear white, whether directly viewed or seen in a good photographic reproduction. At the other extreme, objects that reflect less than 4 or 5 percent of the incident light appear black. Therefore the range of intensities that a photographic print must provide, which corresponds exactly to the range of reflectances that it can produce, need not be greater than about 20:1 in order for the lightnesses of the original scene to be reasonably well depicted.

If the illumination falling upon all scenes were constant, the design of cameras—and eyes—could be greatly simplified. Because such a constant illumination would yield a fixed range of object and background luminances, the camera could be designed with a fixed lens opening and shutter speed, allowing the film always to be exposed within its most sensitive range. But as already noted, the actual range of illuminations under which cameras and eyes must function is enormous. A highly reflecting surface in the sunshine would have a luminance of about 20,000 cd/m^2 whereas the same surface by moonlight would register at about 0.02 cd/m^2. This implies a ratio of incident illuminations of about 1,000,000 to 1.

A typical curve for photographic film is shown in Figure 6.1. The ordinate shows the density[3] of the exposed and processed negative. The abscissa represents, at the plane of the film, the luminance of an external scene. This film, like all such materials, is most sensitive to illuminance variations in a mid-range. Here the slope of the curve is highest, being less so at the extremes labeled "toe" and "knee." Any luminance less than about 2 cd/m^2 fails to increase the density of this film above its unexposed value; a photographic negative thus exposed will be virtually transparent, and if printed in the usual way, the picture will be black. Any exposure greater than about 2,000 cd/m^2 will expose the film to its maximum processed density of about 2.4; this corresponds to an almost

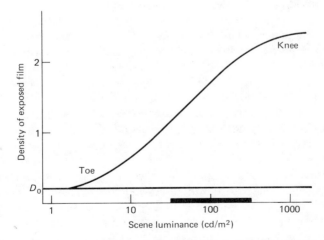

FIG. 6.1. This curve shows how the density of a photographic negative increases as a function of log exposure. Plotted here is the luminance of the external scene, assuming a fixed diaphragm at the camera lens. The black rectangle at the bottom corresponds to a 20:1 range of luminances; the density of the exposed film increases rapidly and nearly linearly through this range.

opaque negative that transmits less than 0.5 percent of the light incident upon it. When processed in the ordinary way, the print will reflect more than 90 percent of the incident light, and it will appear white.

This range of 1000:1 is broader than the 20:1 required to depict a flat scene. But the most useful range is far less than this, because both the toe and knee of the characteristic curve yield only small density changes relative to the middle portion; this implies a loss of information in these regions. Excellent photographic reproduction results only from exposures constrained to the middle portion of the curve, corresponding roughly to the 20:1 variations of discriminable luminances in the original scene. This range is shown in Figure 6.1 as a black rectangle along the abscissa.

In order to take good pictures, then, it is necessary to keep the illuminance level at the film plane, corresponding to the mid-range of scene luminances, at the appropriate level. If the external level of illumination is too low to permit this, then longer exposures can be used. But once the longest practical exposure is reached, no solutions are possible other than to seek a more sensitive film or a larger lens opening. On the other hand, as the level of external illumination is raised, it is easily possible to keep the film exposure constant by progressively reducing the lens opening, decreasing the exposure time, or both. These are familiar procedures, used by millions of photographers.

LIGHT AND DARK ADAPTATION

The term *adaptation* has the general meaning of "adjusting to," or "getting used to" some kind of situation. The expression is used in diverse scientific contexts ranging from the evolution of species characteristics to the tendency of neurons to fire at a constant rate following an initial transient discharge. Even within the much more restricted domain of visual science, the term unfortunately has more than one technical meaning. In contexts outside our concern, the word may refer to adjustments that one makes following prolonged observations of slant, tilt, prismatic distortion, or gratings.

Perhaps the most common theme running through all these examples is the notion that adaptation is not immediate; instead, the process takes time. The change in sensitivity that the eye undergoes in response to changes in luminance level, as we have seen, is no exception. Dark adaptation can be extremely slow, whereas the reverse process of light adaptation, although faster, is by no means instantaneous. These facts permit the following generalization: although a high level of visual information transfer is possible over an enormous range of intensities, the range at *any particular time* is much more restricted.

Measurement of Sensitivity

Sensitivity is defined as the reciprocal of the stimulus energy required to elicit a fixed response (often called a "criterion response") from an observer. The strength of a visual sensation (called *brightness*) is of variable magnitude, ranging from something just barely visible to the brightest light that one can imagine. Its investigation is rendered difficult by the inaccessability of subjective response magnitude. Brightness is not directly measurable in the same sense that physical quantities are, because a sensation is a private, unshared experience. Although numerical estimates of brightness have been attempted with surprising success in many sensory scaling experiments,[4] these methods have not often proved useful for those whose interests include the underlying mechanisms of perception. For example, it would be possible to do an experiment where brightness ratings were recorded as a function of wavelength for a series of equal-photon stimuli. At photopic energy levels, the peak of the resulting curve could be identified without much ambiguity. But the meaning of all other points on the curve would be obscure, and impossible to relate, say, to the action spectra of cone photopigments. The methods of classical psychophysics yield data that plot entirely along physical scales, which makes them much easier to relate to underlying mechanisms (as in the example in Chapter 5 of scotopic spectral sensitivity and its relation to the very similar action spectrum of rhodopsin).

The classical methods may be introduced with the help of another analogy. Imagine that you are given a photocell and a microammeter, but no information about the linearity of either instrument. To make matters still more difficult, suppose that the face of the meter is blank and that, in the absence of any illumination of the photocell, there is a steady dither of the meter needle over some low but finite range. Let us assume that there is a monotonic relation between the intensity of a light delivered to the photocell and the magnitude of mean needle deflection of the meter, analogous to the relation that also exists between light intensity and brightness.

Suppose the task is to find the spectral sensitivity of the system. One could start by delivering equal numbers of photons of light to the photocell at various wavelengths. Just as in the visual case, the wavelength of peak response could be identified but the meaning of all other values would be ambiguous, due to the lack of a scale on the meter (inaccessibility of response magnitude) and the possible nonlinearity of the system.

The preferred solution requires first that some arbitrary point on the scale of the meter be identified and marked. One then takes a calibrated monochromator and irradiates the photocell at some wavelength until the needle is driven to the arbitrary point. Because of the dither (response variability) it would be necessary to make several such estimates. One could then determine the energy required, at each wavelength tested, to produce a 0.50 probability of producing the criterion deflection.

Assessing the spectral sensitivity of the eye requires very similar measurements. Substitute the eye for the photocell, the remainder of the organism for the microammeter, subjective magnitude for needle deflection, and the analogy is complete. Measuring the spectral sensitivity of the eye this way will yield more useful and reliable results than those derived from sensory scaling.

The results of such psychophysical experiments are expressed entirely in physical units, because the aim has been to find combinations of physical variables that interact to produce some criterion response. In the case just cited, the two variables were photon-based intensity and wavelength. In a dark-adaptation experiment, they would be stimulus luminance and time in the dark.

Thresholds

One criterion point on the response scale that has proved particularly useful is the *threshold*. In terms of the photocell analogy, a threshold response would be represented by a just-barely-measurable movement of the needle. In the visual case, it would be a just-barely-percptible flash of light. In each case there is a similar ambiguity. Somebody (or some device) must observe the needle and decide whether the mean deflection has raised it reliably above the baseline dither. Moreover, the needle may move very slowly at first: at just what point can the change be said to be significant? One solution would be to take a small but definite change as a criterion in each case. This is essentially what is done to determine a "threshold" in many electrophysiological experiments, where the response scale is accessible. In the psychophysical experiment, the difficulty is even more subtle.

There is a general problem in science that the act of measuring a state or process often interferes with the state or process being examined. It is therefore desirable to use the weakest possible probe to test the state of a system. A brief test flash that is in the vicinity of threshold fits this description very well. But anyone who has ever observed dim light flashes will realize that merely to judge whether a flash is seen (or not seen) involves a process of decision that goes far beyond the immediate sensation. The observer must therefore adopt some criterion according to which he will say "yes" or "no" in response to a given sensation. Different subjects adopt different criteria, and a given subject's criterion may vary from one time to another. This has been shown in experiments where some of the "flashes" randomly presented are "blanks"; that is, no light is delivered to the eye, though care is taken to produce all of the preparatory signals and usual shutter noises. Some subjects report as many as 30 or 40 percent "false positives" under these conditions, others virtually none. These methods allow the experimenter to record whether a response is "correct" or "incorrect" rather than merely to note whether the subject reports "yes" or "no." Many variations on these methods have been developed, and these are discussed in standard texts.[5]

Mechanisms of Light Adaptation

When the visual messages reach the retinal ganglion cells, they become encoded for the first time in terms of nerve impulse frequency (see Chapter 7). The useful range of frequencies within each cell is not great, ranging from zero to about 100 spikes per second, and there is no convincing evidence that the pattern of the spikes, for any mean frequency, carries any information. Such a range of frequencies seems about right for encoding the range of luminances present in a scene, provided that the illumination level does not change. But it is obviously all wrong for encoding a million-to-one variation in light input. Because the photopic visual system nevertheless handles such a range, some form of gain control is necessary to keep the frequency of optic nerve discharge within the useful range.

Suppose that adaptation were fully compensatory and took place entirely at the level of the individual photoreceptor. If the process worked with perfect spatial and temporal precision, this would mean that the output from each receptor would always be adjusted so that, no matter what the input, the output would be the same. But vision begins with a spatio-temporal pattern of retinal illuminance. Just as in the photographic analog, this pattern contains all the information that is available to be detected and transmitted. A perfectly precise adaptive mechanism, because it would render the output of all photoreceptors constant, no matter what the input, would thereby eliminate all transfer of information.

The foregoing tells us what *not* to look for. We might expect instead to find regions of the retina that are interconnected for purposes of adaptation, and we can anticipate also that adaptation should be a process that has sluggish temporal characteristics.

Could the adaptive machinery operate to attenuate the light input in the manner of an automatic exposure control on a camera? If it could, this would serve to keep average retinal illuminance constant over the whole scene despite changes in external scene luminance, without wiping out the information contained in the point-to-point illuminance variations. It might seem that the pupil of the eye could serve this function because it does admit light and therefore affects retinal illumination in proportion to its area, just as the iris diaphragm of a camera similarly affects the exposure of the film. Moreover, the pupil automatically becomes smaller as the amount of light incident upon the eye is increased.

In a camera, the only mechanism of "adaptation" for a fixed duration of exposure is the size of the camera's "pupil"—the diaphragm whose opening controls the amount of light reaching the film plane. This control is designed to be completely compensatory, to keep the illumination at the film plane constant no matter what the external scene. But in the eye the total range of pupillary constriction, over the millionfold range of photopic luminances, reduces the effective retinal illuminance of the brightest lights by only a factor of about seven. Therefore, as external luminance increases, so does retinal illumination, though not quite in proportion.

BLEACHING AND REGENERATION KINETICS

It is certain that the bleaching and regeneration of photopigments is an important factor in adaptation. Probably the most important application of retinal densitometry has been to the study of the rates of bleaching and regeneration of visual photopigments. As we saw in Chapter 5, the bleaching of photopigments increases the amount of light in the test beam reflected from the fundus. When the bleaching light is extinguished, the test light (itself too weak to bleach significantly) is exposed to monitor the amount of unbleached rhodopsin in the retina. The test-beam intensity declines as expected toward the unbleached level, indicating that the retina's supply of unbleached rhodopsin is being replenished.

Regeneration

A relationship between recovery from bleaching and rod dark adaptation had long been expected; some of the earliest work on retinal densitometry was concerned with this. As already noted in Chapter 5, there was less bleaching than expected. The replacement of rhodopsin, it was found, is a relatively slow process, but not as slow as the recovery of sensitivity in dark adaptation as measured psychophysically: most of the rhodopsin returned in about 5 minutes, whereas dark adaptation takes at least 30 minutes. The precise time course of rhodopsin recovery offers some insight into the process involved. Initially, 0.25 percent of the rhodopsin returns with every second spent in the dark after the bleaching exposure. If recovery were maintained at this rate, one might think that all of the rhodopsin would return in 400 seconds. But this is not how recovery works: the rate of recovery is not constant, but rather it is proportional to the deficit that remains to be made up. Instead of 0.25 percent of the total rhodopsin supply returning every second, it is 0.25 percent of the amount remaining to be replenished that appears each second. For example, if 50 percent of the rhodopsin has already regenerated at some particular time in the dark, only 0.125 percent of the total will be added during the following second.

Mathematically this behavior may be described by a simple differential equation

$$\frac{dp}{dt} = \frac{(1-p)}{400}, \tag{6.1}$$

where p is the amount of unbleached rhodopsin (assigned a maximum value of 1) and the left-hand side of the equation stands for the rate at which p changes with time t measured in seconds. To satisfy this differential equation, p must vary in time in accordance with an exponential function:

$$p = 1 - e^{(-t/400)}, \tag{6.2}$$

which is what Rushton observed (Fig. 6.2). When only a part of the rhodopsin was initially bleached, the same differential equation is found to hold, with the same time constant of 400 seconds, and the pigment returns along the same time course shown in Figure 6.2, except that it starts at some larger value of p, appropriate to the amount of unbleached pigment immediately after the bleaching exposure.

This behavior of rhodopsin during recovery from bleaching exposure strongly suggests that the bleached rhodopsin itself is the source for replenishing

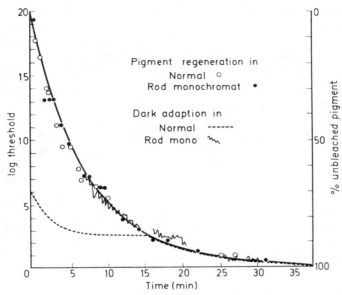

FIGURE 6.2 The points represent retinal densitometric measurements of the fraction of unbleached pigment (right-hand scale) as a function of time in the dark following an exposure that bleaches almost all of the rhodopsin in the eye. The smooth curve drawn through these points is similar to Equation (6.2). The uneven line represents psychophysical threshold settings, obtained by method of adjustment; this should be referred to the left-hand scale. Most of the psychophysical curve cannot be seen in a normal subject, whose sensitivity during the early phase of dark adaptation is controlled by cones, as is suggested by the dotted line. (Adapted from Rushton, 1972, p. 377.)

the store of unbleached rhodopsin. The rate of recovery would then be expected to slow down as recovery approaches completion, as implied by Equation (6.2), because the store of bleached rhodopsin is now much less abundant than it was soon after bleaching. For this reason the restoration of rhodopsin to its 11-cis unbleached form is termed the *regeneration* of rhodopsin, on the assumption that it is produced in the retina by a reisomerization and recombination of the products of bleaching. This implies that the retina has a fixed total pool of ingredients for manufacturing rhodopsin.

Bleaching

In other experiments, Rushton investigated the time course of bleaching during exposure to light. Quite high light levels were required to bleach a large fraction of rhodopsin, a fact which at first seems hard to reconcile with the high sensitivity of rod vision. Indeed, only in bright daylight would as much as 50 percent of rhodopsin be bleached. The quantitative study of bleaching is made easier by the slowness of rhodopsin regeneration, for if the bleaching light does not last longer than a few seconds, only a very small and insignificant fraction of the rhodopsin will regenerate during the exposure (regeneration occurs in the presence of light, as well as in its absence). It is therefore relatively easy to measure the amount of rhodopsin bleached after various intensities of exposure to light, provided that the fraction of rhodopsin bleached is directly proportional to the number of photons in the bleaching exposure, a result in agreement with the expectation that each absorbed photon bleaches only one pigment molecule—the molecule that absorbs it.

This proportionality between the number of incident photons and the number of bleached molecules of rhodopsin cannot continue indefinitely, since there are only a finite number of rhodopsin molecules present in the retina (though it is a very large number, as we saw on p. 82). Thus the situation is formally similar to the regeneration process. For example, if at a particular moment the bleaching photons have converted half the rhodopsin into the bleached state, there are then only half as many molecules as before ready to absorb subsequent photons; at this point in time bleaching should therefore proceed at only half its initial rate. The corresponding differential equation is

$$\frac{dp}{dt} = \frac{-Ip}{N} \qquad (6.3)$$

where I is the intensity of the bleaching light and N is a scaling factor that has a value depending, among other things, upon the units in which the light intensity I is measured.

Because the rate of bleaching decreases with the fraction of pigment remaining to be bleached, Equation (6.3) implies that the amount of unbleached pigment will also decline exponentially as

$$p = e^{(-It/N)} \qquad (6.4)$$

Notice that in this case, where the duration of exposure is short enough to make regeneration negligible, bleaching depends only on the intensity-time product It. This represents the total amount of light delivered during the bleaching exposure, without regard to its distribution in time. This "intensity-time tradeoff" is characteristic of many visual functions. For most of these, however, the limits within which this tradeoff holds true are much shorter than for bleaching. Although exceptions have been found, a visual function that does seem to depend upon the total pigment bleached is the loss of sensitivity caused by previous exposure to strong light.

Bleaching and Regeneration Kinetics Combined

With light exposure longer than a few seconds, the regeneration that occurs during the light exposure can no longer be ignored. In the general case, the behavior of the pigment can be described by adding together the changes that are produced, moment by moment, by both bleaching and regeneration:

Bleaching and Regeneration Kinetics   173

$$\frac{dp}{dt} = \frac{1-p}{400} - \frac{Ip}{400I_0} \qquad (6.5)$$

This equation is achieved by adding together the right hand sides of Equations (6.1) and (6.3). The scaling factor N has been replaced in the bleaching term by $400\,I_0$: the value I_0 is the intensity that bleaches 1/400th of the pigment per second, and that would bleach all of it in 400 seconds if the initial rate of bleaching could be maintained. In fact, however, regeneration always acts to prevent bleaching of all the pigment, and it can easily be shown that, if the eye is exposed indefinitely to light of constant intensity, p will adjust itself toward some steady value. The resulting "steady state" value of p can be found by setting the left-hand side of Equation (6.5) to zero, which is equivalent to saying that the net rate of bleaching, dp/dt, is zero. This yields

$$1 - p = I\,(I + I_0), \qquad (6.6)$$

which shows that the percentage of bleached pigment is not substantially increased until the intensity I approaches the value of I_0, the intensity for which the fractions of unbleached and bleached rhodopsin are 0.5, known as the *half-bleach constant*. This very important equation is shown graphically in Figure 6.3. Among other things, it states that

- At low intensities, where I is small relative to I_0, there is a very nearly linear relationship between I and the fraction of unbleached (and bleached) pigment.
- At high intensities, where I is very large relative to I_0, the rate of photon absorption Ip becomes nearly independent of I and is equal to the maximum

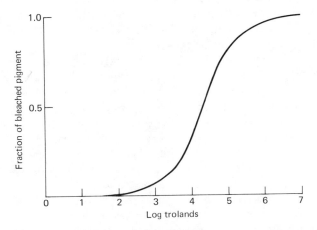

FIGURE 6.3 Proportion of photopigment bleached as a function of log trolands of retinal illuminance. This is a plot of Equation (6.6) in the text, with a half-bleach constant $I_0 = 4.3$ log td.

rate of regeneration that is reached when nearly all the pigment has been bleached.
- The range over which p goes from about 99% to 1% is restricted to about a hundredfold (2 log unit) range of intensities, centered upon I_0.

Cone Photopigment Kinetics

Similar experiments carried out with foveal measurements, using normal subjects as well and protanopes and deuteranopes, have established that the same principles apply as have been outlined for rhodopsin. The following are the main points to be noted:

- There is again no evidence concerning the blue-cone pigment, cyanolabe.
- The bleaching and regeneration kinetics of erythrolabe and chlorolabe appear to be identical.
- The following equation applies:

$$\frac{dp}{dt} = \frac{1-p}{120} - \frac{I_p}{120 I_0} \tag{6.7}$$

The meaning of Equation (6.7) is that cone bleaching and regeneration proceeds more rapidly than that of rods. The value of I_0 is around 20,000 td and is not very different from that for rods. Equation (6.6) describes also the steady state bleaching for cones.

The primary and direct effect of bleaching upon the sensitivity of the eye is easy to understand. If, for example, 90 percent of the initial supply of pigment is bleached away, leaving only 10 percent of the photopigment molecules available to absorb photons, then ten times as many photons would be required in a test flash to achieve the same visual effect as in the dark-adapted state. In other words, sensitivity is proportional to p, the fraction of unbleached pigment. Such loss of sensitivity because of the direct effects of bleaching will hereafter be called the *depletion effect of bleaching*.

An important fact about the depletion effects, true both for rods and for cones, is that the rise in threshold associated with bleaching is enormously greater than depletion alone could cause. This is most evident in rods. The output of the rod system appears to saturate at about 1000 td, implying that the rods and/or the pathways to which they connect are responding with a maximum signal. All discrimination based on rods is lost. Yet the amount of rhodopsin bleached at saturation is only about 2 percent, which would by itself raise the rod threshold by such a small amount that it would be very difficult even to measure by psychophysical methods.

Fortunately, cone vision normally takes over by the time 1000 td is reached. But what about the upper levels of cone vision: do cones also saturate and thereby produce a total loss of visual information? The answer is that they do not: they are protected from saturating by the depletion effects of bleaching.

RECEPTOR ADAPTATION BY RESPONSE COMPRESSION

There are logical grounds for believing that a significant amount of adaptation must take place in the cone photoreceptors. As will be shown in Chapter 7, the cones are "analog" devices, in the sense that they generate signals of graded amplitude, quite unlike the "digital" spikes that are recorded from ganglion cells. We will shortly see that, after bleaching and pupil size are accounted for, the cones still must handle light inputs covering about a 3,000-fold range. To suppose that the cones do so without adapting is to imply that their responses should be linearly related to the rate at which they absorb photons. If so, equal increments of stimulation would yield equal increments of response, regardless of the existing level of stimulation to which the increment is added. We have already seen that the overall system does not work this way (remember the stars in the daytime). Moreover, if the cone responses were linear and nonadapting, the problem of interpreting their signals by horizontal and bipolar cells would be very much like trying to make accurate voltage measurements from 1 to 3,000 volts by using an analog voltmeter without change of range. Although it has not been very popular until fairly recently to suppose that very much of the "gain control" takes place in the receptors, it seems impossible to understand how a receptor could transmit a useful analog signal over such a range, without losing information in the "toe" and "knee" of its characteristic curve.

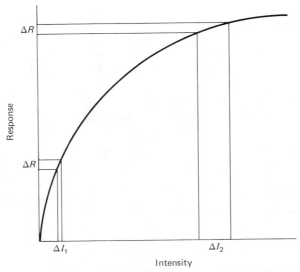

FIGURE 6.4 If the criterion response for perception is ΔR, and the relationship between response and stimulus intensity is nonlinear as shown, then the threshold intensity needed to arouse that criterion response increases from ΔI_1 to ΔI_2 for the two examples shown. Sensitivity is inversely related to the slope of the function.

A mechanism of receptor adaptation has been found by D. Whitten and myself in the receptor potentials of macaque monkeys, whose vision is very similar to that of man (Boynton & Whitten, 1970). We determined by electrophysiological experiment that there is a nonlinear relation between light input and receptor output, even at very low light levels, of a type shown in Figure 6.4. When brief flashes were used, this nonlinearity was accentuated at high light levels by the impending saturation of the cones—a phenomenon analogous to reaching the maximum density of a photographic negative. Depletion prevents such saturation from occurring in the steady state. How this happens will now be elucidated.

HOW THREE FACTORS SHRINK THE RANGE OF CONE RESPONSE

The problem begins to come into proper focus when we again consider the luminance range that cones must handle. Toward the upper end of that range, Stiles (1959) reports constant contrast thresholds ($\Delta I/I$) against backgrounds of approximately 10^5 cd/m^2 that are not different from those obtained for much weaker adapting fields (Weber's law applies). He almost certainly could have gone higher without finding any change in contrast thresholds, but he ran out of light. The highest light level used by Stiles is already three or four times higher than what one sees when looking at a diffuse white surface under direct summer sunlight, and is taken here as a practical upper limit of field luminances with which cones are normally concerned.

According to Stiles, background fields do not begin to affect increment thresholds below about 0.3 cd/m^2 (6 td for a 5-mm pupil). This fact indicates that steady stimuli weaker than this, although visible if presented as flashes, exert a negligible adaptive effect upon the cone system. Moreover, they fade from view very readily and probably can be presumed to produce very small receptor responses in the steady state. For the purposes of the calculations to be done in this section, a value of 0.3 cd/m^2 is taken as a lower limit of luminances that produce significant responses in cones, and the response produced at this level, for a linear nonadapting receptor and fixed pupil, is defined as a unit response.

The results of the calculations are shown on the log scales of Figure 6.5, where the ordinate represents relative cone response amplitude. The abscissa shows the external luminance that would be required to produce these responses, which vary from curve to curve, depending upon what assumptions are made.

Three factors are included in the calculations: (1) dilation of the pupil; (2) bleaching of cone photopigments; (3) cone response nonlinearity. The straight line (1) shows what happens if none of these are considered: this is the hypothetical response of cones that (a) do not bleach, (b) respond linearly, and (c)

The Range of Cone Response   177

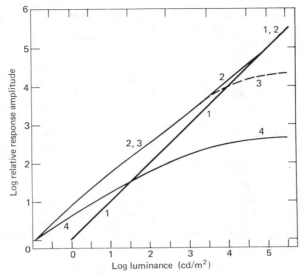

FIGURE 6.5 How three factors combine to shrink the range of cone response. Curve 1 is for a linear, nonadapting receptor, and fixed pupil. Curve 2 results from the enlargement of the pupil as the luminance level is reduced. When the effects of photopigment depletion due to bleaching are added, Curve 3 results. Response compression in the receptor brings Curve 3 down to Curve 4.

are stimulated through a fixed and maximally constricted pupil. Because the real pupil dilates as luminance is reduced; this produces curve 2, which is significantly higher than curve 1 at low intensities, and which also extends the range of stimuli that are able to elicit a unit response or one that is larger. Next, when the reduction of response amplitude that is attributable to the loss of bleachable pigment molecules is also taken into account, curve 3 results. This differs imperceptibly from curve 2 at low and moderate intensities, but bends over and approaches an asymptote caused by bleaching at high intensities. Taking the first two factors into account reduces the response range from 5.5 to about 3.5 log units over the original luminance range of from 0 to 5.0 log cd/m².

But the cone response is not linear, both because of inherent nonlinearities in the lower part of its response range, and saturation that occurs at high intensities. Taking this into account produces curve 4. The original response range (above 0 on the abscissa) has now been reduced from 5.5 to 2 log units. The pupil has extended the stimulus range by 0.82 log unit at low luminances, and there is an additional response range of about 0.6 log unit associated with this. If this is included, the three factors combine to reduce the response range from 5.5 to 2.6 log units, while extending the stimulus range from 5.5 to 6.32 log units.

The calculations are very simple. (Some values used to plot the curves of Figure 6.1 are also shown in Table 6.1)

TABLE 6.1 Calculated log relative response amplitude values for some of the values of log luminance plotted on the abscissa of Figure 6.6. Symbols are defined in the text equations.

log 1	R_1	A	R_2	p	R_3	R_4	log R_4
−0.82	0.15	7.18	1.08	~1	1.08	1	0
0	1	6.56	6.56	.99995	6.56	3.71	0.57
1	10	5.18	51.8	.9995	51.8	15.45	1.19
3	100	3.09	309.	.995	307.	50.4	1.70
3	1,000	1.87	1,870.	.952	1,780.	145.	2.16
4	10,000	1.31	131,000	.667	8,738.	300.	2.48
5	100,000	1.09	109,000	.167	18,203.	380.	2.58
6[a]	1,000,000	1.00	1,000,000	.020	20,000.	390.	2.59

[a] Not plotted

For curve 1, where L represents luminance in cd/m²,

$$R_1 = \alpha L \tag{6.8}$$

The constant α is taken as 3.16 so that a stimulus of $1/(3.16) = 0.316$ cd/m² is said to elicit a response R_1 of 1 unit.

For curve 2,

$$R_2 = AR_1 \tag{6.9}$$

where A is relative pupillary area, taken as 1.0 for a retinal illuminance of 6 log td (5.5 cd/m²). Table 14 from Le Grand (1968) has been used to obtain these values.

The fraction of unbleached pigment p has been calculated from the equation $p = I_0/(I+I_0)$ where I_0 is the half bleach constant (taken as 20,000 td after Rushton and Henry, 1968). The effect of bleaching is given by

$$R_3 = pR_2 \tag{6.10}$$

and this is shown by curve 3.

According to Boynton and Whitten (1970), the nonlinearity of the receptor response R can be calculated, if the pupil is fixed and there is no bleaching, by

$$\frac{R}{R_{max}} = \frac{L^{0.7}}{L^{0.7} + k_r^{0.7}} \tag{6.11}$$

where k_r is a half-saturation constant. Here k_r is taken as 10,000 td, directly from our work, so that $k_r^{0.7} = 631$.

In order to calculate R_4, the nonlinear response, the value L must be multiplied by A (pupil) and p (bleaching):

$$R_4 = \beta \frac{(LAp)^{0.7}}{(LAp)^{0.7} + 631} \tag{6.12}$$

By manipulation of Equations (6.8), (6.9), and (6.10), $L = R_3/(pA)$. Substituting this for L in Equation (6.12) and simplifying gives

$$R_4 = \beta \frac{R_3^{0.7}}{R_3^{0.7} + 631} \tag{6.13}$$

This equation plots as curve 4, which takes all three factors into account. The value β is a scaling constant. Curve 4 has been scaled relative to curve 3 by making the assumption that $R_3 = R_4$ when $L = -1.32$ cd/m².

It should be emphasized that these calculations apply strictly to the steady state. If this is not kept in mind, one could get the impression from looking at the upper end of curve 4 that the eye has become very insensitive to increments. As Boynton and Whitten (1970) showed, the eye in such a case has indeed become less sensitive to increments, but only to an extent that allows Weber's law to hold, as well as to provide an approximately linear range of responses to increments and decrements above and below the steady-state value. (There is no way that these additional facts can be gleaned from Figure 6.5.)

OTHER MECHANISMS OF RECEPTOR ADAPTATION

In addition to the three mechanisms just discussed, there are certainly other processes entering into the control of sensitivity of human cones. Evidence for these comes entirely from nonprimate vertebrates, mainly cold-blooded ones, including lizards, skates, turtles, crayfish, and mudpuppies.[6] The degree to which these other processes apply to primate cones is not known, and probably cannot be established for certain until such time as stable intracellular recordings from such receptors are accomplished.

Studies of the lower vertebrates have clearly shown a settling down of the receptor potential in response to a steady light that takes place over an extended time period. Although superficially similar to changes that can be produced by the depletion effects of bleaching, such changes have been shown to occur under conditions where such depletion is known to be negligible. Therefore estimates that Whitten and I made of the "steady state" potential, which were based upon responses to flashes of only 150-ms duration, could be very wide of the mark, and the agreement we found between our results and the model may be fortuitous, resulting from compensating errors.

Other studies show clearly that response compression cannot, in the preparations used, account for the full adaptive effect that is observed or, in some cases, even very much of it. Many investigators find, for example, that the receptor response is linear at low intensities. A linear response means that there can be no reduction in sensitivity due to response compression over the range where such linearity holds. We will see in Chapter 9 that in the absence of significant bleaching, the visual system tends to behave linearly when reacting to flickering stimuli at high frequencies, no matter what the level of adaptation.

Nothing in the response compression model is capable of accounting for this high-frequency behavior.

There are other important temporal characteristics of the receptor potential that are not dealt with by a response compression model. For example, as adaptation level is increased, the intensity required to elicit a response of a given magnitude also increases: this of course is the prime manifestation of adaptation. But for a response of a particular size, the higher the level of adaptation the sooner the response leaves the baseline, the quicker it rises to a peak, and the more rapid is its decline to the original baseline. Responses to flashes often show an overshoot, or sharp peak before settling down to the plateau level; the percentage of overshoot is adaptation-dependent. It is not entirely clear whether changes in response shape are directly due to the changing state of adaptation, because they could result mainly from the higher intensities of test flashes that are needed to arouse a response of a given magnitude as the adaptation level is increased. In any event it is clear that neither pupil, bleaching, nor response compression can account for these significant changes in the shape of the receptor response.

A number of other models have been proposed to account for the adaptive properties of photoreceptors. Some of these are strictly mathematical in nature; others speculate about possible underlying mechanisms. At least three different models agree that some sort of diffusion process is probably involved (Baylor & Hodgkin, 1974; Ives, 1922; Kelly, 1969). The absorption of a photon is supposed to trigger the release of a packet of material of some kind, which diffuses to the membrane of the outer segment of the receptor and, upon arrival there, blocks the flow of sodium ions across the membrane. It is also necessary to suppose that there is a back reaction capable of removing some of the blocking substance; otherwise a receptor could not continue to function under steady illumination. Although such forward and backward reactions are quite reminiscent of the processes of bleaching and regeneration, they should be carefully distinguished from them. Highly quantitative models of the diffusion process have been worked out, based on psychophysical and electrophysiological evidence, which account well for a range of observed data.

It has been proposed that there may be mechanisms related to bleaching that control the sensitivity of receptors, or possibly of pathways downstream, in a manner more complicated than the straightforward depletion effects that we have discussed so far. If *log* threshold elevation is plotted against the fraction of photopigment bleached in the steady state, the exponential relation that exists between threshold and bleaching translates into a straight line, as shown in the lower part of Figure 6.6. This type of function has been documented empirically in human psychophysical experiments, and it has been shown also to hold for the rat and skate. In the human case, retinal densitometry was used to measure the bleaching of photopigment; in the rat, bleaching was estimated by direct extraction techniques and the gross electroretinogram (see Chapter 7) was used as a response indicator. The relationships are so regular that one is tempted to impute a causal link between the two variables, even though to do so would,

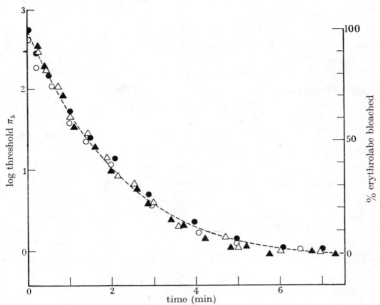

FIGURE 6.6 The top curve, from Rushton (1972), shows a psychophysical cone dark-adaptation curve (left ordinate) and the percentage of erythrolabe bleached (right ordinate). Circles are bleaching, triangles are threshold. Note that the threshold scale is logarithmic.

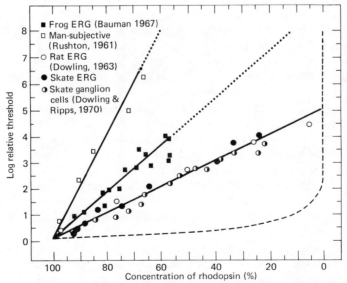

FIGURE 6.6 (Continued) In the bottom curve, the linear relation between log scotopic threshold and rhodopsin concentration is shown for frog ERG (filled squares), human scotopic threshold (open squares), rat ERG (open circles), skate ERG (filled circles) and ganglion cells (half-filled circles). Dotted curve shows how threshold would increase due to the depletion effects of bleaching. (From Dowling and Ripps, 1970.)

for example, imply (in the human case) that bleaching 50 percent of the pigment somehow causes the threshold to rise 25-fold—12.5 times more than the depletion effects of bleaching would predict. How might this work?

Suppose that there were a mechanism in the receptors capable of sensing, somehow, the level of "free" opsin (liberated by bleaching). If so, it could transmit a signal that would be proportional to the fraction of molecules in the bleached state. This would be useful information that could be used, in one way or another, to adjust the gain and other characteristics of the system. This idea has a very bad feature: it requires that the photoreceptors must generate two kinds of signals, one related to the *rate* of light absorption (leading to visual sensation) and the other to the *state* of bleaching (to be used for controlling adaptation). To avoid such an awkward notion, an alternative proposal states that there is but one signal used to adjust system gain, but that it has two sources. Depending upon the source, the signal reflects either the bleaching state ("dark light") or the bleaching rate ("real light"). Although there is some psychophysical evidence consistent with each of these notions, contrary evidence also exists, and there is no direct physiological support for either of them.[7]

MECHANISMS OF ADAPTATION BEYOND RECEPTORS

We move now to even less certain ground, to consider possible mechanisms of adaptation beyond receptors. There is one experimental fact which above all proves that such mechanisms must exist. This is the observation that the ratio of threshold change that takes place, when increments are flashed against steady backgrounds of increasing luminance, depends upon the *area* of the test probe.[8] Of special significance is the fact that changes in area have much larger effects upon thresholds in the dark-adapted eye than they do when the probe is flashed against a bright background. This result implies that the retinal area over which light can be integrated in order to produce a threshold response becomes smaller as the eye becomes more light adapted. This implies a functional reorganization of the retina, which could result either from larger pools of neural summation, or a change in surrounding areas in the center-surround organization (to be discussed in Chapter 7) such that surround-inhibition drops out at low light levels. In either case, the retina would require some kind of information related to the actual level of retinal illumination in order for it to control its own organization as a function of that variable.

Where could such information come from? If the mechanisms of pupillary constriction, bleaching, and response compression were the only ones responsible for receptor adaptation, then Figure 6.5 shows that there is a nonlinear but nevertheless monotonic relationship between input and output where cones are concerned. Given any level of response, the stimulus level that could produce that response can be inferred. Therefore the outputs of the receptors would carry the necessary information.

The most extensive study of the control of retinal sensitivity beyond the receptors has been by F. Werblin and coworkers (Normann & Werblin, 1974; Werblin, 1974; Werblin & Copenhagen, 1974). Because the experiments were carried out on the mudpuppy, the degree to which the results and conclusions can be generalized to humans is uncertain. These studies show clearly that adaptation does occur in both the inner and outer plexiform layers. A prime accomplishment of the additional stages of processing seems to be to keep the system functioning within the most sensitive part of its response range. By the time the ganglion cell level is reached, much of the information about absolute levels of input to cones seems to have been lost. To a degree, the same is true of human vision, but this is not completely so. With practice, one can make judgments about absolute levels that correlate fairly well with the actual level of illumination, even if the sources are shielded and there is no change in the geometry of the situation. This ability tends to be lost with large diffuse fields (although not completely so even then) and at luminance levels where the depletion effects of bleaching have taken over as the principal mechanism of adaptation.

RAPID ADAPTATION AND RESPONSE COMPRESSION

There have been many studies of changes in the sensitivity of the eye that occur within the first few hundred milliseconds following a change in the prevailing luminance level. A precursor to all of them was an experiment by Crawford, published in 1947, which is described and illustrated in Figure 6.7. These threshold changes are substantial, and they continue to be of considerable theoretical interest. It has become conventional to refer to such changes as due to "masking" rather than adaptation, which is very reasonable nomenclature if the processes of adaptation are considered to be those that take an appreciable amount of time to develop. In any event, masking experiments will not be given much consideration in this book.

The sensitivity adjustment implied by the effects of response compression, as illustrated in Figure 6.6, also occurs rapidly and perhaps for that reason also should not be called "adaptation." But this is more a matter of semantics than physiology. An important distinction can be drawn between masking and response compression. Whereas the former is finished in a fraction of a second, and thus its effects are transitory and relatively unimportant for practical vision, the latter is relatively permanent, so long as a prevailing level of adaptation is maintained.

CHROMATIC ADAPTATION

Color Constancy

We have now seen that visual adaptation serves to keep the mechanisms of the eye in balance and within range. To the extent that adaptation is selective

184 Sensitivity Regulation

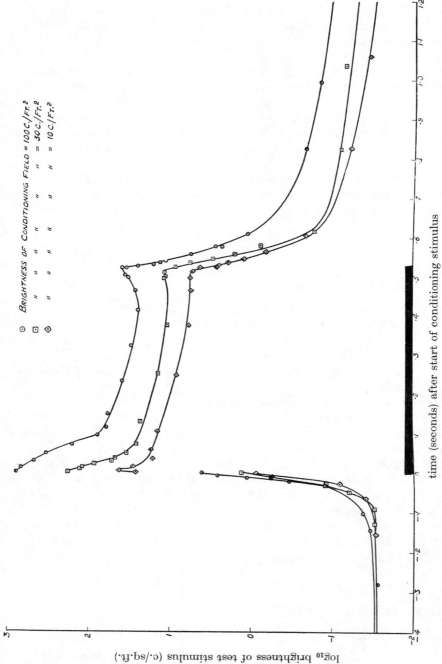

FIGURE 6.7 Results of experiment by Crawford (1947) showing what is now known as "Crawford-type masking." A conditioning flash lasting a little over half a second was repeated every 7 seconds. On each presentation, a superimposed, smaller test flash was delivered at one of the many times indicated, relative to the onset of the conditioning stimulus. The duration of the conditioning stimulus is shown by the black rectangle.

within receptors and their associated pathways, color constancy will be enhanced. Suppose, for example, that the prevailing illuminant is unusually strong in the long wavelengths. If so it would, in comparison with white light, adapt the R cones more than the G cones. Objects in the environment, reflecting more of the long wavelengths than they would under white light, will be mediators of the selective adaptive effect.

The light reflecting from these objects would, if the eye were neutrally adapted, make them appear more yellowish or reddish than normal. But the eye is not neutrally adapted: the selective chromatic adaptation of the R cones, relative to the G cones, will tend to restore the appearance of such surfaces toward the same hue that would have prevailed under white light. Under a red light, surfaces that normally look white tend to retain that appearance.

Two-Color Thresholds

In the laboratory, conditions can be contrived that seldom if ever occur in the everyday world, and the phenomenon of chromatic adaptation can be used to probe the visual system. The remainder of this chapter will emphasize such studies of selective chromatic adaptation, particularly those that utilize the two-color threshold method.

If a test-tube of rhodopsin in solution is irradiated with light, some of the molecules bleach and the transmittance of the solution will be increased. If the solution is pure, the bleaching can be done with light of any wavelength, since precisely the same effect can be produced by adjusting the various wavelengths to take account of the action spectrum of rhodopsin. If the solution is dilute enough to preclude a significant amount of self-screening (see Chapter 5), the normalized spectral absorption curves for all solutions, whatever their concentrations, will be identical. A convenient way to plot such data is on an ordinate of log absorption, in which case the curves will all have the same shape prior to normalization and if shifted vertically they will superimpose. Chemists sometimes take such unchanging curve shapes as evidence that they are working with a pure solution, one that contains only one kind of labile pigment.

Suppose it were possible to extract R, G, and B cone pigments, mix them, and then subject them to the same kind of test. The curve shapes would change, depending upon the wavelength and intensity of the adapting lights. A longwave light, for example, would begin to bleach the R pigment before the B and G pigments were significantly affected; the spectral sensitivity curve would therefore narrow as a result of being selectively reduced in the longwave spectral range.

Since it is not possible to extract human cone pigments and measure their transmittance in solution, similar experiments have been done in situ by means of retinal densitometry (see Chapter 5), and with similar results. But here we consider the consequences of obtaining analogous measures using psychophysical techniques and intact human subjects. The purpose of such psychophysical experiments has been, in the view of some workers, to isolate and measure the properties (particularly the spectral sensitivities) of the R, G, and B cone pigments. Other investigators, led by W. S. Stiles, have taken a more conservative view, reasoning that, to the extent such procedures are successful, they merely measure the characteristics of unspecified cone "mechanisms" whose exact nature cannot be deduced from psychophysics alone.[9] According to this more conservative view, mechanisms are first operationally defined through the use of certain psychophysical procedures. Their characteristics may then be compared with those of cone photopigments, cone action spectra, electrophysiological data, or whatever.

The common feature of all such psychophysical procedures is that the test probes are small, weak, brief, and centrally fixated. Therefore they stimulate only cones in the rod-free foveal area of the retina, doing so without materially affecting the state of the system being assessed. The task of the subject is to detect the presence (or signal the absence) of each test probe, so that threshold radiances can be obtained as a function of wavelength. The reciprocals of these values are plotted and these constitute cone-mediated spectral sensitivity curves. We will see that the absolute height of such functions (on a logarithmic ordinate) is easily manipulated by varying the intensity of an adapting field upon which the test probe is superimposed. More importantly (and quite unlike the case for rods) the shape of the curve is also easy to alter, which is not surprising considering that (1) three different photopigments must be involved, and (2) like our hypothetical pigments in the test-tube, they probably can be selectively "adapted" by bleaching.

Unlike the case of the test-tube pigments, however, bleaching is only one of many adaptive effects that may occur in the eye. Any or all of the adaptive mechanisms already discussed may be operative, together with others that may remain to be discovered. The problem is further complicated by mechanisms of interaction, whose properties cannot be assumed but that must be uncovered by experiment. For example, suppose that an intense red-adapting light were used. Some of this light will be absorbed in G cones as well as in R cones, and the relative amounts may or may not be known. For purposes of exposition, assume that all of the light is absorbed in R cones. Now we may ask: is the desensitization of the eye, as revealed by lowered sensitivity and altered curve shape, necessarily a consequence only of direct adaptation of the R cones, or even of an R-cone "system"? Not necessarily, because there are many mechanisms of adaptation, and many lateral connections are known to exist among cones and cone pathways. It is therefore perfectly possible that the absorption of light in R cones might also alter the sensitivities of G and B cones, even if these other two types do not absorb a single photon. Moreover, although G and B cones themselves might not be so affected, the channels into which they feed could be.

Similar interactions may occur also with respect to the test probe. Suppose it to be of short wavelength, and suppose also that it is absorbed only by B cones. Would it then be safe to assume that only the B cones are affected by the test probe? Since the test probe (being at threshold) is weak and brief, the assumption may seem safer than the analogous assumption with respect to an adapting field. Nevertheless, the assumption must be tested, because the responses of individual cones (in turtles, at least) are now certainly known to be affected by what their neighbors are doing.

Most of the time, a test probe can be expected to stimulate cones of at least two different kinds. In the two-cone case, does the threshold simply depend upon the total amount of light absorbed, regardless of how it is distributed between the two cone types? Or does it depend only upon the responses of the type of cones that are most strongly stimulated? Or are the responses of the two cone types treated as if they came from totally independent mechanisms? Unfortunately for those who like things simple, all of these things and more apparently occur, depending upon circumstances; some of the evidence will be reviewed later.

SPECTRAL SENSITIVITY: VARIATION OF TEST WAVELENGTH

In 1933, Stiles and Crawford measured foveal spectral sensitivity curves, some of which are shown in Figure 6.8. Their adapting fields were of moderate intensity and surrounded the area of the test probe without including it. Such surround fields were found to have a profound effect upon the spectral sensitivity of the eye, based on the reciprocal of threshold energies of test flashes of various wavelengths delivered to the central area. The curves seemed to have three humps, and the possible connection of these with three types of cones immediately suggested itself. This study launched a 25-year series of investigations, mostly undertaken by Stiles alone, leading to the isolation of what he originally called R, G, and B mechanisms, later to be named "π-mechanisms."

In Stiles's subsequent work, the adapting fields typically subtended about 10 degrees and they always included the test area. The test probes subtended 1° and were usually flashed for about 100–200 ms every 3 s. Stiles measured many spectral curves by the method already discussed, where curve shape was altered by selective adaptation to various wavelengths. A set of such functions, obtained under many different adapting conditions, is shown in Figure 6.9. These curves, which represent the outcome of many hundreds of hours of experimental work, are based on the mean data of four subjects, obtained in a British standards laboratory under unusually well controlled experimental conditions. Thresholds were obtained in each case by determining frequency-of-seeing curves and interpolating the 50-percent point (method of constant stimuli). Each subject's threshold was estimated from the mean of from four to eight such determinations.

The most obvious and striking feature of the curves of Figure 6.9 is that their shapes have been grossly altered by the use of chromatic adapting fields. Compare, for example, Curve Y 4.29 (obtained with 19,320 td of yellow adaptation) with the curve for the dark-adapted eye.[10]

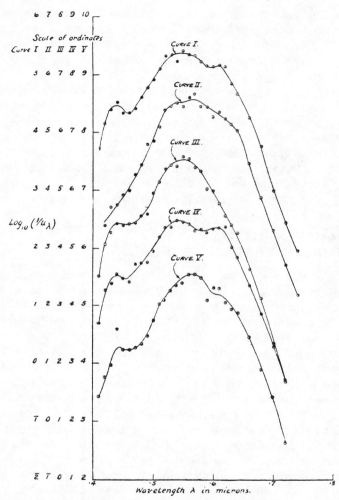

FIGURE 6.8 Results from Stiles and Crawford (1933). The ordinate shows log relative threshold sensitivity of a central test flash as affected by an annular adapting field. Intensities varied between about 2500 and 4400 td, and the curves (arbitrarily displaced vertically) are for filtered lights whose appearance, from top to bottom, was white, blue, red, yellow, and blue-green.

As a result of adaptation to Y 4.29, sensitivity has been reduced only by about 0.5 log unit at the shortwave end of the spectrum, but by about 2 log units at the longwave end. Therefore the adaptation has been *selective*, in the sense that 30 times more sensitivity loss has occurred in the region of the spectrum occupied by the background stimulus.

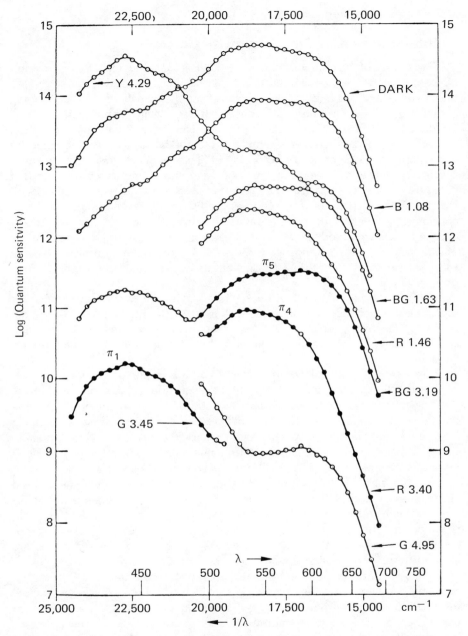

FIGURE 6.9 Test sensitivity curves of Stiles (1964) for a wide variety of conditions of adaptation. Chromatic appearance of the adapting fields was yellow, blue, blue-green, or red. The numerical values following the chromatic symbols represent the retinal illuminance produced by each adapting field, in log trolands. Vertical displacement of the curves is arbitrary. These curves are for quantum sensitivity, plotted on a scale which is linear with frequency, but reversed so that wavelength increases from left to right. See text for explanation of π_1, π_4, and π_5.

Interpretation of Test Sensitivity Curves

The shapes of the curves of Figure 6.9 suggest that they might be understood by assuming that the overall (measured) spectral sensitivity curve, as determined under each condition of adaptation, results from the activity of three underlying processes, each of which has a different spectral sensitivity. Three such functions are defined in Figure 6.9 as portions of three experimental functions where the symbols have been filled. For example, the curve labeled π_1 was obtained by adaptation to a 548-nm field of 3.45 log td. This seems to have brought out a spectral sensitivity that peaks in the shortwave end of the spectrum, one that could be due to the activity of B cones, or at least of a system or "mechanism" fed mainly by such cones. Inspection of the figure will reveal the conditions of chromatic adaptation necessary to reveal the curve shapes of π_4 and π_5, which are the other two underlying functions shown. It should be noted that the levels of adaptation used to bring out these underlying functions are modest, the strongest being sufficient to bleach only about 12 percent of the R- and G-cone photopigments.

From these data alone, there is really no objective way to know whether the three π functions are sufficiently well isolated to represent completely different "mechanisms." Nevertheless, some part of an answer to this question can be obtained by attempting to fit all of the experimental curves with underlying functions.

Curve (a) of Figure 6.10 is an attempt to do this for the dark-adapted curve. The π_1 function seems to account well for the left side of the shortwave hump. The longwave end of the curve can be fitted with the π_5 function, and the middle of the spectrum is well fitted with π_4. But this leaves some problems in between. In the blue-green spectral region (marked with an arrow) the obtained function seems to lie well above both underlying curves. And a similar, though less dramatic, problem is observed in the yellow-orange spectral region.

An attempt to do this kind of fitting for the high-intensity yellow-adapted curve (curve Y 4.29, Fig. 6.10) is more successful. Here the upper envelope of the underlying functions does an excellent job of fitting the obtained curve provided that they are properly positioned vertically. These two examples represent extreme cases; all of the other curves can be fitted, if assumptions are allowed to vary concerning how the underlying mechanisms interact.

It may seem unpleasant and arbitrary to suppose that, depending upon the adapting condition, the rules according to which underlying mechanisms pool their activities to determine the overall sensitivity curve should be allowed to vary. There is however independent evidence to show that such rules of combination are in fact not fixed. An attempt was made by Boynton, Ikeda, and Stiles (1964) to isolate the R and B mechanisms by exposing the eye to moderate to high intensities of steady green light. Pairs of test flashes were presented, one of long wavelength designed to stimulate only the π_5 mechanism, the other of short wavelength, intended to stimulate only π_1. Use of a high level of green

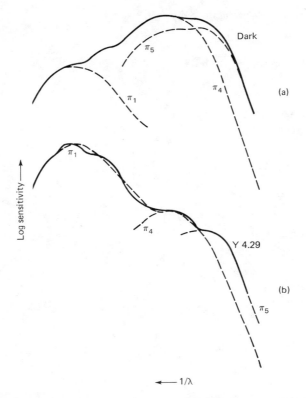

FIGURE 6.10 Attempt to account for two of the functions shown in Figure 6.9 in terms of π_1, π_4, and π_5 (whose shapes are defined by the portions of the three curves drawn through the filled circles in that figure).

adaptation tended to produce data that obeyed the upper-envelope rule, but a half-dozen other possible rules of combination were defined and tested, and the results showed that different rules definitely must be applied under varying circumstances.

Sensitivity Peaks Attributable to Interactions

Although it is not particularly obvious in Stiles's data, other experiments have seemed to provide evidence of a "mechanism" with a peak sensitivity near 610 nm. Clear evidence for this is shown in Figure 6.11, from the work of Sperling and Harwerth. The result is interesting because it is now established that there is no photopigment in the human eye peaking at so long a wavelength (Chapter 5). The curves of Figure 6.11 were obtained by assuming that sensitivity is determined by a signal derived from the *difference* between inputs from the R and G cones as shown by the equations to follow:

Sensitivity Regulation

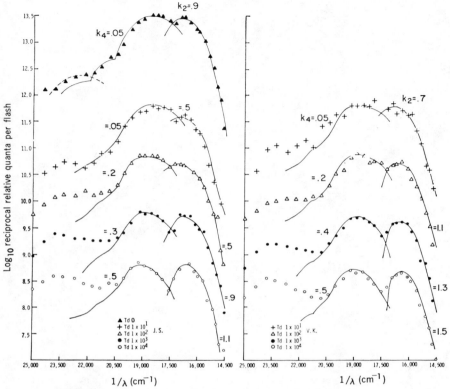

FIGURE 6.11 Effect upon spectral sensitivity of white-adapting fields of varying intensity. Curves are fitted by assuming an inhibitory interaction between R and G cones. (Sperling & Harwerth, 1971.)

$$1/Q_r = k_1\alpha - k_2\beta \tag{6.14}$$

$$1/Q_g = k_3\beta - k_4\alpha \tag{6.15}$$

In these equations, Q_r and Q_g represent the quantal requirements for threshold perception as mediated by R or G cones. The threshold is assumed to be determined exclusively by the more sensitive of these. The quantities α and β represent the action spectra of the R and G cones, assumed to be Dartnall-template pigments peaking at 575 and 535 nm respectively. Although we saw in Chapter 5 (p. 151) that Dartnall pigments do not exactly describe human R and G cones, the changes in this model that would be required by the selection of slightly different cone-pigment curves would not seriously alter the fit of theory to data.

In Figure 6.11, the constants k_1 and k_3 have been set at unity, and the values of k_2 and k_4 are assumed to vary as a function of adaptation level. (The model does not explain why or how adaptation level should cause the values of these "constants" to change.)

The experimental conditions that produced these functions included the use of 45-min foveally fixated test fields, viewed either in the dark (topmost curve) or against white adapting fields at four intensities, ranging from 10 to 10,000 td.

The sensitivity of a mechanism, in the longwave portion of the spectrum, is assumed to be reduced by an inhibitory signal caused by activity of the second and less sensitive member of a R, G cone pair. This inhibitory effect would be maximum where the R and G cone sensitivities are equal, producing a deep notch in the function at about 580 nm. It also accounts for the peak at about 610 nm.

There is only a hint of such a notch in Stiles's data of Figure 6.9, and we may ask why this phenomenon shows so much more clearly in the data of Sperling and Harwerth. The answer probably is to be found in differences among experimental conditions. In addition to using higher adaptation levels, Sperling and Harwerth used small, brief flashes, whereas Stiles used larger, longer ones. Ikeda and I (1962) showed that exposure affects the shape of spectral sensitivity curves but not in a manner that would necessarily bring out the notch. Sperling and Lewis (1959) compared 2° and 45' test areas with the results shown in Figure 6.12. Here the notch is clearly evident with the 45' test, much less so with the larger one.

In a study given wide publicity because of its inclusion in his Nobel address (1968), Wald claimed to isolate the spectral sensitivities of the R, G, and B cones by the use of very high intensities of steady chromatic adaptation. The R curves were obtained with 5.35 log td of blue-adapting light, the G curve with 5.42 log td of purple light, and the B curve with 7.01 log td of yellow light (Fig. 6.13). Wald believed that he was able to isolate photopigment sensitivities by this method. But this seems highly unlikely, because once high bleaching adapting levels are reached, the constituent mechanisms all achieve a constant and limiting Weber fraction (see next section). There is no further selective chromatic adaptation with further increases in retinal illuminance. It is also unlikely that the interactions found by Sperling and Harwerth somehow disappear at very high intensities. This is best understood by looking back at Figure 6.5; in the steady state, all lights brighter than the half-bleach intensity are very nearly equal in their visual effects. High bleaches therefore do not provide the high road to the psychophysical isolation of cone photopigments. Wald's curves, which do not agree very well with other estimates of cone sensitivity functions, remain unexplained.

All of the work so far described required the use of steady background fields. In 1956, I showed that large changes in spectral sensitivity could be produced by the use of very weak (about 2.3 log td) adapting fields, provided that the background field was presented as a *flash* of light presented to the dark-adapted eye. The background flash, lasting for 0.56 s, and the test flash, of 0.04-s

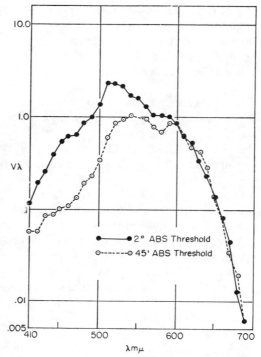

FIGURE 6.12 Spectral sensitivity is markedly altered by changing the size of the test stimulus. Stimuli were concentric with the point of fixation and there was no adapting field. Changes in the short wavelengths are probably due to rods, but the "notch" around 580 nm, which shows clearly only for the small test flash, is probably due to inhibitory interactions between R and G cones. (From Sperling & Lewis, 1959.)

duration, appeared each time 50 ms after the onset of the background flash. The results for yellow and green adaptation are summarized in Figure 6.14. The Sperling-Harwerth type of "notch" at about 580 nm is more evident than in Stiles's steady-state data.

We can conclude that the psychophysical method of overall spectral sensitivity, based upon foveal thresholds determined in the presence of various chromatic adapting stimuli, brings out some evidence of the three underlying cone mechanisms. However, the rules of combination of the underlying activities appear to be exceedingly complex, depending upon (1) the level of the adaptation, (2) which mechanism is most active, and (3) temporal and spatial parameters.

Field Sensitivities

For the purpose of attempting to isolate underlying mechanisms, we have seen two disadvantages of the test-sensitivity method just described. One of these was the problem of isolating underlying mechanisms in the first place:

Variation of Test Wavelength

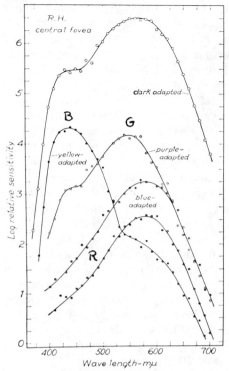

FIGURE 6.13 Attempt by Wald (1964) to determine the spectral sensitivities of R, B, and G cones using very high intensities of adapting lights.

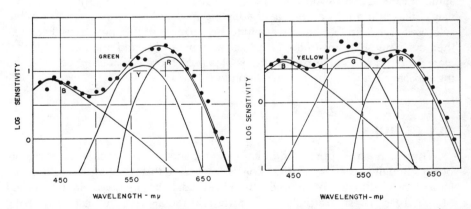

FIGURE 6.14 Transient adapting flashes, whose onsets occurred just before the test stimuli are delivered, produce marked alterations in spectral sensitivity. The peak near 610 nm cannot be due to a cone pigment; a notch near 580, like that seen in Figures 6.11 and 6.12, is evident under a condition of yellow adaptation (right). (From Boynton, 1965.)

only portions of any of the underlying spectral sensitivity curves can be seen in Figure 6.9. For example, it is virtually certain that the shortwave portion of the function that yielded π_5 for long wavelengths (curve BG 3.19) is due to the π_1 mechanism. The second problem was the varied nature of the interactions that must be assumed to occur between these mechanisms in order to account for the overall spectral sensitivity curves.

To get around such problems, Stiles developed what he called the *field-sensitivity* method. For example, to isolate π_5 (the red mechanism) he selected a test stimulus of 667 nm and used that wavelength throughout the experiment. The procedure was to evaluate spectral sensitivity according to the intensities of *adapting* stimuli required to produce a criterion effect upon the test stimulus. Specifically, in the example cited, Stiles determined dark-adapted sensitivity to 667 nm, and then determined, for each of a large number of wavelengths, the field energy required to elevate the threshold of the test flash by a factor of 10 (one log unit) above the dark-adapted threshold. By doing this, he was able to trace out the curve shown as π_5 in Figure 6.15. Over the region where comparison is possible, it closely resembles the π_5 curve of Figure 6.9. But the shortwave spectral region, missing there, has now been uncovered. The relative success of the field method depends in this case upon the fact that the extreme longwave light used as the test stimulus can reasonably be assumed to stimulate only the π_5 mechanism, no matter what the wavelength of the adapting stimulus. In this connection it should be remembered that the adapting stimuli used were usually rather weak—only what was required to elevate the dark-adapted threshold by a factor of 10.

Where the other mechanisms are concerned, the assumption that the test flash stimulates only a single mechanism is not as safe. For example, shortwave light, if delivered to the dark-adapted fovea, tends (although it looks blue) to stimulate the G cones more than the B cones. To get the G cones out of the way, Stiles introduced an auxiliary adapting field of long wavelength, one that selectively reduced G-cone sensitivity relative to that of B cones. Sensitivity was then evaluated in terms of the reciprocal radiances of *added* adapting lights that were required to elevate B-cone thresholds (which are otherwise unaffected by the auxiliary field) by the criterion tenfold.

TVI CURVES

There is a general problem of knowing for sure which mechanism is mainly being stimulated by a test flash. In order to analyze this problem, Stiles used an indirect procedure to obtain his criterion field radiances; he determined so-called "tvi" curves. These are plots of log threshold radiance of the test flash vs log adapting field intensity. The method will be explained by dealing first with conditions that favor stimulation of the rod system. Figure 6.16 shows a hypothetical tvi curve obtained from an eye having only rods. As the radiance of the background field is raised, there is at first no change in the threshold of

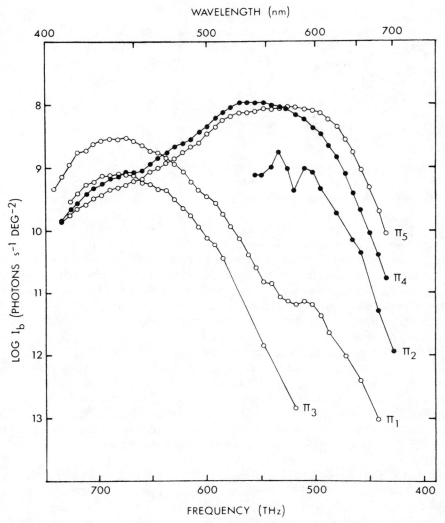

FIGURE 6.15 The field sensitivities of Stiles's five π-mechanisms. From Rodieck (1973), plotted from the data given by Wyszecki and Stiles (1967), p. 579, Table 7.6.

superimposed test flash, but when the background is roughly 10 times the radiance of the dark-adapted threshold of the test stimulus, the threshold begins to rise. The rise is very gradual at first, but soon approaches linearity with a slope of 1. When this slope is reached, the system operates in accord with Weber's law: the ratio of threshold to background radiance is constant. By taking any point along the unit-slope portion of the curve, and projecting to the abscissa and ordinate, the contrast threshold (or Weber fraction, as it is sometimes called in this limiting case) can be determined.

Sensitivity Regulation

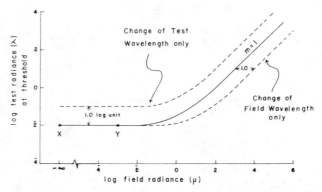

FIGURE 6.16 Hypothetical threshold-vs.-intensity (tvi) curve for rods. (From Boynton, 1963.)

Suppose now that the wavelength of the background is changed from 505 nm to, say, 423 nm. It is known from other experiments that, in order for two scotopic fields to match exactly, about 10 times as many photons would be required for this new wavelength compared to the original one. The reason for this relates, as we saw in Chapter 5, to the probabilities of photon absorption by rods: photons at 505 nm are 10 times more likely to be absorbed by rods than are those at 423 nm. Therefore, to cause equal rates of absorption, which in turn will make the fields match exactly, 10 times as many photons will be required, per unit time, at the wavelength of lesser sensitivity. Moreover, this should be true no matter what the response criterion. For example, if the two equally bright, scotopically matched fields were gradually reduced in radiance, in exactly the same ratio, both fields would become dimmer, but both would continue to match. When reduced further, they should reach threshold together. This is because absorption probabilities are unchanged as a function of absorption rate.

As a consequence of the foregoing considerations, changing the wavelength of the background from 505 to 423 nm should simply shift the tvi curve to the right, without changing its shape. No matter what the threshold radiance of the test stimulus, 10 times as many photons per unit time would then be required to drive the threshold to that level. By analogous argument, changing the wavelength of the test stimulus from 505 nm to 423 nm should raise the entire tvi curve *upward* by one log unit.

Stiles has used the concept of "mechanism" to account for the behavior of a tvi curve of fixed shape that is shown experimentally to obey these "displacement" rules. He did not intend to suggest that the mechanism should necessarily be identified with photopigments, receptors, or any other structural or neurophysiological entity. The definition is strictly operational: a "mechanism" is said to be identified when "it" obeys the displacement rules.

In the case of scotopic vision, which has for simplicity been used so far for

TVI Curves

illustrative purposes, the spectral sensitivity of a mechanism could be said to relate equally to rhodopsin, to rods, to a collection of rods, or even to ganglion cells. But the psychophysical experiment actually measures only the behavior of a large collection of rods; it is these that determine the shape of the tvi curve and the limiting Weber fraction. The Weber fraction can be altered by a change in the area of the test flash, or by changing its duration. In almost all of his work, as noted earlier, Stiles used a large-area, long-duration test flash. His "mechanisms" must therefore be regarded as potentially involving the behavior of all receptors stimulated by such a test flash, as modified by the behavior of the receptors stimulated by the adapting field. (Although the adapting field was considerably larger than the test, much evidence exists to show that regions of the adapting field lying well outside the test area nevertheless importantly affect the threshold of a test flash.)

To further illustrate Stiles's approach it is instructive to consider the function of Figure 6.17. It consists of two branches that are formally equivalent to the rod–cone sections of the classic dark adaptation curve. The two branches have

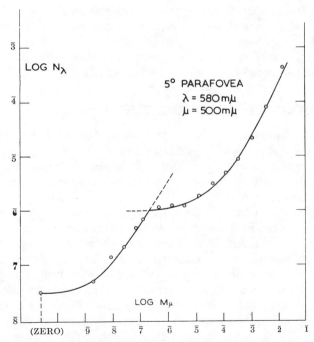

FIGURE 6.17 Data from Stiles, for a background of 500 nm and a test wavelength of 580 nm. The lower branch of this duplex tvi curve is due to rods; the upper branch is due to cones. Dashed portions show that at low adapting luminances the cone threshold is too high to contribute appreciably, so that sensitivity depends upon rods alone; at high intensities the situation reverses. (From Stiles, 1959.)

been well separated here by using a relatively longwave test light (which favors adaptation of rods). As before, when intensity is increased, adapting lights at first have no effect upon the threshold, then elevate it slightly, and finally they drive it up at a unit slope. Under other conditions, the rod branch of the curve will continue to rise for another two or three log units without departure from unit slope, until finally the curve rises almost vertically and "rod saturation" sets in. The condition of Figure 6.17 is designed instead to bring in the cone branch relatively early, and to show a good portion of it. At a background intensity of about -6.5, the threshold rise is halted and the curve goes almost flat; a second curve is traced out that looks similar to the lower one, but which in this case is ascribable to a cone mechanism. To illustrate the essence of how Stiles's method achieves isolation of various branches, suppose that there is but one photopic mechanism and that the wavelength of the test stimulus is shifted from 580 nm to 531 nm. The new wavelength has been chosen so that photopic relative luminous efficiency is the same as before (87 percent of peak). But the scotopic luminosity factor rises from 0.121 at 580 nm to 0.795 at 531 nm. The ratio of these values is 6.57, meaning that the rods are now more than six times as sensitive to the test flash.

What is the predicted consequence of this change? From Chapter 5 the principle of univariance should be recalled, and from it we can deduce that, if 6.57 times less test energy is used than before, then this is equivalent to lowering the entire rod branch of the curve by $\log_{10}$ (6.57) or 0.82 log unit. Doing so would reveal less of the cone branch, and more of the rod branch, than before.

π MECHANISMS: WHAT ARE THEY?

Actually, however, there is no unitary "cone branch," because there is more than one cone mechanism. Stiles's main task was in fact to isolate and explore the various cone branches in an effort to determine their number, their spectral sensitivities, their absolute thresholds, and their tvi curves, including the limiting Weber fraction.

The photopic mechanisms identified by Stiles have the spectral sensitivities shown in Figure 6.15. The limiting Weber fractions for π_4 and π_5 are nearly equal at about 2 percent. That for the π_1 mechanism is nearly 9 percent. A limited spatial and temporal resolution of the B-cone system has also been demonstrated by isolation of π_1; this will be discussed further in Chapter 9.

Figure 6.18 shows a scalloped tvi curve, the test-flash threshold for a 476-nm test as a function of background intensity for a 578-nm field. Although Stiles used a tenfold threshold increase as criterion, any other increase could be used as a criterion so long as the shape of the tvi curve, on a double-logarithmic plot, remains invariant. In some cases, it was necessary to extrapolate to a tenfold criterion, because (as in the case of π_1 in Figure 6.18), it cannot quite be observed. By manipulating test and adaptive wavelengths, Stiles could test the displacement rules, and deduce to which mechanism a particular segment of such a complex tvi curve should be ascribed.

π Mechanisms: What Are They?

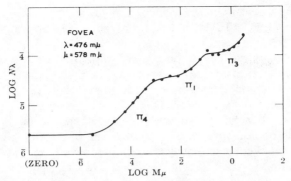

FIGURE 6.18 Here the blue test flash is foveal, and a behavior analogous to that of Figure 6.17 occurs as the intensity of a yellow adapting field is varied. But the branches of the curves are now due entirely to cone activity. By following the displacements of branches such as these, while changing the wavelengths of test and adapting fields, Stiles deduced the spectral sensitivities of his π mechanisms. The mechanism believed responsible for each branch is indicated. (From Stiles, 1959.)

It is the shapes of these tvi curves, as well as the relative sensitivities of the mechanisms that are partially defined by them, that underlie the phenomenon of selective chromatic adaptation. Referring again to Figure 6.18, note that there is a range of background intensities from about -5 to -3 log units where only π_4 is significantly affected. The threshold of this mechanism is being driven up whereas the other mechanisms are at first totally unaffected. Then as field intensity is further increased, the threshold of π_1 is reached but is not at first affected; for this reason the threshold of π_4 becomes higher than that of π_1 and for about a 1 log unit range of adapting intensity, π_1 determines the threshold. Finally, π_3 takes over. It was from analyses of this kind that Stiles was able to follow the spectral sensitivities of his "mechanisms" over the entire spectrum.

Stiles deduced altogether three mechanisms seemingly associated with the B cones. When the tvi curve of π_1 was followed to very high adapting intensities, the function leveled off and then rose again to form an additional scallop, as in Figure 6.18. Had the spectral sensitivity of the mechanism defined by the new scallop been exactly the same as π_1, Stiles could have concluded that the top two scallops related to only one mechanism (although this would have implied that π_1 had a very peculiar tvi curve). But this was not the case for field wavelengths longer than about 500 nm. There π_3 lacks the secondary maximum near 600 nm that is exhibited by π_1.

The adapting stimuli that have been used to follow the spectral sensitivity of π_1 to very long wavelengths are very heavily absorbed by the R and G cones. It seems possible that the stimulation of these cones has an indirect effect upon the B cones. If so, the effect might be to add to the adaptation normally caused by absorption of light by B cones. Mechanism π_2 is deduced from a breakdown of the displacement rules for π_4, not attributable to π_1, when the conditioning field is of a long wavelength and the test stimulus less than 460 nm. The notch at 580 nm for π_2 (Fig. 6.15) is reminiscent of the data of Sperling and Harwerth in Figure 6.11.

If the spectral sensitivities of the π-mechanisms were those of cone photopigments, then the displacement rules obeyed by their corresponding tvi-curve segments would be entirely understandable. But this is not possible, for at least two reasons. First, there are five π-mechanisms (or even seven, if special high-intensity versions of π_4 and π_5, not discussed here, are admitted). There can be only three cone photopigments. Second, the data of color-defective observers, upon which derived cone sensitivity curves are largely based, present a serious problem. Protanopes (see Chapter 10) lack the red-sensitive pigment, erythrolabe. When tested under conditions that discourage a significant contribution from rods or B cones, the resulting sensitivity curve is narrower than π_4. A similar problem exists for the relation between π_5 and the sensitivity of deuteranopes.

It is possible that π_1, π_4, and π_5 have spectral sensitivities equivalent to those of the B, G, and R cones respectively. If so, the color-mixture behavior of normal observers must be correctly predicted by the π-functions. Stiles (1959) did a careful analysis to show that this is nearly so, but he was not satisfied with the extent of agreement; recently Estévez and Cavonius (1977) have shown that if the two kinds of data are taken on the same observers, the agreement is good.

But this still leaves the two other problems—the breadth of the curves and the excess number of π-mechanisms. Pugh (1976) has shown that π_1 consists of two components, only one of which (the shortwave part) appears to reflect the spectral sensitivity of B cones. Using additivity experiments, involving mixtures of long- and shortwave conditioning fields, he has clearly shown that the low-sensitivity, longwave "hump" in the π_1 sensitivity curve comes from some other source, and that, overall, π_1 is not univariant. The same is very probably true of π_2, which shows a notch at 580 nm, has a very strange shape, and cannot even be examined over much of the spectrum. The high-intensity variants on π_4 and π_5 could be explained away as artifacts caused, in one way or another, by driving the system beyond its physiological levels.

The foregoing has rationalized everything except the excess breadth of the π-mechanism curves. Somehow, π_4 and π_5 seem to receive input from both R and G cones. One possibility is that each type of cone contains a small amount of the "wrong" photopigment (for example, R cones might contain a small amount of chlorolabe). But there is no evidence for this. More likely, both types of cones feed very unequally into both the π_4 and the π_5 mechanisms. In experiments where field sensitivities have been measured with flickering as well as with flashing lights, Ingling and Tsou (1977) have attempted to analyze possible contributions to π_5 from a weighted vector sum of inputs from R cones and, in addition, a signal delivered through red-green opponent channels (whose description will begin in the next chapter). Yet Bowmaker, Dartnall,

Lythgoe, and Mollon (1978) believe that the results of their recent retinal densitometry indicate that π_5 and R-cone absorption spectra are the same. However, quite a few assumptions must be made to make the calculations that justify that conclusion, which seems difficult to reconcile with the narrower R function of Figure 5.21, based mainly on data from dichromats. The issue remains unsettled.

Whatever the π-mechanisms may be, it is becoming progressively more customary to design experiments, both psychophysical and electrophysiological, that are designed to isolate one or another of them. Even though there is some ambiguity about what it means to do this, the procedure is a vast improvement on an earlier custom of treating photopic vision as if it were a unitary phenomenon.

SOME EVIDENCE FOR POSTRECEPTORAL CHROMATIC ADAPTATION

This chapter will be concluded with a brief discussion of an interesting kind of experiment that has been attempted several times in an effort to isolate the spectral sensitivities of the three types of cones by a psychophysical technique. The method assumes, first, that adaptation takes place independently in the two eyes. This makes possible a comparison of the appearance of fields that are delivered separately to the two eyes (dichoptic viewing) but which appear to lie side by side in space. As mentioned in Chapter 2 (see also the exercise on p. 161 of this chapter), two such fields, if physically identical, will appear different if the two eyes are differently adapted.

With such asymmetric adaptation of the two eyes, the subject is given control of the chromaticity of one of the fields—for example, by manipulation of the amounts of three spectral primaries in an additive mixture. His task is to produce a dichoptic color match. Assume now that there are only three mechanisms in the eye, each with a different spectral sensitivity, each obeying the principle of univariance. It is further assumed that, if the two test fields can be made to match when viewed by the asymmetrically adapted eyes, the outputs of corresponding mechanisms will be the same for the two eyes. (Unless the eyes are symmetrically adapted, the physical input required to get these outputs differs.)

If this experiment is done for many different adapting and test fields, it should be possible to describe all of the results in terms of the behavior of a unique set of three spectral functions, each representing the action spectrum of one of the three types of mechanisms that were adapted (the full argument is not presented here). This experiment does not succeed. If one grants all of the assumptions, it is necessary to conclude from the results of these studies that the spectral sensitivity of at least one of the three mechanisms varies considerably from one condition to another. Thus no unique set can be derived. We can conclude from this that some or all of the initial assumptions are incorrect. Quite possibly all of them are.

If the mechanisms under test whose action spectra are invariant are types of cones, it is nevertheless likely, as already noted, that there are mechanisms downstream from the cones which also adapt. If so, there is no reason to suppose that test lights that produce the same outputs from the cones of the two eyes will yield the same sensations after being passed through pathways that are differentially adapted in the two cases.

It is quite probable that some of the adaptation that does occur downstream involves sensitivity changes of opponent-color mechanisms.[11] If so, this would be expected to lead to extremely complicated predictions about the effects of chromatic adaptation on color appearance. Moreover, color appearance depends not only on the conditions of stimulation of a test area, and the adaptation that occurs there, but also upon the nature of surrounding fields. At this time, there are empirical equations that are fairly useful for predicting such effects, but most of these are essentially without any theoretical basis. Especially if the complications of surround fields are included, we are a long way yet from having a general theory of chromatic adaptation that will account for the appearance of colored fields.

SUMMARY

Because the eye must operate over an enormous range of external light levels, mechanisms exist that automatically adjust its sensitivity to permit good vision at all levels. Color constancy is somehow preserved despite the existence, in each eye, of three parallel mechanisms that must remain precisely balanced during sensitivity adjustments that occur independently within each.

Because adaptation is such a complicated process, the problems that physiological mechanisms of adaptation are "designed" to solve are introduced in this chapter with a photographic analog, with the admonition that camera and eye solve their common problems in very different ways. Light and dark adaptation are discussed in relation to the bleaching and regeneration kinetics of rod and cone photopigments, because these changes correlate with, and may cause, some of these changes in visual sensitivity. The extent to which steady-state photopic adaptation can be understood in terms of three factors (bleaching, pupillary constriction, and receptor response compression) is considered, and although these factors go some distance toward an explanation, other mechanisms of adaptation are also known to exist, and some of these are discussed.

In the laboratory, the phenomena of adaptation can be deliberately used to help understand some of the characteristics of color vision under extreme conditions of selective chromatic adaptation where color constancy breaks down very badly. As a prime example of this, the two-color threshold technique of Stiles is discussed, which leads to "mechanisms" that can be isolated and studied by psychophysical methods. It is uncertain whether these mechanisms might describe the behavior of the R, G, and B cones.

NOTES

[1] This statement is on page 117 of Adler's translation (1966) of Fechner's *Elements of Psychophysics*, Volume 1.

[2] The equation for this relationship is $E = LA_p$, where E is retinal illuminance in trolands, L is the luminance of the viewed surface in cd/m^2, and A_p is the area of the pupil in mm^2. Discussions of photometric concepts are available in many places. Walsh (1958) tells more about the subject than most readers will want to know. Shorter treatments are available in Boynton (1966), LeGrand (1968), and Wyszecki and Stiles (1967).

[3] Density (D) is related to transmittance (t) as follows: $D = -\log t$, or $D = \log (1/t)$. Transmittance refers to the fraction of incident light that passes through a filter, or photographic film; this can vary from zero (in which case D approaches infinity) to 1.0 (100 percent), in which case $D = 0$. The following table of examples may help:

t	D
1.00	0
.50	0.3
.25	0.6
.10	1.0
.05	1.3
.025	1.6
.001	3.0
.0001	4.0

The placement of a curve like that of Figure 6.1 will depend upon the exposure duration, the numerical aperture (reciprocal f number) of the lens, and the type of film used.

[4] For many years, the chief proponent of the utility of subjective scaling was S. S. Stevens of Harvard University. Interested readers are referred to a collection of papers planned as a *Festschrift* in his honor (Moskowitz, Scharf, & Stevens, 1974).

[5] In the old days, "blank" trials were used in an effort to keep the subject honest and alert, and the attitude in the laboratory was that "false alarm" responses, as these are now called ("yes" responses to "blank" stimuli), were undesirable, if not downright sinful. A more modern view, embedded in signal detection theory, holds that if false alarm data are properly dealt with, it should be possible to derive an estimate of sensitivity (called d') that will remain invariant, for a particular stimulus intensity, despite changes in a subject's criterion. This estimate works, to the extent that it does, because a subject who uses a low criterion for "yes" responses will also generate large numbers of false alarms, whereas a high-criterion subject will produce relatively few. In practice, the criterion problem turns out not to be very serious for the class of visual psychophysics treated in this book, and large bodies of data (such as those of Stiles, discussed in the second part of this chapter) based on simple "yes" and "no" judgments, without adjustment for criterion changes, have proved to be extremely useful. For a recent treatment of signal detection theory and related data analysis, see Egan (1975).

[6] As examples of some of this literature, see Dowling and Ripps (1970), Glantz (1971), Kleinschmidt and Dowling (1972), Normann and Werblin (1974), and Werblin and Copenhagen (1974).

[7]See Barlow (1972) for a discussion of these issues, and for additional references.

[8]This observation proves the point only if receptors behave independently. Although Baylor, Fuortes, and O'Bryan (1971) showed, in the turtle, that they do not, the degree of summation of cone signals is far too small to account for the psychophysical result.

[9]See Stiles (1978), for the most recent summary. The work is reported in detail in Stiles (1939), Stiles (1949), and Stiles (1953). Summaries of his approach written by others are available by Brindley (1970), Enoch (1972), and Mariott (1962).

[10]The numbers next to the curves specify the retinal illuminance of the adapting fields that were used in log trolands.

[11]See, for example, a study by Scheibner (1966). Also, the theory of Jameson and Hurvich specifically assumes that adaptation occurs partly at the opponent-color stage. This theory has had some success in accounting for color shifts caused by chromatic adaptation. For a summary and entry to earlier references, see Jameson and Hurvich (1972).

7
The Encoding of Color

From the perspective provided by Chapter 5, it would be hard to doubt that the R, G, and B cones are truly "mechanisms" of chromatic vision. Yet the achromatic pattern vision that we experience when looking at a black-and-white photograph must—since there are no other cones—be served initially by the same receptors. Those who probe the monkey cortex with microelectrodes often find cells that appear to carry a chromatic code; yet at the same time many of these same units respond selectively to nonspectral characteristics of the stimulus. For example, a cell may respond only to the longwave end of the spectrum we call "red," but its willingness to do so may also require that the red light be presented as a slit, that the slit be oriented in a certain direction, and that it move in a direction perpendicular to its axis. We therefore appear to be dealing with an interlocking system of neural elements whose collective concern is to process information about intensity, space, time, motion, and wavelength; more often than not, any single unit may be involved in two or more of these functions at the same time.

We know a good deal more about the first stage of chromatic processing than about the last. Obvious as it may be, it must be emphasized that vision does not take place in the eye: an intact optic nerve is required to take the message from the eye and pass it along to the brain. Direct electrical or mechanical stimulation of the eye can lead to visual sensations only if the optic nerve is available to carry the retinal signals thus generated to the brain, in the same way that it carries such signals that are generated by light. But direct electrical stimulation of the visual brain can also lead to visual sensations, whether or not there is an optic nerve, or even an eye. The sensations produced by electrical stimulation are spatially diffuse for ocular stimulation, and though localized in space according to which region of the visual brain is stimulated, these so-called "phosphenes" otherwise lack specificity and do not much resemble ordinary visual perceptions. The pattern of brain activity induced by normal input from the light-stimulated eye is evidently exceedingly subtle and precise, and is not likely ever to be duplicated by direct electrical stimulation of the eye or brain.[1]

OPPONENT-COLOR THEORY

In Chapter 1 we saw that Hering first proposed the idea of an opponent-color code in the nineteenth century. By the middle of the present century, a variety of theories had been suggested that attempted to reconcile the idea of trichromacy at the initial stage of vision with the need for subsequent recoding into (1) red−green and yellow−blue opponent signals, and (2) a univariant channel through which to transmit luminance or brightness information. In Stevens's *Handbook of Experimental Psychology,* Judd (1951b) provided a quantitative summary of such models, intended to account both for the trichromatic nature of color matching and for features of color appearance of the sort described in Chapter 2.

In the 1950s, psychophysical and electrophysiological evidence supporting the opponent-color idea started to appear almost simultaneously. This chapter will stress the physiological evidence; nevertheless it will be worthwhile first to review some of the modern psychophysical work which shows that opponent color signals of some kind almost certainly exist somewhere in the visual system. Next an opponent-color model will be presented. This will not only help to organize the physiological data to be presented in this chapter; in addition the concepts of Chapters 8, 9, and 10 will depend heavily upon this model for their exposition.

Chromatic Cancellation

Jameson and Hurvich (1955) reasoned that it should be possible to cancel the hue components of spectral stimuli by superposing lights having dominant hues opposite to those being canceled. For example, an orange light at 600 nm seems to contain both red and yellow hue components. Using a green cancellation stimulus, it is possible to cancel the red component, leaving a pure yellow; the amount of green light required to do this can be used as a measure of the strength of the red component that is canceled in the original orange light. Then, by using a blue cancellation stimulus, it is possible to cancel the yellow component of the original orange, leaving a pure red. Such cancellation was carried out using lights of the four psychologically unique hues, two at a time in each of four regions of the spectrum (separated by the wavelengths corresponding to the unique hues of the spectrum).

Some additional observations were made in order to specify the units of the cancellation stimuli. Opponent pairs of cancellation stimuli were superposed and the relative energy values required to produce their mutual cancellation were taken as equal intensities of these two stimuli. The intensities of red and yellow were taken to be equal when presented in amounts that produced a balanced orange mixture.

The results of this experiment for one observer are shown in Figure 7.1. "Chromatic valence" on the ordinate refers to the amount of the cancellation component, expressed in relative energy units, required to cancel the opponent hue of test stimuli presented at equal energy at various wavelengths. The resulting functions provide a remarkably good description of the appearance of spectral colors. The graph shows the longest wavelengths to be slightly yellowish red, corresponding to a large amount of green that was required to cancel the red component and a much smaller amount of blue to cancel the residual yellow. As explained above, a balanced orange must occur at 600 nm. Unique

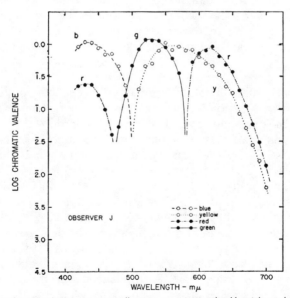

FIGURE 7.1 Results of a chromatic cancellation experiment by Hurvich and Jameson (1955a) in which the perceived amounts of red, green, yellow, and blue hues in spectral colors were assessed in terms of the amounts of complementary colors required to cancel each hue component.

yellow is represented at about 580 nm, where the red-green function crosses the zero baseline. At this wavelength, neither red nor green is seen and neither cancellation component is needed; only blue is used to cancel yellow and thereby produce a white.

In the midspectral region, yellow-greens are flanked by unique yellow to the right, and unique green at about 500 nm to the left. As wavelength is further shortened, a small blue-green region appears that terminates at unique blue at 475 nm. Although the shortest wavelengths are seen as predominantly blue, red reappears in this part of the spectrum, and it is canceled, just as for the long wavelengths, by adding green.

Hurvich and Jameson (1955) went on to show that functions like those of Figure 7.1 can be derived from linear transformations of color-mixture data. In their theory (and others similar to it) the outputs of R and G cones are assumed to subtract from each other to produce the red-minus-green opponent-color function. Similarly a yellow signal was assumed to be in opposition to the B cones. More recently, Larimer, Krantz, and Cicerone (1974, 1975) reexamined chromatic cancellation. They were able to replicate the main features of the Jameson-Hurvich experiment. In addition they demonstrated that, although the red-green cancellation process is linear with intensity, yellow-blue cancellation is not. Therefore the hue should vary somewhat with intensity at most wavelengths, as it does (the Bezold-Brücke hue shift; see, for example, Nagy and Zacks, 1977, for some recent work on this topic). Their result may imply that red-green opponency occurs earlier than yellow-blue cancellation in the chain of events related to color coding in the retina.

Color Naming

A type of experiment that permits a more direct gauging of the appearance of spectral colors utilizes direct color scaling, or color naming. In Figure 7.2 I have replotted color-naming data of Boynton and Gordon (1965). Briefly, subjects were presented (25 times, in random order) with monochromatic lights at 1000 td at each of the wavelengths shown in the figure. They were required to judge the appearance of each stimulus by using only the color names "red," "green," "yellow," and "blue." Either one or two names could be used on each trial. For example, if the subject saw a unique yellow, he simply reported "yellow." If he saw a slightly reddish yellow, he reported "yellow, red," in that order. An important outcome of the experiment was that, (excepting in a few instances involving an 8-year-old subject) responses of "red, green," "green, red," "yellow, blue," and "blue, yellow" were not given, although there was no proscription against using them. A comparison with the Jameson-Hurvich data of Figure 7.1 shows that the correspondence is good in the sense that the relative amplitudes of the Jameson-Hurvich functions predict which color names will be used, how they will be apportioned at each wavelength, and where the various curves cross to indicate unique hues and balanced blends. See Boynton (1975) for a more quantitative comparison of the two sets of data.

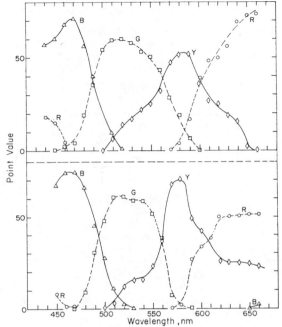

FIGURE 7.2 Results of a color-naming experiment by Boynton and Gordon (1965) as re-potted by Boynton (1975), for the average of three subjects at 1000 td of retinal illuminance.

In summary, two procedures have been described by which it proves possible to scale the appearance of the spectrum by psychophysical procedures. Red cancels green and green cancels red; similarly, yellow and blue cancel each other and the amount of the cancellation stimulus can be used to gauge the components of spectral colors. When direct color naming is used, opponent hues are virtually never seen together, and the appearance of the spectrum as derived from this procedure agrees in important respects with that obtained by the cancellation method.

AN OPPONENT-COLOR MODEL

Before launching an examination of physiological evidence, it will be helpful to have a brief look at an opponent-color model of chromatic vision that seems reasonable to many color-vision experts today. Figure 7.3 illustrates the general idea. The three types of cones at the top of the figure provide the initial stage of the *achromatic* visual system. Output from R and G cones summates and passes out of the retina as an achromatic message, delivered through a "luminance channel." (Note that the B cones deliver no signal to be used for ach-

The Encoding of Color

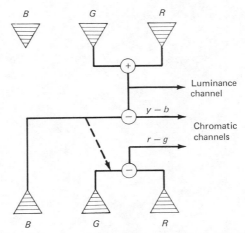

FIGURE 7.3 An opponent-color model of human color vision. The B, G, and R cones at the top are intended to represent the same three cones that are also shown at the bottom. The achromatic (broad-band, nonopponent) pathway is activated by the summated output of R and G cones. The r-g opponent pathway is activated by the difference in output of these same cones. The y-b opponent pathway receives a signal that is the difference between the output of B cones and that of the luminance channel.

romatic purposes.) Although the luminance channel has a dual input, it behaves in many respects almost as if it received information from only a single cone type, containing erythrolabe and chlorolabe in about equal proportions. In particular, it has a "broad band" sensitivity—broader than that of any photopigment—and shows no capacity whatever for wavelength discrimination. The three triangles at the bottom of the figure are intended to represent the same cones that are shown at the top, but they are now to be regarded as the initial elements of the *chromatic* visual system. For this purpose, the outputs of the R and G cones are differenced, and a message related to this difference is passed out of the retina along one of two chromatic pathways. This one is called the "r-g opponent channel." A critically important feature of this model is that, unless some means is found completely to silence the contribution of either the R or G cone, no signal is received by the brain concerning the unique contribution of either. Only the sum and difference of their outputs is registered.

The second chromatic pathway, called the "y-b opponent channel," carries a difference that is taken between the output of the B cones and the luminance signal derived from the R and G cones.

A device built in this way, with only three cones in it, would of course be useless for spatial vision. Therefore we must imagine millions of such cones of the required three types, organized so that they feed into hundreds of thousands of pathways (channels) of the luminance and opponent-color types. The model obviously lacks anatomical and neurophysiological specificity; also there are points about it, even in this very simple form, that are under dispute. At long wavelengths of stimulation, the r-g opponent channel is fed only by R and G cones. The electrophysiological evidence suggests, as we shall see, that the proportion of input from these two types of cones varies considerably from channel to channel, so that a quantitative version of the model, like that represented in Figure 7.4, must represent the average response of many channels

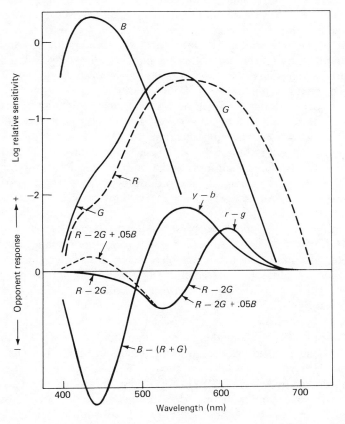

FIGURE 7.4 A quantitative representation of a specific opponent-color model. The curves R, G, and B represent the relative spectral sensitivities of the three kinds of cones. The vertical placement of the R and G curves is such that they cross near 570 nm. Opponent curves are calculated as shown by the labels attached to them in the bottom part of the figure. The cone-sensitivity curves were kindly furnished by Dr. Vivienne Smith. The B curve has been positioned so that it crosses the arithmetic sum of the R and G curves near 500 nm, causing the balance of the y-b opponent system to occur near that wavelength in the lower part of the figure.

of the same general type, and therefore disguises a large degree of underlying variance. The y-b channel is very controversial. There is little agreement about its longwave input: some would prefer to have it come only from R (or G) cones; others prefer their sum.[2]

The current belief in chromatic difference signals rests upon the direct evidence which is now available showing that they exist. But, beginning with Hering, there have been those who have believed in them for less direct reasons. One such reason is that difference signals seem necessary to explain the appearance of colors, especially the dimensions of color experience described here and in Chapter 2. For example, the model explains why we don't see red and green in the same place at the same time: it is because messages meaning "red" and "green" are transmitted through exactly the same pathways. Implicit in this arrangement is the requirement that the signals of the r-g pathways must exist in two qualitative states; otherwise a brain receiving such a message could not use it to distinguish one sensation from the other.

Until direct evidence began to accumulate in the 1950s, few physicists or neurophysiologists wanted to believe this. The physicists' intransigence was related to the focus of their training and concern, which was mainly color matching related to the behavior of the cones—the class of experiment stressed in Chapter 5. Neurophysiologists, in their turn, had long been conditioned by the so-called "law of specific nerve energies," according to which a single nerve fiber was not allowed to carry messages having more than one kind of qualitative significance.

It is interesting to speculate about the possible advantages of computing a red-green difference signal, as compared to the trichromatic alternative that Helmholtz and many other theorists have favored. In linking receptors directly to sensations, Helmholtz implied that signals from R and G cones are kept separate from receptors to brain. A problem with this scheme stems from the large degree of overlap between R and G cone sensitivity curves. Especially in the region where these curves cross (which for chromatic purposes is assumed to be at about 570 nm), wavelength discrimination requires that relatively small differences between signals of nearly equal strength must be reliably discriminated.

Many years ago, Hecht (1932) proposed a theory of color vision in which color-mixture data were transformed so that his resulting triad of curves seemed nearly to lie upon one another. Yet they differed sufficiently that, in a mathematical sense, they made the correct predictions about metameric color matches. Although the overlap between modern R and G cone sensitivity curves is much less, some remarks made by Guild (1932) about Hecht's theory nevertheless apply:

... It is perfectly easy to start with the known properties of ordinary colour-vision ... and then work out a system, such as [in Hecht's] paper, which will be in exact agreement with these properties: it is only necessary to carry the arithmetic to a sufficient number of significant figures in order to do so.

Nature, however, begins at the other end. She first constructs the visual mechanism, not on a calculating machine, but from flesh and blood and protoplasm, and the visual properties which any individual possesses are determined by the particular example of this mechanism with which he is provided.

On any system of the type suggested by [Hecht], all the qualitative properties of vision, as exemplified in the colour-match relations, depend upon small differences in large and nearly equal quantities . . . The slightest deviations from a standard pattern in the various parts of the visual apparatus would alter the colour vision to an enormous extent. . . .

Thus there is no problem about small differences between large signals, provided that one has a digital computer and can carry the computations to a sufficient number of decimal places. But the initial cone signals of vision exist in analog form and, moreover, depend upon the statistical properties of light. The farther such signals are carried through the visual system before being compared, the less reliable they become. Therefore, to keep the signal-to-noise ratio as high as possible it is better to compare the signals early. A differencing process taking place near the receptors constitutes such a comparison.

A related issue concerns the dynamic range of subsequent neural elements, especially the bipolar cells that receive signals from cones and pass their outputs along to ganglion cells. The three factors examined in Chapter 5 proved capable of shrinking the responses of cones to something like 300 to 1 over a millionfold range of stimulus intensities. But 300:1 is still a large ratio of activity to be carried reliably by the analog responses of bipolar cells, or for that matter in the subsequent impulse-frequency code of ganglion cells. But the *ratio* of red to green cone activation varies only from about 1:4 at 465 nm to perhaps 8:1 at the longest wavelengths. Ratios of this order can be reliably encoded, at a given luminance level, without exceeding the dynamic range of bipolar cells.

The Re-emergence of Red at Short Wavelengths

It is clear from Figure 7.4 that the simple subtraction of G from R cone outputs cannot account for the redness of the short-wave end of the visible spectrum. A plausible way to account for it is to suppose that a relatively weak signal from B cones is somehow able to influence the balance of the r-g opponent color system. The dashed line in Figure 7.3 is intended to suggest this interaction. Evidence (cited later in this chapter) that some ganglion cells receive a trichromatic input, is consistent with this hypothesis. Ingling (1977) argues that the interaction is specifically inhibitory, with B cones acting upon G cones. A reduction in the G cone signal would tend to bias the r-g difference signal in the r direction, and this would happen only for the short wavelengths where B cones are activated. Another possibility, for which there is no evidence, is that a small number of R cones might contain cyanolabe, the pigment normally found only in B cones (see Boynton, 1971).

SOME METHODOLOGICAL NOTES

In recent years it has proved possible to impale single cone photoreceptors of fish and turtles with very fine microelectrodes, in order to measure the voltage difference between the inside of each such cell and its surrounding medium. Because this work must be done with excised eyes it is obviously not feasible to use human subjects. Nor has it proved possible as yet to do this class of research in a species more closely related to man than are turtles and fish. It would be particularly helpful to have such evidence from macaque monkeys, because they have a visual system much like that of the human, and there is ample behavioral evidence to document that they have a human form of trichromatic vision. But monkey cones, like our own, are much smaller than those of fish and turtles. Even the finest electrode, by penetrating the cell membrane of such a cone, would probably destroy the cell as a functional unit.[3] Retinal electrophysiology is therefore especially difficult to do when using warm-blooded animals.

For all these reasons, recordings from inside primate cones have not yet been obtained. So, despite the probability of important species differences, work with frogs, turtles, fish, and rats is important to consider as the best evidence that we have. Although not intracellular, microphysiology undertaken with rat rods has permitted a detailed examination of the currents that flow in and around them. It seems likely that the lessons learned from this elegant work have applicability to statements about human cones. Nevertheless it should be kept firmly in mind, as a picture is presented in subsequent paragraphs about how human cone photoreceptors might work, that most of the important concepts upon which such a discussion is based have their origins in physiological studies of cold-blooded animals. Later in this chapter, where responses of ganglion cells and higher brain centers are considered, data are available from the macaque monkey, so we will not need to consider similar data from less closely related creatures.

Electrical records in response to light stimulation can be obtained from the human retina by placing an electrode in contact with the cornea of the eye. Although these records, known as electroretinograms (ERGs), are complex and much more difficult to analyze than are microelectrode recordings from single cells, they do have the important advantage of coming from human eyes.[4] The ERG is based on activity of neurons in the retina, including the photoreceptors. Human ERGs have been obtained for more than 100 years, during which time there has been a gradual improvement in stimulating conditions, in recording procedures, and in the interpretation of data. ERG recording has recently received a powerful assist in the form of procedures that permit the recording of a local electroretinogram (LERG) from monkeys.[5] These improved records are not obtainable from humans, because the technique requires the insertion into the eye of a microelectrode whose tip nestles among (not in) the receptors.

Although records obtained in this way come from thousands of cells, the response is much more localized than the ordinary ERG, which comes from millions of them.

During the 1950s, K. T. Brown achieved the first recordings of receptor potentials from macaque monkeys. He did this by recording a special kind of local ERG, in an eye where the primary circulation of the retina had been "clamped" by putting pressure on the optic disc, where the major vascular supply of the retina passes into the eye along with the optic nerve fibers. Because the receptors are nourished by blood supplied by a different route to the choroid, their responses survive this clamping procedure. Being a local ERG, and not an intracellular record, the response arises from many receptors, but probably from receptors alone.

The techniques for recording brain waves in humans (the electroencephalogram, or EEG) have been available for a long time. But only in recent years has it proved possible to record those variations in the EEG that are related to activity in the brain elicited by stimulation of the eye by light. In response to light flashes, a component of the recording specifically related to the stimulus, sometimes known as the *visually evoked cortical potential* (VECP), is elicited.[6] The magnitude of such evoked potentials is in the microvolt range, and because they are so small, they are ordinarily not visible in the EEG; instead they are swamped by the background activity of the brain and unavoidable sources of noise in the recording. The trick that is required to observe the VECP is called *response averaging*. Although small, the potential fluctuations that comprise the VECP are reliably related to the timing of the light flash that produces them. In other words, the visually relevant potentials tend to follow the same time course in response to each repeated presentation of the stimulus. The background activity, on the other hand, bears a random relation to the timing of the flashes. If one adds together a large number of responses elicited by repetitions of the same stimulus, taking care to use the onset of the stimulus as a trigger to begin each recording period, the time-locked VECP is observed to rise majestically from the background in a spectacular triumph of digital electronic wizardry. Another device, called a *lock-in amplifier*, can accomplish much the same aim when a flickering input is used; by selectively amplifying only those response components whose frequency is close to that of the stimulus, signals are extracted from background activity. Signal-averaging procedures are also used to advantage in ERG recording.

HUMAN VISUAL ELECTROPHYSIOLOGY

Although the use of electrophysiological methods with humans shows considerable promise, it does not seem that these procedures have yet revealed anything new about color coding that was not already known from inferences based on psychophysical experiments. Nevertheless the electrical experiments can serve to confirm and reify such conceptions. Moreover, if the relatively gross electrical records that can be recorded from humans are eventually obtained also with old-world monkeys, which have color vision similar to humans, a comparison of such records with those obtained using microelectrodes inside the visual system could help clarify the exact meaning of human records, particularly with respect to the sources of the externally recorded potentials.

As examples of the sorts of electrophysiological experiments that can be done with humans, studies from three different laboratories will be mentioned briefly.

- Riggs, Johnson, and Schick (1966) studied electrical responses of the human eye to changes in wavelength of the stimulating light. Because the human ERG is strongly influenced by stray light falling outside the image proper (Boynton & Riggs, 1951), spatially alternating stripes were used that could be exchanged for one another at equal luminance. Fifteen wavelengths in 15-nm steps from 450 to 660 were compared in all 210 possible combinations; the magnitude of the average response to the shifting pattern, alternated at about 10 displacements per second, was recorded. The results were summarized, using three functions that resemble constant-luminance output curves for R, G, and B cones. The results suggest that R, G, and B cones contribute linearly to the recorded responses, and that response magnitude is predictable in terms of the total amount of change, for all three types of cones combined, that occurs for a particular wavelength shift at constant luminance.

- Using the visually evoked cortical potential (VECP), Estévez, Spekreijse, van den Berg, and Cavonius (1975) demonstrated that spectral sensitivities essentially identical to psychophysically obtained π-mechanisms could be measured. For example, in order to study the electrophysiological analog of π_5, a longwave test stimulus was used that was alternated with a lesser amount of green light designed to keep the flickering component of G-cone stimulation at a zero level. Because VECPs are much more vigorous when patterned rather than uniform stimuli are used (Harter & White, 1970), a checkerboard with elements 15' on each side was employed, and adjacent squares were exchanged six times per second to elicit what was termed a "contrast EP."

    The experiment consisted of determining the intensity of adapting lights of various wavelengths required to drive the recorded response down to a criterion level of $2\mu v$, which was smaller than the response to the checkerboard would have been in the dark-adapted state. The same apparatus was also used to obtain π_5 with the same subjects using psychophysical methods. Similar procedures were also used to examine π_1 and π_4. The authors conclude that "the close agreement between our data and the π-

mechanisms of Stiles suggests to us that the color coded channels as seen through the contrast EP are mediated through such mechanisms." This conclusion, which implies that signals from R, G, and B cones are preserved in separate channels all the way to the cortex, is probably wrong. After all, since special techniques were used so that, for example, the entire red-green opponent-color variation resulted only from alterations in R cone output, it is not surprising that only R-cone output was reflected. This point will be examined again in Chapter 9 in connection with a psychophysical experiment by Kelly and van Norren (p. 320).

- Regan (1973) studied the effect of purely chromatic contours on the VECP by using checkerboards in which the adjacent squares were of different chromaticity. In a deuteranope presumably lacking G cones (see Chapter 10), Regan found that a relative intensity of the adjacent red and green checks could be found that reduced the response to zero as expected, since two equally effective lights, for the remaining R cones, would be exchanged. For normal subjects, on the other hand, a clear response was always recorded no matter what the relative intensities of the adjacent checks. Although Regan favors the idea that his results are due to red and green signals transmitted over independent pathways to the cortex, his data are also consistent with the possibility (as he admits) that "the human visual system contains *both* chromatic contrast and luminance contrast channels (p. 2398)."

RECEPTORS

In the dark-adapted state, each vertebrate photoreceptor actively generates an intracellular current that flows outward from the base of the cell toward the tip of the outer segment. To complete the circuit, a return current flows outside the cell from the outer segment toward the inner segment (Figure 7.5). This so-called extracellular current, which underlies the receptor component of the ERG, reflects the state of activity of the cell. In the absence of light, the flow of current in the circuit (in and around the cell) is believed to depend mainly on two variables: (1) the activity of a *sodium pump* located somewhere in the inner segment, and (2) the impedance of the outer segment membrane.[7]

Some of the details of the extract pattern of current flow are obscure. Many years ago the famed Swedish neurophysiologist and Nobel laureate Ragnar Granit had concluded that the leading edge of the ERG had its origin in the photoreceptors, but the sign of the response was such as to imply a hyperpolarization of the receptors in response to light. This was not an appealing idea, because all neurons then known were passively hyperpolarized, depolarizing only when stimulated.[8] But evidence about photoreceptors of vertebrates strongly indicates that, in the dark, the electrical impedance of the outer segment

220 The Encoding of Color

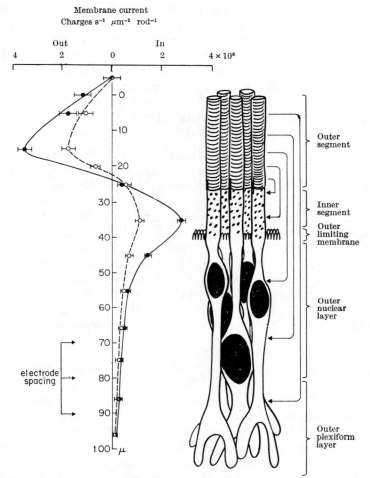

FIGURE 7.5 Direct measurements of current flow external to rat rods (Penn & Hagins, 1969). From the measurement of current flow, in and out of the rods at various points along their length, the pattern of current as indicated by the arrows at the right is inferred. Basically, the extracellular current flows from the outer to the inner segment. Current inside the cells (not shown) must therefore flow in the opposite direction.

membrane is at its minimum, so that the flow of current in and around the cell is consequently at its maximum. The absorption of a photon by a molecule of photopigment somehow causes an increase in membrane impedance which in turn reduces the flow of current. Exactly how this happens is not yet known, but probably soon will be, for this is an area of very intense investigation.

We have here a picture of a most unusual receptor mechanism, one which is active even when totally unstimulated by light. In the light-adapted eye, decrements of light are as effective as increments, since both modulate activity that is perpetually in progress. In addition to acting as a detector and transmitter, the receptor also acts as an amplifier: the energy contained in an incident photon is trivial compared to the response amplitude of the receptor. The action of a photon, when absorbed by a photopigment molecule, is to trigger, not to drive.

Receptors are connected to their postsynaptic elements, the horizontal and bipolar cells, by chemical synapses. The postsynaptic bipolar (or horizontal) cell therefore "knows" what the receptor is trying to tell it only in terms of the rate at which it receives packets of some chemical transmitter. (Exactly what transmitters are involved in vision is another unknown that is under very active investigation.) It is very unlikely that the postsynaptic cell knows anything directly about the current that flows in and around the receptor. Nevertheless it seems likely that these currents play a direct role in vision, because a message signaling that a single photon has been absorbed in the outer segment must somehow be transmitted to the cone pedicle. The modulation of extracellular current flow carries such information in amplified form, and might play a role in liberating the presynaptic transmitter substance.

Microelectrode studies of fish and turtle cones have revealed a number of very significant facts:

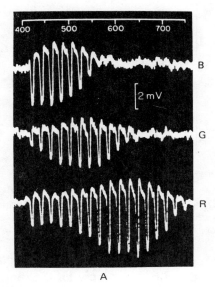

FIGURE 7.6 A: Sample recordings from single cones of the carp retina, for the three types of cones that were found. (Continued on page 222.)

222   The Encoding of Color

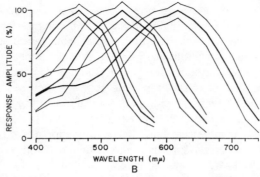

FIGURE 7.6 (Continued)   B: Average curves, with the variability attached to each (± 1 standard deviation) for the three cone types.

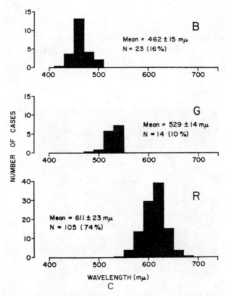

FIGURE 7.6 (Continued)   C: Histograms showing the number of cells peaking at each wavelength, for cells classified as belonging to the R, G, and B categories. (From Tomita et al., 1967.)

1. There are three classes of such cones, which differ according to their spectral sensitivities. Figure 7.6 shows these for the carp, from the pioneering work from Tomita's laboratory (these were the first published intracellular recordings from photoreceptors). The agreement between the electrophysiological sensitivities and those obtained by microspectrophotometry is gratifyingly good,

constituting a further verification in this species that three types of cone with three photopigments provide the initial basis for trichromatic vision. Note, on page 222, that there is considerable variability of spectral sensitivity within each class. This variability seems similar to what has been found by microspectrophotometry, suggesting that a single cone has a spectral sensitivity that is a noisy version of the action spectrum of its constituent photopigment. One possible cause of this variability relates to the dimensions of receptors, which are very small and act like light antennas, or waveguides, as they direct light to the inner segment where the pigment is located. Such waveguide properties are extremely complex and they are wavelength-dependent.[9] Alternatively, both techniques are stretched to the limits of their sensitivity and so are noisy. Some of the noise in the records therefore comes from the recording systems and is not of physiological origin.

2. The hyperpolarization of cones in response to light occurs in the same way for all three types of cones. This means that there is no basis for color opponency in the behavior of individual receptors. A variable degree of hyperpolarization can be accomplished with light of any wavelength, simply by using an intensity that is inversely proportional to the sensitivity of the cell. This provides an electrophysiological expression of response univariance at the receptor stage; no single cone is capable of wavelength discrimination.

3. The degree of hyperpolarization depends upon light intensity, which in turn is related to the rate of photon absorption. (It is this fact that makes possible the examination of the spectral sensitivities of the cones.) To a first approximation, the response of the cell (degree of hyperpolarization) follows the following rule, which relates the relative response R to the stimulus intensity I:

$$R = \frac{I^n}{I^n + K^n} \qquad (7.1)$$

(This equation, with an exponent n of 0.7, is the basis for the response compression discussed on page 175 in the previous chapter.) Theoretically this behavior can be related to the fact that there is a finite number of elements that contribute to the increase of membrane impedance that controls the response. When the light intensity is low, only a trivial fraction of these elements is activated and the response rises almost in proportion to intensity (I is very small compared to K). When the light intensity is very high, I becomes very large relative to K and the value of the fraction approaches 1. This behavior relates theoretically to the idea that all the response elements have been exhausted. When this happens, the cell is then said to be "saturated" in a sense that is similar to the photographic analog discussed in the previous chapter.

4. To a first approximation, the cell hyperpolarizes to a level related to the intensity of the light, and then retains that level indefinitely so long as light

continues to be supplied. Probably the best way to think about this is to imagine that each absorbed photon releases an element of response that lasts for a millisecond or two, rising gradually from a baseline, cresting, and then returning to its initial level. A steady light produces a continuous and overlapping series of such events, and the steady level of the response depends on the mean number of such events that occur within each small slice of time. This view is an oversimplification, because receptor potentials show an overshoot at light onset, and in some species there is a slow decline of the potential over time, followed by a decay at light offset that can be very prolonged, especially for rods. Even with these complications, the response is totally different from the all-or-nothing nerve impulses that have long been known to carry information over long distances in the nervous system. Neurons of that more conventional type always depolarize when stimulated; they require a threshold level of activation and then they fire; the size of the impulse is quite unrelated to the strength of the stimulus; each impulse propagates along the nerve fiber without decrement. In the retina, the only cells that respond in this way are the ganglion cells (see p. 92). Unlike the propagated impulses that run along such fibers, receptor potentials are also decremental, becoming smaller as a function of distance from the source of their generation.

Receptors do not function independently of one another. This means that the response of any particular receptor depends not only upon the rate at which photons are being absorbed in its own outer segment, but also upon the activity of neighboring receptors. At the present time, more questions can be raised than answers definitely given about these interactions. Psychophysical evidence from humans has been brought to bear on these issues and some of it will be considered in Chapter 9. For now, the best we can do is state two of the most important questions, and provide some possible answers.

1. *What is the mechanism of cone–cone interaction?* For excitatory interactions, where (because of the conjoint responses of its neighbors) the response of a cone is larger than it would be in isolation, there seem to be two possibilities. There are so-called gap junctions between adjacent cones. When microelectrode recordings are obtained intracellularly from turtle cones, the size of the response increases with the area of the stimulus, provided that the stimulus is not too large. This result shows that excitatory interactions occur over small distances, and also seems to implicate a role for the gap junctions that exist between cones, both in turtles and in primates.

For inhibitory interactions, horizontal cells seem to be the most likely candidates. Anatomically they cover the larger distances over which such interactions occur, and they feed back upon the receptors, flanking the receptor–bipolar contacts in the invaginations of the cone pedicles (Chapter 4). Although this arrangement might seem to suggest that the action of horizontal cells is merely to modulate the signal that is allowed to pass from receptor to bipolar, the turtle evidence indicates that there is an active inhibition of receptor activity per se. Although there is no direct evidence in primates about the function of gap junctions or horizontal cells, it is not unreasonable to suppose that the monkey retina may work in much the same way as that of the turtle, since the anatomy is fairly similar.

2. *What differences are there, aside from the photopigments, among the three types of cones?* We have already seen (Chapter 4) that there are no anatomical distinctions known to exist among R, G, and B cones sampled from the same region of the retina. However, there probably are many more R and G cones than B cones, with the density of B cones being especially low at the center of the fovea. Although the manner in which the R, G, and B cones are distributed within regions small enough to be regarded as homogeneous is not known, a pattern something like that of Figure 7.7 is not an unreasonable speculation for the central retina. Even if this pattern were random, it is unlikely that the sparse B cones would have direct contact with other B cones, whereas

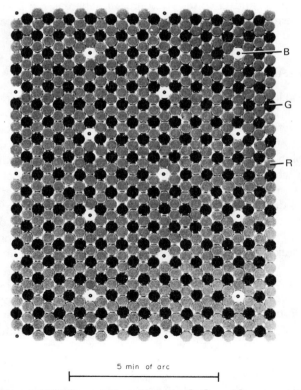

5 min of arc

FIGURE 7.7 Walraven's (1974) conception of how the R, G, and B cones might be arranged in the human retina.

R and G cones have ample opportunities to contact cones of their own or different kinds.[10]

In many ways, the B-cone system appears to differ from that of R and G cones. The B-cone system responds more slowly and with greater spatial diffuseness. As a consequence it cannot mediate a high level of flicker sensitivity or visual acuity. B cones seem not to make any contribution to the luminance channels, they do not contribute importantly to the perception of contour, and they adapt relatively slowly. There is also a good deal of evidence that the R and G cones are highly similar to each other in all respects save for their photopigments and detailed connections. Both contribute to achromatic channels and both are important for good acuity and contour perception. These matters will be dealt with in more detail in Chapter 9.

Whitten and I showed that the receptor potential reacts to the effects of chromatic adaptation in a manner that indicates, not too surprisingly, that the overall response comes from cones having different spectral sensitivities, and that these can be differentially adapted with chromatic light.[11] Using a variation of this preparation, Baron and I later found evidence that the temporal response properties of the R and G cones are identical, whereas the B cones are more sluggish.[12] These results agree to some extent with psychophysical observations to be discussed in Chapter 9.

HORIZONTAL CELLS

In 1956, an investigator in South America named Svaetichin published some landmark records that were obtained using microelectrodes in fish retinas (Fig. 7.8). These were the first intracellular slow potentials ever recorded from the visual system, and some of these recordings also reveal for the first time direct electrophysiological evidence of opponent-color responses. Svaetichin used an apparatus in which interference filters, used to supply monochromatic light, were mounted in a bicycle wheel, connected to a potentiometer that actuated the horizontal deflection of a spot on an oscilloscope. The responses that he recorded, which were actually sustained potentials lasting for the duration of the stimulus, were (because of a very slow sweep speed) exhibited on the scope as spikes, automatically plotted as a function of wavelength for an equal-energy spectrum.

This finding of an opponent-response in horizontal cells has been replicated many times since, but so far only in cold-blooded animals. The opponent-color units (called C-units) responded by hyperpolarizing over part of the spectrum and depolarizing over the remainder. Other units, called L (for luminosity) units, gave a consistent response of one type or another across the entire visible spectrum. (Recordings of this kind from horizontal cells have since been called S—for Svaetichin—potentials.) Although Svaetichin thought at first that his recordings were from cones (which if true would have verified Hering's wildest

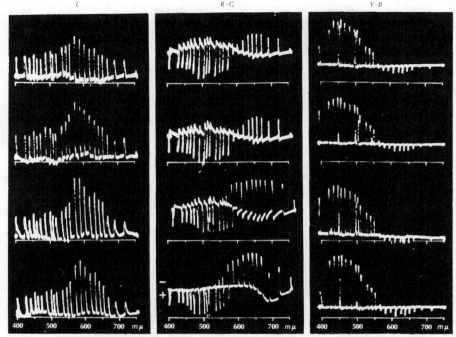

FIGURE 7.8 These are the first opponent-color curves obtained by electrophysiological methods. Sample responses from the nonopponent (luminosity) units are also shown at the left. (Svaetichin, 1956.)

speculations), the use of intracellular dye injection a couple of years later in a study by MacNichol and Svaetichin indicated that the recordings were in fact coming from horizontal cells.[13]

The C potentials divided themselves statistically into two classes, which Svaetichin was quick to label r-g and y-b. He was also quick to see the relation of what he had discovered to opponent-color theory. It has now been established in cold-blooded vertebrates that horizontal cells of the C type receive inputs from more than one type of cone; this has been shown by chromatic adaptation, which selectively eliminates almost all of the input to the cell excepting that from one of the two cone types.

It seems almost self-evident that the C-type horizontal cells must play an important role in creating opponent color responses by somehow extracting the difference in the outputs of the two types of cones to which they apparently connect. But how? The answer is not really known, but a plausible scheme for the goldfish has recently been worked out by Stell and his colleagues. (In goldfish, unlike primates, the different cone types have a distinct morphology, so that it is anatomically possible to distinguish them.) Figure 7.9 shows Stell's conception of how the opponent signals might be extracted in his preparation.

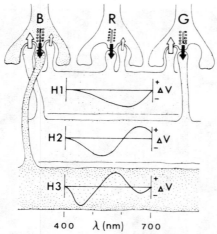

FIGURE 7.9 Stell's (1976) conception of how C-type horizontal cells in the goldfish acquire their response characteristics. The black arrows from the R, G, and B cones are intended to represent the input from cones to horizontal cells H1, H2, and H3. The broadband horizontal cell H1 in this model receives input only from R cones and shows no opponency. But H1 feeds back upon all three types of cones and this action is assumed to be inhibitory, of a magnitude suggested by the size of the white arrows. Consequently for long wavelengths the inhibitory action (mediated by H1) of the R cones upon the G cones results at long wavelengths in a net reduction in the response of G, and therefore H2. This produces the spectrally opponent response of H2, which is a C-type horizontal cell. Similar principles produced a triphasic response of H3. (From Stell, Lightfoot, Wheeler, & Leeper, 1976.) Stell and Lightfoot (1975) show a similar model, except that the feedback is directly from one horizontal cell to another and is not assumed to alter the response of the cones. That model is easier to reconcile with the unidirectional responses of Fig. 7.6.

Presumably there are C-type horizontal cells in the human retina, where they also play a similar role. But there is unfortunately no direct evidence whatsoever of this. Also lacking are records from bipolar and amacrine cells of the sort displayed for the mudpuppy in Figure 4.10. What can be said for certain is this: in primates, there is no evidence of an opponent response in the receptors. There is clear evidence, as we shall shortly see, of such responses in the firing patterns of the retinal ganglion cells. Somehow the outputs of the three cone types are processed by the intervening neural network to create this opponency, as well as nonopponent responses, which are found in many other ganglion cells. Moreover, the receptive field properties of the ganglion cells, to be discussed shortly, do not arise full blown because of inherent properties of ganglion cells alone. These properties demand that the outputs of the various cone types be assembled across a lateral extent of the retina, and then that they be highly organized by the intervening neurons to produce the fields of excitation and inhibition that ganglion cells display. To say any more about this, where the human retina is concerned, would be to indulge in idle speculation. This is an area where intracellular records from primates are badly needed to fill an important gap in our knowledge about the basis of human color vision. So far, such records have proved impossible to get.

PROJECTIONS TO THE BRAIN

The general outlines of organization of the visual brain have been known for a long time and are available in many standard texts. Very briefly, it goes like this. Optic nerve fibers, which are the axons of the retinal ganglion cells, run to four major places in the brain before terminating at a synapse. About 70 percent of these fibers go to the lateral geniculate nucleus (LGN) of the thalamus (Fig. 7.10). This is an important place for color vision, and it is the only terminus for ganglion cell axons that need concern us here.

At first glance, the LGN looks like a simple "relay station" and historically it has often been so considered. About half the optic nerve fibers from each eye cross the midline of the head at the optic chiasm, and each of the lateral geniculate nuclei (one on each side) receives input from both eyes. The LGN has a laminated structure, whose alternate layers also contain cell bodies of the postsynaptic elements that receive input from optic nerve fibers. Messages from the two eyes are segregated in separate layers, and there appears to be little or no interocular interaction. The number of postsynaptic fibers emerging from each LGN, heading for the visual cortex, is of the same order—a million or so—as the number that enter from both eyes.

On purely logical grounds it must be assumed that the idea of the LGN as a simple relay station is false. Long axons of nerve cells are capable of carrying impulses over very long distances without decrement. (In a tall person, for example, axons carrying efferent [motor] messages from the spinal cord, to activate muscles in the feet, may be a meter in length.) The function of the LGN remains stubbornly obscure. It probably does provide the first opportunity in the major pathways of the primate visual nervous system for the afferent sensory message to be altered by feedback from other centers in the brain, presumably "higher" ones. There is little evidence to show whether or how chromatic messages might be altered, although cooling the visual cortex has been shown to produce some quantitative changes (Hull, 1968).

The LGN is "topologically organized." This means that it is possible to predict with some accuracy where messages initiated in a particular region of the retina will be received at the LGN. This high degree of organization of the LGN is surely a boon to the electrophysiologist who wishes to sink his electrode so as to encounter a cell connected to a particular region of the retina. Since the visual system surely did not evolve for the convenience of electrophysiologists, the topography of the LGN must have some other but as yet unknown significance.

Fibers from the LGN project to a region of the occipital cortex (outer layer

230 The Encoding of Color

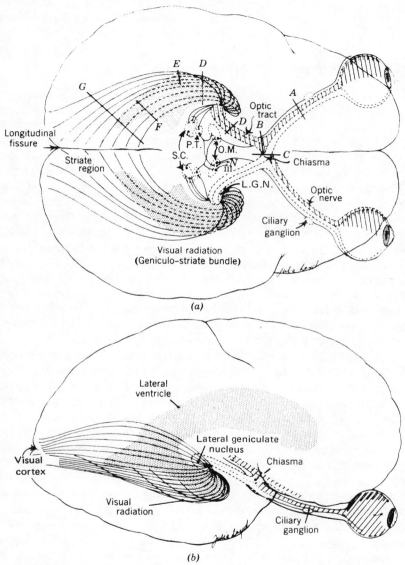

FIGURE 7.10 **Top:** Central visual pathways as seen from above (or below) with the outline of the brain also shown. L.G.N. represents the lateral geniculate nucleus. Pathways involving the pretectum (P.T.), superior colliculus (S.C.) and the oculomotor nuclei (O.M.) subserve visual functions not believed to mediate sensation (such as control of the pupil and eye position). These are not discussed in this book. **Bottom:** side view of the sensory pathways. (From Brown, 1965, as modified from Fox and German, 1936.)

of the brain at the back of the head) known variously as "area 17," "primary visual cortex," or "striate region." Although this area of the brain might seem to be very high up in the cerebral scheme of things, it probably is not. For example, it is known that a cell in this area cannot tell the difference between whether the eye or the external world has moved (Wurtz, 1969). Yet our perception of a stable external visual world survives despite very complicated movements of our head and eyes. Similarly, the activity of units that carry a chromatic code in area 17 seems unlikely to be directly related to the immediate precursors of consciousness. Nevertheless, area 17 has a very specific topological relation to areas of the LGN and consequently also to the retina and the visual field. In particular, it seems to be the place where messages from the two eyes are brought together for comparison, because many of the cells there respond to stimuli to either eye delivered from the same location in visual space. However, none of the few chromatic units (see below) that have been tested for binocularity responds to stimuli delivered to both eyes.[14]

The visual cortex provides a kind of map of the retinal image, but a complex and greatly distorted one. For example, an enormous cortical area corresponds to the miniscule portion of the retina that constitutes the foveal region (recall from Chapter 4 that this is the region where cones are packed at a very high density, and which is most critical for detailed spatial vision). If a given distance in the primary visual cortex were related to a just-discriminable distance in the lateral visual world, the existing arrangement is roughly what would be expected.

SINGLE-UNIT ELECTROPHYSIOLOGY

We have seen that there is only modest variability within the three subclasses of cone types whose slow potentials can be recorded intracellularly in the fish.(This is fortunate, because such records are very difficult to get.) Ganglion cell responses, and those of the LGN and cortex, are quite a different matter. The diversity of firing patterns from cell to cell is astonishing. Little if any appreciation of how information is processed in any part of the visual nervous system can be obtained by looking at the behavior of just a few cells. Instead, hundreds of them are typically sampled, even to produce one publishable study. This permits the determination of a statistical distribution of cells of various types. The problem is complicated by the diversity of stimuli (sometimes called "trigger features") that must be tried in order to obtain a maximum response from cell to cell. For example, when a large field of light is delivered to the eye, a particular unit very well might fail to respond at all. In other words, its resting level of discharge (which is seldom zero) simply does not change when such a field is flashed on and off. But the cell is not blind: it might, for example, respond vigorously to a green slit moving in a particular direction within a restricted region of the visual field.

Because not all experimenters use the same criteria for classifying cells, the interpretation of single-unit data is often very difficult. Yet *some* kind of classification scheme is desperately needed; otherwise the experimental reports would become an endless litany of individual records. In most publications, sample data and records are shown that are believed to be representative of cells of particular types. The numbers of such cells of this-and-that type are reported. There is no way that the reader of the literature can see the raw data. Where classification is concerned, the judgment of the experimenter must be relied upon, and the procedures used are seldom totally objective.

Fortunately for those who need to record from hundreds of cells in order to report a single "experiment," it is not necessary for the microelectrode to penetrate such units in order to record the activity of only one of them. The spikelike discharge of such a cell can be recorded if the electrode tip is merely near to it. Moreover, even if the electrode should pick up activity from two or more cells, the amplitude of the spikes as "seen" from the particular position of the electrode is likely to be quite different, and the probability of exactly superimposed spikes fairly low. Either electronically or by eye, the responses of the constituent units can usually be picked out of such a record. Moreover, a series of cells is often encountered on a single electrode penetration, as the electrode tip is advanced very slowly through the tissue.

One more caveat about single-unit records must be mentioned. There is unquestionably a sampling problem to worry about. The larger a cell, the more likely it is to be found. Moreover, the complete analysis of a unit—for example, the determination of its spectral sensitivity and other properties—may take half an hour or even longer. Many units are "lost" before such procedures can be completed, and there may be a selective bias regarding which cell types can be "held" for long periods. It is therefore likely that many more data have come from large rather than from small cells in the visual system. If the small cells have particularly unique roles to play in visual processing, those roles might not be well studied. Considering all of these problems, the agreement among various studies of chromatic units is more impressive than are the discrepancies.

CHROMATIC MECHANISMS IN THE LATERAL GENICULATE NUCLEUS

The essential feature of a "chromatic mechanism" is that it should display a capacity to react differently to two stimuli having unequal spectral distributions, regardless of their relative intensities. Figure 7.11 shows an excellent example of this, recorded from a single cell in the LGN of a macaque monkey. In this experiment, a standard wavelength of 593 nm was suddenly changed to one of four other test wavelengths. (Shifting from the standard to a test field of the same wavelength, delivered through a second optical channel, was also included as a control, since in the absence of substitution artifacts this procedure should be equivalent to steady presentation of the standard.) For this cell, substitution

Chromatic Mechanisms in the Lateral Geniculate Nucleus   233

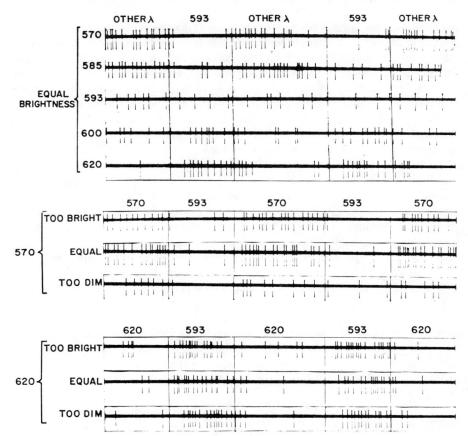

FIGURE 7.11 Firing pattern of a single cell in the LGN, probably of the r-g type, which reacts well to shifts in wavelength but is indifferent to shifts in luminance. (From De-Valois, Jacobs, & Abramov, 1964.)

of a shorter wavelength caused an increase in the firing rate when the test light was present, whereas substitution of a longer wavelength caused a decrease. These effects survived a ninefold range of relative intensities, without showing any significant change in the response pattern; equal luminance (as established behaviorally in the monkey) is near the middle of that range.

Although it is not absolutely certain that a cell responding in this manner has any role to play in the monkey's color perception, such an inference is not unreasonable. Indeed, once the behavior of such a cell is established and correlated with the stimulus, the experimenter can tell, by looking at the spikes on his oscilloscope, in which direction the wavelength shift occurred. At the same time, however, there are other units that behave in just the reverse fashion, showing a decrease in response rate to a shift toward shorter wavelengths, and vice versa. Therefore, if an experimenter were to encounter such a unit for the first time in a random penetration of the LGN, assuming that he knew nothing about the stimulating conditions, he would have no idea what the response might mean. Indeed, it could have come in response to an intensity change from a "broad band, nonopponent" cell (to be discussed below). The same thing must be true from the perspective of the unit of Figure 7.11.

The LGN is in no sense the "seat" of chromatic sensation. We know this, because removal of part of area 17 of the visual cortex, to which the LGN postsynaptic fibers project, results in virtually complete blindness to stimuli in the corresponding region of visual space, and color vision is lost even though the LGN may be intact and functional. (This finding does not make area 17 the "seat" of anything either, since, for all we know, its output may have to go somewhere else in order for visual sensations to take place.) Somewhere, it must be asssumed, there are cells whose activity somehow directly underlies conscious visual experience. But such units are surely not in the LGN, and therefore the single unit of Figure 7.11 cannot by itself reveal anything about the properties of the stimulus that caused it to become excited.

Most of the early work on chromatic cells was done in the LGN. Subsequent research has revealed no important differences between LGN and retinal ganglion cell responses to light (De Monasterio & Gouras, 1975; Marrocco, 1972). Because no obvious alteration in the form of chromatic information occurs at the LGN, evidence from retinal ganglion cells and LGN can be considered collectively. Because evidence from macaque monkeys is both available and relevant, only this evidence will be considered here.

Pioneering Work of DeValois

The pioneering work in this field was done by R. L. DeValois and his collaborators.[15] Almost all of the early work from his laboratory was undertaken with large diffuse fields of monochromatic light, to which LGN single units were found to be marvelously responsive. It proved possible to fit most of the results into a scheme essentially like that of the model presented earlier in this chapter. Some cells were found that apparently carried a red-green code. By comparison with their level of activity in the dark, such a cell might, for example, discharge more vigorously in response to long wavelengths delivered to the eye and less so for short ones. DeValois called these "+R −G" cells. A plot of spike frequency vs wavelength from such a cell exhibited a pattern something like a single cycle of a sine or cosine wave, with a "crossover" wavelength somewhere intermediate in the spectrum, where the stimulus was ineffective no matter what its intensity. For the r-g cells, this wavelength was most often in the neighborhood of 600 nm.

Figure 7.12 is from a major study based on diffuse field stimulation and recordings from the LGN of the macaque monkey; the legend gives the classification scheme. The procedure used was to irradiate the retina with spectral

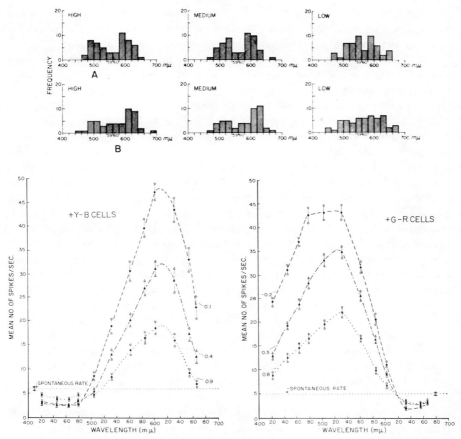

FIGURE 7.12 **Top:** Frequency distributions of crossover wavelengths for LGN single units. **Bottom:** Firing patterns for +Y −B and +G −R units, based on average data for cells with crossover wavelengths of less than 559 nm (left) or 560 nm or greater (right). (From DeValois et al., 1966.)

light for one-second intervals, separated by equal intervals of darkness. Counts were made of the firing rates in a number of such intervals and averages were taken. A total of 147 cells was sampled. About two thirds of these displayed opponent-color characteristics, many of the sort just described; the remainder responded in the same way to all wavelengths—some cells by increasing, and some by decreasing their spontaneous discharge rate. These were called "broadband, nonopponent cells."

In order to produce the curves of Figure 7.12, it was first necessary to decide into which of six categories a particular cell belonged. For the opponent cells, there was never any ambiguity about deciding whether a cell was excitatory to long wavelengths or inhibitory to short ones. Both classes were in fact found, in about equal numbers. But a problem exists regarding the classification of cells into r-g and y-b categories.

We have seen that for each cell there is always some intermediate wavelength for which no reliable change in impulse frequency occurs relative to what is recorded during the dark interval. This crossover wavelength divides the spectrum into two regions having an opposite effect, so that curves like those of Figure 7.12 cross the spontaneous-rate baseline. Operating in isolation, such a cell would be capable of discriminating whether the stimulus that produced its response was longer or shorter than the crossover wavelength. Within each of the spectral regions divided by that wavelength, however, any further change in wavelength could be mimicked by a change in intensity, so that the chromatic discriminating capacity of such a cell would be very gross. But if such cells existed in as few as two classes, corresponding to the r-g and y-b opponent processes of the model presented earlier in this chapter, then trichromacy and full color discrimination could be preserved in the form of only three signals: one from r-g opponent pathways, a second from y-b opponent pathways, and a third from the achromatic, nonopponent pathways, assuming that each is delivered to higher centers that know, somehow, what they are supposed to be looking at. Is this how it really works?

Not quite. The top of Figure 7.12 shows that the crossover wavelengths are in fact widely distributed throughout the spectrum. The distribution is, however, bimodal, especially for units excited by wavelengths at medium and high intensities of stimulation. There is one mode at about 500 nm, which defines the most probable crossover wavelength for y-b opponent units, and another at about 600 nm, which characterizes the r-g opponent cells. DeValois et al. chose 560 nm as a criterion for deciding into which of these two categories to place a particular unit. Any cell having a crossover wavelength of 560 nm or greater was assigned to the r-g category, while a unit with a crossover wavelength of 559 nm or less was placed in the y-b group.

Units of each type were driven with stimuli of three energy levels, as shown in Figure 7.12, which displays average data for all of the units assigned to each class. (The curves for +B −Y and +R −G cells are similar, but much flatter.)

If the data of Figure 7.12 are taken at face value, they say the following: The intensity and color of a particular light is signalled by a change in the resting level of activity in six kinds of units at the LGN. These fit into three categories (if the sign of the change is ignored) corresponding to the r-g, y-b, and L components of the opponent-color model described earlier.

Now is the time to ask some further questions about the meaning of this important work. Imagine yourself locked up in the LGN, surrounded by meters indicating the frequency of spike activity in a million neural units there. Would you be able to deduce the color of an external stimulus on the basis of changes in the readings of those meters? Surely not, unless they were organized, grouped, and tagged in some reasonable way. No certain conclusion could be drawn from the sampling of two units, one from each side of 560 nm. Only if large populations of them were sampled could any deductions be made. If this were the case, an individual locked up inside the LGN would be able to gauge the luminance and the wavelength of any monochromatic light, and in general the chromaticity and luminance of any light in general. Given the spread of crossover wavelengths actually observed, which could result from different proportions of R and G cone input to various ganglion cells, such judgements could still be made, but surely with somewhat reduced accuracy.

It is hard to decide whether the large spread of crossover wavelengths found by DeValois is a attributable to an error in nature's design or in DeValois's technique. We are left with no clear understanding of the functional significance, if any, of such variability.

Another question about this work relates to the types of cones that provide input to these cells. In a study in which the techniques of chromatic adaptation and silent substitution (see p. 322) were employed, Abramov (1968) concluded that the r-g units received their input from only R and G cones, and that the y-b units receive input from only R and B cones. This arrangement differs from that of the model presented in this chapter, where the longwave input ascribed to the y-b system arises from the luminance signal which, in turn, is derived from both R and G cones. Although there is little dispute about the nature of the r-g pathways, the physiological evidence for the y-b system is at best equivocal. Neither of the two techniques used seems capable of providing a definitive answer. We saw in Chapter 6 that chromatic adaptation works at more than one level: therefore it is not clear exactly what a spectral sensitivity curve means, when obtained from a given LGN unit, if the eye is strongly adapted to chromatic light. It is not necessarily to be expected that such a curve will reveal the spectral sensitivity of only one of the contributing cone types. The problem is made very difficult by the spread of crossover wavelengths that has been described, and the fact that, because of the overlap in the spectral sensitivities of the R and G cones, the difference in relative spectral sensitivity between the sum of R + G function and that of R or G alone is not very great. Moreover, the proper use of the silent substitution technique requires that the spectral sensitivities of the cone-type that is silenced must be exactly known. Unfortunately, this was not the case at the time this work was undertaken by Abramov.

Finally, the conclusions to be drawn from these studies are limited by an important complication to be discussed in the next section, concerning the complex interactions between spatial and chromatic vision that are noticed only when stimuli smaller than those used in DeValois's early work are employed.

Phasic vs Tonic Cells.

Gouras (1968) has pointed out an important difference between opponent and nonopponent cells in addition to their receptive field organizations and responses to color. Nonopponent cells (the broad-band units of DeValois) tend to produce responses that are phasic in character. This means that the recorded spikes occur transiently after the onset or extinction of the test stimulus. Opponent cells, on the other hand, are tonic, meaning that they tend to respond continuously in the presence of an appropriate stimulus. Gouras believes that messages from the cones that are delivered to tonic cells get there by way of the midget-bipolar-cell system, whereas signals going to phasic ganglion cells are delivered through the diffuse bipolars, which receive input from a large number of receptors over a relatively large area. This dichotomy is based on the following observations: (1) midget bipolars are more numerous in the central fovea, where color vision is most highly developed; (2) the central receptive field of opponent units is very small; (3) their spikes tend to be of a lower amplitude than those from nonopponent cells. The tonic–phasic dichotomy should be kept in mind, for it helps to explain certain observations concerning temporal differences when achromatic and chromatic pathways are isolated psychophysically (Chapter 9).

RECEPTIVE FIELD ORGANIZATION

The concept of the "receptive field" has its origin in a paper published by another Nobel laureate, H. K. Hartline, in 1938. Recording from ganglion cells in the retina of the frog, Hartline discovered that such a cell was responsive to a wide region of the retina. For each cell, a location on the retina could be found for which the cell responded most vigorously. As a small light probe was moved away from the region of optimal response, the intensity required to maintain the response increased. For the most distant spots used, 1000 times as much light was required to elicit a given level of response. The nature of the preparation was such that stray light could not have caused such a result. The conclusion drawn was that a particular retinal ganglion cell was connected, via interneurons, to many receptors. Today we would call this an "excitatory receptive field." It can be represented graphically as a bell-shaped curve of sensitivity (reciprocal of the radiance required to elicit a constant response) plotted as a function of location on the retina or in the visual field.

The discovery by Kuffler, and independently by Barlow (both in 1953) that ganglion cell responses of the cat and frog could be either excitatory or inhibitory, depending upon the placement of the light in the visual field, was another landmark in the history of visual science. These findings have subsequently been extended to a wide variety of species, including the macaque monkey, and to recordings from the visual brain as well as the retina. The basic findings are ubiquitous, so much so that it has proved possible to work out the quantitative principles of receptive field organization on the lowly *Limulus;* this work

Receptive Field Organization   239

by (Ratliff and Hartline) still stands as the most comprehensive quantitative treatment of the subject.[16]

Briefly, the story goes as follows: After a single cell is isolated (say a retinal ganglion cell) the experimenter moves a small flashing spot around in the visual field until he locates the region of maximum activity. For a train of light pulses of 1-s duration, separated by equal intervals of darkness (as used by DeValois in his experiments just reviewed), this activity occurs either when the light comes on, or after it is turned off. If the first of these occurs, the unit is said to have an "excitatory center," the second is called "inhibitory." If, for an excitatory center, the stimulus spot is concentrically enlarged, the response at light onset grows more vigorous until some optimal spot size is reached. Beyond this size, the vigor of the response decreases with further increases in spot size. In some cases it may cease altogether; in other instances very large spots may cause the response to occur to the onset of darkness, rather than to the onset of the light pulse itself.

Another way to explore the receptive field organization is to maintain the small size of the test spot, while systematically moving it around in the visual field. Consider as an example a spot of optimal size for center excitation. Any movement of the spot reduces the response. A position can be found where

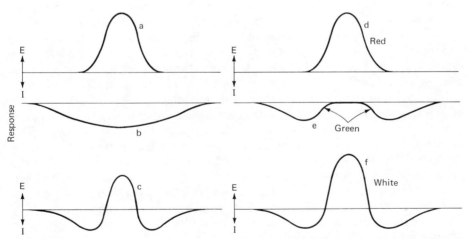

FIGURE 7.13 Two ways in which a receptive field with an excitatory center and inhibitory surround can be constructed. For a nonopponent unit, at the left, all wavelengths reveal an excitatory center (top), a broad inhibition that includes both center and surround (middle), and a resultant "Mexican hat" sensitivity (bottom) with the classical excitatory center and inhibitory surround. A red-green cell, at the right, shows an excitatory center (but only to longwave light) and an inhibitory surround (which does not include the center) only to shortwave light. A large red field of any size will produce excitation, due to the center, and a large green field of any size will produce inhibition, due to the surround.

the response disappears altogether. Then a relatively large surrounding area is discovered in which the "sign" of the response definitely reverses and the discharge is in response to darkness, rather than to light.

What has just been described is an example of a cell having an "excitatory center and inhibitory surround." Cells of the opposite sort are found, with about equal frequency, that have "inhibitory centers and excitatory surrounds." The implication of these findings is that each receptor is functionally connected to many ganglion cells and also that each ganglion cell receives input that begins in the activity of many receptors. It may be assumed that one of the functions of the horizontal and amacrine cells is to provide these connections.

The functional significance of these arrangements is illustrated schematically in Figure 7.13 where a cell with excitatory center is used as an example. The figure shows two overlapping receptive fields—one (a) excitatory with a high central peak and narrow lateral extent, and a second inhibitory one (b) with a poorly defined central peak and broad lateral extent. These combine to produce what has been called a "Mexican hat" function (c).

What is the purpose of this arrangement? A great deal of theory and experiment has led to a consensus: the purpose is to provide a neural enhancement of contour. Suppose that, instead of a circular spot, we have an edge function on the retina, with light on one side of the edge and darkness on the other. The response of an on-center ganglion cell to such an edge can be predicted as the edge is moved across the retina. When the edge is far away, the response of the cell is minimal, since both its excitatory center and inhibitory surround are equally unstimulated. As the bright edge enters the inhibitory surround field of the cell, the resting level of activity of the unit will be reduced. As the bright edge intrudes further into the cell's receptive field, so that a portion of it now stimulates the excitatory center, the inhibition will be canceled and the response rate will return to its resting level. Further incursion increases response rate as the central receptive field is progressively filled with light. This rate reaches a maximum as the bright edge moves across the excitory center to fill it completely and then, as it begins to irradiate the surround field on the other side, the response is reduced again. Finally, as both the center and surround fields are fully filled with light, the activity level will decrease again and may not differ appreciably from what the cell "sees" during darkness. The details would depend on the relative areas under curves of the sort shown in Figure 7.13.

Even if the edge of light does not literally move, the consequence of this receptive field organization is to provide a neural enhancement of such an edge represented as a series of messages, each coded in terms of impulse frequency, in a lateral series of ganglion cells. (Each cell is assumed to have a more or less similar receptive field organization, although such fields are smallest for foveal stimuli and are larger in the periphery.) We know that edges fade from view if the retinal image is artificially stabilized, and we also know that the eye is nor-

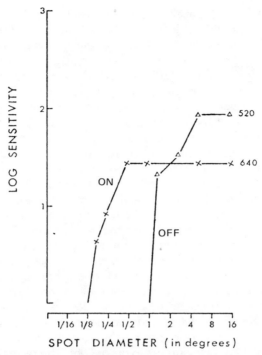

FIGURE 7.14 Behavior of a LGN cell exhibiting a red excitatory center and a green inhibitory surround. Figure at left shows how an on-response (excitatory) grows with spot diameter, levelling off after ½°. The off-response (inhibitory) to green light cannot be recorded until the spot is 1° in size; it then increases as the spot is further enlarged to 4°, stabilizing thereafter. (From Wiesel & Hubel, 1966.)

mally always in motion, even during attempted fixation. Therefore it appears probable that the edge enhancement provided by receptive field organization results in part from the increased activity of each cell as the image sweeps across it.

RECEPTIVE FIELDS AND THE CHROMATIC CODE

Although large white fields do not elicit much of a response from a retinal ganglion cell, large chromatic ones do, as we saw in the work of DeValois, who used very large fields. Why is this? The answer, which to a first approximation at least turns out to be rather straightforward, was first suggested by the results of an important experiment by Wiesel and Hubel (1966). Many—probably most—of the opponent cells in the LGN (and retinal ganglion cells as well) have a chromatically as well as spatially opponent organization. For example, suppose the basic experiment initially described above is repeated, but now with a red rather than a white test spot. As the area of the spot is increased, the vigor of the response increases until it reaches a maximum that defines the limit of the excitatory center for the cell being examined (Fig. 7.14). But unlike the case for white light, a further enlargement of the test spot has little or no additional effect. Probing the field with a spot exactly the size of the excitatory center would probably reveal that the surround is essentially uninterested in such a spot; it fails to react to it one way or another. Recall that this situation is very different from that for a white spot, where probing the surround would cause an inhibitory response.

Now repeat the experiment, this time using a green rather than a red probe. This time it is found that the central field, of a size that was defined by the red spot, is not interested in green light. But as the spot is enlarged (or the smaller probe is moved into the surround field) the resting level of activity is reduced: this same unit is inhibited by green light in the surround field.

Now we can understand DeValois's success with large stimulus fields, and why a particular unit responds in the way it does. If red light is used, an excitatory response is obtained that comes from the central field (Fig. 7.13d). The red light present in the surround field has no effect one way or another. However, as the wavelength is shifted and a large green field is used, an inhibitory response is recorded. This response comes from the surround field only (e), since the central field is unresponsive to green light. The receptive field structure is shown in Figure 7.13, at the right. The resulting "Mexican hat" (f) is not very different from that produced by white light from a nonopponent unit (c).

Suppose now that we have a contour formed by a chromatic, rather than a luminance, difference. Visualize a large field that is red on one side and green on the other, with the relative radiances adjusted for equal luminance. (Electrophysiologically, this could in principle be confirmed by locating one of DeValois's broad-band cells, and showing that it has no response as the chromatic contour is moved through its receptive field.) How will the cell described above, with its excitatory red center and inhibitory green surround, react to the movement of this contour through the field?

Consider that the red side of the split stimulus fills the entire receptive field of the cell and that the green side of the field is still very far away. The result will be an excitatory response, mediated by the red center of the cell's receptive field. As the edge is moved, the green region will eventually begin to encroach on the cell's surround field. Since the surround is inhibitory to green light, the excitatory response, still mediated by red light on the central field, will be reduced somewhat. As the chromatic edge moves farther and includes part of the central field, the response will be further reduced not only by added surround inhibition, but also because of excitatory loss as red is removed from the center. As the edge moves farther to include all of the central field, the net response will be inhibitory, since the excitatory contribution from the center is completely eliminated. Finally, as the edge moves to include the remainder of the inhibitory surround, the response becomes fully inhibitory.

The change just described will be smooth and gradual, with no basis for an edge enhancement of the sort described for white light. Nevertheless, this cell has accomplished something very important. It has signalled the presence of a border which, in a color-blind system (or cell, as in the case of a broad-band nonopponent unit) would not be visible. In addition, if the field is large, it carries a message about color: excitation for long wavelengths, and inhibition for short ones.

There is reason to believe that *all* information about chromatic contour may be mediated by red-green cells of the sort just described, if their counterparts with green excitatory centers are also included. The evidence for this, which is mainly psychophysical in nature, will be given in Chapter 9. For any reader who may have felt that in a book supposedly devoted to color too much emphasis has been placed on spatial vision, it should be pointed out that we have now arrived at the clearest reason yet why it is absolutely necessary to do so. For what we are discussing here is a situation where cells apparently have the dual function of signaling contour as well as color.

A cell like the one just described can respond equally well to a small white spot or large red field. It will not respond well to a large white field. It will respond in an inhibitory fashion to a large green field, or a white (or green) annulus. And, as described above, it will respond to a chromatic edge with either excitation or inhibition, depending upon the location of a red-green contour that is presented anywhere in its visual field.

How can such a cell tell which of these various events has caused its re-

Table 7.1. Classification of responses from two cells.

Characteristics of the spot	Response of a red–green cell	Response of a broad-band cell
Small white	+ (−)	+ (−)
Small green	0 (−)	+ (−)
Small red	+ (0)	+ (−)
Large white	0 (0)	0 (0)
Large green	− (−)	0 (+)
Large red	+ (+)	0 (0)

The red-green cell has an excitatory red center and an inhibitory green surround. The broad-band cell has an excitatory center and an inhibitory surround to all wavelengths. Small spots are assumed just to fill the center of the excitatory fields. Large spots include the center and the surround as well. A + indicates that the cell will respond by increasing its firing rate to the stimulus indicated; a − indicates that the response will be inhibitory (decreased rate), and a 0 means that there will be no change in the resting level of response. Conjointly, the two cells can differentiate all of these, excepting small red vs small white spots. But if these are allowed to move slightly (symbols in parentheses) even these conditions can be discriminated.

sponse? As noted on page 236, it cannot. Although such a single cell is probably a chromatic "mechanism," in the same sense as the receptors are, it nevertheless suffers from color-blindness much as does a single type of cone. The meaning of its message, for form and for color, must require a comparison of its activity with that of its neighbors. The simultaneous presence of broad-band nonopponent cells gives us a clue as to how this might happen. Consider a comparison of the outputs of a red-green cell of the type just described and a broad-band cell having an excitatory center and inhibitory surround. A small white spot will excite both cells. A large white spot will excite neither cell. A small red spot will excite both cells. A small green spot will excite only the broad-band cell. A large red spot will excite the red-green cell and fail to activate the broad-band cell. Just these two cells, if their outputs can be compared, can tell whether the spot is large or small. If the spot is large, it is now possible to deduce whether it is red or green. If the spot is small, it may be red, or white. These various possibilities are summarized in Table 7.1.

There are, in truth, other kinds of cells besides those that have been described that are found both in LGN and the ganglion cell layer of the retina. Only a few of these complications will be discussed here because it is difficult to understand the function of most of them, except in the most general terms. By various techniques, especially through the use of chromatic adaptation, De Monastario, Gouras, and Tolhurst (1975) have shown that many cells that might be classified as pure red-green opponent units actually receive an input from B cones, usually operating in concert with an input from R or G cones in the surround field of the unit. Gouras (as well as Padmos and van Norren, 1975) questions DeValois's division of opponent cells into red-green and yellow-blue categories, suggesting instead that units receiving input from B cones always receive input from both R and G cones as well. Wiesel and Hubel also find many cells with a blue-cone input that fail to fit the y-b opponent-cell model of DeValois. Padmos and van Norren also show that, with chromatic adaptation, many of the so-called nonopponent cells in fact show clear opponent-color properties. It seems clear that DeValois's classification scheme will require substantial revision in the years ahead.

Somehow, at some level of the brain, comparisons among the outputs of the various cell types must be made, and in these comparisons is contained the information whereby the spatial and chromatic codes, still entwined at the single cell level in the LGN, can be unraveled.

VISUAL CORTEX

In an early study of units in area 17 of the monkey, Hubel and Wiesel (1968) were surprised to find that less than 10 percent of the cells sampled seemed to show any chromatically specific characteristics. A number of studies carried out since that time indicate that this figure must be revised sharply upward. In a recent study (as yet unpublished)[17] Gouras and Kruger used a red square against a green background; the red square was moved across the background and it was determined whether some relative luminance of square and background could be found such that the cell would cease to be responsive to the motion. For some cells this is exactly what happened, but there were many others that responded to all relative radiances, so long as the chromatic difference remained, and still others that actually responded much *more* vigorously to chromatic differences at equal luminance than even to huge intensity differences. Overall, 54 percent of the cells sampled responded to either brightness or color differences and of these 71 percent were excited more strongly by brightness than by color contrast. Whereas 40 percent responded only to brightness and not at all to color, there were only 6 percent that responded to color and not brightness. These percentages are in substantial agreement with figures from a study of Dow and Gouras (1973), who examined 122 cortical units in the foveal striate cortex, finding 58 percent that displayed chromatic characteristics. About half of these exhibited a joint color and spatial specificity, responding to slits only when they moved in specific direction, while showing a strong preference for only a restricted region of the spectrum as well.

In a similar study, Yates (1974) also reported on cells that are spatially selective, but which exhibit what he called "pure hue" sensitivity. Yates's stimuli were 470, 500, 540, 570, 600, 640, and 660 nm. These cells responded only to restricted spectral regions that tended to correspond with portions of the spectrum that a human observer would identify as the range covered by one of the four unique hues. One of Yates's cells, for example, responded only to 540 and 500 nm stimuli; another only to 600 and 640 nm stimuli, whereas all other stimuli proved incapable in each case of eliciting any response at all. In addition, Yates (as well as Dow and Gouras) found numerous opponent-color cells that (excepting their preference for moving slits of light) closely resembled such units in the geniculate or retina. Yates also found some cells that responded with chromatic specificity to full-field illumination; Dow and Gouras also report a few of these. Yates found that about half of the 51 units that he studied showed chromatic specificity; this is in reasonable agreement with Dow and Gouras.

The most extensive study of the distribution of cell types in the cortex is that of Gouras (1974), who sampled 317 cells. Of these units 59 percent were broad-band and 41 percent were narrow-band, opponent-color cells. Of the chromatic cells, 72 percent had nonoriented, nondirectional receptive fields, 9 percent had simple receptive fields, and about 4 percent had complex, nondirectional fields. Gouras included, in his opponent-color classification, an unspecified number of "pure hue" cells (by Yates's classification). Gouras also reported good data showing where, in the various layers of the striate cortex, cells of the various types are located.

It is hard to make sense of all this. Despite his vast experience in the field, the best that Gouras has been able to come up with so far is the following:

> What role a cell plays in pattern vision and what role it plays in colour is difficult to ascertain. The tendency for color opponency to diminish as spatial selectivity increases suggests that opponent-colour cells are converging on broad-band cells with higher orders of spatial complexity. Following this path opponent-colour cells would have little to contribute to colour vision although they could be useful for detecting the contrast of edges or contours formed by differences in either luminance or wavelength. Some opponent-colour cells must not follow this route but lead instead to cells involved in colour recognition and naming, but what fraction do this and how confined they are to striate cortex are questions for the future.

Part of the answer may then lie in the pursuit of color cells in other cortical areas. Zeki (1974) has found a region of the prestriate cortex where "cell after cell in a single [electrode] penetration is color coded." This work has not proceeded very far yet, but it has lead Zeki to conclude:

> ... the prestriate areas are a "single functional unit" (Lashley and Clark, 1946) only in the sense that they are visual areas. Within them, a subdivision of labour exists which is reflected in the anatomical mosaic of areas each with a different functional emphasis dependent upon the anatomical input to it. Within the mosaic of these areas there is a finer mosaic of visual field representation and re-representation, for colour after colour in some areas, contour after contour in other areas. ...

Because of its relation to some speculation that was published a long time ago, I am especially intrigued by the "pure hue" cells of Yates, which show up also (but with other names) in the similar research of others. If it is true, as Yates's results suggest, that such cells are responsive to those regions of the spectrum to which we assign one of the basic hue names, then all blends of hues could in principle be built upon the ratios of activation of such cells, assuming that all refer to the same region of visual space. If there is any truth to this viewpoint, then the majority of the cells exhibiting a chromatic code, particularly the opponent cells, are probably concerned mostly with pattern vision. They permit the perception of contours that otherwise would disappear at equal luminance.

A number of investigators have pointed out that the organization of the red−green opponent cells in the LGN is all wrong for explaining simultaneous color contrast (Chapter 10). What is required instead is a "double-opponent, red−green" cell with an excitatory red center, inhibitory green surround, and an inhibitory green center with an excitatory red surround. Recently Michael (1978) has reported clear evidence of such cells in the visual cortex of monkeys, which comprised 16 percent of the cells that he sampled that had concentric receptive fields.

The use of new stimulus patterns is producing results that are novel and difficult to relate to the kinds of stimuli to which investigators were formerly limited. For example, Thorell, Albrecht, and DeValois (1978) have equipped their laboratory with a computer-controlled color TV display upon which virtually any conceivable pattern can be generated. They have chosen to use sinusoidal patterns in space that can be comprised of pure luminance variations, pure chromaticity variations, or combinations of both. They report that 85 percent of their cells respond both to color and luminance, 10 percent respond only to luminance variations, and 1 percent respond *only to color differences*.

Twenty years ago I wrote (Boynton, 1960, p. 944):

It should not be long before the electrophysiologists, already capable of recording from single cortical cells in mammals, will turn their attention to color and begin in earnest to gather this evidence. We know ahead of time that their findings will be confusing; that single cells in the cortex generate patterns of activity that are not readily interpretable except as they relate to patterns of neighboring cells. . . ."

This prediction seems amply confirmed. Now it seems likely to me that the nature of color coding in the primate visual system will become greatly clarified within the next twenty years.

SUMMARY

Experiments are described that employ chromatic cancellation and color-naming techniques for the description of spectral colors. The remainder of the chapter is concerned with evidence regarding the neurophysiological signals that mediate these perceptions. The chapter is organized around an opponent-color model, one that will be relied upon in the remaining chapters of the book.

Intracellular records from photoreceptors and other nerve cells of the retina have been obtained from cold-blooded animals, but so far only the spikes of ganglion cells have been recorded from single units in the eyes of primates having color vision similar to that of humans. The major kinds of electrical records that can be obtained from human subjects (electroretinograms and visually evoked cortical potentials) seem too crude, at least at present, to provide critical insights. Nevertheless, they help to reify and confirm concepts that have been developed via human psychophysics and animal single-unit electrophysiology.

Photoreceptors are unusual because they are continuously active in the dark. To a first approximation, each receptor hyperpolarizes to a level related to the intensity of the light. Increments and decrements are signaled relative to that level. The three types of human cones do not differ very much from one another, although the B-cone system has response characteristics that differ greatly from the luminance channels, fed by R and G cones.

Based upon opponent-color responses that have been recorded from horizontal cells for a quarter of a century, these cells seem to have an important role to play in chromatic encoding, but the exact nature of this role is still obscure. The lateral geniculate nucleus (LGN) has been a favorite recording site in old-world primates, whose color vision, as established behaviorally, is virtually impossible to distinguish from that of man. Single units in the LGN respond well to large, diffuse chromatic stimuli, whereas large white fields are relatively ineffective. This behavior reflects a center-surround receptive-field organization that is chromatically organized.

An attempt has been made to organize evidence derived from diffuse stimulation of the retina and spike responses from the LGN into an opponent-color scheme consistent with the opponent model introduced earlier in the chapter. It is emphasized that no single cell of the LGN, or elsewhere in the brain, can carry a chromatic message unless the category to which that cell belongs is somehow specified. Many cells that appear to exhibit chromatic specificity may be as much, or even more, concerned with spatial vision. It is not known where cells are located whose activity might directly underlie chromatic sensations. The cells of the visual cortex, many of which have chromatically specific properties, are far from certain candidates.

At the present time, the evidence concerning the chromatic code of the visual nervous system is incomplete and difficult to interpret. This is seen as an area of research which, in the context of a bright and prolonged future, has barely begun.

NOTES

[1] Good discussions of the effects of electrical stimulation of eye and brain are given by Brindley, in his monograph (1970) and his technical papers (Brindley, 1962; Brindley & Lewin, 1968).

[2] There are many variations on this basic model. Some of these are summarized in the following list:

Author	Input to Luminance Channel	Input to y-b Channel
Walraven (1962)	R + G + B	(R + G) − B
Guth et al. (1969)	R + G	R − B
DeValois & DeValois (1975)	R + G	R − B
Ingling & Tsou (1977)	R + G	L − B
This chapter	R + G	L − B

[3] Predictions such as this one are always dangerous, since the technical advances of the future are probably no more predictable than those that have surprised us in the past. For a thorough summary of modern electrical recording techniques, see Thompson and Patterson (1973−1974).

[4] An excellent textbook by Armington (1974), describing all aspects of the human ERG, is now available.
[5] For a summary of this work see K. T. Brown (1968).
[6] An outstanding book on evoked potentials is that of Regan (1972). For a briefer treatment, see MacKay and Jeffreys (1973).
[7] For an up-to-date and thorough treatment of retinal neurophysiology, see Arden (1976).
[8] In referring to this issue, Granit (1947) stated, in reference to the "P-III" component of the ERG (which includes the leading edge): "Even if the retina is removed from the bulb and placed between the electrodes the direction of PIII remains the same; the inner surface of the retina becomes negative and the outer surface positive. This means, if the receptors are involved, that their free ends become positive relative to their bases when they are subjected to illumination. If we accept this conclusion we must believe that P-III differs from all the isolated receptor potentials hitherto discovered with respect to its electrical sign (p. 112, in the 1963 reprinted edition)."
[9] The first record of a waveguide pattern in a receptor was published by Enoch (1961a) from the outer segment of a macular monkey cone. Later that year (Enoch, 1961b), Enoch published a color plate showing highly chromatic patterns produced by irradiating receptors with white light. He summarized the work in 1963. At a symposium published in the *Psychological Bulletin* (1964), he cautiously suggested that these patterns might play a role in physiological color separation. As a discussant in that symposium, I (Boynton, 1964) suggested that waveguide effects result because receptors are small, which they must be for good spatial vision, and that they are just noise so far as color vision is concerned. I still hold this view, and feel that this is a major reason why chromatic signals must be averaged over substantial retinal areas in order to yield stable color perception.
[10] The first direct evidence of the distribution of R, G, and B cones in the primate retina was reported by Marc and Sperling (1977), based on a selective reaction of cones treated with nitro-blue tetrazolium chloride when stimulated with lights from various spectral regions. For the peripheral retina they found a rhomboidal pattern of B cones, and very few of them, just as Walraven had speculated. R and G cones were, however, irregularly distributed, with about twice as many G as R cones, just the opposite of Walraven's prediction.
[11] Boynton and Whitten (1972). See also van Norren and Padmos (1972).
[12] Boynton and Baron (1975).
[13] MacNichol and Svaetichin (1958). Early dye markers were crude. Dyes are now available that serve as excellent conductors in micropipette electrodes, which can be injected electrophoretically into the impaled cell and then viewed by the fluorescence induced by ultraviolet radiation. For many cells, including horizontal cells, the dye migrates into even the smallest processes of the cell without penetrating adjacent cells.
[14] Lu and Fender (1972) have made the fascinating observation that random-element stereograms (see Julesz, 1971), which are formed of elements whose contours are provided by purely chromatic differences, do not give rise to the perception of depth. The same elements, if formed by achromatic contrast differences, do elicit depth perception. This difference might imply that the stereoscopic depth caused by systematic displacement of a set of elements in one stimulus relative to another is mediated by a correlational process that requires the activity of binocularly-driven cells in the visual cortex.

[15]The first report from DeValois's laboratory was that of DeValois, Smith, Kitai, and Karoly (1958). For summaries of the extensive work of this laboratory, which moved over the years from Michigan to Indiana to California, see DeValois (1965a, 1965b, 1973) and DeValois and DeValois (1975).

[16]In a volume put together to celebrate Hartline's seventieth birthday, the papers of Hartline and his collaborators have been assembled by Ratliff (1974). The material added by Ratliff helps to make this not only the most convenient, but also the best source for Hartline's important papers.

[17]I thank Dr. Peter Gouras for permission to describe these experiments.

8
Chromatic Discrimination

This chapter will be concerned with three interrelated topics that can be expressed as questions:
- In order for two colors to be barely distinguishable as different, how different must they be?
- What is the physiological basis for such thresholds of color difference?
- Can large color differences be measured and, if so, how?

These concerns relate to problems with which many readers will have had personal experience. Anyone who has tried to replace a broken ceramic tile will know that to match it for color may be nearly impossible. Experienced painters will not permit a batch of paint to run out in the middle of a wall, even if it is a standard commercial mix, because the eye will probably see a difference between the two areas, even though the label on the replacement can reads identically to that of the original.

Another more detailed example may serve to remind readers of similar problems while pointing up the difficulty of defining a detectable color difference. I once had some carpet installed in my home, most of which was of the same blue-green hue. But at a division between hallway and dining room, the installers switched to a new roll and there was an obvious color difference—greener in the hall, bluer in the dining room. When the areas being compared are very large, as in this instance, the *eye is extremely sensitive to such color differences*. Small fields are a different matter. When I looked at the dividing line through a paper towel roll, in order to reduce the field size, the difference was barely discernible. But it fairly leapt out at me when I removed the tube and looked at the carpet in the normal way.

Suppose that I had insisted that the match between the two carpeted areas be "made right." Who then would decide when the match was close enough to be acceptable? The matter might well have landed in a small claims court, where the following scenario can be imagined.

Me: "Your honor, the carpet in my dining room does not match that in the rest of the house. I find this offensive and feel that it is my right to have it match properly."

Judge (to installer): "How do you regard the match?"

Installer: "It looks okay to me."

Me: "Judge, would you be willing to come to my home and look for yourself?"

Judge: "Your suggestion is impractical." (to installer): "Can you show me a sample of the two sections of the carpet?"

Installer: "Not without tearing them off the floor. We threw the scraps away." (I would be grateful for this, since very small scraps from the two sections might not have looked different enough to impress the judge.)

Judge: Can either of you give me some *measurement* of the amount of the color difference?"

Me: "As a matter of fact, I can. I have run a spectrophotometric curve on each section and have computed the tristimulus values for each. From this I calculated their chromaticity values on the CIE chart."

Judge (perplexed): "I must admit that I don't exactly follow what you are saying. Can you show me such a chart?"

Me: "Yes, your honor. I just happen to have one with me. (I haul it out.) This is a standard chart, one certified by the International Commission on Illumination as the proper way to represent all possible colors."

Judge: "Can you show me where the colors of the two sections of your carpet would be represented on this chart?"

Me: "Yes I can. I have done the measurements and calculations. The two points plot here and here" (I point to the chart and draw two X's on it).

Judge (astutely): "How far apart do your X's have to be, in order for the color difference to be noticeable?"

Me: "About *this* far" (I hold my thumb and forefinger very slightly apart).

Installer (reddening): "I don't understand any of this mumbo-jumbo. Believe me, your honor, the difference isn't very great. It happens all the time when we're forced to switch to a new roll. We do the best we can, and besides the difference will fade out after a while."

Judge (to installer): "Apparently then, you admit that there is a color difference. How much would it cost to eliminate it?"

Installer: "We'd have to recarpet the whole house because we'd never find another roll exactly like the first one! We thought we had enough to do the whole job, but it was hard to figure, with the crooked stairway and all. . . ."

In a case like this, even though the difference could be calculated and displayed on the CIE chromaticity chart, the judge would be in a very difficult position. We will see that, depending upon the region of the chart, equal differences are represented by very unequal distances. Moreover, if the judge were willing to inspect the difference for himself, how would he know that his perception of the difference would be the same as that of the average individual?

Manufacturers of ceramics, fabrics, paints, yarn, food, cosmetics, and other products would much prefer that incidents like this one (which are by no means rare) never occurred. The fact that such problems arise very often is only partly due to the lack of quality control of manufactured products. Because of the almost incredible sensitivity of the eye to color differences, color-sensitive devices still cannot match human vision for detecting small differences. The problem is compounded by the fact that the only safe match is a physical one, because (1) metamers may fail when the illuminant is changed and (2) different observers will not agree entirely about metameric matches under the same illumination.

CHROMATIC VS ACHROMATIC COLOR DIFFERENCES

Color differences come in two varieties and also in a combined form. *Achromatic* differences occur when the relative spectral distributions of light in the two fields being compared do not differ. In other words, the two fields differ only in luminance. As an example, imagine a circular field of light and suppose that a thin, borderless neutral filter of 50 percent transmittance is moved halfway across that field. The part of the field with the filter in front of it will have the same relative spectral radiance as the uncovered part, but only half the energy will reach the eye at all wavelengths. The main difference in appearance caused by inserting the filter will be a change in the brightness of the field, although in general (especially if the brightnesses are very different) there will also be a small associated change in hue and saturation. Whether or not these secondary changes occur, we define the difference between two such fields as an *achromatic color difference*. (An achromatic color difference will also occur for fields that match metamerically, except for the special case where their relative radiance levels yield fields of equal brightness.) Although the concept of "achromatic color" may seem strange and contradictory, it makes sense if color differences in general are said to include brightness differences as well as those of hue and saturation.[1]

A *chromatic color difference* occurs whenever the relative spectral distributions of two lights are sufficiently different that, no matter what their relative

Chromatic Discrimination

intensities, they always look different. One of the two lights may appear brighter than the other, or it may not. As an example, visualize two fields, one of which is distinctly green and the other red. Place them side by side so that they are perfectly aligned. Suppose that, to begin with, the green side is obviously very much brighter than the red one. By reducing the intensity of the green side (for example, by placing neutral filters in front of that side only), it becomes possible to make it look very much dimmer than the red. Or by placing filters in front of the red side, the green could be made relatively brighter. Throughout the entire range of such adjustment, there will be no point where the fields look alike, nor will the border that separates them ever disappear.

When this experiment is repeated with two fields having the same relative spectral energy distribution, or that match metamerically, a different result will occur. For example, remove the red field and replace it with the same physical green that is on the other side. Make one side very much brighter than the other; then gradually reduce its intensity so that it eventually becomes much dimmer than the other side. Somewhere between, the two fields will match exactly. The dividing line between them will disappear at this point, and only a single circular green field will be seen.[2] In this second example, we have a range of achromatic color differences; somewhere within this range, the two fields have equal luminances that are based upon their physical identity.

Returning now to the red-green pair, repeat the experiment. This time, pay strict attention to the border separating the fields, while trying to ignore the color difference. When the green side is very much brighter than the red, the border separating them will be very distinct. As the intensity of the green side is reduced, the distinctness of the border between the two fields grows less. At some point it becomes *minimally distinct*, but it does not disappear. Further decreases in the intensity of the green field will again cause the border to appear more distinct. In this second example, the color differences are in general comprised of both chromatic and achromatic components; the difference that remains at the minimally distinct border setting is purely chromatic.

The observed sequence:

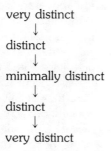

is the same as that observed for an achromatic color difference, except that, in the chromatic case, some border is usually seen at the minimally distinct point, whereas in the achromatic case the border will disappear completely.

Now suppose we pick lights of two wavelengths that are only very slightly different, such as 650 nm and 651 nm; we would like to know whether or not they are visually different. If the 650-nm field is much brighter or dimmer than the 651-nm one, there will be an obvious brightness difference and the border between the two fields will be clear and sharp. The experimental question now becomes this: at the minimally distinct border setting, will any visible difference remain? We will see later (Fig. 8.1) that, for this particular example, the answer is "no." But if we were to repeat the experiment, using 589 nm and 590 nm as the stimulus components, the answer would probably be "yes." This tells us that chromatic discriminations based on wavelength differences are more acute in the neighborhood of 590 nm than around 650 nm. But this conclusion could not be drawn unless the relative intensities of the fields being compared were carefully controlled, as in the example given. Setting a minimally distinct border is one operation that can be used to define equal luminance between any two fields. To test for a chromatic difference between two fields, it is necessary to ensure that they are equated for luminance, since this is when they differ least.[3] Only then is the difference between them a purely chromatic one.

The opponent-color model introduced in Chapter 7 provides a framework within which the concepts of achromatic and chromatic color differences can be readily interpreted. A luminance difference occurs whenever there is a difference in the output of the achromatic pathways associated with the two stimuli being compared. This difference might or might not be a discriminable one, depending upon its magnitude. A chromatic difference will occur whenever there is a difference in the outputs of at least one of the opponent-color channels, and this becomes a purely chromatic difference in the special case where there is no difference between the outputs of the luminance channels. We define a *chromatic discrimination* as depending upon purely chromatic differences; such differences will be the major concern of this chapter.

INTRODUCTION TO WAVELENGTH DISCRIMINATION

Consideration of experimental data will be postponed until the second half of this chapter, to be preceded by a discussion of some fundamental theoretical issues. But theory cannot be discussed in vacuo; as an aid to discussion, the basic experiment on wavelength discrimination will now be described. This is not intended as a description of any particular experiment, but it does indicate how such an experiment can be done, together with the expected result. Real experiments on wavelength discrimination have used many methods and have varied many parameters; accordingly they have produced many different results. But the main features of results to be described here have been noted in most such experiments.

Given a reference wavelength, λ, the problem is to determine the smallest variation in this wavelength that can just barely be detected. This amount is called $\Delta\lambda$. If this experiment is repeated for a large number of λ's, a large number of $\Delta\lambda$'s will be generated. When these are plotted, they appear to fall upon a smooth (if complicated) curve; a continuous curve drawn through these points describes the wavelength discrimination function. Results for five subjects are shown in Figure 8.1.

However, before starting such an experiment, a large number of decisions must be made.

What psychophysical method will be used? The method of adjustment has been the usual choice, although other methods have sometimes been employed. With this method, the subject could vary the wavelength by turning a knob connected to the wavelength drum of a monochromator. The wavelength drum turns a prism (or sometimes a diffraction grating) so that a slit in the projected spectrum permits the choice of a narrow band which passes out and irradiates the field of view. In the ideal case (which can be closely approached though never actually achieved), the field will be strictly monochromatic and completely uniform over its entire extent. Two such fields are required. One is the reference field, in terms of which λ is defined; the other is the variable field, to be set so that it looks just barely different from λ. It is not easy to establish and maintain a criterion of just-noticeable difference. For this reason, an alter-

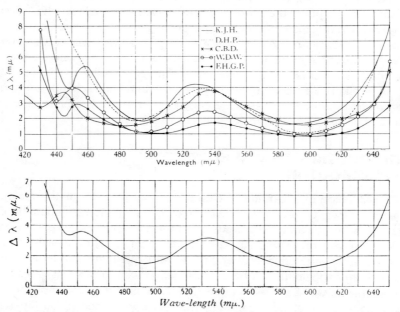

FIGURE 8.1 Wavelength discrimination functions obtained by Wright and Pitt (from Wright, 1946). The method of adjustment was used, and the intensity of the spectrum was "of the order of 70 photons [td] but was somewhat fainter in the blue." The bottom curve, which is for the mean of the five observers, is frequently reproduced as a "typical" wavelength discrimination function.

native procedure has sometimes been used, where the experimenter sets the variable field off from the reference by a substantial amount, and the subject attempts to make a match. On repeated trials, the matches he makes will vary slightly from one trial to another. A measure of dispersion of many such matches (for example, their standard deviation) can serve as an index of discriminability.

How will luminance be controlled? Ideally, when the method of adjustment is used, the luminance of the variable field should remain constant as its wavelength is changed throughout the full visible spectrum. The amount of light coming from the monochromator can be adjusted, at each wavelength, by connecting a moveable variable neutral filter (wedge) to the wavelength control in such a way as to keep the luminance constant. In an earlier era, this could only have been done mechanically, for example, by using specially devised cams and linkages. Today it could be done by programming a digital computer and interfacing it with the neutral density wedge that is used to vary intensity. Most of the older experiments did not in fact control very well for luminance. The results of such flawed experiments are nevertheless of value, because it turns out that the chromatic variation caused by changing the wavelength of light emerging from a monochromator is usually much more potent than the small luminance change which may accompany it.[4]

What values should be chosen for other parameters, such as field size, stimulus duration, relative position of the fields, and the basic luminance of the standard wavelengths? Most often, viewing has been continuous, the field size is small—on the order of a degree or two—and the fields are close together, but some dividing line usually remains when the two parts are physically identical.

Many tests of chromatic discrimination are possible other than those that depend upon variations of the wavelength of monochromatic light. For example, *saturation discrimination* experiments have tested the amount of monochromatic light required, when added to white, in order to produce a just-noticeable tinge of color difference. In general, *chromatic discrimination* can be investigated starting at any point in a chromaticity plane (recall the color triangles of Chapter 5), and chromaticity discrimination can be tested in any desired direction. Such experiments will be considered later in this chapter.

THEORETICAL DEVELOPMENT: PRELIMINARIES

Although there exists a general agreement that the initial basis for the perception of a color difference lies in the differential stimulation of three types of cones, many ideas have been proposed about the exact manner in which a threshold difference is determined. Theoretical suggestions fall generally into two classes. In the first class are theories which assume that the brain has direct access to signals reflecting the outputs of each class of cone separately, or that the receptors themselves limit the discrimination. In order for two colors to look different, according to this view, cones of at least one of the three types are required to produce differential signals that are above some kind of a threshold. Many specific versions of this class of theory are possible, depending upon how the changing outputs of the three types of cones are assumed to interact. Helmholtz favored this class of theory and gave it a geometrical form.[5] The outputs of three types of receptors can be represented as points in three-dimensional space (Fig. 8.2). In the simplest possible model used to characterize the relation between two stimuli, discrimination threshold would be reached for any change in receptor activities caused by these stimuli that yield the same distance dS between the representations of their response loci in Euclidean three-dimensional space. Such a distance is called a *line element*, and it is the aim of discrimination theories of this type to determine a set of relations that will generate line elements of the same length between just-discriminable pairs of stimuli plotted anywhere in the space, oriented in any possible direction. (A complete treatment of line-element theory is given by Wyszecki and Stiles, 1967, p. 511.)

In attempting to bring the results of line-element theory into concordance with experimental data, the chief manipulations are concerned with (1) the assumed receptor input-output relations, (2) the kind of space (Euclidean, Riemannian, and so on) in which the sensory vectors are imagined to plot, and (3) the rules according to which the distances between vector ends may be measured.[6]

On the basis of the physiological evidence that was reviewed in Chapter 7, and psychophysical evidence to be covered in Chapter 9, purely trichromatic theories of color discrimination seem highly implausible. Nevertheless, because of their historical interest, we will deal a bit further with them later in this chapter. Opponent-color theory, which will be emphasized here, does not deny the trichromacy of the first stage. As noted above, trichromatic theories assume either that (1) the higher visual centers have direct access to information about

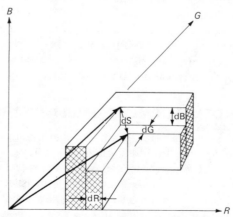

FIGURE 8.2 In this simplest possible line-element model, the threshold of color discrimination is taken to be **dS**, regardless of its position or orientation in three-dimensional Euclidean space. If **R**, **G**, and **B** represent the outputs of the R, G, and B receptors respectively, then $(dS)^2 = (dR)^2 + (dG)^2 + (dB)^2$.

the responses of the three classes of cones—the Helmholtzian view—or (2) the level of processing that limits discriminability is that of the receptor—the view of Stiles. Alternatively, by the opponent-color view, higher centers have access only to what is delivered through the three kinds of channels shown in Figure 7.3: these are the luminance channels (reflecting the summed outputs of the R and G channels) and the two kinds of chromatic channels, r-g and y-b.

CRITICAL QUESTIONS ABOUT CHROMATIC DISCRIMINATION

The topic of chromatic discrimination will now be further developed in the form of a series of questions, each to be followed by the kinds of answers that are suggested by the class of theory that includes an opponent-color stage.

1. *What activation of the R, G, and B cones is produced by an initial stimulus of spectral energy distribution $E_{1\lambda}$ (to be compared later with a second stimulus, $E_{2\lambda}$)?*

The initial action of light in vision occurs, as we saw in Chapter 5, as a result of the absorption of light by the three classes of photopigments. To the degree that the absorption spectra of the three cone classes are known, it becomes possible to translate statements about retinal illuminance distributions into a set of three absorption rates, one for each type of cone pigment. We will assume that these pigments are uniquely isolated by cone type, so that, for example, R cones contain only erythrolabe. Moreover, we will ignore bleaching, so that the relative action spectra of the three cone pigments can be assumed to be invariant. Granting these assumptions, absorption rates can be economically summarized by a set of three equations:

$$\rho = k_r \int E_{1\lambda} r_\lambda d\lambda, \tag{8.1}$$
$$\gamma = k_g \int E_{1\lambda} g_\lambda d\lambda, \tag{8.2}$$
$$\text{and } \beta = k_b \int E_{1\lambda} b_\lambda d\lambda. \tag{8.3}$$

The symbols in these equations have the following meanings:

- ρ, γ, and β (rho, gamma, and beta) are the absorption rates for photons incident upon the three classes of cones, R, G, and B.
- r_λ, g_λ, and b_λ are the relative absorption rates for the red-sensitive, green-sensitive, and blue-sensitive photopigments (erythrolabe, chlorolabe, and cyanolabe) for lights of unit energy.
- $E_{1\lambda}$ is the spectral irradiance of the retina.
- k_r, k_g, and k_b are constants.

In a limited sense, absorption is equivalent to activation, but since the receptors respond nonlinearly (and it is only their responses to which the post-receptoral neurons have access) this nonlinearity should be taken into account. Although this fact should be kept in mind, we will ignore it for now. A simple proportionality will be assumed, one which is not too far from the truth, at least

Chromatic Discrimination

for modest levels of perturbation around a mean adaptation level for a receptor. On this basis, we can substitute R_1, G_1, and B_1 (the magnitudes of the responses of the three cone types) for ρ, γ, and β in Equations (8.1) through (8.3) so that

$$R_1 = k'_r \int E_{1\lambda} r_\lambda d\lambda, \tag{8.4}$$
$$G_1 = k'_g \int E_{1\lambda} g_\lambda d\lambda, \tag{8.5}$$
$$\text{and } B_1 = k'_b \int E_{1\lambda} b_\lambda d\lambda. \tag{8.6}$$

The receptor potential would be a measurable aspect of this response. The rate at which a neurotransmitter is liberated at the cone pedicle would be another.

2. *If $E_{\lambda 1}$ is changed to $E_{\lambda 2}$, by what amounts does this change alter the activation of the R, G, and B cones?*

Before this second question can be answered, the constants k'_r, k'_g, and k'_b in Equations (8.4), (8.5), and (8.6) must be evaluated. Because the actual absorption rates are not known, the simplest thing to do is to set these constants equal to unity. Then

$$R_1 = \int E_{1\lambda} r_\lambda d\lambda, \tag{8.7}$$
$$G_1 = \int E_{1\lambda} g_\lambda d\lambda, \tag{8.8}$$
$$\text{and } B_1 = \int E_{1\lambda} b_\lambda d\lambda. \tag{8.9}$$

By using these equations, and a similar set for a second energy distribution $E_{2\lambda}$, we are now in a position to answer the second question concerning the changes produced by a wavelength shift. If ΔR, ΔG, and ΔB represent the change in responses of the R, G, and B receptors caused by the change of energy distribution, then

$$\Delta R = R_1 - R_2 = \int E_{1\lambda} r_\lambda d\lambda - \int E_{2\lambda} r_\lambda d\lambda, \tag{8.10}$$
$$\Delta G = G_1 - G_2 = \int E_{1\lambda} g_\lambda d\lambda - \int E_{2\lambda} g_\lambda d\lambda, \tag{8.11}$$
$$\text{and } \Delta B = B_1 - B_2 = \int E_{1\lambda} b_\lambda d\lambda - \int E_{2\lambda} b_\lambda d\lambda. \tag{8.12}$$

Because we are concerned with wavelength discrimination at equal luminance, the receptor output functions must each be divided by $R + G = L$.[7] If we call these new quantities R', G', and B', we may calculate them as follows for $E_{1\lambda}$:

$$R'_1 = \frac{\int E_{1\lambda} r_\lambda d\lambda}{L}, \tag{8.13}$$

$$G'_1 = \frac{\int E_{1\lambda} g_\lambda d\lambda}{L}, \tag{8.14}$$

$$\text{and } B'_1 = \frac{\int E_{1\lambda} b_\lambda d\lambda}{L}. \tag{8.15}$$

These values, which have been calculated for monochromatic lights at 10-nm steps centered on wavelengths chosen at 10-nm intervals from 400 to 680 nm, are given in Table 8.1 and are plotted in Figure 8.3. They are based upon the

TABLE 8.1. Calculations Pertaining to Hypothetical Wavelength Discrimination Mediated at Constant Luminance by Differential R-cone Responses

A Wavelength	B $R'=\dfrac{R}{R+G}$	C$_1$ $\Delta R'$ 10 nm	C$_2$ $\Delta R'$ 1 nm	D $J = 1 + \|R'-2G'\|$	E $\Delta R'/J$	F $\Delta\lambda = .004\, J/\Delta R'$
400	.600			1.20		
		.009	.0009		.00074	5.41
410	.591			1.23		
		.014	.0014		.0012	3.33
420	.577			1.27		
		.032	.0032		.0024	1.67
430	.545			1.37		
		.039	.0039		.0027	1.48
440	.506			1.48		
		.038	.0038		.0025	1.60
450	.468			1.59		
		.030	.0030		.0018	2.22
460	.438			1.68		
		0	0		0	
470	.438			1.68		
		.029	.0029		.0018	2.22
480	.467			1.60		
		.029	.0029		.0018	2.22
490	.496			1.51		
		.023	.0023		.0016	2.50
500	.519			1.44		
		.017	.0015		.0011	3.63
510	.536			1.39		
		.016	.0016		.0012	3.33
520	.552			1.34		
		.019	.0019		.0014	2.86
530	.571			1.29		
		.019	.0019		.0015	2.67
540	.590			1.23		
		.021	.0021		.0018	2.22
550	.611			1.17		
		.025	.0025		.0022	1.82
560	.636			1.09		
		.032	.0032		.0031	1.29
570	.668			1.00		
		.038	.0038		.0036	1.11
580	.706			1.12		
		.047	.0047		.0040	1.00
590	.753			1.26		
		.049	.0049		.0037	1.08
600	.802			1.41		
		.047	.0047		.0032	1.24
610	.849			1.55		
		.038	.0038		.0022	1.82
620	.887			1.66		
		.027	.0027		.0016	2.50
630	.914			1.74		
		.020	.0020		.0012	3.33
640	.934			1.80		
		.014	.0014		.0008	5.00
650	.948			1.84		
		.006	.0006		.00032	12.5
660	.954			1.86		
		.005	.0005		.00027	14.8
670	.959			1.88		
		.006	.0006		.00032	12.5
680	.965			1.90		

Column B: Computed R-cone output by Equation (8.13). Column C: Computed difference in R-cone output, specified for intermediate wavelengths (Equation [8.16]). Column D: "J-factor," the relative output of the r-g opponent channel. Column E: Difference in R-cone output attenuated according to the J-factor appropriate to the intermediate wavelength. Column F: Proportional to the reciprocal of Column E, used to convert threshold cone output to threshold of wavelength. The scaling factor .004, by which it is multiplied, is arbitrary.

262   Chromatic Discrimination

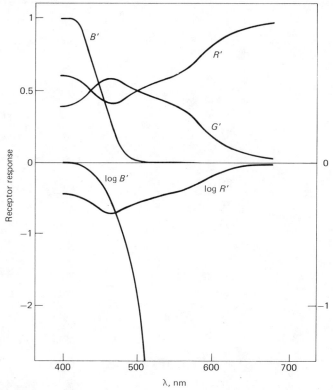

FIGURE 8.3 **Top:** Computed responses of the three types of cones, at equal luminance, shown as a function of wavelength. Note that the **R'** and **G'** functions are mirror images of each other. **Bottom:** log **B'** and log **R'** plotted as a function of wavelength.

Smith-Pokorny curves of Figure 7.4. (At this point, the reader is advised to return to that figure and study it again, because in the modeling to follow, the values of the R, G, and B functions plotted there, which are also tabulated in Appendix III, page 405, will be used.)

The corresponding difference function $\Delta R'$ between R-cone outputs at wavelengths 1 and 2 is given by

$$\Delta R' = R'_1 - R'_2 = \frac{\int E_{1\lambda} r_\lambda d\lambda}{L} - \frac{\int E_{2\lambda} r_\lambda d\lambda}{L}. \qquad (8.16)$$

These values have been calculated for 10 nm-steps centered on intermediate wavelengths chosen at 10-nm intervals from 405 to 675 nm. The results of these calculations are given in Table 8.1 and are plotted in Figure 8.4, together with similar calculations for $\Delta B'$ (Table 8.2). Values have been calculated for monochromatic lights using ±5-nm steps centered on wavelengths chosen at 10-nm steps from 405 to 675 nm. The results of these calculations are given in Table 8.1 and Figure 8.3, for a unit-luminance condition.

An example will help. Suppose we are concerned with the consequences of changing from 620 to 630 nm. The Smith-Pokorny sensitivity values (see page 405) for these wavelengths are as follows:

	$\lambda = 620$	$\lambda = 630$
S_R	.3377	.2421
S_G	.0432	.0229
$S_R + S_G$	.3809	.2650

For unit luminance, the values of S_R and S_G are in each case divided by their sum, $S_R + S_G$. This gives:

	$\lambda = 620$	$\lambda = 630$
R'	.887	.914
G'	.113	.086

To calculate $\Delta R'$, $.914 - .887 = .027$. This value is shown in column C_1 of Table 8.1 and is referred to $\lambda = 625$ nm, the wavelength midway between, which for a linear approximation is the appropriate wavelength to which this value of $\Delta R'$ should be associated. In column C_2, the values of column C_1 have been divided by 10 to provide an estimate of $\Delta R'$ for 1-nm wavelength shifts.

3. *If the activation of B and G cones were held constant, how much change in activation of the R cones would be required for a just-noticeable chromatic difference?*

This is a "trick" question, because it is not possible to vary only the stimulation of R cones to cause a purely chromatic change. By definition, a chromatic discrimination is one that occurs at constant luminance; in terms of the opponent-color model, this implies that the signals in the L channels are fixed; therefore, R + G must be constant. But if R varies and G does not, then R + G will vary as R does, producing output changes in both the r-g and L channels. To avoid this "Catch 22" situation, Question 3 needs to be asked in a different way, as in what follows.

4. *What is required to produce a change that occurs only in the r-g channels?*

To accomplish this objective, one can vary wavelength over the longwave region of the spectrum (to which the B cones are virtually insensitive) while holding luminance constant. This can be done experimentally by calibrating the spectrum for relative luminance at all wavelengths and then proceeding as discussed in the section on "Introduction to Wavelength Discrimination."

264 Chromatic Discrimination

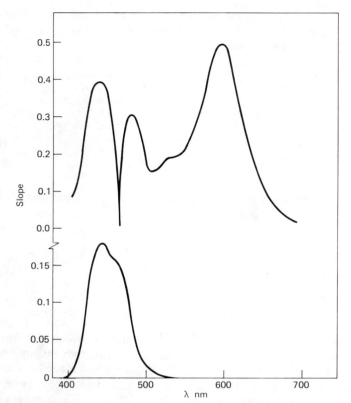

FIGURE 8.4 Top: Slope of the **R'** (cone output) function depicted in Figure 8.3. The calculations, which are based upon Equation (8.16) and shown in Table 8.1, are based on 10-nm segments straddling the points plotted in Figure 8.3. The results are plotted at intermediate wavelengths. **Bottom:** Slope of the **B'** function similarly calculated. The results of these calculations are also given in Table 8.2.

5. *Assuming that only the r-g signal varies, how much variation of it is required to produce a just barely noticeable change?*

There is no simple answer to this question. Here and in Chapter 9, we will see that the threshold for such r-g chromatic discriminations depends importantly on spatial and temporal parameters. But a simple analysis can give the general idea. One would expect discrimination to be good when, as wavelength varies, the rate of change in output of r-g channels is high, and that it would be poor when this rate of change is low. The slope of the function of Figure 8.3 represents that change.[8] In Figure 8.4, the slope segments of Figure 8.3 are plotted (for a continuous function, this would correspond to the first derivative). Where this value is high, a relatively small change in wavelength should be required to produce a given change in the value of r-g. Where the slope value is low, a larger change is required to produce the same effect.

6. *Does the threshold signal of the r-g difference depend upon the value of L?*

The answer to this question is definitely "yes." L, the value of luminance, depends upon the summed outputs of R and G cones. Using the simplified equations (8.7) and (8.8), we can calculate L by adding them together:

$$L = R + G = \int E_{1\lambda} r_\lambda d\lambda + \int E_{1\lambda} g_\lambda d\lambda. \qquad (8.17)$$

At moderate luminances, at least for long wavelengths, wavelength discrimination is virtually independent of luminance. At long wavelengths, discrimination depends only upon ΔR (or ΔG), which by assumption is directly proportional at any wavelength to the intensity of the stimulus. The value of L must have the same property. Therefore, if it is experimentally true that wavelength discrimination is independent of luminance, then the fraction $\Delta R/L$ must be a constant. Therefore the threshold signal for the r-g channels, which is directly proportional to ΔR, must depend upon L; indeed, it would be directly proportional to it in this example.

The idea that threshold values of $\Delta R/L$ are constant is similar to the idea that $\Delta L/L = C$ for achromatic discrimination (Weber's law, Chapter 5). It is to be expected, and indeed it is found, that this relation holds only for moderate intensities, so that the value of $\Delta R/L$ required for a threshold of chromatic discrimination becomes larger as the intensity is reduced (and sometimes when it is increased). If it did not, then our ability to perceive color differences of reflecting samples would be independent of all variations of illumination. Instead, chromatic discrimination, like luminance discrimination, becomes relatively poor at low luminance levels. An exception that occurs at short wavelengths will be discussed later in this chapter.

7. *Does a threshold change in r-g differences depend upon the initial value of r-g?*

The experimental evidence is much less striking in this case, but it indicates a positive answer. As the activity level of the r-g opponent channels increases, they apparently become relatively insensitive to differential signals as wavelength is changed. The load on the r-g channels is minimal at 570 nm, where the signal is zero no matter how bright the light.

8. *What are the rules of operation for the y-b opponent channels?*

All of the questions that have been asked about the r-g channels can be repeated for the y-b case. For the most part, there is no need to do this, since the answers will be about the same. There is however one important exception, since the "Catch 22" situation related to the third question does not arise for the y-b case:

9. *If the activation of the R and G cones were held constant, how much change in activation of the B cones would be required for a just-noticeable chromatic difference?*

"Catch 22" does not apply here because the B cones are assumed to make no contribution to luminance. Therefore, if some means can be discovered to vary the stimulation of B cones without altering that of the R and G cones, an empirical answer can be found. From the standpoint of the y-b opponent channels, such a change manipulates the B input while holding constant the y input (which is proportional to luminance).[9]

Note, in Figure 8.4, that the slope of the B' function is highest for wavelengths near 445 nm. But wavelength discrimination in the shortwave end of the spectrum is keenest at about 490 nm,[10] and it is probable that B cones mediate wavelength discrimination there. So ΔB alone makes a very poor prediction. If $\Delta B/B$ were the controlling variable, the prediction would become even worse. This is also shown in Figure 8.4, where the logarithm of B' is plotted as a function of wavelength. Since the slope of this function *increases* as log B' decreases, the function implausibly and incorrectly predicts that the closer the B-cone response is to oblivion, the better is the discrimination mediated by such cones. The truth must lie somewhere between these assumptions.

One approach to solving this problem is to assume an expression of the form $\Delta B'/(B' + K)$ that is constant for a threshold discrimination mediated by B cones. The use of such an equation has been very frequent in the history of the visual discrimination literature because it seems necessary also for a quantitative description of what is known about luminance discrimination. A quantity like K has been called the "self-light" of the retina (or "dark" light), since K has the same units as B, and behaves as a real light of K units would in a system where $\Delta B/B$ is strictly constant, but with all measurements made against a constant background of intensity K. The exact value of K in the denominator of the fraction $\Delta B/(B + K)$ is critically important. (A similar model is described by LeGrand, 1968, p. 487.)

10. *What are the rules of interaction between the two types of opponent-color channels?*

As wavelength is changed at constant luminance, a simultaneous change usually results in the signals of the r-g and y-b channels. The rates of these changes are shown by the slopes of the curve segments that are plotted in Figure 8.4. Because of the requirement of constant luminance, the y-b system contributes almost no information at long wavelengths: the y value is constant and the B cones are insensitive to these long wavelengths. In the short wavelengths, it might seem likely that the varying y-b signals are so dominant that a smaller contribution from the r-g system could be ignored; but we will see that this prediction is false.

In regions where the rates of change of the two systems are nearly equal, the interaction rules become important for an exact prediction of wavelength discrimination. These rules of combination are not known, but are nevertheless worth discussing theoretically. Somewhat paradoxically, an assumption of total independence between two mechanisms leads to the requirement of "probability summation." Assume that the r-g and y-b channels operate independently as they signal evidence of a wavelength change. At some later stage where such signals are detected, suppose that the detector will signal "yes" whenever either of the two contributing systems indicates that a threshold of wavelength change has occurred. For example, imagine that on any particular trial of the experiment, for some particular wavelength shift, the probability that either the r-g or the y-b system will detect the change is exactly 0.5. If so, the probability that neither system will detect it is $(0.5)^2 = 0.25$. This means that the probability that one or both of these systems will detect the change is $1 - 0.25 = 0.75$. Therefore, in order to reduce this combined probability to 0.5, a smaller wavelength shift would be needed, with both systems active, relative to that required for only one.

Another possibility is that the outputs of the two systems combine fully (complete summation). If this were the case, the wavelength shift with both systems operating would have to be small enough so that the total signal from both systems would be just large enough to detect. Partial summation is also possible. A general empirical rule for specifying such interactions is the following:

$$S = \left[(r-g)^n + (y-b)^n \right]^{1/n} \tag{8.18}$$

Linear summation occurs when $n = 1$, since the total signal S in this case is equal to the linear sum of r-g and y-b. Although probability summation cannot be exactly expressed by this equation, a value of $n = 2$ is not too far from an adequate description. (This same value describes another related model, according to which the r-g and y-b values are treated as orthogonal vectors in a Euclidian plane.)

As the value of n in Equation (8.18) approaches infinity, the "upper envelope" rule mentioned earlier in connection with the data of Stiles, discussed on page 190, is described. According to this rule, sensitivity depends only upon changes in the most active system, regardless of changes in less active ones. In the present context, the upper envelope rule predicts that wavelength changes are signaled either by the r-g or by the y-b system, depending upon which system shows the largest change with wavelength. Even if the other system is changing very nearly as much, it makes no contribution by this rule.

By any of these rules, the contribution of the less sensitive channel is for all practical purposes negligible if it is very much less sensitive (about five times or more) than the more sensitive channel. This is probably the case for wavelength discrimination in most regions of the spectrum.

MODELING WAVELENGTH-DISCRIMINATION FUNCTIONS

Adjustment of the Smith-Pokorny G Function

Unique yellow should be seen at a wavelength corresponding to the crosspoint of the R and G receptor sensitivity functions. These functions (called S_R and S_G in Appendix III, p. 405) were instead positioned by Smith and Pokorny so that their sum would be proportional to the photopic luminous efficiency function. Doing so causes the curves to cross twice at short wavelengths (see Figure 7.4, p. 213). An implication of the failure of these functions to account for luminance when they cross at 570 nm, near where yellow is seen, is that the relative contributions of R and G cones to the r-g opponent-color channels differ when compared to their relative contributions to the luminance channels. In order to make the curves cross near 570 nm, all that is required is to double the relative weight of the G-cone input to the opponent channels. Physiologically this could mean that, relative to their contributions to luminance channels, (1) G-cone signals are amplified for purposes of chromatic balance, (2) R-cone signals are attenuated as they contribute to chromatic channels, or (3) only half the G cones contribute to luminance, whereas all of them contribute to color balance. In the calculations to follow, assumption (1) has been used. In Figure 7.4, assumption (2) is depicted instead. (The choice of assumption does not alter the relative vertical positioning of the two functions.)

The r-g System

From Figure 8.4, it will be seen that the predicted maximum of the $\Delta R'$ function is approximately at 600 nm (this can also be seen in Table 8.1, where the largest value of $\Delta R'$ occurs at 595 nm). Figure 8.1 shows this to be near the minimum of empirical wavelength discrimination functions but the experimental minimum is at wavelengths a bit less than this. (A weighted average of data from four studies[11] suggests a minimum close to 580 nm.) Although discrimination in the long wavelengths seems mostly dependent on $\Delta R'$, an additional assumption is needed to resolve this small yet significant discrepancy.

The J-Factor

Suppose that the "base" against which a change is seen includes a component derived from the r-g channel. Specifically, assume that L is replaced by a value that we will call the J-Factor. For a unit value of L, $J' = 1 + |R' - 2G'|$. J has a unit value at the wavelength of minimum spectral saturation near 570 nm. This wavelength should also correspond closely to unique yellow and to the intersection of the R- and G-cone sensitivity functions, as these contribute to chromatic balance.

In the context of some theories, the difference between unity and J would be related to the extra brightness produced by R and G cones via the r-g channels.[12] Perhaps it is this extra brightness, added to that supplied by the luminance channels, that tends somehow to mask the perception of chromatic differences. Values of J have been tabulated in Column D of Table 8.1, where it will be seen that J is minimum at 570 nm and is maximum for short wavelengths near 460–470 nm and for the long wavelengths at the spectral extreme.

Procedure for Calculating Discrimination Due to R and G Cones

As noted earlier, values of $\Delta R'$ have been approximated for 1-nm wavelength changes in column C_2 of Table 8.1, by dividing the values of column C_1 (which are for 10-nm shifts) by 10. Scanning column E, where the values of column C_2 have been divided by J, reveals that wavelength discrimination is best at 585 nm, where the value of $\Delta R'/J$ is .004 for a 1-nm wavelength change. From Figure 8.1, it will be seen that $\Delta \lambda \approx 1$ nm in this region of the spectrum. Apparently, then, the r-g channels can discriminate .004 parts of increase or decrease in R' (with the aid of a concomitant converse change in G') per unit of J. If we assume that this same proportion of change is also just barely discriminable elsewhere in the spectrum, then we can determine, for various starting wavelengths, how much of a change in λ is required to generate the threshold value of 0.004 in $\Delta R'/J$. For example, at 535 nm, a 1-nm change produces a value for $\Delta R'/J$ of only 0.0015, which is below threshold. To achieve threshold, $\Delta \lambda$ must be increased by a factor of $(0.004)/(0.0015)$, which is 2.67 times the value for 580 nm. Therefore $\Delta \lambda = 2.67$ nm. In general, $\Delta \lambda = \dfrac{0.004 J}{\Delta R'}$; the values are listed in Column F of Table 8.1, and are plotted in Figure 8.5.

Discontinuity at 465 nm

At 465 nm, the R' vs λ function has a zero slope, corresponding to the maximum separation of the log sensitivity curves of G and R cones that causes R' to reach a minimum at this wavelength. This in turn causes the function of Figure 8.5 to become discontinuous at 465 nm. At shorter wavelengths than this, there is an indication that wavelength discrimination improves greatly and may once again be mediated by the r-g system. In Chapter 10, we will see that the form of this function is very similar to that observed experimentally in tritanopes, a class of color-defective individuals who are believed to lack B cones while retaining normal red-green function.

Relation between Receptor and Opponent-Process Differentials

By Equations (8.13) and (8.14), $R' = R/(R+G)$ and $G' = G/(R+G)$, so $R' + G' = 1$. For wavelengths λ_1 and λ_2, $R'_1 + G'_1 = R'_2 + G'_2 = 1$. For a given change in wavelength, $\Delta \lambda$, say from λ_1 at some long wavelength toward λ_2 at a shorter one,

$$R'_2 = R'_1 - \Delta R'_{12} \tag{8.19}$$

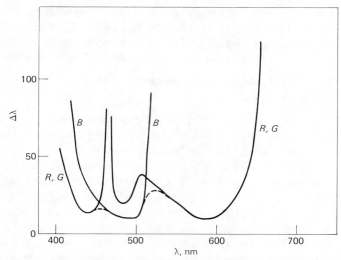

FIGURE 8.5 The values on the ordinate are the reciprocals of the amounts of change caused in two hypothetical systems assumed to determine wavelength discrimination. The U-shaped curve represents discrimination mediated by B cones at constant luminance. The other function, which crosses the B-cone function twice and is discontinuous at 465 nm, represents the discrimination mediated by the r-g opponent color system at constant luminance. The dotted portions of the curve are intended to represent probability summation between the two systems. The lower envelope, including the dotted portions, describes wavelength discrimination for the combined systems.

Because of the mirror symmetry of the R' and G' functions as a function of wavelength,

$$G'_2 = G'_1 + \Delta G'_{12} \tag{8.20}$$

If Equations (8.19) and (8.20) are added, remembering that $R'_1 + G'_1 = R'_2 + G'_2$, it follows that

$$\Delta R'_{12} = \Delta G'_{12} \tag{8.21}$$

It is assumed that the brain receives its signals from the r-g channels, and not from the R and G cones independently. Therefore, for a threshold change of wavelength, $\Delta \lambda$,

$$k \cdot \Delta \lambda = (r-g)'_1 - (r-g)'_2 \tag{8.22}$$

where, for example, $(r-g)'_1$ refers to the opponent color signal at unit luminance for wavelength 1. Substituting $(R'_1 - 2G'_1)$ for $(r-g)'_1$ and $(R'_2 - 2G'_2)$ for $(r-g)'_2$, we have

$$k \cdot \Delta \lambda = 3\Delta R'_{12} \tag{8.23}$$

By combining Equations (8.22) and (8.23),

$$\Delta R'_{12} = \frac{(r-g)'_1 - (r-g)'_2}{3} \tag{8.24}$$

This result shows that the form of the wavelength discrimination function is equally well predicted either by the rate of change in output of R cones or of the r-g opponent system.[13]

Discrimination of Short Wavelengths

To be complete, the model just presented must be expanded to account for the possible improvement of wavelength discrimination caused by the reemergence of red, which gives the appearance of violet to the shortwave end of the spectrum. In Chapter 7 (p. 215) it was suggested that there may be a B-cone contribution to the r-g opponent channels which throws the r-g balance in the r direction.

In Figure 8.6, the theoretical wavelength discrimination curve of Figure 8.5 has been replotted as the dashed curve (1). Recall that this curve was calculated as $.004J/\Delta R'$, so that it represents the wavelength change required to produce a criterion change in R', the output of R cones at constant luminance. The solid curve (2) at the bottom of Figure 8.6 is based instead on changes of $(r-g)'$, the red-green opponent-color function (see the formula near the curve). This curve would have exactly the same shape as the dotted one except that, to account for the reemergence of shortwave red, $0.5B'$ has been added to $R' - 2G'$ in

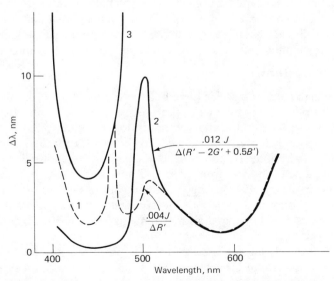

FIGURE 8.6 Curves 2 and 3 show the effects of assuming B-cone input to the r-g opponent system. See text for assumptions used.

the denominator. If the $0.5B'$ term were removed, curve 2 would be everywhere identical to curve 1.

With the $0.5B'$ term included, the predicted discrimination in the shortwave region of the spectrum (curve 2) is much better than that observed experimentally. A possible explanation of this discrepancy requires attention to the larger Weber fraction of B cones, previously assumed to be 0.08 at high luminances, compared to 0.004 for the R and G cones—higher by a factor of 20. Probably this poor discrimination capacity applies also to the fraction of B-cone output that is diverted to the r-g channels. Physiologically this would imply, quite plausibly, that the relatively poor intensity discrimination mediated by B cones is due either to the B cones themselves or to a limit imposed by their pathways prior to the point at which signals from B cones enter into the r-g opponent process. A recalculation of the shortwave section of curve 2 has been made by multiplying each ordinate value by 20 and the result is shown as curve 3 in Figure 8.6. This branch is now so high as to suggest that, although B-cone input to the r-g opponent channel has an important effect upon color *appearance*, it nevertheless may not result in a sufficient rate of change of the B-cone signal to aid *discrimination* very much.

This conclusion is subject to at least a pair of provisos. In the first place, the assumption of a 5-percent contribution of B-cone output to the r-g opponent channel is arbitrary and in any event it is luminance-dependent, as experiments by McCree (1960), to be described later in this chapter, show. At very low photopic levels, there is little appearance of violet at short wavelengths; the sensation grows to a maximum at intermediate levels, and then disappears again at very high levels; similarly McCree finds an optimal intensity for discrimination. In the second place, the 20:1 ratio of Weber fractions assumed for the calculations of this chapter is only approximate, very probably subject to change as a function of stimulus parameters such as area, duration, and intensity.

The y-b System

The calculations made so far have been intended to suggest only what the r-g opponent process contributes to the process of wavelength discrimination. We now turn our attention to the second opponent-color system.

Protanopes and deuteranopes, who are believed to lack R and G cones respectively (see Chapter 10), are able to make wavelength discriminations only in a narrow range of the spectrum near 500 nm. (In this region, they do about as well as normal subjects.) But they fail utterly at the shortest wavelengths and over the entire longwave region of the spectrum. This suggests that the y-b system mediates the discrimination that remains, and that such discrimination is best at about 500 nm.

From Figure 8.4, one can see that the slope of the B' function, which is tabulated in Table 8.2 at 10-nm intervals, is greatest at about 445 nm; this is also apparent in Figure 8.3. As previously noted, $\Delta B'$ is a very poor predictor of the wavelength discrimination that is mediated by the y-b system, even when

TABLE 8.2 Calculations Pertaining to Hypothetical Wavelength Discrimination Mediated by Differential B-cone Responses at Constant Luminance

A Wavelength	B $B' = \dfrac{B}{R+G}$	C_1 $\Delta B'$ 10 nm	C_2 $\Delta B'$ 1 nm	D $\dfrac{\Delta B'}{B' + 0.016}$	E $.08 \left[\dfrac{B' + 0.016}{\Delta B'} \right]$
400	1.000				
		.009	.0009	.00088	90.9
410	1.009				
		.033	.0033	.0033	24.2
420	.975				
		.120	.0120	.0128	6.25
430	.855				
		.173	.0173	.0225	3.56
440	.682				
		.177	.0177	.0290	2.75
450	.505				
		.155	.0155	.0350	2.29
460	.345				
		.148	.0148	.0516	1.55
470	.197				
		.109	.0109	.0688	1.16
480	.088				
		.053	.0053	.0684	1.17
490	.035				
		.021	.0021	.0523	1.53
500	.0132				
		.011	.0011	.0468	1.71
510	.0018				
		.001	.0001	.0057	14.03
520	.00076				

Columns B, C: Analogous to the same columns in Table 8.1. Column D: Weighting of differential B-cone output according to a modified Weber's law, including a "dark-light" factor. Column E: Proportional to the reciprocal of Column D, used to convert threshold B-cone output to threshold wavelength.

y is held constant by the constant luminance criterion. The bottom graph of Figure 8.3 shows, as previously mentioned, that using the log response curve leads to an equally bad prediction, namely that wavelength discrimination should still be improving, for the y-b system, as wavelength is lengthened to 520 nm and even beyond.

Unlike the r-g system, the "base" against which changes in B' are perceived at constant luminance varies dramatically with wavelength, as shown by the thousandfold range of B-cone output for constant luminance shown at the bottom of Figure 8.3. A "self-light" constant is needed, but it must be a small one with a value similar to that of B' at the wavelength of best discrimination, near 500 nm. Column D of Table 8.2 shows that the value of the expression $\Delta B'/(B' + 0.016)$, which reaches a maximum near 475 nm, remains high to 505 nm. The reciprocal of this function should be related to the change in wavelength required for a constant value of $\Delta B'$. The expression in Column E is the reciprocal value multiplied by 0.08, to make $\Delta \lambda$ equal to about 1 nm, (as empirical data suggest it should be) in the region of best discrimination. The U-shaped curve of Figure 8-5 is the function $\Delta \lambda = 0.08 \, [(B' + 0.016)/\Delta B']$.

In a manner analogous to that already used for calculating r-g discrimination, this function is used to calculate wavelength changes, $\Delta \lambda$, required to produce the same value of $\Delta B'/(B' + 0.016)$ as that required for a threshold discrimination of 1 nm at the wavelength of best wavelength sensitivity. The fact that $\Delta B'/(B' + 0.016) = 0.08$ implies that a change in the rate of B-cone activation of 8 percent is required, at high intensities, in order to cause a just-perceptible change of hue.

INTERACTIONS BETWEEN r-g AND y-b CHANNELS

If it is assumed that probability summation is the only "interaction" between the r-g and y-b systems, the dotted lines of Figure 8.5, shown near the regions of nearly equal sensitivities for the two opponent-color mechanisms, are suggestive of what this effect might be. The lower envelope of the function would characterize the predicted result with negligible error for all other wavelengths. All major features of a typical experimental wavelength discrimination function are qualitatively accounted for.

Looking again at the data of Figure 8.1, we are now in a position to speculate about sources of individual differences. Some of these could be caused by variations in the relative number of R and G cones, which are known to differ among subjects (Rushton & Baker, 1964). Observers might also vary in the degree to which the "base" of the r-g system is influenced by the brightness component implied by the J-factor variation. In spectral regions where the two curves of Figure 8.5 cross, subjects may vary according to how these two systems interact. The relative effectiveness of the r-g and y-b systems may also vary from subject to subject. Field size, exposure duration, retinal location, and stimulus intensity are known to affect these differentially for a given subject, and possibly also among subjects. Preretinal absorption, which differs in different subjects, has minimal effect on r-g discriminations, since it does not alter the crucial difference ratio between R- and G-cone outputs. But the B-cone system is highly luminance-dependent, so that preretinal reduction of light will affect it.

Wright and Pitt were not able to maintain their full values of retinal illuminance at the shortest wavelengths. It may be that subject C.B.D. (Fig. 8.1) suffered less preretinal absorption than the other subjects, permitting the short-wave limb of his r-g discrimination function to be sufficiently activated for him to maintain good discrimination there. Finally, there may be large individual differences related to discrimination of violet.

The model just described is not offered as literal truth, but only as something for the reader to hang his hat on. The literature is full of discrimination models, and all of them can "predict" the wavelength discrimination curve, more or less. It is suggested that the present model be kept in mind in the discussion of the empirical literature that follows.

EXPERIMENTAL DATA: CHROMATICITY DISCRIMINATION

Prior to 1942, many experiments on wavelength discrimination (some of which have been mentioned in preceding sections) had been executed and reported. If described in chromaticity space (Chapter 5), such experiments constitute measures of just-discriminable steps along a line that describes the locus of spectral colors.

Such experiments sample only a miniscule part of the total range of chromaticity variation for which one could ask the question: "Starting with point p_1, what distance change, ds, between p_1 and another point, p_2, is required in order to produce a significantly noticeable difference?" Viewed in this way, the size of the problem becomes immediately obvious. The question just posed must be expanded to include the following additional considerations.

- Chromaticity space is continuous, being related to the ratios of cone outputs, each of which is in turn a continuous function of intensity. Accordingly, not all possible points in chromaticity space can be tested and only a few may be sampled. How might it be possible to generalize from such a sample to untested regions?
- A similar problem exists with respect to an infinitude of possible directions of change that are testable around each point. How many directions should be tested? How does one extrapolate to predict results for untested directions?
- By what method should the just-noticeable difference in chromaticity be tested, at each of the points and for each of the directions that have been decided upon?

Wright's Experiment

W. D. Wright (1941, 1946) studied discrimination for variations in chromaticity along lines connecting 15 monochromatic stimuli and 3 extraspectral purples (although not all possible combinations were tested). As an example, consider the data for four observers shown in Figure 8.7. The abscissa is related to the percentage of 570-nm light in a mixture of 460 and 570 nm. For various proportions (for example, those indicated for subject R.A.L. by the filled circles) Wright obtained a measure of the amount of variation in this proportion that was required for a clearly noticeable difference in color.

To make the settings, a subject was required to manipulate two controls, one of which changed the proportion of the two spectral components while the other changed the brightness of the variable field, which the subject attempted to hold constant.[14] A reference field was always present, set to the mixture ratio

276   Chromatic Discrimination

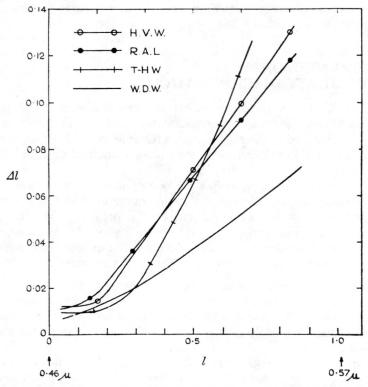

FIGURE 8.7 Color-discrimination data of Wright (1941) for mixtures of 460- and 570-nm light. The abscissa shows the fraction of the mixture that is comprised of 570 nm, and the ordinate shows the chromaticity change required (CIE system) for a just-noticeable difference at constant brightness.

under test, and the subject was free to view it and compare it to the field that was being varied.

The criterion of a noticeable step in Wright's experiment was rather vague. He states: "It was decided that in making a step the difference should be rather larger than that usually understood by a just-noticeable step. In recording the latter, something akin to a sporting instinct can be introduced in an attempt to discern as minute a difference as possible, but this takes time and imposes a considerable strain on the observer. If the standard is made less exacting, the strain is reduced and a lengthy investigation can be completed more successfully." There were some problems concerning the repeatability of such measurements. In averaging data, criterion differences between subjects were reduced by adjusting the values for one subject's data by as much as a factor of three with respect to those of another subject. All subjects showed the same general trends, although the individual differences in curve shapes, even after normalization, were considerable.

Experimental Data: Chromaticity Discrimination 277

No subsequent study has sampled so large a region of chromaticity space as the one tested by Wright. In Figure 8.8, his results are represented in the CIE chromaticity diagram.[15] The "dashes" represent the just-noticeable differences as obtained in the regions of chromaticity space designated by their midpoints. The same data are also shown in Figure 8.9, in a chromaticity diagram that uses a different set of imaginary primaries. (This second diagram is one of a number of so-called "uniform" chromaticity diagrams that have been devel-

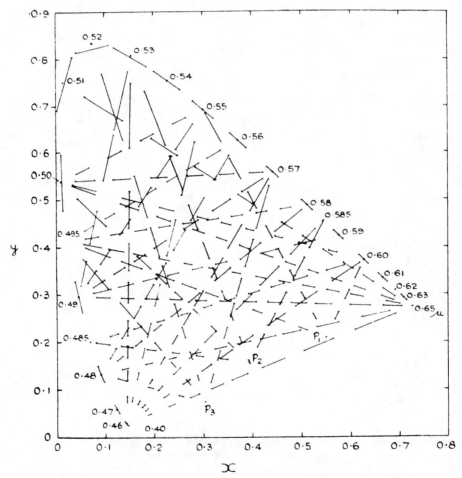

FIGURE 8.8 W. D. Wright's (1947) threshold of chromaticity discrimination plotted in the CIE chromaticity diagram. Note the line connecting 460 and 570 nm, based on the data of WDW in Figure 8.7. The "dashes" grow longer along this line as the chromaticity shifts from that corresponding to 460 nm to that corresponding to 570 nm. A given distance on the CIE chart represents very different chromatic change, depending upon its location and orientation.

278   Chromatic Discrimination

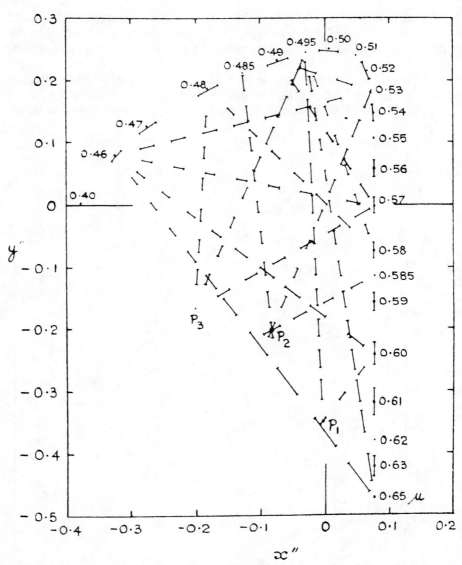

FIGURE 8.9 Wright's just-noticeable differences of Figure 8.8 are represented as dashes on a chromaticity diagram that utilizes different primaries in an effort to make all dashes of the same length. Although there is an improvement, the effort obviously fails.

oped in an unsuccessful effort to reduce Wright's dashes to lines of the same length, or to cause the ellipses of MacAdam, to be discussed next, to become circles of the same size.)[16]

MacAdam's Experiment

An experiment having a similar aim, but differing methodologically, was reported in 1942 by D. L. MacAdam of the Eastman Kodak Company. One impetus for his study was to provide a scientific basis for obtaining a patent on "Kodak yellow" as a trademark for Eastman photographic products. The problem was similar to that described earlier in this chapter in the parable of the carpet. How can one say that two yellows are, or are not, sufficiently similar to be legally identical? Physical measures cannot tell, since metameric matches are possible. It also would be unreasonable to require that, for the chromaticities of two colors to be called the same, they must be identical to 17 decimal places. Where does one draw the line? The experiment that MacAdam chose to conduct examined the problem in a very general way and eventually led to the "MacAdam unit" of discrimination, in terms of which the amount of difference between the Kodak yellow and that of imposters can be stipulated.

MacAdam used more than 100 carefully calibrated color filters to provide his stimuli. His 2° colorimetric field was of similar size to Wright's, though of different orientation and shape. Wright used no surround field; MacAdam used a large uniform surround. Wright's observers had to adjust intensity in an effort to maintain equal brightness as they varied chromaticity; MacAdam's apparatus had the important virtue that it maintained equal luminance automatically. In MacAdam's instrument, as in Wright's, the two halves of the colorimetric field could be set to a physical match. But whereas Wright had started with the match and set it off to determine a discriminable change, MacAdam elected instead to use the dispersion of repeated attempts at making matches as his index of discrimination.

Figure 8.10 shows the results of MacAdam's experiment for one of 25 regions of chromaticity space that he tested. The symmetry of the figure may be somewhat misleading: only one independent test was made along each axis because the results of repeated attempts to match the center point were symmetrically plotted as one standard deviation on either side. Therefore only half an ellipse was independently measured. Given this caveat, the fit to an ellipse is remarkably good, and the figure selected for illustration here is in no way exceptional among the 25 that were obtained and reproduced in MacAdam's paper. Figure 8.11 shows all 25 ellipses, plotted (as MacAdam did it) at 10 times their actual size in the CIE chromaticity diagram.

THEORETICAL CONSIDERATIONS FOR EXTENDING MACADAM'S RESULTS

In 1920, the German physicist Erwin Schrödinger published a classic paper bearing the title (translated) "Outline of a theory of color measurement for daylight vision."[17] In this paper, Schrödinger utilized the idea, discussed earlier

Chromatic Discrimination

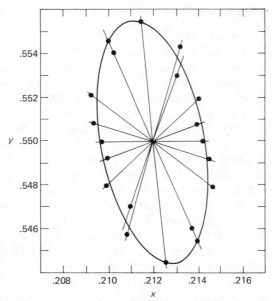

FIGURE 8.10 One of the 25 ellipses of chromatic discrimination measured by MacAdam (1942), plotted in CIE chromaticity space. Data points are shown.

in this chapter, that color can be represented by the direction of a vector in a "color space," with the length of the vector representing the intensity of the color. Viewed in this way, the difference between two colors depends upon the distance between the ends of the vectors which represent them, but not in the simple way that might be imagined for the metric of ordinary Euclidean space such as that of Figure 8.2, where the appropriate measure of the distance between the vector ends is simply the linear distance between them. But different, longer distances could instead be measured along various curved paths—for example, where the vector ends lie upon the surface of an impenetrable sphere. What is usually taken as the appropriate distance to measure is the shortest possible one, called the *geodesic*.

In a Euclidean plane the measure is simply made along a straight line connecting two points. Given the considerations discussed earlier in the context of opponent-color theory, it should come as no surprise that color space is much more complicated than this. Consider the two-dimensional projection of the three-variable Euclidean space that is a chromaticity diagram. If the laws of color discrimination could be represented adequately in this space, then the least number of discriminable steps between any two points in the diagram would lie along a straight line connecting them. Although this prediction has not been extensively tested, it seems clear that it does not generally hold. Schrödinger

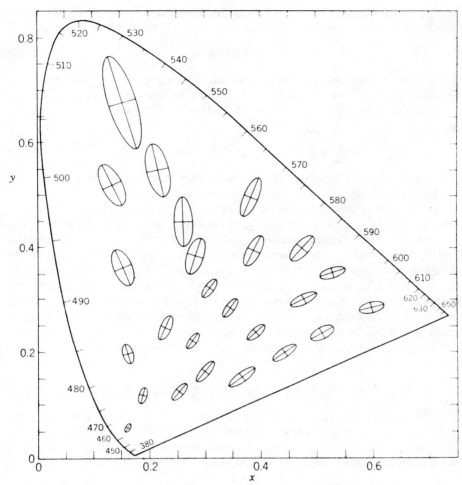

FIGURE 8.11 MacAdam's ellipses of chromatic discrimination, plotted at 10 times their actual size in the CIE chromaticity diagram, with data points omitted.

discussed the problem explicitly with respect to variations in chromaticity that occur from white to a spectral color. As monochromatic light is substituted for white, saturation of course increases. But in general the perceived hue of such a stimulus also changes. Schrödinger suggested that the color geodesic, or the line containing the least number of discriminable steps, should lie along a curve of constant hue.

A kind of space that permits greater flexibility for the representation of local color differences is Riemannian space. In two-dimensional Euclidean space, the square of the distance between two points is calculated, by the Pythagorean rule, as the sum of the squares of the component distances between them:

$$(ds)^2 = (dx)^2 + (dy)^2. \tag{8.19}$$

Here ds is the distance between the points, and dx and dy represent the component distances along the orthogonal axes of this ordinary plane. In Riemannian two-dimensional space, which can be used to represent colors at constant luminance,

$$(ds)^2 = g_{11}(dx)^2 + 2g_{12}(dx \cdot dy) + g_{22}(dy)^2. \tag{8.20}$$

The coefficients g_{11}, $2g_{12}$, and g_{22} are themselves functions of the values x and y, defining the region in space where discrimination is tested.[18]

On a strictly theoretical basis, which includes not only factors discussed here, but several others as well, Schrödinger concluded that "the totality of the geodesic lines . . . is the totality of ellipses inscribed in the color triangle." MacAdam, having found that ellipses, when plotted on a chromaticity diagram, did in fact describe the thresholds of color difference in the 25 regions of measurement, quickly took it as his task to calculate from his data the Riemannian coefficients of Equation (8.20) and to determine smooth curves, looking much like contour maps, which described the course of coefficients of fixed values as they wiggled through the chromaticity plane. The *MacAdam unit* of color difference (M), which has been rather widely applied, is calculated by substituting, in the equation

$$M = [g_{11}(dx)^2 + 2g_{12}(dx \cdot dy) + g_{22}(dy)^2]^{1/2}, \tag{8.21}$$

the values of g_{11}, $2g_{12}$, and g_{22}, as interpolated from contour lines plotted in the CIE chromaticity diagram (see Wyszecki & Stiles, 1967, pp. 531–533). The standard deviation of matching corresponds to a unit value of M, and something on the order of $3M$ is generally regarded as a just-noticeable difference.[19]

ADDITIONAL STUDIES OF CHROMATIC DISCRIMINATION

Since the pioneering work by Wright and MacAdam in the 1940s, a number of additional studies of chromatic discrimination have been carried out in MacAdam's laboratory at the Eastman Kodak Company and in the laboratory of G. Wyszecki at the Canadian National Research Council laboratories in Ottawa. A significant change in methodology was adopted in both laboratories in order to permit the simultaneous evaluation, not only of chromaticity differences at constant luminance, but also of luminance differences at constant chromaticity. It will be recalled that, in MacAdam's original experiment, the observer varied chromaticity along only one dimension at a time, with luminance automatically being held constant. In the late 1940s, MacAdam built a new binocular colorimeter in which comparisons could be made between a reference field comprised of mixed light from three primaries and a comparison field based upon a second set of the same three primaries. The task of the observer was to attempt a complete color match, based upon the manipulation of three controls, each of which varied the intensity of one of the primaries. Later, Wyszecki constructed a colorimeter in his laboratory that permitted the same kinds of measurements.

Results for one subject using one test color are shown from an experiment by Wyszecki and Fielder (1971) in Figure 8.12. The basic result of the experiment is a cloud of points that may be represented in three-dimensional color space. (In this example, x and y refer to the chromaticity coordinates of the CIE system, and l refers to luminance variation.) The ellipse fitted to the points in the y vs x plot corresponds to a criterion such that the ellipse contains, on the average, 95 percent of any random set of color matches.

Using similar procedures, Brown (1957) had earlier tested the color discrimination of 12 observers; before that, Brown and MacAdam (1949) compared two subjects (and occasionally three) in a lengthy investigation. MacAdam (1959) investigated small field effects and Brown (1951) studied the effect of

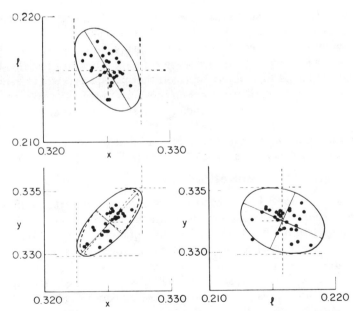

FIGURE 8.12 Some results from a color-matching experiment by Wyszecki and Fielder. Shown here are projections of a cloud of points, each of which represents an attempt to make an exact color match. Chromatic discrimination is gauged by the spread of data in a cross section of the x-y plane shown at the lower left.

reducing luminance to low photopic levels. In the Wyszecki and Fielder paper an attempt was made to compare their newer data with some of those already in the literature. Reductions in field size or luminance have the effect of (1) increasing the size of ellipses in all directions, and (2) selectively increasing them in a direction of discrimination that implies a selective loss of differential B-cone stimulation.

Comparisons between different observers, whether in the same or a different experiment, present a discouraging picture. Although observers agree in certain major trends, individual differences are best described as enormous. Unfortunately, the methods used make it difficult if not impossible to understand these differences, which are doubtless due to an interplay of the kinds of factors discussed theoretically earlier in this chapter. Moreover, as Wyszecki and Fielder note: "The question arises whether the use of three fixed primary colors in producing color matches inadvertently introduces a bias in the distribution of the color matches for a given test color. We notice the tendency of the color-matching ellipse to orient itself toward the chromaticity point of the nearest primary." This finding casts a shadow upon many of the results that have been obtained subsequent to the original studies of Wright and of MacAdam.

METHODOLOGICAL NOTES

Is it sound policy to assume that the dispersion of attempted color matches yields a valid index of discrimination? What one is really interested in, it would seem, is how different two colors must be before they just appear to be different. MacAdam's method of repeated matches certainly does not test this directly, since in each instance the subject reported that no difference was seen at the completion of his setting. The dispersion measure therefore works only to the extent that it consistently relates to meaningful subjective differences by a constant factor, and it is not clear why it should. (Recent tests of the relationship in my laboratory, as yet unpublished, indicate that the relation between these two measures varies as a function of the level of B-cone activation.)

Wavelength Discrimination

The data of Figure 8.1 reflect the serious extent of individual differences in wavelength discrimination functions measured under similar conditions. Over much of the spectrum the differences are more quantitative than qualitative, but below 480 nm, the various curve shapes in the literature are so wildly discrepant that the shortwave segment of an average curve is of very dubious value. As illustrated in Figure 8.5, these short wavelengths encompass a region in which chromatic discrimination is probably controlled by variations both in R-G-cone output and B-cone output.

Figure 8.13 shows some selected results of a well-controlled study by Bedford and Wyszecki (1958), which included deliberate manipulations of stimulus size, configuration, and retinal illuminance. The form of the curves is reasonably

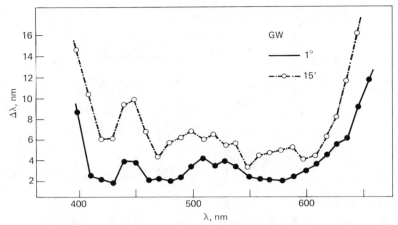

FIGURE 8.13 Wavelength discrimination data of Bedford and Wyszecki (1971). The solid points refer to a 1° field at 100 td; the open points are for a 1.5' field of 2000 td. The larger field, which provides less total flux, nevertheless yields the better discrimination.

similar to those from Wright's laboratory. They confirm that, in addition to the two principal minima at about 580 and 480 nm, there is a third one around 440 nm. It is of interest to note that an 800-fold reduction in area (from a 1° half-circle to a 1.5' spot) is by no means compensated by a 200-fold increase in the illuminance of the small field relative to the large one.

McCree (1961) used small contiguous fields, viewed in Wright's colorimeter. The behavior of his functions in the vicinity of 460 nm is of special interest; it will be recalled that, in the absence of discriminations based upon B-cone activity, there is a discontinuity for wavelength discrimination near this wavelength. McCree's results show (Fig. 8.14) that discriminations mediated by B cones improve as luminance is *reduced*, up to a point, and as area is increased. His worst condition is for a 15' field at the highest intensity used (150 td); the best discrimination occurs for the largest (75') field at an intermediate intensity (8.5 td).

Saturation Discrimination

Another special case of chromatic discrimination that has been extensively investigated is the first step from white. An example of this is shown in Figure 8.15 from Wright's laboratory. The experimental measure is the luminance of the monochromatic component needed, when added to white, in order to produce a discriminable change in color at constant luminance. The fraction of the mixture that is comprised by the monochromatic component is calculated; in Figure 8.15 the reciprocal of this fraction is plotted. It will be seen that discrimination is poorest at 570 nm, which seems to make sense because the slightly greenish yellow seen by most observers at this wavelength is the least saturated

286   Chromatic Discrimination

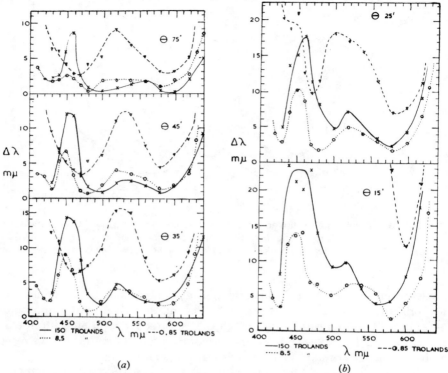

FIGURE 8.14 Wavelength discrimination data obtained by McCree (1960), who used small fields of different sizes at three intensity levels.

hue in the spectrum, being most like white. Small luminances at the spectral extremes have a much higher coloring power. There are many other data on saturation discrimination in the literature, virtually all of which agree that 570 nm is the least saturated spectral color.

Parra (1972) has transformed similar saturation-discrimination data of Priest and Brickwedde (1938) into chromaticity terms. On the basis of MacAdam's work, one would expect an ellipse surrounding the white point (although that part of the ellipse associated with chromaticity changes in the direction of the extraspectral purples would be missing). Parra's calculations instead yield a strange shape having a very long, pointed projection toward 450 nm and a shorter, broader lobe in the opposite direction. Moreover, there is evidence of *concavity* in the shape of the resulting figure. As Parra notes: "The concave shape of the threshold contour predicts that a mixture of A and B, both non-discriminable from O, can produce a color C outside the contour and thus noticeably different from O." In experiments of his own, involving at last count 20,000 color matches, Parra has produced discrimination contours with shapes that he calls "whimsical." LeGrand's (1971) view of Parra's data is that the

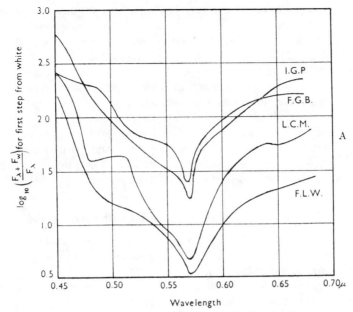

FIGURE 8.15 A purity discrimination function (Wright, 1946). The first discrimination step from white is measured and its reciprocal is plotted to yield a sensitivity plot.

projections point toward the copunctal points (see Chapter 10) of protanopes and tritanopes. The discrepant nature of Parra's results in comparison with those of MacAdam is not currently understood, but it is likely that the much higher intensities used by Parra (about 1000 td) have something to do with it.

A Gap Effect

As we have seen, the r-g and y-b dimensions of chromatic discrimination differ in many ways. Differences in the r-g direction relate not only to color, but they also can support a contour between two fields of equal luminance. Differences in the y-b direction seem related only to hue (see Chapter 7, p. 212). In Chapter 5 we reviewed evidence that B cones are sparsely represented in the retina, which also contains, in addition to rods, R and G cone receptors. It is therefore to be expected that signals from B cones must be averaged over extensive regions. Yet we do not see fuzzy blue edges around things, a fact which suggests that some kind of averaging mechanism works within regions that are defined by contours, even though the contours are exclusively defined by the activity of R and G cones.

With these thoughts as background, we conducted a study (Boynton, Hayhoe, & McLeod, 1977) in which it was predicted that discriminations which depend only upon B cones would be improved by slightly separating (and thus introducing a gap between) the two fields to be compared. The prediction depends upon the idea that, if the fields are precisely juxtaposed, there will be no contour dividing them despite their color difference—a fact that we had already established. The hypothetical averaging mechanism, not knowing where to stop, would therefore tend to derive its signal from the full field (both halves). By separating the two halves of the field, a clear luminance contour is provided between them so that the averaging mechanism should be able to work independently for each half of the field. The prediction was confirmed. By contrast, we found, in agreement with many other studies, that a slight field separation had a significantly deleterious effect upon discriminations that depended only upon luminance differences. Discriminations depending upon r-g differences were little affected by field separation over the range tested.

MEASUREMENT OF LARGE COLOR DIFFERENCES

When two colors differ by a large amount, how is it possible to specify, in a quantitative way, just how different they are? What might be the theoretical or practical importance of being able to do this?

Starting with the second question, it may be replied that, on a practical level, all people concerned with color—whether scientists or artists—seem to agree on the need for a system for the orderly representation of the domain of subjective color experience, more or less similar to the psychological color plane that was described in Chapter 2. Colors lying very close together in such a diagram are to be regarded as similar, whereas those that lie far apart should be judged as dissimilar. When judgments are confined to a single quadrant of the color plane, it is easy to imagine that a given distance on the diagram might be able to represent a fixed sensory difference, regardless of the orientation or location of that distance within the quadrant. For short segments perpendicular to radii of the diagram, a change in hue at nearly constant saturation would be implied, one which we may presume is associated with a large change in the outputs of opponent-color channels, but with their overall response-magnitude unchanged. For radial segments of the same length, discrimination should depend instead upon a change in the magnitude of opponent-color responses, but with their ratios unchanged. For a segment perpendicular to a radius, but near the white point at the center of the diagram, the level of activation of the opponent channels would be weaker than at the rim, and therefore a larger change in hue values would be needed to produce the same amount of sensory change.

It is when one crosses the boundaries from one quadrant to another that comparisons become especially difficult. For example, is a unique red really more different from a unique green than from a unique blue (which is only 90° away and therefore closer to red)? In the sense that red and green are opposites which cancel and cannot be seen together, perhaps they are more different than red and blue, which can coexist. But in terms of judged sensory difference, is green actually seen as more different from red than is blue?

Measurement of Large Color Differences   289

One way to find out is to attempt some kind of direct scaling of large color differences. We will consider one such study as an example, but before doing so we can anticipate that validating the result will be difficult. Indow and Ohsumi (1972) report an investigation where their result is validated against the spacing of stimuli in the Munsell system. In order to interpret this method of validation, it is necessary first to know something about that system.

Albert H. Munsell, an artist born in Boston in 1858, remarked in 1905 that he deplored "the incongruous and bizarre nature of our present color names." He noted that "music is equipped with a system by which it defines each sound in terms of its pitch, intensity, and duration. . . . So should color be supplied with an appropriate system, based on the hue, value, and chroma of our sensations, and not attempting to describe them by the infinite and varying colors of natural objects" (Nickerson, 1976). Initially using rather subjective and intuitive methods, Munsell embarked upon an effort to arrange color chips along the three dimensions that he described. (This effort continued for many years, eventually being carried forward by his descendants.) *Value*, in the Munsell system, is essentially the same as lightness and is correlated with the reflectance of a sample, which Munsell actually measured using a special visual photometer that he developed for the purpose. *Chroma* means about the same thing as saturation (see Chapter 1) and *hue* has its usual meaning. Eventually, through the development of the Munsell Color Company, and later the Munsell Foundation, a *Munsell Book of Color* was produced in which a huge gamut of reflecting samples is displayed on diagrams on which equal distances purport to represent equal sensory differences. Munsell divided the color circle into ten segments as shown at the left in Figure 8.16. In this diagram, white is at the

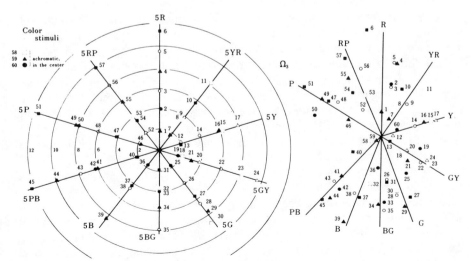

FIGURE 8.16 Results of an experiment on large color differences by Indow and Ohsumi (1976). See text for description.

center, hue varies circumferentially, and chroma increases from the center outward.

Indow and Ohsumi worked with a set of 60 reflecting colors, equal in lightness, or Munsell value, and 26 grays. Subjects were given from 5 to 8 color chips at a time. One of these was designated as a standard and subjects were instructed to order the remaining chips from most to least similar to the standard. Gray samples were then used in an attempt to represent, via the analogy of a series of grays, the degree of perceived sensory difference that lay along the series of colors.

This experiment thereby produced a series of difference scores among many combinations of pairs of colors, represented by the known reflectances of the series of grays. These differences were subjected to a multidimensional scaling procedure known as *analysis of proximities*. With this method a computer algorithm attempted to arrange points in two-dimensional space so that the difference between sampled pairs of points in that space was as highly correlated as possible with the experimentally obtained difference scores.[20] The result of this analysis of Indow and Ohsumi is shown at the right in Figure 8.16. There is a fair agreement between the outcome of this experiment and the arrangement evolved by Munsell and his associates. But there are also important differences, as in the size of the PB segment. The result is hard to interpret. It would be rash to assert (Indow and Ohsumi are careful not to do so) that the Munsell scaling is wrong because it does not agree with the outcome of their experiment; there simply is too much uncertainty concerning what the subjects are actually judging in so complex a task. Nevertheless, this study affords an interesting and instructive example of one modern attempt, among many, to scale large color differences.

A completely different attempt to scale large color differences, undertaken by several of my associates and myself, will be briefly mentioned.[21] Instead of asking subjects to judge color per se, we instead asked them to judge the distinctness of the border that remained between two juxtaposed colors when their relative intensities were adjusted to make that border minimally distinct (p. 254). At first it seemed to us that colors which differed a lot made up very distinct borders, whereas those which differed little produced indistinct borders. (In the limit, those that do not differ at all form no border.) Perhaps, we thought, the judgment of border distinctness would be easier and somewhat more objective than that of color difference, especially when the color difference was large.

In experiments where monochromatic stimuli were compared with white, the method seemed at first to work well. Spectral colors produced a border distinctness with white that was minimal at 570 nm and grew stronger toward the spectral extremes, very much like the saturation-discrimination functions of Figure 8.15, discussed earlier in this chapter. When subjected to the analysis of proximities, the stimuli plotted along a curve as if to define the limits of a color space. A further step was to deal with a large constellation of nonspectral colors.

We compared these in all possible combinations and subjected the distinctness data to the same kind of analysis used by Indow and Ohsumi. We were surprised to find that the additional nonspectral stimuli did not fill in the center of our color space as we had expected, but instead located themselves along the spectral locus. The cause of this discrepancy is that the B cones have no role to play in determining border distinctness under our experimental conditions. Instead, border distinctness depends only upon the differential R- (or G-) cone stimulation supplied by the two juxtaposed stimuli. From this one predicts that any two stimuli which are seen as the same by both R and G cones should fail to support any contour between them, even though, because of differential B cone activation, they may appear very different in color. This prediction has been amply confirmed for the small (less than 2°) stimulus fields that we used.

This result should be considered in the context of the discussion of receptive fields and the chromatic code starting on page 238 of Chapter 7. The distinctiveness of the minimally distinct border is probably a manifestation of activity mediated by the chromatic opponent cells of the r-g variety found in primate brain cells. It seems probable that the y-b pathways signal mainly chromatic information and have little to do with the production of contour.

It is possible (though not proven) that for a tritanope (Chapter 10), who lacks B cones, border distinctness is a valid measure of the color difference that is seen between any two fields. If so, and if some means could also be found for scaling the sensory differences mediated by B cones alone, it might prove possible to combine the two in a system of chromatic difference specification. The advantage of such a system, relative to Munsell space (or to the outcome of an experiment like that of Indow and Ohsumi) would be the relative ease with which it could be related to what is known about underlying chromatic mechanisms.

SUMMARY

Although the difference between two colors depends in the first instance upon differential stimulation of the three kinds of cones, their responses are transformed into two opponent-color signals and one kind of achromatic signal. It is these signals that probably should be examined in order to understand chromatic discrimination.

A model for wavelength discrimination is presented in which the outputs of r-g and y-b opponent systems are utilized. At constant luminance, the first of these reduces to red (or green) cone output alone, and the second to blue cone output only, provided that the probable influence of B cones upon the r-g system at short wavelengths is ignored. In both cases, consideration is given to the "base" activity against which discrimination must be judged. In the r-g case, a "J-factor" is introduced to account for the worsening of discrimination as the red-green balance is upset. In the y-b case, a modified Weber-law relation, which includes a Helmholtzian "self-light" term in the denominator, seems necessary to account for the behavior of the blue-sensitive cones at low intensity levels.

Experimental data on wavelength discrimination, purity discrimination, and generalized chromaticity discrimination are reviewed. It is concluded that there is a need for more data on chromatic discrimination against which to better test further theoretical efforts. Experiments conducted since the pioneering studies that generated the ellipses of MacAdam have added surprisingly little to our understanding of the subject, mainly because the newer methodologies have proved inferior to procedures that were originally used by MacAdam.

Red-green and yellow-blue discriminations follow different rules, as revealed, for example, by different effects when a gap is introduced between the fields being compared. Red-green and yellow-blue discrimination need to be better understood in experiments where one of these two dimensions of variation is held constant while the other is investigated. Only then can the rules of combination, which are not yet known, be understood.

The measurement of large color differences presents some very difficult problems. Two very different attempts at scaling large color differences, which have in common the use of multidimensional scaling procedures, are described. One of these, based on estimates of color differences, succeeds to a degree but is difficult to validate. The other, based on judged border distinctness, fails because the blue-sensitive cones are found not to contribute to the perception of contour.

NOTES

[1] Wyszecki and Stiles (1967) give the following definition, which is similar to that adopted by the International Commission on Illumination and the Optical Society of America: "*Color* is that aspect of visible radiant energy by which an observer may distinguish between two structure-free fields of view of the same size and shape, such as may be caused by differences in the spectral composition of the radiant energy concerned in the observation." This definition includes both the chromatic and achromatic aspects of the stimulus.

[2] It is not easy to set up fields so precisely that the dividing line will disappear when the two halves of the field are of identical color. This observation relates to the fact that, in the world outside the laboratory, achromatic contours usually divide regions of different color. These may be caused by luminance differences, diffraction of light by edges of objects, or sometimes (as in the Sunday comics) by the deliberate introduction of dividing lines between otherwise adjacent regions of differing color.

[3] The term *luminance* has been used in two ways. The term was invented and defined by the CIE; it was briefly discussed on page 164 and will be further treated in Chapter 9. Consider first its strict use: Imagine a univariant detector with spectral sensitivity V_λ. This could be accomplished with a photocell receiving light through a suitably constructed filter, with the output of the photocell delivered to a digital voltmeter. If such a photometer is pointed in turn at two fields that are different in color, and if each field elicits the same reading of the photometer, then the luminances of the two fields are equal.

The V_λ function, which applies to no particular individual, refers to a "standard observer," best regarded as being equivalent to the photometer just described. The V_λ curve is based on the data of many subjects, obtained mainly by the operation of flicker photometry, which is explained in the next chapter (p. 301). But for any real observer, two fields of equal luminance as defined by the photocell may not be equally effective. When two lights are equated for visual effectiveness for a particular observer, using flicker photometry or another method that yields the same result, these lights will generally be of slightly different luminance in the strict sense. It is, however, not unusual to refer to them as being equal in luminance *for that observer*. In the present context, the term is used in this second sense, and should be understood to refer to a particular human observer where it relates theoretically to an assessment of stimuli with respect to their effectiveness for the achromatic (luminance) channels of vision.

[4] An exception occurs at the spectral extremes, where discrimination based upon differences in hue and saturation becomes very poor. Alternatively, the *method of constant stimuli* could be used (see Siegel, 1962). Here the experimenter selects in advance, usually on the basis of some preliminary observations, a set of five or six comparison wavelengths that have previously been equated for luminance relative to a fixed standard with which they are to be compared. For example, the standard might be 580 nm and the comparison stimuli 578, 579, 580, 581, and 582 nm. The five comparison wavelengths are presented many times in random order, and the subject is required to judge whether the comparison field appears greener or redder than the standard. When percent "redder" judgments are plotted as a function of a wavelength, a psychometric function results showing about 50 percent redder judgments at 580 nm and a smooth curve passing through that point, rising from left (578 nm) to right (582 nm). The more acute the wavelength discrimination, the steeper will be the slope of such a curve. One way to gauge the threshold of wavelength discrimination would be to determine the wavelength separation between wavelength values corresponding to the 25 percent and 50 percent values of the curves. (See Engen, 1971, for a summary of classical psychophysical methods.)

[5] The English translation of Helmholtz's *Physiological Optics* (1924) does not contain the discussion of line elements that he developed in 1891 and 1892 and that was included in the second edition. Discussions of Helmholtz's approach are given by Stiles (1972, pp. 1–7), and Wyszecki and Stiles (1967, p. 514).

[6] For example, Bouman and Walraven (1972) employ a space in which the coordinates represent the square roots of R, G, and B. Discrimination is then imagined to take place according to distances measured on the surface of a spherical section whose radius depends upon luminance.

[7] The assumption that the outputs of the R and G cones combine linearly to produce luminance relates to the issue of additivity discussed in Chapter 5 (p. 112) and Chapter 9 (p. 308).

[8] In Figure 8.3, $R' + G' = 1$, so that $G' = 1 - R'$. Therefore any change in R' resulting from a change in wavelength is exactly mirrored by an opposite change in G'. Predictions about wavelength discrimination can therefore be based upon the shape of either function. In this example, $\Delta G' = .113 - .086 = .027 = \Delta R'$.

[9] A reader of a preliminary draft of this chapter wanted to know why hue becomes less yellowish for long wavelengths, if $y = k \cdot L$. Although redness increases with wavelength, yellowness should, according to the model being used, be constant for all wavelengths presented at equal luminance. This excellent question might seem to

raise an embarrassment for the model, but I think not. Consider that the amount of yellowness that can be achieved at a given luminance is maximum around 570 nm, or perhaps at a wavelength a bit longer than this. This is the least saturated region of the spectrum, where R and G inputs cancel in the r-g opponent-color signal. Either (1) yellow is an intrinsically desaturated sensation, (2) the ratio of activities of the chromatic vs achromatic channels is minimum in this region, or both. When aperture colors are viewed, the yellowness of the wavelength that is maximally yellow is in fact remarkably weak. As wavelength is increased at constant luminance, the yellow signal should remain unchanged, but the r-g opponent system should generate a progressively stronger redness signal. The judgment of hue is assumed to be essentially a judgment of the ratio of redness to yellowness. As wavelength increases, redness predominates progressively more, and the field becomes redder and more saturated. Provided that luminance is not too low, a tinge of yellowness still remains at the longest wavelengths, assumed to be the same as that seen at the wavelength of unique yellow. At low luminances, where the spectrum appears nearly achromatic at the r-g balance point, the longest wavelengths would appear more nearly pure red, as they in fact do.

[10] We will see in Chapter 10 that red-green color-defective observers, whose wavelength discrimination depends upon B cones, enjoy their most acute and essentially normal discrimination only in the region of 490 nm. It therefore seems safe to assume that wavelength discrimination in this region of the spectrum depends upon the differential activity of B cones, rather than of R and G cones.

[11] For this purpose, data were weighted and averaged from the following experiments: Bedford and Wyszecki (1958) (data of subjects RE and GW from their Fig. 5, p. 134, for 1° data); Pokorny and Smith (1970); Siegal (1964); Siegal and Dimmick (1962).

[12] Additivity failure for brightness, to be discussed in the next chapter, indicates that when hue is canceled in a mixture of complementary colors, there occurs as well a partial cancellation of brightness. This finding is understandable if it is assumed that brightness depends upon a weighted sum of activity delivered through both the achromatic and opponent-color channels.

[13] The value 3 in the denominator of Equation (8.24) results from the fact that the opponent signal involves the combined action of signals from R and from G cones, and is therefore larger than that of R or G cones alone. Had the R- and G-cone sensitivities been defined initially for a 570-nm crosspoint of the two curves, the denominator would have been 2 instead of 3. The difference reflects the doubling of the G cone signal that is assumed for chromatic purposes, relative to the positioning of the R and G functions required for their sum to be proportional to the luminous efficiency function.

[14] From the standpoint of the theoretical ideas adopted in this book, luminance, and not brightness, must be held constant in order to investigate purely chromatic discrimination. To the extent that brightness depends upon activity in both achromatic and chromatic channels, then constant luminance implies, in general, a slightly different brightness as chromaticity is changed.

[15] See the Appendix for a discussion of the derivation of the CIE chromaticity diagram. The general points being made here apply to any chromaticity diagram, including the triangular variety introduced in Chapter 5.

[16] Judd and Yonemura (1970) begin their paper with the following (p. 23): "In a paper on 'Recent Developments of Thomas Young's Color Theory,' delivered in 1886 before the British Association in Birmingham, A. König stated that 'it ought not to be difficult in the construction of a chromaticity diagram to so modify the adopted arbitrary assumptions that the separation of two points on it would give a measure for the difference in sensation between the colors corresponding to them.'" This has proved to be a much harder task than König had imagined.

[17] See MacAdam (1970) for a translation of this work.

[18] Euclidean space will be recognized as a special case of Riemannian space where
$$g_{11} = g_{22} = 1 \text{ and } 2g_{12} = 0.$$

[19] This is controversial. For example, Friele (1972) indicates that "industrial tolerances are mainly well within 5 MacAdam units."

[20] This statement is an oversimplification of the actual method. See Shepard, Romney, and Nerlove (1972) for further details about methods of multidimensional scaling.

[21] This work has recently been summarized (Boynton, 1978); additional references can be found in that paper.

9
Some Temporal and Spatial Factors in Color Vision

A limiting case of spatial vision occurs in the *Ganzfeld*, which is achieved by filling the entire visual field with light that is uniform in both luminance and chromaticity. Under these conditions, chromatic perception is very poor; colors fade markedly and often disappear entirely.[1] Another limiting case occurs when a point of light is seen in an otherwise dark field; for example, when a signal light is viewed at night at a great distance. Here also color perception is poor—especially if the point of light is of low intensity. Optimal conditions for color perception lie between these extremes.

If a flash of light is bright enough, there is no duration too short for it to be seen. Even complex scenes can be perceived in full color by the light of a photographic flash tube whose illumination lasts for only a few microseconds. This finding does not, however, imply that the physiological activity that is required to mediate such complex perceptions occurs with such lightning-like speed. When the stimulus is brief, both the physiological responses and the sensations that it produces far outlast the stimulus in time. Neural activity concerned with hue, such as color-specific waves of the human evoked cortical response, probably take longer to register than do the components associated with luminance changes (Regan, 1972, pp. 91–109).

The perception of color depends importantly upon which region of the retina receives the image of the perceived object. In general, peripheral color vision is less well developed than that mediated by central vision; this goes hand in hand with the inferior spatial abilities of eccentric vision. Small peripheral targets appear desaturated and, except for red, of uncertain color. Large targets, especially if bright, can mediate good color perception similar to that of central vision. Especially as an aid to speed the search process, peripheral color vision is probably very important.[2]

Both the size of a colored patch, and the sharpness of the boundary that encloses it, can affect its perceived hue and saturation. We saw in Chapter 2 that colors normally are seen as inherent surface properties of objects. The color of an object appears much more uniform than would be expected from a detailed photometric examination of the substantial luminance variations across its surface that most lighting produces.

The perceived color in one part of the visual field depends so importantly upon the remainder of the field that Land and McCann have (incorrectly) suggested that perceived color is unrelated to the physical spectral radiance distribution.[3] Although it is true that the effects of context are important, their underlying physiological basis is not yet well understood. For now, the emphasis will be upon what experiments concerned with spatial and temporal variables can tell us about mechanisms of color vision. Although the stimuli used in the experiments of this chapter are less complex than those used by Land and his associates, they nevertheless include a variety of weird and wonderful arrangements that would never occur in the ordinary world. Of special importance are lights that flicker.

At this point, the reader needs to refer once again to Figure 7.3, which depicts the opponent-color model of human color vision that was used to aid an earlier discussion of relevant electrophysiology. Much of the present chapter will be concerned with experiments and speculations related to the features of that model.

SPATIAL AND TEMPORAL BEHAVIOR RELATED TO R, G, AND B CONES

The visual literature is replete with experiments where the wavelength variable seems to have been tossed in as an afterthought. For example, an investigator who has studied visual acuity as a function of luminance may wonder what would happen if he were to vary the color of the light. Suppose this investigator first does an experiment by illuminating a Snellen acuity chart (of the sort that everyone has seen in doctors' offices or at the Motor Vehicle Bureau) with white light from a slide projector. By dropping neutral filters in front of the projector, the luminance against which the black letters are seen can be controlled, and the results will show that acuity becomes poorer as luminance is reduced: letters on the 20/20 line, which formerly could be resolved, now drop below the threshold of recognition and only the larger letters above can be recognized.

To investigate "color," the experimenter drops an interference filter in front of the projector which, say, passes only a narrow band of blue light centered at 450 nm. An observer, who formerly could read the 20/20 line, now finds that he or she can recognize only those letters corresponding to 20/60 acuity or worse. What can be legitimately concluded from this experiment? The answer is, nothing at all, because luminance has been thoroughly confounded with the chromatic variable. By dropping in the blue filter, the experimenter may have reduced the luminance of the chart to 10 percent or less of what the unfiltered projector light had provided. A control experiment is needed, where the same reduction in luminance is achieved using a neutral filter that does not alter the spectral distribution of the light.

When such controls are used, it is typically found that varying spectral distribution has remarkably little effect upon visual acuity.[4] There may be a small loss in the short wavelengths, but even this probably could be avoided if the myopia of the normal eye for blue light were optically corrected. An unsophisticated interpretation of this result would be that it demonstrated no difference in the spatial resolving power of the three classes of cones in human vision, or of the systems with which they interconnect. This conclusion turns out to be wrong because one cannot assume, just because a light appears blue, that B cones are absorbing very much of the light captured by the photoreceptors. The ability of B cones to transmit signals having a powerful chromatic effect turns out to be extraordinarily high relative to the percentage of photons that they absorb. In other words, despite its blue appearance, it is probable that shortwave light is mostly absorbed by the R and G cones, whose action spectra (it should be remembered) extend across the entire visible spectrum.

Only R and G cones contribute to luminance signals of the achromatic pathways concerned with detailed spatial vision. Light absorbed by B cones therefore is wasted so far as critical spatial vision is concerned. Yet apparently so little of it is lost that it is rather difficult to show that visual acuity is worse in shortwave than in longwave light, where nothing is lost to the B cones.

There are various ways to isolate the behavior of B cones. When this is done, they are found to be both spatially and temporally inferior to the other two cone types. One procedure for isolating B cones is the "test sensitivity" method that was discussed in Chapter 6. Recall that the R and G cones are strongly stimulated by a longwave adapting light. One can then strongly adapt the eye to longwave light, thereby increasing the fraction of visually effective shortwave test light that is absorbed by B cones (Brindley, 1954; Green, 1969; Kelly, 1974; Stiles, 1949). Another technique, called "silent substitution" (to be elaborated below), permits variations of the stimulus that are effective for B cones but fail to produce any change in the steady absorption rate for either R or G cones (Boynton, Hayhoe, & MacLeod, 1977).

The R and G cones work intimately together in a fashion already discussed in Chapter 7. Their output is summed to produce an achromatic, or luminance, signal, and it is also subtracted to generate an opponent-color signal. Almost never is the visual brain permitted to see activity resulting from R or G cones acting in isolation. R and G cones seem to have nearly identical spatial and temporal characteristics. But in order to generate signals for the opponent channels, the sign must be reversed for one of these. Possibly this relates in some way to temporal differences that have been noticed experimentally in connection with alternations between red and green lights at constant luminance.[5]

The temporal properties of the two classes of channels into which R and G cones feed seem to be very different; the opponent channels are more sluggish than the luminance ones. This point will be elaborated later in this chapter.

DIRECT HETEROCHROMATIC PHOTOMETRY

The practical importance of being able to specify which of two lights is visually more effective has long been recognized. Where there is no spectral difference between them, the problem is merely one of physical measurement: whichever light discharges more photons per unit time in the direction of the eye will be the winner. But suppose the lights differ in color: then how can the specification be made? If all vision were scotopic then the spectral radiance distributions of the two stimuli could simply be integrated with the scotopic luminous efficiency function V'_λ (Fig. 5.3), and the larger product would determine the more effective light. But for photopic vision, because there are three kinds of cone receptors, serious problems arise.

Suppose, for example, we wish to compare two fields of light, one a 555-nm green, the other a 465-nm blue. If presented in equal physical amounts (whether specified in energy or in photon units) the green field would look so much brighter than the blue one that there could be no doubt which was the more effective. Indeed, if equal physical amounts of these two lights were used for almost any purpose imaginable, ranging from reading lamps to the illumination of athletic fields, everyone would agree (and it could be shown experimentally) that visual performance[6] under the green light is better than under the blue.

A more subtle question is to ask by what factor the physical intensity of the blue light must be raised in order to equate it for visual effectiveness with the original green light. By what criterion shall visual effectiveness be judged? One approach is to choose a dimension of subjective visual experience that correlates most closely with the physical intensity of the light. This dimension, obviously, is *brightness*.

The procedure by which two fields are compared for brightness, when their colors differ, is called *direct heterochromatic photometry*. Consider again a 555-nm green light on one side of a bipartite field, with the 465-nm blue field immediately adjacent to it. We ask an observer to adjust the intensity of the blue field until it looks "equally bright" as the green one. This turns out to be rather difficult. Although everyone has an intuitive idea of what "brightness" means, the task requires abstracting brightness from a complex sensation—one that may involve large hue and saturation differences in addition to the brightness component. It is found that an observer can choose a criterion and hold it fairly well for a short series of measurements, but when he returns later to repeat the experiment he tends to adopt a different criterion (Walsh, 1958, p. 293). Thus he produces two sets of settings, each with a small variance, but where the mean of the first set differs very significantly from that of the second.

Additivity Failures

These problems could be overcome with enough measurements, many subjects, and good experimental design. But another problem that cannot be so overcome led to the abandonment of direct heterochromatic photometry and to the search for other methods. The problem is that of *additivity failure*.

Consider the following experiment. A white field at the left is compared with a red one at the right. An observer adjusts the red field to appear equally as bright as the white one, and this is done enough times to ensure a stable measure. Now the red field is replaced by a green one and the subject again makes a brightness match. After this has been done, the fields of the two parts of the experiment are optically superposed. Now the field at the left, whose intensity has been doubled, is compared on the right with an additive mixture of red and green (some kind of yellow or white, depending upon the specific spectral distributions of the red and green components).

The surprise is that the right-hand field now appears appreciably dimmer than the white one at the left (Boynton & Kaiser, 1968; Guth, 1967; Tessier & Blottiau, 1951). To show that this is not some kind of an intensity artifact, the mixed fields can be viewed through a 0.3 neutral density filter which absorbs half the light from each field. This returns the left field to the original luminance of each of its equal components. The white or yellow field at the right, being similarly dimmed, still looks much less bright than the white field at the left.

Such additivity failures are not trivial. To restore a brightness match, in a case like that just described, some observers will require that the dimmer field at the right be increased in intensity by a factor of two or even more. This is not a tidy situation upon which to base a photometric system. One would like instead to predict brightness matches by means of an equation having the following form:

$$L = k\int E_\lambda V_\lambda d\lambda. \tag{9.1}$$

Here L is photopic luminance, E_λ represents the energy distribution of a stimulus, V_λ is a unitary photopic luminous efficiency function, and k is a constant.

Because the integral sign means additivity, an equation of this form could never account for additivity failure of the sort just described. Two options suggest themselves. One is to write a more complicated equation that will predict relative brightnesses. The other is to adopt some other criterion for the visual experiment, one that does not lead to additivity failure. *Flicker photometry*, to be discussed next, has met this criterion. As important as this fact has been for practical photometry, its importance for understanding the temporal properties of the visual channels is becoming at least as great.

FLICKER PHOTOMETRY

The Sensation of Flicker

Imagine a spot of light, in front of which is placed a revolving sector disc. When rotated, the disc alternately exposes and occludes the light for equal periods. If the rotation of the disc is slow enough, one sees the spot flashing on and off discretely. A further increase in the rate of rotation produces an ambiguous situation where subjectively the light fails to extinguish completely: in the waxing and waning of the subjective impression, the overall brightness of the pulsing light is greater than it would be if the disc were stopped in the open position, permitting the light to be viewed continuously (the so-called Brücke-Bartley effect: Bartley, 1938, 1941; Brücke, 1864). As rotation rate is further increased, this enhancement of brightness is lost and eventually the field comes to appear almost, but not quite, steady. There remains a sensation of flicker which is just as definite as it is difficult to describe verbally. This sensation is very poorly correlated with the physical flash rate; to the extent that it can be measured, the subjective rate of flicker is lower than the physical one (Forsyth & Chapanis, 1958). As the disc is spun still faster, the sensation of flicker abruptly disappears. All that is seen then is a steady light, and it turns out that the perceived brightness of that light is exactly the same as if the interrupted light were viewed continuously at half intensity, as could be achieved by stopping the disc and placing a 50-percent-transmitting filter between the eye and the spot of light.

The rate of presentation at which flicker disappears is called the *critical flicker frequency* (cff). The phenomenon of flicker disappearance at high presentation rates is called *flicker fusion*. The special case just described can be extended to say that any rapidly repetitive stimulus, no matter how complex its luminance fluctuations in time, will if fused have a brightness equal to a steady light having a luminance equal to the mean luminance of the complex stimulus, calculated for an integral number of cycles. This relationship is known as the *Talbot-Plateau law* (Plateau, 1835; Talbot, 1834).

The Effect of Intensity

Critical flicker frequency is strongly dependent upon luminance. Suppose, for example, that cff has been established in an experiment like the one just described, at a fairly high luminance of the test spot. Decrease the frequency slightly, so that flicker is clearly perceived. Next, place a 50-percent-transmitting filter in front of the eye, and the flicker disappears. Flicker can once more be recaptured by reducing the flicker rate. In systematic studies, cff is found to increase over a wide range approximately as a linear function of log intensity (the Ferry-Porter law).[7] This is a substantial effect: for every tenfold increase in stimulus intensity there is a 10- to 15-Hz increase in cff until very high intensities are reached, where cff stabilizes for large flashes somewhere above 60 Hz.[8]

Preliminary Theoretical Considerations

Why should an increase in intensity cause a change in cff? We should recall that the pathways of the visual system have time constants that make them unable to follow a square-wave input with a square-wave response. This fact also implies that, if an impulse stimulus is delivered to the eye (which can be physically approximated with a xenon flash), the resulting response will not be a spike, but rather a rounded waveform of some kind.

Electrophysiological evidence indicates that some of this "rounding" of the response waveform takes place in the responses of the receptors themselves. Probably the response of the entire receptor has a waveform that is an inherent characteristic of each response element triggered by single-photon absorptions. But the characteristic of the elemental response depends upon the state of adaptation of the receptor. If the eye is light-adapted by the presentation of a steady field upon which a xenon flash is superposed, the response is crisper than in the dark-adapted state. It exhibits a shorter latency before rising from the baseline, its rate of rise is faster, and so is its rate of extinction. This is illustrated by some intracellular responses from the cones of the turtle at different levels of adaptation that are shown in Figure 9.1. Primate receptor potentials exhibit similar changes with adaptation.

But the state of adaptation of the eye need not be controlled only by steady fields; a flickering field will also adapt the eye, and the Talbot-Plateau law holds, in the limit, for adaptation also. Indeed, the precision with which the law holds under most conditions makes it likely that it is determined very early in visual processing, probably in the receptors. If so, a light that is flickering very fast leads to the summation of elemental receptor responses that cannot be distinguished from those produced by a steady light that generates the same mean rate of such responses.[9]

If a light is flickering at a frequency that is not too far below cff, it is convenient to consider it as being comprised of two components. One of these is the steady Talbot-Plateau equivalent, which may be regarded as determining the state of adaptation of the eye. The other is the modulation of light intensity, both above and below that level. For square-wave stimuli of the sort so far considered, the physical modulation is the maximum possible. But the modulation that is produced in the responses of photoreceptors is less than this, and the response associated with the dark phase of each cycle will not fall all the way to the baseline that would be achieved by extinguishing the light for a long time. The higher the intensity of a fully modulated flickering light, the more light-adapted is the eye, the crisper are the elemental responses, and the greater is the physiological modulation that results.

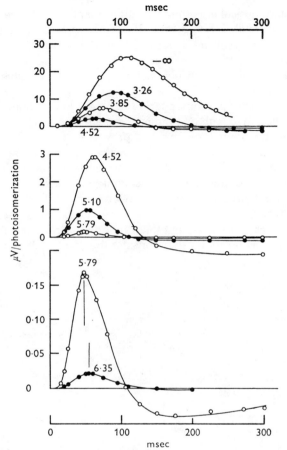

FIGURE 9.1 The effect of increasing the intensity of a background light upon the response to a test flash of constant intensity, measured intracellularly in turtle cones (Baylor & Hodgkin, 1974). Values on the curves are the logarithms of the adapting light (calculated photoisomerizations per cone per s), and responses are scaled in terms of microvolts per photoisomerization. Note that the rise time and time to peak are shortened as the adapting level is raised, and that different scales are used for the three parts of the figure in order to depict clearly the shapes of the curves.

Two Methods Where Flicker Is Used

Since cff depends upon the intensity of the light, one way to specify the relative effectiveness of lights of different colors is to determine the energy required, for various wavelengths in the visible spectrum, for the light to appear just fused (or flickering) when the light is flickered against darkness at some fixed rate. This method has, for example, been used by DeValois to determine the spectral sensitivity of macaque monkeys, and occasionally it has been employed in psychophysical experiments with humans as well (DeValois, Morgan, Polson, Mead, & Hull, 1974; Heath, 1958; Marks & Bornstein, 1973). Since it is possible to work with one wavelength at a time with this method, difficult heterochromatic comparisons are eliminated, and the less ambiguous judgment of "flicker" or "no flicker" can be used instead. Let us call this the method of *single-stimulus flicker*.

Conventional flicker photometry, on the other hand, requires the use of two lights that are alternated with one other. Although technically more difficult than the single-stimulus procedure, this has proved to be an extremely sensitive method, exploited many years ago by practical physicists who recognized the need to develop a standard sensitivity curve by means of which the "relative luminous efficiency" of any pair of lights could be calculated.

Figure 9.2 will help to explain the conventional method. An optical system is required that allows two fields to be presented in the same place in rapid alternation. It is very important that there be no physical artifact at the moment of substitution. As a control for this, consider the train of alternating light pulses

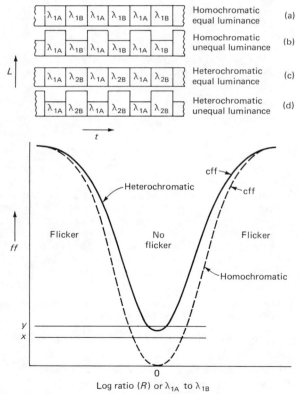

FIGURE 9.2 Flicker frequency (ff) as a function of the ratio of luminances in alternating components. (Adapted from Boynton and Kaiser, 1978.)

represented by (a) in Figure 9.2. Lights of wavelength 1, delivered by field A, are substituted for those of the same wavelength from field B. If the fields are physically equated for radiance, a steady light will be seen, provided that the substitution is temporally and spatially precise. Conventional heterochromatic photometry cannot legitimately proceed until this condition is met.

If the intensity of one of the component fields is reduced, while that of the other is increased by a like amount, the situation represented as (b) in Figure 9.2 will result. This procedure differs from single stimulus flicker because light is now continuously present in the flicker train, whereas for single stimulus flicker, the luminance of component 1B would be zero, producing an alternation between light and darkness. As the luminance of component B is varied relative to A, the expected result is suggested by the dashed curve at the bottom of Figure 9.2. When the two luminances are equal, no flicker will be seen at any frequency, and the function must reach the abscissa of the graph. When component A is reduced to zero, the single-stimulus cff for B will be established as the limit of the asymptotic left-hand branch of the function. At intermediate luminance ratios, the dashed curve is traced out, and there will be a second asymptote at the right, where the luminance of A is much higher than that of B.

Suppose now that the wavelengths of the two components are different. The expected result is depicted as the solid curve in Figure 9.2; the experimental condition that produces this function is depicted as (d) in the upper part of the figure. In general, one would expect that the added chromatic difference would increase cff relative to the achromatic case (b). Of special interest is the minimum of the function (c). Provided that the flicker rate is not too fast, the spectral difference will make it impossible for any ratio of the two field intensities to eliminate the perceived flicker when one field is substituted for the other. Nevertheless, flicker will be minimized when the alternating stimuli are most similar in visual effectiveness. The location of the minimum of the curve on the abscissa may be used to define equal luminance of the two spectral components. (This is the principal experimental operation used in the experiments selected by the CIE for the specification of luminance for the standard observer.)

Also of interest is the value of cff that is represented by the ordinate value corresponding to the minimum of the solid curve. Intuitively it would seem reasonable that the larger the color difference between the two components of the stimulus, the larger should be this minimum value. (At least we know this to be true for the limiting case of no spectral difference, where the ordinate value drops to zero.) Actually, functions of this sort have seldom been obtained, since to do so for a large combination of stimulus wavelengths would comprise a very long and tedious experiment.[10] Instead, the typical procedure for conventional heterochromatic photometry uses a short-cut. A frequency of flicker is selected that is in the vicinity of those rates corresponding to the minimum of the solid curve of Figure 9.2, usually in the range from 10 to 15 Hz. The subject is given control of a knob which varies the intensity ratio of the two components of the field. By a method of adjustment, he determines the knob position which either (1) minimizes the sensation of flicker, or (2) bisects the range within which no flicker is seen. Which judgment is required depends upon the flicker rate chosen. For frequency x in Figure 9.2, flicker will always be seen and the task will be to minimize it. For frequency y, there is a range where no flicker is seen and this range must be bisected. Ideally, a frequency between x and y could be selected that would produce a condition where flicker just barely disappears at the ratio corresponding to the minimum of the solid curve.

Transitivity, Additivity, and Conventional Flicker Photometry

The results obtained by conventional flicker photometry are especially useful because the data conform, at least approximately, to the laws of transitivity and additivity. Transitivity is established in the sense that, if the radiances of wavelengths A and B are adjusted for equal luminance by conventional flicker photometry, and if B and C are similarly equated, then A and C produce minimum flicker when directly exchanged (LeGrand, 1968, p. 75). Additivity experiments have already been described in another context (p. 300). For flicker measurements, suppose that red is flickered with white, green is flickered with white, and then the additive combination of red plus green is flickered with twice the intensity of the original white. Provided that minimum flicker is perceived in each component case, the additive combination still yields a condition of minimum flicker without the need for any further adjustment.

Important advantages accrue when the rules of additivity and transitivity are obeyed. The choice of reference wavelength does not matter, in the sense that a relative luminous efficiency function can be derived by comparing many wavelengths with various fixed references, and the shape of the curve will not change from one reference to another. A further advantage results from the finding that flicker matches are independent of radiance over a wide photopic range. Therefore, since luminance is defined as being proportional to radiance, it becomes legitimate to calculate luminance for a mixture of lights simply by adding the luminances of the components of that mixture. For a continuous distribution of radiance, luminance can then be calculated by Equation (9.1) on page 300, and any two fields having the same calculated value of L should be equal in luminance by the criterion of conventional heterochromatic flicker photometry. In a nutshell, this is the basis of our current photometric system.[11] When defined for a standard observer, V_λ represents the function of *relative luminous efficiency* for photopic vision, better known as the *photopic luminosity curve*.

THEORETICAL BASIS OF FLICKER PHOTOMETRY

Behavior of the sort just described, where additive and transitive relations are obeyed and comparisons are resistant to change with luminance, is exactly what is expected from a univariant mechanism (Chapter 5, p. 109). But at least two classes of cones must supply input to whatever system is being examined by the operations of conventional photopic flicker photometry. If this were not so, the solid curve of Figure 9.2 would reach the x-axis, implying perfect substitution of effectively identical stimulus components, similar to what would be expected if the experiment were performed under scotopic conditions, where only rods are operative.

Examination of the shape of the photopic luminosity curve indicates (Figure 9.3) that it is too broad to be that of a single cone type, and moreover shows that it can be adequately fitted by assuming an additive contribution from only two types of cones, R and G.[12] If so, two fields will be of equal photopic luminance provided that the rate of photon absorption, spread across both R and G cones, is the same for each field, without regard to how the rates are distributed between the two types of cones.

Additional evidence in support of this concept of luminance will be considered later in this chapter. But now we must consider the issue of the apparent univariance of luminosity relationships. This could be accounted for if the outputs of the R and G cones sum linearly as they feed into the luminance channels. But we saw in Chapter 6 that the input–output relations of the photoreceptors are basically nonlinear. How then is it ever possible for their outputs to sum in a linear fashion?

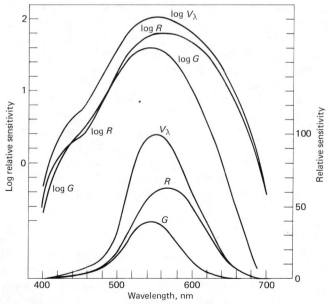

FIGURE 9.3 These graphs show how the Smith-Pokorny **R** and **G** fundamentals sum to produce V_λ, the photopic luminosity function as modified by Judd. The information is given on a logarithmic ordinate (top curves, left scale) as well as on a linear one (bottom curves, right scale).

The answer to this question is not known for certain. One possibility is that, in a steady state of light adaptation, receptor responses are very nearly linear with intensity. Therefore the additivity failures may be too small to measure, and for all practical purposes, linearity is therefore to be expected if the responses of the R and G cones are combined to produce the luminance signal.[13]

A Physiological Basis for Defining Luminance

It would seem desirable to *define* luminance as being related to the linear sum of R and G cone sensitivities. What is required is an agreed-upon pair of R and G receptor sensitivity curves. A decision must be made about how their sensitivities should be set relative to one another. The R and G curves of Figure 9.3 are adjusted vertically so that their sum is proportional to Judd's modified photopic luminosity function. The viewpoint underlying this proposal differs considerably from that of some physiologists. For example, Rodieck (1973, p. 734) states that "The notion of luminance is not much discussed [in this book] for we have no good physiological correlate of it." On the contrary, as shown here, two lights may be said to be of equal luminance when each causes the same rate of photon capture in the combined population of R and G cones, without regard to their relative distribution.

To obtain an experimental measure that correlates with luminance, an operation must be found that does not allow the opponent channels to significantly interfere with a comparison based on activity in the luminance channels. It is only the latter that receive summed inputs from R and G cones. Conventional flicker photometry apparently does this fairly well; the minimally distinct border procedure (p. 290) may do so even better. Both procedures are little influenced by B cone activity, as desired, since on theoretical grounds B cones should deliver their signals to the brain only through y-b opponent channels and therefore make no contribution to luminance.

With the foregoing as background, what remains as a theoretical explanation of the results of conventional flicker photometry is straightforward. The only additional assumption required is to suppose that the opponent-color channels have a more sluggish temporal response than do the luminance channels, and for this reason cannot follow even the moderate rates of flicker that are used in flicker photometry. Ample evidence in support of this assumption now exists; some of it will be reviewed in subsequent sections of this chapter.

SINUSOIDAL FLICKER

The year 1952 separates the literature on flicker into two eras. In that year, Hendrik deLange, working with primitive equipment in a home laboratory in the Netherlands, produced the first of a series of papers that were to revolutionize the study of the response of the visual system to flickering light.[14] What deLange did was to investigate the feasibility of applying *linear systems analysis* to this class of visual phenomena.

The mathematician Jean Baptiste Fourier had shown a century and a half earlier that any repetitive waveform could be replaced by the sum of a series of sinusoids having suitably chosen frequencies and phase relationships. Fourier's analysis applies strictly to linear systems. Among other things, linearity implies that the principle of superposition must be obeyed. For vision, this would mean that the size and shape of responses produced in the visual system must be the same regardless of the level of background luminance upon which the test stimuli are applied. As we saw in Chapter 6, where response compression and other mechanisms of adaptation were discussed, the visual system does not behave in such a linear fashion (see also Fig. 9.1). How then is it possible to apply linear analysis to the nonlinear visual system?

The grossest nonlinearities in vision are those associated with changing adaptive states, produced by overloading the system with stimuli that are much too bright relative to the initial level of adaptation. The solution to the problem of linearity is straightforward; it is to deal with the eye in only one adaptive state at a time, and then to take care not to overload the system.

By allowing the eye to become completely adapted to the level being tested, the resulting response is nearly linear. This has already been discussed in the previous section in connection with the quasi-additivity of the signals from R and G cones. By using the threshold of flicker perception as a response criterion, the visual system is by definition perturbed to the smallest measurable extent, which further serves to negate any residual nonlinearities that might be a problem for stronger test probes.

To test the frequency response of a linear system, an appropriate stimulus to use is one having a sinusoidal modulation. Many readers will be familiar with the use of sinusoids in the evaluation of audio amplifiers and associated components. When the frequency response of such a system is plotted, it usually shows that the output becomes progressively more attenuated as input frequency increases, in which case the system is said to act as a low-pass filter, because it transmits the low-frequency components of the signal better than higher ones. Often there may be a loss of response at low frequencies as well, and it is possible to build electronic filters that pass only a rather narrow band of input frequencies.

If the visual system behaves linearly at a fixed adaptation level, and if the responses of the visual system to sinusoidally varying luminances of all frequencies can be established—including the phase lag between stimulus and response as a function of frequency—then linear systems analysis permits the calculation of responses to any arbitrary stimulus waveform. Because phase information is lacking in psychophysical data, it is important to measure the sensitivity of the eye to sinusoidal inputs directly, doing so at enough frequencies for a smooth function to be fitted to allow an interpolation of sensitivities to frequencies not actually tested. Such a curve is called a *modulation sensitivity function* or a *deLange curve*.

We will not go into detail about the calculations of Fourier analysis, or attempt to develop the formalisms of the method which are second nature to physical science and engineering students, and to which most visual scientists have by now been exposed. Nor will any attempt be made here to cover the whole of a vast recent literature on visual flicker, most of which has relatively little to do with color vision.

In addition to the use of sine waves in recent years, an important difference between flicker studies of the two eras has been the decision to abandon the rather mindless use of full modulation, which had been the standard practice. For sine-wave stimuli, *modulation, M,* is defined as

$$M = \frac{I_{max} - I_{min}}{I_{max} + I_{min}} \tag{9.2}$$

Modulation is thus a relative index that depends in no way upon the value of I. Modulation of 1.0, or 100 percent, is achieved when $I_{min} = 0$. Modulation of 0 occurs when the numerator, $I_{max} - I_{min}$, is zero.

In the older work, as noted above, pulses of light were almost always alternated with periods of complete darkness, as shown in Figure 9.4b. Figure 9.4a shows an example of a 100-percent modulated sinusoid. In the old days, when full modulation was used, the dependent variable of the experiment was cff. Nowadays, in determining a modulation sensitivity function, the frequency is usually set at a fixed value and modulation is varied to find the smallest perturbation that will give rise to a sensation of flicker. Figure 9.4c and d provide examples of 10 percent modulation for sinusoidal flicker and for square wave stimulus at the same adaptation level, having the same absolute amplitude as its sine wave counterpart.

Sensory vs Adaptational Responses

It will be helpful at this point if we can separate our thinking about visual mechanisms into two classes—*adaptational* and *sensory.* As we saw in Chapter 6, mechanisms of adaptation determine sensitivity and certain other characteristics of the visual system. We do not ordinarily have direct sensory access to the behavior of adaptational systems. For example, a field that has completely faded from view under conditions of retinal image stabilization continues to exert its full adaptive effect.[15] By contrast, sensory signals should be regarded as directly responsible for the transmission of information from eye to brain, leading to visual sensations and perceptions.

For any modulation, the state of adaptation of the eye is determined by the mean luminance of the periodic stimulus. Recall that, in the limit where flicker is no longer seen, this value specifies exactly the intensity of a steady light that would be required to match the physically flickering one. To the extent the linear systems analysis is successful, it suggests that the same law applies for the adaptive effects of stimuli that are perceived as barely flickering.

Steady state flicker is an expression that refers to the condition of equilibrium

Sinusoidal Flicker 311

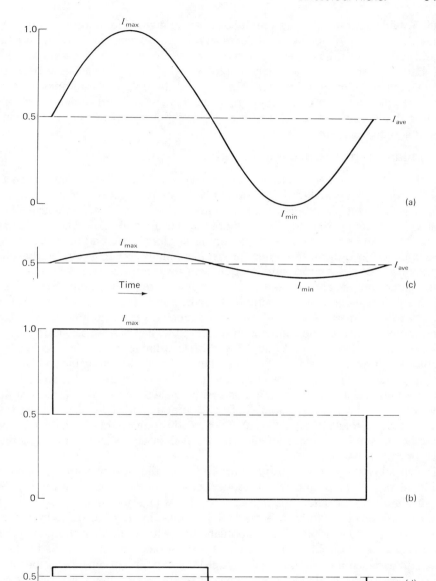

FIGURE 9.4 Examples of sinusoidal and square-wave modulation. In (a) modulation is 100 percent and sinusoidal. In (b), a square wave of the same amplitude is shown. For a linear system, the fundamental sinusoidal component corresponding to this square wave would have 127 percent contrast. To be as effective for the production of visual flicker as (a), the amplitude of (b) must be reduced to 78.5 percent of (a). In (c), sinusoidal modulation is reduced to 10 percent. Panel (d) shows square wave modulation of the same amplitude as (c).

that a stable system achieves after it has been stimulated for a long time by any periodic input, whether or not a fluctuating response remains. For vision near the threshold for the perception of the flickering component of a stimulus, it is probable that the state of adaptation of the eye is literally steady. This is because the adaptational mechanisms are more sluggish than the sensory ones, so that the periodic effects of a flickering input are fully attenuated under conditions where the sensory component of the visual response can follow the flickering input somewhat more faithfully.

Measuring Modulation Sensitivity

If one had direct access to the responses of the visual system, the effects of flicker could be evaluated by measuring the response that results from an eye that is stimulated by 100-percent modulated flicker at various frequencies. Because this is not possible for the psychophysical examination of flicker, the usual "trick" (Chapter 6, p. 169) is employed: flicker frequency and modulation are manipulated in order to determine a just-perceptible flicker. Provided that the system is linear, this procedure is equivalent to the one where a 100-percent modulated input is always used, and a variable response is measured.

To produce curves that resemble those of purely physical measurement, it has become conventional to define the modulation sensitivity function by plotting the *reciprocal* of the modulation threshold, which is a sensitivity measure, as a function of frequency. (When a logarithmic ordinate is used, the modulation sensitivity function is simply the modulation threshold curve plotted upside down.) One way to achieve modulations of less than 100 percent, is to add two stimulus components, one of which is steady while the other one flickers at full modulation.[16] To control adaptation level as modulation is decreased from 100 percent to lower levels, the intensity of the steady component must be increased so that the sum of the steady light and the Talbot equivalent of the flickering component is held constant.

Typical results are shown in Figure 9.5. The ordinate shows threshold modulation, plotted as a function of frequency, with both scales logarithmic. The curves are for four different adaptation levels. At high frequencies, modulation sensitivity declines sharply at each adaptation level. In other words, as frequency is increased, progressively more modulation is required to keep the perception of flicker at a threshold level. When 100 percent modulation is reached (where the curves reach the abscissa of the graph) the experiment must cease because it is physically impossible to produce modulations greater than this. This limiting case is like the measurement of cff in the older studies, and confirms that cff increases with luminance. The remainder of the function provides new and important information.

The high-frequency behavior is not hard to understand in qualitative terms. As frequency increases, the response to each stimulus pulse overlaps progressively more with the one elicited by the next cycle of the stimulus; the responses smear together and if the frequency is high enough, there is insufficient ripple

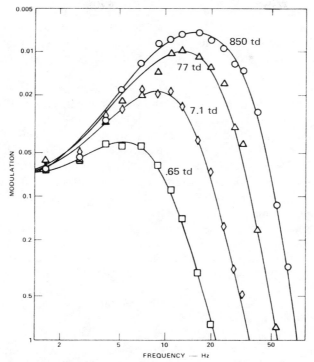

FIGURE 9.5 Threshold flicker modulation in a large field, with adaptation level held constant at the values shown for each curve. (After Kelly, 1961.)

remaining in the sensory channels for flicker to be perceived, even at full modulation. Intermediate and low-frequency behavior is more subtle.

It is clear from Figure 9.5 that there is an optimal frequency for the perception of flicker. For example, at an adaptation level of 850 td, less than 1 percent modulation is required to see flicker at a frequency of about 15 Hz. This modulation cannot be seen at 5 Hz, but 3 percent modulation can. This result seems paradoxical because reducing frequency should allow the responses to be better separated in time at 5 Hz than at 15 Hz. What could be responsible for this inversion of a reasonably expected result?

Explaining the Low-frequency Sensitivity Loss

In order to perceive flicker, a mechanism somewhere in the visual system must be able to detect that there is a difference between the magnitude of the peak of the response to flicker and that of the trough. It is conceivable that the hypothetical detector might have difficulty remembering how large a peak response had been, in order to compare it with the response to the ensuing trough, if too much time were to elapse between the two events. If such peaks and troughs of responses were separated by many seconds, such an explanation might be plausible. But even the slowest frequencies used in most flicker experiments, in the vicinity of 1 Hz, are sufficient to separate the peak and trough of the stimulus, and presumably also of the responses thus produced, by only a half second. Memory over this time period is known to be good (Massaro, 1975).

An alternative explanation (see Kelly, 1972) hypothesizes a sluggish inhibitory process. At low frequencies, inhibition tends to cancel the effectiveness of the flickering component, which otherwise could be seen. But the inhibitory process cannot follow rapid flicker, so high frequencies remain effective. The inhibitory process may be regarded as a property of the adaptation mechanism not specifically discussed in Chapter 6; recall that, in order to work effectively, adaptational mechanisms must have more sluggish temporal characteristics than the more transient sensory signals; otherwise the visual message would be homogenized and information would be lost.

The exactness of the Talbot-Plateau law at very high frequencies suggests that neither the sensory nor the inhibitory machinery is able to react to the fact that the light is physically flickering at these rates. At intermediate frequencies, where flicker is more easily perceived, the inhibitory machinery may continue to respond only to the equivalent Talbot level without being able to follow the undulations of the stimulus. The sensory message, although generally attenuated by the effects of essentially steady adaptation, is therefore not selectively subject to inhibition within a cycle of the stimulus. As frequency is reduced still further, the inhibitory mechanisms begin to follow the flicker, only slightly at first, but progressively better as frequency is further reduced. At extremely low rates of flicker, the inhibitory mechanisms have time to follow almost perfectly, and their effect is to seriously attenuate the differential sensory response to variations in the stimulus.

In other words, inhibitory processes tend to reduce responses of varying magnitude to a common level. These inhibitory processes have their own temporal characteristics, which are somewhat more sluggish than those of the sensory channels of the visual system. At high frequencies, where the adaptational mechanism cannot follow at all, flicker is registered only to the extent that the sensory pathways can follow the action. At low frequencies, where the sensory channels could otherwise follow the flicker very well, adaptation reduces their response to flicker. As a consequence, flicker is easiest to see at intermediate frequencies, where the two factors are in optimum balance.

Effects of Different Luminance Levels

At low flicker rates, the curves of Figure 9.5 converge in conformity with Weber's law. This implies that, in order for Weber's law to apply, the stimulus must last long enough for adaptation to catch up with it, and thereby attenuate the response before the response has had time to run its course. At very high frequencies, there is no adaptation at all, a surprising finding that is best visualized by plotting the same data, as Kelly did, in another way (Fig. 9.6). Here

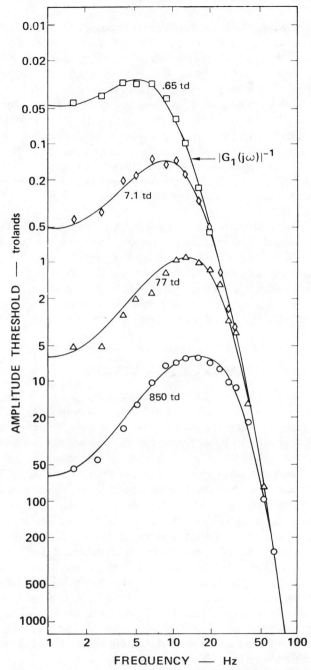

FIGURE 9.6 The data of Figure 9.5 replotted in terms of the absolute amplitude of modulation required for the threshold perception of flicker.

it is the absolute amplitude of modulation, in trolands, that is plotted on the ordinate instead of the relative modulation of Figure 9.5. The curves of Figure 9.6 are related to those of Figure 9.5 by a downward sliding of all of the functions, without change of shape, by amounts which are proportional to the adaptation level. (If A is amplitude, L is mean luminance, and M is modulation, $M = A/L$ by definition—this is equivalent to Equation [9.2]. Accordingly, log L = log A + log M, and since log L^{-1} is plotted, log L^{-1} = log M − log A.) The fact that the functions converge to a common high-frequency asymptote in Figure 9.6 implies that, no matter what the adaptation level, the adaptational machinery is incapable of attenuating a threshold response to flicker that is modulated at 100 percent, or nearly so. (For example, in the neighborhood of 30 Hz, the amplitude of just-perceptible flicker is the same for adapting levels of 7 td and 77 td.)

Another important feature of these functions is their changing shape with adaptation level. The low-frequency sensitivity loss, which is very large at 850 td, is very slight at 0.65 td. This finding is consistent with the idea that the responsible processes of inhibition have temporal properties that are intensity-dependent, also showing a crisper response at high levels than at low ones. Therefore, as the intensity of adaptation increases, inhibition becomes more effective, which causes the optimum sensitivity to move toward higher frequencies.

FLICKER CURVES AND COLOR VISION

Instead of modulating a light by varying its luminance, it is possible instead to produce a chromaticity exchange at constant luminance. To simplify the experiment, one can keep the B cones out of the way by choosing a pair of longwave monochromatic lights that are ineffective stimuli for these receptors. The results of the earliest experiment of this type are shown in Figure 9.7, where they are compared with an achromatic curve from the same study. Two features of the chromatic curve stand out in comparison to the achromatic one: (1) the high-frequency response is inferior; (2) there is no attenuation of sensitivity at the lowest frequencies tested. The chromatic curve describes behavior like that of a low-pass filter, rather than the tuned frequency response of luminance flicker. Why should this tuning be absent for chromatic flicker?

We can begin to answer this question by first posing another. What sort of response is expected to a square-wave chromatic exchange? By such an exchange we mean, for example, the sudden substitution of a red light for a green one, at constant luminance. From the R cones we predict an increase in response level; from the G cones, a decrease. There should also be a definite shift in the output of r-g channels in the r direction. There should be no change in either the luminance or the y-b channels.

The use of a sinusoidal flickering stimulus does not alter these basic relationships: it will still be the case that only the r-g channels will be active, along

Flicker Curves and Color Vision

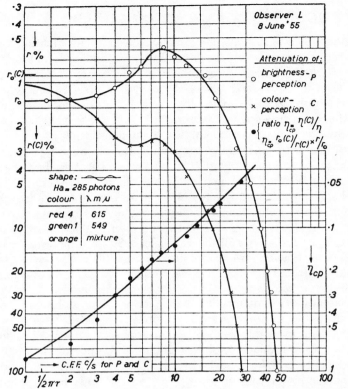

FIGURE 9.7 Results of the pioneering study of deLange (1958), as he displayed them. The ordinate values represent modulation in percent, either for luminance flicker (circles) or chromatic flicker (x's) obtained by shifting the phase of the stimulus components. The ascending curve at the bottom is based on an index of the ratio of flicker sensitivities represented by the two conditions of the experiment.

with the R and G cones which feed them. When compared to luminance flicker, the different behavior of the visual system in response to chromatic flicker cannot be explained by the behavior of the R and G cones themselves, because these receptors feed both kinds of channels. Therefore we must look to the behavior of the r-g channels for an explanation of the chromatic flicker function.

Let us consider first the high-frequency difference between the luminance and chromatic flicker functions. At one level of analysis the explanation is simple: the luminance channels apparently have a high-frequency response superior to that of the r-g chromatic channels. A fuller explanation would require a physiological demonstration of exactly why this is so; detailed evidence of this sort is lacking.[17] Whatever the detailed physiological explanation may be, the general conclusion is clearly consistent with the results of conventional heterochomatic flicker photometry as reviewed earlier.

INTERACTIONS BETWEEN R AND G CONES

The R and G cone systems are spatially as well as chromatically opponent. The perception of a contour may depend upon a luminance difference alone, a chromatic difference alone, or both of these together. In all three cases, R and G cones work together symbiotically in ways that are now beginning to be understood; the background physiology has already been examined in some detail in Chapter 7. An experiment by Kelly (1975) will be help to illustrate this.

Using low-frequency sinusoidal flicker, Kelly investigated modulation sensitivity to temporal variations in luminance and chromaticity, using fields that were either uniform, as shown in Figure 9.8b and c, or vertically divided and modulated in counterphase, as shown in Figure 9.8a and d. For 1-Hz flicker, he found that splitting the field greatly enhanced sensitivity for luminance modulation (Figure 9.8a), but reduced it considerably for chromaticity modulation—see Figure 9.8d. This result can be interpreted on the hypothesis that sensitivity to low-frequency luminance flicker is reduced by an inhibitory process that operates strongly between R and G cones. The inhibitory messages themselves are assumed to follow the low temporal frequencies well and are therefore in phase with the excitatory signal. As a consequence they normally serve to limit the perception of low-frequency luminance flicker—Figure 9.8b. But when the two parts of the field are flickered out of phase—Figure 9.8a—the inhibitory mechanisms cannot operate in their normal way along the border, and sensitivity to flicker there is relatively enhanced by the absence of the inhibition that occurs throughout a uniform field.

In chromatic flicker with uniform fields, on the other hand, repeated exchange of chromaticity does not permit the inhibition between R and G cones to operate optimally, presumably because the inhibitory signals are out of phase with respect to the mechanisms that they would otherwise inhibit, as illustrated by Figure 9.8c. In this case splitting the field, shown in Figure 9.8d, restores the appropriate phase relationships for inhibition along the border, and thereby reduces the sensitivity to chromaticity flicker. These effects were very large. The

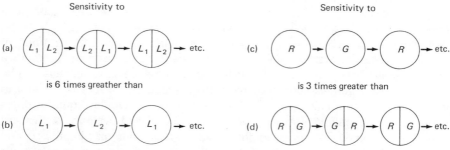

FIGURE 9.8 Summary of experimental conditions and main results of an experiment by Kelly (1975).

introduction of the split field and counterphase flicker improved luminance discrimination by a factor of about 6, while it reduced chromaticity discrimination by a factor of 3—an 18-fold ratio of the combined effects.

A plausible explanation of the different low-frequency behaviors of the achromatic vs chromatic flicker curves relates to this interesting hypothesis that lateral inhibition takes place more between R and G cones than between cones of the same type. In the case of flicker produced with white light, the low-frequency loss of sensitivity is explained by the fact that the R and G cones are working in phase. As the excitation of a particular R cone increases, so does that of neighboring G cones. The activity engendered in these G cones is transmitted to the central R cone as an inhibitory signal, reducing the size of R-cone response relative to that observed without such an inhibitory influence. Conversely, as the excitation of G cones increases, surrounding R cones exert an inhibitory effect upon them.

Two questions may be raised about this scheme. The first is teleological in nature: from a "design" standpoint, why require lateral inhibition to occur between receptors of different kinds, rather than between those of the same type? If the eye did not generate and transmit chromatic signals, there would seem to be no point in such an arrangement. But for an eye that sees color, it is very important, as has been stressed previously, that the difference signal between the outputs of the R and G cones should be extracted as quickly as possible. We have seen that cones are interconnected by horizontal cells, some of which seem somehow to be involved in the generation of r-g opponent signals. If R and G cones are interconnected for that purpose, it surely would be difficult to disconnect them, in a functional sense, in order to provide lateral inhibition only between cones of the same type.

The function of lateral inhibition is apparently to enhance contours. Most contours result from luminance differences. Therefore, so long as there exists a luminance difference to be enhanced (given that this same machinery is also required for chromatic purposes to mediate lateral inhibition between receptors of different types) then why not use it also for this essentially achromatic purpose?

A second question about this scheme relates to the behavior of dichromats (Chapter 10). For example, protanopes (who are believed to lack R cones) show a lack of red-green discrimination as well. One may legitimately inquire: if R cones are lacking in protanopes, what (if anything) takes their place? Is it possible that the protanopic retina is riddled with holes where R cones normally would be? The anatomical evidence is to the contrary (Kalmus, 1965, p. 53), and such a situation would be a structural disaster. A very simple hypothesis is to assume that protanopic R cones are still present, but that they are filled with chlorolabe, the pigment normally found only in G cones. If in addition these "R" cones of the protanope were otherwise normal, then "R" and G cones would mediate achromatic lateral inhibition in the usual way, although the r-g opponent signals would always be balanced at zero. Excepting a reduced sensitivity to long wavelengths and an inability to make color discriminations that depend upon r-g difference signals, protanopes would be expected to exhibit normal vision. This is consistent with observation (see Chapter 10).

A study by Kelly and van Norren (1977) was designed as a further test of ideas similar to those just discussed. Their stimulus configuration is schematized in Figure 9.9. Three optical channels were used.[18] Two of these produced sine-wave flicker, in this case of red and green lights out of phase. Because the green (G) component in this illustration has a higher luminance than the red (R) one, there is an achromatic component of the stimulus whose amplitude is represented by fluctuations around the dashed lines at the top of each part of the figure. The contrast of the flickering component can be altered, without altering adaptation level, by manipulations depicted by the difference between the left- and right-hand diagrams. At the right, the R and G flicker components have been increased in proportion, resulting in a higher amplitude of chromatic and achromatic flicker. To keep adaptation level constant, a steady yellow (Y) field is used, whose intensity is manipulated so that the sum of Y and the average of the $R+G$ flickering components of luminance remains fixed at the level shown by the dashed line.

The special case of purely chromatic flicker is shown in Figure 9.10a. Here the G and R components have the same amplitude; since they are out of phase, there is no luminance fluctuation. Figure 9.10b shows an example of pure luminance modulation produced merely by altering the phase relationship without changing amplitude: now the R and G components are in phase. Because the total excitation of the R and G components of flicker is the same in each case, the level of photon absorption in R and G cones is also unchanged. In Figure 9.10c, the G component of b has been replaced by an equal luminance of R. If the chromatic component of the flickering stimulus is regarded as being proportional to the difference between R and G, then the chromatic flicker of c is the same as that of a, except that it is now initiated only by activity of the

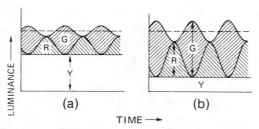

FIGURE 9.9 Examples of stimulus waveforms used by Kelly and van Norren (1977). Here the green/red ratio of two sinusoidal stimulus components is kept constant while the modulation depth is increased in (b) relative to (a). To keep the adaptation level of the eye constant, the luminance of a steady yellow component (Y) in (a) is reduced in (b), so that the sum of the steady Y component and the red-green flickering components produces the same mean luminance in each case. This is shown by the horizontal dashed lines.

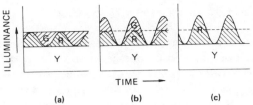

FIGURE 9.10 Luminance profiles of stimulus waveforms used by Kelly and van Norren (1977). In (a), modulation is purely chromatic, because a constant luminance is maintained as the red component replaces the green, and vice versa. By shifting the phase of one component relative to the other (b), pure luminance flicker is obtained. In (c), the green component of (b) has been replaced by an equal luminance of red, to produce a stimulus that includes both the chromatic component of (a) and the luminance component of (b).

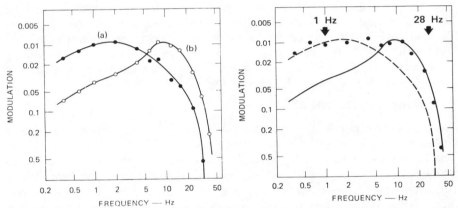

FIGURE 9.10 (Continued) Experimental results obtained for these three conditions. The results for the complex condition (c) are accounted for by the upper envelope of component functions derived from the other two conditions of the experiment.

R component. Since the luminance component of c is the same as that of b, then c can be regarded as combining both components of modulation in a single waveform.

The graph on the left in Figure 9.10 shows the results of an experiment where conditions a and b were tested. The chromatic flicker curve, shown by the filled symbols, is not completely flat at the lowest frequencies tested.[19] This result implies that not all inhibition occurs between R and G cones; there apparently is a certain amount that takes place also within cones of the same type. The achromatic flicker curve, shown by the open symbols, has an entirely different shape. It shows a marked low-frequency attenuation and a substantially better sensitivity to higher frequencies.

When stimulus c is used, it produces the result shown at the right in Figure 9.10. Here the same two curves from the figure at the left have been drawn through the data points for condition c without any vertical or horizontal adjustment. The conclusion seems clear: since stimulus c contains both components of flicker (achromatic and chromatic) that a and b contain individually, and at the same level of modulation for each, then sensitivity for c is governed by the component having the greater sensitivity at each tested frequency. Below 5 Hz, this is the chromatic component; above 5 Hz, it is the achromatic one.

This experiment, and others from the same study, indicate that the achromatic channels of the visual system are clearly separable from the chromatic ones.[20] Under most viewing conditions, chromatic signals passing from eye to brain are represented by the differences between cone outputs, so that activity related only to G cones cannot generally be expected to reveal itself in single-unit responses (whether of ganglion cells, at the LGN or in visual cortex) any more than it does in psychophysical experiments. The only way to reveal the responses of R or G cones in isolation would be somehow to wholly negate the contribution of the other class of cone by some experimental technique. Stiles's field-sensitivity method (Chapter 6, p. 196) represents one attempt to do this, but it works only if one can safely assume that there is no transfer of adaptive effect from one type of cone to another. There is another method, to be described next.

Silent Substitution.[21]

Consider the hypothetical sensitivity curves of R and G cones that are shown in Figure 9.11. Choose an arbitrary sensitivity level S, and draw a horizontal line that intersects each curve twice. The intersection with the R curve occurs at the wavelengths marked λ_1 and λ_2. Suppose that that these two wavelengths are alternated with one another at equal radiance. Since we know that the R function has equal values at these wavelengths, then (by definition of what is meant by spectral sensitivity) they will have identical effects upon the R cones.

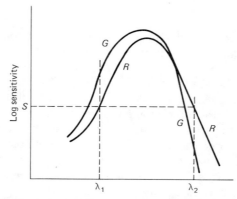

FIGURE 9.11 These hypothetical sensitivity curves are used to illustrate the principle of silent substitution. By choosing two wavelengths, λ_1 and λ_2, to which the R cones are equally sensitive, alternation between them will silence the response to flicker in R cones. Because the G cones are much more sensitive to λ_1 than to λ_2, the same alternating stimulus will be an effective flicker field for them.

Therefore an R cone could not "see" a sudden switch from one of these wavelengths to the other. This is what is meant by a "silent" substitution, or flickerless exchange. On the other hand, the G cones are considerably more sensitive to λ_1 than to λ_2. Therefore the same equal-radiance substitution that is silent for R cones will produce a significant transient change in the stimulation of G cones, with an increased level of stimulation in going from λ_2 to λ_1.

It must be emphasized that the R cones are stimulated by this procedure, but only by a steady light. Therefore, if a flicker experiment is undertaken that uses a rapid alternation between these wavelengths at equal radiance, only the G cones will be able to respond to the flicker.

Actually there is no need to choose a pair of wavelengths to which cones of one type have exactly equal sensitivity. Sensitivity differences can easily be compensated by inverse adjustment of the radiances of the alternating components. The only requirements to be met are (1) that the two sensitivity curves be significantly different, and (2) that the spectral sensitivity of the class of cones to be silenced is known. In Chapter 5, the current status of our knowledge of cone action spectra was discussed. Although these curves are still being refined, they are now fairly well established; recall that we needed to know these shapes in order to analyze chromatic discrimination in Chapter 8.

The result of Kelly and van Norren's application of the silent substitution procedure is shown in Figure 9.12. In this experiment, a red light alternated

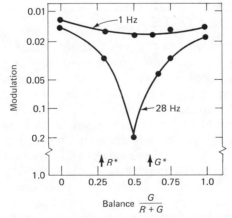

FIGURE 9.12 Results from Kelly and van Norren's (1977) experiment, which in the ratio of red and green components of a flickering stimulus was varied in such a way as to keep r-g chromatic flicker constant as luminance flicker was varied. At 1 Hz, where the chromatic visual channels are most sensitive, the ratio of the two components has little effect. At 28 Hz, where the achromatic channels are most sensitive, flicker sensitivity is minimized when the luminances of the counterphase components are equal.

The arrows at the bottom represent the calculated ratios of the stimulus components: pure R cone activity (R*), with G cones silenced, and pure G cone activity (G*), with R cones silenced.

with a green one. These investigators worked over a range of balances of their stimulus components designed to keep chromatic flicker constant as luminance flicker was varied. The abscissa of the figure refers to the fraction of the total luminance of their stimulus that is made up of the green component. A value of zero indicates that all of the sinusoidal flicker is in the red component; unity indicates that it is all in the green. (Both R and G cones respond, though differentially so, to both components.)

The curve labeled "28 Hz" shows a sharp drop of modulation sensitivity when the luminances of the two components are balanced. Because this is a condition of steady luminance, this curve would drop to zero if the 28-Hz stimulus were effective only upon the luminance channels. The fact that it does not do so indicates that the chromatic channels are capable of following at this frequency, but only rather poorly.

The curve labeled "1 Hz" is for an identical stimulus condition at a lower frequency. For the conditions of this part of the experiment, chromatic flicker does not vary much across the entire range of ratios that were studied. If only the chromatic channels were capable of responding to 1-Hz flicker, the curve would be horizontal. Perhaps there is a slight sag in the middle; if so, this may reveal that the achromatic channels are capable of following this frequency to a slight degree for the low levels of modulation to which the chromatic channels are mainly sensitive.

SPATIAL PROPERTIES OF THE THREE KINDS OF CONES

Evidence was presented in Chapter 7 to show that both chromatic and achromatic pathways mediate the perception of contour. Except possibly for discriminations of the grossest sort, spatial vision at photopic levels depends only upon the activity of R and G cones. These, as we have seen, feed their signals into both luminance and r-g opponent channels. It is sometimes stated that the contours formed by luminance differences are necessarily more salient than those caused by chromatic differences, but this may be an incorrect generalization. In my laboratory we have shown[22] that the strength of a chromatic contour depends upon the differential amount of R (or G) cone activity related to the two parts of the visual field whose junction forms the contour. By a variety of methods (to be discussed below), we have found it possible to determine the amount of luminance contrast needed to produce a contour of the same strength as that caused by any particular chromatic difference at constant luminance.

Border Distinctness

The most distinct contour that a purely chromatic difference can produce is formed between fields of 465 and 700 nm. The first of these elicits the maximum possible ratio of G/R cone activity, whereas the second is optimal for R/G.[23] The amount of achromatic contrast required to mimic this maximum chromatic contour varies from one observer to another, but it is on the order of 30–40 percent. An achromatic contrast of this amount comes very close to what is needed to mediate the highest levels of spatial discrimination.

My associates and I have used three methods to specify an equivalent achromatic contrast which produces the same strength of border as that produced by a purely chromatic difference. In all three cases, the procedure is first to ask the subject to set a minimally distinct border between the two chromatically different fields being tested. For the subject under examination, we believe that this equates the activity of his achromatic pathways over the entire field.[24]

The first method for estimating border distinctness uses a direct comparison. Two juxtaposed fields of uniform chromaticity are presented slightly above, but clearly separated from, the chromatic fields that are being gauged. The observer adjusts the luminance of one side of the upper field in order to produce a contour which, in his judgment, is as distinct as the chromatic border seen below. A second method requires the use of only the chromatic pair: after having set the minimally distinct border, the subject simply rates its perceived strength along a 7-point scale, where zero means no border at all, 7 indicates a very strong contour, and 4 is intermediate (other integers are also used). A similar procedure can be used with borders formed by luminance differences only. The third method measures the tendency of steadily fixated borders to fade in terms of the percentage of time, during five minutes of intense staring, that a border is not seen. Results based upon the three methods agree well.

At a given luminance level, it proves possible to write an equation that relates the two kinds of contrast. But at low luminances, the achromatic contrast required to mimic a certain amount of chromatic border strength is greater than it is for high luminances. A plausible interpretation of this differential dependence upon luminance points up an essential difference between chromatic and achromatic borders that was discussed earlier in this chapter and also in Chapter 7. Border enhancement by lateral inhibition occurs only for achromatic borders (Fiorentini, 1972, p. 194). Assuming that the enhancement process is intensity-dependent, being more effective at high intensities than low, then a higher achromatic contrast would be needed at low luminances than at high in order to mimic a border of fixed chromaticity difference. This hypothesis is consistent with the increased low-frequency inhibition that is found with increasing intensity in the experiments of Figure 9.5.

In experiments where borders divide small, centrally fixated fields, B cones appear to play no spatial role. Any two stimuli that are equivalent for R and G cones will fail to produce a contour no matter how different the B-cone activity level may be in response to the two halves of the field. This leads to a curious situation, where a split field (for example blue on one side and green on the other) has no sharp division between its parts, which seem instead to melt together. If the field is masked down so that only an area of about 12' of width is seen, with the physical border dividing it, the field becomes homogeneous in appearance, with its hue depending upon the location of the physical border, which, as it moves, alters the percentage of the two components. When a similar border is formed by a luminance difference, or by a chromatic difference mediated by R and G cones, it is easily seen as moving within the masked area.

It was pointed out earlier in this chapter that visual acuity is not markedly dependent upon wavelength. However, if the activity of the B-cone system is isolated by the use of intense longwave adapting light, thereby selectively depressing the sensitivities of R and G cones, the true spatial inferiority of the B cone system becomes evident. The physiological basis for this B-cone inferiority, where spatial vision is concerned, almost certainly relates to their sparse distribution in the retina, especially in the central foveal region, where they may be entirely absent in a region of 8' to 20' of arc or thereabouts.[25]

Why Is the B-cone System So Different?

It may be instructive in this case to think teleologically and ask, what is the purpose of this seemingly curious arrangement? In other words, why design the retina this way, rather than to use equal numbers of R, G, and B cones? We may speculate that a principal job of the visual system is to localize regions of space, and then to provide sufficient spatial resolution within these smaller regions to permit a high level of visual acuity. The foveal region of the retina evolved to mediate high spatial resolution, as we saw in Chapter 4. In the fovea, the diffusing layers of the retina needed to process and carry visual messages are swept aside, and almost the entire thickness of the retina is made up of the receptors. Despite the thinness of the foveal retina, the outer segments of the receptors are longer and skinnier than elsewhere, achieving a peak density of about 150,000 receptors per square millimeter.

Rods are excluded from the select group of receptors that is found here, and in addition, B cones are discouraged. There are some B cones in the outer zones of the fovea, but probably not any in the central bouquet with which we do our most critical seeing (Wald, 1967).

The R and G cones have a dual function, as has been repeatedly stressed: to mediate both spatial and chromatic vision. To do this properly, it is likely that they are functionally interrelated, as in the turtle, by way of horizontal cells and probably also by gap junctions (Chapter 7). The difference signals derived from them are of two kinds, spatial and chromatic. It seems clear that these two kinds of cones must have very similar spatial and temporal properties in order to work together properly. They probably differ structurally in no way. They differ only in the photopigments they contain, and the connections that they make.

B cones, on the other hand, seem to have only a chromatic function. They have not as yet been distinguished structurally from other cones in the human retina. Since there are so few of them, they capture relatively few photons and the intrinsic sensitivity of the B-cone system in central vision must be very low. To compensate for this, signals from B cones summate over very large regions. The purpose of this summation is to gain sensitivity, but this gain is achieved at a cost of low spatial resolving power.

The blueness that B cones help to initiate appears to be well integrated within contours that the R, G cone system is responsible for rendering. The process of integration seems to stop, or at least is severely discouraged, beyond these contours. Thus, the blueness of an object appears to terminate at its edge and does not seem to spill into the space beyond. The gap effect, which was mentioned in the previous chapter (Boynton, Hayhoe, & MacLeod, 1977), shows that discriminations which depend only upon differential activity of B cones are improved by contours which serve to confine the averaging within each half of a split field.

Much remains to be learned about the functions of the separate chromatic and achromatic channels that seem to have evolved in human vision. The general outlines, however, seem already to be clear. Because spatial vision is its main assignment, the problem of design is to provide chromatic information without reducing spatial acuity or adding an excessive number of fibers to the million or so neurons of the optic nerve, which seems to be the principal bottleneck for information transmission from eye to brain. Most of these transmission lines probably are concerned with achromatic messages, fed by both R and G cones, the same ones that generate the chromatic difference signals. Fewer channels probably are devoted to these chromatic signals, which means that something must be sacrificed. Temporal resolution seems mainly to be what is lost, as we have seen by comparing chromatic and achromatic modulation transfer functions in time.

The y-b Opponent System

Little has been said here about the y-b opponent channels, which have so far been much less studied psychophysically. To the extent that the physiological dichotomy between r-g and y-b cells (Chapter 7) is accepted as convincing, these signals exist at the ganglion cell level in primates. Therefore, the y-b message, like the r-g, must be extracted in the retina. The rivalrous perception of blue and yellow lights, when these are presented to opposite eyes, also tends to support this contention (deWeert & Levelt, 1975). However, it seems less likely that the y-b signal is extracted in such intimate relation to receptor activity as is the case for the r-g signals. There are, in the first place, no Y cones with which B cones can subtractively interact. Rather, B cones probably interact with signals representing the sum of R and G activity—the luminance signals. The B-cone spectral sensitivity is very different from the photopic luminosity function, so there is much less overlap between R+G and B signals than between R and G; this reduces the need for an immediate extraction of a difference signal. Finally, psychophysical evidence (Larimer, Krantz, & Cicerone, 1975) that the r-g signal is much more linear than the y-b message is consistent with the idea that more stages of visual processing are completed, in the y-b case, prior to the extraction of a difference signal.

TEMPORAL RESPONSES OF CONES AND THEIR PATHWAYS

When a temporal modulation sensitivity function is established by psychophysical procedures, the measurement will reveal the properties of photoreceptors only if it can safely be assumed that the pathways into which receptors feed have a much better frequency response curve than that of the receptors. Otherwise the frequency response of the pathways will interact with that of the receptors in determining the overall ability of the system to follow a flickering input.

We have already seen evidence that the r-g chromatic pathways are limiting in this sense. Flicker photometry apparently succeeds because the r+g pathways, concerned with luminance, have a flicker response superior to that of the r-g pathways that are concerned with color. Because both pathways receive their inputs from the same R and G cones, it cannot be the receptors per se that determine the flicker response in both cases.

The graph of Figure 9.13 provides a further illustration of the effects of adaptation level on the response to flicker. The upper curve (solid circles) shows the threshold amplitude of a sinusoidal stimulus of 100 percent modulation, which of necessity is measured with no added background. The adaptation level for 100 percent modulation is therefore determined solely by the mean luminance of the sinusoidally varying field, which varies along the curve, increasing downward. For example, at a mean luminance of 10 td, the maximum frequency that can be resolved is about 18 Hz. The lower curve (open circles) is for a constant adaptation level of 25,000 td, produced mainly by a steady

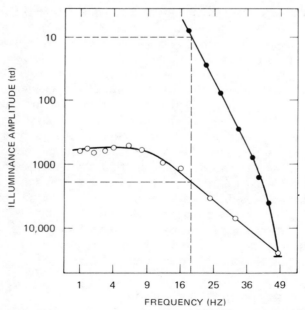

FIGURE 9.13 Results of an experiment by Kelly, Boynton, and Baron (1976). The solid points refer to a condition of 100 percent modulation and variable adaptation level; they specify the maximum frequencies of flicker that can be perceived at these levels. The open circles at the bottom represent flicker thresholds under a condition of 25,000-td adaptation level, which is held constant for all frequencies.

background upon which a smaller flickering component is superposed (except at the highest frequency tested). To see 18 Hz flicker in this case, a larger amplitude of modulation is required than before—about 1500 td. But for an adaptation level of 25,000 td, this large amplitude of modulation nevertheless represents only about 3 percent relative modulation, which means that much greater modulation is yet possible. The limit is reached at the lower right-hand point on the graph, where flicker at nearly 50 Hz can be resolved for 100 percent modulation at 25,000 td.

If the visual channels can handle nearly 50 Hz at a high adaptation level, it seems likely that they can also resolve better than 18 Hz at the lower adaptation level. The message probably fails to register at higher frequencies than this because of two effects associated with low adaptation levels: (1) the lower absolute amplitude of stimulation that physically can be provided by a fully modulated field, and (2) temporally less well defined responses of the receptors. Although light-adapting a receptor reduces its absolute sensitivity, it has the beneficial effect of crispening the temporal characteristics of responses having a given amplitude. Therefore, although a higher absolute amplitude of modulation is required for the light-adapted receptor to achieve a given amplitude of response, still higher modulations are available and these enable the flicker to be followed to very high frequencies.

The foregoing analysis does not rule out the possibility that some of the effects of adaptation are attributable to changes in the ability of the visual pathways to follow what the receptors deliver. It would in fact be extravagant to design a system in which the temporal resolution of the conducting pathways was far superior to that of the receptors themselves. At low adaptation levels, where there is very little light available, the primary task of the visual system is to provide vision that is as good as possible, given the shortage of photons. As an aid to this, the sensitivity of the eye can be improved by permitting the integration of light over longer time periods than might otherwise be optimal. As the adaptation level is increased, the intensity of an added stimulus must be made greater in order for it to be seen. The extra photons in the adapting field can be used to good advantage if they somehow lead to an improved temporal response of the eye. Such improvement occurs in the photoreceptors, as we have seen, but this would be of no use unless the pathways could take advantage of it. So the process of temporal reorganization is probably not limited to the receptors, but very likely extends also to the pathways to which they connect.

This hypothesis about the temporal reorganization of pathways could be tested if the response of the entire visual system, as determined psychophysically, could be compared with that of receptors alone. When this is done by comparing monkey receptor potentials to human psychophysics, the high-frequency asymptotes of the psychophysical R and G modulation-sensitivity functions are identical to each other and to those obtained electrophysiologically. A reasonable but not certain conclusion is that with high-intensity chromatic adaptation of the sort that is normally used to isolate R and G cones, the temporal response of the visual pathways does not limit the psychophysical measurement, which therefore taps the behavior of the receptors.

Frequency Response of R, G, and B Cones

When 100 percent modulation is used to test the maximum frequency that monkey receptors can follow, the use of long- and middlewave light yields essentially identical results, as shown by the solid and open circles of Figure 9.14. By use of longwave adapting stimuli of various intensities, it has proved possible to deduce the frequency response of the B cones, and this curve is also plotted in Figure 9.14. If the curves are adjusted to fit at low frequencies, the response of B cones falls off more abruptly than that of the R or G cones as frequency increases. It may be concluded that, despite any known structural differences between the three kinds of cones in the primate eye, the temporal

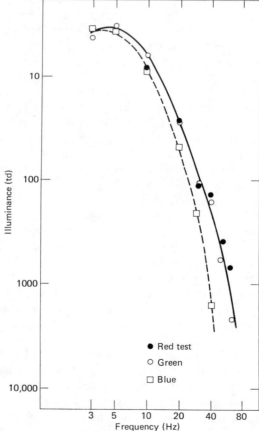

FIGURE 9.14 Absolute amplitude of modulation required to elicit a 10-uv criterion response to flickering lights under conditions designed to isolate responses of the R, G, and B cones of macaque monkeys. (After Boynton and Baron, 1975.)

response of the B cones at high frequencies is for some reason inferior to that of the other two types.[26]

At the lower frequencies normally used for flicker photometry, the R, G, and B cones have more nearly comparable sensitivities to flicker. It therefore seems likely that the failure of B cones to contribute to luminance, as measured by flicker photometry, results largely from a limited frequency response of the y-b pathways. If so, both kinds of chromatic opponent pathways have an inferior temporal resolution relative to that of the cone photoreceptors or the achromatic pathways.

COLOR INFORMATION FROM EDGES

This chapter began with mention of the lack of color perception in a *Ganzfeld*, which suggests that, without contour, there is no color. In Chapter 8 it was suggested that, if the blue cones are excepted, the distinctness of a chromatic border might serve as a valid index of the color difference between the fields being compared. Repeatedly it has been stressed that the same R and G cones that are responsible for initiating contour perception also feed the r-g opponent pathways. These ideas suggest that the perceived color of an area depends heavily upon messages associated with the contour which serves to define a region, and less upon signals coming from within the region so defined.

Contour is necessary for any kind of visual perception. When the retinal image is immobilized, thus eliminating even the smallest eye movements that are present in normal vision, all visual perception fades away after a few seconds.[27] Krauskopf (1963) reported an experiment having special relevance to the role of contour in chromatic perception. He arranged his apparatus so that a central spot, and the region surrounding it, was seen as a stabilized image. The hue of the central spot differed from that of the surround. When the entire stimulus, including the outer edge of the surrounding annulus, was stabilized, the entire target faded from view. But when only the outer edge of the annulus was freed from stabilization, the target once again could be seen. From the standpoint of color vision, the most interesting finding was that the hue of the entire field became that of the annulus. Evidence of a discontinuity of hue between annulus and central spot was apparently lost, along with information about the presence of the contour between spot and annulus. The hue of the central spot then became determined by the action of the unstabilized, and considerably remote, outer edge of the annulus.

A TEMPORAL CODE FOR COLOR?

In this chapter, as well as in Chapter 7, it has been assumed that color is coded in terms of which cells in the brain are active, and that the spatial separation of color signals, which begins in the three kinds of retinal cones, is preserved in multiplexed form in order to provide the brain with the information that it needs for color.

A completely different viewpoint turns up from time to time in the visual literature. It has been proposed that the cones are all fundamentally alike, but that they generate responses which, rather than being univariant, are "tagged" in some way depending upon the wavelength of the exciting light. In addition to contradicting the principle of univariance, which we found in Chapter 7 to be essential for understanding known visual physiology, the "tagged" response concept also fails to explain the facts of color mixture (Chapter 5) and discrimination (Chapter 8).

Most often, similar ideas have been proposed to account for the encoding of chromatic information at postreceptoral stages of visual processing—for example, in the optic nerve. It has been proposed that the chromatic messages are temporally encoded; if so, all nerve fibers could conceivably carry messages about all colors, represented by the pattern of impulses which is presumed to vary depending upon the relative inputs delivered by the three kinds of cones.

A major basis for these ideas lies in the observation that colors can be seen in response to certain black and white patterns. The prototypical example is that of Benham's disc. Half the disc is black; the other half contains 45° triads of arcs drawn with various radii. When this pattern is rotated at the proper speed, various colors are seen at the leading and trailing edges of the arcs. Another demonstration of color in response to a black-and-white stimulus occurs when looking at the noise pattern on an empty black-and-white television channel.

There is no logical connection between such observations and the conclusion that color vision results from the transmission of information according to a temporal code. Rather, in the r-g pathways there may be differential delays depending upon which way the balance is changed, and in addition the y-b and luminance pathways probably have their own temporal characteristics. Given all this, it would be surprising if one could *not* find ways to generate chromatic signals with black-and-white inputs, which, after all, stimulate all three kinds of cones. To ensure achromatic vision it is necessary to keep the r-g and y-b opponent pathways perfectly balanced. If these "illusory" colors are ever to be explained, it seems likely that the proper interpretation will come from a fuller understanding of the kinds of pathways that have been discussed in this book. To start instead with illusions, and then to work backwards in an attempt to postulate perceptual apparatus which might conceivably account for them, has been singularly unproductive throughout the history of the scientific study of perception. Illusions in the domain of color seem to be no exception, especially if one is tempted to extend the ad hoc explanation of the illusion far enough to account for normal color perception.

SUMMARY

Flicker photometry was developed as a procedure to equate the visual effectiveness of lights of different colors. It was used because direct procedures, such as those involving brightness matching, produced unreliable and nonlinear results. The theoretical basis of flicker photometry was originally obscure. The modern view, resting on theoretical conceptions rooted in psychophysical evidence, is that achromatic (luminance) channels of the visual system exhibit a temporal response superior to that of the opponent-color channels. Flicker photometry succeeds because, at intermediate frequencies, only the luminance channels are capable of following the flickering input. Luminance depends only upon signals from R and G cones. Their spectral sensitivities overlap sufficiently for departures from linearity to be very small, and the luminance channels exhibit nearly univariant properties despite their dual input.

The application of linear-systems theory to the study of the temporal response of the visual system has led to the view that adaptational mechanisms cannot follow luminance flicker at high frequencies that the sensory channels can handle. The inhibitory activity associated with adaptation tends to cancel the perception of low-frequency flicker, producing an optimal frequency for achromatic flicker perception. Chromatic channels exhibit little of this low-frequency attenuation of sensitivity. The overall evidence suggests that the inhibitory effect may stem more from interactions between R and G cone systems, than from within systems of the same type. Evidence is presented to show that the visual brain normally does not receive input from R and G cones individually, but instead sees only summed luminance signals and subtracted chromatic signals that carry the red-green code. This is consistent with the opponent-color model first presented in Chapter 7.

The R and G cones play a critical role in spatial, as well as color, vision. Contours can be seen at equal luminance if differential R-G cone activation is present. B cones, on the other hand, have no role to play in spatial vision in the foveal region, where they are sparsely represented. Their role is to mediate the blue input to the yellow-blue opponent channels.

The notion that color information might also be carried by a temporal code is considered and rejected as both unnecessary and implausible.

NOTES

[1] See review by Avant (1965).
[2] A useful discussion of peripheral color vision is that of Moreland (1972). See also Gordon and Abramov (1977). A thorough review of the role of peripheral color vision in search is given by Christ (1975).
[3] Land and McCann (1971) state (p.1): ". . . when we measure the amounts of light in the world around us, or when we create artificial worlds in the laboratory, we find that there is no predictable relationship between flux at various wavelengths and the color sensations associated with objects." On the contrary, when one measures this relationship under controlled conditions, data of astonishing reliability can be generated (Boynton, 1975, p. 322–333; Boynton & Gordon, 1965; Boynton, Schafer, & Neun, 1964).

[4] As will be explained later in this chapter, the concept of *luminance* depends mainly upon the procedures used in flicker photometry; these are not concerned with the spatial resolving power of the eye. Therefore it is not preordained that the relative weights of the contributions from R and G cones, as these enter into the channels that mediate acuity, will be the same as for those channels concerned with the perception of flicker. Nevertheless, when visual acuity is tested with gratings, the luminance required just to resolve a very fine grating is found to be independent of the spectral distribution of the light (Brown, Kuhns, & Adler, 1957). Another approach to the problem, which obviates the need for an independent luminance scale, is to find a task where, unlike the case for gratings, acuity first improves with luminance and then becomes poorer again. Foxell and Stevens (1955) found this to be the case for Landolt Cs. Berbert (1955, 1958), using pairs of luminous dots, was able to determine the minimal separation of the dots required for them just barely to appear as double. He found small differences favoring optimal acuity for broad spectral distributions and narrow bands of light near the center of the visible spectrum, with some loss of resolution at the spectral extremes. Campbell and Gubisch (1967) found slightly better spatial resolution with monochromatic light at 578 nm in comparison with white light. For other references, see Riggs (1965), p. 331.

[5] deLange (1958) was the first to show that small phase adjustments are necessary to produce minimum flicker when there is a sinusoidal exchange of one wavelength for another. Walraven and Leebeek (1964 a, b) demonstrated that this effect is strongly dependent upon intensity, being clearly evident at 1 td but becoming absent at about 20 td and higher. In extending deLange's approach, their results were very complicated, particularly in regard to the influence of the frequency at which the phase shift was measured. A different approach is that of Weingarten (1972), who substituted red and green lights, each in an exposure of 1 s at 2 td, for parts of a white background field. The onset of a shift to 549 nm had to occur about 20–25 ms prior to a shift to 621 nm in order for the two events to be perceived as simultaneous. This difference disappeared when the luminance of the test fields was made three times greater than that of the background. The results can be explained by assuming that, when luminance does not change, the r-g opponent channels must carry the signals. A change toward green for some reason takes longer to register than does one toward red. But when the same spectral changes are introduced together with a luminance change, the r + g nonopponent channels carry signals that probably register centrally before those carried by the slower opponent channels.

[6] *Visual performance* is an expression used mainly in illuminating engineering to refer to any kind of human activity whose efficiency is importantly controlled by the quantity and distribution of illumination. An important example is reading.

[7] Ferry (1892); Porter (1902). This "law" is obeyed much more approximately than the Talbot-Plateau law.

[8] The limiting frequency for flicker perception depends importantly upon the area of the stimulus. Under some experimental conditions, for example those of Figure 9.12, this value will be lower than 60 Hz.

[9] Even steady lights may be regarded as flickering in a statistical sense. Each photon emitted from such a light, when absorbed, is capable of generating an element of response. The apparently steady response of a receptor that results from a high rate of such events actually exhibits some variability due to the statistical nature of this process.

[10] Some such measurements were made for the special case where white and mono-

chromatic lights were alternated, in the early days when the method of flicker photometry was being developed (Ives, 1917; Ives and Kingsbury, 1914; Troland, 1916). See also the more recent work of Truss (1957).

[11] The full story is more complicated than this. See Wright's comments in the Appendix, and also LeGrand (1968, Chapter 4). In determining the CIE photopic luminosity function, some data based on heterochromatic comparisons were used, and a good deal of smoothing was done. Judd (1951a) proposed a modified curve that differs from the original one mainly in showing an elevated sensitivity at short wavelengths. Wyszecki and Stiles (1967, p. 436) have summarized these data.

[12] Very possibly (see the previous chapter) different weights must be attached to the effectiveness of photon absorptions in the R vs G cones depending upon whether they contribute to luminance or to the red-green color balance. The present discussion assumes that the curves of Figure 9.3 represent the true relative ordinate positions of the R and G cone sensitivity curves; no adjustment of the Smith-Pokorny data is required to achieve this. To obtain a balance of R and G activity near 570 nm, as required for color balance, the upper G function in Figure 9.4 must be raised 0.3 log unit relative to the position shown, and all values on the lower G curve must be doubled.

[13] Sirovich and Abramov (1977) have shown how behavior indistinguishable from that for a univariant mechanism could result exactly despite the contributions of nonlinear components. For this to happen, each component must obey the same power law $R = kI^p$, then the sum of the two response components must be raised to the p^{-1} power.

[14] These papers were mainly published in the *Journal of the Optical Society of America*. References to this and other relevant literature may be found in a review chapter by Kelly (1972). In 1964, a collection of papers from a symposium on *Flicker*, which was held the previous year in honor of deLange, was published (Henkes & van der Tweel, eds.). The first chapter of that volume, by G. Sperling, provides an excellent introduction to the theory of linear systems analysis. A more extensive treatment is given by Cornsweet (1970).

[15] Sparrock (1969) showed that increment thresholds are the same, whether or not the adapting field is visible to the observer. He used the technique of image stabilization (Ditchburn, 1973) to render the adapting field invisible on some occasions.

[16] For example, to produce the 10 percent modulation of Figure 9.5 (c), the steady component of the adapting field must be 90 units, and the maximum intensity of the fluctuating component, .1 unit. $I_{max} - I_{min} = .1; I_{max} + I_{min} = .45 + .55 = 1$.

[17] There is, however, clear evidence of separation of these two channels at the LGN, where nonopponent units are found in the magnocellular layers and opponent units are found in the parvocellular ones. The magnocellular units show a superior transient response (Dreher, Fukada, & Rodieck, 1976).

[18] Kelly and van Norren also used a fourth field; to keep the discussion as simple as possible, its function is not described here.

[19] There is a general similarity between these functions and the ones originally obtained by deLange (Fig. 9.5). Two differences are that (1) Kelly and van Norren's stimuli were filtered lights of dominant wavelenghts 632 and 535 nm, which would produce a higher chromatic contrast (R/G ratio) than deLange's monochromatic 615-nm and 549-nm components, and (2) Kelly and van Norren's data include measurements at three frequencies (1 Hz and below) not tested by deLange.

[20] See also King-Smith and Carden (1976).

[21] The procedures discussed in this section were developed independently by Rushton, Powell, and White (1973) and by Estévez and Spekreijse (1974). Such an exchange must be accomplished with excellent spatial and temporal precision. A control condition that is useful requires the exchange, through separate optical channels, of two fields that are spatially superimposed and of the same spectral distribution and radiance. If the apparatus is working adequately, nothing will be seen, other than a steady field.

[22] The work described in this section began with the paper of Boynton and Kaiser (1968) and has subsequently been summarized in two reviews (Boynton, 1973, 1978), which may be consulted for additional references.

[23] For all practical purposes, the R/G ratio is constant beyond 700 nm. Actually, it reaches a maximum at about this wavelength and then declines, but only very slightly. See Brindley (1955), Stiles (1957), and Wyszecki and Stiles (1967, p. 561).

[24] Wagner and Boynton (1972) have shown a good agreement between spectral sensitivity curves obtained by the minimally-distinct-border (MDB) technique and those measured on the same subjects using flicker photometry. Tansley and Boynton (1976) have demonstrated that B cones are not involved in the determination of MDB settings, or in the strength of the residual chromatic contour. Therefore it seems safe to assert that the B cones do not contribute to luminance; if luminance is assumed to be controlled by the achromatic visual pathways, as in the model of Figure 7.3, then the MDB procedure apparently results in an equation of activities in the achromatic pathways that receive their inputs from retinal areas upon which stimuli of different colors are imaged.

[25] Wald (1967). References to earlier work by König and Köttgen and by Willmer and Wright (1945) are given in this paper, which is based on Wald's Ives Medal address to the Optical Society of America. See also Brindley (1954), Green (1968), Kelly (1974), and Stiles (1949), and a paper by Marc and Sperling (1977) that provides the first direct evidence about cone distributions in primates (baboons).

[26] Krauskopf and Mollon (1971) tested and confirmed this indirectly by measuring the critical duration of flashes under conditions designed to isolate Stiles's π_1, π_4, and π_5 mechanisms.

[27] The literature of this field has been summarized in a book by Ditchburn (1973).

10
Variations and Defects in Human Color Vision

In 1794, shortly after his election to the Manchester Literary and Philosophical Society, John Dalton presented the first of 116 papers that he would eventually deliver to that group. He spoke on "Extraordinary Facts Relating to the Vision of Colours," emphasizing his own abnormal color vision. Although Dalton's talk was not the first scientific communication about color defect or *color blindness* (as his condition later came to be called in popular literature) its influence was retroactively enhanced when Thomas Young chose to discuss Dalton's observations in *Lectures on Natural Philosophy* in 1807. Dalton's place in the history of color science was doubtless assured by the reputation that he later developed as the father of atomic theory.[1] In 1827, the term *Daltonism* was coined to describe red-green color deficiency, but this is rarely heard in English-speaking countries today.

Since Dalton's time, the literature on color blindness has become enormous. By 1896, the second German edition of Helmholtz's *Physiological Optics* already listed more than 1,200 references. Today, each issue of the quarterly newsletter *Daltoniana*, published by the International Research Group on Colour Vision Deficiencies, typically includes some 30 to 40 abstracts of relevant new books and papers.

This chapter emphasizes the varieties of relatively common red—green color defects as these relate to their genetic and physiological underpinnings. This discussion will require frequent use of concepts developed in earlier chapters and will serve also to constitute a useful review of some of those ideas. Before dealing with color-defective vision, however, a few introductory remarks will be made about variations in normal color vision.

VARIATIONS IN NORMAL COLOR PERCEPTION

Consider these two cases:

- There are certain shades of turquoise that I see as predominantly green, but which my wife insists are bluer than they are green. Which of us is correct?
- If many normal observers are asked to judge the spectral wavelength that appears as uniquely yellow, there will be a spread of estimates, each quite reliable, covering about 10 nm in the spectrum.[2] In this region of excellent wavelength discrimination, such a range implies that a distinctly greenish-yellow, as seen by one observer, may appear as definitely reddish when viewed by another. Who is right, and who is wrong?

To some extent, such disputes about color names might seem to reflect problems associated more with labels than with sensations. But this is surely not always so. Recall, for example, the exercise described on page 161 of Chapter 6. By selectively adapting only one eye, it is evident that the color sensations subsequently experienced by looking at objects with first one eye and then the other can be different. Such variation occurs in some people without the need for selective adaptation, occasionally in forms so extreme that one eye is essentially color-normal and the other color-blind. Leaving these special cases aside for later consideration, we may speculate about the possible causes of normal variations. Where blue-green is concerned, my wife's retina might contain a higher proportion of B cones than mine. Where yellow is concerned, perhaps there are normal variations among humans in the proportions of their R and G cones. If these simple possibilities are granted, even if all normal visual systems were otherwise identical, we would probably expect the reported results. From this point of view, my wife and I are both correct in our color naming, and there is no wavelength of the spectrum that should be expected to appear as unique yellow for all observers (Fig. 10-1).

In Wald's study described on page 193 of Chapter 6, his star subject for isolating the blue mechanism was R.H., whose sensitivity was about three times higher than the average observer for that mechanism. This could reflect the presence of more B cones and/or more summation of B-cone signals in the eye of R.H. than for other subjects. Rushton and Baker (1964) provide clear evidence that there are substantial variations in the proportions of R and G cones among normal observers. But the question of how color balance is affected by variations of cone populations in different people is a tricky one. Consider, for example, a case where an individual has twice as many R cones, relative to G cones, as the "normal" individual represented by a crossover of the R and G

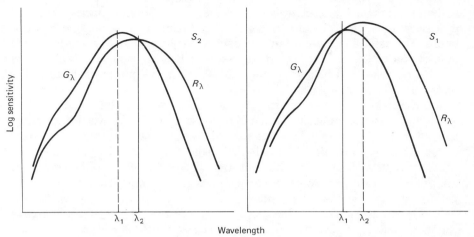

FIGURE 10.1 If a sensation of yellow arises when the numbers of R and G cones are equally stimulated, then subject S_1 at the right, with relatively more R cones than subject S_2 at the left, will see unique yellow at a somewhat shorter wavelength of the spectrum.

cone sensitivity curves at 570 nm as shown in Figure 7.4. By the simplest view, this should cause the R curve at 570 nm for this individual to be raised by a factor of 2 above his G curve, causing 570 nm to appear decidedly orangish; the unique yellow wavelength would be decreased to about 490 nm. But reality may be more complicated than this. In the course of exposure to stimuli in the real world, such an individual would, relative to the "normal" person, receive a steady excess excitation of R over G cones. This would be expected to cause selective adaptation at the cone level, and probably also in the r-g opponent pathways. Such adaptive mechanisms would probably serve to reduce the effects of excess R-cone stimulation in this individual. The adaptational adjustment might be short-term, based upon the immediately prior history of exposure of the eye to various parts of the visual field, as discussed in Chapter 6. However, there could also be a long-term component related to permanent changes in the visual system during critical stages of visual development caused by the relative excess of R over G cone stimulation (see footnote 6).

Sensations are private, so it is impossible to compare them directly among observers. All of us may agree that a 650-nm light appears red, but it is meaningless to ask whether my sensation of red is the same as yours. What we can often agree upon is color names. For example, as I write this sentence I see a red book on my shelf and I am fully confident that a thousand observers, provided they have been screened as "color normal" by the sorts of tests to be described later in this chapter, would each call it "red" if limited to only a single color term. All of us have learned this name in association with objects that have been experienced in the presence of other people with whom we can communicate. Such objects reflect light and, by means of mechanisms and processes described in earlier chapters, certain patterns of activity arise in our brains. The association that we make between a color that we see and the name that we give to it is obviously learned, as are such color names themselves. Yet there is no reason to believe that the *sensation* caused by the activity of the brain has been acquired.[3]

All normal observers seem to agree that red, green, yellow, and blue are words that describe qualitatively different sensations. Where we do not agree so well is upon the assignment of secondary-hue names to blends of these colors, where we must decide whether the balance between two hues of nearly equal strength is exact, or instead leans one way or the other. In the context of the principles of human color vision that have been elucidated in this book, various physiological bases for such differences are easy to imagine. What is unimaginable is that such differences would not exist. After all, quantitative variations between individuals must occur at all stages of information processing throughout the complex chromatic visual system.

The Concept of Color-Blind People

Because they are far from rare, most of us have had experience with *color-blind* people. Some readers will themselves suffer from this condition, so for them the problem is firsthand and very personal. We may have been amused by their inability to name colors "correctly." Yet when they disagree with us, are they really wrong? This time the answer is both "yes" and "no." They seem to err because there are too many color names in the normal vocabulary to suit their needs. But we normals would be similarly "wrong" if we constituted in turn only 4 percent of a much larger population of individuals who, because they possess a more complex visual system than ours, would insist on the use of additional terms that we, given our limitations, could not reliably associate with particular spectral reflectance distributions. Analogously, in a world populated only by color-defective observers one may rest assured that a color vocabulary would have evolved that could be used reliably and consistently, although it would be less rich and would differentiate fewer color differences than the ones that we, as normals, are capable of naming. Therefore, if color-blind subjects are often "wrong," it is only because we normals confuse them by giving them too many names to use. They cannot be accused of being incorrect about what they see, any more than we are wrong in what we see, however limited our perceptions might be in comparison with those of some hypothetical visual Superman with six kinds of cones and three varieties of opponent-color pathways. The deficiency of most "color-blind" observers is therefore only partial, and relates to that of normal observers in the same way that the color vision of the normal relates to the hypothetical visual Superman.

It is perhaps more important that, quite apart from whatever color names are used, such individuals make incorrect color *discriminations* by failing to discern differences that others can report without any difficulty. If a color-blind employee produces defective electrical equipment by connecting color-coded wires inappropriately, it seems certain that his employer will think that the employee is *wrong* and would feel justified not only in excluding that troublemaker from the assembly line, but also in attempting to screen out, in advance, others who might cause similar problems.[4]

Learning from Color Blindness

One can hope to learn something about how a system normally works by studying its behavior when it malfunctions. In this sense, the color-defective observer can be important for understanding normal color vision. Recall, for example, that the best estimates we have of the spectral sensitivities of the R and G cones, whose shapes must be precisely known in order to understand chromatic discrimination (Chapter 8), have depended heavily upon psychophysical studies of observers believed to possess just one of these cone types, while lacking the other. Color blindness also has something to say about human genetics and vice versa, as will be seen later. But not all color blindness has a genetic basis; some forms can result from insults to the body in the form of accident, disease, or drugs. By examining the nature of color defects inherited or acquired, information can sometimes be uncovered suggesting which parts of the visual pathways have probably been affected, thereby helping to diagnose disease or to assess theoretical ideas about the organization of the visual pathways. The study of color blindness also raises subtle questions concerning the relation between perception and the neurochemical mechanisms of the brain whose activity underlies it. These concerns relate to what color-blind people really see and how their perceptions can best be gauged and understood.

HOW COLOR VISION CAN GO WRONG

Once again it is time to look at the opponent-color model of Figure 7.3. This time we will consider the logical consequences of assuming that various components of that model have been altered in ways that might impair the normal system of chromatic information processing.

Loss Systems

Suppose that the B cones were missing, but that the visual system were otherwise normal. Because there are few B cones and they do not contribute to the luminance channels, there should be no change in the spectral sensitivity of the eye as measured, for example, by flicker photometry (Chapter 9). There should also be negligible loss of contour perception, because B cones are scarce and contribute little to contour. But the y-b chromatic channels would be perpetually biased in the y direction. Chromatic discrimination therefore would become dichromatic, mediated only the by the r-g channels. The color triangle would be reduced to a line because only two components—one of long, the other of short wavelength—would be needed to match all possible colors. Observers with this type of color vision exist and are included in a class called *dichromats*. These are defined by the fact that, for them, only two stimuli need be mixed in order to make any color match. They are sometimes called *tritanopes* when the defect relates to the loss of B cones, or to a malfunction of the pathways into which B-cone signals are fed (another class, called *tetartanopes*, will be discussed later).

If the R cones were missing, the sensitivity of the luminance channel would become that of G cones, resulting in a serious loss of sensitivity to long wavelengths. The r-g channels would be perpetually biased in the g direction. A sensation of green would be added to those of yellow or blue that are mediated by the y-b channels, but the defective r-g signal would provide no basis for color discriminations. Such subjects would also be dichromats. A loss of visual acuity might also be expected because of (1) the loss of R cones in the retinal mosaic, which would leave gaps and cause disarray among the remaining G cones, and (2) the elimination of edge-sharpening lateral inhibition of the sort that, in the normal observer, may take place more between the R and G cones than within a system comprised of cones of the same type (Chapter 9).

Only part of this syndrome ever occurs. Because their spatial vision is essentially normal,[5] *protanopes* probably do not lack the R receptor, although they do display the expected loss of longwave sensitivity. It is more probable that their R cones are inappropriately filled with chlorolabe, the photopigment found only in normal G cones. We may call this *loss with replacement*, a special form of loss system. Lateral inhibition between R and G cones could then occur in the presence of luminance differences, and there would be no inactive or missing receptors in the retina. The luminance channel would reflect the action spectrum of chlorolabe, just as it would on a pure loss hypothesis. The difference signal from R and G cones would always be zero. The r-g opponent pathways would probably not develop normally,[6] but in any event there could be no discrimination mediated by them. The predicted color sensations would be yellow and blue.

Similarly, if the G cones of *deuteranopes* were filled with erythrolabe, these subjects would exhibit essentially normal spatial vision, their spectral sensitivity would be that of erythrolabe, no color discrimination could be mediated by their r-g channels and, like protanopes, dichromatic color discrimination would be based only on the activity of y-b opponent channels. They also would see yellow and blue only, and sensitivity to midspectral wavelengths would be reduced, though only slightly.

Losses could occur in channels as well as receptors. A loss of luminance channels would result in the perception of hues of uncommonly high saturation. No such cases seem to have been reported. Loss of the r-g channels would imply dichromatic color vision and normal spectral sensitivity. If such observers exist, and they probably do not (see below), they would be classified as deuteranopes and would be expected to differ only slightly from the loss-deuteranopes described above. Finally, the loss of y-b channels would result in a tritanopia difficult to distinguish from that caused by loss of B cones.

Recall from Chapter 5 that color matches depend upon a physiological identity at the receptor level. It would therefore be characteristic of all loss systems that those afflicted should accept color matches made by normal observers. This prediction follows because a match for all three types of receptors should remain a match for each member of the remaining pair if only one type is removed. The converse is not true because dichromats would usually make matches, identical for their two remaining classes of normal cones, that would be detected as different by way of the third type of cone possessed by normals. Only by chance would such a match be metameric for the missing receptor.

Altered Systems

Suppose instead that all systems existed in their normal states except that some of the spectral absorption curves of cones were modified. Since all photopigments have action spectra of approximately the same shape when plotted on a frequency basis, the most probable altered systems would feature one or more altered types of cone photopigment, showing a shift of λ_{max}. Consider the relation between the R and G cone sensitivities. If the wavelength separation between peak sensitivities were to be increased so that the overlap of the two absorption curves became less than normal, sensitivity to wavelength changes might be improved somewhat in the middle region where the curves cross, but the opposite would be true in the flanks. In the limit, if two such curves were pulled apart until they failed completely to overlap, wavelength discrimination would be almost entirely lost (recall Figure 5.9). There is evidence that alteration by an abnormally great separation of R and G curves may occur (Smith & Pokorny, 1978), but this is not among the common defects that appear to relate to the opposite case where the two curves have peaks that are closer together than is normal. Here, too, it is predicted that wavelength discrimination should get worse, and in the limit will be lost as the two curves overlap completely.[7] Trichromatic color matches are predicted, but with decreased precision of trichromatic settings as the curves overlap more and more completely.[8]

Another interesting prediction results from such curve shifts, namely that subjects so affected would not be expected to accept the color matches of normal observers, and vice versa. These conditions are met in subjects called *anomalous trichromats*, who appear to exist in two classes, *protan* and *deutan*, depending upon whether it is the R-cone or the G-cone sensitivity that is altered.

Weak Systems

A modification of protanopia can be imagined, where most (but not all) of the R cones are filled with chlorolabe, leaving some with the normal R-cone pigment, erythrolabe. Such subjects would make normal color matches, but with increased variability, and a very large change in the unique yellow setting would result, unless compensated during development or by adaptation. This does not describe any known condition, nor does its counterpart for G cones. A reduction in the number of functional R and G cones would, if their proportions remained the same, leave the average unique yellow setting in its normal location, with increased variability both of the unique yellow settings and of color matches. Similarly, a partial loss of B cones could impair discriminations mediated by the y-b channels, but this would predict a shift of unique green to shorter wavelengths; this too is not observed. On the whole, there is little evidence to support the idea of weak systems of this type.

Many other classes of color defect can be imagined, combining two or more of the losses or alterations that have been considered. For example, a protanope, with his R cones filled with chlorolabe, might also lack functional y-b channels. If this happened he would be fully color-blind and would be called a *monochromat*. Even in the context of an oversimplified opponent-color model, the number of theoretically possible combinations and gradations of chromatic defect is extremely large.

Table 10.1 summarizes the categories into which most color-defective observers fall. Additional criteria for classification will be described later in the chapter.

DICHROMACY ON A CHROMATICITY DIAGRAM

Recall from Chapter 5 that it is possible to construct a chromaticity diagram in which colors are specified in terms of *physiological primaries*. For normal observers, there is a unique triad of such reference stimuli, each of which can be imagined to activate only one type of cone.

Figure 10.2 is a chromaticity diagram, in Cartesian coordinates, based on the Smith-Pokorny (1975) estimates of these cone sensitivities.[9] The origin represents a color that would be produced by unique activation of B cones. The point (0,1) corresponds to unique activation of G cones, and (1,0) is for unique activation of R cones. We can refer to these as the B, G, and R "corners" of the diagram. If a protanope were lacking R cones (or if they were filled with

Table 10.1. A 2 × 2 classification scheme for common types of red-green color deficiency

		Dichromats	Anomalous trichromats
Deutans	Normal or nearly normal spectral sensitivity	*Deuteranope* (lacks chlorolabe)	*Deuteranomalous* (abnormal "green" pigment)
Protans	Reduced sensitivity to long wavelengths	*Protanope* (lacks erythrolabe)	*Protanomalous* (abnormal "red" pigment)

Dichromats confuse all colors that are equally bright for them, and that stimulate B cones identically, whereas anomalous trichromats do not. Deutans have a spectral sensitivity that is nearly normal, whereas protans exhibit a severely reduced sensitivity to long wavelengths.

Dichromacy on a Chromaticity Diagram 345

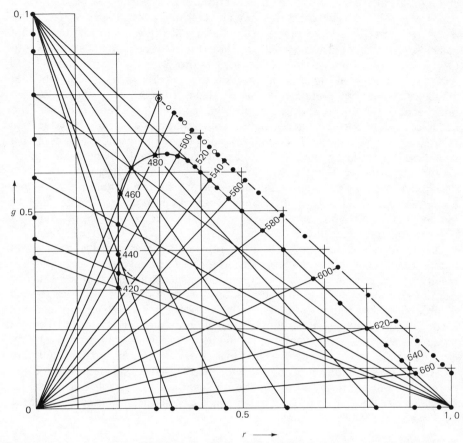

FIGURE 10.2 A chromaticity diagram based upon physiological reference stimuli derived by Smith and Pokorny (1975). Stimuli having chromaticities that plot at the corners of the chart would, if they physically existed, uniquely excite R, G, or B cones. The locations of spectral lights from 420 to 660 nm are indicated in 10-nm steps by the points along the spectral locus. A protanope confuses any two colors that lie upon a line radiating from the "red" corner at (1,0). Similarly, a deuteranope confuses any two colors lying upon a line radiating from the "green" corner at (0,1), and tritanopic confusion lines radiate from the "blue" corner at the origin. The filled circles along the ordinate represent spectral colors on a one-dimensional chromaticity diagram for the protanope, obtained by projecting lines from the "red" corner through the spectral locus at 10-nm intervals. Analogous points lie along the abscissa for the deuteranope. For the tritanope, these points are shown on the slanted line at the upper right. The uppermost part of the tritanopic line is double-valued; open circles refer to the shorter wavelengths. See footnote 10 for an explanation of the alternative dotted portion of the spectral locus at short wavelengths.

chlorolabe), then any two stimuli that cannot be distinguished either by B or G cones would be indiscriminable. A straight line drawn from the R corner of the diagram represents a locus of such stimuli, for which the ratio of B- to G-cone activation is constant at some level. One limit for this level is the abscissa, where $G = 0$; the other limit is the $-45°$ line, where $B = 0$. As an intermediate example, consider a line passing through the spectral locus at 450 nm that intersects the ordinate between B and G. This is the locus of all stimuli (mostly nonspectral) that are as effective as 450 nm for both the G and B cones. The ability of normal observers to distinguish colors that plot along this line depends entirely upon the differential capacity of such stimuli to excite R cones. For a protanope, if he lacks normal R cones, all such stimuli at equal luminance should appear alike. For a fan of lines radiating from the R corner, each line describes a locus of such indistinguishable stimuli for the protanope. Similarly, a deuteranope, lacking normal G cones, would confuse colors lying along lines fanning out from the G corner, and a tritanope would confuse colors that plot on lines radiating from the B corner.[10]

It should be borne in mind that this representation is possible only to the extent that dichromatic vision is a reduced form of normal color vision, with the result that dichromats accept the trichromatic matches of normal observers. The normal chromaticity diagram contains an excess degree of freedom for the dichromat, whose remaining vision, at least insofar as it affects color matching, is conceived to be the same as that of normal observers. A chromaticity diagram applicable strictly to the protanope, having no extra degrees of freedom for him, is represented along the ordinate of Figure 10.2. Monochromatic lights are located at points determined by the projection of lines that pass through the spectral stimuli represented along the horseshoe locus of spectral colors for normal observers. This type of construction is also shown in Figure 10.2 for the other two classes of dichromats.

THE ANALYTICAL ANOMALOSCOPE

The color-matching behavior of normal, dichromatic, and anomalous observers is neatly characterized by a device called an *analytical anomaloscope* first described by Baker and Rushton (1963) and again by Mitchell and Rushton (1971). It is shown very schematically in Figure 10.3. The field at the left receives monochromatic light supplied by a variable wavelength filter, M_λ, which passes light whose wavelength depends upon the lateral position of the filter in a light beam that supplies the left field. The intensity of that field can be adjusted by means of a neutral density wedge W_λ.

The field at the right receives a mixture of red and green light supplied through the fixed filters F_G and F_R, which pass light of wavelengths 550 and 635 nm. These beams are polarized orthogonally so that, when a polaroid analyzer A is turned, one component is gradually exchanged for the other as these are mixed in the right-hand field (red + green). The neutral wedge W_R

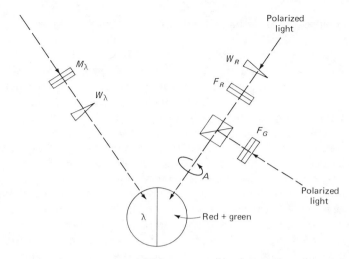

FIGURE 10.3 A schematic drawing to illustrate the principles of the analytical anomaloscope. Light in the left field is controlled for wavelength by a variable wavelength filter M_λ, and for intensity by neutral wedge W_λ. The right field contains a mixture of red and green light supplied through filters F_R and F_G. The polarized light transmitted by these filters is superimposed by the mixing cube. The mixed beam passes through a polaroid analyzer **A**. As **A** rotates, there is a continuous exchange of **R** for **G** or vice versa. The instrument is used in two **modes**, depending upon how protanopes and deuteranopes must set neutral wedge W_R in order that rotation of **A** does not vary the appearance of the right field for them.

is used to vary the amount of red light and thereby alter the relative strengths of the polarized beams *before* they enter the analyzer. This device is conceptually a modification of the simpler, commercially available *Nagel anomaloscope*, which is widely used for color-vision testing (see below).[11]

To use the device as an *analytical* anomaloscope, a protanope is invited to adjust W_R so that, when A is turned, there is no change for him in the appearance of the right-hand field. He can do this because he sees the field using only G cones, and his setting of W_R will allow the two components of the mixture to produce a constant total absorption rate for his G cones no matter what the position of A. Now, with M_λ set in turn for various wavelengths, the protanope makes settings of W_λ to control the brightness of the left field so as to match it with the right one. Because the two halves of the field match exactly at each wavelength used, the left field must also produce a constant absorption rate for the protanope's G cones. Given the appropriate calibration data, the settings of W_λ can be converted into a spectral sensitivity curve which should describe the action spectrum for chlorolabe (and of G cones) in the protanope.

This method is suitable only for wavelengths of F_G that are about 550 nm or longer, because B-cone intrusion otherwise vitiates the results. The part of the spectrum that can be measured extends from 550 nm to the wavelength supplied by filter F_R (635 nm). As far as it goes, the resulting curve resembles that of chlorolabe as deduced by various other methods described earlier in this book.

The setting of W_R by the protanope, so that rotation of A produces no change for him in the right field, is called the *prot mode* of the instrument. When a deuteranope performs the same task, a much higher density of W_R is required in order to produce the desired result. His spectrum, as deduced from W_λ settings, resembles that of erythrolabe. The setting of W_R appropriate for the deuteranope is called the *deut mode* of the instrument.

When a normal observer uses the instrument there will be no setting of W_R that will cause the right-hand field to remain invariant for all positions of A because, as A is turned, the field changes in appearance—for example, from red through yellow to green. W_R could be set to maintain equal luminance, but it is much more instructive to set it either in the *prot* or *deut* mode.[12]

Consider the *prot* mode as an example. As A is turned, there should be no change in the degree to which photons are absorbed in chlorolabe, because the normal subject has the same chlorolabe as the protanope whose settings were uncontaminated by a second pigment.[13] Compared to a field at the left that matches the other one for a protanope when the right field is set fully for W_R, that field will look very bright to the normal observer because of the extra photons absorbed by his R cones, which the protanope lacks. Nevertheless, a wavelength of M_λ can be found that will provide a match for hue, and an appropriate setting of W_λ can be made that will increase the brightness of the left field to yield an exact match.

The experiment is more conveniently done the other way around; for each setting of M_λ selected by the experimenter, values of A and W_λ are set by the subject, who thereby makes a dichromatic match. When the W_λ values for various wavelengths are converted to a spectral sensitivity curve, it is found to be the same chlorolabe curve as that of the protanope. This is because, no matter what the setting of A, the right field has a constant effect upon chlorolabe. In analogous fashion, using the *deut* mode, the spectral sensitivity defined by W_λ is found to agree with that of the deuteranope, revealing the action spectrum of erythrolabe. The obtained experimental agreement is very good.

The settings of A that are reliably made by a normal observer cannot meaningfully be compared with those of dichromats because A-settings are arbitrary for the dichromats. But color-anomalous observers, like normals, require specific adjustment of A as well as W_λ in order to make matches. Consider a protanomalous subject with the instrument in the *prot* mode. We know that the protanomalous observer has some abnormal pigment. If his *green*-absorbing photopigment differs from that of normal chlorolabe, then his spectral sensitivity, as determined by settings of W_λ, should also differ from that of normal and protanopic subjects. But this does not happen. Instead, the data of protanomalous observers are the same as for normals and protanopes. Similarly, in the *deut* mode, deuteranomalous observers produce results that agree with those of normals and deuteranopes. The almost inescapable conclusion is that only the red pigment in protanomalous observers is abnormal; his chlorolabe must be normal. Similarly, it is only the green pigment in deuteranomalous observers that is abnormal, so his erythrolabe must be of the normal variety.

Because anomalous observers must adjust A as well as λ to make a match, a comparison of A values between normal and anomalous subjects is possible. Figure 10.4A shows the result of such a comparison made by Pokorny, Smith, and Katz (1973) using data furnished by D. Mitchell on several anomals of each class. Circles represent the *deut* mode, squares, the *prot* mode. Filled symbols are for normal subjects, open squares represent protanomalous data, and open circles are for deuteranomalous observers. For intermediate wavelengths, the normal observer (black squares) needs little of the red component in the *prot* mode because W_R has been set by the protanope to admit a very high intensity of red light. For the *deut* mode, the normal curve is more nearly linear but bulges upward because the deuteranope lacks middle-wavelength sensitivity and must set W_R at a lower intensity than normal in order to match green. The curves for the two classes of anomalous observers lie between those of normals, differing only slightly from one another. This result suggests that their anomalous pigments may not differ very much from each other.

A recent assessment of the shapes and locations of the anomalous pigments has been made by Pokorny, Smith, and Katz (1973). In their analysis, they used the results of a study by Schmidt (1955), who had tested 883 recently drafted male recruits in the 17–23 year age range. In this population she found 5 protanopes (0.6 percent), 11 deuteranopes (1.2 percent) and 3 *extreme deuteranomals*. (The latter are nearly dichromatic, but will reject matches between

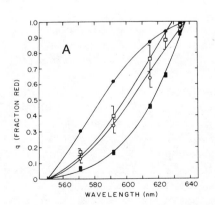
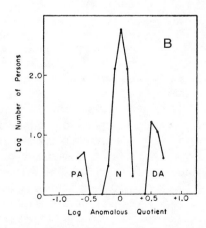

FIGURE 10.4 A. Settings of analyzer A (Fig. 10.3) for normal and anomalous subjects on the analytical anomaloscope of Mitchell and Rushton (1971). This figure is from Pokorny, Smith, and Katz (1973); the vertical lines represent 2 standard errors of the mean for anomals; the symbol heights include 2 s.e.m. for normals. Symbols are explained in the text. B. Distributions of anomalous quotients on the Nagel anomaloscope as found by Schmidt (1955). (See p. 350.)

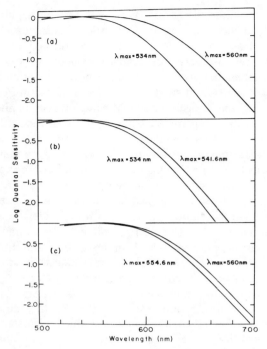

FIGURE 10.4 (Continued)   C. Results of an analysis by Pokorny, Smith, and Katz (1973) showing (a) normal G and R curves, (b) protanomalous curves, and (c) deuteranomalous curves.

the reference yellow and extreme red/green ratios on an anomaloscope.) There were no *extreme protanomals* in her sample, although these have often been observed (they show a reduction in longwave sensitivity similar to that of the protanope).

To compare normals with the remaining anomalous subjects of her sample, Schmidt used an *anomalous quotient*, which is the relative amount of green/red in the Nagel anomaloscope (see p. 347). Using this instrument, subjects matched a 589-nm field with a mixture of 670 nm (red) and 536 nm (green). A value of 1.0 was defined by the average setting of Schmidt's normal observers. She found 10 protanomalous, 822 normal, and 32 deuteranomalous subjects, with no overlap between the three distributions (see Figure 10.4B).

Figure 10.4C shows the longwave portions of curves derived by Pokorny, Smith, and Katz. Starting with their R and G functions for normal observers, they assumed that only one of the normal curves is shifted for an anomalous observer, that the shifted curve has the same shape (on a frequency abscissa) as the normal, and that the concentration of pigment in the anomalous receptors is about the same as for normals. By a trial-and-error procedure, they determined the curve shifts required for a best fit of the Schmidt mean data; the resulting curves are shown in Figure 10.4C.

As a further test of the resulting functions, Pokorny, Smith, and Katz calculated the q-values to be expected for Schmidt's average anomalous observers on the analytical anomaloscope. The curves that are drawn through the Mitchell and Rushton data of Figure 10.4A constitute the results of these predictions, and the agreement is good. This result implies that there is no overlapping range of the two anomalous pigments, contrary to an hypothesis of Schouten, revived by MacLoed and Hayhoe (1974), whose analysis was based on Wright's data. This issue remains unresolved, although it appears that the anomalous pigments of most protanomalous and deuteranomalous observers probably differ from one another.

Other evidence against the Schouten hypothesis lies in estimates of anomalous pigment sensitivities obtained with two-color threshold procedures (Piantanida & Sperling, 1973a, 1973b; Watkins, 1969a, 1969b) or an "exchange" threshold technique designed to cause increments or decrements in the activation of one type of pigment while holding the stimulation of the second pigment at a constant level (Rushton, Powell, & White, 1973a, 1973b, 1973c).

GENETIC BASIS OF COLOR BLINDNESS

The tendency for color blindness to "run in families" and skip generations had been noticed long before there was a science of genetics. Equally obvious was the fact that color deficiency is much more widespread among males than females. A family pedigree illustrating these characteristics, shown in Figure 10.5A, was originally presented by Horner in 1876. According to Kalmus

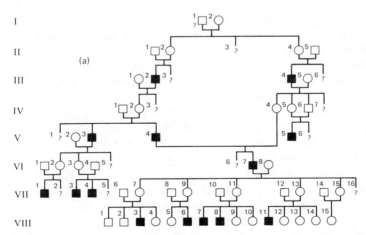

FIGURE 10.5 A. Horner's original pedigree of deuteranopes, first published in 1876. Squares: males; circles: females. Successive generations represented top to bottom. Filled symbols represent deuteranopes. Originally published by Bell (1926); this figure is reproduced from Kalmus (1965, p. 62).

352   Variations and Defects

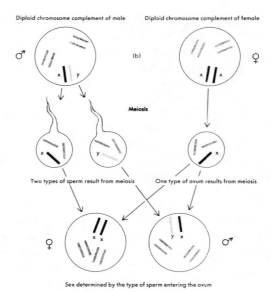

FIGURE 10.5 B. Prior to fertilization, meiotic division of germ cells results in two types of sperm, but only one type of ovum. Depending upon which sperm is effective, the fertilized ovum will have two X cells and be female, or one X and one Y cell and be male. This diagram shows why the X cell of the male offspring can come only from the mother. (From Watson, 1976, p. 14.)

(1965), Horner was the first to recognize the mode of inheritance. Note that all of the deuteranopes are male and that the condition skips generations, demonstrating "Horner's law of inheritance."

A genetic characterization of human red-green color blindness is given in a model proposed by Piantanida (1974, 1976). It will be the primary purpose of this section to attempt a description of his model. (Readers are referred to his papers for references to the primary literature.) First, we need a brief review of some basic genetic principles.

Every human cell contains 23 pairs of chromosomes, each of which in turn contains large numbers of genes. Each gene is comprised of DNA molecules arranged in the now-famous double helix. Provided that the appropriate chemical environment is available, a particular gene is able to instruct a cell to express itself structurally so as to form a specialized part of the organism. A trait such as protanopia is an example of that genetic expression and is called a *phenotype*. Expression of the phenotype is dependent upon the underlying genetic constitution called the *genotype*.

When a cell divides, chromosomes are duplicated and each member of the resulting pair carries an identical genetic message to the daughter cells. Ultimately every one of the 60 trillion or so cells in a fully developed human contains the same genetic information. All 23 pairs of chromosomes in the human female are *homologous*; that is, the members of each of the pairs are identical. During meiotic division these paired chromosomes divide to form ova of just one type, as shown in Figure 10.5B. Both ova therefore have the same morphology and contain genes that govern the same characteristics. This is true of only 22 chromosomes in the male. The exception is the X chromosome, which has a morphologically disparate mate, the Y chromosome. Following meiotic division, these sperm are of two types, one containing an X chromosome, and the other a Y chromosome. At fertilization, when chromosomes derived from those of the parents are recombined into pairs, exactly half of the genetic material is received from each parent. If an X-chromosome-bearing sperm is effective in fertilizing the ovum (Figure 10.5B), the offspring will be female and her twenty-third chromosome will be homologous. But if a Y-chromosome-bearing sperm is effective, the fertilized ovum will contain the X-Y chromosome pairing and the offspring will be male.

Just prior to the meiotic split, a recombination of genes occurs called *crossing over*. This is a pseudo-random process with contingent probabilities. Genes located close together along a chromosome are more likely to remain together (either be included or excluded together from the collection of genes in the new organism), whereas those located far apart along a chromosome behave more independently, with complete independence being the rule for genes located in separate chromosomes.

Genes controlling the same general trait exist at specific loci along the chromosome. From one organism to another, within a given species, genes at a specific locus exist in different types, called *alleles*. When the alleles differ at the same locus on each chromosome of a homologous pair (heterozygous gene pair), the tendency is for one allele to dominate the other in its phenotypical expression. Probably the most familiar example is eye color. By the simplest model, if both alleles were homozygous (brown-brown or blue-blue), then the phenotype would necessarily be brown or blue respectively. But the two heterozygous combinations of brown-blue and blue-brown would lead to brown eyes. By inference the allele for brown eyes is *dominant*, while that for blue eyes is said to be *recessive*. A person carrying the brown-blue gene combination is said to be a *carrier* of the blue-eyed gene. A quarter of the time, two brown-blue carriers, both of whom have brown eyes, would produce a blue-eyed offspring. This expression is probabilistic, so there would be a finite probability that two such blue-eyed carriers could produce, say, 10 blue-eyed offspring in succession, although the odds against it would be about one in a million.

Dominance relations are not really this simple. Eye color is not well described by the model just given; for example, more than just one gene must be involved to account for hazel eyes. Blends occur, phenotypes may be virtually continuous, and complex behavior, such as that mediated by human color vision, can express itself in various ways and may be related to many aspects of underlying anatomy and physiology. Much more is known about the genetics of the fruit fly *Drosophila* or of the bacterium *Escherichia coli* than about that of humans.

354   Variations and Defects

To a considerable extent, therefore, any statements about the genetics of human traits, including those concerning human color blindness, must be taken only as provisional models of reality.

Color-deficient vision is of special interest to the human geneticist because it is *sex linked*, being carried on the X chromosome. As an example of what this implies, consider protanopia relative to the combinations of six parental unions of Table 10.2 (adapted from Kalmus, 1965). In each case the normal allele is dominant. The father has only one X chromosome, which is assumed to carry either the normal (p) or protanopic (p°) genotype at the protan color-vision locus. The mother has two X chromosomes, leading to three possible combinations (pp, pp°, and p°p°). In the female, when one of the alleles is for normal color vision (p) and the other is for protanopia (p°), the normal one dominates. For the male, the phenotype is determined by whatever allele is present, since there is no homologous second member that could dominate it.

Consider two examples from the table. If the father is p (normal) and the

Table 10.2 Color vision of children in the six possible combinations of parental unions that are possible with respect to a particular near-recessive sex-linked color deficiency

Father		Mother		
	p normal	pp, normal	pp°, carrier, usually normal	p°p°, color-deficient
		p sons, normal	½ p sons, normal. ½ p° sons, color-deficient	p° sons, color-deficient
		pp daughters, normal	½ pp daughters, normal. ½ pp° daughters, carriers, usually normal	pp° daughters, carriers, mostly normal
	p°, color-deficient	p sons, normal	½ p sons, normal. ½ p° sons, color-deficient	p° sons, color-deficient
		p°p daughters, carriers, usually normal	½ pp° daughters, carriers usually normal. ½ p°p° daughters, color-deficient	p°p° daughters, color-deficient

After Kalmus, 1965, p. 61.

mother is pp° (a carrier), there are two possible combinations in the female offspring (pp and pp°) which should occur with equal probability. The pp° combination leads to normal color vision, but these females are carriers. So, on average, half the female offspring are fully normal, whereas the other half are phenotypically normal but are carriers.[14] For males, since their only X chromosome is of maternal origin, half will carry the p° allele and will be protanopes, the other half will carry the p allele and be normal. As a second example, consider the color-deficient father (p°) and a mother who is a carrier (pp°). Here the two possible combinations for female offspring are pp° and p°p°; one is a carrier, the other herself a protanope. Again, half the male offspring will be protanopes.

An overall result is that there can be no protanopic offspring of either sex without a mother who is either a carrier or a protanope. A father passes the defect along only through his daughters, most of whom are carriers with essentially normal color vision. For protanopic daughters there is the added requirement of a protanopic father, which severely reduces the probability of color deficiency in females relative to males. Finally, all offspring of parents who are both protanopes will also be protanopes, regardless of sex.

Piantanida's model rests upon these basic principles of inheritance, but it is expanded to take into account six (rather than just one) kinds of color defects. These fall into two groups as follows:

Protan class	*Deutan class*
normal (p)	normal (d)
protanope (p°)	deuteranope (d°)
extreme protanomalous (p^{ae})	extreme deuteranomalous (d^{ae})
simple protanomalous (p^a)	simple deuteranomalous (d^a)

The loci for protan and deutan defects have been established to be at separate sites along the X chromosome. At least one genetic trait (a metabolic condition entirely unrelated to color vision) is known to be expressed at a locus between them. One color locus is assumed to be concerned with the generation of the red-sensitive photopigment, erythrolabe, and the other with that of chlorolabe. Consider first the erythrolabe site to see how the relations of Table 10.2 can be extended to include the two additional forms of protanomalous vision. The gene at the protan site is believed to influence the protein microstructure of the photopigment molecule (this, rather than the vitamin-A-related chromophore, is believed to determine the kind of visual photopigment that develops). The "normal" R-cone pigment has its λ_{max} at 575 nm.[15] The allele for simple protanomaly produces a pigment with λ_{max} at 545 nm. The allele for extreme protanomaly leads to a pigment with $\lambda_{max} = 538$ nm, which is nearly the same as that of chlorolabe, the pigment normally found in G cones.

It is assumed that the B and G cones of protan observers are all normal.

356   Variations and Defects

Protanopia therefore results in the replacement, in R cones, of erythro... ...e by chlorolabe. This causes R and G cones to be of identical spectral sensit... ...ty and produces the total lack of red-green discrimination required for "textbook" protanopes.

To account for the incidence of anomalous protan vision, it is assumed that a hierarchy of dominance of the four possible alleles exists at the protan site, in the order

(p)   Normal (575 nm)
(p^a)   Protanomalous (545 nm)
(p^{ae})   Extreme protanomalous (538 nm)
(p^o)   Protanope (535 nm).

The rule is that the superior form of color vision (the one closest to normal) will always dominate in the phenotypical expression of color defect in the heterozygous female (who carries two of these alleles that are different). Using the symbols shown above, a pp^o female will be a normal carrier, as we saw earlier, and a $p^{ae}p^o$ female will be extreme protanomalous and also a carrier for protanopia, and a pp^a female will be normal and a carrier for protanomaly.

All of what has just been said applies independently also to the state of affairs at the deutan locus along the X chromosome. Here the dominance hierarchy is

(d)   Normal (535 nm)
(d^a)   Deuteranomalous (560 nm)
(d^{ae})   Extreme deuteranomalous (572 nm)
(d^o)   Deuteranope (575 nm).

When the genetic events of both loci are considered together, this leads to the 16 possible genotypes in the male that are represented in Table 10.3, where the values in parentheses along the margins are the estimated frequencies of each genotype as reported by Pickford (1951,1959). For example, the fraction of the population for which the normal gene (d) occurs at the deutan locus is 0.9474, while the normal gene (p) at the protan locus occurs with a slightly higher probability of 0.9746. The product of these is 0.9233, which is the value given in the upper-left cell. Immediately above it, the "575/535" represents the λ_{max} values of the normal photopigments that are controlled by genes at the protan and deutan loci respectively.

It might be thought that a male carrying the defective alleles for both protanopia and deuteranopia (p^o and d^o) would be a monochromat, but an examination of the cell at the lower right shows that, to the contrary, he should have normal color vision. Piantanida calls this predicted condition "pseudonormal" since it is characterized by the fact that the R and G cones both contain

Table 10.3 Sixteen hemizygous genotypes that apply to males

<table>
<tr><th colspan="6">Alleles at the protan locus</th></tr>
<tr><th rowspan="2"></th><th>d(0.9474)</th><th>p(0.9746)</th><th>p^a(0.0060)</th><th>p^{ae}(0.0113)</th><th>p^o(0.0081)</th></tr>
<tr><td></td><td>575/535
0.9233
Normal</td><td>545/535
0.00568
Simple protanomalous</td><td>538/535
0.0107
Extreme protanomalous</td><td>535/535
0.00767
Protanopic</td></tr>
<tr><td>d^a(0.0213)</td><td>575/560
0.0208
Simple deuteranomalous</td><td>545/560
0.000128
Simple deuteranomalous with some loss of red sensitivity</td><td>538/560
0.000241
Slight protan defect</td><td>535/560
0.000173
Slight protan defect</td></tr>
<tr><td>d^{ae}(0.0265)</td><td>575/572
0.0258
Extreme deuteranomalous</td><td>545/572
0.000159
Slight deutan defect</td><td>538/572
0.000299
Pseudonormal</td><td>535/572
0.000215
Pseudonormal</td></tr>
<tr><td>d^o(0.0048)</td><td>575/575
0.00468
Deuteranopic</td><td>545/575
0.0000288
Slight deutan defect</td><td>538/575
0.000542
Pseudonormal</td><td>535/575
0.000389
Pseudonormal</td></tr>
</table>

Alleles at the deutan locus

From Piantanida, 1974, p. 401.

Table 10.4. Eighteen selected heterozygous genotypes that apply to females

	Genotype	Photopigments	Phenotype
(1)	PD/p^aD	575/535/545/535	Normal
(2)	$PD/p^{ae}D$	575/535/538/535	Normal
(3)	PD/p^oD	575/535/535/535	Normal
(4)	p^aD/p^aD	545/535/545/535	Simple protanomalous
(5)	$p^aD/p^{ae}D$	545/535/538/535	Simple protanomalous
(6)	p^aD/p^oD	545/535/535/535	Simple protanomalous
(7)	$p^{ae}D/p^{ae}D$	538/535/538/535	Extreme protanomalous
(8)	$p^{ae}D/p^oD$	538/535/535/535	Extreme protanomalous
(9)	p^oD/p^oD	535/535/535/535	Protanope
(10)	PD/Pd^a	575/535/575/560	Normal
(11)	PD/Pd^{ae}	575/535/575/572	Normal
(12)	PD/Pd^o	575/535/575/575	Normal
(13)	Pd^a/Pd^a	575/560/575/560	Simple deuteranomalous
(14)	Pd^a/Pd^{ae}	575/560/575/572	Simple deuteranomalous
(15)	Pd^a/Pd^o	575/560/575/575	Simple deuteranomalous
(16)	Pd^{ae}/Pd^{ae}	575/572/575/572	Extreme deuteranomalous
(17)	Pd^{ae}/Pd^o	575/572/575/575	Extreme deuteranomalous
(18)	Pd^o/Pd^o	575/575/575/575	Deuteranope

From Piantanida, 1974, p. 399.

the "wrong" pigment. Such an observer would be expected to have normal color vision except that the sensations of red and green would be reversed—something that would be difficult, if not impossible, to prove. A prediction of cone monochromacy would follow only if dichromacy were assumed to be a loss, rather than a replacement, condition. The observer would possess B cones and rods. Actually, although such a condition exists (it will be discussed below), it is rarely associated with red-green defect, and is itself a unique form of incomplete total color-blindness.

For females, with X chromosomes and therefore two alleles at each locus, there are many more combinations to be predicted by Piantanida's model. Eighteen of these are given in Table 10.4. It is mainly from a consideration of these myriad combinations, relative to the actual incidence of color defect in the male and female population, that the notion of a dominance hierarchy of two allelic series has been derived.

SOME CONTROVERSIAL ASPECTS OF RED-GREEN DEFICIENCY

Fusion Deuteranopia

Protanopes lack erythrolabe and consequently suffer a marked sensitivity loss at the longwave end of the spectrum. Deuteranopes lack chlorolabe but their luminosity curves are difficult to discriminate from those of normal subjects. The concept of fusion deuteranopia was introduced by Fick and Leber in the 1870s (and has been championed by many others since) in an effort to account for this seeming discrepancy.[16] The argument is that some deuteranopes may exist whose cones each contain both R and G pigments. Or perhaps the signals generated by their R and G cones, which themselves may be normal, are combined in some way so that there is no differential signal related to wavelength. In the context of an opponent-color model, a simple way to visualize this possibility is to assume that the R and G cones are normal but that the r-g pathways are nonfunctional. The fusion of R and G cone signals would then occur in luminance channels in the same way as for normal observers.

There is little difference between normal observers and deuteranopes in the luminous efficiency functions as obtained by brightness matching, threshold measurements, or flicker photometry. Yet, if their G cones were missing (along with the chlorolabe that they contain) there should be a deficiency of sensitivity in the midspectral region, analogous to the longwave sensitivity loss of protanopes. Recall that on the basis of retinal densitometry, Rushton unequivocally concluded that "there is no chlorolabe in the deuteranope." The fusion idea has no place either in the genetic scheme of Piantanida. And the evidence of the analytical anomaloscope is also contrary to the fusion hypothesis.

The R cones make such a dominant contribution to normal luminosity, according to the analysis of Vos and Walraven (1971), that the expected sensitivity loss occasioned by missing chlorolabe would be much less than that predicted if erythrolabe were absent. There is also substantial variation in normal luminosity functions.

Is it possible that only a small minority of deuteranopes are of the fusion variety? Considering the relatively small numbers of subjects that have been used in retinal densitometry and analytical anomaloscopy, fusion deuteranopes might exist who have not been examined by these methods. The analysis that follows depends on data collected from 38 deuteranopes; it too leads to a negative conclusion relative to the possibility of fusion deuteranopia.

Spectral Neutral Points

For the normal observer, all monochromatic lights are chromatic; that is, they differ in appearance from what would be judged as white. Recall (p. 285) that the least saturated spectral region is near 570 nm and appears as greenish-yellow. When asked to judge the appearance of the spectrum, protanopes and deuteranopes see it as chromatic except for a region near 500 nm that appears achromatic to them, although it is a highly saturated blue-green for the normal observer.

The theoretical basis for the chromatically-neutral spectral colors of these dichromats is easily visualized with the aid of a chromaticity diagram. The chart of Figure 10.6 is based upon the same Smith-Pokorny fundamentals that were used to construct Figure 10.2, but with a tenfold increase in the relative weight assigned to B cones (compared to G and B), which permits a more accurate visualization of relations that otherwise would lie too close to the spectral locus to be seen clearly.

Consider the point C, one of the standard "whites" of the CIE system. If protanopia were a loss system, then all colors on a line from the R corner passing through C should be confused for the protanope. Because an extension of this line intersects the spectral locus at about 492 nm, that wavelength should match C and also appear achromatic, or nearly so.[17] Similarly for the deuteranope, all colors along a line drawn from the G corner through C should be confused; in this case the spectral light equivalent to C lies at about 498 nm.

The existence of a neutral region in the part of the spectrum that looks blue-green to the normal observer is a generally accepted index of dichromatic red-green color defect. Much more controversial is the question of whether protanopes can actually be separated from deuteranopes on the basis of a mere 6-nm difference in their predicted neutral points. The controversy is worth reviewing in some detail.

Figure 10.7 shows the results of dichromatic neutral point determinations from five different laboratories. The procedure used in three of these (unfilled symbols and filled circles was to compare a broad-band white field with one supplied from a monochromator whose wavelength was adjusted by the subject to match. The predicted result depends upon the chromaticity of the particular white chosen; because this differs between studies, perfect agreement cannot

360   Variations and Defects

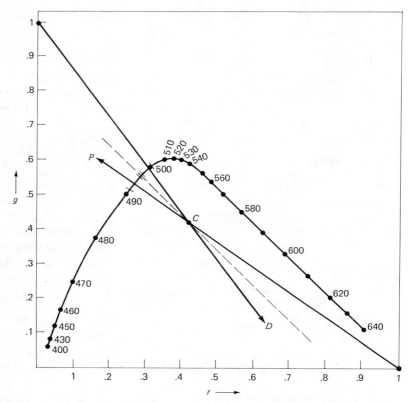

FIGURE 10.6 The full ranges of neutral points for 39 protanopes (P) and 38 deuteranopes (D) as determined by Walls and Heath (1956) are shown along the spectral locus of this diagram. This chromaticity chart uses the same physiological primaries as that of Figure 10.2, except that relatively more weight has been assigned to the B cones. Point C represents the white with which colors were compared having the dominant wavelengths represented by the matching bands. The dashed line is predictive of colors that fusion deuteranopes should confuse. Because this line passes through the gap defined by the P and D distributions, it fails to provide support for the idea of fusion deuteranopia.

be expected. All three studies nevertheless agree fairly well, showing that protanopes and deuteranopes differ, on the average, in the theoretically expected direction. But there is substantial overlap between groups, even within studies, so it would not be possible to classify a subject as protanope or Deuteranope on the basis of this kind of neutral point test.

Possible sources of variability that could contribute to the overlap between the two populations are these:

- Subjects might differ in the prereceptoral absorption of their ocular media.

- They might have a residual red-green discrimination based on a small number of cones of the putatively missing type.
- Subjects may differ slightly with respect to their remaining longwave pigment, which could be slightly anomalous.

If the remaining pigment of a dichromat were anomalous, this would invalidate the use of the chromaticity diagram to predict the achromatic wavelength, leading to an uninterpretable spread of data if it were used anyway. Residual red-green discrimination would cause the match between white and the spectral color to become inexact, thus contributing to variance. Nevertheless, if sufficient numbers of settings were made, a reliable mean setting should be possible for each subject. With too much residual red-green discrimination, accurate settings would not be possible. (In the limit, a normal subject, if given control of the wavelength and intensity of the test light, would have a terrible time trying to "match" a saturated blue-green with a white.)

These three studies probably all suffer from the problem of differential prereceptoral absorption for the various subjects that were tested. Recall, from Chapter 5 (p. 147), that if the normalizing system developed by W. D. Wright is used, the location of a broadband stimulus (such as white) will shift in the chromaticity diagram relative to an invariant spectral locus as the ocular pigmentation is changed. A shifting white point, based on known variations in ocular pigmentation between human subjects, probably could account for much of the variation in the three original studies of Figure 10.7.

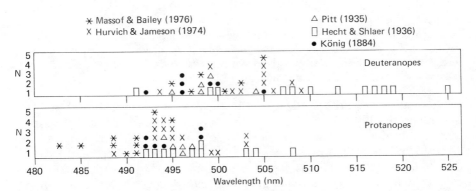

FIGURE 10.7 Spectral neutral points for protanopes and deuteranopes as determined by König (1894), by Pitt (1935), and Hecht & Shlaer (1938), using a match with a broad-band stimulus that appears achromatic to normal observers. Also shown are data from Hurvich and Jameson (1974) and Massof and Bailey (1976). The subjects of these studies set the wavelength drum of a monochromator to produce the "least amount of color" (Massof & Bailey) or "until the color in the test field is the transition color between two hues that differ markedly from each other" (Hurvich & Jameson). (Adapted from Hurvich and Jameson, 1974, p. 208.)

Walls and Mathews (1952) carried out experiments on dichromatic neutral points that largely circumvented the problem of individual differences in ocular pigmentation. Instead of using spectral colors to be compared with white, they used instead a color wheel similar to that originally introduced by Maxwell (see p. 18). Their 7° disc contained sectors of blue and green papers whose proportions could be varied. The resulting mixture color was compared with an overlying mixture of black and white papers of smaller radius, similarly adjustable. After a match was made, the junction of the chromatic and achromatic fields was viewed through a reduction screen that cut the field to about 3.5° with a slightly curved junction; the subject made his final match with this smaller field. The resulting protanopic and deuteranopic neutral-point distributions, though they differed by only about 5 nm in mean values for 19 protanopes and 14 deuteranopes, were so tight that they failed completely to overlap. This work was extended in a study by Walls and Heath (1956). For 39 protanopes the mean matching wavelength was 492.3 nm, with a standard deviation of only 0.70 nm; for 38 deuteranopes the corresponding values were 498.4 ± 1.21 nm.[18] Again there was no overlap despite the large populations used. The following is their comment about how they achieved such a clear separation where others had failed:

Walls and Mathews did not understand why their protanopes and deuteranopes were grouped so closely that they pulled apart from each other and left a 1.6 nm no-man's-land between them. This was later explained by D. B. Judd in a personal communication. . . . Judd pointed out that with this [Maxwell disk] method the effect of scattering the apparent neutral points is practically eliminated. The Munsell papers reflect such broad spectra that an interposed yellow filter shifts the chromaticity of the blue-green zone of the mixer about as much as it does the gray zone. If these shifts were exactly equal, a match made by a dichromat would remain a match even if his ocular pigmentation magically increased or magically disappeared (p. 641).

Another procedure for attempting to circumvent the problem of preretinal absorption has been to eliminate the use of a comparison stimulus altogether. Instead, observers are asked to adjust (or to judge) spectral wavelengths in an effort to find the center of the least saturated, most achromatic band. Hurvich and Jameson (1974) did this and their data are included in Figure 10.7. They report a difference of mean values in the expected direction between protanopes and deuteranopes, but with a much wider spread, 12 of 22 observers falling in an overlapping range. Since their standard deviations were about five times those of Walls and Mathews, it might seem that the absolute-judgment method is either less precise than the matching method, or taps other sources of variation between individuals of the same general type. However, Massof and Bailey (1976), using similar procedures but with extremely large numbers of settings by each subject, obtained essentially nonoverlapping distributions.

The imagined achromatic stimulus, with which the spectral light was being compared in the more recent studies, is not comparable to the physical stimulus

C used by Walls and Mathews in their matching experiment. In the latter case there is no requirement (or even likelihood) that C arouses the same achromatic percept for protanopes and deuteranopes, or even that it should necessarily appear white to members of either group. Indeed, if white for the red-green dichromat results from the y-b opponent signals being set to zero, the mixtures of short and long wavelengths required to achieve this balance in the protanope would be expected to differ because of the serious loss of y input.

The Walls and Heath data, which seem to be excellent, can be used to drive a final nail into the coffin containing any possible remains of Fusion Deuteranopia. If a dichromat suffers from the loss of only the r-g opponent system, but not from a loss of R or G cones or from any other abnormality, then any two equiluminous stimuli that are equivalent for B cones should match for that dichromat. On a chromaticity diagram with physiological primaries, such as those of Figures 10.2 and 10.6, lines of negative unit slope describe this condition. The dotted line in Figure 10.6 is drawn through C with a slope of -1 (parallel to the longwave spectral locus). Note that this line neatly "shoots the gap" between the protanopic and deuteranopic neutral point ranges. This version of fusion dichromacy therefore predicts neutral points that are not found to exist within a very large population of red-green dichromats of both classes. It seems most unlikely that such dichromats exist and have merely been missed.

Varieties of Red-Green Anomaly

In an unusually thorough study of fairly large numbers of red-green anomalous observers, Wright (1946) measured wavelength discrimination curves and found that they covered a fairly continuous range from nearly normal to almost dichromatic. Figure 10.8 shows his results for six subjects classified as deuter-

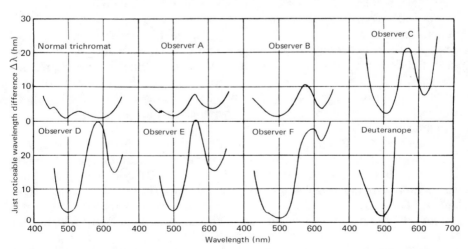

FIGURE 10.8 Wavelength discrimination curves of 6 deuteranomalous observers (from Wright, 1946, p. 313) shown with normal and deuteranopic functions as end-points.

anomalous and for a normal trichromat and deuteranope, whose data anchor the endpoints of the series. (Similar data were obtained for a sample of eleven protanomalous observers.)

It is almost possible to convince oneself that the variations measured by Wright can be explained by Piantanida's model. If the color vision physiology of the anomalous observer is normal except for the anomalous pigment, then discrimination will suffer because the range of R/G cone-stimulation ratios will be truncated compared to that of the normal observer. In extreme deuteranomaly, by Piantanida's model, only a 3-nm separation exists between the λ_{max} values of the deuteranomalous pigment and that of erythrolabe, so that the curves would virtually overlap but with just enough separation to permit the (very poor) performance of subjects C through F. Observers A and B could be simple deuteranomalous observers. But Wright's protanomalous observers are less dichotomous than this, suggesting that the varieties of protanomaly are many, and that there may be more protanomalous alleles than merely the two postulated by Piantanida. Indeed, it seems possible that the peak sensitivities of these pigments may vary from the extreme anomalies to the limiting case that was first suggested by Schouten.

RESIDUAL RED-GREEN DISCRIMINATION IN DICHROMATS

For most observers diagnosed as dichromats, it seems likely that a modest ability to discriminate among long wavelengths of constant brightness persists. Although color matching may not be the most sensitive test of such residual function, Smith and Pokorny (1977) have found that dichromats become trichromats when large fields are used; they ascribe the alteration to the intervention of rod vision. Careful determinations of protanopic and deuteranopic copunctal points, using spectral lights that obviate the problem of preretinal absorption, do not reveal an ideal clustering of such estimates, as would be expected if dichromacy were complete. To the extent that a third pigment is present and functional, the prediction of converging confusion lines in trichromatic chromaticity space is violated; in practice the presence of a third pigment may yield an influence so slight that the general scheme nearly works, but only with limited precision.

Scheibner and Boynton (1968) found that, with 3° fields flanked with a 1000 td surround, most dichromats could name equally bright spectral stimuli of wavelength greater than 530 nm in a manner which, though highly deficient, was nonrandom and revealed a surplus of "red" responses to the longer wavelengths. The possibility that differential rod stimulation was responsible for the residual discriminations could not be ruled out absolutely. Very recent data collected by A. Nagy in our laboratory in San Diego indicate that most dichromats make residual red–green discriminations, given large fields, even when stimuli are presented during the "cone plateau" phase of dark adaptation, from the fifth to ninth minute after exposure to a bright bleaching light. During this period, cone sensitivity has recovered, but that of rods is still far above threshold. The stimuli used were virtually ineffective upon B cones; therefore the R and G cones appear capable of differential stimulation that translates into weak color differences. In this experiment, a color-naming technique was used in response to brief flashes which probably do not permit residual color differences to adapt out as they may during the steady examination of fields like those used during color matching.

Selective Chromatic Adaptation

Studies mf dichromats agree in showing that, unlike normals, there is no selective chromatic adaptation to pairs of longwave stimuli. A heterochromatic threshold-reduction factor (HTRF) test[19] was applied by Boynton and Wagner (1961) and Scheibner and Boynton (1968) with that result. Similar conclusions can be drawn for studies of Speelman and Krauskopf (1963) and Boynton, Kandel, and Onley (1959). This result is exactly what is predicted on the assumption that dichromats have only one longwave pigment. It would be expected that ordinary anomalous observers, with R and G curves separated by as much as 15 nm, would show a significant degree of selective chromatic adaptation. Watkins (1969a, 1969b) found such an effect, but the shortwave member of his HTRF pair was at 480 nm, too short a wavelength to exclude a contribution by the B cones. In the study by Boynton and Wagner (1961) no such effect was found either for flashed or steady background fields. Mean HTRF values, expressed as arithmetic factors, were as follows (for transient adapting conditions that produced the largest effect for normals):

Subject	Type of HTRF	Mean HTRF
Normal ($N = 29$)	RG	4.1
	RB	11.3
Protanope ($N = 6$)	RG	1.0
	RB	2.3
Deuteranope ($N = 5$)	RG	1.0
	RB	8.1
Protanomalous ($N = 2$)	RG	0.9
	RB	2.7
Deuteranomalous ($N = 5$)	RG	1.1
	RB	9.1
Extreme deuteranomalous ($N = 2$)	RG	1.1
	RB	11.3

In this study, red, green, and blue gelatin filters were used. That the red-green pair did not pass light that was effective on B cones was indicated both by the physical characteristics of the light and the HTRF values of 1.0 for the

RG pair, found both for protanopes and deuteranopes. The value of 4.1 for normal observers means that heterochromatic thresholds for the red-green filter pair are on average more than four times lower than their homochromatic counterparts. The results for 9 anomalous observers for the red-green filter pair do not differ from those of the dichromats. For the red-blue pairs, normals and all types of deutans agree that there is a substantial selective effect, averaging about tenfold, which must be due to the participation of B cones and longwave cones that selectively adapt. The protans show a much smaller amount of red-blue selectivity, probably because of the reduced effective intensity of the longwave light for them (the same objective field intensities were used for all subjects). Watkins (1969b) found an HTRF for protanomalous observers less than normals but significantly greater than 1.0; again this can be interpreted in terms of the probable participation of B cones. On the other hand, Piantanida and Sperling (1973a, b) found that, provided the exactly right adapting wavelengths were used, selective chromatic adaptation of anomalous observers could be demonstrated.

It may be concluded that the R and G cones of deuteranomalous and protanomalous observers, in addition to having spectral sensitivities whose peaks are closer together than those of normals, may not adapt as selectively as their relative sensitivities would predict. Or their spectral sensitivities may lie close enough together that the ratio of R/G cone stimulation is simply not sufficiently different to sustain the selective adaptation. Smith and Pokorny estimate this ratio, for anomalous observers, to be no greater than that elicited by stimuli of 570 and 600 nm for normals. The red-green HTRF for normal observers has not been tested for these wavelength pairs, although for some normals it is not significantly different from zero even for wavelengths more separated than this (Boynton, Scheibner, Yates, & Rinalducci, 1965).

Other failures to achieve selective chromatic adaptation of anomalous observers have been reported by Wald (1964), using the two-color threshold techniques, and by Alpern and Torii (1968a, b), using brightness-matching procedures. Their failure to selectively adapt anomalous observers is particularly intriguing in that sufficiently high adapting levels were used to have achieved significant photopigment bleaching.

OTHER FORMS OF COLOR BLINDNESS

Rod Monochromacy

This form of color blindness is total, apparently caused by an absence (or near absence) of all cone function. It is considered to be congenital and autosomal recessive, that is, not sex-linked. Rod monochromats exhibit a foveal scotoma (blind spot) and frequently a related nystagmus (involuntary eye movements). Such subjects are often photophobic (dislike moderate to bright lights that do not bother normal observers very much) and they always show very low acuity, around 20/200. They have often proved useful as subjects for the study of rod vision at relatively high levels, where cone vision normally intrudes to make such investigation difficult. The rod monochromat has no color discrimination, as would be predicted on the basis of arguments advanced about rod vision in Chapter 5. A postmortem anatomical investigation by Glickstein and Heath (1975) has revealed the presence of cones in a "rod" monochromat, despite the lack of any such evidence as based upon psychophysical testing.[20]

Tritanopia

Congenital tritanopia has been shown by Kalmus (1965) to be an autosomal dominant trait that is extremely rare (less than 1 in 10,000). In 1952, W. D. Wright reported on a substantial population of tritanopes, obtained following the publication in the widely circulated *Picture Post* magazine of pseudo-isochromatic plates (see below) that had been designed by Farnsworth. A similar plate is shown in Kalmus, 1965, as Plate I. Luminosity curves were found to be virtually identical to those of normals, color-mixture data were dichromatic, and the chromaticities that were confused tended to fall along lines radiating from a single tritanopic copunctal point. Their unusual wavelength discrimination functions were also measured. These are compared in Figure 10.9 with data from a similar study by Fischer, Bouman, and ten Doesschate (1951) and a theoretical prediction by Walraven, 1962, similar to that generated by the model of Chapter 8 (p. 270). For comparison, wavelength discrimination functions for normals as a function of area are shown; these show clearly that the normal subject tends toward tritanopia for the smallest field used.

A blue-yellow dichromacy based on a loss of the b-y channels would predict two neutral points in the spectrum, one at unique yellow around 575 nm and the other at unique blue around 465 nm. Although such an observer has been called a tetartanope, there is no evidence from Wright's sample that such people exist; other investigators seem to believe that they do. Tritanopes, on the other hand, come close to having a second neutral point only at the shortest perceptible wavelengths, as is predicted in Figure 10.2, if a line is drawn from the blue corner to 575 nm.

Cone Monochromacy

As pointed out earlier, if protanopia and deuteranopia are replacement rather than loss systems, then the simultaneous occurrence of the two conditions in a single individual, which is theoretically possible, will result in normal color vision (pseudonormal by Piantanida's classification). The simultaneous occurrence of protanopia or deuteranopia with tritanopia could result in cone monochromacy characterized by vision that is otherwise quite normal.

In his Friedenwald Award lecture to ARVO, Alpern (1974) reported the discovery of R-cone monochromacy.[21] His subject was capable of matching all spectral colors to a single standard, yielding a spectral sensitivity curve matching that of deuteranopes, except for wavelengths below 500 nm where the R-cone

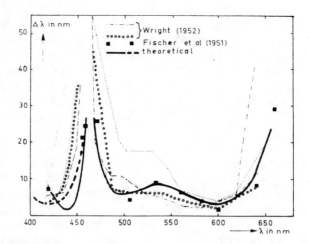
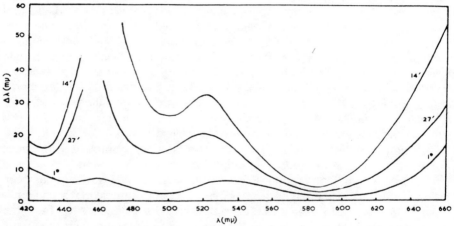

FIGURE 10.9 **Top:** Wavelength discrimination data of tritanopes (from Walraven, 1962, p. 63). **Bottom:** Similar data for normal observers as a function of field size (data of C. R. Forshaw from Weale, 1960, p. 127). Note the similarity between the trianopic data and the small-field data of the normal subject.

monochromat's sensitivity was higher. Curiously, his spectral sensitivity under conditions of strong yellow adaptation was that of π_3, one of Stiles's "blue" mechanisms. Apparently Alpern's subject has B cones, but for some reason they are not useful for purposes of color discrimination; possibly his y-b opponent pathways are inoperative. G-cone monochromats were reported by Weale (1953b), who found that the spectral sensitivities of these subjects were a bit too high in the long wavelengths to match those of protanopes, so in his case there appeared to be some R cones contributing. Like Alpern's B cones, these did not mediate chromatic discrimination; perhaps in Weale's subjects the r-g opponent pathways were nonfunctional.

B-cone monochromacy is relatively the most common type, although it is still exceedingly rare.[22] Such observers have about 20/60 acuity at best, roughly consistent with predictions based on normal subjects under conditions of B-cone "isolation" that may be achieved with strong yellow adapting lights and blue test stimuli (Brindley, 1954). Their photopic spectral sensitivity is essentially that of B cones, as inferred from human color mixture and two-color threshold work. Their modulation sensitivity is close to what has been inferred for normals under conditions of B-cone isolation. Of special interest is the fact that, over a remarkably small range of luminance reduction, as judged from spectral sensitivity analysis, their vision switches from B cone to rod. Many of these subjects have a rudimentary form of dichromatic color vision in the transition range; this is significant because it indicates that the sensations mediated through the B-cone system and those mediated by rods are qualitatively different.

Although it is difficult to be certain, it seems likely that the distribution of B cones in B-cone monochromats is about the same as in the normal retina, and that their function is normal. They exhibit a normal Stiles-Crawford effect, which would not be likely if the remainder of the foveal cones were missing, and rod sensitivity can be obtained for small fixated stimuli. Although these facts suggest that the R and G cones may contain rhodopsin (a possibility which has also been entertained in the case of total rod monochromacy), rhodopsin-mediated vision is not found at intensities above rod saturation, and one cannot be certain that these subjects use their foveas in a normal way.

Acquired Color-vision Deficiencies

Injury or diseases of the eye or optic nerve, which frequently can be diagnosed by procedures not requiring color-vision testing, are often the cause of defects of color vision. That a condition is acquired rather than congenital is signaled, not only by the presence of other abnormality, but by the awareness of the patient that there has been a change in his color perception. In addition, careful testing may reveal losses in color discrimination that mimic the congenital forms, but which differ from these in detail.

Not very much has yet been learned about normal color vision by the study of acquired *dyschromatopsia*, so only a few brief remarks about this class of defect will be made to round out this section of the chapter. For more information, readers are referred to a monumental study of some 400 patients by Verriest (1963) and to an excellent summary chapter by Grützner (1972).

The most common form of acquired loss of color discrimination occurs as a natural part of the aging process, as the lens of the eye absorbs progressively more light at the short wavelengths (Lakowski, 1962; Weale, 1960, 1963). The effect is predominantly optical, as may be proved by tests using monochromatic lights that, if intense enough, can be made to reach the retina. For example, most of the changes with age in the chromaticity of the spectral locus can be elminated by using the normalizing technique of Wright, described in Chapter 5. The loss of discrimination is therefore similar to what the young, normal observer would experience if looking through an attenuating filter that mimics the prereceptoral absorption of light in the older eye.

Most other acquired loss of color vision involves problems either with the retina or with the optic nerve. Figure 10.10, from Grützner (1972), shows that

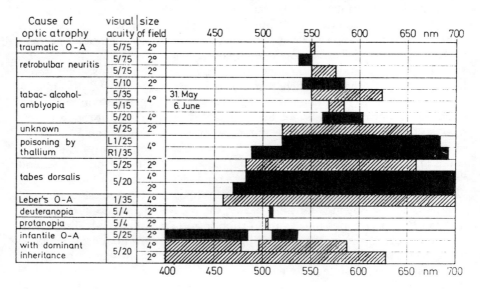

FIGURE 10.10 Wavelengths having a neutral appearance for patients with various diseases of the optic nerve. The much narrower bands of congenital dichromats are also shown. (From Grützner, 1972, p. 654.)

the spectral band that appears neutral is typically much wider and tends to be centered at longer wavelengths than for congenital protanopia or deuteranopia. Retinal disease is more likely to lead to tritanlike defects than to abnormal red–green discrimination; yet both occur and are specific to particular disease states. Acquired optic nerve dichromacies may resemble congenital ones, but there are important differences. Verriest (1963) puts it this way:

> ... the color discrimination is (as with congenital defects) reduced to a twofold function of wavelength and the confusions can be checked in the chromaticity diagram by an infinity of confusion axes, which are parallel or are convergent to a point outside the spectrum locus. However, the acquired defectiveness is not quite as clear-cut as the congenital, because the direction of the neutral axis varies from case to case, because there is always some impairment of discrimination at right angles to the neutral axis, and because the discrimination often becomes much better when the visual angle is increased (p. 191).

The latter is also true of congenital dichromacy, more so than is commonly realized (Pokorny & Smith, 1977). In any event, these complications make acquired color deficiencies, especially in their early stages, much harder to detect and to diagnose than the congenital form. It is probable that some disease states could be diagnosed earlier by color-vision testing than by any other procedure, if baseline data existed for the patient and sophisticated tests were used. But most ophthalmologists and optometrists rely only on the pseudoisochromatic plates, which are not very adequate for detection and diagnosis of acquired defects, and baseline data using more sensitive tests probably seldom exist. Grützner (1972) provides a table indicating which tests constitute the preferred methods of investigation according to the retinal disease that causes the deficiency.

COLOR-VISION TESTING

Quick Tests

It is remarkable that some people are able to reach adulthood without being aware that they have a serious red–green color deficiency. Pickford (1951), who personally tested the color vision of many hundreds of subjects using a wide variety of devices, relates the following anecdote concerning one such individual:

A . . . subject was not aware of any difficulty with colours until he failed in a test for the R.A.F. [Royal Air Force]. In this test he once mistook fawn [a variable color averaging a light-grayish brown] for green, and was very annoyed at being rejected. In the laboratory he spent five minutes trying to make quite sure that a green and a fawn skein of wool were not the same colour. Losing patience a little, I asked him what his difficulty might be, but he replied that he had no difficulty and was merely trying to be very exact. I explained to him that if in five minutes he had been trying to be very exact over the colour of a green signal at night in a fog, he might have crashed his aircraft into a hangar and killed a number of people. He does not believe that he is colour blind, but has a marked difficulty in distinguishing reds and greens from each other and from yellows, when there are no brightness differences, though he has no weakness in blues or yellows. This is an example of moderate red-green blindness, and this sort of man is liable to call certain fawn or yellowish colour "reddish-green." He would not be failed in a colour vision test with any injustice, however, because his sensitivity to the difference between red and green is at least ten times less than that of 90 per cent of men (p. 24).

People of this sort are rather sensitive about their color defect and do not wish to admit, even to themselves, that they are abnormal. Because there are many form and brightness cues that a clever person can use (wittingly or unconsciously) to make educated guesses about color names, the condition may go undetected. This is of course especially true for anomalous color vision where good hue discrimination may remain.

For the screening of large masses of people, a quick test is an absolute necessity. Such tests are desirable not only for restraining people from entry into the Royal Air Force or some other occupation where good color discrimination is necessary; they should be used also as a routine part of any optometric or ophthalmic examination in order to provide a full description of the patient's visual capacity. Moreover, as we have seen, such tests can have diagnostic value for ophthalmic disease. It would be desirable to have school children routinely tested for color defect, just as is commonly done for visual acuity deficit and hearing loss. Difficulty with colors can otherwise be embarrassing, whether the victim is a kindergartner who seems stupid to others because he does not learn his color names properly, or a high school chemistry student who fails in his qualitative analysis because he cannot tell red from yellow in a flame test.

The type of quick test in common use consists of a series of *pseudoisochromatic plates*. Each such plate is composed of a large nuimber of small discs of various colors. The test takes advantage of one of the Gestalt laws of organization, the *law of similarity*.[23] According to this principle, elements having the same appearance tend to be apprehended as a pattern, as in the black-and-white example at the top of Figure 10.11. By manipulating the chromaticities of such elements at constant luminance, they can form a figure and a background. It is possible to develop a test plate in which figure and ground fall along a confusion line in chromaticity space for a certain dichromat, whereas they look very different for the color normal who will see the figure that the dichromat misses.

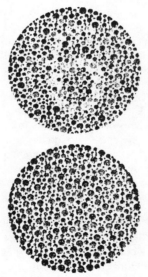

FIGURE 10.11   These pseudo-isochromatic plates, from the American Optical Company set, were originally reproduced in color, where the number 12 stands out clearly in the lower plate. In this black-and-white reproduction, the camera had equal sensitivity to the orange dots that made up the number and the blue ones that formed the background. The red-green color differences forming the 6 at the top were translated into lightness differences. (From McConnell, 1977, p. 178.)

Such tests were originally developed mostly by trial and error. A number of them have been examined by Lakowski (1969a,b), whose papers on the theory and practice of colour-vision testing provide an excellent summary. An example of a particularly interesting and tricky kind of test is illustrated in Figure 10.12.

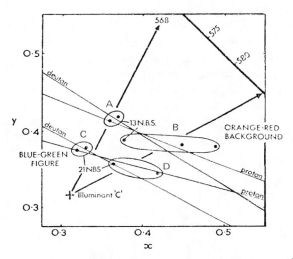

FIGURE 10.12 This diagram depicts the chromaticities in CIE space (see Appendix) of the 9 colors used in a particularly complicated isochromatic plate where normals and dichromats see different numbers. (From Lakowski, 1969, p. 267; Ishihara plate from the fifth edition.)

This plot shows the chromaticities of the elements of a test plate where normals and dichromats usually see different numbers. In this plate the elements consist of four groups of colors labeled A B C D. The Gestalt number 74 is represented by dots formed by colors AC against a background of dots formed by colors BD, seen by normals as blue-green against orange-red. From inspection of the protan and deutan confusion lines that are shown in the figure, it is clear that neither class of dichromat can discriminate A from B, or C from D, with any precision. Although they can tell B from C and A from D (because in each case these are differentially effective for B cones) the coarse spacing of such dots contained within the number 74 seen by normals makes that configuration hard to discern relative to a number 21 provided when dots AB form the figure against CD as the background. But A and B do not look alike for the color normal, nor do C and D, and therefore the grouping that stands out for the dichromat exists at only half density for the normal. For him, the number 74, based upon a substantial difference in R vs G cone activation, is much more apparent. (Most plates are not this complicated.)

If properly administered, the best of such tests can discriminate normals from color-defective observers with reasonable accuracy. However, they are not dependable for discriminating protans from deutans. Nor is this a suitable type of test for separating dichromats from anomalous observers, because an anomalous subject may or may not pass the test, depending upon the severity of his defect. Nevertheless, there is a correlation between performance on the test and ability to perform other tasks that require red−green color discrimination.

Because the degree of defect is hard to quantify, such tests are better used as "go, no-go" screening devices to separate color normals from the red−green defectives. Because such a test consists of a number of plates of varying difficulty, one possible measure of degree of defect lies in the number of plates that are misread. But subjects who are color normal by more stringent tests also make some errors; for example the color normal usually *can* see the number 21 in the plate explained in Figure 10.12, if it is pointed out to him, and despite normal vision he might fail to read a number because of an inability to achieve the necessary Gestalt organization. In this context, the results of Figure 10.13

FIGURE 10.13 Frequency of "wrong numbers" seen on the Dvorine isochromatic test shown for groups of subjects divided according to ranges of age. (From Lakowski, 1969, p. 272.)

are of interest. It is probably not true, as the graphs seem to suggest, that subjects in the 5−15 year age group have poorer color vision than those in the 16−35 year age group. On the other hand, the increase in errors in the older age groups probably *does* represent, for the most part, a real deterioration of color vision. Apparently the higher-order requirement of Gestalt apperception, which may depend on age, intelligence, or perceptual aptitudes unrelated to color vision, may confound the result.

Why not then simply put two colors side by side? These could be chosen to look alike for the dichromat but different for the color normal. They could be presented admixed with pairs that are physically the same, and which therefore must match for both groups, and with other pairs that should differ for everyone. Forced-choice discriminations of same and different could be used and these could be objectively scored "correct" or "incorrect."

In principle, the foregoing could be done, but in practice it probably would not work out. The reasons for this have relevance also for the proper administration of the pseudoisochromatic tests. One problem relates to the practical difficulty of controlling the printing process that determines the spectral reflectances of the colored discs. Known differences exist, for example, in the chromaticities of discs that are supposed to be the same across various editions of the Ishihara plates that comprise one of the most widely used pseudoisochromatic tests. So it is possible that a number not seen by a dichromat on one edition of the test might be discriminable in another, although this is much less likely than if discriminations were based upon contiguous comparisons. A second problem concerns individual variations among color-blind subjects of the same class, for example, differences attributable to preretinal absorption in the eye media. These differences can make one dichromat's match for reflecting samples slightly different from another's. A third problem concerns the choice of illuminant to be used. Recall from Chapter 5 (p. 155) that reflecting samples that are metameric under one illuminant will not generally match under another. Although these problems exist also for the pseudoisochromatic plates, the lack of contiguity of the discs, and a range of color differences between similar dots, which is deliberately built into such plates, allow the test to achieve a robustness that would not be possible with comparisons of contiguous fields.

Pseudoisochromatic plates have also been developed for testing tritan deficiencies, but these are much less used. A tritanope would probably be classified as color-normal most of the time by pseudoisochromatic tests as currently administered.

Farnsworth-Munsell 100-Hue Test

This test was developed by a Navy captain, Dean Farnsworth. (According to an unconfirmed report, he got the idea for it from an Englishman named Pierce at the National Institute of Industrial Psychology.) It is probably the best test of color discrimination available for general use. In its completed form, the test uses only 85 cylindrical objects. Because these resemble small bottle caps with pieces of Munsell-colored papers recessed into them, the test objects are usually called "caps."

The chromaticities of the 85 caps, shown in Figure 10.14, were chosen to form a continuous hue circle of about equal chroma relative to a white point ("C" in the diagram). Starting with color number 1, the hues shade from red through orange to yellow, then from yellow through green to blue-green, to blue, purple, and back to red. Colors numbered 1, 22, 43, and 64 are used as anchors at the ends of four wooden trays. The subject's task is to deal with one tray at a time. For example, the subject attempts to order caps 2 through 21 in the manner shown in the figure, "to form a continuous series of colors." The steps are very small and the task is not easy. A complete test requires the use

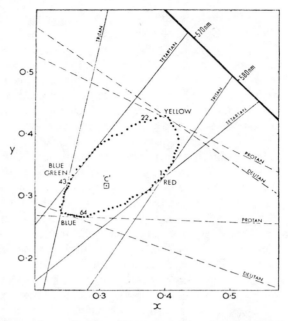

FIGURE 10.14 Chromaticities of the 85 caps of the Farnsworth-Munsell "100-hue" test represented in CIE chromaticity space (see Appendix). Confusion lines for 4 kinds of dichromats are shown. Where the elliptical configuration described by the chromaticities of the samples of the test is tangent to a dichromatic confusion line, poor discrimination is predicted. (From Lakowski, 1969, p. 273.)

of all four trays. Each cap contains its number on its reverse side; when the subject finishes arranging the caps of a tray, the cover of the tray is closed, the closed tray is inverted, and the bottom is lifted to expose the underside of the caps, showing their numbers. An error score for each cap is computed as the sum of the differences between the number of that cap and the numbers of the adjacent caps. For example, if the ordering were 4-6-5, the error score for position 6 would be 3.

It is important that the error scores be localized in some way, rather than just averaged overall, because the pattern of such scores around the hue circle is of diagnostic value. The reason for this is clear from Figure 10.14, which shows confusion axes for various classes of color defect. When error scores are plotted on such a standardized polar diagram, the resulting lobes are characteristic of the major forms of color blindness. Because the discriminations require sensitivity to very small steps, few subjects obtain a perfect score and the test is useful also as a means to assess variations in color discrimination among color normals.

As with the pseudoisochromatic plates, the 100-hue test must be used with the appropriate illuminant. As the illumination level is reduced below the level

Color-Vision Testing 377

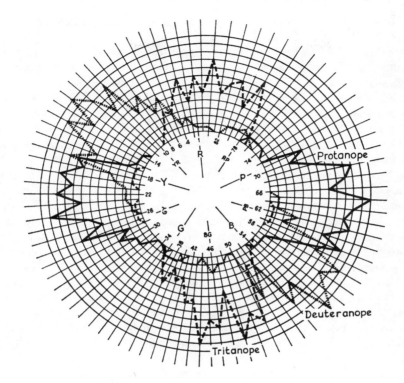

FIGURE 10.15 Illustrative data to show how the results for three kinds of dichromats are plotted on the polar diagram used for the Farnsworth-Munsell 100-hue test. No mistakes would be represented by the innermost circle; a normal observer does not produce an error score of more than two or three at any location, and sometimes will show no errors at all. (From Kalmus, 1965, p. 48.)

that is recommended for the test, all normals make more errors, and in the limit, as scotopic levels are reached, a characteristic scotopic axis is achieved. Apparently most caps, of equal value (lightness) for cones but not for rods, can be ordered according to a scale of scotopic lightness, except for two regions around the circle where their scotopic lightnesses are nearly equal.

Because the 100-hue test takes about 15 to 30 minutes to administer, it is not a "quick test." It is considered too difficult to be used with young children, and the scores are influenced to some degree by psychological variables, such as the motivation of the subject.

Anomaloscopes

The undisputed queen of all color-vision testing instruments is the anomaloscope, the only device in common use (despite its high price) that is able to discriminate reliably between dichromats and anomalous trichromats. As normally used, it is a red—green test only, although some anomaloscopes exist that test also for tritan defects.[24]

The *Rayleigh equation* refers to color matching using nearly spectral colors, leading to the anomalous quotient previously discussed with respect to the analytical anomaloscope. In the Nagel Model I anomaloscope, which is probably the most widely used in this country, a semicircular yellow field is seen at the bottom. Its lateral subtense is about $1°-3°$ of visual angle, depending upon telescope focus. A red−green mixture (670 nm and 545 nm) is seen at the top, and the overall field is circular. The instrument is constructed so that one knob, when turned, varies the intensity of the yellow (589 nm) field while the other varies the ratio of red to green in the mixture field without altering its luminance. The color-normal individual therefore can make an exact match by (1) varying the red−green mixture to form a yellow and (2) also varying the intensity of the monochromatic yellow field to make the two fields match for brightness. Some iteration may be required, but for normal observers the match is easy and precise. Because longwave lights are used, the comparison does not involve the B cones.

When a deuteranope attempts the match, he has one degree of freedom too many. The examiner can set the red−green knob to any position, and the subject can make a match by means of the yellow knob alone. If given use of both controls, the deuteranope might by chance make a normal match, but on repeated occasions his matches will vary over a wide range of the red−green scale.

When a protanope attempts a match, he behaves similarly to the deuteranope except that the brightness of the red−green field depends for him upon the ratio of the two components. In the Nagel Model I the full red looks very dim, while full green looks brightest. Therefore, if the red−green ratio is set toward red by the examiner, the protanope's setting of the yellow knob, as needed to produce a color match, will produce a field of lower luminance than if the red−green ratio is set toward green.

When a protanomal attempts a match, he behaves similarly to the protanope with respect to the yellow setting that he makes, providing that his red−green setting, which he must also be allowed to make in order to produce a perfect match, is the same one used to test the protanope. The settings of anomalous observers will be reasonably exact (as exact as those for normals in some cases), although on repeated matches most anomalous observers will show more variability of the red−green ratio, and their matches will not be acceptable to normals. An ordinary deuteranomal behaves like the ordinary (simple) protanomal except that his yellow setting is in the normal range. Extreme protanomals and deuteranomals have matching ranges so wide as to include both normal and anomalous matches.

Figure 10.16 summarizes, in a graphical form, these generalizations about anomaloscope matches.

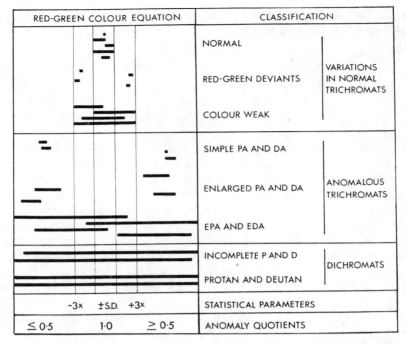

FIGURE 10.16 Ranges of anomaloscope settings, when subjects are allowed to manipulate both the red-green and the yellow intensity controls, for normal and color-defective observers. (Originally from Lakowski, 1969, p. 278; slightly modified and furnished by V. Smith and J. Pokorny.)

Other Tests

The analytical anomaloscope, previously discussed, is not a conventional test for color blindness. Nor are measures of wavelength discrimination or spectral neutral points useful, because these require apparatus too elaborate for general use. Many other tests have been suggested from time to time, but new tests are unlikely to be used unless they are diagnostically superior to those that have already become established. An example of such a procedure that remains unused is the HTRF test that was developed and tested nearly 20 years ago in my laboratory (Boynton & Wagner, 1961) and pursued also by Ikeda and Urakubo (1968), who developed a flicker version of it.

In addition, there are a variety of tests designed for specific vocational purposes, where color theory is not at issue, and the closer the test is to the actual task, the more valid it is likely to be. Examples include the sorting of skeins of wool and the naming of the colors of signal lights. A number of other tests are described by Burnham, Hanes, and Bartleson (1963).

WHAT DO RED-GREEN-DEFECTIVE OBSERVERS REALLY SEE?

The color perception of a red-green anomalous observer can most easily be understood by first calculating the R/G cone activation ratio for any particular stimulus, based on his longwave cone sensitivities, which are too close together to be normal. Next, determine for a normal observer the wavelength that would be required to produce that same R/G ratio. Assume that B-cone activity is normal for both. Anomalous observers would be expected to see all of the hues that normal observers see, except for the most saturated reds and greens, which cannot be simulated because of the limited R/G cone ratios of the anomalous observer caused by the abnormal closeness of their cone absorption spectra. A protanomalous observer would in addition see the more saturated red colors as being much darker than they are for the normal or deuteranomolous subject.

On the basis of the opponent-color model that has been presented, one can make reasonable predictions about what dichromats should see, assuming that the replacement hypothesis is correct and that the visual pathways are normal except for the r-g channels. For spectral colors, there is a division at the neutral wavelength that should cause shorter wavelengths to appear blue and longer ones yellow. For a short distance on either side of the neutral point, there is a rapid increase in saturation. This corresponds to the range within which the U-shaped wavelength discrimination functions of protanopes and deuteranopes can be measured. Outside this range, on each side of the zone of good discrimination, a dichromat should experience little or no difference in the appearance of spectral colors.

For the normal observer, spectral colors are the most saturated. For the deuteranope, spectral stimuli should have no such special quality. As plotted upon the chromaticity diagram of the normal observer, any nonspectral color can be matched by the protanope or deuteranope by a spectral color that lies on the protan or deutan confusion line passing through the point representing the chromaticity, for a normal observer, of the nonspectral stimulus. Therefore, if the appearance of spectral colors is known, that of any nonspectral color can readily be predicted.

The expected color perception of the protanope is essentially the same as that of the deuteranope, except that different spectral colors must be chosen to match nonspectral ones, and colors which are equivalent to long-wavelength spectral lights will appear very dim.

Color names, for the dichromat, describe salient properties of objects other than hue. For example, a protanope learns that objects that would be described as "dark yellow" or "brown" by normal observers (if they could see them with a protanope's eyes) must be called "red" if the color identification is to be "correct" in the sense of agreeing with that of normal observers. Few dichromats can be convinced that their color vision accords with the theoretical description just given. Moreover, there is no proof that the descriptions just given are accurate characterizations of what red—green defective observers actually do see. A major problem, as noted at the outset of the chapter, is that sensations are not logically comparable between different individuals. Therefore it is not really meaningful to state dogmatically that a deuteranope sees the long spectral wavelengths as yellow. Perhaps the closest that one can come to a solution of this dilemma is to study a *unilateral dichromat*, a person who is color defective in one eye and color normal in the other. Some unilateral dichromats have been discovered. Judd (1948) stated that 37 cases had been reported by that time, but Hsia and Graham (1965) note that "only about 8 of these have proved useful for theory." Some unilateral subjects (for example, one studied intensively by Graham and his colleagues) seem to see colors in much the way that the opponent-color model predicts. But according to Walls (1958), no bona fide unilateral protanope has ever been discovered. This was a matter of great interest to him because he predicted, as a trichromatic theorist, that protanopes should see blue and green, not blue and yellow.

Walls pointed out that Graham's subject was not classically deuteranopic, probably being heterozygous for the deuteranopic gene so that the defect expressed itself in unusual ways. Besides the unusual asymmetry of the defect, it also seems likely that the deuteranopia was incomplete because wavelength discrimination in the supposedly dichromatic eye was not completely lacking in the longwave end of the spectrum.

MacLeod and Lennie (1974) discovered a man who was classically deuteranopic in one eye and deuteranomalous in the other. As previously noted, a deuteranomalous observer enjoys most of the normal color experiences; surely he has had sensations of red, green, yellow, and blue and should therefore be in a position to name the hue seen in the deuteranopic eye, using the relatively normal eye and his (presumably) normal brain as a gauge. It is embarrassing for opponent-color theory that the color he reported in response to long wavelengths, seen by his deuteranopic eye, was not yellow, but orange. These authors conclude:

> By providing such a clear exception to the rule that yellow and blue are the only colors perceived by the red-green blind, these observations of R. H. destroy the last remaining support for "opponent process" interpretations of color blindness and particularly of deuteranopia. But the support afforded to opponent process interpretations by the earlier unilateral cases was in any case flimsy. Binocular matches can lead to rigorous conclusions about retinal events only if a binocular match is a match at the retinal level, and this cannot be guaranteed unless the afferent pathways from left and right eyes are similar. The necessary assumption of afferent identity is difficult to justify in unilateral cases, for it is clear . . . that different "stimulus histories" for left and right eyes may bring about differences of organization in the afferent pathways at stages prior to binocular combination (pp. 132—133).

In other words, it is possible that a message from the deuteranopic eye that would have been interpreted as "yellow" if transmitted through normal pathways, and moreover received by a brain with normal, chromatically-rich, and binocularly-balanced input, might instead register as orange. Although this interpretation might seemingly help to save opponent theory (especially since some other unilateral color blinds do see the predicted colors) it logically implies that the issue of what dichromats "really" see probably can never be fully resolved.

VARIATIONS IN NORMAL COLOR VISION

Two different kinds of variations among normal observers will be discussed in this final section: (1) those that apply to any particular observer as a result of changes in stimulating conditions other than spectral distribution, and (2) those that occur between observers under similar or identical stimulating conditions.

Effect of Field Size

Much of the emphasis in this book has been upon the perception of color in centrally fixated fields subtending about 2° or so of visual angle. A number of interesting changes occur when the field is made either larger or smaller than this.

As field size is reduced, the relative contribution of the y-b opponent system becomes progressively less important until, with very tiny centrally fixated fields, normal color vision becomes tritanopic. Only two primary stimuli are then required to make a color match, and lights are confused if they lie along tritan lines in chromaticity space (Willmer & Wright, 1945). The most likely interpretation of these results is that there are few B cones in the fovea and probably none at all in its very center. Despite this lack, a very small shortwave light, when directly fixated, will appear blue. The explanation for this may relate to scattered light that excites some B cones in the immediate surround. The stimulus is correctly localized at the foveal center because the light is seen there as a result of its action upon R and G cones which are present there in high density. Perhaps the blueness becomes attached to the percept by mechanisms related to those discussed in connection with the "gap effect" on page 287.

As field size increases, color discrimination improves, probably almost without limit. With large fields at mesopic and moderate photopic levels, rods as well as cones are stimulated. Nevertheless, color matching does not become tetrachromatic. (The subject's task is made more ambiguous by the selective influence of the macular pigment, which affects only the central region but not the more peripheral parts of the field. In large-field matching studies, subjects are typically instructed to ignore the center, which they seem able to do; sometimes an annular field may be used instead.) Although the matches are trichromatic, the rods nevertheless can have an effect. The mathematical laws of color mixture (Chapter 5), which allow the transformation of color-matching data from one reference system to another, are not fully obeyed for large fields. Additivity often breaks down for such matches, and incompatible data may be generated depending upon details of experimental procedure (Crawford, 1965).

It is probable that the nonlinearities of large-field color matching are attributable to rod intrusion (Clarke, 1963). Because unique matches are made with only three variable reference stimuli, only by chance would the resulting match for cones also be a match for rods. When the rod activity generated by the two matching stimuli is different, it could have an effect on the relative appearance of the fields. If so, large-field trichromacy results from a limitation imposed by three pathways (luminance, r-g, and y-b) rather than one set by three pigments. No assurance remains that large-field color matches are physiologically identical at the cone stage. Implicit in this argument is the notion that the rods are not capable of generating any new sensations that differ from those mediated by the cone systems by themselves.

Trezona (1976) has reported a procedure whereby it is possible to make large-field color matches that are exact for rods as well as for the three types of cones. A fourth primary, chosen so as to be especially effective for rods, is added to the usual three. After a subject makes a trichromatic match with the usual three primaries at a photopic luminance level, the halves of the field will then not match at scotopic luminances. By altering the fourth primary, the subject then makes an adjustment to permit a scotopic match. The intensities of the fields are then increased again, all in proportion, to photopic levels where the match again fails. By iterating between the two levels (a slow and tedious process) it proves possible finally to satisfy both the cones and rods. Therefore, when considered in terms of the numbers of reference stimuli required to cause such an overall physiological identity, four primaries are needed and human large-field color matching becomes tetrachromatic. Nevertheless, because the rods, lacking private pathways to the brain, cannot induce a novel scotopic quality of sensation, large-field color matching is trichromatic in the sense that three controls suffice to make color matches.[25]

These results have interesting implications for color-defective observers. Recall, for example, that blue-cone monochromats exhibit a form of dichromatic vision over a mesopic range. This result implies that, in the case of these unusual observers, signals generated by rods lead to sensations that are qualitatively different from those attributable to what their cones alone can provide. A plausible interpretation is to suppose that rods are capable of generating signals that are transmitted through the r-g opponent pathways, and that this may happen also for normal subjects. At mesopic levels, this input would for normal observers alter only slightly the ongoing activity of the r-g pathways that is largely determined by input from the R and G cones—a minor effect and one that causes no new sensations. For the blue-cone monochromat, on the other hand, such variable rod input might be sufficient to keep the r-g pathways functional, and to induce novel sensations (red and/or green) compared to what the blue-cone monochromat would see without rod intrusion. Recently, Smith and Pokorny (1977) have made a strong case that the residual red-green vision that dichromats exhibit for large fields may have a similar cause.

Effect of Retinal Location

As the size of a centrally-fixated field increases, progressively more rods are recruited and the cone population simultaneously changes to include the fatter and more sparsely distributed peripheral cones. Therefore, the effect of field size per se is confounded with changes of central vs peripheral retinal characteristics. To obviate this confounding, it is better to compare fields of modest size in different retinal regions. When this is done, small changes in color mixture result that seem attributable to the different densities of cone pigments to be expected in foveal vs peripheral cones (Pokorny, Smith, & Starr, 1976). Much larger changes occur in color appearance, as shown by an excellent color-naming study reported by Gordon and Abramov (1977). These authors conclude that previous reports of color deficiency in the peripheral retina have been misleading: "The quality of color vision in the periphery depends critically on stimulus size. If the stimulus is sufficiently large, subjects see a full range of well saturated hues.... [T]his principle also holds for the fovea.... [S]mall colored stimuli anywhere on the retina will be perceived in much the same way."

Variations among Normal Human Observers

Large variations in the wavelength and chromatic discriminations of normal subjects were mentioned in earlier chapters. There is a substantial range of normal scores on the Farnsworth-Munsell 100-hue test. All observers show poorer discrimination as illumination is reduced, but some show this influence sooner and more precipitously than others.

A chief cause of variations among normal observers lies in prereceptoral absorption differences, beginning with a wide range of densities of macular pigment. Secondly, the yellowing of the eye lens with age leads to predictable changes in color vision that are associated with the selective absorption of shortwave light. As noted in Chapter 5, most of this change can be eliminated by using Wright's system of normalizing mixture primaries, which boosts the intensity of the shortwave mixture component as much as may be required to keep the stimulus at the retina at normal levels.

SUMMARY

Substantial variations in color perception exist among normal individuals, as exhibited by differences in unique yellow settings and disagreements about secondary color names, both of which probably have a physiological rather than a cultural basis. So-called color-blind individuals, with a few exceptions, are not really color-blind but are more properly called *color-defective*. Although they confuse many colors that normals would see as different, and misname some of them because the color vocabulary of the normal observer is for them needlessly rich, most color-defective observers nevertheless see many colors as different from one another.

Various possibilities exist for the alteration of the normal opponent-color model that was proposed in Chapter 7 and used in the last four chapters of this book. Only some of these possibilities seem to be expressed in color-blind human observers. These include: (1) loss defects (where a single cone type, or—less certainly—one of the opponent pathways, may be missing or nonfunctional), (2) weak systems, and (3) shifts in the spectral location of one of the three types of cones. The latter seems required to account for anomalous color vision, which is trichromatic but different from (and usually inferior to) that of normal observers.

Because the remaining types of dichromatic cones appear to be those of normal observers, it becomes possible to represent the color confusions of dichromats in the chromaticity diagram of the normal observer. If a physiologically based diagram is used, these lines radiate from the "corners" of the diagram which represent unique activation of normal R, G, and B cones. The contribution of one type of cone to the color perception of each type of dichromat is apparently missing, although a weak residual capacity to discriminate colors along these "confusion lines" can be demonstrated in most such observers.

To further elucidate the relations among normal, dichromatic, and anomalous color vision, the analytical anomaloscope is discussed. This is followed by a brief consideration of the genetics of color deficiency. The most common forms, protanopia and deuteranopia, are most easily explained as sex-linked congenital losses of normal R and G cone function. The cones probably are not literally missing, but the abnormal ones may contain pigments of the other class, or ones very nearly like those. Anomalous observers probably have replacement pigments that differ from the normal ones by being shifted in the spectrum so as to overlap abnormally with the remaining, unaltered pigment.

An analysis of spectral neutral points provides further evidence that fusion deuteranopia does not exist. The varieties of red-green anomaly, ranging from pure dichromacy to normal trichromacy (with simple and extreme anomalies in between) is probably too continuous to be characterized by genetic models that deal with only seven categories (protanope, extreme protanomal, protanomal; deuteranope, extreme deuteranomal, deuteranomal; normal).

Color defects actually exist in many varieties, most of them quite rare. Rod monochromacy, tritan defects, cone monochromacy, and acquired color deficiencies are discussed.

Accurate conceptualization of the nature of defects of human color vision requires methods of classification that are fast and accurate. Pseudoisochromatic tests are fast, but inaccurate. The Farnsworth-Munsell 100-hue test is the best of those that use surface colors. The best of the screening devices, the anomaloscope, is fast, accurate, but relatively expensive.

The chapter concludes with a discussion of possible bases for variations in the color vision of normal observers.

NOTES

[1] Parsons (1924, p. 170) and Boring (1942, pp. 183–184) cite Turbervil in 1684 as reporting a case of total color blindness, and Huddart in 1777 as reporting the first case of partial color blindness.

[2] A summary of such data is given by Judd (1951) and has been reprinted by Boynton (1975). An excellent study not cited in those references is that of Thomson (1954).

[3] Evidence supporting this assertion exists in crosscultural studies by Berlin and Kay (1969) and in the use of hue categories by human infants (Bornstein, Kessen, and Weiskopf, 1976). See also Bornstein (1973).

[4] Although hard to prove, there seems to be an almost perverse tendency for color-blind individuals to gravitate toward occupations where good color vision is a necessity. In any case it seems certain that such people do not necessarily screen themselves out. Often this is due to a lack of awareness that their color vision is abnormal.

[5] In the last paper published by Selig Hecht (1949) he compares a sample of 6 normals, 3 protanopes, and 3 deuteranopes. He concludes that, compared to normal observers, protanopes need twice as much light (and deuteranopes about 60 percent more) in order to achieve the same visual acuity. There seems to be no other supporting evidence for this result, which apparently is an accident of small-sample statistics. In general, dichromats do not seem to suffer any loss of visual acuity when compared to normals.

[6] A growing body of evidence suggests that, in order to develop normally, the neurons of the visual system must be exercised by reacting to the kinds of environmental inputs to which the eye is normally exposed. The literature on this subject has mainly been concerned with spatial vision (e.g., Hirsch & Spinelli, 1970). Pettigrew and Freeman (1973) report that kittens raised in a planetarium-like visual environment lacking straight-line contours develop cortical neurons that respond mostly to spots, rather than lines, quite in contrast to such cells in the normal cat. Anatomical changes may be associated with stimulus deprivation during development. It therefore seems unlikely that the r-g pathways, if they receive zero input during development (or one that is strongly biased in one or another direction) would exhibit normal activity if normal receptor function could somehow be restored to them as adults. However, it seems likely (see p. 215) that the r-g pathways receive input from B cones in response to short wavelengths; the possibility that they may also receive excitation from rods is examined later in this chapter.

[7] Are the R and G cone-absorption spectra for normal human vision separated by an optimal amount? This question is much easier to state than to answer. The hypothesis cannot be tested without a full description of how the cone signals are utilized by the remainder of the visual system. Even if this were known—for example, if the simplified scheme of Chapter 8 were an accurate description of reality—a thorough ecological study would still be needed to determine what kinds of spectral differences are most important for us to discriminate in the real world. In addition to the degree of separation between them, the absolute placement of λ_{max} values for the two longwave cone photopigments would also be important. For example, discrimination between 700 and 750 nm is necessarily poor because the R/G cone activation ratio remains nearly constant as wavelength is varied over this range. By shifting the sensitivity curves of both classes of cones 150 nm toward longer wavelengths, discrimination would be improved in the neighborhood of 725 nm. But because of the

high rate of spontaneous thermal decomposition and the low photon energy, it might be difficult to achieve reliable signals from receptors in response to such long wavelengths (recall the argument on p. 106). Shifting the B-cone sensitivity to shorter wavelengths would not be useful unless the high absorption of light by the optical media could be reduced, along with the fluorescence of the lens that occurs when it is stimulated with ultraviolet radiation. Although the problem of what is optimal is very complicated, it nevertheless seems likely that the action spectra of the cones actually posessed by normal human observers reflect an optimization of many factors, one that has been achieved through the process of evolution.

[8] The midpoint of the range, if enough settings are made to establish it reliably despite the variability of individual settings, is related to and serves as an index of the nature of the shift of λ_{max} of the anomalous pigment.

[9] Figure 5.14 represented the same conception, but was plotted in triangular coordinates, using a set of hypothetical spectral sensitivity curves that approach, but do not duplicate, the more realistic set of Smith and Pokorny.

[10] The first use of this type of construction was by Maxwell (1855), followed by König and Dieterici (1893), who were the first to represent Maxwell's triangle with corners based on their best estimate of the physiological primaries. See also Helmholtz (1924, pp. 145–150 of Vol. 1). Pitt (1944) (see Wright, 1946) did empirical studies of confusion lines for dichromats and plotted these in Wright's chromaticity diagram. Many texts feature the same information on the CIE chromaticity diagram (e.g., Wyszecki & Stiles, 1967, p. 406; LeGrand, 1968, p. 348). Rodieck (1973, p. 743) shows a diagram with physiological primaries, as does Rushton (1975, p. 69) but a triangular plot is used in each case. Pitt attempted this in 1944 using Cartesian coordinates. Only in a diagram based upon physiological primaries do the dichromatic confusion lines radiate exactly from the corners of the diagram. Otherwise, the copunctal points from which such lines radiate must be located elsewhere. Whatever system of reference stimuli is used, the locations of copunctal points specify imaginary stimuli capable of uniquely exciting R, G, and B cones. Smith and Pokorny (personal communication) feel that, in a diagram such as that of Figure 10.2, the shortwave spectral locus should bend around as indicated by the dotted line, rather than to continue its downward plunge as shown by the solid line that is based upon their data. This change would provide pairs of very shortwave confusion colors for deuteranopes, as shown for example by the line from the G corner that passes through 440 nm and cuts the spectral locus again at a shorter wavelength. Much of this modified spectral locus falls upon one of the protan confusion lines, suggesting a range of short wavelengths which, like longwave ones, should be confused by protanopes. The failure of the Smith and Pokorny data to show these relationships is believed to result from the requirement that they be transformations of Judd's modification of the CIE color mixture functions, which are probably not exactly correct. Accurate color-matching data for protanopes and deuteranopes at very short wavelengths, which are hard to produce at sufficient radiance, are not abundant. Ultimately, in order to settle upon a set of functions that are physiologically accurate, it will be necessary to abandon the requirement that they should be transformations of CIE-based data.

[11] There are a number of differences between the instrument described here and the one actually developed by Mitchell and Rushton, but these are not fundamental to the theory of the instrument.

[12] To simulate the behavior of the Nagel device, W_R would be set so that the fields R and G are of equal *luminance* when the analyzer is rotated 90° to display first one component and then the other. Given this, the field changes, as A is turned, from red to green (or the reverse) without variation in luminance. A single wavelength in the yellow region of the spectrum is used in the left field. By varying W_λ, protanopes and deuteranopes can each match the right field no matter what the setting of A. Protanopes require less light in the left field to make a match if the right field is fully R; normals and deuteranopes require approximately the same amount no matter how the analyzer is set. Normal subjects must be allowed to vary M_λ as well as A in order to make a color match.

[13] For this to work exactly, it is also necessary that the protanope's cones have the same optical density of photopigment, and the same prereceptoral absorptions as those of the normal observer.

[14] Heterozygous females who are carriers of color defect are not normal in all respects. For example, carriers of protanopia have a somewhat decreased sensitivity in the long wavelengths, although they are trichromats (known as *Schmidt's sign*). Others exhibit patches of dichromatic retina which is an aspect of the *Mary Lyon* Syndrome (see Wooten and Wald, 1973). Although these conditions are trivial from the standpoint of the color vision of the female carrier, they are important to the human geneticist working on family pedigrees, and for validating the idea that the color deficiency is transmitted to a male offspring from the mother.

[15] This wavelength is somewhat too long relative to the various estimates that have been made. The principles of Piantanida's model are not affected by the exact wavelengths chosen, so long as the separations between the λ_{max} values of the various photopigments are of the same order as those assumed for his model.

[16] See Hurvich (1972), p. 604. Professor D. MacLeod has called my attention to an obscure publication by Aitken (1872) in which the fusion idea is mentioned.

[17] Stimulus C presumably appears achromatic to the normal observer because it elicits a nearly zero output from both the r-g and y-b opponent systems. For protanopes and deuteranopes, the r-g system could be balanced because of photopigment replacement and therefore not biased in the g direction. But the y input to the y-b opponent system cannot be normal, if it depends upon the summed input from both R and G cones, one of which is missing in each class of red-green dichromat. Nevertheless, when some of Walls and Mathews's subjects were asked to name the hue of the mixture field that matched C, most of them said that it looked gray. Almost as many saw it as greenish, and 5 subjects (4 of 27 protanopes and 1 of 32 deuteranopes) called it pink. One said that it was "greenish with a little pink in it." For normal observers, there is a substantial region in chromaticity space that appears white, although if two colors were chosen from the extremes of this region they surely would not match, and hues would be reported. It seems probable that stimulus C falls within this region both for normals and dichromats. Because colors called "green" by normals look very desaturated to protanopes and deuteranopes, who probably lack the *sensation* of green entirely, little importance can be attached to the application of that name to the appearance of illuminant C. See Hurvich and Jameson (1951 a,b) and Jameson and Hurvich (1951) for a psychophysical study of white.

[18] Nonspectral colors, such as those provided by reflecting surfaces, do not have "a wavelength." The values provided by Walls and Heath are the so-called *dominant*

wavelengths. In the CIE system (see Appendix) these are determined by drawing a line from a white point in the CIE chromaticity diagram through the nonspectral color to be specified, in order to determine the wavelength of the spectral locus where an extension of that line intersects. Roughly speaking, the dominant wavelength is a spectral color that nearly matches the (usually less saturated) nonspectral color with which it is being compared.

[19] The heterochromatic threshold-reduction factor (HTRF) is a measure of the degree to which two-color thresholds for heterochromatic pairs are lower than those for homochromatic ones (Boynton, Scheibner, Yates, & Rinalducci, 1965). For a univariant mechanism, the factor will be 1; larger values imply selective chromatic adaptation of two or more chromatic mechanisms.

[20] It is common for these subjects to show other evidence of cones in their retinas (Alpern, Falls, & Lee, 1960; Falls, Wolter, & Alpern, 1965); but it is possible that their cones contain rhodopsin.

[21] Alpern called this π_5 *cone monochromacy*; rod monochromacy was numed π_0, and red and green cone monochromacies were designated as π_5 and π_4 types respectively. Such a designation imples that the conditions are explicitly related to Stiles's π-mechanisms, which seems far from certain.

[22] Statements in this section about B-cone monochromacy are based on evidence from the following studies: Alpern, Lee, and Spivey, 1965; Blackwell and Blackwell, 1961; Daw and Enoch, 1973; Green, 1972; and Pokorny, Smith, and Swartley, 1970. See also Alpern's Friedenwald Lecture to ARVO (1974).

[23] See Hochberg and Silverstein (1956) for a rare experimental test of this law, which is often cited but seldom quantified.

[24] These include the Nagel anomaloscope Model II, the Pickford-Nicolson anomaloscope (Lakowski, 1969), and a new instrument under development by Moreland and his associates.

[25] See Brindley (1970) for a discussion of a possible, though controversial, exception reported by Bongard and Smirnov (1956).

390 Appendix

APPENDIX

The CIE system of colorimetry, mentioned in an historical context in Chapter 1 (p. 19) has been employed as little as possible in this book. The system has served a very valuable purpose, and will doubtless continue to be used into the indefinite future for practical work, but in this book—where emphasis has been upon physiological mechanisms of color vision—its use would not generally have been helpful. Nevertheless, the use of the CIE system is so widespread that the literature on human color vision (including some of the figures in this book) cannot be appreciated without knowing something about it. The purpose of this appendix is to furnish the needed information. As background, the concepts developed in Chapter 5 should be reviewed.

The first part of this appendix reproduces some material previously published as part of a chapter in a multiauthored textbook (Boynton, 1971). This will provide some needed background for the second part, which consists of remarks by W. David Wright that are "based on a tape recording of a very informal and highly personal account of the CIE system given to the Colour Group [of Great Britain] on 5th February 1969." Thanks are given to Dr. Wright, and to Mr. David J. McConnell (Secretary, The Colour Group) for permission to reproduce an abridged version of this material, which was originally transcribed for the *Colour Group Journal*, which has now ceased publication. Part III gives the Smith-Pokorny sensitivity curves in tabular form.

PART I: CIE SYSTEM

Color Equation

The results of a color match using three spectral primaries may be described by an equation:

$$c(C) + r(R) \equiv g(G) + b(B) \tag{A.1}$$

Equation (A.1) should be read as follows: c units of the test color (C) plus r units of the red primary (R), additively mixed to one half of the field, exactly matches ($\equiv$) g units of the green primary (G) plus b units of the blue primary (B), additively mixed to the other half of the field.

For a test wavelength of 490 nm, the equation reads (from the curves of Figure A.1):

$$0.082\ (C) + 0.058\ (R) \equiv 0.057\ (G) + 0.083\ (B) \tag{A.2}$$

From J. W. Kling and Lorrin A. Riggs (Eds.) *Woodworth and Schlosberg's Experimental Psychology* (3rd ed.), pp. 352–358. (New York: Holt, Rinehart and Winston, 1971). Copyright © 1971 by Holt, Rinehart and Winston, Inc. Reproduced by permission.

This is an empirical statement about an experimental operation, not a formal statement of mathematics. The plus sign is borrowed to indicate colorimetric addition by superposition of lights; the symbol "≡" is deliberately used to make it clear that an experimental match is implied, rather than a mathematical equality. Nevertheless, if the analogous mathematical statement is written and is manipulated in accordance with the rules of algebra, it is found experimentally (within fairly wide limits) that such calculations predict the results of new color matches when translated back into the experimental analog.

As an example, suppose we multiply Equation (A.2) by a constant factor of 2. It will then read

$$0.164 \,(C) + 0.116 \,(R) \equiv 0.114 \,(G) + 0.166 \,(B) \qquad (A.3)$$

After manipulating our wedges to produce these trichromatic amounts, we can then check to see whether there is still a match between the two halves of the field. There will be. Or we could add a given quantity to both sides of the match—let us call the quantity X. Then, mathematically,

$$0.082 \,(C) + 0.058 \,(R) + X \equiv 0.057 \,(G) + 0.083 \,(B) + X \qquad (A.4)$$

An easy way to check this out is to add a uniform light to the entire field—perhaps reflected off a glass plate in front of the colorimeter. The match will remain.

Generally, the additive, multiplicative, associative, and distributive laws of algebra all work, so that we can predict color-matching behavior using the powerful tool of algebra. This is consistent with the model of color vision that has been presented in this book, and in fact constitutes one of the primary reasons for believing that equal absorptions in photopigments are responsible for color matches.

There are some algebraic manipulations that cannot be exactly duplicated in the laboratory, namely those that require negative amounts of light. However if a positive quantity is added to the opposite side of the field, as previously explained, the predicted color match will hold.

The values r_λ, g_λ, and b_λ shown in Figure A.1 are known as *distribution coefficients* and the curves are called *color mixture functions*. The values have been adjusted so that the area under each of the three functions is 1.0.

In order to provide a colorimetric specification of any stimulus light, it is necessary to evaluate its effectiveness with respect to each of the three color mixture functions. (This is directly related to its effectiveness upon each of the three types of cone photopigment.) For this purpose, the concept of the *tristimulus value* is introduced. There are three of these defined as follows:

$$\begin{aligned} R &= \int E_\lambda \, r_\lambda \, d_\lambda \\ G &= \int E_\lambda \, g_\lambda \, d_\lambda \\ B &= \int E_\lambda \, b_\lambda \, d_\lambda \end{aligned} \qquad (A.5)$$

Here E_λ is the radiance distribution in the stimulus; E must be measured in

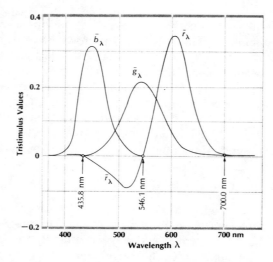

FIGURE A.1 Color-matching functions (tristimulus values for an equal energy spectrum) in the primary system where R = 700 nm, G = 546.1 nm, and B = 435.8 nm. (From Wyszecki & Stiles, 1967.)

physical energy units for every wavelength λ throughout the visible range of the spectrum. If we have two stimuli such that $R_1 = R_2$, $G_1 = G_2$, and $B_1 = B_2$, even though physically different values of E had to be used to produce them, they will match for the standard observer. Such matches are called *metameric* and the matching pairs are called *metamers*. (Physical matches are called *isomers*.)

The Chromaticity Diagram

Tristimulus values can have any magnitude, depending upon the radiance levels of the stimuli. Everyday experience tells us that if we double the amount of light (as for example by adding a second light bulb to a lamp) the color appearance of a surface illuminated by the lights changes very little. Because hue and saturation are approximately independent of luminance, it would be convenient to develop a two-variable scheme that deals with relations among trichromatic units, while at the same time factoring luminance out of the system. This is done by specifying *chromaticity coordinates*, defined as follows:

$$r = \frac{R}{R + G + B}$$
$$g = \frac{G}{R + G + B} \quad (A.6)$$
$$b = \frac{B}{R + G + B}$$

Tristimulus values, R, G, and B, show the absolute amounts of the three primaries required to make the match being specified. The chromaticity coordinates tell us the ratio of each of the three trichromatic amounts to the sum of the three. (Their sum must total unity and therefore any two of them will provide a complete specification. In practice, a plot of g versus r is most often used.)

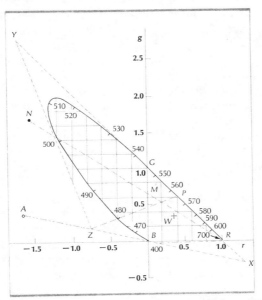

FIGURE A.2 Chromaticity diagram based on the spectral primaries of Figure A.1. X, Y, and Z represent the primaries of the CIE system, as represented in the RGB chromaticity space. (LeGrand, 1957.)

A *chromaticity diagram* for the set of primaries of Figure A.1 is shown in Figure A.2, in which each spectral stimulus plots as a point. For example if λ = 490 (for which the tristimulus values were specified in Equation [A.2]), the following chromaticity coordinates are produced:

$$r = \frac{-.058}{.082} = -0.707$$
$$g = \frac{.057}{.082} = +0.695 \quad \text{(A.7)}$$
$$b = \frac{.083}{.082} = +1.012$$

Other spectral stimuli, calculated and plotted in the same way, form a *spectral locus* connected by a continuous curve that includes all possible intermediate wavelengths.

System of Imaginary Primaries

The chromaticity system for specifying color, worked out by Maxwell (although in a triangular coordinate system) more than 100 years ago, proved so useful that an international standardizing organization, the Commission Internationale de l'Éclairage (CIE) in 1931 established an international system. A major point to be decided upon was the choice of primaries, for an infinity of chromaticity charts can be prepared, depending upon the colors that are taken as primaries. Whatever the choice, the red primary on an r versus g chart will plot at $r = 1.0$, $g = 0$, the green primary will plot at $r = 0$, $g = 1.0$, and the blue primary at $r = g = 0$ (note that this is the case in Figure A.2). It works out that the spectral locus defined by one system of primaries is a projective transformation of that defined by any other system of primaries, a projection which places the three primaries in a relation that forms a right triangle with equal sides adjacent to the right angle.

A straight line in one chromaticity chart will transform into a straight line in another chart based on different primaries, but the lengths of such lines relative to one another will change from chart to chart, as will also their angular relations to one another.

In developing the CIE system, a decision was made to utilize a set of imaginary primaries. In essence, this amounts to an extrapolation in the mathematical domain beyond what can be realized physically. Probably the easiest way to visualize what was done is in terms of the chromaticity diagram of Figure A.2. This diagram, it will be recalled, is based upon a set of real primaries.

The imaginary primaries that were chosen are shown in Figure A.2 as the

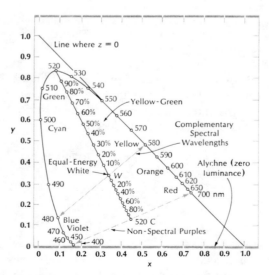

FIGURE A.3 Chromaticity diagram based upon the imaginary primaries of the CIE system. (Boynton, 1966.)

points X, Y, and Z. In this diagram, note that the angle YZX is not a right angle, X does not plot at an abscissa value of 1.0, Y does not plot at an ordinate value of 1.0, and Z is not at the origin. These positions are accomplished in the diagram of Figure A.3, which is the appropriate transformation to produce a chromaticity diagram specified in terms of the imaginary primaries X, Y, and Z indicated in the original chromaticity space of Figure A.2. In both projections, X, Y, and Z are well outside the spectral locus; this is what makes them imaginary. They were deliberately chosen this way so that the chromaticity coordinates of all real stimuli would have positive values. In other words, the entire domain of real colors in the transformed diagram falls in the all-positive quadrant.

There are, of course, many sets of three points in the diagram of Figure A.2 that could accomplish this objective. The ones that were selected have several advantages. In the first place, the lines connecting them just barely graze the spectral locus. This means that there is little waste space near the axes of the transformed diagram. The line XY, furthermore, is coincident with the locus of long-wave spectral stimuli from about 550 nm onward. Second, the line XZ was chosen to fall on the *alychne*, the zero-luminance line. A consequence of this is that both the X and Z primaries in this imaginary system have zero luminance. Calculations pertaining to luminance can therefore be based upon the Y primary alone. To finish the job, the line between Y and Z was drawn to be almost, but not quite, tangent to the spectral locus in the neighborhood of 500 nm.

It will be recalled that the chromaticity diagram in Figure A.2 was based upon the set of color-mixture curves of Figure A.1. It is possible to go the other way: Given the location of three primaries, such as X, Y, and Z in Figure A.2, and the luminance of each, a set of color mixture curves can be derived which correspond to these. This has been done for the CIE primaries, and these curves, called $\bar{x}$, $\bar{y}$, and $\bar{z}$, are shown in Figure A.4.* As would be expected, all values are positive. Values of $\bar{z}$ are zero beyond 560 nm. This corresponds to the fact that these stimuli fall on the line where $\bar{z} = 0$ in the chromaticity chart. Values of $\bar{x}$ form a double-humped curve as a function of wavelength. It reaches close to zero near 500 nm, where the spectral locus of the chromaticity diagram nearly touches the ordinate. The left-hand hump of $\bar{x}$ corresponds to the bending of the spectral locus away from the ordinate in the chromaticity chart as the wavelength is shortened from 500 nm. The $\bar{y}$ function is exactly proportional to the V_λ function (the luminous efficiency function of the standard observer in the CIE system). As previously noted, this results from a choice of X and Z primaries which puts both of them on the alychne.

The curves of Figure A.4 are known as the distribution curves for an equal-energy spectrum in the CIE system. These are widely used in order to calculate chromaticities in a standard way, given that the physical characteristics of a

---

* The CIE dropped the subscript λ on these symbols, which should be regarded as implicitly including them.

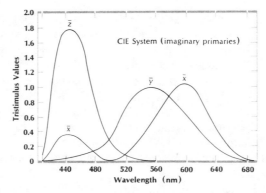

FIGURE A.4 Color-matching functions (tristimulus values for an equal-energy spectrum) in the primary system of the CIE. (Boynton, 1966.)

stimulus to be evaluated are known; and to predict which stimuli will match other ones.

Suppose that we have two physical samples and we wish to know whether they match. To find out, we determine the tristimulus values X, Y, and Z in the CIE system, defined as follows (see Equation [A.5]):

$$\begin{aligned} X_1 &= \int E_\lambda \bar{x} d\lambda \\ Y_1 &= \int E_\lambda \bar{y} d\lambda \\ Z_1 &= \int E_\lambda \bar{z} d\lambda \end{aligned} \qquad (A.8)$$

We do the same for the other sample to obtain X_2, Y_2, and Z_2. If $Y_1 = Y_2$, the two samples have the same luminance, but may not match for hue and/or saturation. If additionally $X_1 = X_2$ and $Z_1 = Z_2$, the two samples will match in all respects.

To determine chromaticity in the CIE system, calculate

$$\begin{aligned} x &= \frac{X}{X + Y + Z} \\ y &= \frac{Y}{X + Y + Z} \end{aligned} \qquad (A.9)$$

and plot the result in the standard diagram.

The development of the CIE system has been described here by graphical means. (For a discussion of the corresponding algebra, see LeGrand [1968] or Graham [1965] or Wyszecki and Stiles [1967].)

An alternative scheme for specifying chromaticity may be made in terms of *dominant wavelength* and *excitation purity*. To determine the dominant wavelength of a sample, draw a line from the white point through the point which represents the chromaticity of the sample, extending it until it intersects the spectrum locus. This intersection point defines the dominant wavelength. Excitation purity is defined (see Figure A.3) as the distance of the sample point from the white point, expressed as a percentage of the distance all the way from the white point through the sample point to the spectrum locus. For samples lying between the white point and the line of extraspectral purples (see above) excitation purity is similarly defined as a percentage of the distance from the white point to the purple line. The dominant wavelength of such a sample is specified by the complementary spectral wavelength, followed by a lower-case c; for example, $\lambda = 540$ c.

PART II: THE ORIGINS OF THE 1931 CIE SYSTEM

By W.D. Wright (Imperial College, London, England)

I happened to be at the committee meeting when it was suggested that I might give this talk on the origins of the 1931 C.I.E. system. I was a little taken aback by this suggestion and I was not quite sure why I was asked to do this. I had half a feeling that they thought this dreadful C.I.E. business was all my fault! (laughter) I also got a distinct impression that they thought I was not looking too healthy and if they did not hurry up it might be too late. (laughter) Well, anyway, I have made it today, but how much longer I will last I do not know.

Now, the question is really where to start. The most active period was obviously in the 1920's but I thought it would be a good thing to go back a little further to pick out one or two historic landmarks, because, as you will see, some of the work done in the last century played quite an important part in the discussions. Now, the target we were aiming at in the 1931 system was the spectrum locus in the chromaticity chart, leading to a set of colour mixture curves (or colour matching functions). We had to derive standard data for an average observer and then establish a co-ordinate system for practical colour measurement and specification.

I think I should first make a brief reference to the pioneer work done by Maxwell. Among the various papers I have managed to collect, I am fortunate to have a reprint of Maxwell's 1860 paper[1] in which he describes his colour box and colour mixture curves which he produced. I was not around at that time, as you understand, but G. F. Thompson, Sir George Thompson, who was head of this Department, passed this reprint over to me when he left Imperial College. He himself had received it from his father, J.J. Thompson, so that it is really a sort of holy relic. Anyway, that was a beginning, and I think Maxwell's curves were the first set of colour mixture curves that were produced. The colour box itself consisted of a prism system, three entrance slits, the widths of which could be varied, and when they were illuminated they produced three overlapping spectra. Depending on the separation of the slits, you could choose the three particular wavelengths that were focused on the exit-pupil and entered the observer's eye. You made your colour match by varying the slit widths, and the curves he derived were in fact obtained from a series of matches on the white using various combinations of wavelengths.

The basic colour arithmetic had been established earlier by Grassmann's Laws and, to some extent, by Helmholtz.

The next experimental work I must refer to is the work of König and Dieterici. They measured the colour mixture curves using Helmholtz's colour mixing apparatus as described in his "Physiological Optics."[2]

This apparatus was used in the experiments by König and Dieterici in 1892. I have here my most precious possession, namely, König's collected works published in 1903.[3] It includes the paper in which he reports the colour mixture curves which they recorded and a number of others, including, of course, his paper on small field tritanopia.

At about the same time, Sir William Abney, using his colour patch apparatus at Imperial College, also measured the colour mixture curves. The results are included in Abney's "Researches in Colour Vision," published in 1915.

Now I must move on to two papers by R.E. Ives, which I have here, published in the Journal of the Franklin Institute in 1915 and 1923.[4] In these papers he made some adjustments to the König mixture curves and produced what came to be known as the König-Ives colour-matching data. Then in 1920-21 another American, E.A. Weaver, combined König's and Abney's results to produce a set of mixture curves which were recommended by a colorimetry committee of the Optical Society of America for colour measurement work. There was also a report in 1921 by the O.S.A. Colorimetry Committee.[5] I think this really marks the beginning of modern colorimetry, and certainly led the way to the 1931 C.I.E. system. As you can see, it is quite a massive report and it covered a variety of topics. It included a long section on nomenclature, and other sections on standard psycho-physical data, physical standards, methods of colorimetry, and their inter-relations, and so on.

I would like to quote from the opening paragraph of this report. It says: "That the nomenclature and standards of Colour Science are in an extremely unsatisfactory condition is manifest to practically all workers in this field. It is the purpose of the present report to take an initial step towards remedying this state of affairs. That the result cannot be final as regards either nomenclature or standards is a natural consequence of the pioneer character of the effort."

This was the beginning of the very fruitful 1920-1930 period. Again in the section on the colour mixture problem, they said: "probably the most fundamental of all the psycho-physical data relating to colour are the three colour excitation curves" (which is what the colour mixture curves of colour matching functions were then called) "which represent the laws of three colour mixture. Extant data on these relationships are due to Maxwell, Abney, König and Dieterici."

This report had some really valuable information in it and it gives the tables and curves which Weaver derived by combining König's and Abney's results. And also, incidentally, it contains on one of its pages a diagram of the chromaticity chart or colour triangle. It is the first time, as far as I know, that the Maxwell triangle was produced on rectangular co-ordinates; it was also an all-positive system. So that was really quite a landmark.

This O.S.A. report and the two Ives' papers triggered off a series of quite outstanding papers by Guild published in the Transactions of the Optical Society in this country.[6] Ives' papers had shown that colour mixture data could be expressed in terms of any three stimuli. Usually they would be red, green and blue, but having recorded the results in terms of one set of stimuli you could transform them to another set if you wished. And there was no need to use the so-called fundamental sensation curves, representing the actual sensitivities of the processes in the eye, at least not for colorimetric purposes. Guild took up this theme of the transformation of data and produced simplified transformation formulae. He laid particular emphasis on the possibility of using a two dimensional chromaticity chart, although he did not call it that at that time. I have Guild's papers here and perhaps I could comment that these were my Colorimetric Bible when I started. You can see how tattered they are, and the most tattered numbers are the issues which have papers by Guild in them.

In addition to this theoretical work on transformations, Guild also carried out much experimental work. In the Transactions of the Optical Society there are important papers describing his visual spectrophotometer, his criticism of the monochromatic-plus-white method of colorimetry, his vector method of colorimetry and also, of course, his trichromatic colorimeter. In his colorimeter the red-green-blue mixture was produced by means of a prism rotating in front of segments of red, green and blue colour filters. You obtained a colour mixture as the rapid pulses of red, green and blue light were focused on the retina. You varied the amount of red, green and blue by changing the sector openings. This, of course, is the instrument which he used to measure his colour mixture curves.

All this was in the period 1924, 1925 and 1926, then came the very important survey which he gave at the Optical Convention of 1926, which was held in this College. This long paper of some 80 pages summarized the situation not only as far as colorimetry was concerned, but also photometry. He makes a reference to the conditions under which heterochromatic photometry should be carried out, because in 1924 (I shall come back to this) the C.I.E. had standardised the V_λ curve, then called the visibility curve, again partly on the basis of studies made by Ives, who established the conditions under which flicker photometry was additive.

I apologize that I must now be rather personal since this Optical Convention and the paper by Guild were very important events for me, as they led, through the influence of Sir John Parsons, the ophthalmologist, to my being offered a grant from the Medical Research Council to undertake research on colour vision. I was at the convention as a student, and demonstrated some experiments there, although I did not go to hear Guild's paper. At that time I was just about to look for a job in the optical industry. However, the optical industry was then suffering from a severe depression and, although I was not at all interested in doing colour work, when the M.R.C. grant became available, it was offered to me and I was glad to take it up. So this was how I first came into colour research. I think it was very fortunate for me that I was around at that time looking for a job and that I was given the opportunity to work at such a critical moment in the subject. I would also say that I was very fortunate as far as the literature which I could consult. The books that I used as a research student were Helmholtz's *Physiological Optics*, König's *Collected Works*, Abney's *Colour Researches*,[7] Guild's *Survey*, the book on *Colour Vision* by Sir John Parsons,[8] Martin's own book on *Colour and Methods of Colour Reproduction*,[9] Walsh's *Photometry*,[10] the two Troland Reports, and, most of all, the papers that Guild had published in the Transactions of the Optical Society—the ones to which I have already referred. Because, although I had got the grant and I knew what the project was called, I really hadn't a clue what it was about except that my first job, I knew, was to build a colorimeter. This I set about doing, but the first thing I had to do was to dismantle Abney's colour patch apparatus. I pulled this to pieces, used some of the parts to build mine and I used also the same special room which Abney had built for his colour research. I decided in building my new colorimeter to stick to spectral matching stimuli, no doubt because Abney's colour patch apparatus used these (but I imagine also on the advice of Dr. Martin) whereas Guild of course had used filters in his colorimeter. I am embarrassed that I must once again describe my colorimeter because I have done it so many times before. As you know, it uses a prism system to form two spectra. From one spectrum you pick out the red, green, and blue matching stimuli and from the other the monochromatic test colour. The selected wavebands are reflected back through the system and the dispersion which originally separated the light out into the spectrum is used in reverse to re-combine the red, green and blue stimuli. The amounts of red, green and blue are controlled with photometer wedges mounted in front of the matching stimuli. To add a little bit of human interest, in this first model I had to use a fairly narrow prism about ¾" thick with a face about 3" or so to select the strip of light which formed the test colour spectrum. Professor Conrady, who was on the staff then, suggested that I cut a slice from a larger prism which we had in the Department. I said "Well, how do I go about doing that?" and he said "You get a hack saw, fit it with a copper wire and feed it with carborundum powder and saw away." And this, in the end, I did.

I really must have worked rather hard because I not only assembled the colorimeter and used it but I made the bits and pieces or a lot of them. I don't know how I managed to do it in the time, (October 1926 to March 1929) especially as I had to spend two and a half days sawing prisms!

In the meantime, Guild was carrying on with his programme using his colorimeter and I want to make it quite clear that he had probably almost completed his project before I had hardly started, certainly before I had got my colorimeter working. I remember visiting his laboratory with Professor Martin, probably in 1927, when I saw curves which Guild had already obtained of the spectrum locus in the colour triangle. He was using his filter colorimeter and obtained his monochromatic test light independently from two Hilger constant deviation spectrometers in series as a double monochromator. I was fortunate to be able to discuss the problem with Guild and must obviously have obtained some very valuable advice from him as well as from Professor Martin.

I described my colorimeter in 1927–28 and then in 1928–29 brought out a paper on the trichromatic coefficients and the spectrum locus, as well as a Medical Research Council Report which came out about the same time.[11]

I keep referring to Mr. Guild because I owe so much to him but not only did he write a number of very important papers, but he also took the trouble to discuss other people's papers at very considerable length. I benefited a lot from several pages of discussion on the papers which I gave—first of all on the one describing my colorimeter and then on my redetermination of the trichromatic coefficients.

I must apologise for all this personal history but it does have some bearing on the 1931 C.I.E. system. Having done this work I got a job in America with Westinghouse in Pittsburgh working on television. I was in fact only there for a year. For domestic reasons I had to come back after a year but while I was there and during my spare time in the evenings, I had a shot at working out the spectral mixture curves. So when I returned to England I presented another paper to the Optical Society, in which I reported this work. But in addition, I did something that Guild had previously asked me to do; I transformed my spectrum locus into the N.P.L. 700, 546.1, 435.8 primary system. Now this enabled Guild to make a comparison of my results with his and again I got about three or four pages of discussion from him which was terribly helpful. He appreciated that I had given the information in this way and went on to say: "I have compared these with my own figures at various critical parts of the chart, and am pleased to say that no discrepancies exceeding the colour limen in the neighbourhood were found at any of the points checked. This agreement adds enormously to the value of his data and mine because it must be remembered that the two determinations were made by two different groups of observers and using entirely dissimilar apparatus". I think I can fairly say that it was when he realised that his curves and mine were so close together that he was encouraged to press on with the idea of getting standard data adopted by the C.I.E. which was due to meet in England in 1931.

Guild then went ahead and presented a paper to the Royal Society called "The Colorimetric Properties of the Spectrum".[12] He read this in April 1931 giving his own curves which, as I have tried to make clear, he had measured a year or two before I had even got cracking but he had not published them. He then went on to compare his and my results. He also showed how the old König/Abney spectrum locus which Weaver had derived differed very significantly from our loci. He then made plans to submit our mean data for adoption by the C.I.E. at the meeting which was due to be held in Cambridge, England, in September 1931, only a few months after he produced this paper.

In 1931, colorimetry really burst on the C.I.E. and in the 1931 Proceedings we have several pages of discussion reported and, of course, the resolutions which determined the 1931 system. Two people were particularly involved in these discussions: Priest from America and Guild from this country. Priest was the official American delegate and I think it was quite clear that he had come briefed to delay the adoption of any standard observer, since he thought we were rushing things too much. He in fact raised a succession of objections—he had a week's visit to the N.P.L. before the C.I.E. meeting and during that time (I only know this from hearsay) he raised a succession of objections. Then overnight, T. Smith, who was Head of the Light Division and who involved himself in the subject, and Guild would recalculate a lot of data to meet Priest's criticisms,[13] and Priest would turn up next morning with something else to object to. In the end they wore Priest down and he accepted most of the proposals that Guild was going to put forward at the C.I.E meeting. As you can imagine, there was quite a bit of discussion but they eventually approved the standard observer data. However, when you come to look at the resolutions you find that, whilst approval was given at the meeting, subsequently France reversed all its decisions and opposed all the resolutions—shades of de Gaulle!—and Germany reversed their vote, but as long as Britain and America agreed that was really all that mattered. (laughter) Having approved the standard observer data, they then approved the transformation of the data to the present all-positive X, Y, Z system.

In addition to adopting an all positive co-ordinate system, the decision was taken to follow a suggestion of Judd's in 1930 of locating X and Z on the alychne, that is the locus of colours in the chromaticity chart which have got zero luminance and which had been described by Schrödinger in 1925. This was done and the data were also combined with the 1924 V_λ curve. Interestingly enough, some fiddling had to be done with the actual relative luminances of the R, G, B stimuli in order to make the whole thing consistent. This was [a] procedure of mine that Guild had criticised. Also, I was rather pleased in looking through some of these papers recently to come across a paper of Judd's[14] in which he was prepared to support my approach and be critical of Guild. So we stood up to Guild from time to time but he was obviously the dominant person.

The C.I.E. produced their set of distribution curves in terms of x, y, z. The y curve was identical with the V_λ curve because of the particular choice of X and Z to have zero luminance. They also recommended the three illuminants, S_A, S_B and S_C, S_A a tungsten light, S_B tungsten light plus liquid filter to correspond to about 4800°K to simulate sunlight and S_C about 6500°K to correspond to north skylight. The filters that were used were those recommended by the work that Davis and Gibson had reported.[15] They had made a big study on the reproduction of sunlight and daylight at various colour temperatures. At the N.P.L. itself, Guild had also produced some daylight liquid filters and he would no doubt have liked to have had those adopted, but he recognised that Davis and Gibson had done much more work on it, so he accepted the American filters. No doubt there was a bit of horse trading here so that, as Priest had yielded on the standard observer data, Guild could yield on these filters. In addition to the C.I.E. Proceedings, a full description of the system was given by Judd in the Journal of the Optical Society of America and by Smith and Guild in the Transactions of the Optical Society.

I must stop in a moment but I would like to look back and ask the question

"Did we do a good job?" Well, one limitation, as you know, is that the 1931 C.I.E. observer refers to 2° field viewing conditions. This was quite inevitable because in the climate of the time the data had to fit in with the conditions under which the 1924 V_λ curve had been determined and this was under 2° viewing conditions. As far as Guild's and my data are concerned, I think that we can claim that the 2° spectral chromaticity co-ordinates have stood the test of time rather well and hardly differ at all from the results which Dr. Stiles obtained on his more elaborate instrument some twenty-five years or so later. There is in fact no major difference between the 1931 2° and Stiles' 10° spectral chromaticity co-ordinates. It is only when you incorporate the V_λ curve that you get the difference. Now I want to make it clear that in the distribution curves (or colour matching functions), there is a true difference between the 1931 C.I.E. 2° and 1964 C.I.E. 10° observers, especially in the blue-green.

I do not know whether everyone likes this alychne device with X and Z having zero luminance; I think it is hard to understand but it is a rather clever device and really rather convenient. Probably one of the biggest criticisms of the choice of co-ordinates is that they did not lead to a chromaticity chart with a more uniform distribution of discriminable colours across the chart. But the necessary discrimination studies had not been carried out in 1931.

We have come a long way from 1860 with Maxwell's paper and just to indicate how far we have got, we might compare the information in Maxwell's paper with the vast amount of information given, for example, in this very excellent book *Color Science* by Wyszecki and Stiles.[16] When you see all the data that has been accumulated over the years, you realise that quite a lot has happened. I hope my defence and description of the 1931 system has been adequate. If you do not like the actual X, Y, Z co-ordinate system, I would only say that, whilst I knew a good deal about the R, G, B system, when I attended the C.I.E. meeting in 1931, I had only the vaguest idea what the X, Y, Z system was. But personally I think that Guild and Priest, and I would want to include Judd for his influence behind the scenes, did a very good job indeed.

I would make one final comment before I stop. The C.I.E. Colorimetry Committee recently in their wisdom have been looking at the old 1931 observer and have been smoothing the data to obtain more consistent calculations with computers. This has also involved some extrapolation and, in smoothing, they have added some additional decimal places. When I look at the revised table of the $\bar{x}$, $\bar{y}$, $\bar{z}$, functions, I am rather surprised to say the least. You see, I know how inaccurate the actual measurements really were. (Laughter) Guild did not take any observations below 400 nm and neither did I, and neither did Gibson and Tyndall on the V_λ curve, and yet at a wavelength of 362 nm, for example, we find a value $\bar{y}$ of .000004929604! This, in spite of the fact that at 400 nm the value of $\bar{y}$ may be in error by a factor of 10. (Laughter) I can not help wondering what Mr. Guild thinks if he happens to see these tables. I know we can put the blame on the computer but we must not abdicate our common sense altogether.

I think on that note I had better stop!

PART III. SMITH AND POKORNY (1975) CONE SENSITIVITY FUNCTIONS

R- and G-cone functions are based on transformations from Judd's (1951a) color-matching functions ($\bar{x}_\lambda$, $\bar{y}_\lambda$, $\bar{z}_\lambda$) as follows:

$$S_R = +0.15514\bar{x} + 0.54312\bar{y} - 0.03286\bar{z}$$
$$S_G = -0.15514\bar{x} + 0.45684\bar{y} - 0.03286\bar{z}$$
$$S_B = 0.00000\bar{x} + 0.00000\bar{y} + 0.001608\bar{z}$$

Wavelength	S_R	S_G	S_B[a]
400	.0027	.0018	.00450
410	.0055	.0038	.00938
420	.0101	.0074	.01708
430	.0149	.0124	.02336
440	.0192	.0187	.02583
450	.0219	.0249	.02367
460	.0263	.0337	.02071
470	.0399	.0511	.01790
480	.0650	.0740	.01214
490	.1032	.1047	.00717
500	.1675	.1555	.00425
510	.2696	.2334	.00247
520	.3930	.3170	.00123
530	.4926	.3694	.00063
540	.5629	.3911	.00032
550	.6078	.3871	.00014
560	.6329	.3621	.00006
570	.6355	.3164	.00003
580	.6146	.2554	.00003
590	.5697	.1872	.00002
600	.5063	.1247	.00001
610	.4271	.0759	.0000
620	.3377	.0432	.0000
630	.2421	.0229	.0000
640	.1634	.0116	.0000
650	.1014	.0056	.0000
660	.0582	.0028	.0000
670	.0307	.0013	.0000
680	.0164	.0006	.0000
690	.0079	.0003	.0000
700	.0040	.0001	.0000

[a] Scaled so that B/(R + G) = 1.0 at 400 nm.

BIBLIOGRAPHY

The following is a list of books and journals referred to in the article and which were on display at the Colour Group meeting when the paper was presented.

[1] J. C. Maxwell, "On the theory of compound colours and the relations of the colours of the spectrum", Phil. Trans. Roy. Soc. Lond. v. 150, p. 57, 1860.
[2] H. v. Helmholtz, *Handbuch der Physiologischen Optik*. (Various parts of first edition appeared between 1856 and 1867). Translation of third edition published by Opt. Soc. Am., 1924.
[3] A König, *Gesammelte Abhandlungen Zur Physiologischen Optik*, (Barth) 1903.
[4] H. E. Ives, "The transformation of color-mixture equations from one system to another". J. Franklin Inst., v. 180, p. 673, 1915. "The transformation of color-mixture equations from one system to another. II. Graphical Aids". J. Franklin Inst., v. 195, p. 23, 1923.
[5] L. T. Troland, "Report of Committee on Colorimetry for 1920–21", J. Opt. Soc. Am., v. 6, p. 527, 1922. "The present status of visual science", Bull. Nat. Res. Counc., v. 5, Part 2, No. 27, 1922.
[6] J. Guild, "An equipment for visual spectrophotometry", Trans. Opt. Soc. Lond., v. 26, p. 74, 1924–25. "The transformation of trichromatic mixture data: algebraic methods", Trans. Opt. Soc. Lond., v. 26, p. 95, 1924–25. "The geometrical solution of colour mixture problems", Trans. Opt. Soc. Lond., v. 26, p. 139, 1924–25. "A trichromatic colorimeter suitable for standardisation work", Trans. Opt. Soc. Lond., v. 27, p. 106, 1925–26. "A criticism of the monochromatic-plus-white method of colorimetry", Trans. Opt. Soc. Lond., v. 27, p. 130, 1925–26. "On a new method of colorimetry", Trans. Opt. Soc. Lond., v. 27, p. 139, 1925–26. "A critical survey of modern developments in the theory and technique of colorimetry and allied sciences", Proc. Optical Convention 1926, Part. 1 p. 61.
[7] W. de W. Abney, *Researches in Colour Vision*, (Longmans, Green) 1913.
[8] J. H. Parsons, *An Introduction to the Study of Colour Vision*, (Cambridge University Press), 1st Ed. 1915, 2nd Ed. 1924.
[9] L. C. Martin and W. Gamble, *Colour and Methods of Colour Reproduction* (Blackie) 1926.
[10] J. W. T. Walsh, *Photometry* (Constable), 1926
[11] W. D. Wright, "A trichromatic colorimeter with spectral primaries", Trans. Opt. Soc. Lond., v. 29, p. 225, 1927–28. "A re-determination of the trichromatic coefficients of the spectral colours", Trans. Opt. Soc. Lond., v. 30, p. 141, 1928–29. "A re-determination of the trichromatic mixture data", Medical Research Council Spectral Report Series No. 139, 1929. "A re-determination of the mixture curves of the spectrum" Trans. Opt. Soc. Lond., v. 31, p. 201, 1929–30.
[12] J. Guild, "The colorimetric properties of the spectrum", Phil. Trans. Roy. Soc. Lond., Ser. A. v. 230, p. 149, 1931. Proceedings, Commission Internationale de l'Éclairage, vols. for 1924, 1928, 1931.
[13] T. Smith and J. Guild, "The C.I.E. Colorimetric Standards and their use", Trans. Opt. Soc. Lond. v. 33, p. 73, 1931–32.
[14] D. B. Judd, "Reduction of data on mixture of colour stimuli" U.S. Bur. Standards J. of Research, v. 4, p. 513, 1930. "Comparison of Wright's data on equivalent colour stimuli with the O.S.A. data". J. Opt. Soc. Am., v. 21, p. 699, 1931. "The 1931 I.C.I. Standard Observer and co-ordinate system for colorimetry", J. Opt. Soc. Am., v. 23, p. 359, 1933.
[15] R. Davis and K. S. Gibson, "Filters for the reproduction of sunlight and daylight and the determinations of color temperature", U.S. Dept. Commerce. Misc. Pub., Bur. Standards No. 114, 1931.
[16] G. Wyszecki and W. S. Stiles, *Color Science* (Wiley) 1967.

REFERENCES

Abramov, I. Further analysis of the responses of LGN cells. *Journal of the the Optical Society of America 58*, 574–579 (1968).

Aguilar, M., & Stiles, W. S. Saturation of the rod mechanism at high levels of stimulation. *Optica Acta 1*, 59–65 (1954).

Aitken, J. On colour and colour sensation. *Royal Scottish Society of Arts, Transactions, Edinburgh, 8*, 375–418 (1872).

Alpern, M. What is it that confines in a world without color? *Investigative Ophthalmology 13*, 648–674 (1974).

Alpern, M., & Dudley, D. The blue arcs of the retina. *Journal of General Physiology 49*, 405–421 (1966).

Alpern, M., Falls, H. F., & Lee, G. B. The enigma of typical total monochromacy. *American Journal of Ophthalmology 50*, 996–1011 (1960).

Alpern, M., Lee, G. B., & Spivey, B. E. π_1 cone monochromatism. *Archives of Ophthalmology 74*, 334–337 (1965).

Arden, G. B. The retina—neurophysiology. In Davson, H. (Ed.), *The eye* (2nd ed.). New York: Academic Press, 1976.

Armington, J. C. *The electroretinogram*. New York: Academic Press, 1974.

Avant, L. L. Vision in the Ganzfeld. *Psychological Bulletin 64*, 246–258 (1965).

Baker, H. D., & Rushton, W. A. H. An analytical anomaloscope. *Journal of Physiology 168*, 31P–33P (1963).

Barlow, H. B. Summation and inhibition in the frog's retina. *Journal of Physiology 119,* 69–88 (1953).
Barlow, H. B. Dark and light adaptation: Psychophysics. In Jameson, D., & Hurvich, L. M. (Eds.), *Handbook of sensory physiology* VII/4. New York: Springer-Verlag, 1972.
Bartleson, C. J. Brown. *Color Research and Application 1,* 181–191 (1976).
Bartley, S. H. Subjective brightness in relation to flash rate and the light–dark ratio. *Journal of Experimental Psychology 23,* 313–319 (1938).
Bartley, S. H. *Vision.* New York: Van Nostrand, 1941.
Baylor, D. A., Fuortes, M. G. F., & O'Bryan, P. M. Receptive fields of cones in the retina of the turtle. *Journal of Physiology 214,* 265–294 (1971).
Baylor, D. A., & Hodgkin, A. L. Changes in time scale and sensitivity in turtle photoreceptors. *Journal of Physiology 242,* 729–758 (1974).
Beare, J. I. *Greek theories of elementary cognition from Alcmaeon to Aristotle.* Oxford: Clarendon Press, 1906.
Bedford, R. E., & Wyszecki, G. Wavelength discrimination for point sources. *Journal of the Optical Society of America 48,* 129–135 (1958).
Bell, J. Colour blindness. *Treasury of human inheritance,* v. II, part II, 125–268. Cambridge, England: Cambridge University Press, 1926.
Berbert, J. H. Visual acuity as a function of luminance for different hues. *Journal of the Optical Society of America 45,* 902 (1955).
Berbert, J. H. Visual acuity as a function of intensity for different hues. *NRL Report 5104,* Naval Research Laboratory, Washington, D.C. (1958).
Berlin, B., & Kay, P. *Basic color terms: Their universality and evolution.* Berkeley: University of California Press, 1969.
Biernson, G. Uni-receptor theory of color perception. *Journal of the Optical Society of America 53,* 520 (1963).
Biernson, G. A feedback-control model of human vision. *Proceedings of the Institute of Electrical and Electronics Engineers 54,* 858–872; 1226–1229 (1966).
Blackwell, H. R. Contrast thresholds of the human eye. *Journal of the Optical Society of America 36,* 624–643 (1946).
Blackwell, H. R., & Blackwell, O. M. Rod and cone mechanisms in typical and atypical congenital achromatopsia. *Vision Research 1,* 62–107 (1961).
Boll, F. On the anatomy and physiology of the retina. Translated by R. Hubbard. *Vision Research 17,* 1253–1265 (1977).
Bongard, M. M., Smirnov, M. S. & Friedrich, L. The four-dimensionality of the human eye. In *Visual problems of colour,* pp. 325–330. London: Her Majesty's Stationery Office (1958).
Boring, E. G. *Sensation and perception in the history of experimental psychology.* New York: Appleton-Century-Crofts, 1942.
Bornstein, M. H. Color vision and color naming: A psychophysiological hypothesis of cultural difference. *Psychological Bulletin 80,* 257–285 (1973).
Bornstein, M. H., Kessen, W., & Weiskopf, S. Color vision and hue categorization in young human infants. *Journal of Experimental Psychology (Human Perception and Performance) 2,* 115–129 (1976).
Bouman, M. A., & Walraven, P. L. Color discrimination data. In Jameson, D., & Hurvich, L. M. (Eds.), *Handbook of sensory physiology* VII/4. New York: Springer-Verlag, 1972.

Bowmaker, J. K., Dartnall, H. J. A., Lythgoe, J. N., & Mollon, J. D.   The visual pigments of rods and cones in the rhesus monkey, *Macaca mulatta*. *Journal of Physiology 274*, 329–348 (1978).

Boycott, B. B., and Dowling, J. E.   Organization of the primate retina: Light microscopy. *Philosophical Transactions of the Royal Society of London 255B*, 109–176 (1969).

Boynton, R. M.   Rapid chromatic adaptation and the sensitivity functions of human color vision. *Journal of the Optical Society of America 46*, 172–179 (1956).

Boynton, R. M.   Theory of color vision. *Journal of the Optical Society of America 50*, 929–944 (1960).

Boynton, R. M.   Contributions of threshold measurements to color-discrimination theory. *Journal of the Optical Society of America 53*, 165–178 (1963).

Boynton, R. M.   Discussion: Competing theories of receptor excitation. *Psychological Bulletin 61*, 262–267 (1964).

Boynton, R. M.   Vision. In Sidowki, J. B. (Ed.), *Experimental methods and instrumentation in psychology*. New York: McGraw-Hill, 1966.

Boynton, R. M.   Color vision. In Kling, J. W., & Riggs, L. A. (Eds.), *Experimental psychology*. New York: Holt, Rinehart and Winston, 1971.

Boynton, R. M.   Implications of the minimally distinct border. *Journal of the Optical Society of America 63*, 1037–1043 (1973).

Boynton, R. M.   The visual system: Environmental information. In Carterette, E. C., & Friedman, M. P. (Eds.), *Handbook of Perception*, v. 1. New York: Academic Press, 1974.

Boynton, R. M.   Color, hue, and wavelength. In Carterette, E. C., & Friedman, M. P. (Eds.), *Handbook of perception*, v. 5. New York: Academic Press, 1975.

Boynton, R. M.   Ten years of research with the minimally distinct border. In Armington, J. C., Krauskopf, J., & Wooten, B. (Eds.), *Visual psychophysics: Psychophysics and physiology*. New York: Academic Press, 1978.

Boynton, R. M.   Color in contour and object perception. In Carterette, E. C., & Friedman, M. P. (Eds.), *Handbook of perception*, v. 8. New York: Academic Press, 1978.

Boynton, R. M., & Baron, W. S.   Sinusoidal flicker characteristics of primate cones in response to heterochromatic stimuli. *Journal of the Optical Society of America 65*, 1091–1100 (1975).

Boynton, R. M., & Gordon, J.   Bezold-Brücke hue shift measured by color-naming technique. *Journal of the Optical Society of America 55*, 78–86 (1965).

Boynton, R. M., Hayhoe, M. M., & MacLeod, D. I. A.   The gap effect: Chromatic and achromatic visual discrimination as affected by field separation. *Optica Acta 24*, 159–177 (1977).

Boynton, R. M., Ikeda, M., & Stiles, W. S.   Interactions among chromatic mechanisms as inferred from positive and negative increment thresholds. *Vision Research 4*, 87–117 (1964).

Boynton, R. M., & Kaiser, P. K.   Vision: The additivity law made to work for heterochromatic photometry with bipartite fields. *Science 161*, 366–368 (1968).

Boynton, R. M., & Kaiser, P. K.   Temporal analog of the minimally-distinct border. *Vision Research 18*, 111–113 (1978).

Boynton, R. M., Kandel, G., & Onley, J. W.   Rapid chromatic adaptation of normal and dichromatic observers. *Journal of the Optical Society of America 49*, 654–666 (1959).

Boynton, R. M., & Riggs, L. A.   The effect of stimulus area and intensity upon the human retinal response. *Journal of Experimental Psychology 42*, 217–226 (1951).

Boynton, R. M., Schafer, W., & Neun, M. E. Hue-wavelength relation measured by color-naming method for three retinal locations. *Science 146*, 666–668 (1964).

Boynton, R. M., Scheibner, H., Yates, T., & Rinalducci, E. Theory and experiments concerning the heterochromatic threshold-reduction factor (HTRF). *Journal of the Optical Society of America 55*, 1672–1685 (1965).

Boynton, R. M., & Wagner, M. Two-color threshold as test of color vision. *Journal of the Optical Society of America 51*, 429–440 (1961).

Boynton, R. M., & Whitten, D. N. Visual adaptation in monkey cones: Recordings of late receptor potentials. *Science 170*, 1423–1426 (1970).

Boynton, R. M., & Whitten, D. N. Selective chromatic adaptation in primate photoreceptors. *Vision Research 12*, 855–874 (1972).

Bridges, C. D. B. Visual pigments of the pigeon *(Columba livia)*. *Vision Research 2*, 125–137 (1962).

Brindley, G. S. The summation areas of human colour-receptive mechanisms at increment threshold. *Journal of Physiology 124*, 400–408 (1954).

Brindley, G. S. The colour of light of very long wavelengths. *Journal of Physiology 130*, 35–44 (1955).

Brindley, G. S. *Physiology of the retina and the visual pathway*. London: Edward Arnold, 1960.

Brindley, G. S. Beats produced by simultaneous stimulation of the human eye with intermittent light and intermittent or alternating electric current. *Journal of Physiology 164*, 157–167 (1962).

Brindley, G. S. *Physiology of the retina and the visual pathway* (2nd ed.). Baltimore, Md.: Williams & Wilkins, 1970.

Brindley, G. S., & Lewin, W. S. The sensations produced by electrical stimulation of the visual cortex. *Journal of Physiology 196*, 479–493 (1968).

Brindley, G. S., & Willmer, E. N. The reflexion of light from the macular and peripheral fundus oculi in man. *Journal of Physiology 116*, 350–356 (1952).

Brown, J. L. The structure of the visual system. In Graham, C. H. (Ed.), *Vision and visual perception*. New York: Wiley, 1965.

Brown, J. L., Kuhns, M. P., & Adler, H. E. Relation of threshold criterion to the functional receptors of the eye. *Journal of the Optical Society of America 47*, 198–204 (1957).

Brown, K. T. The electroretinogram: Its components and their origins. *Vision Research 8*, 633–677 (1968).

Brown, W. R. J. The influence of luminance level on visual sensitivity to color differences. *Journal of the Optical Society of America 41*, 684–688 (1951).

Brown, W. R. J. Color discrimination of twelve observers. *Journal of the Optical Society of America 47*, 137–143 (1957).

Brown, W. R. J., & MacAdam, D. L. Visual sensitivities to combined chromaticity and luminance differences. *Journal of the Optical Society of America 39*, 808–834 (1949).

Brücke, E. Über den Nutzeffekt intermittierender Netzhautreizungen. *Akadamie der Wissenschaften, Mathematisch-Naturwissenschaflichen classe, Wien 49*, Part 2, 128–153 (1864).

Burnham, R. W., Hanes, R. M., & Bartleson, C. J. *Color: A guide to basic facts and concepts*. New York: Wiley, 1963.

Cajal, S., Ramon y The vertebrate retina. Translated by R. W. Rodieck & D. Maguire. Appendix A in Rodieck, R. W., *The vertebrate retina*. San Francisco: Freeman, 1973.

Campbell, F. W., and Gregory, A. H. Effect of size of pupil on visual acuity. *Nature 187*, 1121–1123 (1960).

Campbell, F. W., & Gubisch, R. W. The effect of chromatic aberration on visual acuity. *Journal of Physiology 192*, 345–358 (1967).

Christ, R. E. Review and analysis of color coding research for visual displays. *Human Factors 17*, 542–570 (1975).

Clarke, F. J. J. Extra-foveal colour metrics. *Optica Acta 7*, 355–384 (1960).

Cooper, G. F., & Robson, J. G. The yellow colour of the lens of man and other primates. *Journal of Physiology 203*, 411–417 (1969).

Cornsweet, T. N. *Visual perception.* New York: Academic Press, 1970.

Crawford, B. H. Visual adaptation in relation to brief conditioning stimuli. *Proceedings of the Royal Society 134B*, 283–302 (1947).

Crawford, B. H. Colour matching and adaptation. *Vision Research 5*, 71–78 (1965).

Crombie, A. C. Helmholtz. *Scientific American 198* (3), 94–102 (1958).

Dalton, J. Extraordinary facts relating to the vision of colours: With observations (read in October, 1794). *Memoires of the Literary and Philosophical Society* (Manchester) 5, 28–45 (1798).

Dartnall, H. J. A. The interpretation of spectral sensitivity curves. *British Medical Bulletin 9*, 24–30 (1953).

Dartnall, H. J. A. Extraction, measurement, and analysis of visual photopigment. In Davson, H., (Ed.), *The eye.* New York: Academic Press, 1962.

Daw, N. W., & Enoch, J. M. Contrast sensitivity, Westheimer function, and Stiles-Crawford effect in a blue cone monochromat. *Vision Research 13*, 1669–1680 (1973).

deLange, H. Experiments on flicker and some calculations on an electrical analogue of the foveal systems. *Physica 18*, 935–950 (1952).

deLange, H. Research into the dynamic nature of the human fovea → cortex systems with intermittent and modulated light: II. Phase shift in brightness and delay in color perception. *Journal of the Optical Society of America 48*, 784–789 (1958).

De Monasterio, F. M., & Gouras, P. Functional properties of ganglion cells of the rhesus monkey retina. *Journal of Physiology 251*, 167–197 (1975).

De Monasterio, F. M., Gouras, P., & Tolhurst, D. J. Trichromatic colour opponency in ganglion cells of the rhesus monkey retina. *Journal of Physiology 251*, 197–216 (1975).

DeValois, R. L. Behavioral and electrophysiological studies of primate vision. In Neff, W. D. (Ed.), *Contributions to sensory physiology,* v. 1. New York: Academic Press (1965a).

DeValois, R. L. Analysis and coding of color vision in the primate visual system. *Cold Spring Harbor Symposia on Quantitative Biology 30*, 567–579 (1965b).

DeValois, R. L. Central mechanisms of color vision. In Jung, R. (Ed.), *Handbook of sensory physiology* VII/3A, New York: Springer-Verlag, 1973.

DeValois, R. L., Abramov, I., & Jacobs, G. H. Analysis of response patterns of LGN cells. *Journal of the Optical Society of America 56*, 966–977 (1966).

DeValois, R. L., & DeValois, K. K. Neural coding of color. In Carterette, E. C., & Friedman, M. P. (Eds.), *Handbook of perception,* v. 5. New York: Academic Press, 1975.

DeValois, R. L., Jacobs, G. H., & Abramov, I. Responses of single cells in visual system to shifts in the wavelength of light. *Science 146*, 1184–1186 (1964).

DeValois, R. L., Morgan, H. C., Polson, M. C., Mead, W. R., & Hull, E. M. Psychophysical studies of monkey vision: I. Macaque luminosity and color vision tests. *Vision Research 14*, 53–67 (1974).

DeValois, R. L., Smith, C. J., Kitai, S. T., & Karoly, S. J. Responses of single cells in different layers of the primate lateral geniculate nucleus to monochromatic light. *Science 127*, 238–239 (1958).

Dirac, P. A. M. *The principles of quantum mechanics* (4th ed.). London: Oxford University Press, 1958.

Ditchburn, R. W. *Eye-movements and visual perception*. Oxford: Clarendon Press, 1973.

Ditchburn, R. W. *Light* (3rd ed.). New York: Academic Press, 1976.

Dow, B. M., & Gouras P. Color and spatial specificity of single units in Rhesus monkey foveal striate cortex. *Journal of Neurophysiology 36*, 79–100 (1973).

Dowling, J. E. Organization of vertebrate retinas. *Investigative Ophthalmology 9*, 655–680 (1970).

Dowling, J. E., & Boycott, B. B. Organization of the primate retina: Electron microscopy. *Proceedings of the Royal Society of London 166B*, 80–111 (1966).

Dowling, J. E., & Ehinger, B. Synaptic organization of the amine-containing interplexiform cells of the goldfish and Cebus monkey retina. *Science 188*, 270–273 (1975).

Dowling, J. E., & Ripps, H. Visual adaptation in the retina of the skate. *Journal of General Physiology 56*, 491–520 (1970).

Dreher, B., Fukada, Y., & Rodieck, R. W. Identification, classification, and anatomical segregation of cells with X-like and Y-like properties in the lateral geniculate nucleus of old-world primates. *Journal of Physiology 258*, 433–452 (1976).

Egan, J. P. *Signal detection theory and ROC Analysis*. New York: Academic Press, 1975.

Engen, T. Psychophyisics: I. Discrimination and detection. In Kling, J. W., & Riggs, L. A. (Eds.), *Experimental psychology*. New York: Holt, Rinehart, and Winston, 1971.

Enoch, J. M. Wave-guide modes in retinal receptors. *Science 133*, 1353–1354 (1961a).

Enoch, J. M. Nature of the transmission of energy in the retinal receptors. *Journal of the Optical Society of America 51*, 1122–1126 (196lb).

Enoch, J. M. Optical properties of the retinal receptors. *Journal of the Optical Society of America 53*, 71–85 (1963).

Enoch, J. M. Physical properties of the retinal receptor and response of retinal receptors. *Psychological Bulletin 61*, 242–251 (1964).

Enoch, J. M. The two-color threshold technique of Stiles and derived component color mechanisms. In Jameson, D., & Hurvich, L. M. (Eds.), *Handbook of sensory physiology VII/4*. New York: Springer-Verlag, 1972.

Estévez, O., & Cavonius, C. R. Human color perception and Stiles' π mechanisms. *Vision Research 17*, 417–422 (1977).

Estévez, O., & Spekreijse, H. A spectral compensation method for determining the flicker characteristics of the human colour mechanisms. *Vision Research 14*, 823–830 (1974).

Estévez, O., Spekreijse, H., van den Berg, T. J. T. P., & Cavonius, C. R. The spectral sensitivities of isolated human color mechanisms determined from contrast evoked potential measurements. *Vision Research 15*, 1205–1212 (1975).

Evans, R. M. *An introduction to color.* New York: Wiley, 1948.
Evans, R. M. Variables of perceived color. *Journal of the Optical Society of America 54,* 1467–1474 (1964).
Evans, R. M. *The perception of color.* New York: Wiley, 1974.
Evans, R. M., & Swenholt, B. K. Chromatic strength of colors: Dominant wavelength and purity. *Journal of the Optical Society of America 57,* 1319–1324 (1967).
Falls, H. F., Wolter, J. R., & Alpern, M. Typical total monochromacy. *Archives of Ophthalmology 74,* 610–620 (1965).
Fechner, G. *Elements of psychophysics, vol. I.* Translated by H. E. Adler; D. H. Howes, & E. G. Boring. New York: Holt, Rinehart and Winston, 1966.
Feinberg, G. Light. *Scientific American 219* (3), 50–59 (1968).
Ferry, E. S. Persistence of vision. *American Journal of Science 44,* 192–207 (1892).
Fick, A. Die Lehre von der Lichtemfindung. In Hermann, L. (Ed.) *Handbuch der Physiologie,* pp. 139–234. Leipsig: Vogel, 1879.
Fiorentini, A. Mach band phenomena. In Jameson, D., & Hurvich, L. M. (Eds.), *Handbook of sensory physiology* VII/4. New York: Springer-Verlag, 1972.
Fischer, F. P., Bouman, M. A., & ten Doesschate, J. A case of tritanopy. *Documenta Ophthalmologica 5,* 73–87 (1951).
Forsyth, D. M., & Chapanis, A. Counting repeated light flashes as a function of their number, their rate of presentation, and retinal location stimulated. *Journal of Experimental Psychology 56,* 385–391 (1958).
Fox, J. C., & German, W. J. Macular vision following cerebral resection. *Archives of Neurology and Psychiatry 35,* 808–826 (1936).
Foxell, C. A. P., & Stevens, W. R. Measurements of visual acuity. *British Journal of Ophthalmology 39,* 513–533 (1955).
Friele, L. F. C. FMC-metrics: What next? In Vos, J. J., Friele, L. F. C., & Walraven, P. L. (Eds.), *Color metrics.* Soesterberg, Netherlands: Institute for Perception TNO, 1972.
Glantz, R. M. Peripheral versus central adaptation in the crustacean visual system. *Journal of Neurophysiology 34,* 485–492 (1971).
Glantz, R. M. Visual adaptation: A case of nonlinear summation. *Vision Research 12,* 103–109 (1972).
Glickstein, M., & Heath, G. G. Receptors in the monochromat eye. *Vision Research 15,* 633–636 (1975).
Gordon, J., & Abramov, I. Color vision in the peripheral retina. II. Hue and saturation. *Journal of the Optical Society of America 67,* 202–207 (1977).
Gouras, P. Identification of cone mechanisms in monkey ganglion cells. *Journal of Physiology 199,* 533–547 (1968).
Gouras, P. Opponent-colour cells in different layers of foveal striate cortex. *Journal of Physiology 238,* 583–602 (1974).
Gouras, P., & Kruger, J. Personal communication.
Graham, C. H. (Ed.) *Vision and visual perception.* New York: Wiley, 1965.
Graham, R. E. Communication theory as applied to television coding. *Acta Electronica 2,* 333–343 (1957–1958).
Granit, R. *Sensory mechanisms of the retina.* London: Cambridge University Press, 1947. (Reprinted in 1963 by Hafner Publishing Co., New York.)
Green, D. G. Sinusoidal flicker characteristics of the color-sensitive mechanisms of the eye. *Vision Research 9,* 591–601 (1969).

Green, D. G. Visual acuity in the blue cone monochromat. *Journal of Physiology 222*, 419–426 (1972).

Green, D. G., Dowling, J. E., Siegel, I. M., & Ripps, H. Retinal mechanisms of visual adaptation in the skate. *Journal of General Physiology 65*, 483–502 (1975).

Gregory, R. L., & Wallace, J. G. *Recovery from early blindness*. Experimental Psychology Society (England) Monograph No. 2, 1963.

Griffin, D. R., Hubbard, R., & Wald, G. The sensitivity of the human eye to infra-red radiation. *Journal of the Optical Society of America 37*, 546–554 (1947).

Grützner, P. Acquired color vision defects. In Jameson, D., & Hurvich, L. M. (Eds.), *Handbook of sensory physiology*, VII/4. New York: Springer-Verlag, 1972.

Guild, J. The colorimetric properties of the spectrum. *Philosophical Transactions of the Royal Society of London 230A*, 149–187 (1925–1926).

Guild, J. Discussion in *Report of a joint discussion on vision held on June 3, 1932, at the Imperial College of Science by the Physical and Optical Societies*, p. 157. London: Physical Society, 1932.

Guth, S. L. Nonadditivity and inhibition among chromatic luminances at threshold. *Vision Research 7*, 319–328 (1967).

Guth, S. L., Donley, N. J., & Marrocco, R. T. On luminance additivity and related topics. *Vision Research 9*, 537–575 (1969).

Harter, M. R., & White, C. T. Evoked cortical responses to checkerboard patterns: Effect of check-size as a function of visual acuity. *Electroencephalography and Clinical Neurophysiology 28*, 48–54 (1970).

Hartline, H. K. The response of single optic nerve fibers of the vertebrate eye to illumination of the retina. *American Journal of Physiology 121*, 400–415 (1938).

Harwerth, R. S., & Sperling, H. G. Prolonged color blindness induced by intense spectral lights in Rhesus monkeys. *Science 174*, 520–523 (1971).

Heath, G. Luminosity curves of normal and dichromatic observers. *Science 128*, 775–776 (1958).

Hecht, S. A quantitative formulation of colour-vision. In *Report of a joint discussion on vision held on June 3, 1932, at the Imperial College of Science by the Physical and Optical Societies*. London: Physical Society, 1932.

Hecht, S. Brightness, visual acuity and colour blindness. *Documenta Ophthalmologica 3*, 289–306 (1949).

Hecht, S., Ross, S., & Mueller, C. G. The visibility of lines and squares at high brightness. *Journal of the Optical Society of America 37*, 500–507 (1947).

Hecht, S., & Shlaer, S. The color vision of dichromats: I. Wavelength discrimination, brightness distribution, and color mixture; II. Saturation as the basis for wavelength discrimination and color mixture. *Journal of General Physiology 20*, 57–82; 83–93 (1936).

Hecht, S., Shlaer, S., & Pirenne, M. H. Energy, quanta, and vision. *Journal of General Physiology 25*, 819–840 (1942).

Helmholtz, H. *Physiological optics* (edited by J. P. C. Southall; 3 volumes). Rochester, New York: Optical Society of America, 1924.

Helson, H. Fundamental problems in color vision: I. The principle governing changes in hue, saturation, and lightness of non-selective samples in chromatic illumination. *Journal of Experimental Psychology 23*, 439–476 (1938).

Helson, H. Studies of anomalous contrast and assimilation. *Journal of the Optical Society of America 53*, 179–184 (1963).

Helson, H., & Michels, W. C. The effect of chromatic adaptation on achromaticity. *Journal of the Optical Society of America 38,* 1025–1032 (1948).

Henderson, S. T. *Daylight and its spectrum.* (2d ed.). Bristol, England: Adarm Hilger, 1977.

Henkes, H. E., & van der Tweel, L. H. (Eds.), *Flicker.* The Hague: W. Junk, 1964. [Also published as *Documenta Ophthalmologia 18* (1964.)]

Hering, E. *Outlines of a theory of the light sense.* (Translated by L. M. Hurvich & D. Jameson.) Cambridge, Mass.: Harvard University Press, 1964.

Herrnstein, R. J., & Boring, E. G. (Eds.), *A source book in the history of psychology.* Cambridge, Mass.: Harvard University Press, 1965.

Hirsch, H. V. B., & Spinelli, D. Visual experience modifies distribution of horizontally and vertically oriented receptive fields in cats. *Science 168,* 869–871 (1970).

Hochberg, J., & Silverstein, A. A quantitative index of stimulus similarity: Proximity vs. differences in brightness. *American Journal of Psychology 69,* 456–458 (1956).

Horner, F. Die Erblichkeit des Daltonismus: Ein Beitrag zum Vererbungsgesetz. *Amtl. Ber. Verwaltung d. Medizinalwesens Kanton Zürich* 1876, 208–211.

Hsia, Y., & Graham, C. H. Color blindness. In Graham, E. H. (Ed.), *Vision and visual perception.* New York: Wiley, 1965.

Hubbard, R. Preface to the English translations of Boll's *On the anatomy and physiology of the retina* and Kühne's *Chemical processes in the retina.* *Vision Research 17,* 1247–1248 (1977).

Hubel, D. H., & Wiesel, T. N. Receptive fields and functional architecture of monkey striate cortex. *Journal of Physiology 195,* 215–243 (1968).

Hull, E. Corticofugal influence in the macaque lateral geniculate nucleus. *Vision Research 8,* 1285–1298 (1968).

Hunt, R. W. G. *The reproduction of colour* (3rd ed.). New York: Wiley, 1975.

Hurvich, L. M. Color vision deficiencies. In Jameson, D., & Hurvich, L. M. (Eds.), *Handbook of sensory physiology* VII/4. New York: Springer-Verlag, 1972.

Hurvich, L. M., & Jameson, D. A psychophysical study of white: I. Neutral adaptation. *Journal of the Optical Society of America 41,* 521–527 (1951a).

Hurvich, L. M., & Jameson, D. A psychophysical study of white: III. Adaptation as variant. *Journal of the Optical Society of America 41,* 787–801 (1951b).

Hurvich, L. M., & Jameson, D. Some quantitative aspects of an opponent-colors theory: II. Brightness, saturation, and hue in normal and dichromatic vision. *Journal of the Optical Society of America 45,* 602–616 (1955).

Hurvich, L. M., & Jameson, D. On the measurement of dichromatic neutral points. *Acta Chromatica 2,* 207–216 (1974).

Ikeda, M., & Boynton, R. M. Effect of test-flash duration upon the spectral sensitivity of the eye. *Journal of the Optical Society of America 52,* 697–699 (1962).

Ikeda, M., Hukami, K., & Urakubo, M. Flicker photometry with chromatic adaptation and defective color vision. *American Journal of Ophthalmology 73,* 270–277 (1972).

Ikeda, M., & Urakubo, M. Flicker HTRF as test of color vision. *Journal of the Optical Society of America 58,* 27–31 (1968).

Indow, T., & Ohsumi, K. Multidimensional mapping of sixty Munsell colors by nonmetric procedure. In Vos, J. J., Friele, L. F. C., & Walraven, P. L. (Eds.), *Color metrics.* Soesterberg, Netherlands: Institute for Perception TNO, 1972.

Ingling, C. R., Jr. The spectral sensitivity of the opponent-color channels. *Vision Research 17,* 1083–1089 (1977).

Ingling, C. R., Jr., & Drum, B. A. How neural adaptation changes chromaticity coordinates. *Journal of the Optical Society of America 63*, 369–373 (1973).

Ingling, C. R., Jr., & Tsou, B. H. Orthogonal combinations of three visual channels. *Vision Research 17*, 1075–1082 (1977).

Ives, H. E. A polarization flicker photometer and some data of theoretical bearing obtained with it. *Philosophical Magazine 33*, 360–380 (1917).

Ives, H. E. A theory of intermittent vision. *Journal of the Optical Society of America and Revue of Scientific Instruments 6*, 343–361 (1922).

Ives, H. E., & Kingsbury, E. F. The theory of the flicker photometer. *Philosophical Magazine 28*, 708–728 (1914).

Jameson, D., & Hurvich, L. M. A psychophysical study of white: II. Neutral adaptation: Area and duration as variants. *Journal of the Optical Society of America, 41*, 528–536 (1951).

Jameson, D., & Hurvich, L. M. Some quantitative aspects of an opponent-colors theory: I. Chromatic responses and spectral saturation. *Journal of the Optical Society of America 45*, 546–552 (1955).

Jameson, D., & Hurvich, L. M. Color adaptation: Sensitivity, contrast, after-images. In Jameson, D., & Hurvich, L. M. (Eds.), *Handbook of sensory physiology* VII/4. New York: Springer-Verlag, 1972.

Jones, L. A. (Chairman) Committee on Colorimetry, Optical Society of America. *The science of color.* New York: Crowell, 1953.

Judd, D. B. The 1931 I.C.I. standard observer and coordinate system for colorimetry. *Journal of the Optical Society of America 23*, 359–374 (1933).

Judd, D. B. Hue, saturation, and lightness of surface colors with chromatic illumination. *Journal of the Optical Society of America 30*, 3–32 (1940).

Judd, D. B. Color perceptions of deuteranopic and protanopic observers. *Journal of Research of the National Bureau of Standards 41*, 247–271 (1948).

Judd, D. B. Report of U. S. Secretariat, Committee on Colorimetry and Artificial Daylight. *Proc. CIE I*, part 7, p. 11 (Stockholm, 1951a). Paris: Bureau Central CIE.

Judd, D. B. Basic correlates of the visual stimulus. In Stevens, S. S. (Ed), *Handbook of experimental psychology*. New York: Wiley, 1951b.

Judd, D. B. Some color demonstrations I have shown. *Journal of the Optical Society of America 49*, 322–328 (1959).

Judd, D. B. Appraisal of Land's work on two-primary color projections. *Journal of the Optical Society of America 50*, 254–268 (1960).

Judd, D. B., & Yonemura, G. CIE 1960 UCS Diagram and the Müller theory of color vision. *Journal of Research of the National Bureau of Standards 74A*, 23–30 (1970).

Julesz, B. *Foundations of cyclopean perception.* Chicago: University of Chicago Press, 1971.

Kalmus, H. *Diagnosis and genetics of defective colour vision.* New York: Pergamon Press, 1965.

Katz, D. *The world of color.* Translated in abridged form from the second German edition (1930) by R. B. MacLeod & C. W. Fox. London: Kegan, Paul, 1935.

Kaufman, J. E. (Ed.) *IES lighting handbook* (5th ed.), New York: Illuminating Engineering Society, 1972.

Kelly, D. H. Visual responses to time-dependent stimuli: I. Amplitude sensitivity measurements. *Journal of the Optical Society of America 51*, 422–429 (1961).

Kelly, D. H. Sine waves and flicker fusion. *Documenta Ophthalmologica 18*, 16–35 (1964).

Kelly, D. H.   Diffusion model of linear flicker responses. *Journal of the Optical Society of America 59,* 1665–1670 (1969).
Kelly, D. H.   Theory of flicker and transient responses: I. Uniform fields. *Journal of the Optical Society of America 61,* 537–546 (1971).
Kelly, D. H.   Flicker. In Jameson, D., & Hurvich, L. M. (Eds.), *Handbook of sensory physiology* VII/4. New York: Springer-Verlag, 1972.
Kelly, D. H.   Lateral inhibition in human colour mechanisms. *Journal of Physiology 228,* 55–72 (1973).
Kelly, D. H.   Spatio-temporal frequency characteristics of color-vision mechanisms. *Journal of the Optical Society of America 64,* 983–990 (1974).
Kelly, D. H.   Luminous and chromatic flickering patterns have opposite effects. *Science 188,* 371–372 (1975).
Kelly, D. H., Boynton, R. M., & Baron, W. S.   Primate flicker sensitivity: Psychophysics and electrophysiology. *Science 194,* 1077–1079 (1976).
Kelly, D. H., & van Norren, D.   Two-band model of heterochromatic flicker. *Journal of the Optical Society of America 67,* 1081–1091 (1977).
Kingslake, R.   Refraction. In Bensançon, R. M. (Ed.), *The encyclopedia of physics* (2nd ed.). New York: Van Nostrand Reinhold, 1974.
King-Smith, P. E., & Carden, D.   Luminance and opponent-color contributions to visual detection and adaptation and to temporal and spatial integration. *Journal of the Optical Society of America 66,* 709–717 (1976).
Kleinschmidt, J., & Dowling, J. E.   Intracellular recordings from Gecko photoreceptors during light and dark adaptation. *Journal of General Physiology 66,* 617–648 (1975).
Kling, J. W., & Riggs, L. A.   Woodworth and Schlosberg's *Experimental Psychology* (3rd ed.). New York: Holt, Rinehart, and Winston, 1971.
Kohler, I.   Experiments with goggles. *Scientific American 206* (5), 62–84 (1962).
Kolb, H.   Organization of the outer plexiform layer of the primate retina: Electron microscopy of Golgi-impregnated cells. *Philosophical Transactions of the Royal Society of London 258B,* 261–283 (1970).
König, A.   Über den menschlichen Sehpurpur und seine Bedeutung für das Sehen. *Acadamie der Wissenschaften (Berlin) Sitzungsberichte,* 577–598 (1894).
König, A., and Dieterici, C.   Die Grunempfindungen in normalen und anomalen Farbensystemen und ihre Intensitätsverteilung im Spektrum. *Zeitschrift für Psychologie und Physiologie der Sinnesorgane 4,* 241–347 (1893).
Krauskopf, J.   Effect of retinal image stabilization on the appearance of heterochromatic targets. *Journal of the Optical Society of America 53,* 741–744 (1963).
Krauskopf, J., & Mollon, J. D.   The independence of the temporal integration properties of individual chromatic mechanisms in the human eye. *Journal of Physiology 219,* 611–623 (1971).
von Kries, J.   Theories of vision.   In Southall, J. P. C. (Ed.), *Helmholtz's treatise on physiological optics.* Rochester, N. Y.: Optical Society of America, 1924.
Kuffler, S. W.   Discharge patterns and functional organization of mammalian retina. *Journal of Neurophysiology 16,* 37–68 (1953).
Lakowski, R.   Is the deterioration of colour discrimination with age due to lens or retinal changes? *Farbe 11,* 69–86 (1962).
Lakowski, R.   Theory and practice of colour vision testing: A review. Part 1. *British Journal of Industrial Medicine 26,* 173–189 (1969a).

Lakowski, R. Theory and practice of colour vision testing: A review. Part 2. *British Journal of Industrial Medicine 26*, 265–288 (1969b).
Land, E. H. Color vision and the natural image: Part I. *Proceedings of the National Academy of Sciences 45*, 115–129 (1959a).
Land, E. H. Color vision and the natural image: Part II. *Proceedings of the National Academy of Sciences 45*, 636–644 (1959b).
Land, E. H. Experiments in color vision. *Scientific American 200 (5)*, 84–99 (1959c).
Land, E. H. The retinex theory of color vision. *Scientific American 218* (6), 108–128 (1977).
Land, E. H., & McCann, J. J. Lightness and retinex theory. *Journal of the Optical Society of America 61*, 1–11 (1971).
Landis, C. *An annotated bibliography of flicker fusion phenomena covering the period 1740–1952.* Ann Arbor, Michigan: Armed-Forces–NRC Vision Committee Secretariat, 1953.
Larimer, J., Krantz, D. H., & Cicerone, C. M. Opponent-process additivity: I: Red/green equilibria. *Vision Research 14*, 1127–1140 (1974).
Larimer, J., Krantz, D. H., & Cicerone, C. M. Opponent-process additivity: II. Yellow/blue equilibria and nonlinear models. *Vision Research 15*, 723–731 (1975).
Lashley, K. S., & Clark, G. The cytoarchitecture of the cerebral cortex of Ateles: A critical examination of architectonic studies. *Journal of Comparative Neurology 85*, 223–305 (1946).
Lawson, R. B., Goldstein, S. G., & Musty, R. E. *Principles and methods of psychology.* New York: Oxford University Press, 1975.
Leber, T. Über die Theorie der Farbenblindheit und über die Art und Weise, wie gewisse, der Untersuchung von Farbenblinden entommene Einwände gegen die Young-Helmholtz'sche Theorie sich mit derselben vereinigen lassen. *Klinisch Monatsbläter für Augenhelkunde 11*, 467–473 (1873).
LeGrand, Y. Les seuils différentiels de couleurs dans la théorie de Young. *Revue d'Optique 28*, 261–278 (1949).
LeGrand, Y. *Light, colour, and vision* (2nd ed.). Translated by R. W. G. Hunt, J. W. T. Walsh, & F. R. W. Hunt. Somerset, N. J.: Halsted Press, 1968.
LeGrand, Y. Unsolved problems in vision. In Pierce, J. R., & Levine, J. R. (Eds.), *Visual science.* Bloomington: Indiana University Press, 1971.
Liebman, P. Microspectrophotometry of photoreceptors. In Dartnall, H. J. A. (Ed.), *Handbook of sensory physiology* VII/1. New York: Springer-Verlag, 1972.
Lu, C., & Fender, D. H. The interaction of color and luminance in stereoscopic vision. *Investigative Ophthalmology 11*, 482–490 (1972).
MacAdam, D. L. Visual sensitivities to color differences in daylight. *Journal of the Optical Society of America 32*, 247–274 (1942).
MacAdam, D. L. Small-field chromaticity discrimination. *Journal of the Optical Society of America 49*, 1143–1146 (1959).
MacAdam, D. L. (Ed.), *Sources of color science.* Cambridge, Mass.: M.I.T. Press (1970).
MacKay, D. M., & Jeffreys, D. A. Visually evoked potentials and visual perception in man. In Jung, R. (Ed.), *Handbook of sensory physiology* VII/3B. New York: Springer-Verlag, 1973.
MacLeod, D. I. A. Visual sensitivity. *Annual Review of Psychology 29*, 613–645 (1978).

MacLeod, D. I. A., & Hayhoe, M. Three pigments in normal and anomalous color vision. *Journal of the Optical Society of America 64,* 92–96 (1974).

MacLeod, D. I. A., & Lennie, P. A unilateral defect resembling deuteranopia. *Modern Problems in Ophthalmology 13,* 130–134 (1974).

MacNichol, E. J., & Svaetichin, G. Electric responses from the isolated retinas of fishes. *American Journal of Ophthalmology 46,* No. 3 Part II, 26–46 (1958).

Magnus, R. *Goethe as a scientist.* Translated by Heinz Norden from *Goethe als Naturforscher,* Leipzig, Germany, 1906. New York: Henry Schuman, Inc.; Reprint: Collier Books, 1949.

Makous, W. L. Cutaneous color sensitivity: Explanation and demonstration. *Psychological Review 73,* 280–294 (1966).

Marc, R. E., & Sperling, H. G. Chromatic organization of primate cones. *Science 196,* 454–456 (1977).

Marks, L. E., & Bornstein, M. H. Spectral sensitivity by constant CFF: Effect of chromatic adaptation. *Journal of the Optical Society of America 63,* 220–226 (1973).

Marriott, F. H. C. Colour vision: The two-colour threshold technique of Stiles. In Davson, H. (Ed.), *The eye.* New York: Academic Press, 1962.

Marrocco, R. T. Responses of monkey optic tract fibers to monochromatic lights. *Vision Research 12,* 1167–1174 (1972).

Massaro, D. W. *Experimental psychology and information processing.* Skokie, Ill.: Rand McNally, 1975.

Massof, R. W., & Bailey, J. E. Achromatic points in protanopes and deuteranopes. *Vision Research 16,* 53–57 (1976).

Maxwell, J. C. Experiments on colour, as perceived by the eye, with remarks on colour-blindness. *Transactions of the Royal Society, Edinburgh 21,* 275–298 (1855).

McCamy, C. S. Colors perceived with abridged color projection systems. *Journal of the Optical Society of America 50,* 510 (1960).

McCann, J. J., McKee, S. P., & Taylor, T. H. Quantitative studies in retinex theory. *Vision Research 16,* 445–458 (1976).

McConnell, J. V. *Understanding human behavior* (2nd ed.). New York: Holt, Rinehart and Winston, 1977.

McCree, K. J. Small-field tritanopia and the effects of voluntary fixation. *Optica Acta 7,* 317–323 (1960).

Michael, C. R. Color vision mechanisms in monkey striate cortex: Dual-opponent cells with concentric receptive fields. *Journal of Neurophysiology 41,* 572–588 (1978).

Miller, S. S. Psychophysical estimates of visual pigment densities in red-green dichromats. *Journal of Physiology 223,* 89–107 (1972).

Mitchell, D. E., & Rushton, W. A. H. The red/green pigments of normal vision. *Vision Research 11,* 1045–1056 (1971).

Monty, R. A., and Senders, J. W. (Eds.), *Eye movements and psychological processes.* New York: Lawrence Erlbaum Associates, 1976.

Moreland, J. D. Threshold measurements of the blue arcs phenomenon. *Vision Research 8,* 1093–1106 (1968a).

Moreland, J. D. On demonstrating the blue arcs phenomenon. *Vision Research 8,* 99–107 (1968b).

Moreland, J. D. Retinal topography and the blue-arcs phenomenon. *Vision Research 9,* 965–976 (1969).

Moreland, J. D. Peripheral color vision. In Jameson, D., & Hurvich, L. M. (Eds), *Handbook of sensory physiology* VII/4. New York: Springer-Verlag, 1972.

Moscowitz, H. R., Scharf, B., & Stevens, J. C. *Sensation and measurement: Papers in honor of S. S. Stevens.* Boston: Reidel Publishing Co., 1974.

Müller, G. E. Zur Psychophysik der Gesichtsemfindungen. *Zeitschrift für Psychologie und Physiologie der Sinnesorgane 10,* 1–82; 321–413 (1896).

Nagy, A. L., & Zacks, J. L. The effects of psychophysical procedure and stimulus duration in the measurement of Bezold-Brücke hue shifts. *Vision Research 17,* 193–200 (1977).

Newton, I. New theory about light and colors. *Philosophical Transactions of the Royal Society 6,* 3075–3085 (1671).

Newton, I. *Opticks* (4th ed.). London: William Innys, 1730. Reprint: New York: Dover, 1952.

Nickerson, D. History of the Munsell color system, Company, and Foundation: Parts I, II, and III. *Color Research and Application 1,* 7–10; 69–77; 121–130 (1976).

Normann, R. A., and Werblin, F. S. Control of retinal sensitivity: I. Light and dark adaptation of vertebrate rods and cones. *Journal of General Physiology 63,* 37–61 (1974).

van Norren, D., & Padmos, P. Human and macaque blue cones studied with electroretinography. *Vision Research 13,* 1241–1254 (1973).

Optical Society of America. *The science of color.* New York, Crowell, 1953.

Padgham, C. A., & Saunders, J. E. *The perception of light and colour.* New York: Academic Press, 1975.

Padmos, P., & van Norren, D. Cone spectral sensitivity and chromatic adaptation as revealed by human flicker-electroretinography. *Vision Research 11,* 27–42 (1971).

Padmos, P., & van Norren, D. Cone systems interaction in single neurons of the lateral geniculate nucleus of the macaque. *Vision Research 15,* 617–619 (1975).

Palmer, G. *Theory of colours and vision.* London: S. Leacroft, 1777.

Parra, F. Continuation of the study of colour thresholds. In Vos, J. J., Friele, L. F. C., & Walraven, P. L. (Eds.), *Color metrics.* Soesterberg, Netherlands: Institute for Perception TNO, 1972.

Parsons, J. H. *An introduction to the study of colour vision.* Cambridge, England: Cambridge University Press, 1924.

Penn, R. D., & Hagins, W. A. Signal transmission along retinal rods and the origin of the electroretinographic a-wave. *Nature 223,* 201–205 (1969).

Pettigrew, J. D., & Freeman, R. D. Visual experience without lines: Effect on developing cortical neurons. *Science 182,* 599–601 (1973).

Pfleegor, R. L., & Mandel, L. Interference of independent photon beams. *Physical Review 159,* 1084–1088 (1967).

Piantanida, T. P. A replacement model of X-linked recessive colour vision defects. *Annals of Human Genetics, London 37,* 393–404 (1974).

Piantanida, T. P. Polymorphism of human color vision. *American Journal of Optometry and Physiological Optics 53,* 647–657 (1976).

Piantanida, T. P., & Sperling, H. G. Isolation of a third chromatic mechanism in the protanomalous observer. *Vision Research 13,* 2033–2047 (1973a).

Piantanida, T. P., & Sperling, H. G. Isolation of a third chromatic mechanism in the deuteranomalous observer. *Vision Research 13,* 2049–2058 (1973b).

Pickford, R. W. *Individual differences in colour vision.* London: Routledge and Kegan Paul, 1951.

Pickford, R. W. A practical anomaloscope for testing colour vision and colour blindness. *British Journal of Physiological Optics 14,* 2–26 (1957).

Pickford, R. W. Some heterozygous manifestations of colour blindness. *British Journal of Physiological Optics 16,* 83–95 (1959).

Pickford, R. W., & Lakowski, R. The Pickford-Nicolson anomaloscope. *British Journal of Physiological Optics 17,* 131–150 (1960).

Pirenne, M. H. *Vision and the eye.* London: Chapman and Hall, 1948.

Pirenne, M. H. *Optics, painting, and photography.* London: Cambridge University Press, 1970.

Pitt, F. H. G. Characteristics of dichromatic vision, with an appendix on anomalous trichromatic vision. *Great Britain Medical Research Council, Special Report Series,* No. 200 (1935).

Pitt, F. H. G. The nature of normal trichromatic and dichromatic vision. *Proceedings of the Royal Society of London 132B,* 101–117 (1944).

Plateau, J. Sur un principe de photométrie. *Bull. Acad. Roy. Sci. Bell-let. Bruxelles 2,* 52–59 (1835).

Pokorny, J., & Smith, V. C. Wavelength discrimination in the presence of added chromatic fields. *Journal of the Optical Society of America 60,* 562–569 (1970).

Pokorny, J., & Smith, V. C. Luminosity and CFF in deuteranopes and protanopes. *Journal of the Optical Society of America 62,* 111–117 (1972).

Pokorny, J., & Smith, V. C. Effect of field size on red-green color mixture equations. *Journal of the Optical Society of America 66,* 705–708 (1976).

Pokorny, J., & Smith, V. C. Evaluation of single-pigment shift model of anomalous trichromacy. *Journal of the Optical Society of America 67,* 1196–1209 (1977).

Pokorny, J., Smith, V. C., & Katz, I. Derivation of the photopigment absorption spectra in anomalous trichromats. *Journal of the Optical Society of America 63,* 232–237 (1973).

Pokorny, J., Smith, V. C., & Swartley, R. Threshold measurements of spectral sensitivity in a blue monocone monochromat. *Investigative Ophthalmology 9,* 807–813 (1970).

Polyak, S. L. *The retina.* Chicago: University of Chicago Press, 1941.

Polyak, S. L. *The vertebrate visual system* (edited by Heinrich Klüver). Chicago: University of Chicago Press, 1957.

Porter, T. C. Contributions to the study of flicker: II. *Proceedings of the Royal Society of London 70A,* 313–329 (1902).

Pratt, C. C. *The logic of modern psychology.* New York: Macmillan, 1948.

Priest, I. G., & Brickwedde, F. G. The minimum perceptible colorimetric purity as a function of dominant wave-length. *Journal of the Optical Society of America 28,* 133–139 (1938).

Pugh, E. N., & Sigel, C. Evaluation of the candidacy of the π-mechanisms of Stiles for color-matching fundamentals. *Vision Research 18,* 317–330 (1978).

Purkinje, J. *Beobachtungen und Versuche zur Physiologie der Sinne.* Prague: J. G. Calve, 1823.

Rainwater, J. *Vision: How, why, and what we see.* New York: Golden Press, 1962.

Ratliff, F. (Ed.) *Studies on excitation and inhibition in the retina.* New York: Rockefeller University Press, 1974.

Regan, D. M. *Evoked potentials in psychology, sensory physiology, and clinical medicine.* London: Chapman and Hall, 1972.

Regan, D. Evoked potentials specific to spatial patterns of luminance and colour. *Vision Research 13,* 2381–2402 (1973).

Richards, W. Visual suppression during passive eye movement. *Journal of the Optical Society of America 58,* 1159–1160 (1968).

Riggs, L. A. Visual acuity. In Graham, C. H. (Ed.), *Vision and visual perception.* New York: Wiley, 1965.

Riggs, L. A., Johnson, E. P., & Schick, A. M. L. Electrical responses of the human eye to changes in wavelength of the stimulating light. *Journal of the Optical Society of America 56,* 1621–1627 (1966).

Robinson, D. A. Eye movement control in primates. *Science 161,* 1219–1224 (1968).

Rock, I. *An introduction to perception.* New York: Macmillan, 1975.

Rodieck, R. W. *The vertebrate retina.* San Francisco: Freeman, 1973.

Ronchi, V. *The nature of light* (translated by V. Barocas from *Storia della Luce,* 1939). Cambridge, Mass.: Harvard University Press, 1970.

Ruddock, K. H. Light transmission through the ocular media and macular pigment and its significance for psychophysical investigation. In Jameson, D., & Hurvich, L. M. (Eds.), *Handbook of sensory physiology,* VII/4. New York: Springer-Verlag, 1972.

Rushton, W. A. H. A cone pigment in the protanope. *Journal of Physiology 168,* 345–359 (1963).

Rushton, W. A. H. Color blindness and cone pigments. *American Journal of Optometry 41,* 265–282 (1964).

Rushton, W. A. H. The Ferrier lecture, 1962: Visual adaptation. *Proceedings of the Royal Society of London 162B,* 20–46 (1965a).

Rushton, W. A. H. A foveal pigment in the deuteranope. *Journal of Physiology 176,* 24–37 (1965b).

Rushton, W. A. H. Visual pigments in man. In Dartnall, H. J. A. (Ed.), *Handbook of sensory physiology* VII/1. New York: Springer-Verlag, 1972.

Rushton, W. A. H. Visual pigments and color blindness. *Scientific American 232* (3), 64–74 (1975).

Rushton, W. A. H. A highly speculative eye model. *Proceedings of the Institute of Electrical and Electronic Engineers,* 1130 (1966).

Rushton, W. A. H., & Baker, H. D. Red/green sensitivity in normal vision. *Vision Research 4,* 75–85 (1964).

Rushton, W. A. H., Campbell, F. W., Hagins, W. A., & Brindley, G. S. The bleaching and regeneration of rhodopsin the living eye of the albino rabbit and of man. *Optica Acta 1,* 183–190 (1955).

Rushton, W. A. H., & Henry, G. H. Bleaching and regeneration of cone pigments in man. *Vision Research 8,* 617–631 (1968).

Rushton, W. A. H., Powell, D. S., & White, K. D. The spectral sensitivity of "red" and "green" cones in the normal eye. *Vision Research 13,* 2003–2015 (1973a).

Rushton, W. A. H., Powell, D. S., & White, K. D. Pigments in anomalous trichromats. *Vision Research 13,* 2017–2031 (1973b).

Rushton, W. A. H., Powell, D. S., & White, K. D. Exchange thresholds in dichromats. *Vision Research 13,* 1993–2002 (1973c).

Sabra, I. *Theories of light from Descartes to Newton.* London: Oldbourne Book Co., 1967.

Sakitt, B.   Counting every quantum. *Journal of Physiology 223,* 131–150 (1972).
Salzmann, M.   *The anatomy and physiology of the human eyeball in the normal state* (translated by E. V. L. Brown). Chicago: University of Chicago Press, 1912.
Scheibner, H. M.   Adaptive color shifts. *Journal of the Optical Society of America 56,* 938–942 (1966).
Scheibner, H. M. O., & Boynton, R. M.   Residual red-green discrimination in dichromats. *Journal of the Optical Society of America 58,* 1151–1158 (1968).
Schmidt, I.   Some problems related to testing color vision with the Nagel anomaloscope. *Journal of the Optical Society of America 45,* 514–522 (1955).
Schrödinger, E.   Grundlinien einer Theorie der Farbenmetrik im Tagessehen. *Annalen der Physik und Chemie (iv) 63,* 481–520 (1920).
Scully, M. O., & Sargent, M.   The concept of the photon. *Physics Today 25* (3), 38–47 (1972).
Shepard, R. N., Romney, A. K., & Nerlove, S. B.   *Multidimensional scaling: Vol. I. Theory; Vol. II. Applications.* New York: Seminar Press, 1972.
Siegel, M. H.   Discrimination of color: I. Comparison of three psychophysical methods. *Journal of the Optical Society of America 52,* 1067–1070 (1962).
Siegel, M. H.   Discrimination of color: IV. Sensitivity as a function of spectral wavelength, 410 through 500 nm. *Journal of the Optical Society of America 54,* 821–823 (1964).
Siegel, M. H., & Dimmick, M. H.   Discrimination of color: II. Sensitivity as a function of spectral wavelength, 510–630 nm. *Journal of the Optical Society of America 52,* 1071–1074 (1962).
Sigel, C., & Pugh, E. N.   Evaluation of candidate cone action spectra by a new minimization technique. *Investigative Ophthalmology and Visual Science 16* (Suppl.), 161 (1977).
Sirovich, L., & Abramov, I.   Photopigments and pseudo-pigments. *Vision Research 17,* 5–16 (1977).
Sjöstrand, F. S.   The ultrastructure of the outer segments of rods and cones of the eye as revealed by the electron microscope. *Journal of Cellular and Comparative Physiology 42,* 15–44 (1953).
Smith, V. C., & Pokorny, J.   Spectral sensitivity of color-blind observers and the cone photopigments. *Vision Research 12,* 2059–2071 (1972).
Smith, V. C., & Pokorny, J.   Spectral sensitivity of the foveal cone photopigments between 400 and 500 nm. *Vision Research 15,* 161–171 (1975).
Smith, V. C., & Pokorny, J.   Large-field trichromacy in protanopes and deuteranopes. *Journal of the Optical Society of America 67,* 213–220 (1977).
Smith, V. C., & Pokorny, J.   An unusual color vision defect. *Investigative Ophthalmology and Visual Science 17* (Suppl.), 198 (1978).
Sparrock, J. M. B.   Stabilized images: Increment thresholds and subjective brightness. *Journal of the Optical Society of America 59,* 872–874 (1969).
Speelman, R. G., & Krauskopf, J.   Effects of chromatic adaptation on normal and dichromatic red-green brightness matches. *Journal of the Optical Society of America 53,* 1103–1107 (1963).
Sperling, H. G.   Linear theory and the psychophysics of flicker. *Documenta Ophthalmologica 18,* 3–15 (1964).
Sperling, H. G., & Harwerth, R. S.   Red-green cone interactions in the increment-threshold spectral sensitivity of primates. *Science 172,* 180–184 (1971).

Sperling, H. G., & Lewis, W. G.   Some comparisons between foveal spectral sensitivity data obtained at high brightness and absolute threshold. *Journal of the Optical Society of America 49,* 983–989 (1959).

Stell, W. K., & Lightfoot, D. O.   Color-specific interconnections of cones to horizontal cells in the retina of the goldfish. *Journal of Comparative Neurology 159,* 473–501 (1975).

Stell, W. K., Lightfoot, D. O., Wheeler, T. G., & Leeper, H. F.   Goldfish retina: Functional polarization of cone horizontal cell dendrites and synapses. *Science 190,* 989–990 (1975).

Stiles, W. S.   The directional sensitivity of the retina and the spectral sensitivities of the rods and cones. *Proceedings of the Royal Society of London 127B,* 64–105 (1939).

Stiles, W. S.   Increment thresholds and the mechanisms of colour vision. *Documenta Ophthalmologica 3,* 138–163 (1949).

Stiles, W. S.   Further studies of visual mechanisms by the two-colour threshold method. *Coloquio sobre Problemas Opticos de la Vision 1,* 65–103. Madrid: Union Internationale de Physique pure et appliquée, 1953.

Stiles, W. S.   18th Thomas Young oration: The basic data of color-matching. In *Physical Society Year Book,* pp. 44–45. London: Physical Society, 1955.

Stiles, W. S.   Color vision: The approach through increment-threshold sensitivity. *Proceedings of the National Academy of Sciences 45,* 100–114 (1959).

Stiles, W. S.   Appendix: Foveal threshold sensitivity of fields of different colors. *Science 145,* 1016–1017 (1964).

Stiles, W. S.   The line element in colour theory: A historical review. In Vos, J. J., Friele, L. F. C., & Walraven, P. L. (Eds.), *Color metrics.* Soesterberg, Netherlands: Institute for Perception TNO (1972).

Stiles, W. S.   *Mechanisms of colour vision.* New York: Academic Press, 1978.

Stiles, W. S., & Crawford, B. H.   The luminous efficiency of rays entering the pupil at different points. *Proceedings of the Royal Society of London 112B,* 428–450 (1933a).

Stiles, W. S., & Crawford, B. H.   The liminal brightness increment as a function of wave-length for different conditions of the foveal and parafoveal retina. *Proceedings of the Royal Society of London 113B,* 496–530 (1933b).

Stiles, W. S., & Wyszecki, G.   Colour-matching data and the spectral absorption curves of visual pigments. *Vision Research 14,* 195–207 (1974).

Strong, J.   *Concepts of classical optics.* San Francisco: Freeman, 1958.

Svaetichin, G.   Spectral response curves from single cones. *Acta Physiologica Scandinavica 39* (Suppl. 134), 17–46 (1956).

Talbot, H. F.   Experiments on light. *Philosophical Magazine* (3rd series) 5, 321–334 (1834).

Tansley, B. W., & Boynton, R. M.   A line, not a space, represents visual distinctness of borders formed by different colors. *Science 191,* 954–957 (1976).

Tansley, B. W., & Boynton, R. M.   Chromatic border perception: The role of red- and green-sensitive cones. *Vision Research 18,* 683–697 (1978).

Taylor, E., & Jennings, A.   Calculation of total retinal area. *British Journal of Ophthalmology 55,* 262–265 (1971).

Taylor, J. G.   *The behavioral basis of perception.* New Haven: Yale University Press, 1962.

Tessier, M., & Blottiau, F. Variations des chractéristiques photométriques de l'oeil aux luminances photopiques. *Revue d'Optique 30,* 309–322 (1951).

Thomson, L. C. Sensations aroused by monochromatic stimuli and their prediction. *Optica Acta 1,* 93–101 (1954).

Thompson, R. F., & Patterson, M. M. (Eds.), Bioelectric recording techniques (3 volumes). New York: Academic Press; Vol. 1: 1973; Vols. 2 and 3: 1974.

Thorell, L. G., Albrecht, D. G., & DeValois, R. L. Spatial tuning properties of macaque cortical cells to pure color and luminance stimuli. *Investigative Ophthalmology and Visual Science 17* (Suppl.), 195 (1978).

Tomita, T. Electrophysiological study of the mechanisms subserving color coding in the fish retina. *Cold Spring Harbor Symposia on Quantitative Biology 30,* 559–566 (1965).

Tomita, T., Kaneko, A., Murakami, M., & Pautler, E. L. Spectral response curves of single cones in the carp. *Vision Research 7,* 519–531 (1967).

Trezona, P. W. Aspects of peripheral color vision. *Modern Problems in Ophthalmology 17,* 52–70 (1976).

Troland, L. T. Notes on flicker photometry: Flicker-photometry frequency as a function of light intensity. *Journal of the Franklin Institute 182,* 261–262 (1916).

Truss, C. V. Chromatic flicker fusion frequency as a function of chromaticity difference. *Journal of the Optical Society of America 47,* 1130–1134 (1957).

Verriest, G. Further studies on acquired deficiency of color discrimination. *Journal of the Optical Society of America 53,* 185–195 (1963).

Vos, J. J., & Walraven, P. L. On the derivation of the foveal receptor primaries. *Vision Research 11,* 799–818 (1971).

Vos, J. J., & Walraven, P. L. An analytical description of the line element in the zone-fluctuation model of colour vision: I. Basic concepts. *Vision Research 12,* 1327–1344 (1972).

Wagner, G., & Boynton, R. M. Comparison of four methods of heterochromatic photometry. *Journal of the Optical Society of America 62,* 1508–1515 (1972).

Wald, G. Photo-labile pigments of the chicken retina. *Nature 140,* 545–546 (1937).

Wald, G. Human vision and the spectrum. *Science 101,* 653–658 (1945).

Wald, G. The receptors of human color vision. *Science 145,* 1007–1016 (1964).

Wald, G. Blue-blindness in the normal fovea. *Journal of the Optical Society of America 57,* 1289–1301 (1967).

Wald, G. Molecular basis of visual excitation. *Science 162,* 230–239 (1968).

Wald, G., Brown, P. K., & Gibbons, I. R. The problem of visual excitation. *Journal of the Optical Society of America 53,* 20–35 (1963).

Walls, G. L. Graham's theory of color blindness. *American Journal of Optometry and Archives of the Academy of Optometry 35,* 449–460 (1958).

Walls, G. L. Land! Land! *Psychological Bulletin 57,* 29–48 (1960).

Walls, G. L., & Heath, G. G. Neutral points in 138 protanopes and deuteranopes. *Journal of the Optical Society of America 46,* 640–649 (1956).

Walls, G. L., & Mathews, R. New means of studying color blindness and normal foveal color vision. *University of California Publications in Psychology 7,* 1–172 (1952).

Walraven, P. L. On the mechanisms of colour vision. Soesterberg, Netherlands: Thesis, Institute for Perception RVO-TNO, 1962.

Walraven, P. L. A closer look at the tritanopic convergence point. *Vision Research 14,* 1339–1343 (1974).

Walraven, P. L., & Leebeek, H. J. Phase shift of sinusoidally alternating colored stimuli. *Journal of the Optical Society of America 54*, 78–82 (1964a).

Walraven, P. L., & Leebeek, H. J. Phase shift of alternating coloured stimuli. *Documenta Ophthalmologica 18*, 56–71 (1964b).

Walsh, J. W. T. *Photometry* (3rd ed.) London: Constable, 1958. Reprinted, New York: Dover, 1958.

Watkins, R. D. Foveal increment thresholds in normal and deutan observers. *Vision Research 9*, 1185–1196 (1969a).

Watkins, R. D. Foveal increment thresholds in protan observers. *Vision Research 9*, 1197–1204 (1969b).

Watson, J. D. *Molecular biology of the gene* (3rd ed.). Menlo Park, California: Benjamin, 1976.

Weale, R. A. Photochemical reactions in the living cat's retina. *Journal of Physiology 122*, 322–331 (1953a).

Weale, R. A. Cone-monochromatism. *Journal of Physiology 121*, 548–569 (1953b).

Weale, R. A. *The eye and its function.* London: Hatton Press, 1960.

Weale, R. A. *The aging eye.* London: Lewis, 1963.

Weale, R. A. Vision and fundus reflectometry: A review. *Photochemistry and Photobiology 4*, 67–87 (1965).

de Weert, Ch. M. M., & Levelt, W. J. M. Comparison of normal and dichoptic colour mixing. *Vision Research 16*, 59–70 (1976).

Weingarten, F. S. Wavelength effect on visual latency. *Science 176*, 692–694 (1972).

Weisskopf, V. How light interacts with matter. *Scientific American 219* (3), 60–71 (1968).

Werblin, F. S. Control of retinal sensitivity: II. Lateral interactions at the outer plexiform layer. *Journal of General Physiology 63*, 62–87 (1974).

Werblin, F. S., & Copenhagen, D. R. Control of retinal sensitivity: III Lateral interactions at the inner plexiform layer. *Journal of General Physiology 63*, 88–110 (1974).

Werblin, F. S., & Dowling, J. E. Organization of the retina of the mudpuppy, *Necturus maculosus*: II. Intracellular recording. *Journal of Neurophysiology 32*, 339–355 (1969).

Westheimer, G. The Maxwellian view. *Vision Research 6*, 669–682 (1966).

Westheimer, G. Visual acuity and spatial modulation thresholds. In Jameson, D., & Hurvich, L. M. (Eds.), *Handbook of sensory physiology* VII/4. New York: Springer-Verlag, 1972.

Wiesel, T. N., & Hubel, D. H. Spatial and chromatic interactions in the lateral geniculate body of the rhesus monkey. *Journal of Neurophysiology 29*, 1115–1156 (1966).

Willmer, E. N., & Wright, W. D. Colour sensitivity of the fovea centralis. *Nature 156*, 119–121 (1945).

Wolff, E. *The anatomy of the eye and orbit* (3rd ed.). Philadelphia: Blakiston, 1949.

Wooten, B. R., & Wald, G. Color-vision mechanisms in the peripheral retinas of normal and dichromatic observers. *Journal of General Physiology 61*, 125–145 (1973).

Wright, W. D. A re-determination of the mixture curves of the spectrum. *Transactions of the Optical Society, London 30*, 141–164 (1928–29).

Wright, W. D. The sensitivity of the eye to small colour differences. *Proceedings of the Physiological Society of London 53*, 93–112 (1941).

Wright, W. D. *Researches on normal and defective colour vision.* London: Henry Kimpton, 1946.

Wright, W. D. Characteristics of tritanopia. *Journal of the Optical Society of America* 42, 509–521 (1952).

Wurtz, R. W. Comparison of effects of eye movements and stimulus movements on striate cortex neurons of the monkey. *Journal of Neurophysiology* 32, 987–994 (1969).

Wyszecki, G., & Fielder, G. H. New color-matching ellipses. *Journal of the Optical Society of America* 61, 1135–1152 (1971).

Wyszecki, G., & Stiles, W. S. *Color science.* New York: Wiley, 1967.

Yates, J. T. Chromatic information processing in the foveal projection (*area striata*) of unanesthetized primate. *Vision Research* 14, 163–173 (1974).

Young, R. W. Visual cells. *Scientific American* 223(4), 80–91 (1970).

Young, R. W. The renewal of rod and cone outer segments in the rhesus monkey. *Journal of Cellular Biology* 49, 303–318 (1971).

Young, R. W. Visual cells and the concept of renewal. *Investigative Ophthalmology* 15, 700–725 (1976).

Young, R. W. Visual cells, daily rhythms, and vision research. *Vision Research* 18, 573–578 (1978)

Young, T. On the theory of light and colours. *Philosophical Transactions* 1802, 12–48.

Zeki, S. The mosaic organization of the visual cortex in the monkey. In Bellairs, R., & Gray, E. G. (Eds.), *Essays on the nervous system.* Oxford: Clarendon Press, 1974.

Zoethout, W. D. *Physiological optics* (4th ed.). Chicago: Professional Press, 1947.

Index of Names

Abney, W., 398, 400, 405
Abramov, I., 233, 237, 333, 335, 384
Adler, H. E., 205, 334
Aguilar, M., 93
Aitken, J., 388
Albrecht, D. G., 247
Alhazen (Abu Ali Mohammed Ibn Al Hazen), 5, 6, 22
Alkendi, 5
Alpern, M., 87, 366–368, 389
Arago, D. F. J., 160
Aranzi, J. C., 9
Arden, G. B., 249
Aristotle, 4, 23
Armington, J. C., 249
Avant, L. L., 333

Bailey, J. E., 361–362
Baker, H. D., 274, 338, 346
Barlow, H. B., 206, 238
Baron, W. S., 249, 328, 330
Bartleson, C. J., 42, 379
Bartley, S. H., 301
Baylor, D. A., 180, 206, 303
Beare, J. I., 3, 22
Bedford, R. E., 284–285, 294
Bell, J., 351
Berbert, J. H., 334
Berlin, B., 386
Bezold, 210
Biernson, G., 156
Blackwell, H. R., 389
Blackwell, O. M., 162, 389
Blottiau, F., 300
Boll, F., 106–107, 117
Bongard, M. M., 389
Boring, E. G., 6, 22–23, 386
Bornstein, M. H., 304, 386
Bouguer, P., 160

Bouman, M. A., 293, 367
Bowmaker, J. K., 156, 202
Boycott, B. B., 81, 89, 91
Boynton, R. M., 21, 70, 77, 130, 176, 178–179, 190, 195, 198, 205, 210, 215, 218, 247, 249, 287, 295, 298, 300, 304, 327–328, 330, 333, 336, 364–366, 379, 386, 390, 394, 396
Brewster, D., 16
Brickwedde, F. G., 286
Bridges, C. D. B., 156
Brindley, G. S., 108, 156–157, 206, 248, 298, 336, 369, 389
Brown, J. L., 85, 230, 334
Brown, K. T., 216, 249
Brown, P. K., 82
Brown, W. R. J., 283
Brücke, E., 210, 301
Burnham, R. W., 379

Cajal, S. R. y, 95
Campbell, F. W., 77, 157, 334
Carden, D., 336
Cavonius, C. R., 202, 218
Chapanis, A., 301
Christ, R. E., 333
Cicerone, C. M., 210, 327
Clark, G., 246
Clarke, F. J. J., 158, 383
Conrady, A. E., 400
Cooper, G. F., 156
Copenhagen, D. R., 183, 205
Copernicus, N., 8
Cornsweet, T. N., 89, 120, 335
Crawford, B. H., 68, 183–184, 187–188, 383
Crombie, A. C., 24

Dalton, J., 337

Index of Names

Dartnall, H. J. A., 121, 150–152, 156, 202
da Vinci, L., 5, 6, 22
Davis, R., 402, 405
Davy, H., 15
Daw, N. W., 389
de Gaulle, C., 402
deLange, H., 308, 317, 334–336
Della Porta, G. B., 8
Democritus, 3, 10, 23
De Monasterio, F. M., 234, 244
Descartes, R., 8, 9, 66, 71
DeValois, K. K., 248, 250
DeValois, R. L., 233, 234–238, 241–243, 244, 247, 248, 250, 303–304
De Vries, H., 108
de Weert, C. M. M., 327
Dieterici, C., 387, 398
Dimmick, M. H., 294
Dirac, P. A. M., 49, 70
Ditchburn, R. W., 49, 70, 96, 335–336
Dow, B. M., 245
Dowling, J. E., 81, 83, 89, 91, 93, 96, 181, 205
Dreher, B., 335
Dudley, D., 87

Egan, J. P., 205
Ehinger, B., 83
Eisner, A., 157
Empedocles, 2
Engen, T., 293
Enoch, J. M., 206, 249, 389
Epicurus, 2, 23
Estévez, O., 202, 218, 336
Evans, R. M., 27–28, 32–33, 36–39, 41–42

Falls, H. F., 389
Farnsworth, D., 367, 375
Fechner, G., 160, 205
Feinberg, G., 46, 70
Fendee, D. H., 240
Ferry, E. S., 334
Fick, A., 358
Fielder, G. H., 283–284
Fiorentini, A., 325
Fischer, F. P., 367
Forshaw, C. R., 368
Forsyth, D. M., 301
Fourier, J. B., 309
Fox, J. C., 230
Foxell, C. A. P., 334
Fraunhofer, J., 14

Freeman, R. D., 386
Friele, L. F. C., 295
Fukada, Y., 335
Fuortes, M. G. F., 206

Galen, 4, 5, 23
Gamble, W., 405
German, W. J., 230
Gibbons, I. R., 82
Gibson, K. S., 402–403, 405
Glantz, R. M., 205
Glickstein, M., 367
Goethe, J. W. von, 12–13, 22–23, 114
Gordon, J., 210, 333, 384
Gouras, P., 234, 237, 244–246, 250
Graham, C. H., 381
Graham, R. E., 98, 396
Granit, R., 219, 249
Grassman, H., 157
Green, D. G., 298, 336, 389
Gregory, A. H., 77
Gregory, R. L., 41
Griffin, D. R., 107
Grutzner, P., 369–371
Gubisch, R. W., 334
Guild, J., 19, 144, 214–215, 399–403, 405
Gullstrand, A., 16, 96
Guth, S. L., 248, 300

Hagins, W. A., 157, 220
Hall, E. M., 304
Hanes, R. M., 379
Harter, M. R., 218
Hartline, H. K., 238, 250
Harwerth, R. S., 191–194, 202, 267
Hayhoe, M. M., 287, 298, 327, 351
Heath, G. G., 304, 360, 362–363, 367, 388
Hecht, S., 63, 90, 214, 361, 386
Helmholtz, H. von, 13–18, 21–22, 24, 108, 117, 120, 157, 214, 293, 337, 387, 398, 400, 405
Helson, H., 21
Henderson, S. T., 50–51, 70
Henkes, H. E., 335
Henry, G. H., 178
Hering, E., 13–14, 18, 22, 24, 208, 226
Hernnstein, R. J., 23
Hirsch, H. V. B., 386
Hochberg, J., 42, 389
Hodgkin, A. L., 180, 303
Horner, F., 351–352
Hsia, Y., 381

Index of Names

Hubbard, R., 106–107
Hubel, D. H., 241, 244
Hull, E., 229
Hurvich, L. M., 24, 206, 208–210, 361–362, 388
Huygens, C., 55

Ikeda, M., 190, 379
Indow, T., 289–291
Ingling, C. R., Jr., 202, 248
Ishihara, S., 373
Ives, H. E., 180, 335, 398–399, 405

Jacobs, G. H., 233
Jameson, D., 24, 206, 208–210, 361–362, 388
Jeffreys, D. A., 249
Jennings, A., 80
Johnson, E. P., 218
Judd, D. B., 21, 37, 39, 114, 144, 208, 295, 308, 335, 362, 381, 386, 402–405
Jules, Z. B., 249

Kaiser, P. K., 300, 304, 336
Kalmus, H., 319, 351, 354, 367
Kandel, G., 365
Kaneko, A., 96
Kardy, S. J., 250
Katz, D., 41–42
Katz, I., 349–351
Kaufman, J. E., 70
Kay, P., 386
Kelly, D. H., 180, 219, 298, 313–314, 318, 320–321, 323, 328, 335–336
Kepler, J., 8, 9, 22, 61, 65, 72
Kessen, W., 386
King-Smith, P. E., 336
Kingsbury, E. F., 335
Kingslake, R., 71
Kitai, S. T., 250
Kleinschmidt, J., 205
Kling, J. W., 390
Kohler, I., 68
Kolb, H., 93
Konig, A., 108–109, 111, 118, 295, 336, 361, 387, 398, 405
Kottgen, E., 336
Krantz, D. H., 210, 327
Krauskopf, J., 331, 336, 365
Kruger, J., 245
Kuffler, S. W., 238
Kuhns, M. P., 334

Lakowski, R., 369, 373–374, 376, 379, 389
Land, E. H., 20, 297, 333
Larimer, J., 210, 327
Lashley, W. S., 246
Lawson, R. B., 23
Leber, T., 358
Lee, G. B., 389
Leebeek, H. J., 334
Leeper, H. F., 90, 228
LeGrand, Y., 53, 77, 178, 266, 286, 306, 335, 387, 393, 396
Lennie, P., 381
Levelt, W. J. M., 327
Lewin, W. S., 248
Lewis, W. G., 108, 193–194
Liebman, P., 118, 156
Lightfoot, D. O., 90, 228
Lu, C., 249
Lythgoe, J. N., 156, 203

MacAdam, D. L., 24, 278–284, 286–287, 292, 295
McCamy, C. S., 21
McCann, J. J., 21, 297, 333
McConnell, D. J., 390
McConnell, J. V., 372
McCree, K. J., 272, 285–286
MacKay, D. M., 249
McKee, S. P., 21
MacLeod, D. I. A., 90, 287, 298, 327, 351, 381, 388
MacNichol, E. J., 96, 227, 249
Magnus, R., 23
Makous, W. L., 69
Mandel, L., 49, 70
Marc, R. E., 249, 336
Mariott, F. H. C., 206
Marks, L. E., 304
Marrocco, R. T., 234
Martin, L. C., 400–401, 405
Massaro, D. W., 314
Massof, R. W., 361–362
Masson, V., 160
Mathews, R., 361–363, 388
Maxwell, J. C., 17–19, 117, 128, 132, 142, 155, 362, 387, 394, 398, 403, 405
Mead, W. R., 304
Meyer, T., 15
Michael, C. R., 246
Michels, W. C., 21
Miller, S. S., 157
Mitchell, D. E., 127–128, 346, 349, 351, 387

Index of Names

Mollon, J. D., 23, 156, 203, 336
Monty, R. A., 96
Moreland, J. D., 86–87, 333, 389
Morgan, H. C., 304
Moskowitz, H. R., 205
Mueller, C. G., 63
Muller, G. E., 18, 23
Muller, J., 8, 16
Munsell, A. H., 289–290
Murakami, M., 96

Nagel, W., 16
Nagy, A. L., 364
Nerlove, S. B., 295
Neun, M. E., 333
Newton, I., 10–16, 22–25, 41, 54, 66, 71, 97
Nickerson, D., 289
Normann, R. A., 183, 205

O'Brien, P. M., 206
Ohsumi, K., 289–291
Oldenburg, H., 23
Onley, J. W., 365

Padmos, P., 244, 249
Palmer, G., 24
Parra, F., 286–287
Parsons, J. H., 386, 399–400, 405
Patterson, M. M., 95, 248
Pautler, E. L., 96
Penn, R. D., 220
Pettigrew, J. D., 386
Pfleegor, R. L., 49, 70
Piantanida, T. P., 351–352, 355–358, 364, 366–367, 388
Pickford, R. W., 356, 371
Pierce, 375
Pirenne, M. H., 7, 88, 90, 105
Pitt, F. H. G., 126–128, 256, 274, 361, 387
Plateau, J., 301
Plato, 2–4, 23
Pliny, 15
Pokorny, J., 151–153, 268, 294, 345, 349–351, 364, 366, 370, 379, 383–384, 387, 389, 404
Polson, M. C., 304
Polyak, S. L., 9, 22, 72, 85–86
Porter, T. C., 334
Powell, D. S., 336, 351
Pratt, C. C., 45
Priest, I. G., 286, 401–403

Pugh, E. N., 202
Purkinje, J., 114

Rainwater, J., 23
Ratliff, F., 239, 250
Regan, D. M., 219, 249, 296
Richards, W., 95
Riggs, L. A., 218, 334, 390
Rinalducci, E., 366
Ripps, H., 181, 205
Robinson, D. A., 96
Robson, J. G., 156
Rock, I., 41
Rodieck, R. W., 73, 95, 197, 308, 335, 387
Romney, A. K., 295
Ronchi, V., 14, 22–23
Ross, S., 63
Ruddock, K. H., 156
Rushton, W. A. H., 109, 118, 120, 122–128, 156–157, 170–171, 178, 181, 274, 336, 338, 346, 349, 351, 358, 387
Russell, B., 16

Sabra, I., 65
Sakitt, B., 90
Salzmann, M., 73
Sargent, M., 70
Schafer, W., 333
Scharf, B., 205
Scheibner, H., 206, 364–366
Scheiner, C., 9
Schick, A. M. L., 218
Schmidt, I., 349–351
Schouten, J. F., 351
Schrodinger, E., 18, 279–281, 402
Scully, M. O., 70
Senders, J. W., 96
Shepard, R. N., 295
Shlaer, S., 90, 361
Siegel, M. H., 293–294
Silverstein, A., 389
Sirovich, L., 335
Sjostrand, F. S., 82
Smirnov, M. S., 389
Smith, C. J., 250
Smith, T., 402, 405
Smith, V. C., 151–153, 213, 268, 294, 345, 349–351, 364, 366, 370, 379, 383–384, 387, 389, 404
Snell, W., 65–66, 71
Southall, J. P. C., 16
Sparrock, J. M. B., 335

Index of Names

Speelman, R. G., 365
Spekreijse, H., 218
Sperling, H. G., 191–194, 202, 249, 267, 335–336, 351, 366
Spinelli, D., 386
Spivey, B. E., 389
Starr, S. J., 384
Steinheil, 160
Stell, W. K., 90, 227, 228
Stevens, J. C., 205
Stevens, S. S., 205
Stevens, W. R., 334
Stiles, W. S., 68, 93, 100, 124, 144–146, 149, 151, 176, 186–191, 193–194, 196–202, 204–206, 219, 258–259, 282, 292–293, 298, 335–336, 387, 389, 392, 396, 403, 405
Strong, J., 24, 70
Svaetichin, G., 94, 96, 226–227, 249
Swartley, R., 389
Swenholt, B. K., 32

Talbot, H. F., 301
Taylor, B., 7
Taylor, E., 80
Taylor, G. I., 70
Taylor, T. H., 21
ten Doesschate, J., 367
Tessier, M., 300
Thompson, G. F., 397
Thompson, J. J., 397
Thompson, R. F., 95, 248
Thomson, L. C., 386
Thorell, L. G., 247
Tolhurst, D. J., 244
Tomita, T., 96, 222
Torii, 366
Trezona, P. W., 383
Troland, L. T., 335, 400, 405
Truss, C. V., 335
Tsou, B. H., 202, 248
Turbervil, L., 386
Tyndall, J., 403

Urakubo, M., 379

van den Berg, T. J. T. P., 218
van der Tweel, L. H., 335

van Norren, D., 219, 244, 249, 320–321, 323, 335–336
Verriest, G., 369–370
Volkmann, A. W., 160
von Kries, J., 16, 18
Vos, J. J., 152–153, 358

Wagner, G., 336, 365, 379
Wald, G., 107, 110, 113–114, 156, 193, 195, 326, 336, 338, 366, 388
Wallace, J. G., 41
Walls, G. L., 21, 360, 362–363, 381, 388
Walraven, P. L., 152–154, 225, 240, 293, 334, 358, 367–368
Walsh, J. W. T., 300, 400, 405
Watkins, R. D., 351, 365–366
Watson, J. D., 352
Weale, R. A., 118, 123, 156–157, 368–369
Weaver, E. A., 398, 401
Weingarten, F. S., 334
Weiskopf, S., 386
Weisskopf, V., 54
Werblin, F. S., 93, 183, 205
Westheimer, G., 77
Wheeler, T. G., 90, 228
White, C. T., 218
White, K. D, 336, 351
Whitten, D. N., 176, 178–179, 226, 249
Wiesel, T. N., 241, 244
Willmer, E. N., 157, 336, 382
Wolter, J. R., 389
Wooten, B. R., 388
Wright, W. D., 19, 144, 147–149, 158, 256, 274–279, 282, 284–285, 287, 335–336, 351, 361, 363–364, 367, 369, 382, 384, 387, 390, 397, 405
Wurtz, R. W., 231
Wyszecki, G., 100, 151, 197, 258, 282–285, 292–294, 335–336, 387, 392, 396, 403, 405

Yates, T., 245–246, 366
Yonemura, G., 295
Young, R. W., 82–83
Young, T., 15–18, 22, 24, 49, 117, 154, 295, 337

Zeki, S., 246
Zoethout, W. D., 96

Index of Subjects

Aberration, chromatic, 9, 67, 68
   spherical, 76
Absorption, by blood vessels, 84–85
   chromatic aberration and, 68
   in eye lens, 79, 384
   photoisomerization, 110
Absorption spectrum, see Spectral sensitivity
Accommodation, 79
Achromatopsia, see Monochromacy
Action potentials, 90, 231–247
Acuity, see Visual acuity
Adaptation, chromatic, 136, 160–161, 183–186, 203–204, 365–366
   dark, 121, 166
   and flicker, 302, 310, 312, 314
   light, 168–169
   modulation sensitivity and, 316
   to prisms, 68
   rapid, 183–184
   see also Sensitivity, regulation of
Additivity, in color matches, 112
   failure of, in direct heterochromatic photometry, 300
   Purkinje shift, 114
   flicker photometry and, 300–301, 306
   test of, 300
Afterimage, 37–39
Age, and presbyopia, 79
   and yellowing of lens, 79, 105, 384
Anatomy, amacrine cells, 83, 91, 92, 94
   bipolar cells, 83, 91, 92
   brain, 4, 229, 244–247
   choroid, 80
   cones, 82–83, 87–89, 90, 91, 224–226, 249
   cornea, 74, 75–76
   fovea, 84–89
   ganglion cells, 83–84, 86, 90–91
   gap junctions, 224–225
   horizontal cells, 91–94, 96, 224, 226–228
   iris, 76–77
   lateral geniculate nucleus, 228–238
   lens, 79
   optic disc, 84
   optic nerve fibers, 83–87
   receptor distribution, 88–89
   retina, 80–94
   rods, 82–83
   vitreous body, 79
   see also Cone(s); Rod(s); Retina
Anomaloscope, analytical, 346–349
   anomalous quotient, 350
   Nagel instrument, 347, 350
   test, 377–379
Anomalous photopigments, 348–351
Anomalous trichromacy, see Color blindness
Area effects, in color discrimination, 382–383
   in large field color matching, 383
   in peripheral color vision, 296–297, 384
   rod–cone distribution and, 87–89
   surrounds, effects of, 21, 32–33
   see also Receptive fields
Assimilation, 38

Bezold-Brücke hue shift, 14
Black, 32
Black and white, surface properties and, 3
Bleaching and regeneration kinetics, 169–176
Blue arcs, 86–87
Blue blindness, see Tritanopia
   -sensitive cones, see Cones, types of
   -sensitive pigment, see Cyanolabe
Boundaries, see Contour
Brightness, additivity failure of, 259, 294, 300
   heterochromatic photometry and, 299–300
   versus hue and saturation, 30
   versus lightness, 155
Brain, projections to, 229–231
   as sentient center, 4, 207–208, 230–231
Brown (color), 33, 42
Camera obscura, 5
Chlorolabe, 122, 152

Index of Subjects

Chromatic adaptation, see Adaptation, chromatic
Chromatic discrimination, B-cone variation and, 265–266
  cone activation in, 259–263
  in dichromats, 363–365
  methodological issues, 284
  red-green channels and, 263–265
  questions, critical, 259–267
  yellow-blue channels, 265–266
Chromaticity diagrams, color triangles and, 132–134, 157–158
  center of gravity principle, 136–137
  triangular, 138, 158
  uniformity of, 295
  see also Cone(s), sensitivity curves; Reference stimulus
CIE system, 390–397
  dichromacy in, 344–345
  history of, 19, 397–403
Color(s), chromatic vs. chromatic, 253
  complementaries, 115–117
  context, 20–21, 297
  definition of, 253, 292
  equations for, 134–137, 390–391
  exchange of, 316, 322–323
  naming of, 14, 210–211
  related vs. unrelated, 28
  in retinal image, 9
  space, 280
  of surfaces, 3, 26–27, 42
  and television, 34–37, 98, 157
  theory of, see Theories of vision and color vision
  zones of the visible spectrum, by chromatic cancellation, 208–210
  by color naming, 14, 210–211
Color, appearance of, 25–42
Color blindness, acquired, 369–370
  altered systems, 343
  anomalous, 343, 348–349, 363–364
  B-cone monochromacy, 369
  chromatic adaptation and, 365–366
  chromaticity diagram and, 344–346
  deuteranopia, 342, 345, 348, 355–356, 358–363
  diagnosis of, 346–351, 371–379
  dichromacy, see Dichromatic vision
  discriminations, 340–341
  extreme anomalies, 349–350
  in females, 358
  genetics of, 351–358
  loss systems, 341–342
  missing receptors, 342
  monochromacy, 344, 366–369
  neutral points in spectrum, 359–363
  in normal individuals, 99–100
  R-cone monochromacy, 367–368
  replacement theory, 355–358
  testing for, 371–379
  tritanopia, 367
  unilateral, 381–382
  weak systems, 343
Color constancy, 26, 183–185
Color differences, large, 288–291
  see also Chromatic discrimination
Color equations, 134–137
Color matching and mixture, chromatic adaptation and, 136
  in color-blind observers, 346–349, 378
  complex spectral distributions and, 112–113
  early ideas about, 2, 3
  dichoptic (binocular), 203–204
  intensity, dependence upon, 121–122
  laws of, 20, 21
  Maxwell and, 18
  Newton's views, 12, 41
  in peripheral visual field, 382–384
  physiological basis of, 117–118
  primaries, CIE, 402–404
  primaries, NPL, 401
  primaries, physiological, 142, 149–153
  rods and, 101–104, 111–112, 383
  stimuli versus sensations, 132, 157
  subjective aspects of, 130–132
  by temporal alternation, 157
  trichromatic (cone), 113–117
  unit coordinate system, 147
  units for, 117
Colorimetry, see Chromaticity diagrams; Color matching and mixture
Cone(s), absorption spectra of, 149–153
  bleaching kinetics, 174
  density of photopigment in, 122, 157
  distribution of, 87–89, 225–226, 249
  hyperpolarization of, 223–224
  interactions between, 224–225, 318–324
  intracellular recording from, 216
  peripheral, 88
  photopigments in, see Chlorolabe; Cyanolabe; Erythrolabe
  regeneration of outer segments of, 82
  responses, see Electrical recording
  retinal densitometry and, 122
  sensitivity curves, hypothetical (for color

Cone(s) (cont.)
    matching), 129–130, 138–142
    peaks due to interactions, 191—195
    π-mechanism, 189—191, 196—203
    psychophysical determination of, 123
    tails, importance of, 128
    Smith-Pokorny fundamentals, 153, 404
    see also Retinal densitometry
  spatial properties of, 324—327
  temporal properties of, 327—331
  types of, blue-sensitive (B), 272, 287, 298, 325–327
    green-sensitive (G), 298–299, 318–324
    red-sensitive (R), 263, 298–299, 318–324
    see also Anatomy
  waveguide patterns in, 223, 249
Contour, color discrimination and, 254, 287, 292
  color perception and, 331
  receptive fields and, 240
Contrast, color, 37–39
  defined for flicker, 309–310, 312
  defined for small targets, 162
  successive, 37–39
Cornea, 37–39, 73–76
Critical flicker frequency, 301–302
Cyanolabe, 122, 151–152

Dark adaptation, see Sensitivity, regulation of
Delay in perception, 296
Density, optical, 6.B, 165, 205
Depth of field, 77–79
Deuteranopia, retinal densitometry and, 123, 127–128
  see also Dichromatic vision
Dichromatic vision, chromatic adaptation and, 365–366
  cone absorption spectra and, 150
  confusion lines in, 344–345
  deuteranopia, 342, 345, 348, 355–356, 358–363
  neutral points in spectrum, 359–363
  protanopia, 342, 345, 348, 355–356
  red-green discrimination, residual, 364–365
  tests for, 371–379
  tritanopia, 367
Difference threshold, for color, 253–255, 288–290
  for intensity, 162–163, 288
  see also Threshold vs. intensity curves; Chromatic discrimination; Wavelength, discrimination of
Diffraction, 55

Discrimination, see Difference threshold; Chromatic discrimination; Threshold
Duplicity theory, 19, 81–83
  see also Cone(s); Rod(s)

Eccentricity in visual field, see Area effects
Electrical recording, classification of single unit records, 232
  electroretinogram, 72, 216–218, 219, 249
  evoked cortical potentials, 217–219
  intracellular, from cones, 215–216
  local electroretinogram, 216–217
  methods, 95, 231–232
  single unit, from monkey, 231–232
    sampling problem, 232
Electroretinogram, 72, 216–218, 219, 249
Emanation theory of vision, 2
Erythrolabe, 122–123, 151
Evoked potentials, 218–219
Exchange thresholds, see Silent substitution
Extrafoveal vision, see Area effects
Eye, Greek knowledge of, 2–4
  gross features of, 73–74
  image in, see Retinal image
  movement of, 74–75, 96
  optical elements in, 75–80
  stray light in, 80
  structure of, see Anatomy
Eye–camera analogy, 163–166

Fixation, 75
Flicker, chromatic, 316–322
  photometry and, 301–308
  sensation of, 301
  steady-state, 310
Fluorence, 32, 41–42
Fluorescence, 70
Fourier analysis, 309
Fovea centralis, 75, 84–87, 113
Fundus, 80
Fusion frequency, 301–302

Ganzfeld, 1, 3, 47
Gap effect, 287
Genetics of color blindness, 351–358
Geodesic, 280
Gray content, 32
Green, blindness, see Deuteranopia
  -sensitive cones, see Cones, types of
  -sensitive pigment, see Chlorolabe

History of color science, 1–24
Hue, as abstract sensation, 1
  balanced, 31

Index of Subjects

versus brightness and saturation, 30
change with intensity and, 14
circle to represent, 30–31, 35
code for, 93–94, 207–250
measurement of, 14
Newton and, 14
of object, 1
stimulus size and, 297
unique, 31
wavelength and, 14, 50

Illuminance, see Troland (unit)
Increment thresholds, see Difference threshold; Threshold vs. intensity curves
Individual differences, in normal color vision, 338–340, 384
see also Color blindness
Information, see Visual information
Inhibition, and low-frequency flicker, 313–314
see also Receptive fields
Integrating sphere, 70
Intensity, effect on color perception, 39–41
effect on critical flicker frequency, 301–302
effect on hue, 14
effect on modulation sensitivity, 314
generic use of the term, 156
photons and, 50, 156
see also Luminance; Troland; Units
International Commission on Illumination, see Chromaticity diagrams; CIE system
Ishihara plates, 375
see also Pseudoisochromatic plates
Isomerization, 110
Isomers (physical color matches), 100

J factor, 268

Lens, Kepler's discoveries, 8, 9
of eye, accommodation, 79
presbyopia, 70
spectacles, 8
Light, adaptation to, see Sensitivity, regulation of
definition of, 46
diffraction of, 55
dispersion of, 10, 11, 13, 65–67
frequency of vibration of, 48
interference of photons, 48–50
media of transport, 55–56
mode of perception (vs. surface mode), 27–28
polarization of, 70
quantal nature of, 46, 47
quantity of, specification, 299

as rays, 2, 11
reflection of, 54, 55
role in object perception, 45
scatter of, 57, 58
sources of, 50–54
velocity of, 47, 48, 56, 71
wavelength of, 48
see also Photon(s)
Lighting, 33
Lightness, 155
Line element, 258
Linear systems analysis, 308–310
Luminance, 164, 255, 292, 294
Luminosity function, see Spectral sensitivity

Mach bands, see Receptive fields
Maxwellian view, 77
Metameric matches, 100–102, 155
Metric, color, 279–282
Microspectrophotometry, 118
Mind–body problem, 4
see also Sensation(s)
Minimally distinct border, 254–255, 290–291
Modulation, 310
Modulation sensitivity, 311–316
Monochromacy, 106, 366, 367–369
Munsell system of color specification, 289

Nerve spikes, see Action potentials
Neutral points of dichromats, 359–363
Newton, analysis of the spectrum, 11, 12
prisms, 23
rings, 13, 14, 23, 24
Nodal point concept, 61, 62
Noise, in electrical records, 223
in visual system, 214–215, 249
Nystagmus, physiological, 75

Object color, 25–27
Object perception, 1, 2, 45
Ophthalmoscope, 120
Opponent-color cells, 226–228, 232–246
Opponent-color channels, red-green, 263–265, 298–299
sluggishness of, 308, 316–317, 323
yellow-blue, 265–266
Opponent-color model, achromatic vs. chromatic color differences, 253–255
chromatic discrimination and, 263–266
color blindness, 341–344
Hering and, 18
interactions between r-g and y-b channels, 266–267, 274–275
limitations of, 212–213

Optogram, 106

Parafovea, see Area effects
Pattern vision, see Spatial vision
Perception, modes of, 10–12
　of objects, 1, 2, 45
　speed of, 296
Periphery, see Area effects
Phosphenes, 208
Photochemistry, bleaching kinetics, 171–172
　photoisomerization, 110
　regeneration kinetics, 170–171
　see Chlorolabe; Cyanolabe; Erythrolabe; Rhodopsin
Photochromatic intervals, 114
Photography as visual analogy, 163–166
Photometry, 64, 65, 299–317
　see also Flicker; Units
Photon(s), absorption in rods and cones, 90
　characteristics of, 47
　energy of, 64
　fate of, 58–60
　numbers involved in vision, 161–162
　path of, 47
　wavelength of, 48, 64
Photopic relative luminous efficiency function (V_λ), 300, 306
　and CIE system of colorimetry, 403
Photopic vision, see Cone(s)
Photopigments, see Anomalous photopigments; Chlorolabe; Cone(s); Cyanolabe; Erythrolabe; Rhodopsin; Rod(s)
Photoreceptors, current flow in, 219–220
　distribution of, 87–89
　rods vs. cones, 81–82
　see also Anatomy; Rods; Cones
Physical vs. perceptual reality, 44–46
π mechanisms, 187–191, 196–203
　see also Spectral sensitivity
Pinhole camera, 5
Primary, see Reference stimulus
Protanopia, genetics of, 351–358
　retinal densitometry and, 123–127
Pseudoisochromatic plates, 372–375
Psychophysical methods, 167–168, 205, 256–257, 293
Pupil of eye, 5, 76–77
　artificial, 77
Pure hue, see Hue, unique
Purity, 116–117, 396
Purkinje shift, 40, 114

Quantum of light, see Photon(s)

Rayleigh equation, 378
Receptive fields, border enhancement, role in, 239–240
　chromatic code and, 241–244
　discovery of, 238
　methods to test, 238–240
　pupil size and, 76–77
　of rods, 77
Receptors, electrical records from, 216–217, 249
　opponent differentials, 269–271
　responses and cff, 302
　see also Anatomy; Cones; Rods
Red, blindness, see Protanopia
　-sensitive cones, see Cones, types of
　-sensitive pigment, see Erythrolabe
　shift, 111
　at short wavelengths, 215, 271
Reduction screen, 2, 28
Reference stimulus (primary), change of primaries, 143–144
　CIE system, 390–406
　imaginary, 142–144, 394
　physiological, 149–153
　Wright's system, 147–149
Reflection, 25, 26, 54, 55, 120, 162
Refraction, 56, 76
Refractive index of eye media, 76
Regeneration kinetics, 170–171
Resolution, temporal, 301
　see also Flicker
Resolving power, spatial, see Visual acuity
　temporal, see Flicker
Response averaging, 217
Response compression, 175–176, 223
Retina, 80–94
　see also Anatomy
Retinal densitometry, 118–128, 156–157
Retinal image, animal eye, direct view, 9
　color vision and, 9, 10
　color of, 9
　inversion of, 6, 7, 8, 23, 56–57
　Kepler and, 8, 9
　mechanisms of, 75–79
Rhodopsin, 106–109
Riemannian space, 281–282
Rod(s), in color matching, 383
　connections with cones, 93
　distribution in retina, 87–89
　monochromacy and, 366–367

Index of Subjects

pigment, 82
regeneration kinetics, 120–121
regeneration of outer segments, 82
response, saturation of, 93
see also Anatomy

Saturation, color and, 30
  discrimination of, 257, 285–287
  of physiological response, of rods, 93
  of cones, 223
Scientific method and philosophy, analytic vs. holistic, 12
  limitations of gross electrophysiology, 216–217
  machine view of man, 8
  Newton vs. Goethe, 12, 13
  physiology and sensation, 98–99
  sensory discrimination, 46
  speculative theory, 156
  teleological explanations, 105
  use of simplified stimuli and responses, 99
Scotopic vision, see Rod(s)
Sensation(s), during color matching, 132
  color and wavelength, 21
  of dichromats, 380–382
  dimensions of chromatic experience, 27–33
  of flicker, 301
  measurement of, 14
  photoisomerization and, 110
  private nature of, 339
Sensitivity, defined, 166
  directional, of retina, 68
  regulation of, bleaching and regeneration of photopigments, 169–174, 176–179
    chromatic adaptation, 160–161
    cone pigment kinetics, 174
    light and dark adaptation, 160, 166–169
    mechanisms of light adaptation, 168–169, 182–183
    photons, number of, 161–162
    pupil and, 176–179
    response compression and, 175–179, 223
    spectral, 306, 403, 102–106, 153–154
    two-color threshold and, 185–203
    Weber's law, 160
Sensorium, 4
Signal detection theory, 205
Silent substitution, 237, 322–323, 348
Simultaneous contrast, 39
Sinusoidal stimuli, 308–317
Sky, 57–60
Slow potentials, 90

Snell's law, 65–66, 71
Spatial vision, 1, 2, 9, 10, 47–48, 60–63
  see also Visual acuity
Specific nerve energies, 8, 23
Spectral sensitivity, of cones, 118, 149–153, 405
  energy vs. photon basis, 103
  field method for determining, 195–196
  hypothetical curves, 129
  infrared limitation, 105–106
  lens, absorption and, 105
  logarithmic ordinate, need for, 103–104
  photopigments and, 121–122
  psychophysical methods for determining, 166–168
  of rods, 102
  rod vs. cone, 113–114
  scotopic, 102–103
  test wavelength variation and, 187–194
Spectrum, appearance of wavelengths in, 50
  Newton and, 10
  visible, 104–106
Standard observer, 402–403
Stiles-Crawford effect, 68
Stimulus for vision, flickering, components of, 311
  husk theory of Epicurus, 2
  minimum duration of, 296
  physical definition, important of, 43–46
  see also Light; Photon(s)
Summation, temporal, 301
  see also Flicker
Surrounds, 21, 29, 32–33, 39

Talbot-Plateau law, 301, 314
Tapetum, 119
Tetrachromacy of extrafoveal vision, 383
Theories of vision and color vision, critical flicker frequency, 302
  emanation, 2
  flicker photometry, 306–308
  Hecht, 214–215
  low-frequency sensitivity loss, 313–314
  Newton, 13–15
  opponent color, 18, 208
  speculative models, 156
  temporal coding, 331–332
  trichromatic, 15–18, 24
  wavelength discrimination, 255–275
  Young-Helmholtz, 17
  see also Color blindness; Sensitivity, regulation of

Threshold, absolute, 159, 161—162
  defined, 168
  increment, see Contrast; Sensitivity
  two-color, see Sensitivity, two-color threshold and
  univariance and, 198—199
  see also Difference threshold
Threshold vs. intensity (t.v.i.) curves, 94, 163, 196—203
Touch and vision, 25, 41
Tristimulus value, 396
Tritanopia, 367
Troland (unit), 64, 164, 205
Two-color threshold method, 163, 187—203

Units, cancellation stimuli, 209
  chromatic difference, 282
  illuminance (td), 64, 164, 205
  luminance (cd/m^2), 164
  trichromatic, 137—138
  Wright's system, 147—148
Univariance, principle of, 15—16, 109, 112

Visual acuity, B-cones and, 226
  influence of wavelength upon, 298
Visual adaptation, see Adaptation, chromatic; Sensitivity regulation
Visual angle, 62
Visual brain, 4, 217—219, 229—247
Visual information, coding of, 93—94, 207—250
  and color TV, 34—37, 98
  difference signals, 211—215
  inverted retinal image and, 7
  and photographs, 164
  see also Sensitivity regulation
Visual pathways, centripetal, 83
  states and sensation, 98
  temporal properties of, 327—331
Visual purple, see Rhodopsin

Waveguide patterns in receptors, 223, 249
Wavelength, discrimination of, 259—275
  dominant, 116, 396
  and hue, 14, 15, 50
  see also Light; Photon(s)
Weber fractions of R, G, and B cones, 272
Weber's law, 160
White (color), 11—12, 30, 117

Yellow at long wavelengths, 293
Yellow-blue opponent channels, 272—274, 327
Young-Helmholtz theory of color vision, 17

Zone theory, 18
  see also Opponent colors